# MANAGING RISK

Frontispiece

The risk of the unknown in exploring a new homo-technological system produced the first known prior outcome or fatality caused by humans flying. In the classical Greek myth illustrated here on this platter, Daedalus can be seen helplessly watching Icarus fall to his death below him. Daedalus, the designer of the Minotaur's Labyrinth and imprisoned there, in order to escape had fitted himself and his son, Icarus, with these innovative wings. But during the escape, Icarus became intoxicated by this new power of flight and, despite Daedalus's repeated warnings and his lack of experience, took the risk of flying so high that the sun melted the wax holding his feathered wings. (Photo © John W. Saull.)

# MANAGING RISK
## THE HUMAN ELEMENT

By

**Romney B. Duffey** BSc, PhD, FASME

**John W. Saull** CEng, FRAeS, DAE

**WILEY**

A John Wiley & Sons, Ltd., Publication

ISBN: 978-0-470-69976-8

Library of Congress Cataloging-in-Publication Data

Duffey, R. B. (Romney B.)
 Managing risk : the human element / by Romney B. Duffey, John W. Saull.
   p. cm.
 Includes bibliographical references and index.
 ISBN 978-0-470-69976-8 (cloth)
 1. Industrial safety.  2. Industrial accidents.  I. Saull, John Walton, 1935–  II. Title.
 T55.D816 2008
 363.11–dc22

                                                                    2008033263

A catalogue record for this book is available from the British Library.

Set in 10 on 12 pt Times by SNP Best-set Typesetter Ltd., Hong Kong

# Contents

# About the Authors

**Romney Beecher Duffey**

Romney Duffey, B.Sc. (Hons), Ph.D., FASME, is an internationally recognised scientist, manager, speaker and author, having written more than 200 papers and articles on the risk, safety and design of modern energy systems. Dr. Duffey has also co-authored the book *Know the Risk* concerning the safety of modern technological systems and the role of human error.

He has a distinguished 30-year career examining the safety and performance of nuclear systems in Europe and the USA. He is presently the Principal Scientist for Atomic Energy of Canada (AECL) with a wide range of responsibilities, including advanced and future concepts, advanced product development, advice on overall R&D directions, international collaborations, analysis of global energy and environment scenarios and energy policy, and senior-level reviews.

He is an ASME Fellow, a past Chair of the ASME Nuclear Engineering Division, an active member of the American, Canadian and British Nuclear Societies, and a past Chair of the American Nuclear Society Thermal-Hydraulics Division.

## John Walton Saull

Photo © RB

*John Saull*, C.Eng., FRAeS, DAE, is an internationally known aviation regulator and author, having presented many technical papers on aviation safety, and is the co-author of 'Know the Risk' published in 2003. He has over 45 years of experience in commercial aircraft certification, manufacturing, operations and maintenance. He has taken a specific interest in safety management and human error in technological industries.

He is presently the executive director of the International Federation of Airworthiness (IFA), following a distinguished and fascinating career with the Air Registration Board and the UK Civil Aviation Authority, where he held several senior positions. He retired as head of operating standards division in 1995, with 32 years experience in safety regulation.

His experience includes, 7 years on the development of the Concorde supersonic transport aircraft, responsible for the construction standards. He also held technical advisory positions overseas, in Argentina and the West Indies. He has held a pilot licence for 40 years and is the co-owner of a light aircraft.

He is member of several international safety committees and has organised international safety conferences. He is a Freeman of the City of London and a Liveryman of the Guild of Air Pilots and Air Navigators and, a trustee of UK Confidential Human Factors Incident Reporting Programme. He is chairman of the College of Aeronautics Alumni Association (Alumnus 1967). He has served on the Council of the Royal Aeronautical Society.

John is married with three children.

# Preface

'But indeed, another way is open to us here by which we may obtain what is sought; and what you cannot deduce a priori, you can at least deduce a posteriori – that is, you will be able to make a deduction from many observed outcomes of similar events. For it must be presumed that every single thing is able to happen and not to happen in as many cases as it was previously observed to have happened and not to have happened in like circumstance.'

Jakob Bernoulli, 1713, in his 'Art of Conjecture'

Humans made mistakes, and hopefully we learn from them. Bernoulli pointed that out very, very clearly, nearly 300 years ago. But as part of our lives, we still take risks, which can have good or bad consequences. We need to understand fully the role of the human element in risk prediction.

We are an integral part of modern technology. No matter how we try to spread and define the blame, we humans are responsible for the vast majority of errors and accidents, and most of the mistakes. We are an inseparable part of the entire technological, social and decision-making machine, and of the learning process itself. We make 'good' and 'bad' choices, take 'right' and 'wrong' actions, we 'fail' or we 'succeed', make 'snap' or 'considered' decisions, and cause 'successful' or 'unsuccessful' results. These are the bifurcations or forks in the road along our pathway through life. Those who do not learn are either eliminated, or do not achieve as successful or desired an outcome. Luck and chance can play their part too. To try to bias things in our favour, to reduce the risk, we humans interfere and interface with the technological world using management systems, procedures, rules, training, inquiries, rewards and punishments. But the risk of outcomes, good or bad, is still out there, waiting to happen and continuing to occur, no matter our efforts to ensure that they 'never happen again'.

In our previous book (*Know the Risk*), by looking at the world's accident and event data, we showed that a Universal Learning Curve indeed existed. Inexorably, we are doomed to follow its trend. If we are learning that trend depends on the rate we make mistakes, based on either the conscious and the unconscious, or the known and the unknown risks that we take, and the judgements we make along the way, we are always taking risk. Whether we gamble or invest, go for a drive or a walk, take a medicine or a herbal remedy, avoid an argument or confront, make an instant or a measured decision, open a store or close one, or mend an appliance or not. Indeed, it is the very business, function and role of management to make decisions based on inadequate information, and hence, to take risks.

So risks indeed do still occur: the Shuttle crashed in thousands of pieces; the great ten-million person electricity blackout occurred; aircraft collided in midair; trains still crashed; doctors still made misdiagnoses; companies failed; tsunamis and hurricanes washed away whole towns; anti-missile systems failed; and speculators still made profits. We know they happened because we observed them: so when, where and what is the next one? How successful or not will we be in the future? Is our individual and collective risk less or more? Have we learned anything or are we still doomed to have many more similar or new outcomes? And how many? As Bernoulli said so elegantly, what happened before can be presumed to happen again.

How then do we predict when and what events will happen, whatever they may be, how and to whom? How can we measure and reduce our risk, our personal, social and professional probability of becoming just another statistic? How can we manage the risk?

If outcomes are unpredictable, and risk taking and events occur randomly, how can we make any judgements about the future at all? It seems hopeless, as if we are just the unwilling and unwitting cogs in the wheel of life, subject to the whims of fate.

To gain back control of our future, to provide insight from learning, we have explored the common phases of some of the major events that have petrified and riveted the world. We show exactly how the human actions, behaviours and responses are interlinked and interwoven with technology. Using that knowledge, we suggest how we can measure our risk and improve by using our hard-won experience.

Because predicting is hard, and risk analysis is such a highly emotionally charged arena because lives and money are at stake, there are many false trails already out there. They include studies on human behaviour, risk taking, financial risk assessment, safety analysis, sociological survival trends, management attributes, psychological influences, communications technology, economic learning curves, decisional techniques, sampling statistics and human reliability. Unifying these diverse topics, we provide a new concept and set of ideas based on the very fact that we cannot describe the detailed behaviour of everything anyway. This may seem like a paradox, but overall, we find the very unpredictability of outcomes actually makes it possible to predict their probability, which of course is a measure of their likelihood of occurring. This very randomness and uncertainty are also essential for the appearance of the systematic influence of the human element on risk. We call that predicting the unpredictable, and lies at the very heart of predicting the statistical nature of our world and understanding how we can manage risk successfully.

To undertake the impossible, to try to predict, we stood on the shoulders of past giants of physics and mathematics, such as the legendary pioneers Laplace, Bernoulli, Bayes, Boltzmann, and more recently, Jaynes. They gave us the tools and the insights, the courage and the power, to enable us to sample from the Jar of Life and make a prediction about the future. Sampling also the diverse fields of physics, mathematics, sociology, biology, economics, aeronautics, management, safety and risk analysis, statistics, and psychology, provided us clues to solve the problem of developing a general theory that is derived from, and testable against, data. That data then naturally gave a measure of the uncertainty, the $H$-factor, of how to evaluate risk and characterise the systematic effects of organisational learning and safety management system effectiveness which are so liked by students, consultants and managers of human behaviour in organisation and systems research. We can eliminate the qualitative degree of risk reduction with a real numerical measure of uncertainty based on our experience.

To provide that measure, we had to invent a description of 'experience space' which we humans inhabit, whether we know it or not. We found that the trends for individual learning and skill acquisition within a system are precisely reflected in the emergent patterns, outcomes and learning curves observed for the entire system. We had to find and analyse new data and develop entirely new ways for how we could actually measure and manage risk reduction. Providing new answers to some old problems, we had to create a different way for us all to look at and to manage risk.

So we wrote this book: enjoy *Managing Risk*.

# Acknowledgements

*'The fundamental problem of scientific progress, and a fundamental one of everyday life, is that of learning from experience.'*

Harold Jeffreys, *'Theory of Probability'*

We were inspired by the works of the giants of science, Jakob Bernoulli, Pierre-Simon LaPlace and Ludwig Boltzmann, who left their indelible impressions on the analysis of the physical world; and to Edwin Jaynes, for making all this prior work so useful and highly relevant to the likely future. The pioneering ideas of Professors Henry Petroski and Karl Ott on the essential role of failures in engineering and safety were both important and motivational.

We are indebted to Dr. Phillip Myers, whose insights and untiring questions first lead us directly to the entire idea of adapting engineering reliability and probability estimation to the learning hypothesis, and to our examining in detail the oil and gas industry data. We are particularly grateful to Professor Stellan Ohlsson for having invented the theory of human error correction, and for providing stimulating advice, data and insights on human learning, and invaluable information on the laws of practice in psychology. We especially thank Dr. Vinius Angel and Professor Yuri Kirillov who pointed out the relevance of the advances in entropy formulations, complexity and information theory and, most importantly, where to find them, and also drew our attention to the theorems and methods of machine learning. Professor Joseph Fragola provided invaluable details of the modern applications of risk analysis to space vehicle architecture and design, plus mission launch data sources. Dr. David Varis contributed risk definitions and information on the status of international work on risk standards. We especially thank Professors Cristina Fang and Stellan Ohlsson who gave us access to their learning experimental data, a key piece of real information. Dr. Ann Britt Skjerve provided major encouragement, and a new perspective on the unique application to offshore facilities and newly available risk indicator data. For probabilistic safety analysis, Dr. Tom Hannaman provided useful information, criticism and comments on human reliability. We are particularly grateful to Dr. Stephen Douglas for his keen insights into the mysteries of statistical probability and sampling methods.

In-depth reviews, key discussions, valuable suggestions and insightful critiques were made by Professor Terry Rogers, John Waddington, Dr. Harold Blackman, Ingemar Ingemarson, Bruce Hallbert and by a number of anonymous reviewers. Comments and contributions to our thinking and on sections of draft text were made by Dr. Feng Hsu, Professor James

Reason, Dr. Alistair Miller, Dr. Vaughan Pomeroy, Professor Yuri Kirillov, Captain John Hutchinson and Dr. Ron Lloyd, among many others, who provided corrections, necessary encouragement and helpful commentary, for which we truly thank them. We also thank our technical interactions with Brian McGee, Dr. Victor Snell and Paul Lafreniere on the principles and practices of safety management; and with Michael Stephens on measures in industrial safety and quality management, and for insisting on clarity in the probability definitions. Dr. Trevor Cradduck pointed us to the latest medical error data and to several other sources in that specialised field. We are grateful to Ms. Victoria Duffey for editing and clarity reviews, and to the many colleagues, friends, experts and professionals who have contributed their experience and cajoled, criticised and commented on our text and ideas. Although the work published here is new, we have learned much from many sources. Numerous contacts have provided valuable prior information, sources, data, references, reports and possible connections, many of which are reflected in the References. We also apologise to any of our colleagues and correspondents whom we may have inadvertently omitted mentioning by name.

We remain indebted to the Internet (and its search engines) without which we could not have even begun, allowing us to learn from the experience at official web sites stocked with treasure troves of reports and national datasets. Particularly, excellent information was obtained from the magnificently detailed records of the ATSB (Australian Transport Safety Bureau) and also access to the USCG (US Coast Guard) historical files was granted. Published reports also came from the marvelously complete web sites of the NTSB (US National Transportation Safety Board), CSB (US Chemical Safety and Hazard Investigation Board), OSHA (US Occupational Safety and Health Administration), NHTSA (US National Highway Transport Safety Administration), NASA (US National Aeronautics and Space Administration), HSE (UK Health and Safety Executive), ORR (UK Office of Rail Regulation) and the PSA (Petroleum Safety Authority Norway). We much appreciate both the open and the licensed use of their information and that from the other non-government sources we have listed. We thank those organisations and individuals who granted special permissions for extended use of original source materials, as indicated in the text.

We thank Judy Charbonneau for her diligence, dedication and persistence in turning our many drafts and redrafts into the collated, corrected and organised text. We thank our Publishing Editors, Debbie Cox and Nicky Skinner, at John Wiley and Sons, and Dr. Peter Williams, Academic Director at Professional Engineering Publishing for their professional and caring help in finally bringing this work to print.

Last but really first, we recognise and honour the support of our wives, Vicky Duffey and Silvina Saull, whose patience, resourcefulness and feedback kept us both sane and motivated throughout our entire multi-year journey.

We all managed the risk; and this book happened because of all of you. Any errors that remain are due to the human element and are ours alone.

Romney B. Duffey
John W. Saull

# Definitions of Risk and Risk Management

*'... and nothing is but what is not.'*

William Shakespeare's MacBeth

The literature of the world is sprinkled with a bewildering array of terminology, usage and definitions of risk. We summarise here the relevant ones we have found or been pointed towards[1], simply noting the non-uniformity of usage and definition raises many contrasts and questions, and perhaps occasionally some incredulity.

In the *business* context by Moore, 1983 [1], as derived from the French word *risque*, 'Risk is a portmanteau word, (that) describes a scenario in which possible losses are present ... colloquially, risk is used to cover the combination of an unfavorable result and the non-zero chance of it occurring'.

From a *historical* viewpoint as stated by Bernstein, 1996 [2]: Derived from the early Italian word *risicar*, '... risk is a choice rather than a fate ...'.

In the arena of *decision theory*, as stated by Jaynes, 2003 [3]: 'the notions of risk and admissibility are evidently sampling theory criteria ... as they evoke only the sampling distributions ... the optimal strategy should be sought only in the class of admissible ones'.

In the abstract world of the highly *mathematical theory of machine learning*, expected risk is defined mathematically since 'if we have no knowledge about the test patterns ... we should minimize the expected error over all training patterns'. Theorems and rules are established for successive approximations that will assist convergence, so 'the learning problem then consists in minimizing the risk (or expected loss on the test data)' (Scholkopf and Smola, 2002) [4], meaning ensuring error minimisation in fitting the assumed mathematical functions to the known and existing data.

In *risk communication and societal perception*, according to Bechmann, 2006 [5]: 'technological and ecological dangers are perceived by some as risks and others as dangers and people behave accordingly ... Risks are events that occur without the individual's knowledge, assent or direct involvement'.

---

[1] We are indebted to David Varis, our professional acquaintance and fellow risk analyst, for contributing some complementary and interesting risk definitions from the Czech Republic, found while researching the development of the IES/ISO Risk Standard, to which he also brought our attention.

In *industrial safety*, where the issue is worker protection against injury (UK Health and Safety Executive leaflet, Five Steps to Risk Assessment, http://www.hse.gov.uk): 'Hazard means anything that can cause harm (e.g., chemicals, electricity, working from ladders, etc). Risk is the chance, high or low, that somebody will be harmed by the hazard. A risk assessment is nothing more than a careful examination of what, in your work, could cause harm to people, so that you can weigh up whether you have taken enough precautions or should do more to prevent harm. The aim is to make sure that no one gets hurt or becomes ill . . . you are legally required to assess the risks in your workplace.'

In the vast topic of *industrial health and safety*, major industries and corporations define differing categories of risk (e.g., business, workplace, and process and technical risk) where (BP, 2002) [6]: 'Risk is a function of both frequency and consequence; both are equally important'. 'Risks may be expressed either qualitatively, e.g., high/medium/low, or quantitatively, e.g., dollars or expected mortality/year'. 'Risk management decisions must consider both frequency and consequence'. The risk management process involves the 'activities of identifying hazards or threats; assessing the risk to people, property, the environment, and profits associated with those hazards or threats; evaluating risk elimination/reduction measures; (and) implementing the risk elimination/reduction measures'.

For major industrial facility risk, the *legal definition* of risk adopted in France is comprised of four components being 'the combination of hazard (probability x intensity x kinetic) and vulnerability' (Tremolieres, 2006) [7]. The intent is to link the hazard evaluation with the land, municipalities, buildings and social infrastructure near where the hazard is located, and that can possibly be harmed or affected.

For *serious or severe accidents*, risk is 'a probability of accident occurrence and its possible consequences which might occur during a certain period or under certain circumstances' (Technical University of Liberec, 2003) [8]. According to the same source, a serious accident is 'an extraordinary, partly controllable or totally beyond control event limited with regard to time and space . . . which results in immediate or subsequent serious damage or threat of people's life or health, livestock, the environment or damage to property exceeding limits given by the law'.

In the arena of *safety and risk assessment* in safety critical computer systems, N. Story, 1996 [9]: 'Risk is a combination of the frequency or probability of a specified hazardous event and its consequences'.

In *engineering safety and reliability* fields, we have risk definitions based on the concept of establishing a 'target risk' for the numerical probability of any serious event, as in the aircraft industry (International Civil Aviation Organization (ICAO), 1995) [10] which states:

In assessing the acceptability of a design, it was recognised that rational probability values would have to be established and these were set on the following basis:

a) historical evidence indicates that the risk of a serious accident due to operational and airframe-related causes is approximately one per million hours of flight . . . it is therefore required that the probability of a serious accident from all such failure conditions should not be greater than one in ten million flight hours, i.e., a probability of less than $1 \times 10^{-7}$;

b) the target risk of $1 \times 10^{-7}$ was apportioned . . . thus, the upper risk for an individual failure condition that would prevent safe flight and landing is set at $1 \times 10^{-9}$ for each flight.

This statement has been used to provide a measure for the reliability of engineered structures in an aircraft. These figures have therefore also been considered as a reasonable measure for an acceptable expectation of the probability of operational safety-critical failure conditions in airline operations.

In *environmental risk management*, Steven Milloy, 1994 [11]: 'Risk: the probability of injury, disease or death under specific circumstances'. Meanwhile, at the government level (MEM, 2005) [12], it is defined as 'a probability of occurrence of an undesirable event with undesirable consequences'.

In *health and environmental system risk assessment*, Ricci and Rowe, 1985 [13]: 'Risk to human health is a cost'; and, according to the UK Department of Health, 2000 [14]: 'Risk (is) the likelihood, high or low, that somebody or something will be harmed by a hazard, multiplied by the severity of the potential harm'.

In the hotly debated arena of *global climate change*, the UN International Panel for Climate Change (IPCC) 2001 report [15] states: 'The literature suggests that a prudent risk management strategy requires a careful consideration of the consequences (both environmental and economic), their likelihood and society's attitude toward risk. The latter is likely to vary from country to country and perhaps even from generation to generation'.

In the *social sciences*, where the study of populations and the events they are exposed to is paramount, according to Allison, 1984 [16]: 'A central concept in event history analysis is the risk set, which is the set of individuals who are at risk of event occurrence at each point in time'.

In the world of *financial portfolio* optimisation according to Cormac Butler, 1999 [17]: 'Risk measures how volatile an asset's returns are . . . (where) volatility is a measure of how much the price of an asset fluctuates'.

While correctly defining *risk as a possibility of loss, harm or failure* (MFM, 2005) [18], the Czech government ministry then also defines distinct types of *economic risk*, such as business, financial, and insolvency, where for the latter: 'there is a possibility a debtor is not able to pay off provided finances (to) a creditor in a fixed period', which is a rather nice way of characterising a bad debt.

Indeed, for actual money, *currency risk* is: 'a kind of risk that occurs when a currency is exchanged for another one. A customer is exposed to the risk but he might insure against it' [18].

So we find in the heady field of *business risk*, where decision-making reflects directly on profits and losses, market trading and investment needs have lead to a distinction where, according to Knight, 1921 [19]: 'risk is defined as the measurable uncertainty', to distinguish it from the unmeasurable uncertainty due solely to opinion. This idea later lead Holton, 2004 [20] to state the definition that: 'risk is the exposure to a proposition of which one is uncertain', thus implicitly also capturing the issue of voluntary or involuntary exposure to other human actions with uncertain results.

In the arena of *investment* in power plants, according to the International Energy Agency (IEA), 2005, [21]: 'The level of risk anticipated by an investor . . . will be reflected in the level of return expected on that investment'. The greater the business and financial risks, the higher the return that will be demanded.

In the related business of *asset management* for large capital cost facilities, as stated by David Boath, 1999 [22]: 'Risk is a measure of the probability and consequence of an occurrence leading to an unfavourable change of state . . . for asset management, we can use probabilistic risk evaluation and models to help us predict future events'.

In the business applications of *corporate risk management*, companies and their Executives and Boards implement prudent management systems to avoid incurring excessive liabilities or potential financial loss exposure. According to a typical Policy (Canadian National Railroad Company, 2003)[23], safeguarding the employees' health and safety, protecting the value of the company's assets, and limiting damage to the customers' goods are all part of the aim of the integrated management system, which is implemented 'to minimise risk and optimise loss control'.

In the business of *tourism*, the objective is on providing a safe vacation experience at reasonable cost, while not causing any undue personal or environmental harm and still making money. The emphasis is on establishing the right risk management process for optimising the purchasing and other decisions about insurance, contracts, waivers and limiting liabilities. Here, according to the Canadian Tourism Association, (Fitzgerald, 2003) [24]: 'Risk management is a strategic process that will protect the assets and ensure the financial stability of an organisation from the consequences of competitive business decisions'. 'Risk management will reduce uncertainty and the potential for accidental or unanticipated loss and will provide the basis for maximizing opportunity'. Minimising the potential fiscal and legal liability of tour operators and tourist destinations is the key here. As the notice posted at the main gate to a major private game reserve filled with photogenic wild animals in South Africa says: 'Visitors enter at their own risk'. A tourist can approach and peer over the churning and seething edge of the majestic Victoria Falls in Zambia, when having signed a waiver that: 'I am aware of all dangers and risks . . . I participate in this activity entirely at my own risk . . . I waive any and all claims . . . arising out of any harm, injury or loss suffered . . . whether arising from an act of commission or omission and/or negligence on the part of the organizers'. Taking such risks are fun, good business and relatively dangerous to do.

In the very different world of *governments that deal with people, immigration and refugees*, prior to removal from the country (a euphemism for extradition, forced repatriation, expulsion or refusal of entry) in Canada there is a Pre-Removal Risk Assessment Process. Anyone who alleges there is a risk of persecution, torture, cruel or unusual punishment, or even to their life, will not be removed until the actual risk is formally determined. These conditions, under the so-called diplomatic 'non-refoulement' principle, are given in the Citizenship and Immigration Canada Manual PP 3 (available at http://www.cic.gc.ca/english/resources/mauals/pp). Unfortunately, there is also a risk that such processes can be bypassed. In the well-known Maher Arar case, a Canadian citizen suspected of terrorism was forcibly deported from and by the USA to another country and subsequently tortured, apparently with the prior knowledge and at least silent assent of the Canadian authorities.

For *military defence*, planning for attacks means: 'a certain probability that the event occurs'. 'Risk is always derivable and derived from a specific threat. Rate of risk, or probability of harmful consequences . . . might be assessed according to a risk analysis (Ministry of Interior, 2004) [25] which follows from assessment of our readiness to face threats.'

For evaluating and determining the risk of *terrorist attack*, several levels of threat have even been defined by the US Department of Homeland Security (http://www.dhs.gov), and risk management approached by separately distinguishing between operational risk and strategic risk. Differing relative 'threat levels' based on risk being from 'low' to 'severe' have been defined, which are nationally published and updated in a formal Advisory System. The idea is to advise and protect people and important facilities by alerting them to the probability of random or planned attacks that might cause danger, physical harm and significant disruption.

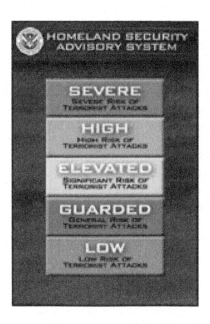

In the important *medical arena*, where human health is of concern, major risk factors are those that research has shown significantly increase the risk of disease and/or death. Thus, the US Centers for Disease Control (CDC) have a Behavioral Risk Factor Surveillance System (BRFSS) available at http://www2.cdc.gov/nccdphp/brfss2/training_ov/default.htm that states: 'High risk health behaviors include: having hypertension or diabetes and not taking medication to control it, not getting enough exercise, eating a poor diet, drinking too much alcohol, having sex with multiple partners and not using condoms'. The American Cancer Society, as one example, defines a risk factor as anything that increases your chance of getting a disease such as cancer. Some risk factors are hereditary and unchangeable, some are environmental in origin, and some due to lifestyle. An attempt to establish uniformity was published by the Canadian Patient Safety Institute in the 'Canadian Patient Safety Dictionary', in October 2003, where it was recommended that: '**risk** be defined as the probability of danger, loss or injury within the health-care system'.

In the *prescription, sale and use of drugs and pills*, there are the risks of possible side effects, with potential for interactions with other ailments and medications, and other factors like patient age, sex and risk perception play a role in the drug effectiveness. According to a recent newspaper report:

> ... *risk is the chance that a patient will suffer from disease or injury over a certain period of time ... risk can be defined in a variety of ways, from odds ratio to ... relative and absolute risk. ... Patients are confused by the numbers surrounding risk.*
>
> Source: *Ottawa Citizen, 19 February 2005, p. B3*

In the *transport sector*, which is concerned over minimising the possibilities of injuries to their passengers as well as to their own staff, we also find explicit warnings about possible physical harm or exposure. In the railways, to help meet rather vague legal requirements: 'it can be helpful to categorise risks as unacceptable, tolerable or broadly acceptable, where . . . an unacceptable level of risk must be ruled out or reduced to make it at least tolerable, except in exceptional circumstances . . . a tolerable level of risk is in-between the unacceptable and acceptable regions and the risk must be reduced . . .; and a broadly acceptable level of risk implies a level of risk that is generally regarded as insignificant, therefore little proactive effort is required to identify measures that reduce the level of risk' (quoted from 'Internal guidance and general principles for assessing whether health and safety risks on Britain's railways have been reduced So Far As Is Reasonably Practicable (SFAIRP)', UK ORR, Doc # 290942.02, available at http://www.rail-reg.gov.uk). For passengers, airlines have standard safety briefings and information cards on evacuation routes for every flight and for every plane. On the London Underground trains known as the Tube, another clear example is the red-lettered sign posted at eye level on the emergency doors that link between carriages: '*Danger: Risk of death if used when train is moving*'.

Finally, of course, in the age-old *risqué world of anonymous limericks*:

> *There was a young man from Bengal,*
> *Who went to a fancy dress ball.*
> *He thought he would risk it*
> *And went as a biscuit,*
> *But the dog ate him up in the hall.*

So the loose and even colloquial use of the term 'risk' has different meanings to both people and specialists, and varies all the way from specific numbers to qualitative feelings that cover the whole spectrum of human activities and interests, and what is an acceptable risk and what is not. This confusing and dizzying array of terminology and usage is the result of specialisation of application in different fields, not generalisation of the basic methods and problems themselves. These have barely changed, and the use of additional decision tools, subjective risk measures and appeals to information theory are merely embellishments to cover up our remaining ignorance about the future.

## References

[1] Moore, P.G., 1983, 'The Business of Risk', Cambridge University Press, p. 152.
[2] Bernstein, P.L., 1996, 'Against the Gods', John Wiley and Sons, New York, p. 8.
[3] Jaynes, E.T., 2003, 'Probability Theory: The Logic of Science', First Edition, Cambridge University Press, Cambridge, UK, Edited by G.L. Bretthorst.
[4] Scholkopf B. and Smola, A.J., 2002, 'Learning with Kernels: Support vector machines, regularization, optimization and beyond', MIT Press, Cambridge, MA, USA, p. 127.
[5] Bechmann, G., 2006, 'The uncertainties in risk communication in knowledge societies', Proc. ESREL 2006 on Safety and Reliability for Managing Risk, Editors, Soares and Gio, Taylor and Francis, London, p. 1253.
[6] BP, 2002, 'Getting HSE Right: a Guide for BP Managers' (Available: www.bp.com).
[7] Tremolieres, A., Merad, M., Rodrigues, N., Propeck-Zimmermann, E. and Saint-Gerand, T., 'Stakes and Vulnerabilities Assessment in Industrial Risk: French Context and Perspectives Offered by Territorial Approach', Proc. ESREL, 2006, Estoril, Taylor and Francis, London, pp. 2041–2046.

[8] Technical University of Liberec, 2003, 'Safety methodology in petrochemical industry', Application Guide, Czech Republic.

[9] Story, N., 1996, 'Safety Critical Computer Systems', Addison-Wesley, p. 60.

[10] International Civil Aviation Organization (ICAO), 1995, 'Continuing Airworthiness Manual', Doc. 9642-AN/941.

[11] Milloy, S., 1994, 'Choices in Risk Assessment, The Role of Science Policy in the Environmental Risk Management Process', National Environmental Policy Institute, Regulatory Impact Analysis Project, Inc., Washington, DC.

[12] Ministry of Environmental Matters, 2005, 'Dictionary of the Ministry of Environmental Matters of the Czech Republic', Prague.

[13] Ricci, P.F. and Rowe, M.D., 1985, 'Health and Environmental Risk Assessment', Pergamon Press.

[14] UK Department of Health, 'An Organisation with a Memory', 2000, Report of National Health Service Expert Group on Learning from Adverse Events, London.

[15] UN International Panel for Climate Change (IPCC), 2001, 'Climate Change 2001: Mitigation – Summary for Policymakers', WMO/UNEP, Available: www.grida.no/climate/ipcc

[16] Allison, P.D., 1984, 'Event History Analysis', USA: Sage Publications, p. 32.

[17] Butler, C., 1999, 'Mastering Value at Risk', Financial Times/Pitman, pp. 2, 6.

[18] Ministry of Financial Matters, 2005, 'Dictionary of Financial Matters of the Czech Republic', Prague.

[19] Knight, F.H., 1921, 'Risk Uncertainty and Profit', Hart, Schaffner & Marx; Houghton Mifflin Company, Boston, MA.

[20] Holton, Glyn. A., 2004, 'Defining Risk', Financial Analysts Journal, Vol. 60, No. 6, pp. 21–25, CFA Institute.

[21] International Energy Agency (IEA), 2005, 'Projected Costs of Generating Electricity', 2005 Update, NEA-OECD, Paris, France, p. 178.

[22] Boath, D., 1999, 'Risk Management Techniques to Support the Asset', Proceedings, 6th International Conference on Probabilistic Safety Assessments in the Nuclear Industry, London, UK, 18–19 May.

[23] Canadian National Railroad Company, 2003, 'Risk Management Policy', (Available: http://www.cn.ca, dated February 2003).

[24] Fitzgerald, P., 2003, 'Risk Management Guide for Tourism Operators', Canadian Tourism Commission, Ottawa.

[25] Ministry of Interior, 2004, 'Terminological Dictionary for Crisis Management and Planning of Defence of the Country', Czech Republic, Prague.

# Introduction: The Art of Prediction and the Creation of Order

*'The uncertainty is killing me.'*

*– Donaldson-Khahn, 'Love me or Leave me'*

## Risk and Risk Management

Risk is caused and measured by our uncertainty, and the measure of uncertainty is probability.

We live in a world full of risks, outcomes and opportunities. As we try to avoid the things that might kill or harm us, we follow the survival of the fittest. If we take a risk, a chance, we hope the outcome will be favourable, whatever it may be. We might trust luck, but there is always a chance, a probability that something nasty, something hurtful might happen, and we might be harmed physically, mentally or financially. Not just by our own actions, but harm from an unexpected failure of any of the technological systems on which we rely. Simply as the result of human decisions, we are just plain uncertain as to how things that happen will play out or if they will even occur.

Risk surrounds us. We also want and need to make a living, so we have a job and carry on our work. Hopefully we are safe doing that job, but there is always a chance we may suffer an injury, perhaps through no apparent fault of our own. Even in our personal lives, there are choices and chances, some with a life-changing risk from a gamble to be taken, or when facing more than one possible or probable outcome. When we choose where to live, we accept the dangers of earthquakes, floods, fires and mudslides as covered by the building codes and standards that apply, and take a chance that we do not have one. Whether we change jobs, take a new responsibility, drive to work, cross a street, stay on a beachfront or travel somewhere, we take both conscious and unconscious risks. We want to make enough money to be comfortable, so we earn money that we can also invest and gamble. Hopefully, these investments will make a profit, and we will not squander our wealth. But a chance exists of a loss, not a gain, and of an expensive, even painful lesson.

How can we reduce the risk?
Should we avoid the risk?
Do we want the risk?
Can we measure the risk?
Can we manage the risk?
Is there an acceptable risk?

Simple questions: difficult answers.

Throughout the centuries, mathematicians, soothsayers, sociologists, psychologists, gamblers, bankers, insurers, and more importantly, ourselves, have all tackled basically the same questions. Using the tools of statistics and of data analysis, we try to use the past history of events to make an informed guess about the future. In that way, and only in that way, can we examine, quantify and predict the risk of what *might* happen. Not what *will* happen, but the 'chance' or the 'probability' of something happening, whether it is good or bad. Failures occur in our technological and societal systems because we humans have a unique and huge role in creating and using them all around us, which then puts us all at some probable or improbable risk.

So simply put, all we have to do is determine the chance or risk of outcomes occurring in the future based on what we have already observed about the probability of occurrence up till now. This apparently simple task turns out to be quite difficult, so this Introduction lays out the ideas and methodology that we believe are needed to succeed.

The societal implications of risk management are immense. As Professor Theo Theofanous states clearly: 'risk assessment is already becoming a dominant force in technology and environment, and through them in economics, politics, and everyday life – indeed, as some issues are of global significance, we can visualise a potential impact on our civilisation as a whole' Theofanous, 1996 [1]. This is not an understatement, but an emerging reality.

We all wish to be able to *predict* both our personal risk and the risk of an entire technological system failing; and in so doing to be able to manage that risk and hopefully avoid it. Assuming only that we learn, and without trying to understand all the inner workings of the human psyche, we want to provide a basis for predicting what will or might happen next.

## Defining Risk

To achieve what we are proposing to manage risk, we need to stray into and explore the fields of risk analysis, risk management, risk valuation and risk prediction. In our book [2], where we were interested in the way humans behave, we gave and used the ordinary and accepted dictionary definitions of risk:

*The possibility or likelihood of danger, injury, loss etc. (Universal English Dictionary)*

*The chance of injury, damage or loss. (Webster)*

We paraphrased the definition as: *'the chance of an error causing you harm, where chance is an undesigned or fortuitous occurrence or cause'*.

To define the chance or possibility of a fortuitous occurrence, or of something unexpected happening, we turn to the classic works. Long ago, Pierre-Simon Laplace in 1814 (See Plate 1) defined probability in his 'Essai philosophique sur les probabilites', which is translated in J.R. Newman's superb compendium of historical mathematical advances [3]:

*The theory of chance . . . consists in determining the number of cases favorable to the event whose probability is sought. The ratio of this number to that of all cases possible is the measure of this probability . . .*

We can and will use this definition of probability *as a measure of the risk* of an outcome. The larger the number of cases, or the larger the number ratio, the more probable or the greater is the risk. For our purposes here, an outcome is any type of adverse happening or undesirable event.

Since it is evident that we do learn from our mistakes, we have already shown the existence of a universal learning curve (ULC) that enables all of us to determine what *rate* outcomes occur in a system as we learn from experience [2]. But such outcomes and events still occur randomly and unpredictably. As one World Cup show jumper reportedly said after a poorer–than-expected performance in the competition: *'If I jumped that same jump one hundred times, I would jump it clean with that horse 99.9% of the time. Sometimes you just get a little unlucky. It is only by competing at this level that you learn these things'.* That percentage is an unexpected error or outcome only once in a thousand jumps, or every nine hundred and ninety-nine successful jumps, being the non-outcomes. The risk probability, or LaPlace's number ratio, based on this prior experience is simply 1/1000, if no more jumps are ever attempted. But what about the performance success in future competitions when making and experiencing even more jumps? Should the risk of failure be the same, or less, or worse?

Simply put, *the Learning Hypothesis is based on the well-known proposition that humans learn from their mistakes.* Therefore, we descend a learning curve as our experience increases and if we are learning. The result is a reduction in accidents, mistakes, errors and events, assuming feedback from learning occurs. That results in a neat and useful way to inter-compare data, and to include the common basis of all outcomes – the human involvement. Rather amazingly, this learning idea turns out to be exactly the physical and mathematical realisation of the concept of the 'Theory of Error Correction' adopted by Ohlsson, 1996 [4] in the psychological literature to explain how knowledge and practice improve individual human performance.

In our book 'Know the Risk', 2002 [2], we examined the influence of human involvement in technological and organisational systems, and how this produced and reduced the risk and outcome trends. We found a universal commonality of the contribution of the human element, which was integral with and inseparable from the entire system. No matter where, whether in design, regulation, construction, operation, maintenance, management, training or repair, the risk was never zero. The observed trend was always of decreasing outcome rates with increasing accumulated experience if, and only if, learning was occurring (as shown in Figure 1 using logarithmic scales).

We reduce our errors exponentially (progressively more slowly) when learning to a finite minimum depending on our accumulated and depth of experience, however that is usefully defined for the system we are in. We can then make predictions about the probability or risk

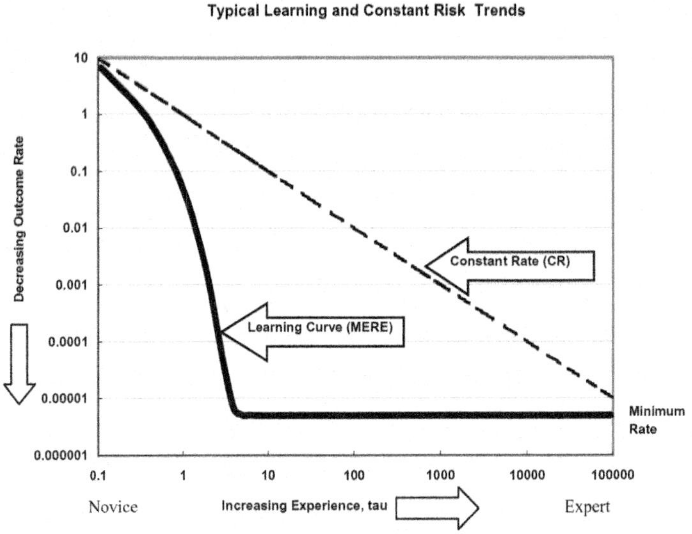

**Typical Learning and Constant Risk Trends**

**Figure 1.** The Universal Learning Curve: data on outcome rates follow the solid learning curve line (MERE), reducing with experience compared to the constant rate (CR) dotted line that occurs without learning as we move from being a novice to becoming an expert

of future accidents or error rates based on the statistical fit of the theory to the data we happen to already have, and our projection of the future experience.

## Managing Risk: Our Purpose, Plan and Goals

The purpose of our book here is to build on that prior knowledge of learning to provide a means to *predict* the chance of when and how many outcomes (defined as events, accidents and errors) will occur, or with what probability. To provide that approach, we cross-utilise the tools of engineering reliability, probability theory, information theory and statistical physics analysis to determine the likelihood and distribution of outcomes with our changing experience, including the very special one-of-a-kind or rare events. This method then determines the risk of an outcome.

*Risk Management is a human activity aimed at defining and predicting limits, procedures or bounds on the **probability** of future injury, loss or damage based on our knowledge of the related outcomes of previous human activities.*

The Risk Management activity can be active or passive, explicit or implicit, personal or collective, a business or a science. It is not only the way we behave, *it is the way we actually proceed.*

Risk and risk management occurs in almost any human, technological, business, management, legal, fiscal, investment, political, medical, contractual and social activity. It has been defined in many different ways for many different circumstances. For completeness and the purposes of showing the sheer breadth and importance of risk, we list and summarise the definitions used in a myriad of applications and their working usages in the Addendum[1].

---

[1] See page xxi.

As far back as Greek civilisation, several thousand of years ago, the role of chance in life and its outcomes was explicitly recognised in their sophisticated and elaborate mythology. The probability of future fame and fortune, and of life and death itself, lay in the hands of the three Fates who determined the outcomes for all human life. There was Clotho forever spinning and creating the thread of Life; Lachesis casting the lots that determine human's destiny in the woven fabric of Life; and blind Atropos whose sharp shears then cut the thread to end that Life.

We, however, wish to reduce the uncertainty, to be more accurate in predicting both occurrence and consequences. We would like to make more confident predictions in order to provide well-defined margins of safety, more precise defense in depth, better financial planning, tighter operational procedures and more effective management controls. These tasks are not easy, particularly with human involvement. If we used purely mechanical devices, we would have purely mechanical failure modes following some physical laws, but not when we are subject to the vagaries and involvement of the human element. Unfortunately, being a technological society, humans are always involved somehow, somewhere, and in some way, so outcomes *always* involve the human element. How hard it is to predict human thinking and responses, let alone its interaction with technology, is well known. The understanding of human behaviour, unraveling its mysteries, is the work of centuries of Psychiatry, Psychology and Psychoanalysis.

The problem we all face was well stated nearly 250 years ago, when Richard Price transmitted the famous posthumous work of Thomas Bayes, 1763 (See Plate 1) [5], '*An Essay towards solving a Problem in the Doctrine of Chances*' to the Royal Society. Bayes wrote with the intent:

> *To find out a method by which we might judge concerning the probability that an event has to happen, in given circumstance, upon supposition that we know nothing concerning it but that, under the same circumstances, it has happened a certain number of times, and failed a certain other number of times.*

In that essay, Bayes developed this key concept that the probability of one event or outcome being observed was coupled to and conditional on the probability of the ones before. In this book, to help make such predictions about what might happen and when, we develop the concept by looking at those technologies and activities where, by our thoughts, actions and mistakes, we have some control of our fate: and by exercising that control, some ability to manage our risk. We examine the possibility of observing future outcomes and non-outcomes using our knowledge of previous 'happenings'. We also examine the situations where we have limited experience on how we might manage even a seemingly unknown risk; or where we have never seen a risk before and there is 'missing information'. Then we are even trying to predict the probability of the seemingly unpredictable.

A successful or an unsuccessful outcome is certain since one or the other must happen. Now the probability of success, $p$(Success), is simply the converse or opposite of the probability of failure, $p$(Failure), so if we know one we will know the other. Since we have made mistakes before, perhaps we should have learned from the failures as well as from the successes. Instead of just relying on Fate, in this book, we analyse what we know about our prior knowledge and what outcomes have or have not occurred before. Using the concept of experience space, in this book we show how we not only accumulate experience as we observe similar outcomes and events, but also that we exhibit varying depths of experience that determine the distribution of outcomes. This enables us to estimate future rates and the distribution of outcomes as to how they vary with our increasing experience.

From that basis, we show that the inherent and apparent disorder can actually be used to provide guidance, to introduce both learning and new habits. We will define the '*H*-factor', a single unambiguous measure of the effectiveness of our much sought after 'learning environment' or 'safety culture', based solely on the outcomes we observe and manage.

## Recent Tragic Outcomes

Recently, the crash of the NASA Space Shuttle *Columbia* and the great blackout of the North East USA and Canada occurred, as well as the giant Asian tsunami and the New Orleans flooding by Hurricane Katrina. Other smaller but also key accidents have occurred: the midair collision over Europe of two aircraft carrying the latest collision avoidance systems; the glider landing of a jet aircraft out of fuel in the Azores; a concrete highway overpass collapsing in Laval, Quebec; (See Plate 2) the fatal oil refinery explosion in Texas; and the huge oil tank fire in England; more ships sinking, more trains derailing, even more cars colliding and evermore medical errors.

We have already examined the worldwide trends for outcomes (measured as accidents, errors and events) using data available for large complex technological systems with human involvement [2]. That analysis was a dissection of the basic available, published data on real and measured risks, for trends and inter-comparisons of outcome rates. We found and showed how all the data agreed with the learning theory when the accumulated experience is accounted for. Here, learning includes both positive and negative feedback, directly or indirectly, as a result of prior outcomes or experience gained, in both the organisational and individual contexts.

Any resulting inability to actually track progress as a function of experience down the learning curve means it is not possible to correctly rank the relative importance of error *rate* and cause *rate* reduction.

As we, and more importantly, the data show, the residual limit of the existence of a finite number of irremovable errors and the ultimate certainty of an outcome may not be particularly likeable, but are: (a) actually realistic and in accord with theory; (b) reflected in *all* the available data; (c) actually and perversely aid the workings of skill acquisition and of the human psyche; and (d) enable measurement of progress in the real world. Setting impossible goals and trying to meet them potentially diverts precious resources from realisable achievements, synonymous with investing for a poor return. *Paradoxically, only by expecting to fail, by making and admitting mistakes, and by learning from them can we actually improve!*

## Power Blackouts, Space ShuttleLosses, Concorde Crashes, Chernobyl, Three Mile Island, and More . . .

We have all seen the headlines, heard the media reports or even read the published government reports of the known accidents, deaths and injuries. The names of some of these events are so famous that we need little more as a descriptor to provoke our thoughts and fears.

Just their utterance conjures up an instant memory, an image or a preconditioned emotional response:

- For Chernobyl and Three Mile Island, of reactors out of control or burning, releasing unknown and threatening radiation.
- For *Columbia*, and for *Challenger*, of the space shuttles spectacularly exploding or disintegrating, causing the deaths of brave crews.
- For *Concorde*, this beautiful streamlined shape falling from the sky in flames.

For the more mundane aspects of daily life, we have power blackouts and power failures, where we and millions of others were faced with sudden loss of our ability to do anything but light candles and walk home or wait in the dark. We have explosions in oil refineries and storage facilities, gas pipelines and chemical plants that kill, maim and destroy. Some major accidents lead to evacuation of thousands of people from their homes due to the dangers from uncontained gas clouds and chemical spills and leaks.

These outcomes are all major disasters. In each case, we understood the causal factors *afterwards*: society and inquiries pointed the fingers of derision and blame, but neglected and forget the underlying reasons. They were all avoidable, if only we had been smart enough to see the warning signs, better manage the situation, and to predict and reduce the risk. These accidents involved our most advanced technologies. Yet they were all preventable: only *after the fact*, when we knew or found out what had happened. A combination of circumstances occurs, unique but unforeseen, combined with very human misunderstandings, mistakes and misperceptions that lead to the observed outcome. Because of the multiple contributing factors, components and causes, in the industrial safety literature these outcomes have already been labeled as 'complex' failures or accidents (H.C. Howlett II, 1995) [6]. The observation of multiple causation is not new: in fact, trying to learn from, understand and eliminate the myriad of detailed minor problems that lead to past outcomes or the *prior* events is at the heart of many of today's safety and management programs.

We hope that we have learned something from the outcome, often in the mistaken belief that it 'cannot happen again'. And if we are thorough or prudent, then it will not, but only if we totally remove whatever it was from misoperating again in the same way, by making a local change so that particular outcome cannot physically happen, or changing out the management and the procedures. We must remove the human element, which is impossible.

So another similar outcome, an event or error, will occur sometime, somewhere, in a random but at the same time a systematic way. Mistakes *will* be made. It will happen because humans and other circumstances will conspire and combine in another unforeseen way to make it happen; with different consequences, in a different place, and at a different time. We observe the frequency of such outcomes, but we really need to estimate their probability of occurrence.

The analysis presented here is designed to definitively make a prediction.

In the past, to estimate risk, the standard statistical approach would be to take the past outcomes as defining the prior information, and average the number or rates over some time interval. So we have a time series, where the observation interval is usually a calendar year or some subset. The number of outcomes in the interval gives some measure of the rate and trend, in, say, traffic fatalities per year, injuries per employee or working hour, stock price change per day, shipping losses per year, train derailments per year, stock market price trends and variability, etc. Plotting these data often allows a trend line to be fitted as a basis for a projection of the future rate, with some uncertainty bounds based on the goodness of fit. However, we attack the prior data and the prediction of risk quite differently.

In this book, we take the statistical variations into account naturally, by explicitly allowing for the random nature of what we observe. In that way, we can also make predictions of the future chance, meaning the *likelihood* of the most and least risk, including what we have learned from both past outcomes and non-outcomes.

## How Events and Disasters Evolve in a Phased Development: The Human Element

We argue that these outcomes (and hence most others) show, demonstrate and contain the same causal factors of human failures and failings, and as a result, the same general and logical development path everywhere. Our experience is flawed, our learning inadequate. Specifically, the observed outcome can be conveniently grouped in Phases which are intertwined and overlapping and contain the common feature of the Human Element:

*Phase (1)* of the early unfolding precursors which were known to happen but unrecognised as to their significance by the humans who built, use, insure and operate the system.

*Phase (2)* where the confluence occurred of developing failures and events where, despite the humans nominally being in control, they actually had no choice but to make decisions based on inadequate data, commercial or fiscal management pressures, and rely on software or instruments that did not provide up-to-date or believable control information for the actual circumstances that existed.

*Phase (3)* results when the escalation occurs during the repeated and continuing emphasis and attempts to ensure that everything remains more or less understood, when it is not and/or far from normal. Suffering from 'pressonitis', we continue on rather than isolating the failed parts of the system, and addressing those first, thus further compounding the situation.

*Phase (4)* finally denial is evident from the humans involved, where they do not realise their full responsibility and contribution, and how it happened. Also management and society believes that actions taken or not, could have saved the day (thus saving the investment), and others are to blame for whatever happened, while in fact *all* were and are an integral part of the shared problem.

We can show by examining these recurring themes and phases for well-known and documented outcomes that they all share the underlying common feature of the *human element*. Embedded in the phases and the mass of detail are the layer upon layer of human actions and inactions, personal understanding and misunderstanding, system errors and mistakes, operational decision and denial, management responsibility and irresponsibility, and corporate strategy and folly.

Tragically, in hindsight, the large tsunami in the Indian Ocean that flooded Asia in December 2004, and also the flooding of the city of New Orleans due to Hurricane Katrina the next year in August 2005, had exactly the same phases. Both terrible tragedies and a monumental disaster for humans, much death and destruction occurred that was still avoidable and preventable. The loss of life and property in a day was huge (perhaps above 300,000 lost lives in the tsunami or 300,000 destroyed homes in the hurricane), but at most still just comparable to the numbers killed in industrial accidents worldwide each and every year (also above 300,000 according to the UN International Labor Organization). We can explain why there is a correspondence: the outcomes are the loss of lives and the destruction of property, in which just as for any other outcome, humans were involved. These natural disasters show inadequate risk preparation, planning and safety measures.

In such ways, human errors and reliability are tightly coupled to and embedded within all technological, organisational and social systems, as we live on the planet and try to harness Nature. Although different specific outcomes, there is no difference physically, psychologically and mathematically. We cannot prescribe all the workings of the human mind, or describe its coupled interaction with a complex technological system. So, we must and do use a general *emergent theory*, where the failure rate is invisible inside the entire human technological system until we observe the errors as outcomes, and then try to correct them by learning. The basic and sole assumption that we make is the 'learning hypothesis' as a physical model for human behaviour when coupled to any system. Simply and directly, we postulate that humans learn from their mistakes (outcomes) as experience is gained. So, the rate of reduction of the outcome rate (observed in the technology or activity as the number of accidents, errors and events) is proportional to the rate of outcomes that are occurring.

Due to the Human Element, despite our best efforts, *we will always still have some outcomes*, and we will still improve further and reduce the future rate by learning from them. This is the principle at the heart of the ULC (Figure 1).

We are seemingly doomed to rediscover event-by-event, case-by-case, inquiry-by-inquiry, accident-by-accident, error-by-error, tragedy-by-human-tragedy, disaster-by-disaster, the same litany of causative factors, the same mistakes, same errors. Perhaps they are not in the same order, or importance, or the same type, but essentially the same, nevertheless.

In fact, Professor Henry Petroski, 1985 [7] has argued forcefully in his extensive writings that we *must* have such errors and mistakes in order to improve. This view is in total accord with the Learning Hypothesis. In essence, the only way forward is to rectify past blemishes and learn from the outcomes, as he clearly states:

> *I believe that the concept of failure – mechanical and structural failure – is central to understanding engineering, for engineering design has as its first and foremost objective the obviation of failure.*
>
> *Thus the colossal disasters that do occur are ultimately failures of design, but the lessons learned . . . can do more to advance engineering knowledge than all the successful machines and structures in the world.*
>
> *Indeed, failures appear to be inevitable in the wake of prolonged success, which encourages lower margins of safety. Failures in turn lead to greater safety margins, and hence new periods of success.*
>
> *To understand what engineering is and what engineers do is to understand how failures can happen and how they can contribute more than successes to advance technology.*
>
> Source: *Professor Henry Petroski, by permission*

In the far removed but apparently related field of medical research where learning is critical, although differently worded, we find exactly the same principle being taught by Judah Folkman, 2001 [8]:

*One of the fundamental lessons . . . passed to young people . . . was that success could often arrive dressed as failure. Success is great . . . but doing experiments that invariably bring the expected results may mean the questions aren't tough enough. To fail, then struggle to understand why, may offer more insights and greater learning.*

Even in politics and war, the same principles apply since according to former US General and Secretary of State Colin Powell:

*There are no secrets to success. It is the result of preparation, hard work, and learning from failure.*

Success is the opposite of failure. In this sense, these inevitable human failures are an essential part of ultimate human success. So our new work brings a basic framework enabling both quantification and prediction to these philosophies, life experiences and insightful observations.


## Our Values at Risk: The Probable Improvement

The quantification of risk provides the challenge, given and including the inherently subjective nature of risk perception by humans. We often seem to take our risk decisions subjectively, based on our feelings, not objectively, using just the facts.

Economists since the days of Bernoulli have assigned the *utility* (the real or perceived value to the individual) of something happening as a measure of whether and how the human will make a specific choice. The utility can be variously defined and situation dependent: such as return on stock, increase in capital asset value, reduced risk exposure, the value of money or an added consumer choice. The theories of human risk-taking behaviour (be it in an impersonal business or a personal choice, or for an investment bought or choosing a marriage partner) try to ascribe some measure of the utility. This highly subjective response may displace or completely overthrow rational decision making based on the prior knowledge and data.

There are whole studies, methods and books on relative risk, comparative risk, voluntary risk and even acceptable risk, which rank the chance of death and injury by both natural and unnatural causes. But we humans do not carry a subconscious ranking or listing of hazards in our heads, or make totally rational choices based on our chance of death, of success or failure, of a good or a bad investment, of buying a bargain or not. We know some things are more dangerous than others, either instinctively or from experience. We make our final and personal risk choices subjectively whatever the objective evidence.

In fact, there is *no natural* absolute measure of risk, in all its myriad forms, and the comparative risks can be quantified only in statistical and numerical terms of the chance of death, the probability of having an accident, or of making a fortune. But we behave and react and make our choices as subjective human animals, *not* as calculating machines that numerically calculate risk versus benefit, relative good or bad outcome ratios, or probability times consequence that many suggest using as risk measures, we make judgements, both consciously and unconsciously. The correct physical and psychological measure of risk is the uncertainty, or as some have said: 'What we do not know about what we do now know'.

In reality, we accept some risks (going to the doctor), and avoid others (like 'bad' neighbourhoods). We take risk in our choices (crossing the road) and hope for the best (buy a lottery ticket). We make decisions (brake the car now) and make mistakes (drive through a stop sign). We invest (in houses or stocks) and sell or lose them at a profit or a loss. How is this myriad of complexity in the human aspect to be dealt with in an inclusive and comprehensive way?

There is a conflict: between the use of statistics, with all their power and technique to quantify probability in the presence of uncertainty and human choice; and the adoption of strategies, techniques and hypotheses to deal with the results of our only being able to sample reality. Nowhere is the unknown effect of the human involvement properly accounted for, since statistical methods alone must focus on the known and the prior data.

The whole field of statistics is a mature and complex field. Based on the outcomes we sample and observe and the distributions they exhibit, we make estimates of their probability of occurrence. Here, we must move from providing purely numerical estimates of the occurrence probability of past events, to the murkier topic of making risk predictions for a future including the human element.

Since the errors inherent in human activities are known and our specialty, and forecasting them in the future is our objective, we are particularly interested in how the influence of experience on and in past failures and outcomes is handled for making *future* risk predictions.

## Probably or Improbably Not

Since the future is always unknown, we still have the odds, probabilities and uncertainties on our future estimates based on our past sample. Whether we use a method to minimise, insure, reduce, gamble or measure future risks, and what limits are taken on the uncertainties, are then our personal, professional, business, legal and societal choices. We are *managing* the risk.

Any risk assessment, despite our best efforts to be complete and comprehensive, is flawed by the uncertainty in the sample or the lack of past and future data, and the impossibility of making accurate predictions. As the UK Health and Safety Executive, or the 'British Nanny' as it is colloquially called, says in its guide: '*A risk assessment is nothing more than a careful examination of what, in your work, could cause harm to people, so that you can weigh up whether you have taken enough precautions or should do more to prevent harm*'.

The definition of the word 'probability' must also be considered. The world of statistics is full of arguments, pedantics, methods and approaches to estimate the future chance, odds and probabilities based on some prior knowledge or previously observed distribution of outcomes. There are extensive discussions, and sometimes quite personal disputes, in the field of statistics about the relationship and distinction between the *frequency* of an outcome, being the number of times something was observed or appears, and the *probability* of occurrence, being the fractional chance of an outcome in the future based on the total number that might have already occurred (see, for example, Jaynes [9]).

Because we are dealing with predicting the future, this discussion cannot be without some controversy and uncertainty itself, and indeed the technical and philosophical debate is still ongoing. One view of probabilities is that they are *objective* and derived from prior data (often held by the so-called Frequentists) and from calculation, and as such obey the rules of statistical analysis that determine the numerical uncertainty of any outcome. Therefore, we need to consider and determine only the possible uncertainty in the representative nature and significance of the past data sampling that are subject to rigorously derived, known or postulated frequency distributions.

The other view of probabilities is that they are *subjective* and derived from prior information (often held by the so-called Bayesians) and from judgement, and as such obey the rules of logical analysis that determine the likelihood and conditional possibility of any outcome. Therefore, we need to consider and determine only the possible uncertainty in the nature of the different beliefs and logical inferences about the past and about the future that are subject to rigorously derived, known or postulated probability distributions.

These two views of the past and of the future, which we shall see later are actually complementary, really collide head-on in the fields of human error, system failures, decision making, outcome prediction and financial portfolio management. If we measure and report the statistics of outcomes like deaths, profits, diseases and accidents, we know about the possible past or observed likelihood of occurrence. We can then try to postulate and determine the likely probable trend or future possibility of similar happenings, by combining what we think we know has already happened with what we think might possibly occur next. We can then predict risk so that we can manage risk.

We usually may know what has actually happened up till now (the past, the prior, the history) and how we observe and interpret that knowledge; but we really need to understand and hopefully predict what might possibly happen next (the likely, the posterior, the future) and how we might act or decide. But there is still uncertainty in doing that. Fortunately for us, we may and do use all these valuable ideas and viewpoints to our advantage as we proceed to understand how we humans are interacting with technology and managing risks, both now and in the future, without our having to take sides.

## How This Book Is Organised

Our reading plan and text development is relatively simple. We approach risk management in a rigorous theoretically based manner that is systematically tested against data. The approach we take here treats technological risk, financial risk prediction and management risk as one related subject, which we believe to be a new idea. The approach is a logical extension of the learning hypothesis and of our prior results.

Before examining four key examples, we give a recap and introduction on the ULC, to explain how it can be used to analyse real data, and extended to show how it implies human reliability (Chapter 1).

To emphasise this (unpredictable and major) human element of risk, we then review the Four Echoes in some more detail (Chapter 2). They are very powerful and highly visible examples of major failures and outcomes in modern technological society.

To give some idea of how these ideas can be applied, we examine the range of risks associated with missile defense effectiveness and the prediction of the probability of rocket losses and industrial accidents (Chapter 3). This interesting diversion gives a hint of how widely the concepts of risk and the new methods we develop can be applied.

Since the role of the human dominates the outcomes, the development turns naturally to the next discussion on the quantification of human error and reliability (Chapter 4) as an integral element of an entire technological system. The analysis and approach parallels equipment reliability, but includes the effects of learning so the natural human and dynamic aspects are allowed for.

We then show how statistical ideas can help with predicting the random nature of observed outcomes (Chapter 5). The distributions derived from the average behaviour are consistent with and reconcile the systematic effect of learning with the unpredictability of our observations of actual outcomes. The concepts of depth of experience and information entropy arise quite naturally from this discussion. In principle, this also allows for the elimination of error states and risk reduction.

These new ideas are then applied to the examples in the world of financial risks in insurance, project failure and investments, and to the learning curves that can and do enhance market share in competitive technological markets (Chapter 6). The key observation is that the reduction in cost and the increase in market share are driven by technological learning, as also observed in the management of risks in stock market portfolio value. We are thus unifying very disparate fields using the same learning hypothesis.

Finally, we show how these concepts and methods can be applied in safety and risk management, a field of importance to wise executive and corporate risk decisions (Chapter 7). The use of safety management systems and performance indicators are reconciled with the Learning Hypothesis in practical examples, all the way from the probability of potential industrial events to the chance of unknown terrorist attacks. We define a single quantity, the $H$-factor, as a measure of information, which unscrambles the degree of uniformity and order from the complexity inherent in the variation of outcomes with experience. This measure is related to safety culture as well as risk management. We tackle the difficult question of risk perception, and how we might actually measure it, thus also providing a rational physical context for our fear of the unknown (Chapter 8). Finally, we summarise the key points (Chapter 9) resulting from this new approach, including the legal as well as the personal ramifications.

In the Appendices A, B, F and H, for the theoretically inclined, we give some more complete and greater mathematical detail on the theory of the chance of outcomes actually happening; and what we might observe as we sample the Jar of Life, to help us make predictions about the future based on that prior knowledge. Also, the Appendices C, D, E and G contain many more details on some selected actual outcomes, which are typical of the major events that society has actually observed, to show what we can learn from them. These outcomes, in all their human detail, are the prior knowledge, which together with the data files for the numbers of events, accidents and outcomes are analysed in the text for their development phases, which always follow a distinct pattern. In Appendices I and J, we consider and show the importance of how disorder gives rise to order and stability as manifested in risk management, error correction, skill acquisition and decision making. Hence, we link the individual human learning behaviour from repeated practice with the observed overall system outcome trends with experience. Finally, in Appendix K, we give an extensive case study using our theory, models and techniques that analyses a complete data set for rocket launch reliability and then predicts the future risk for such a real system.

This is *not* a book about the rigorous statistical analysis of outcomes. It is a book about *risk*, how we can measure and predict risk, and how we can reduce risk by ensuring that learning occurs. The theory is simply meant to be a guide to our thinking, and an aid to our understanding of real data on outcomes and how to manage and reduce them. The data are what really matter here.

To emphasise the influence of the human element, how statistical ideas can help, and why we are seemingly doomed to make the same mistakes over and over both until and while we learn, let us first review the Universal Learning Curve, and then the Four Echoes in some more detail. They are very powerful and highly visible examples of major failures and outcomes in modern technological society. We can then decide for ourselves what is really happening as we manage and take technological risk, trying to learn as we do so. Or not.

# References

[1] Theofanous, T., 1996, 'On the Proper Formulation of Safety Goals and Assessment of Safety Margins for Rare and High Consequence Hazards', Reliability Engineering and System Safety, 54, pp. 243–257.

[2] Duffey, R.B. and Saull, J.W., 2002, *Know the Risk*, First Edition, Butterworth and Heinemann, Boston, MA.

[3] Laplace, P.S., 1814, 'Essai philosophique sur les probabilities', extracted as 'Concerning Probability' in J.R. Newman's 'The World of Mathematics' Vol. 2, p. 1327, 1956.

[4] Ohlsson, S., 1996, 'Learning from Performance Errors', Psychological Review, Vol. 103, No. 2, 241–262.

[5] Rev. Bayes, T., 1763, Th. Bayes Memoir communicated by R. Price, 'An essay toward solving a problem in the doctrine of chances', Royal Society of London, Vol. 53, pp. 376–398.

[6] Howlett II, H.C., 1995, 'The Industrial Operator's Handbook', Techstar/Gary Jensen, Pocatello, ID, p. 5.

[7] Petroski, Henry, 1985, 'To Engineer is Human: The Role of Failure in Successful Design', St. Martin's Press, New York, Preface, p. xii.

[8] Folkman, Judah, 2001, attributed in 'Dr. Folkman's War', Robert Cooke, Random House Publishers, p. 238

[9] Jaynes, E.T., 2003, 'Probability Theory: The Logic of Science', First Edition, Cambridge University Press, Cambridge, UK, Edited by G.L. Bretthorst.

# Technical Summary

'The goal of psychology is to find order in this complexity.'

*Stellan Ohlsson, 1997*

## Defining the Past Probability

We are dealing here with prior events observed and recorded as outcomes in some selected window of the past. Suppose we treat our observations, of $n$ outcomes, as accidents and events occurring in some chosen or even arbitrary interval of experience, whatever it is we happen to have. The outcomes are distributed in some order, they are independent, they appear only when we are there to measure or observe them, and we do not know how many there really are, either observed or in total. There may be more later, but we observe, $n$, outcomes so far out of some total possible number of outcomes, $N$, which could have happened in the past, may or may not have been observed, and might occur in the future. The theoretical details as applied to outcomes and learning can be seen in the later chapters and mathematical Appendices.

First, let us return to Laplace's historical and pivotal definition of probability and how it relates to outcomes. The number of outcomes, $n$, observed or counted in the past is just the number of times something, some outcome has come up until now (the 'number of cases favourable'). Each outcome has a certain value in monetary terms or as numbers, and forms part of some distribution of outcomes. There are also some, $N$, total possible ones (the 'all cases possible'), but we have not observed them all since some are in the future or were not observed or have occurred in the past. The prior probability ('the ratio') based on the past frequency of observations is then equal to small $n$, divided by big $N$, which is our first equation in this book:

$$p = n/N.$$

For the prediction of the future risk, we must estimate how many more 'number of cases' there are of both favourable and the total of 'all cases possible' events. If this ratio in the future is in the same ratio as the past, the future *probability* (the relative chance) is predicted

*Managing Risk: The Human Element*   Romney B. Duffey and John W. Saull
Copyright © 2005 and 2008 Romney B. Duffey and John W. Saull, Published by John Wiley & Sons, Ltd

based on the past *frequency* (the relative number). If *n*, the observed number of outcomes, is also the number of failures then the probability of failure, $p(\text{Failure}) = n/N$; hence the converse is the probability of success, $p(\text{Success}) = 1 - p(\text{Failure}) = 1 - n/N$, since we must have observed outcomes as either failures or successes.

Our personal or societal window on the world is limited to our own experience or observation interval and what has been tested or observed in it. It is only a sample, *n*, out of all the *N* possible outcomes, and they can appear in many, many different sequences.

As Bernoulli and common sense tells us, we can only predict future outcomes with some real, finite and persistent uncertainty! We can only make estimates of future probability based on the past outcomes or some sample of the present observed outcomes. Often these observed outcomes are normally, log-normally, binomially or in some other manner mathematically distributed around some average value. The most usual is the Gaussian or Normal (bell-shaped) curve. The science of statistics has now dealt with this problem of distributions for centuries, providing the tools and terminology to establish the mean, the variance, the standard distribution, the uncertainty bounds, confidence limits, and last but not least, the *probability*.

We do not need to repeat all the excellent work consolidated in the standard statistical texts: for a cross-section, see the books by Bulmer, 1979 [1], Hays, 1988 [2], Fisher, 1932 [3] and Jaynes, 2003 [4]. We can use the good work they have done and apply it anew to the world of risk coupled with human behaviour. We note the following key points as this new development proceeds:

a) standard statistics is based on sampling a subset of what we are interested in, and unchanging characteristics are assumed between that subset and the actual whole: since changes such as *learning are not accounted for*, we need a new approach as the existing methods must fail;

b) the presence of learning gives us a form of distribution which is not distributed normally around the mean in experience space: the trend of the data is to the *minimum* rate of outcomes but *not* to the mean as is traditional;

c) the sampling of outcomes in past *experience space* gives a basis for systematic prediction of future outcomes, based on the dynamic learning behaviour while allowing for uncertainties: this requires that a relevant measure for experience exists; and

d) because outcomes appear stochastically, several powerful and highly useful analogies exist between standard statistics and statistical mechanics and physics: the realisation is that *we cannot describe the instantaneous behaviour of the world* but we can determine the distributions of outcomes that depend on the depth of our experience.

We will show how these points are handled not only in a rational, but also in an improbable way to predict future outcomes. Using the *learning hypothesis*, we combine the estimation of probable outcomes with the improbable world of statistical physics and the unpredictable human psyche. Our problem is slightly different from the usual ones in that we have a dynamic distribution; a time series with a trend that means the mean value is changing as we learn.

## Predicting Future Risk: Sampling from the Jar of Life

Gamblers of old were not all fools. They knew they needed to calculate whether and when the odds were in their favour. The whole history is given eloquently by Jaynes' book and in some detail by Senn, [5], so we only need summarise as far as it is relevant to our present goal of managing risk.

The predictions of the future based on theory also became clear with the posthumously published work of Bayes in 1763, who realised that predicting future events was not only dependent on the frequency of past outcomes but also involved deciding how likely the future was to occur. *Thus, the future is dependent on the past.* The exact wording used by Bayes, 1763 [6] seems a little quaint from our distance of over 200 years, but is worth quoting here as it forms the entire foundation in modern statistics that the chance of a subsequent outcome (event) depends on another outcome (event) having already occurred:

'*The probability that two subsequent events will both happen is a ratio compounded of the probability of the first, and the probability of the 2nd on supposition that the 1st happens*'.

Thus, Bayes' theoretical result is based on the concept of conditional probability, and how it follows from theory has been stated in words and in an elegant symbolic form, for example by Bulmer, 1979 [1] and later by Senn, 2003 [5]:

Posterior probability, $[p(P)]$ is proportional to Prior probability, $[p(\varepsilon)]$ times Likelihood, $[p(L)]$

or, symbolically and clearly,

$$\text{Future } p(P) \propto \text{Past } p(\varepsilon) \times \text{Likelihood } p(L)$$

This simple-looking equation has all the conceptual and practical elements needed for risk management. The past frequency history, $p(\varepsilon)$, is equally weighted by some future probability, $p(L)$. The belief and use of the prior knowledge, outcomes or observations, $p(\varepsilon)$, are tempered and modified by the future gain or loss of the degree of risk summed up by the *undefined* term 'likelihood', $p(L)$, which multiplies our prior observations. The estimate of the future probability of outcomes is conditionally dependent on the observed past frequency of outcomes and how likely they are to occur in the future. Statisticians write out this so-called Bayes Theorem or equation more rigorously and in more complex notation[1], but the basic idea is unchanged. In statistical terminology, the likelihood is derivable from the ratio of the probability that an outcome will occur in some increment of experience, to the accumulated probability of all outcomes. This predictive equation, which was actually not written by Bayes himself, is indeed based on the idea of a conditional probability. As such, it is quite rigorously derivable, but at the same time opens up a whole new debate.

By defining 'likelihood' as a condition on the future, this approach is actually determining *the probability of a probability.*

The analogy is to that of the drawing of coloured balls from a jar, the classic urn of Bernoulli. The game is like the drawing of lots, and we can gamble on both the sequence and colour that the balls appear. This model problem, where we cannot see into the Jar, and do not know what precisely is in it but only make estimates from what we happen to take out, is adopted to inference and induction studies, as shown in Jaynes' book [4]. It is not an exact representation of a technological system and the human minds acting within it, nor is

---

[1] See for example Jaynes Chapter 4, equation (4.3) et seq., and Hayes, Chapter 1, equation (1.13.1).

that required. The Jar analogy is a convenient way to describe how we are observing outcomes and making informed choices and decisions about the future based on what we have observed in the past.

The Jar analogy replaces the Greek image of the thread of life that the three Fates wove and spun, and blindly cut or not the thread according to the casting of lots. The Jar delivers the emergence and occurrence of both known events and unknown happenings into our world of experience, where we can now see them as outcomes. They appear in some random order from a hidden future into which we cannot see, where the unknown remains unseen and not experienced, with some chance or risk of emerging (happening) or not. (See Figure 1.)

In the study of human psychology and the process of learning, the presence of the prior knowledge is critical. Having already seen several outcomes, how and what have we learned? The appearance of the prior outcomes and our knowledge about them is a guide to our future actions and beliefs. As stated clearly by Stellan Ohlsson [7]: 'the role of prior knowledge in skill acquisition is to enable the learner to detect and correct errors'. So the Jar analogy also provides a beautiful conceptual link between the physical and the psychological worlds. We can interrelate the *mathematical* concepts of probability based on the number and distribution of outcomes already observed (the conscious numbering, order and colour of the balls that we might actually observe) to the *cognitive* concepts of learning based on our prior knowledge of those very same outcomes (the subconscious patterns, beliefs and interpretations that we might actually decide).

We observe the pattern of outcomes (the black balls) as if sampled from the Jar and expect to make some prediction about how many more there are and when they will appear – and in what pattern or sequence. Of course, in so doing we are implicitly utilising the non-outcomes too, whatever we observe.

We adapt this conceptual model of the Jar to the world of physically observed outcomes, the Jar of Life, where the number of draws represents the chance of observing and experiencing both known outcomes and non-outcomes. The action of drawing from the Jar is equivalent to just the appearance or not, one by one, of similar events or outcomes. In the Jar, by this

**Figure 1.**   The Jar of Life: the outcome is a black ball, observed somewhere among a sequence of non-outcomes, the white balls, as they emerge from among the unknown contents of the urn (Photo © RB Duffey, private archive)

analogy, there are unknown black balls (which represent outcomes) and white balls (non-outcomes), but we do not know how many of each, but there must be $N$ outcomes in total, where this may be any number. We make choices from the Jar and may pull out many white balls, $m$, representing non-outcomes, so many that the few, $n$, black balls (events) might even seem quite rare. This Jar analogy is clearly a gross simplification for any homo-technological system (HTS), by avoiding describing the complex multitude of possible internal processes in the Jar. We can also think of it as a giant output logic 'OR' gate, or an 'ON/OFF' binary switch, providing the ultimate and integrated output from many such possible internal system, decision or logic processes.

So we have come up with, $n$, discrete outcomes, observed and recorded as a sequence of black balls in our observation interval. There are, $n^N$, different sequences possible in all, which could be a huge number. Presumably, we observe the most probable in our observation interval. There are standard geometric formulas for the probability of a given sequence only if we know something about the number and order of the prior black and white balls.

Straightforwardly, the cumulative prior probability or risk of observing any outcome at some experience, $\varepsilon$, is:

$$p(\varepsilon) = n/N,$$

using the Laplace definition for the prior observed frequency, all outcomes being equally likely. We have not counted or included the non-outcomes, $m$, in this definition as we may or may not have observed or recorded them. This probability is the prior knowledge, the so-called uniform prior, where we have not assigned greater or less chance of occurrence to any one outcome in this set of similar outcomes in our experience window, such as real-life car crashes, aircraft near misses, train derailments, industrial injuries, job moves, stock price changes, oil spills, ships sinking or medical adverse events.

Our jar is the Jar of Life and is limited by our experience. But we do not have to count all the non-events and we may not actually observe or even measure them. Ideally we would, but in reality not. Out there, somewhere, there may be near misses that were not quite outcomes (balls not drawn) and many more non-outcomes outside our observation range (in other jars), outside of our experience (later on), or even not reported (ooops!), and hence, are not in the Jar at all.

Consider if we only removed the outcomes (black balls) as they appear. Then we are purely being reactive, which is what modern safety practice usually does. We observe the outcome and then try to fix it so it cannot happen again: we remove the outcome, just that specific black ball, and hope that magically turns some of the others white. But other black balls are still in the Jar. Our feedback system does not remove those that have yet to occur: we just hope that our measures have increased the number of non-outcomes (white ones) and reduced the outcome probability (the fraction of black ones).

We just do not even know how many non-outcomes or events, $m$, that we have not seen, in addition to those we do, just how many we missed, or how many were not quite events . . . or how many were almost an outcome but were not. They appear as white balls, but go *unrecorded* as non-outcomes. The information and knowledge we have are always incomplete; what the statisticians call 'censored' data. If we did record them all, as near misses, say, we would have perfect learning. Even in regulatory schemes, even the best assessment reports cannot catch all events. Who possibly can collect all the data? No one.

What happens in practice is that we try to fix the number, $N$, by taking a sample or a subset of samples of the things we want to study (components, railway trains, registered voters, airline flights, medical patients, commodity price variations and so on), and assume they are typical of everything and everybody for that set of activities. We then observe the chosen sample under the relevant conditions and observe a subset of $n = N_j$ outcomes (failures, derailments, voter counts, stock price variations, near misses, crashes, shipwrecks or adverse events) in our reduced sample number for our particular or $j$th observation window. In conventional statistics, the sampling estimate, $N_j$, is assumed to be representative of the whole, $N$, and the distribution unchanged by, and independent of the actually observed outcomes. The missing data are treated as typical of the observed data.

Similar and very common situations occur in sampling *any* accident or outcome data. In the modern day analysis of rear-end auto collisions, for example, the issues are still clear:

*Obviously, any effort directed towards crash countermeasures must start from data collection that can provide information about the driver-related parameters. This would further mean deploying vehicles on the roadways, which are equipped with certain recording devices, as well as making the voluntary drivers available. Due to the random nature of these crashes, the number of vehicles required to deploy for observing a certain number of them involved in such crashes may be large. On the other hand, due to budgetary restrictions and operational constraints, the sample size actually required may not be permissible. The effort should be, therefore, to make the best use of the available resources. The problem of estimating the number of vehicles/drivers required (sample size) until a given number of them is involved in rear-end crashes is treated as the 'discrete waiting-time problem'. The sampling in this case is called 'inverse sampling'. In addition, binomial probability distribution is used for estimating the number of vehicles/drivers that would be involved in rear-end crashes out of a certain number engaged in data collection.*

Source: *DOT HS 809 541 April 2003, Technical Report,*
*'Sampling Issues in Rear-end Pre-crash Data Collection', by S. Singh.*

The reality (the 'discrete waiting time problem') is that we can really only count the black balls, the rear-enders, as outcomes that we actually observe and record. This is the 'event history' of all accident reports, incidents, lost time, fatal auto collisions, stock market crashes, technology breakthroughs, train derailments, medical adverse events, etc., etc. This is the reality of human life, of all accident, health, safety and industrial injury reporting, the 'rear-enders' that actually happened, and those yet to occur.

We do not count or report the non-events, all the near misses, the incidents avoided, or the many successes (like braking in time or swerving to avoid a collision), so our dataset is not only censored, it is inherently incomplete *and always will be*. We just do not know how many rear-end crashes we did not observe.

This means the Jar of Life has a constantly changing content, and even $N$, the total number of rear-enders, may be changing. Of course, the Jar may also contain not just black balls, but a myriad of different colours, red ones and blue ones, each representing a different type or class of outcome. The outputs could then be described as sampled from a so-called multinomial distribution, rather than from the simplest binomial choice. In the mathematical Appendices, for completeness, we derive the probability of the distributions of outcomes, $n$, and non-outcomes, m, incidentally linking learning with traditional statistical analysis and binomial sampling.

As we learn, as we take risk and succeed in life, luck is with us if we do not have an adverse outcome. Despite good things happening, only the bad news, the real outcomes, grab the headlines and are entered and reported in the statistics of experience. How typical is this then of the expected future behaviour? Here again, conventional statistical theory comes to our aid, from the premise that the past frequency is indeed conveying information about the *likely* future, ceteris paribus[2] as the authorities on economics would say.

What is the posterior chance? What is our risk of the very next draw being an outcome?

## A Possible Future: Defining the Posterior Probability

Recall that the likelihood is derivable from the ratio of the probability that an outcome will occur in some increment of experience, or uniformly $1/N$, to the accumulated probability of all the past outcomes, $n/N$. Hence, the chance or the likelihood of the very next outcome, a black ball, is always just one more out of the, n, outcomes already observed since for the very next outcome consistently:

$$p(\mathrm{L}) \approx (1/N)/(n/N) = 1/n.$$

We have not changed our sampling or drawing process so the likelihood is a uniform probability based on our prior knowledge of the already observed outcomes, $n$. We have used the approximate sign, written $\approx$, because we do not really know if this is true: it is even an assumption that at least one more outcome still exists in the Jar of Life.

Now, as before, our estimate of the posterior probability for the next outcome is:

$$\text{Future } p(\mathrm{P}) \propto \text{Past } p(\varepsilon) \times \text{Likelihood } p(L)$$

Thus, our future is decided as, having already observed, $n$, outcomes for the very next observed outcome, $n + 1$:

$$p(n+1) = p(\text{next}) = p(\varepsilon) \times p(\mathrm{L}) = (n/N) \times (1/n) = 1/N$$

which, since $N$ is constant, is also a constant probability. The result is exactly the (uniform) chance of any outcome in the first place!! It is our state of prior ignorance.

Unfortunately, as Bernoulli recognised, we do not know $N$, so this result is both interesting but useless. Sampling methods, which form the basis for statistics, assume the past frequency will remain unchanged ($n/N$), that the sample we have observed is indeed typical of all, and that rational choices will be made or some risk-taking behaviour limits are defined. Statistically speaking, the future is determined by the past. Somewhere, lurking out there, is the chance of an unknown outcome occurring.

But as we know, the Jar of Life includes learning: the participants are not Jaynes' highly useful but mindless robot, blindly assuming the same rule to always apply. We have been learning how to reduce outcomes, by feeding back our prior knowledge into changing the number of outcomes. We are learning, so the future distribution of $n$ with experience is *not* the same as existed in the past, if we are learning and/or changing our experience. The most likely *next* outcome will be changed by what we have learned in the past.

---

[2]Other conditions being equal or everything else is unchanged.

So now what do we do?
The answer is to think.

## The Engineers have an Answer: Reliability

The use of 'human reliability analysis' in probabilistic safety assessments (PSA), is one example where the mechanistic approach to human error has already been applied. The method relies again on incremental action data, derived from observing humans making mistakes and taking decisions; but it is basically an approach that does not account for the dynamic integration of the human with the HTS or the influence of learning.

In conventional human error analysis, the actions, decisions and errors are treated as independent events, and models for interactions between human actions are included as links in the event sequences. For any accident sequence that is being analysed, assumptions have to be made about not only the rate of failure, but also the influencing and contextual elements (so-called performance shaping or influencing factors, (PSF)). These are like the ambient lighting, the time of day, the state of crisis, management pressures, the team members' relationships, etc. The aim is to derive a number, say one in a hundred chance ($10^{-2}$) of a failure to perform a task each and every demand, that can be used to multiply related equipment failures and incident rates to derive an overall frequency of outcome or failure occurrence for a given assumed sequence.

But obviously, despite its merits and promise, this approach is doomed to failure itself in trying to predict an actual outcome. The issue of completeness is that *we will never know exactly what the human will do*, out of the infinite variety of what things (actions, tasks, decisions, interactions, mistakes) could really be done. Moreover, the human is acting as an *integral* part of the machine: they are intrinsically not extrinsically linked.

Now another whole arena exists in modern technology to determine the risk of failure, which examines the outcomes from a system to determine the failure rate of components. It is the analysis of equipment *reliability*. Any manufactured system is made up of many components, which themselves may be made of subcomponents, the bits and pieces of products. These include everything from hardware, to firmware to software, the valves, pipes, controllers, power supplies, amplifiers, tuners, cables, switches, handles, CPUs, memory chips, instruction sets, wheels, tires, bearings, solenoids, filters, batteries and motors of the everyday technological world. These can and do fail, due to design, defects, wear, usage, misoperation, overload and sheer aging. The reliability is a direct measure of how often they do *not* fail.

So 'reliability engineering' is the study of failure modes and rates, and is a very large technical field [8]. We even have reputable organisations, like Underwriters Insurance, who deliberately torture consumer items and products to failure just to see if and how they survive standard fire, dropping, impact, mishandling, electrical safety and wear test conditions.

Because the distribution of failures (outcomes) is time, duty cycle and sample dependent, empirical failure distributions are invoked and fitted to the data in order to make predictions about the future 'TTF'. This is exactly risk management applied to engineered systems and is exactly the same statistical problem we have been examining for other systems. In words, remembering our definition of the conditional future, in any experience interval chosen:

Future failure (Posterior) probability, $p \propto$ Past (Prior) probability, $p(\mathrm{P}) \times$ Chance of
future failure (Likelihood), $p(\mathrm{L})$.

So, if we have $n$, observed failures or outcomes, out of some total number of components or systems, $N$, then the probabilities have exactly the same form as we have already discussed.

Our colleague and reader Phil Myers, to whom we are most grateful, suggested that we should examine the extensive set of techniques existing in failure and engineering reliability analysis. The question is: *How well does human reliability mimic, or can be described by the tools and techniques that describe equipment and component failures?*

Conventionally, reliability engineering is associated with determining the failure rate of components, or systems, or mechanisms, not human beings in and interacting with a technological system. However, the most useful concepts are of the probability of failure (error), $p(\varepsilon)$ or the cumulative distribution function (CDF) before or in less than any interval, $\varepsilon$; and the probability density function (PDF, $f(\varepsilon)$), as the probability of failure (error) in any small experience interval, $d\varepsilon$, (Lewis, 1994) [8]. The ratio of these two measures, of the PDF (the differential, fractional or incremental probability) to the CDF (the integral, total or accumulated probability), is again taken as the measure for the 'likelihood' in statistical reasoning since it is the chance of an outcome in the next experience interval divided by the total chance up to then. The 'reliability' is then defined from the fraction that do not fail, being the probability for the outcomes that do *not* happen, as a real measure of success or failure resistance.

To make progress, we adopt and apply exactly the same definitions and models as reliability engineering, thus consistently and coincidentally unifying the theory of failures and errors in both human and mechanical systems in the presence of learning.

## Drawing from the Jar of Life: The Hazard Function and Species Extinction

Just like safety analysts counting the number of outcomes, engineers observe component failures occurring with increasing operating hours, or with the number of duty cycles like 'on' or 'off' for electrical switches. This is equivalent to the risk or outcome rate (errors and accidents), and to our experience with HTS with human involvement and learning. Instead of the elapsed or operating time, $t$, or some number of duty cycles, we actually utilise everywhere the accumulated experience parameter $\varepsilon$, which can be taken as elapsed time only for special cases. In a given or selected observation interval, we have observed, $n = N_j$, outcomes as some sample of the total as from our Jar of Life.

The probability of the outcome or error occurring in or taking less than $\varepsilon$ is the CDF. Conventionally, the CDF is written as the failure fraction, $F(\varepsilon)$, which, of course, is just the prior probability, $(n/N)$ and is related to the observed *outcome reliability*, which can be written symbolically as:

$$R(\varepsilon) = 1 - F(\varepsilon) = 1 - n/N$$

The fractional reliability, $R(\varepsilon)$, thus represents all those outcomes that by chance have *not* occurred by accumulated experience, $\varepsilon$, and conversely the unreliability or failure fraction, $F(\varepsilon) = p(\varepsilon) = n/N$, all those that have occurred. This is exactly the same form as the Laplace outcome probability. The failure rate is defined by the fractional rate of change of the reliability, which is a measure of how fast the outcomes are occurring, so the two are inextricably intertwined.

This rate of outcomes is usually what we record as discrete outcomes such as accidents, errors and events per unit experience. We have termed this the Instantaneous Rate, which represents the observed *rate* of outcomes, $n$, with changing experience. Thus, as stated before, the observed event or outcome rate usually recorded or reported is directly proportional to the failure rate. The probability density function, PDF or $f(\varepsilon)$, which is a measure of how fast the chance of an outcome is changing, is also derived from the rate of change of the incremental failure fraction with experience.

The probability of risk (a failure or outcome) for any experience can now be defined. We simply equate and translate all these different, but standard terminologies to the case of an HTS where we have observed $n$, outcomes out of $N$, total possible. We just switch everything to experience space. The reliability nomenclature appears in many and various forms in many engineering textbooks, which focus on reliability and failure rates of systems and components. This may all sound or seem a little complicated at this stage, but it is actually quite simple and just adopts handy mathematical shorthand that is useful to know, even hopefully without the mind going blank. We give the details later, but for now we can just summarise the relationships and definitions using our new terminology of an experience basis for the symbols:

a) the *hazard function* is equivalent to the *failure rate* at any experience, $\lambda(\varepsilon)$, being the relative rate of change in the reliability or the fractional number of outcomes with experience;

b) the *cumulative distribution function*, CDF, or outcome fraction, $F(\varepsilon)$, is just the fraction of the number of prior outcomes already observed, or the ratio, $n/N$, out of a total possible of $N$;

c) by definition, this fraction of prior outcomes is identical to the observed *cumulative prior probability*, $p(\varepsilon)$, which hence is also the CDF;

d) the *reliability*, $R(\varepsilon) = 1 - n/N$, is a fractional measure of how many outcomes did *not* occur;

e) the future failure chance (or *Posterior probability*, $p(P)$) is proportional to the Prior probability, $p(\varepsilon)$, times the chance of future failure or the Likelihood, $p(L)$;

f) the chance of an outcome in any small observation interval is the *probability density function*, PDF $f(\varepsilon)$, which is just the rate of change of the outcome fraction with experience;

g) the *Likelihood*, $p(L)$, is the ratio $f(\varepsilon)/F(\varepsilon)$, being the probability that an outcome will occur in some interval of experience, the PDF, to the total probability of occurrence, the CDF; and

h) the CDF is directly related to the failure rate, via the sum or integration of the rate at which the outcomes occurred up to the present experience.

We encourage you to reread these (a) through (h), particularly if the terms and definitions seem a little interwoven, *because they are*. The last one (h) cleverly links back to the first one (a) in a loop.

Having mastered them, you have mastered the beginning elements of the whole technical discipline that is at the heart of designing, maintaining and operating modern HTS. Many practicing operators, risk specialists and safety engineers, may use little or no math, so find the exercise a real trial. And the theory may seem heavy going if you do not pause and think about the terminology; just as it did to us when we were making the reliability approach used for components consistent with the learning hypothesis terminology.

This last result (h) for the CDF is of exactly the same form as the extinction rate equations for estimating the population change and longevity of the human or any other species! Basically, in the fields of Biology, Sociology and Anthropology, heartless though it may seem, human deaths are also treated just like equipment and component failures. The analysis can be considerably simplified if the failure (or death) rate, $\lambda(\varepsilon)$, is assumed or is approximately constant, or taken as some average value. This simplification is often the case taken for components with nearly constant or suitably averaged failure rates, or where we do not know the detailed variation in, say, the equivalent observed or excavated outcome, species, historical or geological record.

Thus, the *analysis of the rate at which outcomes occur follows the same basic approach used for the failure rate of components*. The very same model also is applied cold-heartedly in geology, sociology and biology to describe the extinction rate and population changes of species. For us humans, extinction is a risk in which we have a very vested interest, or should we dare say, a lifetime investment.

In that sense, since deaths are just outcomes, the lifetimes of humans and components are mathematically equivalent. This latter analogy may or may not be a comforting comparison, as obviously there must be uncertainty too in how long we, *homo sapiens*, or as a person might be expected to survive (J.R. Gott, 1993) [9]. We need to know if the prior knowledge of species' lifetimes, growth and extinction rates are useful as an estimate of the future probability of life. This makes the Jar of Life analogy even more interesting!

The actual measures taken or assumed as surrogates for the experience, $\varepsilon$, must be justified, and are discussed later.

## Experiencing Failure: Engineering and Human Risk and Reliability

Normally, we would expect there to be early failures as we find initial faults occur; then a drop off in failure rates as we learn and become more robust because these have been eliminated; and then finally a rise in failures again as aging, forgetting and wear-out processes occur.

Hence, as a key result, we find that the risk probability of failure (error), $p(\varepsilon)$, is a double exponential or 'bathtub' due to the exponential form of the failure rate, $\lambda(\varepsilon)$, itself with accumulated experience. We can derive this quickly by substituting this exponential (largely human) failure rate into the probability expression, as mathematically shown in Chapter 2 and Appendix A. The result is sketched in the Figure 2.

Although seemingly a complex expression, the term 'double exponential' or bathtub for the probability is actually simple to understand. It is analogous to the failure rate of components and shows a systematic risk variation. At the beginning, some 'infant mortality' outcomes emerge until, as learning sets in, we descend the learning curve to some minimum or trough value. Eventually, as much more experience is gained, 'aging' also occurs and we start to climb up the curve again. An outcome is inevitable ($p = 1$) at infinite or large experience: we are *doomed* or certain eventually to have one, and can only delay its occurrence to some later experience by having as low a minimum failure or outcome rate as possible. This is because no matter how small the lowest attainable or minimum outcome rate, provided it is not zero, we must ultimately have at least one outcome at large enough experience, despite

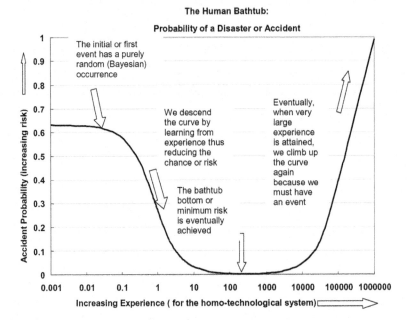

**Figure 2.** The Human Bathtub

implementing defence in-depth, risk reduction and safety improvement measures. Recall now that the probability of success is simply the converse of failure, $(1 - p)$, or an inverted humped-shape curve opposite to that shown in Figure 2.

This formulation and description is equivalent to the 'wear out' problem with components that also follows a bathtub curve. The conventional engineering models use an empirical or experience-based set of exponential functions to construct the 'life curve', to represent infancy, maturity and aging (see, for example, Lewis [8]). The failures inevitably follow an infancy period of high mortality since we do not have large experience, to eventually yield to a similarly high-failure probability later in life. We are damned if we do have experience; and certainly damned if we do not.

What we have shown is that the probability of an outcome risk based on the prior frequency, $p = n/N$, depends only on the experience and the learning rate constant. Assuming that we know or have observed the initial and minimum failure rates, the choice and determination of the total number of outcomes, $N$, is no longer an issue. By recognising the importance of, and switching to experience intervals the total and average number of outcomes is sample-dependent.

We have invariably found that the exponential learning curve form is the preferred choice for fitting event rate data when plotted versus a measure of *accumulated experience*. The statistical software that we use (TableCurve2D) usually picks this as the top choice among the analytical forms; and polynomial fits that may be better in the experience range give much poorer predictions (in Know the Risk) [10].

For the special and interesting ideal limit of 'perfect learning', we learn from all the non-outcomes as well as from all the rare outcomes. The measure of experience is then determined by how many non-outcomes we have, if we know which usually we do not. This Perfect Learning limit fails as soon as we have an event, as it should. But we find that, in principle, we learn from non-outcomes the same way we learn from outcomes. But the perfect learning ends as soon as we have just a single outcome at some finite experience, which it must if it has any chance or probability of occurrence.

## Experience Space

No, this is not a call to take a ride in a spaceship! But we do partially abandon our usual and comfortable time coordinates by substituting experience coordinates for when and what outcomes we observe. As used in Statistical Physics modeling, this aid to our thinking creates an idealised and conceptual 'phase space', in which the observed outcomes are somehow distributed.

Therefore, as we examine in detail in Chapter 5, we translate our world of observed outcomes to a 3D cube of 'experience space', with the three dimensions shown in our sketch Figure 3. Accumulated experience increases in the x–direction; and depth of experience in the z-direction; with the rate of outcomes defining the y-direction. Any outcome appears somewhere at some value of experience, $\varepsilon(i,j)$, scattered around the learning and distribution curves shown. The cube is our 'phase space' defined by our experience, and allows us to visualise what we are both observing and describing theoretically.

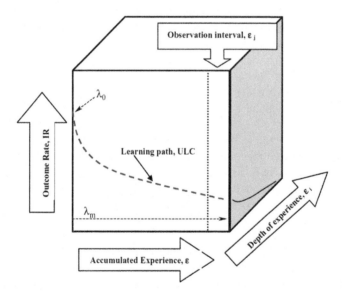

**Figure 3.**   Experience space shown as a 3D cube, with the learning path sketched on the face and the distribution curve on the end or side of the observational slice

As shown in the diagram, as we move from novice to being experienced, we follow a learning path. The rate of errors and outcomes falls if we are learning. The ULC that traces out our progress has few undefined parameters, is well behaved even beyond its fitting range, and is very robust for making prediction, lending itself to analytical formulation.

In any given observational interval or slice of experience, like that shown bounded by the vertical dotted line and the right hand edge of the cube in the sketch, we see and record some apparently random distribution of outcomes. The number of outcomes that we record will decrease with increasing *depth of experience*. Also, being exponential in form, the distribution curve we derive parallels the result and derivation for the physics of the distributions of molecular and atomic systems. There is a relationship between the depth of experience and the accumulated experience, proportional to the number of outcomes in any given observation interval, as we shall show in detail in Chapter 5.

There is a useful and powerful analogy developed here to modern psychological models of mental decision processes where 'consciousness is depth experienced as surface' (Tor Norretranders, 1991) [11]. The observed outcomes represent our *conscious* decision-making activity, as we track a path down the learning curve on the face of the experience-space cube. Meanwhile, our *unconscious* decision-making activity is represented by the (hidden) distribution of outcomes with the depth of experience, shown by the curve traced out on the side of our observed slice of experience space. As we shall see, conceptually, the inherent complexity involved in human mental decision and learning processes is then represented by the *information entropy, H*, which is a measure of the uncertainty, or the number of possible ways the outcomes might be distributed with depth of experience. Translated back to our more usual and familiar 2D experience space, we have to imagine some (vertical) slice at some accumulated experience as our collective or personal observation interval.

The uncertainty in the extrapolation for the future prediction is firmly based on the prior knowledge. So we will show that the prior knowledge indeed gives us an easy and direct way to determine the future probability of failure, and hence, the risk. The result is a direct variant of the Bayesian type of analysis and Jaynes would likely have been pleased with this extension to *human* failure analysis. The future risk that is the most likely as measured by an outcome rate can be derived and bounded. So can the least attainable outcome rate. There is no inconsistency between the uniform probability of observing any given outcome or pattern of outcomes, and having a learning effect that is changing the probability with increasing experience.

Note, the Jar of Life result is *entirely consistent* with the distribution of future outcomes usually assumed or derived for the normal drawing of outcomes (balls) from a jar problem, which follows a binomial, or Poisson distribution (see Appendix F). Instead of being invariant with the draws that are made, for the Jar of Life there is a dynamic behaviour in the probability of observing outcomes with experience, even though we have an equal chance of observing any given pattern of outcomes. *What happens with learning is that we observe a variable distribution and changing probability of outcomes with increasing experience*. Outcomes should decrease, but only as we observe and suffer more of them. As we draw from the Jar of Life, we find that the result changes if and as we learn. The rate of outcomes (the changing risk) and the number fall with increasing experience if we are learning; and depend on the experience level.

Even with *perfect learning*, in the ideal limit where we learn from all the non-outcomes as well as the outcomes, we find the decrease in the probability of an outcome still dependent on our learning rate and experience.

## Managing Safely: Creating Order Out of Disorder Using Safety Management Systems

The more we learn with experience, the lower our risk. Given the new quantification of the importance of the effect of experience, we also proceed to consider the effect on how we can try to manage risk.

In the past, the traditional engineering approach has been to try to Prevent events happening, using safety measures and design features, and to Mitigate the effects of any failures or errors by adding defensive devices that reduce the chance and extent of injury to the humans involved.

For example, buildings are built to (national) Electrical, Fire and Safety Codes, but emergency stairs, evacuation routes and sprinkler systems are added just in case of accidental or even deliberate fire. Similarly, autos are built with multiple mitigation devices to reduce the extent of injury to the passengers in case of a crash (seat belts, air bags, crushable zones and bumpers). Commercial aircraft are designed and maintained to high reliability, but seat belts, emergency slides and smoke detectors are now standard. The only useful device not included so far is a parachute and you are precluded from bringing your own (in part, because of just one prior hijacking and robbery experience). All these mitigating devices and design features were all added as a result of painful lessons learned as a result of outcomes (tragedies) due to failures of the human and the machine. They represent completely ad hoc safety management, usually as a result of regulations, licensing and inspections that mitigate against future outcomes. But despite all the requirements, fire escapes can still remain locked, seat belts left unused and smoke detectors unpowered or battery-less.

Traditionally, as outcomes (errors and risks) occur, Engineers, Managers, Society and Regulators introduce new measures (Rules) to attempt to eliminate their reoccurrence. They examine and try to determine the causes and minimise the consequences of these known outcomes. Appointed or independent Investigators evaluate in detail the 'event sequences' to determine the apparent causes and make recommendations. New 'design guides' or standards are invoked. Measures are taken to try to control the errors caused by the role of humans themselves. New Laws or Procedures are passed that may require different safety measures. Process changes are implemented in design manufacturing or operation, or using other management means (such as safety programs, retraining and/or the reassignment of staff). Fines may be levied as a means of punishment for allowing something to even happen. The inclusion of all these new Rules is an example of learning, which should change the observed distribution of outcomes with experience, and hence, explains the effects of safety management or intervention in the system.

*To put it another way, management, laws, inquiries, regulations and safety systems try to impose order on disorder.* Implicitly, they try to reach a minimum state of disorder, or a maximum state of order, as effectively as possible using Goals and incentives (both rewards and punishments).

Physically, the act of creating order seems to violate the principles of physics behind the inevitability of the generation of entropy. We examine later the behaviour of statistical error states, and their relation to what is known as the Information Entropy, which is a well-known measure of the uncertainty with which signals, which in our case correspond to outcome distributions, are transmitted and received. We can and will show that the distribution of outcomes with experience is consistent with the principles of, and directly derivable from statistical mechanics. The measure of the information content is derived from the number of different possible combinations of the outcomes: distribution patterns representing knowledge and skill emerge naturally as we gain experience. This measure of complexity represents the state of order, or conversely the degree of randomness or uniformity in the distribution of the outcomes, and can also be used to define the stability (or so-called 'resilience') of an entire system or organisation.

Creating order from complexity is exactly also the intent and function of 'Safety Management Systems', which are so popular today. The emphasis is on the creation of a 'safety culture', coupled to an organisational structure that places unending emphasis on safety at every level. We propose and prefer the use of the term and the objective of sustaining a 'Learning Environment', where mistakes, outcomes and errors are used as learning vehicles to improve. Simply put, an effective 'safety culture' requires that there be a good learning environment.

We can seek out 'root causes', assign and partition responsibility, and apply audits and reviews, all to give us the experience and the feedback we need to improve. We must measure where we are on the learning curve, using this experience, and how much we are improving by recording the outcomes in an open and honest manner.

Thus, the inherent disorder is not replaced but is used to ensure reporting, the measure of chaos to provide guidance, and the degree of uniformity of the outcomes to introduce learning and new habits. We define in Chapters 5 and 8 the '$H$-factor', a single unambiguous measure of the effectiveness of our much sought after 'learning environment' or 'safety culture', based solely on the outcomes we observe and manage.

## Describing the Indescribable: Top-Down and Bottom-Up

But we cannot predict precisely *when* an outcome will occur, only that on average it will be with a certain *probability* of occurrence.

Therefore, to solve this impossible problem, we adopt a powerful analogy. In statistical physics, the very impossibility of predicting the instantaneous behaviour of complex physical systems has been solved. It was achieved using Boltzmann's invention (See Plate 3) and Gibb's extension of successful deriving the average observed behaviour from the distribution of unobserved statistical fluctuations. This idea has laid the foundations of modern physics and chemistry, and been extended to the use of the degree of order and disorder in a system as a measure of its probability of occurrence (Bernstein, 1996 [12] and Jaynes, 2003 [4]). Using this same idea, we can derive a physically based theory based on the distribution of observed outcomes (error states) for a system, where the 'error states' define one distribution (or macrostate) out of many possible ones. Using this physical model, immediately we can indeed reconcile the apparently stochastic occurrence of the outcomes that we observe as accidents and errors with the observed systematic trend from having a learning environment. This *emergent* theory is also entirely consistent with the models of human consciousness that invoke the idea of the processing, and more importantly, the discarding or the unlearning of prior information (Ohlsson [7] and Tor Norretranders [11]).

To resolve this apparent paradox of describing the indescribable, we analyse and predict the randomness of outcomes at the bottom-up or microscopic level, consistent with the systematic effect of learning from the top-down or macroscopic trends. To do this, we can adopt and utilise these same and well-known concepts and methods of statistical physics to the prediction of outcomes. These methods seek the rules that govern the behaviour of the science of the natural world, based on the average unobserved and unpredictable statistical fluctuations. Exactly this same (impossible) problem occurs of not being able to describe the instantaneous behaviour of the natural world and the atoms it is made from and their reactions with each other, despite knowing the laws that are being followed. This approach, strange as it may seem, is at the very foundation of modern chemistry and physics.

At the top-down or macroscopic system level, we can say and see that humans by themselves learn from their mistakes. Thus, we observe the outcomes but not the internal workings of the human mind. We see that the rate of learning is proportional to the number of mistakes (errors) that we are making at the technological system level. In that way, we can show and observe that there is a ULC that, on average, we follow in all major technologies. The rate of learning is empirically determined from the data and we can show conclusively that 'zero defects' is not attainable, no matter how desirable or attractive it might be.

Down at the detailed bottom level, the microscopic events or outcomes arise from a confluence of circumstance that is stochastic, unobserved and inherently unpredictable as to its *frequency* of occurrence. We cannot predict the workings of the human mind, or when a component, system or procedure will fail, and how the system and the human will then interact. The use of event trees helps define which outcomes *might* occur, but not which ones actually *will*. As each outcome occurs, we see randomness, unpredictability, uncertainty and statistical fluctuations that we cannot model. The observed distributions of outcomes depend, as we shall show, on the varying depth of experience for each outcome. The individuals in a system form a collective that obeys certain unknown rules as to how they interact and learn together as one 'organisational organism'.

We make a key analogy in accord with applications of statistical mechanics. We adopt the approach of defining distributions of errors (which are the observed outcomes), arguing that we do not and *cannot* know all the error states of the system, and only observe the outcomes based on some statistically average behaviours. We then do not have to know all the 'rules' that may describe the human and machine reliability (the level of complexity that dominates 'cause'), only we must attempt to describe the actual or prior emergent or observed distribution of the real outcomes (accidents, events and errors). The distribution we observe as one out of many possible is then simply the most likely and depends systematically on the *depth* of experience as we show later.

The resulting distribution is the exponential form exactly in the shape of a learning curve, as has previously been found in both classical and quantum physics, which respectively describe the continuous and discrete views of the atomic world. Thus, our new quantitative and general theory of errors examines and predicts the average observed behaviour of a complex system of error states (as observed outcomes). We cannot and do not describe the detailed behaviour of the human(s) or the machine(s) with which it is interacting, only the average distribution of accident outcomes that are observed as a result of the random occurrence and existence of errors.

## What an Observer Will Observe and the Depth of Our Experience

Instead of a complete model of instantaneous behaviour of everything, we invoke the idea that we can describe the average behaviour that we observe (the distribution of 'error states') based on the fluctuations and random outcomes that exist but we actually do not observe.

The hypothesis and results can explain the stochastic occurrence of outcomes (errors and failures) in technological systems, coupled with the systematic key role of human error and learning through experience. The method also potentially quantifies the impact of proposed safety management schemes (SMS), and provides a basis for understanding risk perception and our fear of the unknown.

We assume that we are not special or privileged observers of outcomes. The period over which we happen to observe and/or count the outcomes defines our Observation Range (the experience 'space') or interval. The selection of an interval arbitrarily censors the data since events or outcomes may or may not occur outside of when, in our experience, we happen or are able to observe. The distribution of observed outcomes, $n(\varepsilon) = N_j$ in our jth observation 'window of experience' is just one of many possible but unique distributions that we could have observed. But since it was actually observed, it happens to be the *most likely* distribution, and is the curve sketched on the shaded edge of the observational slice of the experience space cube in Figure 3.

But there is nothing special about the outcomes or how they are distributed in 'experience space'. They just happened to occur when and where they did when we observed them. We know that, on average, they follow some learning curve, both within the jth Observation Range and for the next j + 1 range. This is the prior knowledge, and the randomness or degree of disorder contains the inherent information content we are seeking. We extract the signal from the noise.

We prove the validity of the approach and the mathematical results by comparison to data and by physical reasoning. This work developed here is the first adoption and adaptation of the well-known principles and methods of statistical physics to the measurement and prediction of accidents and the contribution of the human element. In particular, utilising these concepts from statistical mechanics, the observed properties of macroscopic systems, are predicted by the microscopic distributions of outcomes among states. One of the major attractions of this idea is that, together with the learning hypothesis, it is the simplest possible[3], and is an extension of, and consistent with, the derivations used for the known laws of physics. It is also consistent with the Laplace–Bayes definition of probability, $p = n/N$, and with sampling theory when observing a finite number of outcomes.

Using this physical model, we show that we can therefore reconcile the apparently stochastic occurrence (frequency) of accidents and errors with the observed systematic trend from having a learning environment. The top-down and the bottom-up approaches (thankfully) produce the same form of results, and are consistent theoretically and numerically.

Thus, we find that learning rates depend on the depth of experience and that a formal 'experience-shaping factor' emerges naturally from and during the total experience. The 'statistical error state' theoretical result is also consistent with and supports the 'Learning Hypothesis' universal curve model of Duffey and Saull, 2002 [10] and the 'Theory of Error Correction' of Ohlsson, 1996 [7]. In addition, we can show the link between *individual* learning and error correction with repeated trials, with the observed *system* learning behaviour.

The uncertainty is then defined by a new measure of the number of ways the observed distributions of outcomes could occur, and hence, includes *the combination of our accumulated experience and of the depth of our experience*, and is thus determined by how small

---

[3]The scientific principle that simpler is better is known as Ockham's Razor, relevant to the choice between competing hypotheses or theories.

we have defined, measured or 'grained' our painfully earned experience space. Using this measure of uncertainty, called the *information entropy*, we can even estimate the reduction in response time needed as we learn to obtain the correct solution. Hence, we move naturally from being a novice to becoming an expert as we acquire new skills through the accumulation of experience. It is also consistent with the classical ideas behind information theory as applied to signals and communication: the so-called 'missing information' is represented by the entropy in Baierlein, 1971 [13]. In addition, the individual decrease in response times for decision-making errors with repeated trials is shown to be linked to the information entropy, so there is a fundamental connection to cognitive psychology and human learning and the so-called 'laws of practice'.

This new risk approach is a necessary first step in determining, formally and in practice, the quantitative impact of SMS and risk management principles on accident, event and error occurrence probability. It is a testable theory that will make predictions and can be compared against other ideas and refined as needed. For the first time, we can define, quantify and measure what is meant by such concepts as 'safety culture', 'organisational learning' and 'resilience', and hence, establish the basis for the key role and function of management in creating order from disorder. We can even make estimates for the probability of an unknown event happening and of the risk or possible threat of having a repeat occurrence.

*The important point is the new concepts enable a firmer basis for the prediction and management of risk.* Unfortunately, some of the new ideas we develop require physical insight and mathematical knowledge, plus an understanding of statistics, combined with knowledge of statistical mechanics, event data analysis, likelihood estimation, the use of theoretical analogy, and the key concept of information entropy. Out of consideration for those without all these skills or experience, and to help the text flow, we have compressed the details of the maths and the physics into selected chapters. We also have banished some other derivations to the Appendices where the wise and the curious can see for themselves if the results are consistent and derivable. All others can skip them, as they wish, but we hope will at least scan the pages while discerning errors!

We provide examples and test cases as we proceed to illuminate the message from a wide range of HTS, including case studies of particular events and industries.

## References

[1] Bulmer, M.G., 1979, 'Principles of Statistics', Dover Publications, Inc., New York, p. 170.

[2] Hays, W.L., 1988, 'Statistics', Holt, Rinehart and Winston, Inc., Fourth Edition.

[3] Fisher, R.A., 1932, 'Inverse Probability and the use of Likelihood', Proceedings of the Cambridge Philosophical Society, Vol. XXVIII. Part III, p. 257.

[4] Jaynes, E.T., 2003, 'Probability Theory: The Logic of Science', First Edition, Cambridge University Press, Cambridge, UK, Edited by G.L. Bretthorst.

[5] Senn, S., 2003, 'Dicing with Death: Chance, Risk and Health', Cambridge University Press, UK, Chapter 2, pp. 26–49, ISBN 0 521 54023 2.

[6] Rev. Bayes, T., 1763, Th. Bayes Memoir communicated by R. Price, 'An essay toward solving a problem in the doctrine of chances', Royal Society of London, Vol. 53, pp. 376–398.

[7] Ohlsson, S., 1996, 'Learning from Performance Errors', Psychological Review, Vol. 103, No. 2, 241–262.

[8] Lewis, E.E., 1994, 'Introduction to Reliability Engineering', Second Edition, John Wiley and Sons, New York, pp. 61, 112 and 141.

[9] Gott III, J.R., 1993, 'Implications of the Copernican Principle for Our Future Prospects', Nature, Vol. 363, pp. 315–319.
[10] Duffey, R.B. and Saull, J.W., 2002, 'Know the Risk', First Edition, Butterworth and Heinemann, Boston, MA.
[11] Norretranders, Tor 1991, 'The User Illusion: Cutting consciousness Down to Size', Penguin Books, London, UK, p. 290.
[12] Bernstein, P.L., 1996, 'Against the Gods', John Wiley and Sons, New York, p. 8.
[13] Baierlein, R, 1971, 'Atoms and Information Theory', W.H. Freeman and Co., San Francisco.

# 1

# The Universal Learning Curve[1]

*'I think success has no rules, but you can learn a lot from failure.'*

*Jean Kerr*

## Predicting Tragedies, Accidents and Failures: Using the Learning Hypothesis

Is it possible to predict when an accident or tragedy will occur? Is it possible to predict the future price of a product and when that will happen? Up to now, the answer has been no, it is impossible. We only know after the fact.

This is because accidents, like the crashes of the Space Shuttle or Concorde, are stochastic in their occurrence. They can seemingly occur as observed outcomes at any instant, without warning. They are due to a combination of human and technological system failures, working together in totally unexpected and/or undetected ways, occurring at some random moment. Massive inquiries into these crashes and other spectacular events, like the UK Ladbroke Grove railway collision and the USA Three Mile Island reactor, show the cause is due to an unexpected combination or sequence of human, management, operational, design and training mistakes. Once we know what happened, we can fix the engineering or design failures and try to obviate the human ones.

Similarly, taking an item from being a prototype idea to the production of many items in large factories, with optimised labour and manufacturing techniques, and large sales campaigns, is an exercise in cost and price reduction. There is risk inherent in the costing, the market size, the manufacturing costs and the ultimate competitiveness of the product. The homo-technological system (HTS) in this case is the entire complex marketplace, the factory and the technology, with humans designing, operating and producing what is made and sold. The human rules governing the market behaviour, the tug and pull between supply and demand, and the concepts of utility, are the stuff and content of economics textbooks.

---

[1] This Chapter expands on the ideas suggested in R.B. Duffey, 'A New General Accident Theory', Paper # 0759, Proc., International Conference on Probabilistic Safety Assessment and Management (PSAM 7), Berlin, Germany, 14–18 June 2004.

---

We have invented and use technological systems everywhere in the last two centuries or more and our progress is marked by deaths, injuries and fiscal and human disasters, as failures and errors occur. Since technological systems do not usually fail all by themselves – after all we collectively did invent and build them – the major causes are the errors caused by us, Homo sapiens, in the system design, construction, operation, maintenance, control, licensing and management. Be it a bridge collapse, an airplane near miss, an operating room death, a milling machine accident, a train derailment, an automobile collision, a ladder falling, a pipeline fire or a mineshaft collapse, we cannot separate out the human component of the mistakes easily. When looking for cause, or blame, or improvement, we have to consider the entire HTS, of which and where we humans are an integral part.

But so far we have no real physical theory of the way humans behave and make mistakes, so we are seemingly doomed to rediscover them, as humans continue to make errors. We can and must introduce corrective and best practice procedures, training, rules, safety measures and management incentives to minimise the number and chance of mistakes. Without a theory and a prediction, we are faced with making risk and safety estimates based solely on those failures and sequences that we have observed or might imagine. There is a plethora of 'models' for human behaviour and decision making in the psychological and human factors literature, including how we behave under stress, make judgements, take actions, plus how we might train and how we may use our skill, rule and knowledge base to improve. All of this material and literature is largely empirical and qualitative. But apart from the results of repetitive tests on learning and pattern recognition by individual subjects, there is not a measurable and testable prediction about the rate at which mistakes (outcomes or errors) are made or occur.

Even the selected and best rules on how to make decisions and interact (GIHRE, 2004) [1] are really excellent 'best practices'. But nowhere do they provide a genuine risk reduction number or a prediction.

To address the apparently hopeless predictive problem and the impossibility of accurately predicting human behaviour when interacting with an HTS, we still try to reduce the probability of error and mitigate consequences of mistakes. Engineers, regulators, professional bodies, legislators and consultants use a myriad of techniques to continuously improve our technological system designs, ease of operation, safety of performance and the margins to component and system failure. By hypothesising initiating events and conducting hazard analyses, invoking safety and performance standards, and probabilistic risk and safety assessments, we implement design and protective features using safety measures and equipment. We also try to prevent future events by invoking laws, procedures, regulations and penalties for similar actions. By paying attention to features like the human–machine interface (the controls, the alarms, the layout, and the labelling) using human-centred design, we can also try to make the operation less risky, the diagnosis and prevention of failures more simple and intuitive, and avoid blunders in the operation. Automation can be introduced, taking the human out of the control and decision-making loop, although this itself can lead to issues of when, if ever, the human should intervene or take over.

In the fiscal world, risk management techniques are adopted to minimise risk exposure, like varying the portfolio of products, not betting on one outcome or product being successful, or building in margins. The risk that an investor is prepared to take is then estimated by balancing the exposure (the downside) against the gain (the upside), just like trying to make a rational decision about the future when it is uncertain.

As society uses and develops modern technology, we want to be able to predict accidents before they happen, to reduce their number and to avoid failures. If our risk, personal or system, were truly measured by the common idea of event frequency times its consequence, we would have some measure of success. But events and observed outcomes may range from large catastrophic events – like the Space Shuttle – in very expensive technological systems, to the everyday but still personally expensive and embarrassing auto collisions that we almost all have. The number of casualties, deaths or injuries – heart rending though they are – is purely another arbitrary statistic. Some events in our lives, like medical errors, being stuck in a hotel elevator or a fire, experiencing a train derailment or a aircraft near miss, are not due to anything under our real control, as we offer our bodies or ourselves up for transport, diagnosis, treatment, practice and operations. Nothing we do is 'risk free', so as a society we have to tolerate some risk (chance of an accident) and just hope it does not happen to us as an individual. But we do not know if it will and we can simply make a statistical estimate that it is unlikely to happen to ourselves since we are just one person among many risk-exposed people.

This whole issue of personal risk and predicting when and where an event will occur cannot be simply solved using human-centred design to make items and technology safer and simpler to use. It also cannot be solved by inquiries into cause of failure; or meting out punishment for failure; or legal and fiscal assignment of responsibility. These are all case-by-case, item-by-item, after-the-fact, without general application. *Instead, we need to understand how we must and do learn from our mistakes and improve our safety and performance as we go* so we may anticipate and prevent using prior knowledge (Jaynes, 2003) [2].

In all major industrialised societies, like many in Asia, India, Europe or North America, the major mistakes that occur are recorded as outcomes such as failures, accidents, deaths, events, injuries, hospital visits, insurance losses and the like. The events that occur are the subject of investigation for the assignment of cause and blame, and of fiscal, corporate and personal liability and responsibility. They can themselves cause expensive inquiries, regulations and litigation.

But their occurrence is random, not predictable. We may assign or observe a rate of events, deaths or injuries, but we cannot predict when any one event will occur or how much reduction in outcomes that a particular safety measure will provide. So we end up being reactive, in our laws, in our punishment, in our redesigns, in our recalls, and in our training and our knowledge of failure. This inevitability of failure, this lack of knowledge about why and when errors will happen and how they combine, leads us into extensive procedures in the design, testing, training, procedures and safety analysis of our systems, and even more expensive and heart-rending inquiries and retribution when events do occur, as they inevitably do. In fact, Henry Petroski, 1985 [3] asserts that failures are vital and necessary for us to improve, and lack of failures leads to complacency.

But we should not despair. After all, making predictions of outcomes was never easy, be it the score of a sports game, the winner of elections, the chance of an illness or the potential for future fame and wealth, let alone an accident where humans have a role.

## The Learning Hypothesis: The Marketplace of Life

Predicting a future event, or the price of a product, based on past events is inherently uncertain. We need a theory that is a quantitative equation not just a qualitative model in order to make predictions, and hence, have verifiable and testable hypotheses.

The simplest hypothesis we can make and have is the Learning Hypothesis. For any HTS, the basic and sole assumption that we make is the 'Learning Hypothesis' as a physical model for human behaviour when coupled to a technology (an HTS).

*Simply and directly, we postulate that humans learn from their mistakes (outcomes) as experience is gained.*

Although we make errors all the time, as we move from being novices to acquiring expertise, we should expect to reduce our errors or at least not make the same ones. Thus, hopefully, we should descend a 'learning curve' like that shown in Figure 1.1, where our rate of making mistakes decreases as we learn from experience. Remember that this curve is the dotted line drawn on the front face of the cube of 'experience space'.

The past rate of learning determines our trajectory on the Learning path and thus:

- how fast we can descend the curve;
- the rate at which errors occur determines where we are on the curve;
- changes in rate are due to our actions and feedback from learning from our mistakes;
- no reduction in error or outcome rate could mean we have reached the lowest we are able to or that we have not sustained a learning environment; and
- an increase in rate signifies forgetting.

The rate at which we might eliminate events based on our past experience is also akin to estimations of the duration and future of humans overall based on the observation of past species growth and collapse (Goth III, 1993) [4]; or predicting the likelihood (or probability) of a particular outcome in a game of chance (gambling) based on the distribution or prior outcomes, as studied by Bernoulli, 1713 [5] and Laplace, 1814 [6]. (Plate 1)

It turns out, as we shall see later, that the same rules and forces of error correction, goal setting and learning appear in the economic marketplace. As products move from development to full market deployment, a similar learning curve is followed in the decline of cost and/or price. So we are able to argue that the same hypothesis is at work in many fields of

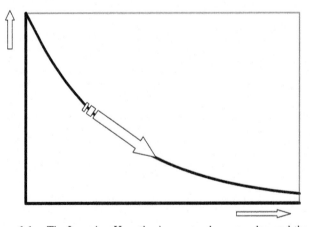

**Figure 1.1.**   The Learning Hypothesis – as we learn we descend the curve

human endeavour where we are working with the machinery of technology and trying to survive in the marketplace of life. We need to be able to predict the risk inherent in producing a competitive product as a result of cost reduction through learning, as exemplified by products as diverse as air conditioners, TV sets, computers, chocolate bars, clothing, ethanol fuel and pre-packaged microwaveable groceries.

The basic set of economic risk assumptions for price reduction we make are the same as those for error reduction by learning. Thus, *the overall rate of production cost or market price reduction (learning) in a technology or market is proportional to the competitive pressure* (as measured by the unit market price or cost). Market forces and competitive pressures both drive the price down, either to a profitable or market-determined value, using both innovation and experience. This effect has been embodied before in empirical 'progress functions' or 'learning curves' describing the reduction in cost observed with increasing production in manufacturing – the mass production effect beloved of industry. In early texts and tests of this approach, it was found that the apparently constant learning rate could be determined by striking a line through the data and using or providing tabulations for the fitting parameters (Andress, 1954) [7] and (Jordan, 1972) [8]. In fact, defense procurement contracts in the USA apparently included requirements for showing price and/or cost reductions through learning, and manufacturers and management used such curves to predict workload and staffing as well as future price. As remarked presciently by Andress, half a century ago, on the basis of these purely empirical observations: *'The learning curve is a device that promises to have many important uses'*.

A general accident and economic risk theory, like the Learning Hypothesis, should be testable, able to provide real predictions and explain actual outcome, error and economic data. Hence, we take the rate of reduction of outcomes (observed in the technology or activity as accidents, errors and events) as proportional to the number of outcomes that are occurring (Know the Risk, 2002) [9].

All humans and engineers, in particular, would like to believe they learn from their mistakes.

## Learning in Homo-Technological Systems (HTSs): The Way a Human Learns

We would have expected there to be a large learning literature, especially for human behaviour and skill acquisition, and indeed there is a huge volume of work. But most of it is related to trying to solve the cognitive and psychological rationale for human learning, whereas we are interested in how this works when the human is an integral part of the machine or technical system. How do humans learn with and from experience? Is there reinforcement and feedback at work? And can we predict it?

We need to somehow couple the individual learning behaviour, whatever it may be, to the observed trend in the outcomes at the HTS level. So far, we have treated the human as inseparable from the HTS in and with which it is interacting. We recently came across one of the key psychologically based concepts related to the Learning Hypothesis for HTS: Ohlsson's Theory of Error Correction for the acquisition of individual skill (Ohlsson, 1996) [10]. Without repeating the entire argument here, Ohlsson's main postulate is the idea that errors are detected on the basis of their outcomes. Analogous to the learning hypothesis that we apply to *systems*, the mistakes or undesired results are corrected by the cognitive processes of alteration of or revision to the *individual*'s prior and overly general knowledge structure that produce the wrong behaviour or unexpected result. Thus, the transition from mistake-prone novice to highly skilled expert is the 'unlearning' of the 'rules' that produce the undesired errors (outcomes).

This qualitative theory of Ohlsson produces insights and predictions that are entirely in accord with the Minimum Error Rate Equation (MERE) quantitative analysis:

a) finite and non-zero errors always remain due to residual rule conflicts, much akin to the minimum attainable error rate (i.e., whether turning right is right at a junction or whether it is wrong depends on the situation relative to other vehicles and local one-way rules, as well as on the particular junction);

b) a learning curve should exist where the number of attempts to get to the desired state decrease with practice (i.e., corresponding to the ULC, the unlearning of errors should be a function of experience);

c) the real importance of prior knowledge is on the human performance, as the feedback from actions corrects the rule structure causing the erroneous actions (i.e., the probability of subsequent error depends on the earlier outcomes);

d) blame assignment, rule revision and specialisation occur, the number of events should be some function of a learning rate (i.e., learning effectively eliminating the errors and changing the distribution with experience); and

e) situation or context are important (i.e., the current rate of learning depends on both the present outcome rate and the experience-dependent distribution of errors).

In private correspondence, Professor Ohlsson raised some key thoughts about individual versus collective learning. At the individual level, some description of the error has to be made in order to unlearn (remove, revise or rescind a prior acquired 'rule'). In addition, this unlearning involves some fundamental process including 'counter-indication', which should be system-dependent to some degree.

So, *in principle*, all we have to assert here is the idea that the same behaviour that drives individual learning and error elimination in skill acquisition by repeated trials is manifested at the collective or system level by the observed reduced rate of outcomes as a function of the total experience with the (particular) system. The correctness of this interconnected equivalence would be buried in the data and behind the vagaries of human nature, as indeed we shall see.

The whole field of corporate and social organisation has also studied this same issue, mainly in a qualitative manner. They grapple with important problems, like this aspect summarised here by J. Denreall et al., 2004 [11]:

> [The] organization literature has explored both the power and the limits of experiential learning. Although learning stemming from prior experience can be associated with performance improvement ... it can also pose difficult challenges of inference. The link between current actions and observed outcomes may be (confused) by noise and interaction with other learners. The link between actions and outcomes can also be obscured by temporal interdependencies, such as competency traps and delays in feedback.
>
> This delay in realizing feedback complicates search behavior because only at the end of a long sequence of actions is there some discernable payoff. More generally, this challenge is known as

*the credit assignment problem – how should one assign the credit arising from the overall sequence of actions to each of the antecedent actions?*

Source: *Denreall, Fang and Leventhal* [11]

Suppose we have a sequence of actions, choices and decisions. It is plainly a difficult, if not impossible, problem to separate all the influences, nuances and factors before, after and during learning. This is very relevant to the errors made in HTS, to risk taking behaviour (as if it is OK if the result cannot harm me until later . . .). The ability of humans includes being able to ignore prior knowledge, written procedures, feedback (both mental and physical) and screen out unfavourable information. This is just what humans do to survive.

As we show here, the 'credit', however it is defined, can actually take many forms: less risk, more knowledge, less errors, improved performance, lower costs, all in conjunction with the technological system. We consider that the feedback process is built in as part of the total system and ignore the problem of describing the individual behaviour, delays and decisions. In effect, we model the external forces that influence the collective whole (like cost pressures and competition) acting *together* with the internal forces that shape the purely human actions (like success, happiness, utility . . .) as one integral but unseen feedback loop.

## Evidence of Risk Reduction by Learning

That we learn is entirely obvious, but has not been fully described before theoretically with a testable model.

So, while it is self-evident that we must learn, if only to survive, it is not obvious how we can distinguish just learning facts (i.e., a vocabulary in a language) from making foolish or wise decisions (i.e., making or not making mistakes). Clearly, many psychological, environmental, social, cultural and mental factors are involved in the rate of learning, the admission of error, the assignment of blame and the corrective measures. These decisions are often taken in real time, on the job, during action and reaction to immediate situations, accompanied by background pressures and situational factors and concerns, being in what is termed the 'context' in cognitive psychology. All this can occur in the presence of and the potential for deliberate risk taking rather than risk avoidance. Add to this, the complication of working with and interfacing with a technological system, no matter how simple (a car, a computer, an instrument signal, an administrative action . . .), and the problem of human decision making attains immense complexity. We cannot describe the inner workings of the human mind from the observed outcomes.[2]

The very first so-called 'Golden Rule' of the Group Interaction in High Risk Environments (GIHRE) exercise is to ask questions early, as the evidence suggests that the subsequent performance is improved. This result and recommendation is stunning in both its self-evidence and that it would need such a high-powered study to disclose its existence. One suspects that successful teachers have known this for millennia. In addition, on contacting the distinguished lead GIHRE authors to see how this approach was being applied, measured and tested against data, we were informed that the work was finished. But, as we really know, learning is a continuous journey that is *never, ever* over.

---

[2]It is known from recent neurological studies that actual physical and dynamic changes occur in the neural structures in the brain because of learning (the so-called 'plastic brain').

We also find as a result of our analyses that there is a special case, which we call 'perfect learning'. Then we learn from all the non-outcomes as well so that in this 'perfect learning' case, we also can take the number of non-outcomes as a measure of the experience. This assumption implies the ideal of learning from all the non-outcomes, not just the (rare) outcomes

## Evidence of Learning from Experience: Case Studies

We have shown before many cases of learning (and forgetting) at work. Even the show jumper quoted in the Introduction was learning.

Now let us look at a case where the human is in more immediate control of a machine. One example is driving a vehicle, where there is direct feedback both ways, from the vehicle to the driver and back in a tightly coupled control loop. There is also clear evidence of learning, through prior knowledge, in the driver's response to tire failures in SUVs. Tread separation events, which was a hot topic at one time and led to millions of tire recalls and replacements (see Know the Risk, 2002) [9]. So the US NHTSA conducted a simulator driving study to see how drivers reacted to a tire failure by separation.

It was found that, not surprisingly, once warned about the risk, the chance of failing to retain control after a failure fell by more than a factor of two. The reason was the prior knowledge affected the subsequent behaviour. In the words of the report:

*Knowledge of the imminent tread separation reduced the overall probability of control loss from 55% to 20%, and that, because they braked and reduced speed, when drivers had prior knowledge of the imminent tread separation, they were significantly less likely to sustain loss of vehicle control following the tread separation.*
*(Source: NHTSA 'Investigation of Driver Reactions to Tread Separation Scenarios in the National Advanced Driving Simulator (NADS)', Report DOT HS 809 523, January, 2003)*

This is learning at work in a real-life situation that can possibly occur once every three years or so. These large factors of risk reduction (ranging from 2 to 10) are what we have come to expect from having a learning environment with strong feedback from experience into the subsequent behaviour.

How about any more direct evidence on, say, human decision making and learning? It is clear our mistakes can and do reduce with learning, as shown in a simple experimental exercise (Christina Fang, 2003) [12]. Utilising a 'treasure hunt' game on a computer, the progress was simply by counting the number of moves needed to find the treasure. It was shown that not only did humans (in this case a sample of 68 of them) follow a learning curve to reach the treasure in fewer moves, but the number of decisions and actions required to find the treasure improved dramatically after only about 2–3 trial attempts. The learning was rapid and effective: people wanted to find the treasure and developed strategies for remembering and using previous trial attempts. In fact, Fang assumed that the improvement was too rapid to be pure learning since it did not follow a classic inverse power law decline with increasing experience (cf. the classic economic elasticity relation).

However, as Figure 1.2 shows, the data do follow a classic MERE learning curve, as derived from the Learning Hypothesis. The minimum number of moves is only about 20% of the initially required attempts, and corresponds to almost the minimum possible of ~6

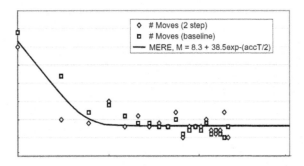

**Figure 1.2.** The evidence of learning

moves in the initial game set-up. This fractional or 5× reduction is of the same order of improvement that has been observed for industrial accidents, near misses, etc.

We consider this experiment of Fang, to whom we are most grateful for the use of the data, *a direct demonstration of the existence of learning as a part of an HTS*, in this case, a stylised computer game. It turns out that the reduction in the number of errors from repeated trials, and hence, an increasing number of successes, $N_S$, as a result of practice at mechanical tasks, is common for humans and individuals and has led to formulating empirical 'laws of practice'. These 'laws' relate the number of successes to the number of trails, $t$, raised to some power or exponent, $m$, where:

$$N_S \propto t^m$$

The subject of the influence of practice and the exact relationship to learning curves and outcome rates are covered in mathematical detail in Appendix J. There, we show that the learning traits and trends observed with repeated trials with individuals fit *exactly* the same learning trends observed in the outcome rates for a myriad of entire systems with increasing experience.

## Evidence of Learning in Economics

We also learn how to reduce the cost of producing an item in a factory and how to take it from the test or prototype stage to full production. Modern computers are a fine example of how dramatically the cost of a consumer good like the PC has plunged, so that now the software is more expensive than the hardware. The performance has improved too and competition has provided a key incentive in the marketplace. Technology has advanced, and costs and prices have reduced as experience of the marketplace has been accumulated. There are extensive analyses of 'learning curves' during mass production with increased operational experience, even to develop an elasticity value between the numbers produced and the unit cost (see below).

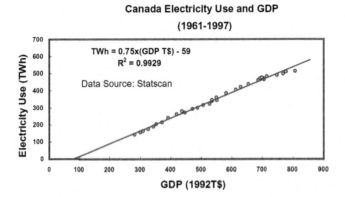

**Figure 1.3.** Canada electricity use and GDP

We will also examine a number of such cases in more and greater detail in Chapter 6, but another unusual case springs to our attention.

In Canada, as a developed country, the use of electricity as a means of energy has increased in lockstep with economic growth. As we learned to grow wealth, we used more electric power, or vice versa. It is just not obvious at first what is the cause and what is the effect. As the country's gross domestic product (GDP) has grown, so has the electric energy use (measured in TWh). The relation from 1961 to 1997 is shown in Figure 1.3.

The relation is so close that at 99% confidence for that 1961 to 1997 interval we could say that the change in electricity usage was given by a straight-line fit of 75% of the change in the GDP. Hence:

$$\text{TWh used} = 0.75 \times (\text{GDP, T\$}) - 59$$

This increase in usage occurred despite large (>10%) gains in overall energy efficiency: we learnt to use electricity more as we learnt to use energy more efficiently. This is somewhat of a paradox, as increasing efficiency implies even greater electricity energy usage, and as more electricity was produced, the price lowered too. Will this electricity growth trend continue indefinitely? What is the risk that we could, by producing less electricity or raising its price, cause an economic recession?

Globally, we have a similar but slightly slower growth rate in electricity usage as shown in Figure 1.4 on a per capita basis (the individual's usage).

Globally, the rate of growth of wealth levels off as we have more and more power: we have learnt to adapt somehow. What these examples tell us is that the factors influencing learning can be intertwined with others, such as economic considerations. The feedback can be in unexpected ways and can change the trends.

## Evidence of Learning in Engineering and Architecture: The Costs of Mistakes

No one wants a human-designed and human-built structure to fail and kill anyone, so mechanical and civil engineers, structural analysts and architects combine their talents and

**Global Economies and Electricity Use**

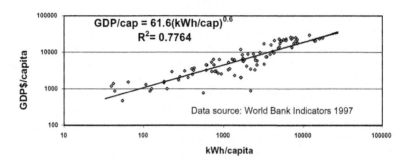

**Figure 1.4.**  Global economies and electricity use

expertise to ensure safe, effective and economic designs. We do not now expect bridges or office towers to collapse, ships to break up and sink, or the wings to fall off an aircraft. Materials have improved and the margins to failures due to stress and fatigue of materials have been refined. Driven by need, by safety and by costs, from when the first steam boilers used to explode, and the first iron bridges collapsed, safety systems and margins have been rigorously refined in their design.

In engineering, in the design of structures like bridges and buildings that we all use, and in the design of ships, trains, drilling rigs and aircraft, there is clear and compelling evidence of learning from mistakes.

But even today, as we move forward in the never-ending quest for perfection and performance, we move from proven technology with known performance to new applications and into realms of the unknown or less explored. We press forward with 'improvements' and 'innovations' in design to reduce cost, to enhance safety, to have a better 'product', or just to produce a new idea. An excellent summary of disasters and failures in engineering systems has been given (Lancaster, 1996) [13], which examined in detail how the refinements in technology changed safety and introduced failures. Just for hydrocarbon (oil, gas and chemical) processing plants, the costs of the explosions, fires and events from 1963 to 1992 were placed at a staggering $6B (his table 1.25) and was rising in losses year by year. The recent Texas City oil refinery explosion shows that such events are not just things of the past and can cost many millions.

In fact, it has been stated eloquently by Petroski [3] that failure is a *requirement* for success in engineering simply because only by learning from our mistakes can and do we improve. The trend for the failure rate with time is generally downward and Lancaster has fitted a whole variety of empirical Weibull curves to a wide range of the failure data that show a downward trend. We show later (in Chapter 4) that the Weibull form, as commonly adopted in fitting data in engineering failure analysis, is actually inapplicable to describing the real trends in the learning data.

Now Lancaster [13] was not aware of our then unpublished work on the Universal Learning Curve (ULC) and the key role of *experience*, any more than we were aware of his intriguing book until very recently. It was actually pointed out to us by an interested reader and colleague in 2006, who remarked that Lancaster's data curves looked much like our theoretical ones and that maybe there were some common features. And so it was proved. Lancaster examined in detail the engineering causes (the key mechanical and physical reasons) behind a large set of catastrophes and accidents in engineering systems and, after some 270 pages of detailed analysis of these multiple failures and events, came to the key conclusion:

*The evidence shows that in most fields of human activity, and particularly those which are the most advanced mechanically, there is general improvement of safety with the passage of time. Such improvement, however, takes the form of a proportional reduction of accident rate. . . . So it never becomes zero.*

And later:*The benefit does not derive from any single cause or activity, it is an evolutionary trend based on the efforts of countless individuals towards making a better product . . . and this trend will undoubtedly continue.*

> *Quoted from 'Engineering Catastrophes', J. Lancaster, pp. 277 and 279*

We would simply substitute the word 'experience' for 'time' in the above statement and emphasise that in our view, the dominant cause of the failures is the *human* contribution found within the entire system. So the rate reduction is due to learning from those same errors, whatever they may be due to.

## Learning in Technology: The Economics of Reducing Costs

Historically, the observed and desirable decrease in cost of any manufactured item with increases in production is well known (Wright, 1936) [14]; (McDonald and Schrattenholzer, 2001) [15]. The decrease parallels the classical economics price/demand relation with increases in quantity produced and these references contain sufficient background that we need not repeat the historical basis here. This decrease is obviously due to a combination of technological and market factors such as:

a) economy of scale with numbers made, repeat orders and standardised processes;
b) streamlined and bulk ordering of supplies, parts and equipment;
c) increasing experience of the labour force and its management;
d) product, process and production improvements;
e) market forces and price pressures; and
f) innovation and technology shifts.

McDonald and Schrattenholzer, 2002 [16] and many others before them point out that because experience accumulates with time, unit costs decrease for a given technology where the important variable is the 'accumulated experience', not time passing. So the measure of experience – or its surrogate – is key, exactly as observed in modern technological systems exhibiting error, accident, event, injury and incident reduction. This basic fact is shown by the theory and data in Duffey and Saull, 2002 [17]. The decrease is non-linear.

   The economic formulae (or 'model') proposed and used to date are empirical and describe a cost reduction rate or trajectory with experience. The simplest are of the form of a power law relating the cost reduction rates to a production parameter, for example, material and/or labour cost. Thus, Wright's (1936) original formula leads to an empirical power law of the form:

$$\text{Cost Reduction Factor, } F = (\text{Quantity, } N)^x$$

where $x$ is an unknown or observed power 'law' factor. Since the cost reduction factor is related to the cost of the first unit, $C_0$, then $F \equiv (C/C_0)$ and the accumulated production quantity can be written as $\varepsilon$, this relation is then of decreasing cost or price with increasing production/experience:

$$C = C_0(\varepsilon)^{-b}$$

where the power law 'elasticity' parameter, $x = -b$, is derived from experience, and $\varepsilon = \Sigma n_i$ $\varepsilon_i$, the accumulated experience or total number or quantity of relevant units produced. The actual observed price or cost or time decrease is then 'piecewise' fitted by a series of values of $b$, which vary with increasing production/experience (i.e., $b = f(\varepsilon)$). The percent cost reduction for a doubling of cumulative output is often used as a measure of the learning rate, $LR$, where,

$$LR = (1 - 2^b) \times 100\%$$

McDonald and Schrattenholzer's, 2002 [16] expression for the 'concept of technological learning' in the capital cost of energy systems is of the similar power law form:

$$\text{Specific Cost, } C = (\text{Initial cost, } C_O) \times (\text{Installed capacity, } C\text{cap})^b$$

where $b$ (like the power law factor, $X$) is termed in economic jargon a 'learning elasticity' and $C$cap is equivalent to experience, $\varepsilon$. The same formulation can hold for Price if market forces are active.

It has been shown that many energy systems can be fitted with b-values. It is actually observed that the cost curves are not of constant slope, so the value of the elasticity, b, varies with accumulated experience too. Thus, continuous learning or experience curves are approximated by a series of piecewise fits, varying b, so that it is a non-unique function with accumulated production. This must also be able to correct for the wrong asymptote with the implication is that the price, $C$, tends to zero at large experience ($\varepsilon \to \infty$), whereas in reality, there is always minimum price/cost for a product in the commercial market – unless it is a loss maker. This has led analysts to introduce the so-called 'kinked' power law models or variants, with an arbitrary change of slope or b-value at some experience, quantity produced or date.

Since the value of $b$ can vary, the choice of the accumulated experience, acc$N$, in this case was predicated by the accumulated (electric) power production potential (accMW) sales for each technology. This measure for the experience was and is relevant to these energy technologies competing in the power market. The technologies are price-takers dependent on the local market price of power sold to consumers and/or wholesalers or marketeers, where the incentive is to reduce unit investment cost (measured in \$/kW installed) as quickly as possible to the value needed for market penetration and electricity sales.

As we gain experience and learn, the rate of decrease in cost (or price) is proportional to the instantaneous cost (or price) above the ultimate market value. This assumption (or hypothesis at this stage) is justified a posteriori by data and model comparisons, and we later show this very same idea to also be at work in portfolio management in the apparent chaos of the stock market.

## Evidence of Learning Skill and Risk Reduction in the Medical Profession: Practice Makes Almost Perfect

We would expect the impact of learning to be commonplace and well recorded, especially where we may have many, many learning opportunities. The medical profession is one such system.

Unfortunately, we all may have to go to see a doctor sometime and, whether we like it or not, sometimes we have to have surgery. There is an outcome risk of death for every surgery. In fact, since 1979, the medical profession has known about the so-called 'volume effect': the more patients that are treated by a hospital or doctor(s) using a specific surgical procedure, the less risk they have of dying as a result. This led to the trend to justify centralisation of health care using regional centres, to ensure enough patients were treated in order to help reduce the death risk.

As an example, we found data available in the literature on a very common procedure, namely, eye cataract surgeries in Ontario (Bell et al., 2007) [18]. Some 290,000 total cataract surgeries were recorded and the data examined for surgeons who performed ranges of surgery 'volume' (none to 250, 250 to 500, 500 to 1000, and above). The number of errors in any volume range was about ~1; and the calculated rate of errors is shown in Figure 1.5 as an adverse rate, $R\%$, versus the volume $V$, being the number of surgeries performed. The standard MERE Learning curve fit is also shown.

These data show clear evidence of learning and that even for such a common and usually simple surgical procedure, there is a large reduction in error rate with increasing experience. The implication is that a minimum number (or 'volume') of surgeries to ensure the competency and skill to achieve the lowest possible error rates. In fact, empirical guidelines based on data have been published in the USA for desirable specific surgical procedure rates per year. These are the so-called 'Evidence-Based Hospital Referral' procedures based on the volumes in terms of numbers of specific operation types performed per year using data on whether a 'volume effect' was observed for the particular procedure (see, e.g., listings in

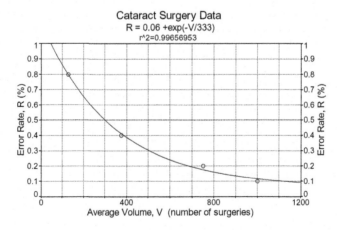

**Figure 1.5.** 'Volume effect': learning in cataract surgery procedures

Urbach et al., 2005) [19]. These guidelines can be used by a physician for a referral of a patient to a specific hospital that satisfies the rate (volume) guidelines. In other words, there is a threshold risk for you, the sick patient, to be sent to a specific hospital that does enough surgeries similar to the one that you need. So well-known medical and surgical centres really do have a reason for being well-known in their field of competency, be it heart, cancer or immune system treatments. They have a lower risk of death.

In 'Know the Risk' [9], we showed how the data for overall medical errors, the so-called adverse events leading to unnecessary deaths, did *not* show any evidence of learning with increased patient numbers and we return to update this analysis of overall medical errors in Chapter 7. But we also showed that the specific case of heart surgery did show significant evidence of learning, with the risk of death reduced by increasing the number of surgeries beyond about 300 to 400. Obviously, more intricate surgeries benefit from performing more of them. How can that be?

As the adverse event data show, many medical errors are being made anyway, so there is one clear explanation. There are overall many potential learning opportunities, but error reduction and skill are key for specialised procedures. Rigorously, learning and re-learning how to perform surgery reduces the errors and increases proficiency and skill. The 'practice makes perfect' hypothesis already exists in the medical profession and is clearly a subset of our MERE learning model. This idea is entirely consistent with our analyses of multiple HTS-like health care, except that we know now that no desirable state of perfection is possible. Low error rates are nearly achievable, but the perfection of zero not quite. For any and all HTS, we would say, 'practice makes *almost* perfect'.

A recent study of all the previous published medical volume effect studies has confirmed the presence of a beneficial risk-reducing volume influence for the vast majority of cases (CIHI, 2005) [20] and (Urbach et al., 2005) [19]. The most commonplace procedures, as they are called, were gastrointestinal, vascular and heart operations. The definition of 'volume' varied study by study, but was generally the total number of cases analysed: our interpretation using the DSM learning curve approach is that volume is equivalent to the accumulated experience. This number should be measured by counting the running integral of the number of patients treated or procedures performed, a fact also noted by Urbach et al. [19], but this was not available for every study.

The CIHI-sponsored review covered a wide range, with some nine major categories of surgical procedures, and multiple subcategories. Because of the variations, no tabulation was given of actual outcome numbers, just whether there existed or not a so-called 'positive association' of risk of death with volume. Of the total 331 studies reviewed, covering over two million cases (2,368,512 deaths to be exact), over 60% showed a statistically significant learning effect of a reduced death rate with increasing 'volume'. This fraction is remarkably, and in our view, not coincidentally also close to the estimated human element contribution for accidents and outcomes. The review report contains a key carefully worded statement that confirms the presence of a learning effect (Urbach et al.) [19]:

*Our review provides considerable evidence for the ubiquity of volume-outcome associations for virtually every health service that has been investigated. Assuming that the lack of negative studies is not due to a publication bias against research with negative results, one might speculate that almost any health service subjected to sufficient scrutiny will be found to have a volume-outcome relationship.*

Just how many of the two million lives lost could have been saved?

We just do not know if the data follow a true learning curve or how much the study samples deviate from a constant risk line. The risk reduction was estimated in the review using the so-called 'odds ratio', which indicates the strength of the statistical association between a predictor and an outcome (for example, age and mortality) so as to be able to compare the 'likelihood' of an outcome between multiple groups of patient types. For expected death rates of between 0.2 and 4% for a given procedure, the *reduction* in death risk with 'volume' increase was estimated as between 0.3 and 4% for every additional procedure performed, the range depending on the exact surgical procedure. Using that rate range means the minimum reduction in the number of deaths per additional procedure is given by:

(Least % reduction in deaths per procedure)×(Number of total deaths reviewed in
   CIHI survey)×(Fraction of procedures reviewed showing a reduction with volume)
   $= (0.003) \times (2.37.10^6) \times (0.68) \sim 5,500$ preventable or less deaths per additional procedure.

Since this strong learning effect is so well known and universal in medicine, and the implications so personal and deadly, what is remarkable is how long it has taken to implement the risk reduction measures. The so-called 'conspiracy of anonymity' is the unspoken pact between patient and physician, the caregiver and receiver, where highly personal details, professional advice and medical history are never released without consent. We all, and not just the medical profession, clearly need to provide a modern and transparent basis for standard reporting for all procedures that we can all have confidence in and learn from. These new data will then show precisely where the HTS of the medical profession stands on the ULC; and would determine the rate of learning and the influence of any measures taken to improve it.

## Learning in HTSs: The Recent Data Still Agree

In our book that established the existence of the learning curve (Know the Risk), we examined many case studies. Since then, even more data have appeared to support and verify the approach, which we can now include. In fact, we continue to discover such data almost by accident, as they are continually reported in year-by-year format in many, many quite obscure places as well as by traditional government agencies.

Particularly interesting, we found data for oil spills at sea from the US Coast Guard that we will analyse in some detail later when we examine risk perception. Since spills are just another accident in an HTS, namely a ship operated by people, it is interesting to see if the usual everyday accidents do exhibit learning. These accident outcomes include groundings, collisions, fires and all manner of mishaps. The most recent data we found were on the web in the Annual Report for 2004 of the UK Marine Accident Investigation Board (MAIB, for short, at www.maib.gov.uk). The MAIB's responsibility is to examine reported accidents and incidents in detail. The MAIB broke down the accidents by type of ship, being the two broad categories of merchant ships that carry cargo or fishing vessels that ply their trade in the treacherous waters off the UK islands.

In both types of ship, the number of accidents were given as the usual uninformative list of tabulations by year from 1994 to 2004, together with the total number of ships in that

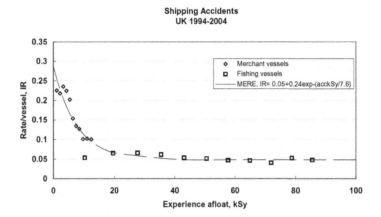

**Figure 1.6.** The learning curve for shipping accidents

merchant or fishing vessel category, some 1,000 and 10,000 vessels, respectively. Instinctively, we think of fishing as a more dangerous occupation, with manual net handling and deck work sometimes in rough seas and storms, but surprisingly it turns out not to be the case.

We analysed these accidents by simply replotting the data as the accident rate per vessel versus the thousands of accumulated shipping-years of experience, kSy. By adopting this measure for experience, not only can we plot the data for the two types on the same graph, we also see if we have a clear learning trend emerging. The result is shown in Figure 1.6, where the line or curve drawn shown is our usual theoretical MERE learning form.

We see immediately that, at least in the UK, not only the (outcome) accident rate is higher for merchant vessels than fishing boats, but also that learning is evident in the data that fit together on this one plot only if using experience afloat as a basis. The other observation is that the fishing vessels are at the minimum rate per vessel that the merchant vessels are just approaching. Perhaps the past few centuries of fishing experience has led to that low rate so that, in fact, fishermen and fisherwomen are highly skilled at their craft. The lowest attained rate of ~0.05 accidents per vessel corresponds to an hourly rate if afloat all day and working all the time, of

$$\sim 0.05/(365 \times 24) \sim 5.10^{-6} \text{ per hour.}$$

That is one accident per vessel every 175,000 hours, which is about the least achieved by any HTS or industry anywhere in the world, including the very safe ones like aircraft, nuclear and chemical industries of 100,000 to 200,000 hours. Even allowing for a duty factor afloat for the vessel or crew of 50% or so, or working at sea half the time, it is still of the same order. That last result is by itself simply amazing and reflects the common factor of the human involvement in HTS. Why is the curve the shape it is? Why does this same minimum value appear and reappear? Can we predict this curve? Let us examine the learning hypothesis analysis again, but in some more detail.

## The Equations That Describe the Learning Curve

We can and will show that the learning curve that described the performance improvement and risk reduction is exactly the one we derive next!! It is the MERE exponential learning curve, which should come as no surprise to us given the wide range of data that it already describes.

We seek the simplest rule that can successfully describe the widest range of data and experience, from the learning hypothesis, in words:

*The rate of reduction of the outcome rate with increasing experience is proportional to the rate at which outcomes are occurring.*

As we have shown before, from this simple rule, writing the conventional symbol $\lambda$ as the outcome (error or failure) rate and $\varepsilon$ for the experience, we have the MERE:

$$d\lambda/d\varepsilon = -k(\lambda - \lambda_m)$$

where $k$ is the learning rate constant of proportionality, positive for learning and negative for forgetting, and $\lambda_m$ the minimum attainable rate. The failure rate as a function of any accumulated experience, $\lambda(\varepsilon)$, is then obtained by straightforward integration from some initial rate and experience, $\varepsilon_0$, out to the present or future with any larger experience. Thus, the error or failure rate, $\lambda$, decreases exponentially with increasing experience, $\varepsilon$, as given by the MERE.

We need to relate this failure rate to the recorded accident, event and error data for outcomes, say as numbers killed per unit experience. We have the proportionality that the failure rate $\lambda(\varepsilon) \propto A$, the observed outcome rate, measured as counts of accidents, deaths, outcomes or errors (see the mathematical Appendix A). That result does not pretend or assume that some errors have no measurable, recorded or observed outcomes, but simply allows use of the multitudinous outcome data reported by the many agencies, administrations, inquiries, safety authorities, industries and investigators.

This MERE solution leads directly to the ULC that is useful for correlating the world's data, which can be written in the non-dimensional form,

$$E^* = e^{-KN^*}$$

This form has been validated by comparison to outcome (failure) rates from two centuries of the available world accident, injury and event data (as shown in Figure 1.7). The data are for a wide range of HTS and all follow the same trend according to the Learning Hypothesis, and the value of the learning rate constant of $K \sim 3$ was chosen to give the best overall fit. Obviously, any individual dataset can be fitted with more accuracy than the entire group, as we shall see later also. It is worth noting that the observed value of $K \sim 3$ (or approximately and perhaps coincidentally, $K \sim \pi$) implies that the characteristic learning scale is about one-third of the maximum experience, and to first order almost independent of the HTS or where it is located.

The learning approach is inherent or implicit in current management approaches, but has been applied in a reactive manner, not predictively. Not using a priori analysis, but adopting apostiori reflection. All engineers, politicians, regulators and designers, being highly

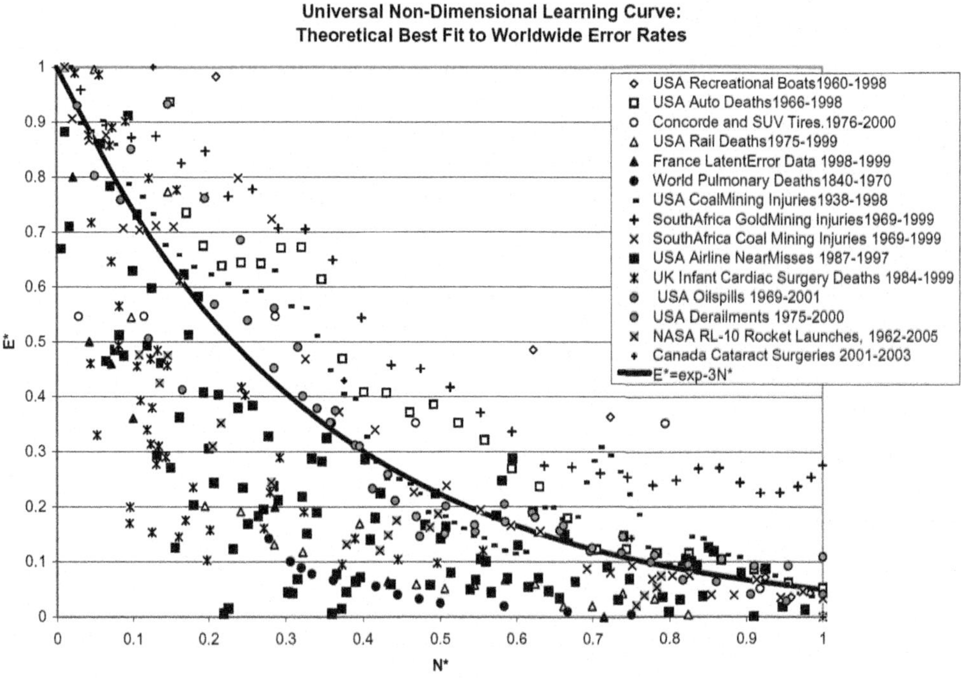

**Universal Non-Dimensional Learning Curve:
Theoretical Best Fit to Worldwide Error Rates**

**Figure 1.7.** The Universal Learning Curve compared to data; many diverse data follow the same trend

professional managers and operators, strive to eliminate the accidents, failures, outcomes and errors we observe from 'ever happening again'. We use Quality Systems to track and improve, providing procedures, report non-conformances to requirements, adopt design and safety standards. Impressive lists of recommendations for improvement and their implementation using empirical safety schemes almost inevitably result as reactive 'Safety Management' and layered 'Quality Management' systems. These are useful, but are all reactive: we would prefer to be predictive, taking advantage of acquired experience and learning trends, and quantify the effect of corrective measures[3].

The exact individual event is indeed unlikely (improbable) of happening again, or recurring, unless there is a repetitive failure mechanism. But since the events themselves occur randomly, we can only eliminate those we actually observe.

Since we are not special observers (the Copernican view) and only observe what we happen to measure or record during our observation interval (or HTS lifetime), we are faced with predicting random events and making only case-by-case improvements. If the events are distributed uniformly in our observation interval, and our elimination of cause or non-failure rate were constant, the number of events and the rate would appear to fall away steadily as an exponential curve.

---

[3]The systematic 'naming', classification or taxonomy for events is another useful example of systematically learning from errors, as advocated by B. Wallace and A. Ross in 'Beyond Human Error: Taxonomies and Safety Science', Taylor and Francis, Boca Raton, FL, USA, 2006.

## Zero Defects and Reality

We have already shown that the world data show conclusively that we can reduce the rate of outcomes through learning, but cannot totally eliminate them. Consistent with the psychological model of individual skill acquisition, residual rule conflicts that cause errors always exist. There is always a finite, residual and non-zero risk. This is despite the best intentions, exhortations and practices of managers, operators and regulators. But all is not lost: we can and must still improve as much as we can.

One major method used for improvement has been to set management targets and invoke specific systems (e.g., based on a zero-defect goal or 6-sigma quality). It has become almost dogma that for continuous improvement (read learning) to occur, we must have a challenging and aggressive goal (read zero events, accidents or non-conformances).

What we argue and what the data say is that we all really need to know:

- where we are on the ULC;
- how can we practically adopt a useful measure for our experience;
- how fast we improve (learn) or not, compared to others;
- what actual reduction in events our measures are achieving numerically;
- how close are we to the nirvana of the lowest possible rate;
- what goals should management set and expect;
- how we should improve our systems, safety and learning environment; and
- how we should measure and report outcomes.

In our investigations and published book ('Know the Risk') [9], we have already shown that the rate of errors depends on the accumulated experience, as we learn from our mistakes and errors.

The key consequence arising from the world's data over the last two centuries of observation is that 'zero defects' is actually unattainable. This residual finite rate is attributed to the non-removable component due to the human element and chance. That means a minimum rate, despite our best efforts, is observed about 1 event per 100,000 to 200,000 experience hours (an outcome frequency of $5 \times 10^{-6}$ per experience hour). This is the lowest that the safest HTS attain.

In any large engineering project, using say a million hours of skilled labour, we can expect there to be a minimum of five design and construction errors. The aim, goal, job and objective of safety management and quality assurance are to find those errors!!

Such is the paradox of learning from experience that the observation of the non-existence of zero defects or events has caused some of our colleagues some genuine conflict and heartburn. This arises because of prior or existing corporate, management, production, quality, legislative or commercial commitments to attain what is almost a Holy Grail of zero mistakes, errors, events or outcomes. Admitting that the least rate is not zero and still finite means that management and safety regulators can be accused of, perceived to be 'wrong'. By admitting they may be setting unattainable goals and unrealistic expectations, relaxing means they are now 'allowing' mistakes to occur. In effect, admitting that failures are expected or inevitable also means admitting that we humans are fallible. Which, of course, we really are: we do make mistakes in the natural course of events (Perrow, 1984) [21].

By examining failure data due to the human element in engineering and technological systems, we have demonstrated the existence of a ULC. This allows both monitoring of past and present performance and of predictions using the solution of the MERE. The learning hypothesis shows that the resulting probability of error agrees with available data as we now show.

We have also provided comparisons to empirical parameter fitting of failure distributions using conventional reliability engineering methods. Hence, we can relate and contrast the techniques used for component failures to that needed for human reliability estimates.

## Predicting Failures: The Human Bathtub

By its very nature, the error probability due to the human element is dynamic and may be predicted using the MERE learning hypothesis and the minimum failure rate. Data from the world's commercial airlines, the NASA Shuttle failures and from nuclear plant operator transient control behaviour show agreement with this theory. The results also agree with the overwhelming contribution of the homo-technological errors to other major engineering and safety catastrophes (e.g., Ladbroke Grove, Columbia and Concorde), as well as to everyday failures (e.g., of pressure vessels, train derailments, oil spills and shipping losses).

Best estimate values and relationships can be derived for both the error rate and for the probability of failure for the entire system. *Moreover, for perhaps the first time, we are in a position to be predictive about the rate and probability of failure in any HTS simply based on our learning history.*

According to the Learning Hypothesis, the event rate falls away exponentially from its initial value as learning occurs with experience towards its minimum value. We can simply relate the failure rate to the probability of an event using conventional analysis.

The result (formally reclaimed and given in Chapter 4 and Appendix A) is a 'bathtub' shaped curve for the human reliability or probability of failure for any HTS.

The curve is sketched in Figure 1.8 using the observed 'best' value for $k$ and an arbitrary measure for experience using a logarithmic scale. The observation is that we learn from experience, reducing the probability of error quickly to $<10^{-2}$, which then remains in a trough until inevitably the probability rises. This rise at large experience occurs, no matter how small the minimum or smallest rate, since eventually we must have an event, even if it is near an infinity of experience on the scale. It is analogous to the wear-out that happens to equipment at large usage.

Clearly, the outcome probability due to the human element is dynamic, changing with experience in a manner defined by the learning rate. Similarly, if we are forgetting, or not learning, the probability does not decrease.

## Experience Space: The Statistics of Managing Safety and of Observing Accidents

We need to reconcile the systematic effects of learning with the fact that events, outcomes, errors and accidents occur randomly. Many years ago, Boltzmann understood this inherent unpredictability of nature and our inability to describe the instantaneous nature of our world,

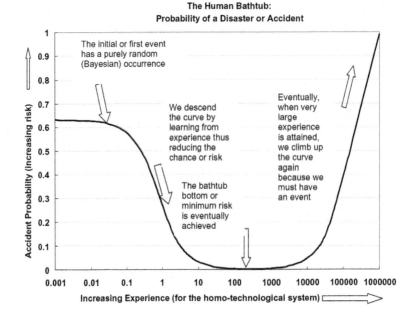

**Figure 1.8.**   The Human Bathtub

but by recourse to statistical arguments, he and others showed how the trends can be reclaimed from considering the microscopic statistical variations.

At a macroscopic level of accidents and errors, this same argument and analysis still holds. In *experience space*, we have the (non-unique) piece of the world's experience interval in which we observe outcomes or events of different experiences that are occurring stochastically.

As errors occur, Engineers, Managers, Society and Regulators introduce new measures (Rules) to attempt to eliminate their re-occurrence. Investigators evaluate in detail the 'event sequences' to determine the apparent causes. New 'design guides' or standards are invoked. Measures are taken to try to control the errors caused by the role of humans themselves. New Laws or Procedures are passed that may require different safety measures. Process changes are implemented in design manufacturing or operation, or using other management means (such as safety programs, retraining and/or the reassignment of staff). Fines may be levied as a means of punishment for allowing something to even happen. The inclusion of these Rules is an example of learning, which should change the observed distribution of outcomes with experience, and hence, explains the effects of safety management or intervention in the system.

These methods, mechanisms and management systems constitute ways of learning from experience. However, to put it another way, management, laws, inquiries, regulations and safety systems try to impose order on disorder. Implicitly, they try to reach a minimum state of disorder, or a maximum state of order, as effectively as possible using Goals and incentives (both rewards and punishments).

## Predicting the Future Based on Past Experience: The Prior Ignorance

How can we predict what might occur, or its chance of occurring again, when we do not know what could happen and when?

However, as noted clearly by Jaynes, 2003 [2], defining probabilities and rates in this way requires a prior knowledge of the total number of outcomes, $N$, which for any predictive purposes we do not know or have. We may know the past frequency, but not the future probability without making some assumptions. As baldly and boldly remarked by Arthur H. Copeland, 1932 [22] long ago, '*The definition of the word probability has never been agreed upon*'.

We show here that the future estimate for the event probability (the likelihood) is solely a function of experience and that the future is hence predictable by the past. The future event probability is determined by the dominant influence of the human element.

The probability of any such event ever 'happening again' (the posterior probability) given the probability of some other prior event having already happened (the prior knowledge that we have observed already), is called the conditional probability. It is usually judged by multiplying the prior occurrence frequency or probability, $p(\varepsilon)$ – a measure of the number of times it has happened up until now in our experience – with its chance or likelihood of it ever happening again, $p(L)$, assuming that the prior exists.

We may, of course, not have a very good estimate for the likelihood, $p(L)$. The frequency of the occurrences may not be the same as the probabilities, particularly for stochastic and rare events, and when corrective measures may or may not have altered the chance. The resulting equation is Bayes hypothesis that:

$$\text{Posterior probability, } p(\text{P}) \propto \text{Prior probability, } p(\varepsilon) \times \text{Likelihood, } p(\text{L})$$

The posterior $p(\text{P})$ is estimated by the chance of it having already happened anyway, $p(\varepsilon)$, which is assumed to be known somehow, weighted by the likelihood, $p(L)$, being an estimate of the probability of another event happening or not.

Generally, we do not know how many events (in part or in total) have occurred or will occur. In our Copernican viewpoint, we just happen to have observed some sample set of outcomes, $n$, out of the possible total, $N$.

If somehow we knew how many events, $n$, had occurred or been observed out of the possible total of $N$, where $n < N$, then it would be possible to link the probability, $p(\varepsilon)$, with the prior frequency of observed events or outcomes. This link can be achieved via the numerical definition of the probability of an already observed sample of outcomes, $n$, namely the prior probability according to the Laplace and Bayes formulation:

$$p(\varepsilon) \approx n/N$$

In general, we can show both from sampling theory and Baysian reasoning that the probability for the very next event to occur, $p(L)$, is simply the chance of the next single event occurring given all those already observed:

$$p(\text{L}) \sim 1/n$$

Hence, the estimate for the posterior probability of the next event is given by:

$$p(\text{P}) \approx (n/N)(1/n) = 1/N \text{, always,}$$

and our state of ignorance remains complete since we do not know the value of $N$.

To avoid this conundrum, we might possibly also assume that the likelihood of the next outcome, $n$, among $N$ total, is based on choosing from a known or assumed prior distribution.

The case often adopted in the literature is to utilise the binomial distribution, which is equivalent to the special case of a large sample, $N$, from the hypergeometric sampling function (see Appendix F). For this limit, we can also reclaim that $p(L) \sim 1/n$, so the result is consistent with the previous purely Bayesian estimate. The same formal result also holds in the limit of vanishingly small probability (the Poisson distribution) as is appropriate for rare events.

Other cases can be used, as a check of these answers, to be sure there is not an error. For example, adopting a uniform distribution given by, say, the Laplace prior, $p(\text{LaP})$. In that special case, the Rule of Succession is:

$$p(\text{LaP}) \equiv (n+1)/(N+2)$$

We can expand this result in an approximation for large $N$:

$$p(\text{LaP}) \approx n/N + 1/N - 2/N^2 + \dots \text{ higher terms}$$
$$= p(\varepsilon) + 1/N - 2/N^2 + \dots$$

In this approximation, the probability can be seen to be simply the prior probability ($n/N$) plus the chance of any next outcome ($1/N$), plus higher order terms. Thus, for the limit of many possible outcomes, $\{n, N\} \gg 1$, $p(\text{LaP}) \rightarrow n/N = p(\varepsilon)$, the usual result discussed above. Conversely, for rarely observed events, $p(\varepsilon) \rightarrow 0$, and $p(\text{LaP}) \rightarrow 1/N$, reflecting the uniform prior probability of our state of ignorance.

For a large sample, $n \rightarrow N$, $n \gg 1$, and so $P(\text{LaP}) \approx 1$, and we must have an event.

When we have not yet even observed the first outcome, $n = 0$, $p(\text{LaP}) \sim 1/N$, as we have seen and derived before for the uniform prior; or when we have no data or prior knowledge, $\{n, N\} = 0$, $p(\text{LaP}) \rightarrow 0.5$, which are odds of 50%, being an equal chance of observing one or not, and so on.

Unfortunately, we usually lack the detailed statistics, prior knowledge or the data on numbers of outcomes or rare events to accurately make such estimates. We often just do not know the values to adopt for $n$, or for $N$, as our observation interval is finite, and we do not know how many total events there might be *in the future*.

## Future Events: The Way Forward Using Learning Probabilities

There is a way forward, despite this lack of knowledge and prior ignorance, based on the learning hypothesis. The probability of an outcome in an HTS and its associated failure or error rate, we expect to be changed only with experience, unless some dramatic or unforeseen technology shifts occur. We can estimate the likelihood of another event, and whether the MERE error rate frequency gives sensible and consistent predictions.

To do this, we return to using conventional statistics and reliability analysis, but applied in experience space. The probability of the outcome or error occurring in or taking less than $\varepsilon$, is just the Cumulative Distribution Function, or CDF, conventionally written as the failure fraction $F(\varepsilon)$ for the failure rate, $\lambda$, for our experience, $\varepsilon$:

$$p(\varepsilon) \equiv F(\varepsilon) = 1 - e^{-\int \lambda d\varepsilon}$$

where the probability of an outcome, $p(\varepsilon) = n/N$. Of course, for small constant rates we can expand and approximate the exponential so that $p(\varepsilon) \approx \lambda \varepsilon$. Recall that for the usual general case, the failure rate is $\lambda = \{dn/d\varepsilon/(N-n)\}$, so that $p(\varepsilon) \rightarrow n/N$, as it should.

More generally, the probability of error is a double exponential or 'bathtub' as shown in the text (Figure 1.8) due to the exponential form of the failure rate. In Appendix A, we derive the exact form, which is obtained by substituting the MERE failure rate into the probability expression and by carrying out the integration from an initial experience, $\varepsilon_0$, to any interval, $\varepsilon$, we obtain the probability as the double exponential:

$$p(\varepsilon) = n/N = 1 - \exp\{(\lambda - \lambda_m)/k - \lambda(\varepsilon_0 - \varepsilon)\}$$

where,

$$\lambda(\varepsilon) = \lambda_m + (\lambda_0 - \lambda_m)\exp - k(\varepsilon - \varepsilon_0)$$

and $\lambda(\varepsilon_0) = \lambda_0 = n/\varepsilon$, at the initial experience, $\varepsilon_0$, accumulated for the initial $n$-outcome(s), and for the first *or for a rare event* $n \sim 1$. This low rate is exactly the form observed in the Space Shuttle and aircraft fatal accident and hull losses.

Let us now look at what happens if we are experienced or not, and what predictions we can make.

## The Wisdom of Experience and Inevitability

Now at larger and larger experience, just by letting $\varepsilon \rightarrow \infty$ in the above formal expressions, the failure rate tends to a minimum, but the probability, $p(\varepsilon)$ tends to unity. *The event is ultimately certain to occur.*

This certainty of an event is independent of how much learning has occurred and the experience at when it occurs only depends on the attainable minimum rate. Thus, we are indeed doomed to failure (the 'normal accident' pessimism), but the event is most likely to occur later if we are learning and not forgetting, or have attained the lowest rate (the 'learning hypothesis' optimism).

*Thus, using good practices and achieving a true learning environment, we can defer the chance of an accident, but not indefinitely. Moreover, by watching our experience and monitoring our rate, understand and predict when we are climbing up the curve.*

## The Last, First or Rare Event

Now consider when we are a novice, when we have some minimal or initial experience, and $\varepsilon \rightarrow \varepsilon_0$, with an initial failure rate, $\lambda(\varepsilon) = \lambda_0$.

The number of events at large experience is asymptotically constant and is actually given by:

$$n \sim N(1 - \exp\{(\lambda_0 - \lambda_m)/k\})$$

Since the probability of an outcome is:

$$p(\varepsilon) = n/N = F(\varepsilon) = 1 - R(\varepsilon)$$

Then the asymptotic Reliability is given by:

$$R(\varepsilon) = \exp\{(\lambda_0 - \lambda_m)/k$$

Now for the other extreme, the very first or rare events, $n = 1$ and the initial failure rate is $\lambda_0 \sim 1/\varepsilon_0$. As shown in Appendix B, this also represents the minimum likelihood (least likely) outcome rate.

For this special case of very low failure rates or rare events, we have a neat approximation that gives the *probability of the event becoming a function only of the initial experience and the learning rate constant.*

Thus, the probability is,

$$p(\varepsilon) = n/N \sim 1/k\varepsilon_0$$

The initial probability tends to a limit of $\sim O(1 - (1/e)) \sim 0.64$, which means about a 60% chance of a novice mistake. Typical human element contributions are cited to be about 65% or more: whether this is a delightful coincidence, a true explanation, or a numerical error we do not know.

If we are lucky or have not yet had an accident but still have some finite experience, for the very first event, $n = 1$. The total possible number of events becomes $N \sim k\varepsilon_0$, and is linearly and solely dependent on our learning rate and our initial (in)experience interval with that HTS. *We just happened to observe that first or rare event/mistake/outcome with the experience we had when we did.*

These are all obvious points, once stated, even if we tend to dislike the answers. What we have done here is reconcile the observation of accidents and tragedies with the formal existence of learning, and demonstrated the utilisation of probability theory applied to human behaviour when using machines.


## Conclusions and Observations: Predicting Accidents

Is it possible to predict when an accident or tragedy will occur? We have now provided an answer: the event rate and probability depend on our experience and how fast we are learning. This should come as no surprise.

Analysis of failure rates in the modern world shows the importance of the rate of learning. The 'learning hypothesis' – that we learn from our mistakes – allows a new determination of the dynamic outcome or error rate in HTS, derived from the available world data. The hypothesis is also confirmed by Fang [12] and other data from actual learning experiments with human subjects; is consistent with Petroski's [3] argument of the need for failures to occur in engineering in order to succeed; and is reflected by Ohlsson's [10] Theory of Error Correction for the psychological processes inherent in individual skill acquisition. It is also in accord with common sense.

The failure rate solution of the MERE defines the probability of an outcome or error as a function of experience. The initial rate is given simply in the limit of rare events by the

Bayesian estimate and is proportional to the inverse of the experience accumulated up to the initial or early outcome(s). In reality, after the initial events or outcomes, the subsequent probability is of a double exponential form and naturally follows a classic 'human bathtub' curve.

The future failure rate is entirely determined by the past experience: *thus, the past defines the future*. This is the classic result and basis of statistical analysis and has been reconfirmed as applying for all the myriads of data that we have examined.

The certainty of ultimately having an event is independent of how much learning that has occurred and the experience at when it occurs only depends on the attainable minimum rate. Thus, we are indeed doomed to failure (the 'normal accident' pessimism), but the event is most likely to occur later if we are learning and not forgetting, or have attained the lowest rate (the 'learning hypothesis' optimism).

*Thus, by using good practices and achieving a true learning environment, we can effectively defer the chance of an accident, but not indefinitely. Moreover, by watching our experience and monitoring our rate, understand and predict when we are climbing up the curve.*

Comparisons of the theory to outcome data for typical HTS from the world's commercial airlines, from the two shuttle failures, and from nuclear plant operator transient control behaviour, show a reasonable level of accord with the learning hypothesis.

The results clearly demonstrate that the error probability due to the human element is dynamic and may be predicted using the learning hypothesis. The future probability estimate is once again derivable from its unchanged prior value, based on learning, and *thus the past frequency predicts the future probability.*

# References

[1] Gottlieb Daimler and Karl Benz Foundation, 2004, 'Golden Rules of Group Interaction in High Risk Environments (GIHRE)' (Available: www.daimler-benz-stiftung.de/home/foundation/en/).

[2] Jaynes, E.T., 2003, 'Probability Theory: The Logic of Science', First Edition, Cambridge University Press, Cambridge, UK, Edited by G.L. Bretthorst.

[3] Petroski, Henry, 1985, 'To Engineer is Human: The Role of Failure in Successful Design', St. Martin's Press, New York.

[4] Goth III, J. Richard, 1993, 'Implications of the Copernican Principle for Our Future Prospects', Nature, Vol. 363, pp. 315–319, 27 May.

[5] Bernoulli, Jacob, 1713, 'Ars conjectandi (The Art of Conjecture)', Basel, Switzerland.

[6] Laplace, P.S., 1814, 'Essai philosophique sur les probabilités', extracted as 'Concerning Probability' in J.R. Newman's 'The World of Mathematics' Vol. 2, p. 1327, 1956.

[7] Andress, F.J., 1954, 'The Learning Curve as a Production Tool', Harvard Business Review, Vol. 32, pp. 87–97.

[8] Jordan, R.B., 1972, 'How to Use the Learning Curve', Third Edition, Cahners Books, Boston, MA.

[9] Duffey, R.B. and Saull, J.W., 2002, 'Know the Risk', First Edition, Butterworth and Heinemann, Boston, MA.

[10] Ohlsson, S., 1996, 'Learning from Performance Errors', Psychological Review, Vol. 103, No. 2, 241–262.

[11] Denreall, J., Fang, C. and Levinthal, D.A., 2004, 'From T-Mazes to Labyrinths: Learning from Model-Based Feedback', Management Science, Vol. 50, No. 10, October 2004, pp. 1366–1378.

[12] Fang, Christina, 2003, Stern School of Business, New York. 'Learning in the Absence of Feedback', unpublished MS.

[13] Lancaster, J., 1996, 'Engineering Catastrophes', Abington Publishing, Cambridge, England.

[14] Wright, T.P., 1936, 'Factors Affecting the Cost of Airplanes', Institute of the Aeronautical Sciences, Journal of Aeronautical Sciences, Vol. 3, pp. 122–128.

[15] McDonald, A. and Schrattenholzer, L., 2001, 'Learning Rates for Energy Technologies', Energy Policy, Vol. 29, pp. 255–261.

[16] McDonald, A. and Schrattenholzer, L., 2002, 'Learning Curves and Technology Assessment', Int. J. Technology Management, Vol. 23, Nos. 7/8, pp. 718–745.

[17] Duffey, R.B. and Saull, J.W., 2002, 'The Physics of Human Error: A New Emergent Theory', Proc. American Nuclear Society, International Topical Meeting on Probabilistic Safety Assessment (PSA), Detroit, MI, 6–9 October.

[18] Bell, C., Hatch, W., Cernat, G., and Urbah, D., 2007, Ophthalmology, 114, No. 3, pp. 405–410.

[19] Urbach, D.R., Stukel, T.A., Croxford, R. and MacCallum, N.L., 2005, 'Analysis of current Research Related to the Impact of Low-Volume Procedures/Surgery Care on Outcomes of Care', Institute for Clinical Evaluative Sciences, CIHI, Canada.

[20] Canadian Institute of Health Information (CIHI), 'Health Care in Canada, 2005', (Available: www.cihi.org.)

[21] Perrow, C., 1984, 'Normal Accidents, Living with High Risk Technologies', Basic Books, New York.

[22] Copeland, A.H., 1932, 'The Theory of Probability from the Point of View of Admissible Numbers', Annals of Mathematical Statistics, American Statistical Association, Vol. 3, pp. 143–156.

# 2

# The Four Echoes

*'You can't change human nature – I've made errors, we all make mistakes, we know we make mistakes.'*

                                                        *Robert S. McNamara 'The Fog of War'*

## Power Blackouts, Space Shuttle Losses, Concorde Crashes, and the Chernobyl and Three Mile Island Accidents

We observe outcomes all the time, and the more spectacular or costly ones are heavily reported in the media. Recent major events are startling, quite complex and diverse, and made headlines and caused huge inquiries. Here, we are truly sampling reality, and because they are supposed to be rare events or outcomes, not happening often, they surprise us. The risk of such a major calamity is meant to be small, which means the probability should be negligible and/or remote. These catastrophes include:

- The Space Shuttle *Columbia* spectacularly disintegrating on re-entry, causing the deaths of the brave crew.
- The supersonic *Concorde* crashing on take-off, this sleek streamlined shape falling from the sky in flames, with no survivors.
- Recent large *power blackouts* over large areas of the USA, Canada and Europe, affecting millions and taking international inquiries to examine why we were suddenly left in the dark.

For these major disasters, and many others, we understood the causal factors afterwards; and we may point fingers of derision and blame, but neglect and forget the underlying reasons. These accidents were in and to our most advanced technologies; to the finest designs we had produced, in major and highly visible applications, often in full view of modern cameras and news stations. Their names provide echoes that still sound in the industries in which they happened; of designs abandoned, staff discredited, managers removed, inquiries conducted, victims mourned, reports produced, and then all fading and forgotten except by those impacted and directly affected by the events.

*Managing Risk: The Human Element*   Romney B. Duffey and John W. Saull
Copyright © 2005 and 2008 Romney B. Duffey and John W. Saull, Published by John Wiley & Sons, Ltd

Yet they were *all* preventable: after the fact we knew or found out what had happened. *A combination of circumstances occurs, unique but unforeseen, combined with very human misunderstandings, mistakes and misperceptions that lead to the observed outcome.* The outcomes are tragic, random and we should hopefully be eliminating their occurrence, not just their reoccurrence. This is the entire basis for implementing, designing and managing industrial safety programs (H.C. Howlett II, 1995) [1], where prior outcomes dominate root cause analysis, management attitudes and safety training.

But another similar outcome, event or error will occur sometime, somewhere, in a random but at the same time systematic way. It will happen because humans and other circumstances will conspire in another unforeseen way to make it happen. With different consequences, in a different place, and at a different time. We observe the historic frequency of such events, but we really need to estimate their future probability of occurrence.

These echoes, these outcomes and their recurrences raise major questions about our institutions, about our society and our use of technology and about their causes, and the responsible and best way forward. Each can or has temporarily paralysed the industry where it occurred, causing inquiries, recriminations, costs, litigation, regulations and heartache.

How do they share a common basis? Should we have expected or even better anticipated them? Are we learning from our mistakes like these and all others that just 'happen'? What should or can we do to ensure these crippling losses are not in vain? How can we predict the next events? Or should we continue to analyse them, event by event, without understanding the real reasons why we have these echoes?

We argue that these events (and hence most others) show, demonstrate and contain the same causal factors of human failures and failings, and as a result, the same general and logical development path.

## The Combination of Events

If there is anything we know, it is that we do not really know anything at all. Our understanding of reality is based on approximate physical 'laws' that describe how the universe we observe behaves. The complexities of the human mind, when coupled with complex technological systems that have been created by that same mind, produce both outcomes we expect (results and/or products) and some that we do not (accidents and/or errors). Since one cannot expect to describe exactly all that happens, and since we only understand the cause(s) afterwards, reactively assigning *a posteriori* frequencies, any ability to proactively predict the probability of outcomes *a priori* must be based on a testable theory that works.

That is true for all the accidents that surround us because of the *overwhelming contribution of human errors* to accidents and events with modern technological systems. The human failings and the failures are what cause them. That is *the* common Human Element in the Four Echoes. But when faced with an error, major or minor, humans always first deny, then blame-shift, before accepting it as their very own. It is a natural survival instinct; it is part of living and our self-esteem. We do so as individuals and seemingly also as part of our collective societies.

Our mistakes are *inseparably* embedded or intertwined as part of a larger 'system', be it a technology, a corporation, a mode of travel, an investment decision, a rule or regulation, or an individual action or responsibility. They arise as and from an unforeseen combination of events that we only understood afterwards. As pointed out by Dr Feng Hsu (private communication) in commenting on our ideas:

> 'There are significant events or accidents which were caused by utilizing immature technology, by improper application of technology, or by lack of implementing risk management technology as part of the overall system technology (often called assurance engineering). For instance, in the aerospace industry, many design technologies that were practiced were flawed simply because (of the) lack of understanding of risk and safety technology, and did not properly incorporate these in the early design stages . . .'.

Their consequences (the outcomes) can be large or small, but all are part of a larger picture of which we humans are the *vital* contributor, invariably in some unforeseen way that was only obvious afterwards.

## The Problem Is the Human Element

The first problem is the human involvement, subtle, all pervading, unrecordable and somewhat unpredictable. We cannot creep inside the human brain to see what drives it: instead we observe externally what happens internally as a result of stimuli, thinking, actions and decisions that are made inside the human technological machine as it interacts with the situation and the technology.

*Conventionally, reliability engineering is associated with the failure rate of components, or systems, or mechanisms, not human beings in and interacting with a technological system.*

All events (accidents, errors and mistakes) are manifested as *observed outcomes* that may have multiple root causes, event sequences, initiators, system interactions or contributory factors. Striking examples of these random confluences are legion in so-called accident sequences with multiple human-based causes, resulting in the interval for the risk of death in the crash of the Space Shuttle *Columbia* being the same as for all industrial accidents; and the interval for commercial airlines being the same as for the *Concorde* crash. The reason is the stochastic and pervasive contribution of the human element.

It is the involvement of the human that causes the outcomes we observe and which determines the intervals: rarely is it simply failure of the technology itself. The Federation Aviation Agency (FAA) has noted:

> 'We need to change one of the biggest historical characteristics of safety improvements – our reactive nature. We must get in front of accidents, anticipate them and use hard data to detect problems and the disturbing trends'.

This is a very clear message to us all, and to be proactive requires a new theory and understanding of the stochastic nature of error causation and prevention. Our fundamental work on the analysis of recorded events in major technological industries shows that when humans are involved, as they are in most things:

- a ULC exists which we can and must use to track trends;
- in technological industries, accidents involving humans are random (stochastic) and hence unpredictable;

- accidents have a common minimum attainable and irreducible value for their frequency;
- apparent disparate events in systems share the common basis of human error; and
- typical intervals for events are 20,000 experience hours, for the commoner outcomes, falling away to a minimum achievable of near ~200,000 experience hours.

This is not new: take the case of the two space shuttle accidents. Embarrassingly, unexpected and in full public view, the USA humbled itself and its technology, first, launching on a too-cold day, and then, attempting re-entry with a damaged vehicle. In the *Columbia* inquiry, it was stated that there were 'echoes' of the previous *Challenger* disaster present. Echoes that the key contributors were the same, the safety practices, internal management structures and decisions, institutional barriers and issues, and lack of learning from previous mistakes and events,

We are doomed to rediscover event-by-event, case-by-case, inquiry-by-inquiry, accident-by-accident, error-by-error, tragedy-by-human-tragedy, the same litany of causative factors, the same mistakes, the same errors. Perhaps not in the same order, or have the same importance, or the same type, but the same nevertheless. So the preventable becomes the unforeseen, the unavoidable, the inevitable, and the unthinkable, the observed, time and time again. We can even show that statistically, if we try often enough, Echoes will occur (see Appendix H), and hence, might almost be expected.

Of those echoes we should take notice. We now take a closer look at the four headline-making cases as illustrative but well-known samples of the wider and huge number of events, accidents and errors that occur everyday, to the human race, as we run a technological experiment on ourselves. We cannot run experiments on the human brain, or being, or psyche, to completely understand all the complex workings. Nor need we. Instead, we can and should observe what is shown by all our data (as psychoanalysts do for the human mind and physicists for the natural world), and from the outcomes, we see, we can invoke theories and draw conclusions.

## The Four Echoes Share the Same Four Phases

The classic accidents, the unthinkable events, the shocking tragedies and the routine injuries share common traits and phases. Complex with differing details, each with their own background, origins, development, scenario and sequence, we can categorise the general trends arising from the human element involvement. We shall show that the same four Phases characterise these most heavily publicised, documented and visible of recent major accidents with our best but still experimental technological systems:

*Phase 1*: the Unfolding of the precursors, the initiators and the preliminaries.
*Phase 2*: the Confluence of events, circumstances and bases of errors.
*Phase 3*: the Escalation, where the unrecognised unknowingly causes the event.
*Phase 4*: the Denial caused by lack of comprehension, followed finally by acceptance.

Of course, this last phase is often followed or accompanied by inquiry, retribution, assignment of blame, liability and responsibility in the name of improving public and personal safety. The tools used are often official inquiries, criminal or civil investigations, commissions, often with court hearings, testimony and litigation, with consequent recommendations, procedural and institutional processes. These allow us as a society to partition the cause and blame, provide cathartic process by which we can feel that we have identified the wrongs and tried to put everything right.

The detailed transcripts of the unfolding events for the Four Echoes are given in full in Appendix C. In the detail given there, carefully extracted from the available records, reports and recorders, the reader can trace the unfolding conversations, events and terror.

Despite the huge differences in technologies, timescales, countries, dates, systems and people, they all share the same riveting features and the same phases, as we now show. They unfold as if in a dream, the players and the sequence inevitably developing, and reinforcing the view that what we observe and when we observe it are truly both predictable but unexpected.

## The First Echo: Blackout of the Power Grid

It was a normal late summer's day in 2003 – the power demand was high because of air conditioning but not excessive in the North East USA and Canada. The electricity markets were and are connected as grid, with different regions and states buying and selling power, as they needed. Margins between demand (the need) and the supply (the generation) were tight but not excessively so, and the grid operators planned out their day as per normal.

Blackouts, meaning loss of power, occur on a smaller scale quite often, as events that occur, cause a temporary problem, are controlled, and then recovered. A major Blackout affecting millions had not occurred since 1977, some 26 years ago, when the East coast of the USA had been plunged into darkness. That was obviously the fault of the regulated power utilities who were largely state-owned and run. A failure in a substation in New York had triggered a chain reaction, overloading and tripping out many others, in a 'domino' effect that just grew larger and larger. Clearly, the owners must have been inefficient and poorly managed to allow such a thing to occur (=blame-shift), having high reserves but no response to market forces. Power prices were fixed and electricity returns on investment were guaranteed or at least assured, and there were no incentives to improve or enhance.

On this day, it was different: power marketers, merchant power plants, commercial companies had formed or been divested from the previous monopolies, and power market prices and supply were now in the hands of literally 'market operators', whose job was and is to ensure supply and demand stay matched, and that prices were at least stable. Excess (or excessive?) power margins had fallen, but then New York could get its additional needed power from sources to the East. Ontario also needed to import power at peak times from South and East of its borders with the USA. So electricity was traded around, like any other commodity, transmitted on the conducting high-voltage wires of the electricity grid.

The only difference from any other commodity is that electricity is *instantly perishable*. Electricity has zero shelf-life and it cannot be easily stored. So the rule is simple: at all times, we must have supply, which must *always* equal demand, or:

$$Supply = Demand + Losses,$$

where the Losses are from the resistance incurred in the lines from moving the power around through the grid wires. The instantaneous matching is the task of the power generators, the power companies and the grid/reliability operators.

As trades and deals were made for power in markets to meet the demand, electricity was moved around by having power plants come on line (attach to the grid) or not as needed or previously agreed by power trades. The plants are needed to provide sufficient voltage across the wires to drive the power through the wires, as needed or consumed.

The 'base' load needed everyday (the Supply) came largely from large coal and nuclear plants, and the 'peaking' or additional from natural gas and coal facilities that often cost more to run. So, Supply being matched to Demand also affected the price since high demand meant more plants on line, more expense and higher prices, which was considered a good way for 'market forces' to moderate demand through price 'signals', i.e., high use = higher price. Now, prices were partly and in fact controlled or capped by some market operators, and the customers have and had no idea where the power is coming from or the price until the bill arrives. That was good provided it all worked out.

The full sequence has been published in transcripts and hearings held by the US Committee on Energy and Commerce; in the reports of the Joint US/Canada Task Force; and in testimony by the system operators[1] and other analysts (see Appendix C). The whole sequence reads as a chronology of a bad day at the office, with multiple faults combining to slowly erode the margins and capacity available to move power around the region to the points that needed it via the grid power lines. Eventually, the lines and the power plants attached to them could not handle the large shifts in power. There was loss of control of the HTS by the human element.

At 4:10 p.m. on 13 August, the lights started going out in parts of the East, as hundreds of power-generating plants started to trip and shut down to avoid trying to power overloaded lines and supply unusual parts of the electric grid. By 4:13 p.m., Ontario, New York, Ohio, New Jersey and New Hampshire were all dark – 15 million or more people without power. In some places, it came back on in only a few hours; in others, it took nearly a week to restore power to the grid. Why? What happened? Where had it gone?

Was it an echo of the earlier blackout? As one CEO said shortly afterwards in Congressional testimony: 'We strongly believe that such a widespread loss of power could only result from a combination of events, not from a few isolated events . . . it is understandable that everyone is looking for the straw that broke the camel's back . . . but there is no one straw – they're all heaped together . . . and the camel's ability to support the load cannot be overlooked'.

The costly and extensive review of cause, and assignment of blame, was carried out and reported by the Joint US/Canada Power System Outage Task Force, 2003 [2]. The Report is very clear in stating the causes of the slowly unfolding event on a power system operating company First Energy (FE) and their related reliability (Control Center) operator (MISO) [3] who did not realise that the failure of its power lines was leading to overloading of the entire system as power tried to reroute around the failed lines.

The initiating (causal) events were due to transmission (overhead electric) lines shorting the electric current to ground by tree growth. This apparently avoidable and not uncommon event is made worse by the subsequent overloading and heating of other lines by any diverted current, as they will sag even more.

---

[1]We are grateful to the Midwest Independent System Operator (MISO) for making the full Control Center dialogue available and for permission to publish the extracts.

The Report claimed multiple failings, which are all in fact very human:

1. Inadequate situational awareness – they just did not know what was happening, as power lines failed, where and why;
2. Failure to perform routine maintenance, in this case, tree trimming close to the lines, which could short out the power line locally, so losing multiple overhead power lines;
3. Failure of others (MISO) to provide effective diagnostic support, due to lack of data, software analysis and inadequate communication (written and verbal) as the failures spread slowly.

Specific violations were also listed:

Violation Number 1: Following the outage of a 345-kV line, FE did not take the necessary actions to return the system to a safe operating state within 30 minutes.

Violation Number 2: FE did not notify other systems of an impending system emergency.

Violation Number 3: FE's state estimation/contingency analysis tools were not used to assess the system conditions.

Violation Number 4: FE operator training was inadequate for maintaining reliable operation.

Violation Number 5: MISO did not notify other reliability coordinators of potential problems.

It is worth noting that during the day, the necessary hardware and software systems used for monitoring and power system status (the so-called State Estimator and the Emergency Management System used to aid decision making by the human operators and the management) were often out of service, were providing what was thought to be misleading information, were disbelieved, and/or taking too long to analyse and not providing timely data about the evolving situations.

At this point, it is easy to blame the operators and the system for not making the right choices, taking the correct actions or analysing fully the options and decisions to be taken.

But this does not change the overall power *system*, the degree of automated control, enable more effective decision making, and allow the technology to be more forgiving in the event of errors, misoperation and accident.

Similar, but not identical, events can still occur anywhere with a loosely interconnected system, run by diverse operators, with sparse instrumentation, insufficient real-time diagnosis and large communication gaps, without adequate contingency analysis and safety margin and management systems.

## Management's Role

It is the role and duty of senior corporate management to know what is happening, to direct the company staff, and take effective leadership actions, to allow for preparedness, prevention and proactive response. The CEOs of the power companies, the grid owners, the market operators and the reliability managers were all quickly summoned to Washington to testify before Congress and answer the leading questions.

Please explain what had happened? So why did parts of the grid go down? So why did you let these failures occur?

What all said was that we need more investment in the grid, better coupled markets with more access and more government or investor money.

But as one key player in the transmission system said:

*An additional and extremely important measure put in place after the 1965 blackout as a means of restoring the balance between load and supply following a major disturbance, was the introduction of the automatic capability to reduce demand (referred to as automatic under frequency load shedding).*

> Source: *'Blackout 2003: How Did It Happen and Why?',*
> *Full House Committee on Energy and Commerce Hearing, 4 September 2003,*
> *Washington, DC, Testimony of National Grid Transco*

Translated, this means customers are disconnected when a problem occurs. But as another independent grid transmission operator noted:

*. . . this blackout did not arise from a lack of electric generation supply. Rather, this blackout was rooted in a disconnect between the use of and the capability of the transmission system to deliver that supply. This disconnect in turn is rooted in institutional failures to properly regulate and monitor such transmission usage such that the transmission system stays within its physical limitations.*

Which condition could not be met because:

*They informed me that there were no records or reports of the line outages which were so critical to this event. Without such information, there is no way for Control Area Operators or Security Coordinators to take actions necessary to mitigate problems, especially those events in other systems which could affect our system.*

And, of course, the worst problem above all:

*On August 14, it was apparent that parties were choosing to operate the grid within their sphere of influence for their own purposes without regard to rules, procedures, or the impact of their actions on other users of the grid. Further, the convoluted (transmission) configurations that major entities have contrived to create virtually guarantees that communication, when it occurs, will be a matter of luck.*

Moreover, it was already known that the electricity market supply system could be manipulated:

*As (one) MISO Market Monitor had warned in a March 2003 MISO market monitor presentation to Federal Energy Regulatory Commission (FERC): 'the electrical configuration between the PJM and the MISO also raises substantial gaming concerns'. Entities will have the means to game the system to their own ends to the disadvantage of all other users.*

> Source: *'Blackout 2003: How Did It Happen and Why',*
> *Full House Committee on Energy and Commerce Hearing, 4 September 2003,*
> *Washington DC, Testimony of International Transmission Company*

Thus, the system was set up to fail due to multiple unrelated events that had not been fully diagnosed or anticipated. The whole system was improperly managed.

## The First Echo: Findings

The major intergovernmental Joint US/Canada Task Force has published the results of its inquiries, and blames one of the power generators and its reliability coordinator for a combination of events. There was plenty of time to perform diagnosis, to take corrective actions and to prevent the event.

The four Phases are all here and are clear:

*Phase 1)* The early *unfolding* precursors were loss of lines that were routine happenings; with data flowing and the routine trading of power that meant some regions supplied power to others in quantities that – if disconnected – could not be made up.

*Phase 2)* The *confluence* occurred when other power plants, lines and operators all conspired inadvertently to ignore the major mismatch between supply and demand as they made decisions based on inadequate data, commercial (market) needs and software that did not provide up-to-date or believable control information ('state estimation').

*Phase 3)* The *escalation* was in the repeated and continuing emphasis and attempts to ensure supply was adequate, rather than isolation of the failed parts of the system, and mending those first, rather than pressing on with the day's seemingly routine tasks.

*Phase 4)* The *denial* is evident in the transcripts from the grid operators, where not only do the grid operators not realise their full involvement, and how it happened, but the companies believe that the domino effect of blackouts saved the day by not damaging equipment (thus saving the investment), while it certainly did hurt the consumer (by abandoning the customer). In addition, early on, many in the USA blamed Canada, and vice versa, while in fact all were and integral part of the shared problem.

Blackouts happened before: precursors exist, and accidental loss of grid is expected, even if not desirable. Larger ones occur less often than small, where the size is determined by the number, $M$, of millions of customers 'affected'.

A reasonable fit to the data shown in Figure 2.1 is given simply by:

$$\text{Rate per year of blackouts, } (\mathrm{d}B/\mathrm{d}y) \sim 0.5 M_c^{-2/3}$$

where $M_c$ is the millions of customers 'affected' (i.e., disconnected). Why the data should have this form is not clear or stated. We may assume that the millions of customers use power uniformly or some average amount such that, $P \propto M_c$. On that assumption, the total number of blackouts, $B$, in a given year then varies roughly as the proportionality $B \propto 0.5(y/P^{2/3})$, or nearly inversely proportional to the amount of power being used. This suggests a learning effect.

Interestingly, this fit also implies, in the limit of very frequent outages, some limited number are without power at any given time, as many homeowners could agree. But for ~1 $M$ people disconnected, the rate is about twice a year. For larger and more major Blackouts of $10M$ or so affected customers, somewhat greater than a single city, the rate is one every 10–20

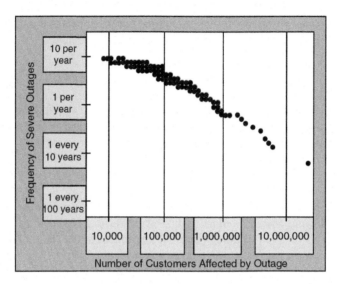

**Figure 2.1.** Blackout outage rate in North America: the prior knowledge [1] (With kind permission of US DOE NE Blackout Report)

years. On an average basis, the interval between such very large Blackouts is one in every 15 years, or one per ~130,000 hours.

This interval result is within the same minimum interval of 100,000 to 200,000 hours that we have found for every major system we humans have designed, operated, maintained and regulated.

Instead of isolating the fault and accommodating it while fixing the problems, the grid operators are trained to 'supply', to work around the system to always try to provide the needed power.

Instead of reducing power and shedding demand, they were continually fixing the system, recovering as they went, without adequate data, control span or capability for load management across boundaries. The conflicts were between the observed data that suggesting failed systems and lines, coping with and relying on a failed analyser, all within the context of the pressing demands and requirements to supply power. This scenario is confirmed by superimposing the timeline of events in the Interim Report with the fascinating and ongoing dialogues between the controllers, which are given in detail in Appendix C.

As the transcripts show, repeated attempts were made to diagnose, to repair problems, to cope with failures by shifting power, to re-analyse the system, and to cooperate and communicate across closed organisational and regional boundaries. The operators had no knowledge of and no means to manage the power outside their own fragmented jurisdiction. Eventually, the system (grid) operators were ineffectively reduced to watching the events unfold outside their control area on television, unaware of the scope and the extent to which the power imbalance problem had already and could spread.

Except that early in the day, fully two hours before the Blackout, a stunning premonition or a deja vu, had occurred to one of the Control Center staff, as he saw the potential for a repeat (an Echo) of the earlier large New York blackout. But the event progressed and finally did repeat, not in the same way, or with the same cause or sequence, but with the same outcome. The error was the same, of millions without power and with billions of dollars lost.

Instead of reducing supply, and hence revenue, by disconnecting customers (demand side reduction) on a smaller scale to solve the problem, they ended up disconnecting everyone, thus automatically and safely protecting the system.

Instead of requiring all connected to have adequate reserves, the grids were using a make-shift network of regional power 'supply = demand' balances, with exporters and importers all believing the grid was stable and fault-tolerant, with connections and supply driven by the desire to sell power.

Instead of investing in new power equipment and grid capacity that might cause an over-supply (and lower prices), there was incentive to maximise revenue from existing equipment and keep margins at their economic minimum.

Instead of 'market failure', since power prices did represent cost, there was 'grid failure' because of the failure to be able to supply the full demand in the presence of a confluence of system failures.

Thus, no one person, system owner, generator or regulator is to 'blame': *they all share the responsibility simply because they were connected, coordinated and managed in such a way as to cause the confluence of unforeseen outcomes.*

## Error State Elimination

Was it predictable?

We would argue, yes. That if the right data had been collected, on events, outages, margins, trades and costs, and analysed versus a chosen and meaningful experience parameter, then we would have seen the trends clearly. We do not know the parameter that can be used today, or even if it is available. But we can guess a few likely candidates, e.g., number and volume of power trades, power transmitted, and grid capability.

The prior knowledge indicates that all was not happening according to the agreed rules and procedures. The North American Electric Reliability Council (NERC), in a letter to the US Congress in October 2003, stated that their 'compliance program' reported 444 violations of the Operating Policies and 97 violations of the Planning Policies just in the year before.

The EPRI Report [4] shows clearly that over the period of few days earlier, a steady decline in minimum system voltage had been occurring. It was not analysed, it was not taken as a precursor, or as a warning sign. No actions were taken, as the 'right' measure had not been defined or analysed. The available data were not considered or acted upon: so the inevitable happened.

The Task Force and the grid operators have now suggested that mandatory, enforceable 'reliability standards' be put in place, with compliance reporting and penalties for transgressions. These standards existed before, as voluntary or as only part of the system. Indeed as just one example, the IMO in Ontario [5], where power shortages had occurred earlier, required in its very own Rules Section 3.2.1 and 4.2.1 issued that very same year:

*The IMO shall direct the operations of the IMO-controlled grid pursuant to the provisions of all applicable operating agreements and shall maintain the reliability of the IMO-controlled grid. The IMO's responsibilities in this regard shall include, but are not limited to, the monitoring of, and the issuing of orders, directions or instructions to dispatch generation, dispatchable loads, distribution facilities and transmission facilities on the IMO-controlled grid.*

*The IMO shall carry out its obligations in accordance with all applicable reliability standards.*

*The IMO shall operate the IMO-administered markets and contract for ancillary services, including by means or within the scope of an operating agreement or another agreement of similar nature, to ensure that sufficient ancillary services are available to ensure the reliability of the IMO-controlled grid.*

In addition, as part of the release of the Final Report with its 44 explicit recommendations, it was stated that: (a) mandatory reliability standards are being implemented in the United States and Canada. Further, (b) the NERC was submitting 118 new standards to the US FERC and appropriate authorities in Canada for review and approval; and (c) the governments of the United States and Canada have also established the Bilateral Electric Reliability Oversight Group as a forum in which the US Department of Energy, FERC, Natural Resources Canada and provincial energy ministries can discuss issues of common concern.

However, the existence of such *explicit and enforceable* Rules, guidance and procedures does not stop blackouts, as the data clearly show. Rather, they define a minimum standard of expectations and requirements that need to be translated into practical power margins and grid transmission. But the IMO is not responsible for actually doing any of that, as they just administer the power market as an auction house would, by matching price, demand and supply.

As the US Secretary of Energy Bodman said on the release of the Joint Task Force Final Report in 2006: '*I appreciate the hard work and diligence that went into this important report. It demonstrates that while improvements are being made to enhance grid reliability, we still have a very complex system that is subject to possible mechanical and human failures. We must remain vigilant*'.

An eerily similar situation then occurred just a few weeks later on 28 September, blacking out much of Italy [6], who depended, like many states, on the import of power. In this case, the power and the lines came in through Switzerland, who was not a member of the European Union, so had no real say and little control over the extra power being traded across their borders (cf. FE and MISO) from France, according to the official Swiss report [7].

As shorts or grounding occurred to trees (again!!), the insufficient reductions in power, and the ineffective response and rebalancing, caused the overloading of remaining lines. In just 28 minutes (much the same time frame as for the US case), the lights went out in northern Italy as, after the Swiss had to disconnect themselves, just a few minutes later the underpowered Italian grid failed in a domino effect again. The usual finger pointing and blame-shifts were evident again (in considerable amounts) between Italy and Switzerland, and new rules are soon to be in place to govern cross-border transmission in Europe. After all, the Swiss argue that they should have some say in what power is moved across their country from France to Italy.

But as we now know, the *existence of rules does not preclude events*. Thus, reliability standards per se cannot eliminate the error states and do not address the issues of decision making in large technological systems. Better to plan for failure of the system, and how to cope with that, than to claim, imply or pretend that it cannot fail. Blackouts (power losses) still have occurred as echoes in seemingly distant cities like London, the UK and Queens,

**Figure 2.2.** Typical grid control centre (With kind permission of US DOE NE Blackout Report)

New York, but which are still connected by a common technological system – the use of electric power grids operated, maintained and supplied by humans. (See Figure 2.2.)

## The Second Echo: Columbia/Challenger

The Space shuttle is a fine piece of engineering, a truly amazing concept to launch humans and materials into space strapped to large booster rockets. Once launched, the tanks are discarded and the shuttle becomes a space plane, able to rendezvous and supply, conduct experiments, park satellites and construct new space 'stations'. Once through with the task, it could glide back to earth, re-entering the atmosphere at supersonic speed, and finally landing again on Earth. One trip is called a 'Mission' and some 112 previous missions had been flown.

It was and is known to be a dangerous technological venture: each launch and Mission had a considerable (or non-negligible, or inherent) risk level, and safety was reviewed and analysed continuously. Previous accidents had occurred, the Challenger exploding on launch as leaking seals allowed explosive propellant to escape. The Inquiry showed the accident was an unforeseen confluence of circumstances; a cold morning for the launch, a known weakness in the design (a seal), a safety warning overruled by management; a desire to proceed with the launch schedule, a lack of safety awareness, inadequate procedures and launch limits, plus insufficient test data for the seal. These were all so clearly evident afterwards.

The usual inquiry, the Rogers Commission, was formal and deeply moving, and showed a distinct lack of safety awareness by management at the time (so-called lack of 'safety culture'), and the need for truly independent (uninfluenced) safety review. Design fixes on the seal proceeded: after all, this leaking seal event 'cannot happen again'. So it did not.

It was known that other problems occurred on launch. Pieces of insulation from the big strapped-on tanks regularly fell off, hitting the Shuttle and damaging its own insulation. That insulation was needed for re-entry to shield the vehicle and crew against temperatures of several thousands of degrees outside. Damage happened so often as to be repaired and reviewed, and determined (dispositioned is the engineering term) as an 'operational concern'. That means insulation damage was not a safety issue. The falling-off insulation issue could be fixed, but that takes time and money, and the incentive to invest in that was reduced provided missions could still occur, and the damage repaired each time. So missions continued.

Columbia STS-107 on 16 January 2003 was one such mission. The launch had seemed the usual spectacular media event, majestically rising into space on a tail of a hydrogen-fuelled flame. Just 16 days later, it disintegrated on re-entry, one wing fatally burnt through, the failure spreading and penetrating from where the leading-edge insulation had been damaged by a piece of foam striking it.

The interval between the two Shuttle accidents (errors) was 17 years, or about 150,000 hours, exactly what was and is found (within the uncertainties) for the minimum interval attained for *all* technologies.

The Mission had proceeded as planned, successfully, while behind the scenes repeated but unsuccessful requests were made by some engineers to understand a problem. They had seen the foam strike, and they asked for damage assessments, for in-orbit imaging and for consequence analyses. The repeated imaging (picture) requests were denied by management and managers continued with their daily duties. The system was proceeding well while the crew was doomed.

Rentry (denoted as EI) was underway on 1 February 2003 and the disaster now unfolded quickly, and it is evident that no one knew what was really happening (cf. the Blackout). (See Plate 4)

## The Results of the Inquiry: Prior Knowledge

The subsequent Columbia Accident Investigation Inquiry Board (CAIB) report [8] published in 2003 was both thorough and in-depth. The accident was stated to be an 'echo' of the same but still unforeseen confluence of circumstances: a known weakness in the design (foam debris), a safety warning overruled by management, a desire to proceed with the launch schedule, a lack of safety awareness, inadequate procedures and launch limits, no in-flight repair process, plus insufficient test data for the effect of impacts. These were all so clearly evident afterwards. The Report makes chilling reading:

> . . . the Board identified a number of pertinent factors, which we have grouped into three distinct categories:
>
> 1) physical failures that led directly to Columbia's destruction;
> 2) underlying weaknesses, revealed in NASA's organization and history, that can pave the way to catastrophic failure; and
> 3) 'other significant observations' made during the course of the investigation, but which may be unrelated to the accident at hand . . . (if) left uncorrected, could contribute to future Shuttle losses.
>
> Connecting the parts of NASA's organizational system and drawing the parallels with Challenger demonstrate three things. First, despite all the post-Challenger changes at NASA and the agency's notable achievements since, the causes of the institutional failure responsible for Challenger have not been fixed. Second, the Board strongly believes that if these persistent, systemic flaws are not resolved, the scene is set for another accident. Therefore, the recommendations for change are not

*only for fixing the Shuttle's technical system, but also for fixing each part of the organizational system that produced Columbia's failure. Third, the Board 's focus on the context in which decision-making occurred does not mean that individuals are not responsible and accountable. To the contrary, individuals always must assume responsibility for their actions. What it does mean is that NASA's problems cannot be solved simply by retirements, resignations, or transferring personnel.*

The CAIB Report [8] summarises the knowledge of physical cause thus:

*Foam loss has occurred on more than 80 percent of the 79 missions for which imagery is available, and foam was lost from the left bipod ramp on nearly 10 percent of missions where the left bipod ramp was visible following External Tank separation. For about 30 percent of all missions, there is no way to determine if foam was lost; these were either night launches, or the External Tank bipod ramp areas were not in view when the images were taken. The External Tank was not designed to be instrumented or recovered after separation, which deprives NASA of physical evidence that could help pinpoint why foam separates from it. The precise reasons why the left bipod foam ramp was lost from the External Tank during STS-107 may never be known. The specific initiating event may likewise remain a mystery. However, it is evident that a combination of variable and pre-existing factors, such as insufficient testing and analysis in the early design stages, resulted in a highly variable and complex foam material, defects induced by an imperfect and variable application, and the results of that imperfect process, as well as severe load, thermal, pressure, vibration, acoustic, and structural launch and ascent conditions.*

It is evident that the precursors were there: why then had they not been seen? *The prior knowledge existed.* The answer is simple and occurs each time – although the data existed, they were not obvious. (See Figure 2.3.)

Board investigators also reviewed Columbia's maintenance, including the prior Mission STS-109 and reviewed the preparation for STS-107, and NASA's Problem Reporting and Corrective Action database. They found it contained 16,500 Work Authorization Documents consisting of 600,000 pages and 3.9 million steps. This database maintains critical information on all maintenance and modification work performed and Corrective Action Reports that document problems discovered and resolved. The Board also reviewed the Lost/Found item database, and the Launch and Flight Readiness Review documentation. Multiple formal meetings had occurred also prior to launch: but a good analysis of the 'reliability' (failure probability) had been made and reported before:

*Shuttle reliability is uncertain, but has been estimated to range between 97 and 99 percent. If the Shuttle reliability is 98 percent, there would be a 50–50 chance of losing an Orbiter within 34 flights . . . The probability of maintaining at least three Orbiters in the Shuttle fleet declines to less than 50 percent after flight 113.*

(Source: *The US Congress Office of Technology Assessment, 1989*)

The other indicators are of course the pre-existing insulation damage (foam debris) incidents. There had in fact, since 1983, been seven known events of foam coming free in the same place as *Columbia*. Despite the high level of concern after the first incidents, and up to the *Challenger*, pieces of foam continued to fall off the External Tank for 65 of the 79 missions with pictures (82%). Over the life of the Space Shuttle Program, Shuttles have had an average of 143 divots in the upper and lower surfaces of the insulation (Thermal Protection System

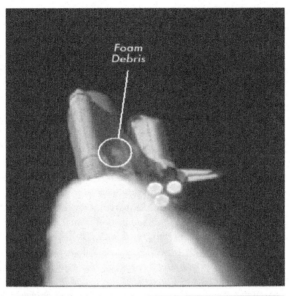

**Figure 2.3.** Photographs of the two shuttles at the moments of seal failure and of foam impact [8] (With kind permission of US NASA)

tiles) with 22% over an inch in one dimension. The lower surface had 121 'hits', also with about 20% larger than an inch in diameter.

The 'foam loss' events were routine enough that mending them was a regular maintenance task and not considered a safety issue, but its cause was never really examined. It was never really solved – the error state persisted.

The strip is the number of 'dings' or 'divots' greater than one inch, for each Mission, which as we know could be about 1/3 to 1/5 of the total number of debris 'hits' (See Figure 2.4.). Two items are of real interest to us here: firstly, there is no evidence of a decline with increasing experience; and secondly, there is a random-like or stochastic structure to the number observed. We can test this observation by replotting the numbers as a distribution of the frequency of having a number of hits in Figure 2.5.

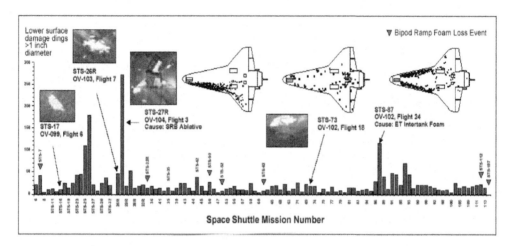

**Figure 2.4.** Typical stochastic trend of debris hits on the Shuttle – the prior knowledge [7] (With kind permission of US NASA)

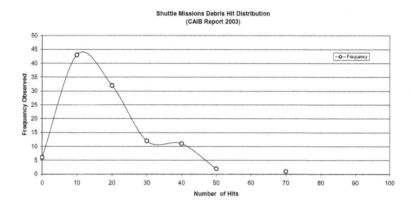

**Figure 2.5.** Distribution of debris impacts – the prior information

## The Second Echo: The Four Phases

The four Phases are here evident again:

*Phase 1)* The early *unfolding* precursors were insulation damage events that were routine happenings; and the routine of launching that meant that deadlines for launch took priority as funds and time could not be made up.

*Phase 2)* The *confluence* occurred when other events conspired to make the damage vital and irreparable, although efforts to characterise and look at the damage region were rebuffed, and instruments did not provide direct information on either the damage or potential re-entry temperatures and failure.

*Phase 3)* The *escalation* was in the repeated and continuing emphasis and attempts to ensure the Mission remained on schedule, rather than isolation of the failure, estimating the effect on the system of the system, and mending those first, rather than pressing on with the day's seemingly routine tasks.

*Phase 4)* The *denial* is evident in the Board report pointing out serious institutional issues, whereas subsequent NASA statements focus on a relaunch schedule for subsequent Missions (of about a year). Not only did the launch managers at the time not realise the full problem, and how it happened, but clearly many still believe that the design is still robust enough for future Missions to proceed again.

## Management's Responsibility

As a result of this analysis, we know that the precursors existed, as observed by the CAIB in their analysis of the physical cause (insulation debris impact). Their criticism of the NASA system was for allowing that Cause to continue to exist [8]:

> *The organizational causes of this accident are rooted in the ... original compromises that were required to gain approval for the Shuttle ... subsequent years of resource constraints, mis-characterization of the Shuttle as operational rather than developmental, of an agreed national vision for human space flight. Cultural traits and organizational practices detrimental to safety were allowed to develop, including: reliance on past success as a substitute for sound engineering practices (such as testing to understand why systems were not performing in accordance with requirements), organizational barriers that prevented effective communication of critical safety information and stifled professional differences of opinion; lack of integrated management across program elements; an informal chain of command and decision-making processes that operated outside the organization's rules.*
>
> *This report discusses the attributes of an organization that could more safely and reliably operate the inherently risky Space Shuttle, but does not provide a detailed organizational prescription. Among those attributes are a robust and independent program technical authority that has complete control over specifications and requirements, and waivers to them; an independent safety assurance organization with line authority over all levels of safety oversight; and an organizational culture that reflects the best characteristics of **a learning organization**.*

Prudence really suggests a full independent safety review and potential (major) redesign, which could take years, and a full review of the measures for experience that are meaningful. We have made an estimate of that risk and the measure.

After all, the Shuttle is designed to fly and commercial airline crashes occur too. So how does the shuttle risk compare to other such commercial risks?

The answer is surprising: the risk to the Shuttle crew, tracked in Mission time, is about the same as that for industrial accidents. We show this in Figure 2.6.

The lines shown in Figure 2.6 correspond to the rare event rate, $CR \sim n/\tau$, where $\tau$ is the chosen measure of experience, which is millions of hours for this case, and $n \sim 1$ for the first or initial outcome. Because of the form of plot used in Figure 2.6, the same actual number of accidents will always fall on the same line with a $-1$ slope ($n = 1, 2, 3 \ldots$).

This has interesting implications:

1. if you doubled or halved your experience, nothing happens relative to the $-1$ parity line – you slide up or down it;

2. if you have a lot more accidents for the same experience, you do move upward from the line, but you need a very big change for it to be visible on a log-log plot – some airlines really do appear to be dreadfully accident-prone relative to their better peers;

3. Concorde was not really one of the safer options for flying but there were worse; and

4. for the Shuttle being high and to the left is that this was technology with minimal experience because the accident rate *per mission or takeoff* clearly was very high.

On this plot, the fatal accident rate for 200 million commercial airlines worldwide are plotted versus the number of flights, and also shown are the Shuttle and *Concorde* supersonic aircraft accidents. These key data are available from commercial aircraft outcomes (fatal crashes) throughout the world. The major contributor is human error not purely equipment failure, although these latter can also be ascribed to the root cause of human failings. Fatal crashes and accidents for the 30 years between 1970 and 2000 are known (e.g., from Airsafe, 2000) [9], for 114 major airlines with ~725 million hours (Mh) of total flying experience. For each airline with its own experience, the fatal accident rate per flying hour can be plotted as an open circular symbol in Figure 2.6 versus the accumulated experience in flying hours (adopting the FAA value of ~$3\frac{1}{3}$ hours as an average flight time).

In addition to airlines with both large and small experience, and to cover four to six orders of magnitude of experience, we also show the data points for two other key events, which might have been expected to be different both in rate and technology but in fact are not. These are (a) the crash of the supersonic *Concorde* with a rate of one in about 90,000 flights shown as a lozenge symbol; and (b) the explosion and disintegration of the space shuttles, *Challenger* and *Columbia*, with a rate for two events out of 113 total missions.

Given the significant apparent differences in the designs, structures and operations, what we have shown here is that we can compare these rare outcomes by adopting some measure of experience as a basis.

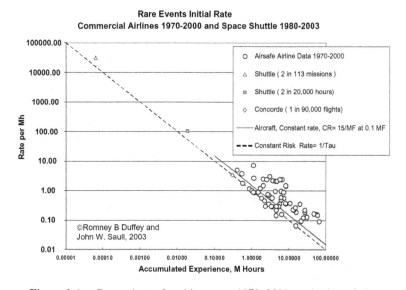

**Figure 2.6.** Comparison of accident rates 1970–2000 – prior knowledge

As they mature, technologies ought to slide down the curve as experience is gained. The rate (of accidents) per experience is what counts and that is very high with a new technology with little experience. 'How high?', in the Shuttle's case, depends on whether you just count the highly dangerous bit in the atmosphere or include the relatively risk-free bit floating in orbit. To include this range of crew-risk exposure, the triangular symbol takes a typical 'flight time' for the shuttle as the 30–40 minutes for re-entry or launch as reported by NASA time-lines; and the square as ~20,000 hours for the entire 113 typical 7- to 9-day missions. As shown, the trend is quite insensitive to the actual value taken.

For all these data and experience, there is a remarkable constancy of risk, as shown by the straight-line of slope $-1$, which as we noted above is given by the equation:

$$\text{Loss rate, } F \times \varepsilon = \text{constant} = n \sim 1$$

where, $n$, is the number of outcomes; $\varepsilon$, the experience measure; and $F$, the rate of losses per unit experience. The rate of fatal events per MFh is on the same constant risk (i.e., chance of a fatal accident) as shown by the extrapolated line given in the book 'Know the Risk', but the shuttle data point is three orders of magnitude higher (Figure 2.6).

Therefore, of course, for the first event the probability is $p(\varepsilon) = 1/\varepsilon$ since $n = 1$, and

$$(\text{Rate of losses per flight}) \text{ times } (\text{Number of flights}) \sim 1$$

Note the interval between major shuttle accidents (Columbia and Challenger) is from 1987 to 2003, so is two in 16 years, or one in 140,000 hours. This is about the maximum interval (or the minimum error rate) obtained for fatal accidents for flight in commercial aircraft, and for major blackouts. On the other hand, using the entire interval from the first (STS-1) to the last launch (STS-107) gives two in 22 years or about one in 190,000 hours.

Note that the measure of experience taken here is for the total *system* experience, from launch preparation and training, through to launch and flight.

## Error State Elimination

To stop such an event happening again, the CAIB report [8] is quite clear in requiring shifts in management, safety culture and operational emphasis in the NASA. Prior failures (due to design problems with a seal and with foam debris) had been allowed to persist, with safety taking a second role to performance and the priority pursuit of the mission. The fact that the event is a 'repeat' in many ways is evidence of a more systematic problem.

Is this coincidence? We believe not.

Thus, these rare accidents occur equally stochastically in these two apparently disparate but actually quite similar (flying) technologies. The common factor is because of the human involvement. It may appear 'fundamentally different' technology, for example, the Concorde and the Shuttle, but of course it is not in the *cause* of its accidents.

The Cause is the human interacting with a technological system.

The modifications being considered for the Shuttle include sensors to detect debris impact; better visualisation and monitoring of the structure to try to assess the extent, if any; and the use of insulation repair kits in space if damage has occurred.

The only way to avoid fatalities in space travel is either (a) not to use humans and/or (b) have a fail-safe design with a 'crew survival' capsule, which is so-called mitigating measure.

**Figure 2.7.**   The Mission Control Center information [8] (With kind permission of US CAIB)

Once again, expecting the unexpected, and planning for it is paramount. But if the cost or weight (payload) penalty is too high, and the system is allowed to operate, then fatalities and accidents will occur, as expected using the 'normal accident theory' approach. (See Figure 2.7.)

## The Third Echo: Concorde Tires and SUVs

On 24 July 2000, a *Concorde* supersonic plane took off from Paris as Air France flight 4590. During the takeoff briefing, the crew had pre-activated their mental picture for a normal takeoff and to face the possibility of a single engine failure.

The first phase of the takeoff was completely normal, and after 38 seconds the speed beyond which the takeoff could not be safely aborted was reached at 100 kt (V1), without any hint of a problem.

In the following seconds, an unusual noise was heard, then almost instantaneously the crew perceived violent lateral and longitudinal accelerations due to the sudden surging loss of thrust on two left engines and the plane deviated towards the left edge of the runway. Forty-one seconds into the takeoff run at a speed of 183 kt, just before the planned 'nose-up' rotation speed VR, the Captain began a slow rotation and applied right rudder for right roll control.

One second later, the FO said: 'Watch out', without any apparent input on the flight controls.

The four jets from the reheats were perfectly visible. During the acceleration, several people heard explosions. The first was followed by the appearance of a flame under the wing, between the left engine nacelles and the fuselage, a few seconds before the beginning of the rotation for takeoff. Now on fire, trailing flames in full view, the fatally impaired plane struggled to rise, then plunged, killing all 109 souls aboard and four on the ground.

The CVR stops recording as the aircraft crashes in flames some 9,500 m (or about 6 miles) from the runway just 1 minute and 18 seconds after the fire started. The crew were all found at their takeoff positions, and the passengers in the seats assigned at boarding, which were all fragmented. All the seat belts found were fastened. The fire and the crash damage to the aircraft meant that the accident was not survivable.

It was not that such crashes are commonplace. *Concorde* was the peak of technological accomplishment at the time of its introduction, the only commercial aircraft faster than sound, and a marvel of engineering and international cooperation and commitment.

The aircraft has diverse control systems and had been subject to rigorous testing, quality assurance and safety analysis before being certified to fly. Shortly after the crash, the Certificates of Airworthiness to fly were revoked, as if the original had been in error, or something unforeseen had occurred. The cause was claimed to be a metal strip, inadvertently left on the runway by another aircraft, which ripped a tire and caused the fuel tank in the wing to be punctured by tire debris. The fuel was released in a massive leak and caught fire, the engine power was reduced by tire debris entering the engine air intakes and the plane crashed. (The details are given in the Official Report, 2001) [10].

As an indirect result of this accident, all the *Concorde* fleet was withdrawn from service as too expensive to fly. The remaining craft, cannibalised and silent, are now parked on the end of runways in London Heathrow and Manchester, at Toulouse and Paris, and in the halls of collections and museums in Barbados, New York, Edinburgh and Bristol, sad reminders of greater days.

## Tire Failures: The Prior Knowledge

Tire failures had occurred before on the Concorde, so the BEA also have analysed this failure data in more detail to see if a precursory indication existed related to such potentially catastrophic tire failures, which could damage fuel tanks and perhaps cause a fire. It did.

Figure 2.8 summarises the random occurrences of tire failures. At least five events with damage due to these tire failures, but without a fire, were known to have occurred before.

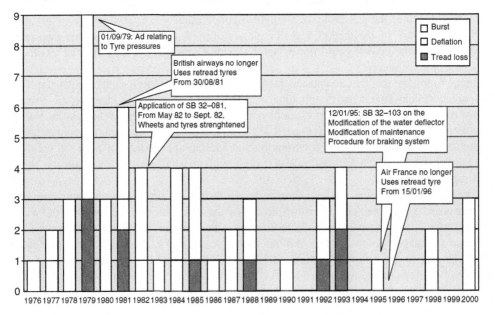

**Figure 2.8.** History of Concorde tire events 1976–2001 – the prior knowledge [9] (BEA by permission. See www.bea.aero)

On 14 June 1979, during takeoff from Washington Dulles Airport, deflation of a tire, followed by loss of tread, led to burst of another tire and the destruction of the wheel. This event caused a variety of damage to the aircraft, including damage to the left main landing gear, to the hydraulic and electrical circuits and slight perforations in fuel tanks 2, 5 and 6, mainly caused by pieces of wheel rim. After some unsuccessful attempts to retract the landing gear and the loss of hydraulic circuits, the crew turned around and landed the aircraft back 24 minutes later.

Four Airworthiness Directives or mandatory corrective action notices were issued as a result, calling for the installation of a system for detection of main landing gear tire under-inflation, for improvements in protection in the normal braking hydraulic system, defining an inspection procedure for the main landing gear tires and wheels before each takeoff, and calling for the installation of new reinforced wheels and tires.

In August 1981, on takeoff from New York, a burst of two tires led to minor penetration of a fuel tank. Then on 15 November 1985, on takeoff from London Heathrow, a burst of a tire caused damage to the landing gear door and minor penetration in a fuel tank, probably by a piece of the door mechanism.

Somewhat differently, on 29 January 1988, on takeoff from London Heathrow, there was loss of 10 lug nuts from a wheel and a bolt punctured a fuel tank. Then, in July 1993, on landing at London Heathrow, burst of a tire led to damage to the gear door mechanism, and a different fuel tank was damaged, probably by a piece of this mechanism.

Finally, on 25 October 1993, while taxiing at London Heathrow, a tire burst led to damage of a fuel tank which suffered minor penetration, probably from a piece of a deflector.

But despite these events, the risk of fire was regarded as small. It was concluded that it was not necessary to install protection for the underside of the wings as a result of studies carried out on the risks of damage from pieces of tire and the integrity of the structure in case of direct penetration. In fact, it was only after the Paris crash that any really substantive measures were taken, by changing the tire type and supplier, changes to electrical systems and internally protecting the exposed fuel tanks against a major leak.

Overall, some 57 failures of tires had occurred before on the *Concorde* fleet; it takes off at over 200 kt (370 km/h). The causes were not all known. The analysis of these data in the BEA *Concorde* report [10] and the events on takeoff only are given in the report, where a failure is defined as a burst or deflation.

We simply note that for these component failures, the rate falls as experience grows. Experience is measured in cycles accumulated, modifications also being made to tires and equipment. The apparent failure rate is also close to the radial tire failure rate for automobiles ($\sim 10^{-4}$), but we still need to know how much the tires were actually used. With about 30 cycles for each tire life and a total of eight main-wheel tires for the entire total of ~83,000 cycles, we have:

$$\{83,000 \times 8 \text{ total tire cycles}/30 \text{ cycles}\} \sim 22,000 \text{ tires used}$$

The failure rate for 57 tire failures with a total 22,000 tires is then the fraction $n/N$ or:

$$57/22,000 = 2.6.10^{-3} \sim 1 \text{ in } 390 \text{ tires}.$$

When we calculate the event rate, the elapsed time in use (one cycle ~ 2.7 hours flying), the average failure rate on takeoff is ~1 in every 30,000 actual tire hours. This is basically the same interval we have found before for industrial accident and injury (outcome) intervals. So the echo is now resounding, in that for tire technology, the outcomes occur apparently just as they do for all other industries.

Tire failures occur in automobiles too, and the US National Highway Transport Safety Administration [11] examined and found tread or belt edge separation occurred on large SUVs, depending on the detail of the design and manufacturing process. The tire failure (claims) rate obtained by back-extrapolating the best-fit exponential line to the claims data rate in for SUVs and radial tires is actually the same as the Concorde non-radial tire failure value of about 1 in 390 again. This correspondence in rates is not likely to be a pure coincidence and furthermore implies the same risk of tire failure at the same accumulated experience.

But something else caused the tire to fail – in this case, the piece of metal. Airport requirements specify three daily visual inspections of runway condition in addition to a lighting inspection. These are spread through the day, before 0700h, around 1400h, then around 2100h local time.

On 25 July, the early morning inspection of the runway was performed in two passes by a runway inspection vehicle. Nothing was reported. Then at around 1430, a partial inspection of the runway was performed in the vicinity of a taxiway, but not the runway, following suspicion of a bird strike.

The DC 10 registered N 13067, operated by Continental Airlines, had taken off 5 minutes before the Concorde (at about 1437), to undertake the Paris–Newark flight COA 55. Since this aircraft could have lost the (tire-puncturing) metal strip, technical specialists visited Houston to examine the aircraft in the presence of representatives of the operator. Only one other aircraft, an Air France Boeing 747, had taken off between the N 13067 DC 10 and the Concorde.

The observations in the USA of the N 13067 aircraft's right engine (engine 3) showed that the lower-left wear strip, about 44 centimetres (just over a foot) long, was missing. Its size, and the paint and sealant used matched that found on the runway in Paris, and in the position of the missing part, the support still possessed several rivets. This strip had been subject to repair, refitting and replacement during previous recorded maintenance.

But, as luck would have it, between 1435 and 1510, an exercise with several fire service vehicles took place on runways 26 right and 26 left. To allow for this exercise, the planned runway inspection (for 1400h) was delayed. The Concorde took off at 1442, hitting the metal strip left lying undetected on the runway, having fallen off this previous aircraft. *This was clearly preventable.*

The BEA Report [10] says that subsequent hindsight confirmed the fragility of tires against impacts with foreign bodies and the *inadequacy of the tests in the context of certification.* Recent examples on aircraft other than *Concorde* have shown that tire bursts can cause serious damage. Also the *Concorde* investigation showed that a shock or a puncture could cause damage to tank from a projectile. Such indirect processes, though known about, are complex phenomena that had never been identified on civil aircraft.

The BEA Report [10] notes that the crew had no way of grasping the overall reality of the situation, reacting instinctively when they perceived an extremely serious but unknown situation, which they were evaluating by way of their sensory perceptions. Each time the situation allowed, they applied the established procedure(s) in a professional way.

The crew were unprepared for such a sequence and combination of events, including double-engine failure and a fire until advised by Air Traffic Control, when the aircraft was past the takeoff decision speed, V1. The hindsight is clear, although aborting the takeoff above V1 speed would have resulted in a crash and fire too, and this eventuality was not covered during crew training.

It is evident that the precursors were there: why then had they not been seen? The answer is simple and occurs each time – although the data existed, they were not obvious.

## The Third Echo: The Four Phases

The four Phases are here evident again:

*Phase 1)* The early *unfolding* precursors were tire failure events that were not considered serious enough to ground the fleets.

*Phase 2)* The *confluence* occurred when other events conspired to cause the tire damage by the undetected metal strip.

*Phase 3)* The *escalation* was enabling the subsequent structural failure and fire to spread uncontrollably.

*Phase 4)* The *denial* is evident in the efforts subsequently to shift the blame to the source of the metal strip and in trying to rectify the plane to make it more resistant to tire failure.

The common factor is the unavoidable involvement of humans in all the stages and uses of the design, manufacturing, production and operation of technology.

## Management's Responsibility

How could such a magnificent piece of technology fail, from a simple tire puncture, and now be doomed to spend its days as a museum curiosity. Safety analyses had been done that considered tire failure. Certificates of Airworthiness had been issued by the best national agencies.

The BEA report [10] says simply:

> *The investigation showed that a shock or a puncture could cause damage to a tank according to a process of transmission of energy from a projectile. Such indirect processes, though known about, are complex phenomena which had never been identified on civil aircraft. Equally, the ignition of the kerosene leak, the possible forward propagation of the flame, its retention and stabilisation occurred through complex phenomena, which are still not fully understood.*

The preparation for the unexpected had never occurred and the lack of defined mechanisms meant that they had not been previously or fully considered. We had only prepared for the known, not for the unknown.

## Error State Elimination

In the BEA report [10], it is clear that several factors contributed to the accident. The approach actually taken to ensure flight continuation was to (a) reinforce the inside of the fuel tanks, using reinforced plastic lining so debris could not cause such large damage and (b) change to a tire with a lower failure rate and hopefully, less debris.

In the special language of bureaucratic formality, the BEA report [10] recommends:

*It was in this context that the airworthiness authorities defined the following measures:*

- *Installation of flexible linings in tanks 1, 4, 5, 6, 7 and 8.*
- *Reinforcement of the electrical harnesses in the main landing gear bays.*
- *Modification of Flight Manual procedures so as to inhibit power supply to the brake.*
- *Ventilators during critical phases of flight and revision of the MMEL to ensure that technical operational limitations cannot be applied for the tyre under-pressure detection system.*
- *Installation of Michelin NZG tyres and modification of the anti-skid computer.*
- *Modification of the shape of the water deflector and removal of the retaining cable.*
- *A ban on the use of volatile fuels and an increase in the minimum quantity of fuel required for a go-around.*

*Consequently, the BEA recommends that:*

*The airworthiness authorities, the manufacturers and the operators of Concorde reinforce the means available for the analysis of the functioning of aircraft systems and in-service events and for the rapid definition of corrective actions.*

   *Recording the engine parameters, which allow engine speed to be determined only every four seconds, slowed down and complicated some work essential for the technical investigation. This characteristic also tends to mask certain facts during examination of incidents for which it would not be possible to devote as much time and effort as for the 25 July 2000 accident. In contrast to Air France's Concorde aircraft on the day of the accident, British Airways aircraft are equipped with recorders that allow the parameters from all four engines to be recorded every second. Consequently, the BEA recommends that:*

   *Air France equip its Concorde aircraft with recorders capable of sampling at least once a second the parameters that allow engine speed to be determined on all of the engines.*

   *The technical investigation brought to light various malfunctions relating to the operation of the aircraft, for example the use of non-updated flight preparation data, the absence of archiving of certain documents or incomplete baggage management. Equally, omitting the left bogie spacer was a consequence of non-respect of established procedures and of the failure to use the appropriate tool. Consequently, the BEA recommends that: the DGAC undertake an audit of Concorde operational and maintenance conditions within Air France.*

There is no attempt to ensure that tire failure cannot occur, or that debris generation is prohibited, or that multiple-engine failure and uncontained fire is acceptable.

However, the result was the same, as within two years, the aircraft had been declared uneconomic to fly, and all the fleet grounded and many donated to museums. The error state was truly eliminated.


## The Fourth Echo: Chernobyl

## An Echo of Three Mile Island

It was a night like any other in the flat, tree-lined Russian countryside in April 1986. The town of Prypiat lay outside Kiev, the major city of the Ukraine, and most everyone worked at the four nuclear plants just outside the town, and the two larger ones with their cranes in place still under construction. The Ferris wheel, the apartments, the streets, were all built to service the plant, and the staff and families there enjoyed a comparatively sure existence in the then Soviet Russia. A short distance from the town was the Chernobyl reactor site, with its four giant square-shaped buildings, tall chimneys and grid wires supplying electric power to a major part of the country. It was a prestigious job, although the plant was designed by and largely dependent on Russians. After all, the Ukraine had no oil, no gas and precious little coal, so nuclear energy was an obvious answer.

On 25 April, before a routine yearly shutdown, the reactor crew at Chernobyl Unit 4 were busy preparing for a test. It was to determine how long the turbines, driven by the steam boiled from the reactor, would still spin and supply emergency power if there was a loss of main (outside) electrical power supply. Such tests had already been carried out at other plants. The rundown time and behaviour were sensible parameters to determine as they set the requirements for how long emergency generators had to start and how long everything took to happen.

Throughout, the operators were to control the plant based on plant instrumentation signals, automatic power control systems and their experience. They planned to start to conduct the low power test, for which there were no operating or training procedures, by tripping the turbine generator. The sequence for the accident is in [12, 13, 14].

As the reactor shutdown proceeded, the reactor operated at approximately half power when the electric load dispatcher refused to allow further shutdown. Power was still needed to the Ukrainian grid (recall the Blackout). As part of the test, to avoid a spurious injection, the emergency core cooling system was switched off while the reactor carried on at half power. At about 2300h on 25 April, the grid controller agreed to a further reduction in power.

The operators made a mistake, forgetting to reset the controller, which caused the power to fall to a power level too low for the test. This is most likely due to the so-called and well-known 'xenon poisoning', where xenon (a neutron absorbing gas) is produced from decay of the products of the fission reaction itself. Eventually, after the approximate eight hours or more before the part- or load-reduced power operation, sufficient xenon was produced with absorption enough to reduce the reactor power. To correct the low power, the RO started to increase power by withdrawing control rods, thus overriding the xenon effect, *but without automatic control being available.*

At about midnight, although the reactor was supposed to be at 1,000 MW(t) prior to the planned shutdown test, the power fell to about 30 MW(t) due to the delay at part power, and an operational error in switching between power control systems. To avoid tripping the reactor and aborting the test, the operators disconnected or disabled several safety trips and emergency water injection systems. They then tried to raise the power manually for the test, matching the steam flow to the turbine with the make-up water (the feedwater flow to the reactor) while maintaining the reactor water inventory, using the water level measured in the huge horizontal steam drums as a guide.

Now, in a reactor like this, there has to be, at steady conditions, a balance between the steam generated by the power from the reactor (using that steam to turn the turbine) and the make-up water (feedwater) needed to replace and replenish that being used. Rather like the electricity grid, with a balance between power production (supply) and power use (demand), there must be a balance between the amount of steam produced (boiling in reactor) and the amount of steam used (condensed in the turbine). So, at any moment in steady conditions, to maintain a fixed water inventory, rather like our electric grid where there must be a power balance:

Thermal power = Reactor power = Steam flow = Feedflow

Since the plant could not make the desired test conditions automatically, the operators took over. They raised the power manually by working the control rods out of the core, so that by 0100h on 26 April, the reactor was stabilised at 200 MW.

Now, in a transient, it is not that simple a balance, for three reasons.

There are time delays of tens of seconds between changing the feedflow to the core, pumping it so that water boils as it passes through the reactor core, and the steam leaving and turning the turbine. In addition, the reactor power depends on how much steam is formed in the core itself (so-called void coefficient of power), so the power varies with the reactor flow, the feedflow and the pressure. The pressure depends on how much steam is going to the turbines, which is controlled to match the electric power output required for the grid. The reactor must always operate between safe limits, on core temperatures, power and have the ability to shut down ('scram') the reactor and overcome any 'power' locked up in the steam in the core. This control of power and shutdown is done using shut-off rods, moving in guide tubes into and out of the core. In addition, power-absorbing materials build up in the nuclear fuel as the fission process occurs, and with changes in the power level (rate of fissions), they change the amount of power that can be raised over timescales of hours.

So the process is more complicated than the steady state case, and as a result, automatic devices are usually used (controllers) to match the power to the steam and feedflow rates, moving the control rods in the reactor. Plainly, symbolically we can write:

Reactor power = Nonlinear Function of (Feedwater flow; Steam flow; Void and Power; and Pump flow)

When the function is known, which it is theoretically true, then automatic control is straightforward using normal control technology of adjustable lags, leads and time constants.

So when the Chernobyl Unit 4 operators took over manual control, they moved into uncharted depths, controlling on their measurements, using their knowledge of plant response, and driven by the need to match the plant to the state needed for the test. They commenced the test, turning off equipment and disabling key safety systems so the test would not abort and have to be repeated or delayed.

Shortly after reaching the new power, an increase in coolant flow and a drop in steam pressure occurred, requiring the withdrawal of nearly all the rods. The reactor then became very unstable and the operators had to make adjustments every few seconds to maintain a constant power. The operators reduced the flow of feedwater to maintain the steam pressure, as the pumps that were powered by the slowing turbine provided progressively less flow to the reactor.

Eventually, the additional steam in the cooling channels (positive void coefficient) meant the operators could not control the plant and they then tried to shut it down by inserting rods. But, as luck would have it, the design meant a short power increase occurred before a decrease due to the shutdown rods: ironically, that increase was sufficient to drive the plant unstable.

A power surge occurred that was estimated afterwards to be over 100 times the normal power. The temperature rise rate caused part of the fuel to vaporise, failing the reactor core piping, blowing open the reactor vault and physically lifting the core. Shortly after, a second explosion caused by increasing power with no control or cooling is postulated to cause the final destruction of the reactor.

It is postulated that this was after the lower reactor channel joints had failed (and possibly much other pipework), allowing steam into the reactor cavity or vault. The vault is only designed to safely vent the steam from one channel, not from many. The resulting unvented steam causes pressure forces that are enough to raise the concrete and steel sealing disc, and the graphite shielding blocks, and lift the entire reactor assembly up and out of its cavity. This tears more pipework apart and lifting up the whole concrete disc, tossing the fuelling machine aside, and much more.

There is another large explosion as the exposed reactor power increases uncontrollably, since the shut-off rods are no longer in the core and it is dry. This second large power increase vaporises some of the fuel and the force of this explosion fails the reactor building and tosses fuel, graphite blocks and core parts directly into the outside night.

Eye witnesses at various locations around the site (two fishermen, an administrator and a fireman) confirm hearing first large steam discharges, then two distinct explosions, one after the other, the second seen sending incandescent pieces of debris 150 m into the night sky.

The operators, skilled, experienced, did not know what had happened. They had not been trained on operation at low power or on the test procedure and limits, and did not have needed instrumentation and/or control capability. Central Control panel, Shift Chief Engineer Boris Rogozkin, who was at control panels for the entire Chernobyl complex, reported afterwards:

*I heard a deafening shock . . . after 1–2 seconds system electrical accident began . . . the lights went out . . . there was a wild noise from the apparatus . . . everything droned, wailed and blinked. A fuel assembly (ejected from the reactor, one of many) had fallen on the bus of the Unit 4 transformer. I heard the shock . . . the cause was the collapse of the turbine hall roof. He continues: 'I received reports from the chiefs of the shift and RO, including Vice-Chief Engineer, A.S. Dyatlov who said: 'Boris, I can't understand anything. We pushed the button for AZ-5 and nothing had happened. Rogozkin asked: Is water going into the reactor? The Shift Chief S. Akimov answered: Water is flowing . . . but we don't know where it is going.*
                                                          Source: *Gregoriy Medvedev, The Chernobyl Notebook, 1989*

The debris burned for days, heated by the fuel, emitting radioactive smoke from a large smouldering mass of steel, graphite and fuel. Thousands of tonnes of boron, dolomite, sand, clay and lead were dropped on the burning core by helicopter to extinguish the blaze and limit the release of radioactive particles. The resulting 'lava' or molten mix formed, flowed and froze in fantastic forms in the basement and substructure of the building where it still resides today. Eventually, a series of concrete and steel 'shelters' were built over the collapsed unit, limiting radioactive release and retaining the debris, while the ground outside could be cleared and cleaned.

## The Consequences

The Chernobyl disaster and its impact on the course of Soviet political events were profound: it could not be covered up, and international outrage and concern was evident. This was the beginning of the era of 'Glasnost' (openness) in Russia, and the decline of the Communist party and the break-up of the Soviet Union followed. No more reactors of this type have been ordered and/or built since, and the others at the site were eventually closed down, and the nearly completed new ones were instantly abandoned.

Thirty-one emergency workers (firemen and plant staff) were killed. Some died in heroic acts, such as determining whether the reactor foundation was intact and ensuring that key valves were open for water to flow inside, and from fighting the radioactive fire and moving burning debris.

In the years following the accident to reduce unnecessary radiation exposure, about 116,000 people had to be evacuated, and up to 1995, an additional 200,000 or so people were resettled from Ukraine, Russia and Belyorus, including those within the 30-kilometre 'exclusion zone' of greatest contamination. The psychological impacts remain the largest on the surrounding people. Many were relocated, suffered from unnecessary fear of radiation, were given inadequate information and suffered from top-down decision making. Many international studies now show that the overall deaths ascribable to radiation effects are insignificant, being probably <0.01% of normal. But the infamy and scaremongering remained, and the finger of blame was pointed at the nuclear plant operation and management for allowing it to happen.

## Echoes of Three Mile Island

The previous large commercial reactor accident was in Pennsylvania, USA. Here, the operators at the Three Mile Island Unit 2 reactor ignored signals that a valve was leaking as it had given false indications before.

The reactor lost water over some hours, but the operators thought it was still full because the level in the pressuriser tank showed full because of the location of the leak at the top of the tank. The overflow tank for the water leak showed full, but was ignored too. So when the emergency core cooling came on, in response to the lower pressure of the leak, *they turned the ECCS off.* Now without make-up, and the water level falling, the core dried out, the fuel overheated and failed, and some melted and slumped to the bottom of the reactor vessel.

There were no instruments to tell the operators what was happening, only many, many alarms based on indirect indications of the dried out core, failed fuel, radioactive release, high temperatures and low water level. The procedures for dealing with this type of accident did not then exist, so it was some time after core melt that the operators guessed the answer and turned the ECCS on again, but it was too late to save the core. The activity was largely contained inside the reactor building, no fuel escaped and the core cooled, but both the power company and the reactor design were discredited.

In the panic that followed, local residents worried about being irradiated. There were in fact no real danger, and no deaths or injuries, but there was a lot of fear. Many claims were made about health damage and possible radiation exposures. The media reporting was extensive, and the subsequent government inquiries and regulations required many changes to plant operations and training afterwards.

In the panic and paranoia that followed Chernobyl, unsubstantiated claims were also made about the bad health effects on huge number (millions) of people. Italy briefly stopped eating salad and the government voted to stop its reactor program, a decision that lasted for nearly 20 years. The psychological damage was extensive, particularly near the plant.

As with many matters nuclear, extravagant claims have also been made regarding the death toll attributable to the Chernobyl disaster, even in a publication by the UN Office [15] for the Coordination of Humanitarian Affairs (OCHA). However, the Chairman of UNSCEAR made it clear that 'this report is full of unsubstantiated statements that have no support in scientific assessments'. Both more balanced and authoritative, the UNSCEAR report of 2000 has confirmed that there is no scientific evidence of any significant radiation-related health effects to most people exposed to the Chernobyl disaster. This is consistent with earlier World Health Organization findings.

The UNSCEAR report points out some 1,800 cases of mostly treatable thyroid cancer among a total exposed population of millions, but apart from this increase, there is no evidence of a major public health impact attributable to radiation exposure 14 years after the accident. There is no scientific evidence of increases in overall cancer incidence or mortality or in non-malignant disorders that could be related to radiation exposure. As yet, there is little evidence of any increase in leukaemia (appearing), even among (the emergency) clean-up workers where it might be most expected. However, these workers remain at increased risk of cancer in the long term.

All this debate and science does not mean that this is an acceptable event: but was it preventable? Again the answer appears to be, yes.

## The Causes

At the Sochi Workshop, just a year after the accident, it was clear that blame-shift was at work. No one, not the designers, the pump makers, the physics staff, the control programmers, nor the operators or managers wanted to take responsibility. That was committing professional and personal suicide, with severe social consequences. After all, their particular equipment had worked as designed, turning on and off as it should. It was only a combination of unforeseen events that caused the accident, as Roger Heider and one of us (RBD) pointed out to the Workshop attendees using a 'fish bone' root cause diagram. No single item caused it, but all acting together did.

After many meetings, hearings and workshops, the usual culprits emerged, some being in the plant design and some the way the plant was operated and the staff trained. Various websites cite a lack of 'Safety Culture' in the Chernobyl Nuclear Power plant organisation, so that known design weaknesses went unchanged and unchallenged despite being known about before the accident. Once secret memoranda from the Russian archives say for example cite construction issues and poor quality, which by themselves did not cause the accident but were perhaps symptomatic. After all, the 'old' Soviet culture was known for poor and shoddy work in many buildings. The memo dated February 1979 states in part:

> According to data in the possession of the KGB of the USSR, design deviations and violations of construction and assembly technology are occurring at various places in the construction of the second generating unit of the Chernobyl AES, and these could lead to mishaps and accidents. The

leadership of the Directorate is not devoting proper attention to the (concrete) foundation, on which the quality of the construction largely depends.

Walking the eerie corridors inside the Chernobyl Unit 4 plant after the accident, one was struck by the generally low standard of the work and finish; and by the women without radiation detectors whose job it was to mop and sponge water on the floors to stop dust (radioactive particles) from being inhaled.

## Error State Elimination

Some 15 or so reactors of the Chernobyl-type (so-called RBMK) have operated in Russia, Ukraine and Lithuania. Of the over 11,000 years of reactor operation worldwide to date (from some 400 plants), this RBMK type has accumulated about 260 years of operating experience from these 11 units in Russia.

Therefore, the approximate outcome rate is 260/11 or one serious accident every 23 years or so, or an interval of ~200,000 hours. That is well within the range for the minimum we have come to expect of 100,000 to 200,000 hours, and close to that for the space Shuttle program overall, the Concorde value and the major blackout interval. Echoes within echoes.

Design faults were also inherent in the reactor, with feedback between the steam void and the power causing instability at low power (arising from a so-called positive void coefficient). Thus, the slow-moving shut-off rods first introduced more power from having a dead entry length, before actually shutting the reactor power down by absorption. This was fixed by changing the rod design.

Also, the steam could not vent from the reactor vault if too many channels failed since the vault could only vent the steam from one broken channel. This was then changed to accommodate at least 10 channels failing.

In addition, there were both violations and lack of procedures during the test by the RO staff, shutting down needed safety systems, such as having insufficient (6–8) control rods available during the test, while a standard operating order requires that a minimum of 30 rods to retain control. The reactor's ECCS was turned off and trip signals for low steam drum level disabled. 'Pressonitis' occurred, as shown by the desire to complete the test almost without regard for the plant state, with no clear test termination criteria.

The design changes discussed above, in the control rods, vault venting and void-power, were made to other operating units of similar (so-called RBMK) type. Also, international support to enhance operator training, provide additional firefighting measures and safety modifications were undertaken. Despite this, the undamaged plants at Chernobyl were all eventually closed, as well as others elsewhere, and no new ones built.

The denials initially evident in the early days after the accident were overwhelmed by the realities and need for full disclosure due in part to international impact and pressures. The social and political consequences of the eventual admission of error at the government level and the impacts of the accident in the larger national and international contexts are comprehensively examined elsewhere [16].

## The Fourth Echo: The Four Phases

The four Phases are here evident again:

*Phase 1* The early *unfolding* precursors were the delays and lack of test procedures and training, events that were routine happenings.

*Phase 2* The *confluence* occurred when other events conspired to cause the plant safety systems to be disconnected and bypassed, without any limit while the plant approached unknown and unstable operating territory.

*Phase 3* The *escalation* was enabling and allowing the subsequent test to proceed even though the conditions were well outside what was needed or desired, and control was being performed manually.

*Phase 4* The *denial* is evident in the official efforts first to deny that anything serious had happened. Then, when the full scope was obvious (due to the uncontrolled release of radioactivity from the burning reactor), subsequently to try and shift the blame to any system or operators other than understand there was a real design issue.

## Regulatory Environment and Practices

Given these major Echo events, and many others, it is reasonable to examine the role and purpose of regulation on safety and on risk. After all, if regulations worked properly, there should be less chance or a lower risk of an accident. By regulation, we mean the legal standards and laws that prescribe the practices, requirements, training, procedures, analyses, design margins, guidelines, inspections and reporting, as well as the issuing of the actual licence(s) for allowing the operation by humans of facilities, factories, financial institutions, equipment and machinery. Safety legislation, associated regulations and best practices are fundamental to the safety control of homo-technological industries (HTS), both from a technical point of view and providing industry-wide *minimum* safety standards. As we learn from errors and also with technology improvements, the legislation and regulations change, always increasing in complexity, to notionally improve the standards of every HTS. This is done using a patchwork of rules, which are unique to each HTS, to each government department, to each licensing authority, and to each legal national or local jurisdiction corresponding to accepted norms, established precedents and acceptable past practices. Generally, the licences are issued for a particular design, operating in a specific region or location, and cover commercial activities which are privately owned, while mandating standards to protect the 'public' from an undue or unacceptable risk of exposure or harm.

The upper echelon of regulation development organisations is those requirements or good practices with internationally agreed status, for example, International Civil Aviation Organisation (ICAO) and International Atomic Energy Authority (IAEA). The ICAO 'Standards and Recommended Practices' (SARPS) are set down for implementation by individual Contracting State regulatory organisations, for example, Transport Canada, Federal Aviation Administration USA and the more recently formed European Aviation Safety Agency (EASA), which will eventually encompass legislation responsibility for over 25 European States national authorities under European Commission developing legislation. International regulatory organisations have technical subject groups comprised of specialists from a range of countries. ICAO Contracting States are obliged to follow the internationally agreed standards, however, they have the opportunity to file a difference, which is required to be registered, stating the reason, for example, a delay in producing the state legislation, or they simply file a non-compliance. Over a global industry, this makes for a complex and uneven situation.

In practice, aviation, being a global activity, means that the overall standards of compliance is generally high as ICAO-recommended standards lead to state legislation of an internationally agreed and harmonised standard, otherwise restricted geographical operation may apply. This often applies to the onboard equipment standards and meeting installation compliance for international airspace operation.

Similarly, in the nuclear industry, the IAEA (available at www.iaea.org) issued Safety Standards, Guides and Codes, as well as Safety Reports, which are adopted as a broad baseline by the member states and their independent national regulatory organisations, for example, the US Nuclear Regulatory and Canadian Nuclear Safety Commissions. However, the individual states promulgate, legislate and retain the right to follow their own detailed practices and standards, within this overarching and more general guidance. Once again, over a global industry, this makes for a complex and uneven situation.

To illustrate this regulatory role for just one HTS out of many, we consider commercial aviation, noting that each industry may have slightly different or additional practices (e.g., to meet OSHA, EPA and other national and local standards).

## Case Study: Regulation in Commercial Aviation

### a) Regulations Development

The two internationally adopted basic requirement codes are those of the FAA and EASA. Most countries mirror image the requirements, developing their own national code that is compatible to international standards, via their own legislation procedures. Since the 1980s, much international effort has been given to the harmonisation of requirements, thus effectively providing a global standard footprint for an improved safety standard. However, there remain some historic differences of approach, in the fields of aircraft design and operation regulatory standards. No doubt these differences will eventually become an agreed standard.

Most of the world regulatory organisations are government departments, for example, Civil Aviation Authorities or Departments, but many are not, and are essentially organisationally independent of government with legislation requiring delegated regulatory functions to be carried out by that organisation, for example, the UK Civil Aviation Authority (CAA) is responsible for the regulatory standards for all its national civil aviation activities. These are now EU (EASA) regulations and standards.

The standards are not necessarily prescriptive in nature and often allow flexibility for the achievement of a standard. In complying with equipment standards, the industry usually develops equipment as an acceptable means of compliance, with manufacturers providing an approved product, e.g., Airborne Collision Avoidance System (ACAS) or Terrain Avoidance Warning System (TAWS), which is mandatory fitment for all aircraft above a specified weight or a specific number of passengers. This was mandated via ICAO legislation in SARP Annex 6 (Operation of Aircraft) for international operations. Further development of this requirement has increased the compliance base: it is now mandated for smaller passenger aircraft.

## b) Compliance Standards

The application and monitoring of regulatory standards by national authorities is variable throughout the world and a major question remains as to competency of the regulatory system in their respective industry (HTS). With the objective of improving compliance with the internationally agreed standards in commercial aviation, ICAO required an audit programme covering each contracting state regulatory compliance standard with the internationally agreed SARPS (All Annexes). These audits have shown a wide variation of standards in the application of regulatory standards. It is not difficult to identify shortcomings, but it is another challenge to obtain the resources, expertise and finances required to rectify the situation.

Industry representative groups have drawn up a Global Aviation Safety Plan for ICAO. Its implementation is aimed at giving 'A reduction of the global risk in commercial aviation'. This will be a long-term project.

Some governments run a 'black list' of airlines, which are not permitted to operate into their state due to identified shortcomings in their regulatory control. Adverse ratings can be reversed once the corrective action has been shown to be satisfactory. The EU has its own list applicable to all EU states.

## c) Accident Investigation

Accident and incident boards conduct the investigation against ICAO standards, SARPS (Annex 13 – Aircraft Accident and Incident Investigation). These investigations are usually carried out with the assistance of experts, such as the manufacturer and appropriate certification bodies. The state where the accident occurred leads the investigation, unless it is transferred to another Accident Board. Most accident investigation boards are quasi-independent of the government with expert technical ability and external specialist expert consultants, such as UK Air Accident Investigation Board, the US National Transport Safety Board and the Australian Transport Safety Bureau, and many such others that we have used for reference and source material. The purpose of the Investigation Boards is to establish the cause and make recommendations, but not to apportion blame.

Every licensed operator, manufacturer and maintenance organisation is responsible for applying the regulatory standards. The regulatory inspecting staff are required to monitor the effectiveness of the compliance standards, including the associated operational procedures.

Some accidents, like these Four Echoes, show clearly that the regulatory standards are not as effective as they should be. The financial and competitive element of the industry can undoubtedly have some part to play in the results achieved. Further, the regulations are set at a minimum standard. This book gives many examples recorded from accident investigations in HTSs, inevitably the human element is involved and accident boards are increasingly focusing on this issue. For example: how well were the procedures followed? Or was there any evidence of flight crew or maintenance engineer or Air Traffic controller fatigue? In the aviation industry, an investigation of error reports from a maintenance point of view has shown that over 70% of contributing factors relate to installation errors.

Accident and serious incident reports will have recommendations that demand a formal response from the appropriate industry organisation and the regulatory authority as appropriate.

## Addressing Human Error

As we have seen, stressed and stated repeatedly, it is the human element that *completely* dominates risk. The human element plays the major part in HTS success or failure as the maturity or experience of the industry develops. It has been shown that approximately 80% of accidents are caused by human error, not necessarily the sole cause but often in a combination of individual events leading to the end result, an accident or incident.

In the early 1990s, ICAO, through the Annexes, introduced requirements for human factors training. This subject has received a considerable amount of attention and regulators have seen that specific awareness training is a necessity in order to try and reduce the numbers of direct or contributing factors recorded human error events. This process will be a continuing event with no end in sight. Similarly, the US Nuclear Regulatory Commission took a leading role in human factors and risk assessment following the Three Mile Island incident, and still does so using probabilistic safety approaches.

In the application of regulatory practices and procedures, individual responsibility is as vital as ever; commercial, schedule and project pressures are often high and employees must be mindful of their individual performance in their work, including personal fatigue considerations. Investigation of data in UK aviation has shown that installation errors are by far the most common human error category. It is vital to have the data on errors in order to analyse what went wrong and why – in order to make adjustments to procedures and training programmes – thereby developing a continual process of best practice, created by a Learning Environment with the application of a 'Just Culture'. A 'Blame Culture' merely leads to mistrust and will reduce the value of reporting. Criminalisation of personnel, often before the results of the investigation are concluded, can be seen as having a negative effect on a sound reporting culture. It follows that if the regulations do not demand a categorised reporting procedure, for example, Mandatory Occurrence Reporting Schemes, then mistakes and errors will not be highlighted and are unlikely to receive corrective action. Some states have a great wealth of defect data, but unless this set of data is systematically investigated with adequate feedback, the reports are of little value and the system can fall into mistrust and disrepute. Datasets can be huge and require a considerable effort to make proper use of them to achieve positive results (as one of our correspondents said, his industry had a DINO system – 'Data In, Nothing Out').

Some states have instituted a confidential reporting programme, covering operational activities of all the aspects of an HTS. For example, in the UK, Maritime and Railways are also included as well as commercial aviation. Implementation of an acceptable confidential reporting scheme to all involved parties is not easy and must have a great measure of trust for a satisfactory outcome, as a contribution to improving safety. Several states have, thus far, failed to implement schemes, apparently due to inadequate safeguards for confidentiality. It is important that confidential reporting schemes are not anonymous as there can be no surety of the information unless the reporter cannot be contacted and the report details discussed and fully understood and investigated before the crucial process of de-identifying the report is carried out.

## Management Responsibilities

Corporate Manslaughter legislation is being introduced in some states regarding HTS safety failings (see also Chapter 8). This trend is a result of increasing legal challenges by involved relatives and public reaction to the findings of some fatal accident investigations, where it is clear that the causal factors are shown not to be the sole responsibility of those employees who were directly involved, but a failing of the organisation and its inherent safety control procedures is to blame. It is the responsibility of senior management to ensure the application of a satisfactory control of safety strategy and sound practices, acting within the regulations and laid-down practices. In this book, we have already shown several examples and will show more where management failings have been identified in accident investigation reports.

## Designing to Reduce Risk and the Role of Standards

The natural question that arises is why not *design* to reduce the risk of such failures and accidents? In fact, in the course of learning from errors that is what is usually done, but on a case-by-case basis: changing power line maintenance practices; redesigning thermal tiles to avoid loss and damage; strengthening aircraft fuel tanks and tires; and changing reactor core design so it is much harder or impossible to explode. The apparent paradox is that we must make the very mistakes we seek to avoid, and hence, to be able to address those same errors by improved design.

The issues and approaches in modern design improvement were well stated by one of our correspondents and a leading risk analyst:

> In the final analysis human error is the fundamental driver of design risk because it is humans who set the design specifications and it is humans who accept that they have been met.
>
> However what is important from a design perspective is what failures have human error as their proximate cause, and therefore are susceptible to process control remediation, and what failures have more remote human errors such as design errors or specification errors, which are better remediated by design, materials, or manufacturing tolerance changes. In our experience it is the latter failures that dominate 'new' developmental designs and weeding them out is the primary driver of the growth in reliability with the former responsible for the residual failures that establish the plateau value. This is how complexity enters into the growth process. This is never more apparent than in the design of software, where the specification becomes the design and the 'mettle' is human thought . . .
>
> Source: *Joseph Fragola, 2008, private communication quoted by permission.*

The design issues that ultimately impede risk reduction are clear: increasing system complexity coupled with the dominating influence of the human element on the inevitable 'residual' risk. As another approach to design requirement that include human contributions, there are International Standards (ISO) under development that set minimum requirements and good practices.

We became aware of the development of a new ISO standard on 'Risk Management – Guidelines on Principles and Implementation of Risk Management'[2]. This standard is an

---

[2] We are indebted to our professional colleague Dr. David Valis for bringing the development of this Standard to our attention.

attempt to apply a general risk management framework, which addresses the management of uncertainty, within a specific organisation. In effect, the standard would mandate the use of an integrated 'risk management system' throughout all activities, which identifies, reviews, records and communicates risk on and for all aspects of the organisation. The processes, criteria, assessment methods and consequences are all supposed to be defined and used as part of risk treatment and minimisation, recording what is or has been done.

The difficulties we have with such a consensus-type approach are of course the:

a)  extreme generality of the concept; hence
b)  lack of specific methods, techniques, data or tools; with
c)  no quantification of uncertainty; plus
d)  absence of risk prediction; that, in effect,
e)  provides no effective guidance.

We know of no effective use or test of such a generalised and non-specific approach, other than in suggesting what is supposedly 'good practice'. In essence, having something is better than having nothing, but it is not clear that identifying and treating uncertainty in such a general manner actually reduces the risk due to the *human* element.

There are other interesting documents under development, consideration or proposed (e.g., International Electrical Commission, Guidance on Human Factors Engineering for System Life Cycle Applications 56/1163/NP) that examine Human Factors (abbreviated HF), which try to include human aspects into the design process. The idea is to ensure that what emerges is not an impracticable, wrong, unusable, risky or dangerous design. However, this guidance is misguided, although well-intentioned, as the difficulty with such general 'standards' is that the focus is on the *design process* when it should really all be about the *product function*. To set our thinking, we can imagine what would happen if these 'guidelines' were applied to Case Studies of design and manufacture of real items of successively increasing complexity that we actually *use*. Consider the 'hi-technology' case of the Blackberry handheld, where the function is to create modern, rapid, handheld communication. The proposed draft Guide could not have produced anything like the amazingly successful designs, but probably something that looked like a phone from the 1930s since *innovation in design is not mentioned.* Typing on a miniature QWERTY with your *thumbs* to respond to e-mail is not conventional HF design, which would have immediately demand, dictate or mandate that fingers and larger keys be used to reduce errors.

For the case of the design of process control room, such as which featured heavily in the NE Blackout, Space Shuttle and Chernobyl events, we have an even more complex system. The required 'Howlett function' is to retain control of the system. The actual design starts by establishing the tasks to be performed to control the evaluation and development of the technology that can be deployed, followed by extensive MMI/HF review, followed again by acceptance testing, validation of procedures and operator training. The proposed Guide alone would keep designers hung up for months without designing anything, when what is needed is the right information, presented in the right form, for the trained operators to do the right thing for control, command and communication.

Hence, the proposed HF Guide is really impracticable because of being too highly qualitative, not supportive of actual design, not addressing the quantification and often competing pressures of risk and cost reduction, and really providing a disincentive for needed innovation and technology change. The argument against such Standards were stated many years ago by the greatest engineer of all, the inventor of the suspension bridge, designer and constructor of the first iron-hulled ships, and builder of bridges, tunnels and major railroads:

> *If the Commission is to inquire into the conditions 'to be observed', it is to be presumed they will ... lay down, or at least suggest, 'rules' and 'conditions' to be observed ... or, in other words, embarrass and shackle the progress and improvement of tomorrow by recording and registering as law the prejudices and errors of today .... No man, however high he may stand in his profession, can resist the benumbing effect of rules laid down by authority .... Devoted as I am to my profession, I see with fear and regret this tendency to legislate and to rule.*
> Source: *Isambard Kingdom Brunel Statement to the Royal Commission on the Application of Iron to Railway Structures, England, 1848*

## Conclusion and Echoes: Predicting the Unpredictable

We have analysed in detail the causes, sequences and lesson learned from four major events, each one echoing the next. They are actually representative of the millions of everyday events that occur around and to us all. These four simply demonstrate the spectrum of outcomes and systems, where the common feature is the human element interacting with and within the entire homo-technological system.

Unique in their sequence, unpredictable in their occurrence and major in their message, they share the errors that humans make as they experiment with technology on themselves.

These four echoes have received more attention simply and only because they were larger, highly reported and extensively documented. They were so visible and unforgettable, yet all were preventable. They cover a wide spectrum of technologies, deliberately chosen and carefully revealed. Thus, though all are different, in fact all are the same. They share the human element in their design, their operation and their cause, however that is assigned.

In fact, we can separate the purely physical cause, which is usually what is so highly examined and unique, from the contributory cause, which is similar, and lastly, the underlying cause which is identical (see Table 2.1).

**Table 2.1.** Comparison of Cause

|  | Physical cause – *different* | Contributory cause – *similar* | Underlying cause – *identical* |
|---|---|---|---|
| Columbia | Insulation debris damage causes re-entry loss | Inadequate information, lack of corrective actions and design flaws | Faulty safety management and no learning: pressonitis |
| Concorde | Metal strip punctures tire, that punctures fuel tank(s) | Inadequate information, design flaws and lack of corrective actions | Inadequate safety management and operational procedures |
| Blackout | Line overload and tree shorts to ground | Inadequate information, loss of vital equipment, lack of corrective actions and design flaws | Lack of safety management and inadequate reliability margins |

So while these appear superficially different, the underlying human and management factor is common to all. Because these events (and hence most others) show and contain the same causal factors, as a result they demonstrate the same general and logical development path. Specifically, they contain a set of four conveniently grouped 'watch out' Phases, which we should now be able to instantly recognise and which are intertwined, interdependent and overlapping:

**Phase 1** Contains the early unfolding precursors that were known to happen but unrecognised as to their significance and/or uncorrected by the humans building, using and operating the system.

**Phase 2** Develops as the confluence occurred of failures and events where, despite the humans nominally being in control, they actually had no choice but to make the wrong decisions. Based on inadequate data, commercial or fiscal management pressure, they relied on software or instruments that did not provide up-to-date or believable control information for the actual circumstances that existed.

**Phase 3** Results as the escalation occurs in the repeated and continuing emphasis and attempts to ensure that everything remains more or less understood, when it is not and/or far from normal. Thus, rather than isolation of the failed parts of the system, and mending those first, effort is devoted to pressing on with the day's seemingly necessary tasks which further compound the situation.

**Phase 4** Finally, denial and blame-shift is evident in the humans involved, where they do not realise their full responsibility, and how the outcome occurred. Management believes that actions taken or not could have saved the day (thus saving the investment), and others are to blame for whatever happened, while in fact all were and are an integral part of the shared problem.

In Appendix A, formally and mathematically, we demonstrate that – in the presence of learning – the future event probability (the posterior) is determined solely by the past (the prior) frequency as it varies systematically with experience. Thus, the stochastic events and confluence of factors in the Phases are well represented by a systematic overlay due to learning from those same mistakes. In Appendix H, this analysis is extended to derive the probability of 'matching' or of having similar outcomes. The results show that, statistically at least, these Echoes are likely to be observed if we try often enough, even if they are themselves rare events with low probabilities of occurrence or have small failure rates.

The future estimate for the probability is once again derivable from its unchanged prior value, and including learning *the past frequency predicts the future probability*.

Therefore, the Four Echoes, in all their apparent complexity, are simply reminders that the Past appears time and again. Perhaps in different disguises, or cloaked in superficially different physical causations. The observations are the outcomes, the major events, being the manifestations of human error inextricably embedded within any given HTS. In fact, as we wrote this book, a Fifth Echo occurred with echoes of these four: this was the catastrophic and very expensive explosion at the BP Texas City oil refinery. Just like the Four Echoes, its occurrence caused multiple reviews, recriminations, findings and fines for the entire organisation, being one of the largest energy companies in the world. This event highlighted and was critiqued for showing a lack of 'safety culture', which is simply a convenient terminology for a widespread corporate, facility, supervisory and personal lack of the necessary management, training, and safety prevention and awareness systems. We will return to probing this Fifth Echo later in Chapter 8.

## References

[1] Howlett II, H.C., 1995, 'The Industrial Operator's Handbook', Techstar/Gary Jensen, Pocatello, ID, p. 5.

[2] U.S./Canada Power System Outage Task Force, 'U.S.–Canada Power System Outage Task Force Final Report on the August 14, 2003 Blackout in the United States and Canada: Causes and Recommendations', April 2004; Interim Report, 12 September 2003; and Final Report on the Implementation of the Task Force Recommendations, Natural Resources Canada, US Department of Energy, September 2006 (Available: http://www.doe.gov)

[3] Midwest System Operator (MISO), Transmission Control Center phone transcripts 'August 14, 2003 Outage Sequence of Events'.

[4] Electric Power Research Institute (EPRI), 'Factors Related to the Series of Outages on August 14, 2003', White Paper, 20 November 2003, (Available: http://www.epri.com.), Palo Alto, CA.

[5] Ontario Independent Market Operator (IMO) Market Rules, Chapter 5 'Power System Reliability', June 2003.

[6] Union for the Coordination of Electricity Transmission (UCTE), 'Interim Report of the Investigation Committee on the 28th September, 2003, Blackout in Italy', 27 October 2003.

[7] Swiss Federal Inspectorate for Heavy Current Installations, 'On the Blackout That Occurred in Italy and Border Regions of Switzerland on September 28, 2003', 12 November 2003.

[8] Columbia Accident Investigation Inquiry Board (CAIB) Report, Volume 1, August 2003. (Available: http://www.nasa.gov).

[9] Airsafe, 2000, http://www.airsafe.com. 'Fatal Events and Fatal Event Rates' from 1970–2000, September.

[10] Bureau d'Enquete Accidents (BEA), 2001, 'Accident on July 25, 2000, at La Patte d'Oie in Gonesse (95) to the Concorde Registered F-BTSC Operated by Air France', Translation f-sc000725a, 2001.

[11] National Highway Transport Safety Administration (NHTSA), 2001, 'Engineering Analysis Report and Initial Decision Regarding EA00-023: Firestone Wilderness AT Tires', Safety Assurance, Office of Defects Investigation, US Department of Transportation, October.

[12] Ukrainian Academy of Sciences, ISTC, 1995, 'The Chernobyl' 4 Accident Sequence: Update-April 1995', Kiev, Ukraine, (edited by Edward E. Purvis III).

[13] Duffey, R.B., 1990, 'Chernobyl Reactor Integrated Accident Process and Timeline', EG&G Report EGG-EAST-8947, Idaho National Engineering Laboratory, Idaho, USA.

[14] World Nuclear Association (WNA), 2003, http://www.world-nuclear.org/info/chernobyl/, London, UK.

[15] Report by the UN Scientific Committee for the UN General Assembly on the Effects of Atomic Radiation (UNSCEAR), Highlights Section C and Table 4, and Section III.

[16] Rhodes, R., 2007, 'Arsenals of Folly: the Making of the Nuclear Arms Race', First Edition, Alfred A. Knopf, Random House, New York.

# 3

# Predicting Rocket Risks and Refinery Explosions: Near Misses, Shuttle Safety and Anti-Missile Defence Systems Effectiveness

*'When you think you can or you cannot do something, you are probably right.'*

*Attributed to Henry Ford*

## Learning from Near Misses and Prior Knowledge

We have shown in Chapter 2 how major events and accidents evolve. We observe that outcomes typically develop in phases. Mistakes, misinformation, mismanagement and malformed mental models all contribute to the escalation and the sequence of events. Traditionally, we investigate these outcomes and their sequences to learn from them and to correct our mistakes. We track the sequence looking for root causes and then fix the things we physically can correct (by removing, say, spalling insulation, failing state estimators, tire debris, tree branches from power lines, and not allowing unauthorised repairs and replacements). We establish new paper rules, procedures and requirements. So we expect that, whatever it was, the particular outcome is even more unlikely to 'ever happen again'. We undertake exhaustive inquiries, plus legal and expert reviews, in order to allocate blame and make recommendations for improvement. This examination and elimination of *cause* is all part of a learning process.

*But how can we actually predict the chance of another event?*

This problem of fixing the causes of observed outcomes on a case-by-case basis is that, unfortunately, this approach only addresses those items that we know about, the ones that

*Managing Risk: The Human Element*   Romney B. Duffey and John W. Saull
Copyright © 2005 and 2008 Romney B. Duffey and John W. Saull, Published by John Wiley & Sons, Ltd

have already occurred. In a sense, we only tackle the easy issues, retroactively and reactively. We are not proactive, except through the continued application of whatever safety management system, rules, training and procedures that already exist. The harder problems of the human failings in operating the homo-technology systems (HTSs) and the randomness and unpredictability of the events still remain, along with their unknown probability. The analogy is to weather forecasting, where only hindcasts are 100% accurate, when we really want and need an accurate forecast. We can prepare for the expected bad weather, but we cannot predict exactly when it will occur, and we continually revise our projections. The natural variability is, in our case, due to the human presence.

To show the strong influence of the human presence, and how such escalation and phases of development exist to some degree in basically all other events, we illustrate two recent and very frightening outcomes in aviation. In Appendix D, the example given is the jet aircraft running out of fuel over the Azores due to a human-caused leak, which luckily was able to glide to an emergency landing without any engine power. In Appendix E, the other example is the mid-air collision (NMAC) of two modern jets over European airspace, again due to human-caused actions, in full view of a distracted ground control and with collision warnings sounding. Not only do these two very recent examples demonstrate the four phases, they also show how already known hazards (faulty maintenance, poor instrumentation and near mid-air collisions) are effectively ignored as we continue to try to continue to operate HTS. We are at risk and have not managed to reduce the risk.

We can illustrate this where we have data. The risk of a NMAC is well known: so-called 'near misses' occurred before and still occur, where the official separation rules were violated. As an illustration of actual outcomes, a recent set of US FAA data for NMACs is shown in Figures 3.1 and 3.2.

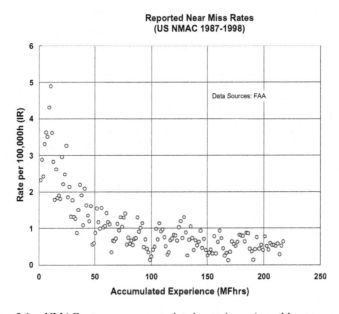

**Figure 3.1.**   NMAC rate versus accumulated experience (monthly average data)

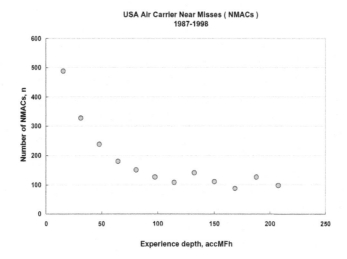

**Figure 3.2.** NMAC number versus depth of experience (yearly average data)

In experience space, the rate of NMACs ($IR = A = dn/d\varepsilon \equiv \lambda$, the failure rate) versus the *accumulated* experience, $\varepsilon_j$, is shown in Figure 3.1. Similarly, in Figure 3.2, we show the total number of outcomes observed ($n = N_j$) versus the *depth* of experience, $\varepsilon_i$. In both cases, the surrogate measure for experience was taken as the millions of actual flying hours (MFh), since NMACs only occur while aircraft are in the air. The *j*th observation interval was randomly chosen as 1987–1998 in which there were some 200 million flights. Because of the chosen observation interval, we take the same experience measure and amount of experience ($\varepsilon_i = \varepsilon_i$) for both plots.

We immediately observe that both the rate and the number decrease with increasing experience, just like a learning curve, towards a finite, non-zero minimum. The outcome rate in Figure 3.1 is clearly both known and predictable: the ratio of the initial rate (*IR*) of ~4.5 per 100,000 Fh to the last or minimum rate (*IR*) of ~0.5 per 100,000 Fh is or order nine. In contrast, the distribution of the number of events with experience, $N_j$, in Figure 3.2 falls from about 500 to near 100, a factor of five reductions. So the increased number of flights overall has caused an increased number of NMACs, which has partly offset the reduction in the rate.

In both representations of the data, we have done a good job of learning, and the reduction effect is clear: there is a clear learning curve. As we will see and illustrate, how we learn from such 'near misses' is relevant to the entire risk management process for *any* system. But events will still happen despite our best technological system, equipment and intent. In the cases given in the Appendices and in this Chapter, the evidence is that the technology as well as the human presence contributed to the outcome.

## Problems in Quantifying Risk: Predicting the Risk for the Next Shuttle Mission

Space flight presents a particular paradox: how can we possibly learn to explore without taking the risk of losing lives? Since we know that space travel is hazardous and largely new for humans, what risk is acceptable and how is it to be managed (Bob Krone, 2006) [1]?

There have been many errors causing risk in the US space program, ranging all the way from launch failures to re-entry losses. The US NASA now conducts detailed 'mishap' investigations of nearly every major event or outcome, in a quest to learn from them and attempt to identify and eliminate the cause(s). As one example, the damage to the $264 M *Genesis* spacecraft in 2004 was due to non-deployment of its parachute on its re-entry after a solar mission of many millions of miles. The impressive and thorough 231-page 'Mishap' report (available at http://www.nasa.gov/genesis) ascribed the problem to the simple design error of installing the release switches backwards and not testing them beforehand. Deficiencies in the pre-launch processes were not only that the design process inadvertently inverted the sensor design, but that the design review process did not detect the design error, the verification process did not detect the design error, and lastly, a detailed final expert or 'Red Team' review (a normal engineering practice for critical projects and designs) also did not uncover the failure in the entire verification process.

So, potential risks and errors are actually probable in complex and new HTSs, despite having multiple systems, procedural barriers, extensive reviews, corrective actions, and modern safety management processes.

*How can we actually estimate the chance of another event when learning effects are not clear?*

For purely illustrative and comparison purposes, let us look again at the Shuttle accidents and losses again. This time, we examine them from the angle of being an example of how to estimate risk when we have a few prior losses, so there may be apparently no learning curve evident but we want to make a prediction about future risk. These 'rare events' occur with a failure rate given by the number of outcomes (shuttle losses) divided by the mission experience, or $\sim n/\varepsilon$. There were a fixed sample of NASA missions of 113 up to and including the *Columbia* event, and we have observed the outcomes as known numbers of either successful or unsuccessful. Historically, there were two losses, $n = 2$, one on launch and one on re-entry, in a total $m + n = 113$ flights or missions, which gives a prior probability of an outcome from the cumulative distribution function (CDF) or failure fraction as:

$$\text{Shuttle loss probability, } p(\varepsilon) = n/(n + m) = 2/113 = 0.018,$$

which is a loss risk per mission of about a 2% chance, or odds of about 50 to 1.

Previous estimates have been made. Richard Feynman, the famous physicist, as a member of the Rogers Commission that investigated the Challenger accident, estimated the likelihood of shuttle failure as about 1% per flight, or one in a hundred launches ($p \sim 0.01$) (Feynman and Leighton, 1988) [2]. The first NASA attempt at comprehensive quantitative risk assessment was derived from prior probabilistic risk assessment methods already developed by the US Nuclear Regulatory Commission for nuclear power plants. Using fault and event trees, according to reports, some components were assumed to contribute negligible risks and some external initiators like micrometeorite impacts were not included (Paté-Cornell and Dillon, 2000; Fragola and Maggio, 1995) [3,4].

The analysis of the probability of the *Challenger* O-ring failures on the external fuel tanks was conducted based on examining all the prior failure data for such seals (Dalal et al., 1989) [5]. This careful statistical analysis derived a seal failure probability estimate of $0.032 < p(\varepsilon) < 0.13$, or somewhere between a 1 in 30 to a 1 in 8 chance. The equivalent prediction based solely on the number of missions is, of course:

Shuttle loss probability, $p(\varepsilon) = n/(n + m) = 1/24 \approx 0.042$,

which also lies within the above range.

Anyway, complete or not, the results apparently showed the probability of shuttle failure as between 1 in 76 and 230 launches (or a probability range of $0.013 < p < 0.0043$). Paté-Cornell and Dillon remark in their conclusions that '... if one wants to assess the risk, the Bayesian approach is unavoidable because there are seldom enough data for a classical statistical analysis'.

For comparison, the Shuttle outcome estimates were one in 140,000 to 190,000 hours, as derived in the previous 'Four Echoes' discussed in Chapter 2. Using an average time between missions of 70 days (~1,700 hours), we have a time-based outcome probability ranging from 1,700/140,000 to 1,700/190,000, or $p(\varepsilon) \sim 0.012$ to 0.009. So the different risk estimates are comparable, based on the prior knowledge and design configuration, and vary at most by a factor of two to three.

Since the *Columbia* loss, NASA has gone to great engineering and management lengths to improve the insulation installation process, examine and ensure insulation integrity, and reduce the chance of debris formation by redesigning and heating of cryogenic tank fittings, eliminating FOD (foreign object debris), and overall reduce the debris impact risk. In addition, there is improved monitoring for potential damage, by instrumentation and checking of wing leading-edge areas, and by physical imaging of the Shuttle with high-power cameras and digital video that also improve the detection of external problems. Nearly 300 design and engineering changes have been made to reduce the risk.

In addition to these physical changes, there has been a major focus on risk identification, evaluation and reduction, such that it permeates throughout the entire readiness-for-launch process. In the NASA 'Implementation Plan for Return to Flight', 2005, [6] one intent is to determine an acceptable level of residual risk that can be achieved. This is to allow 'senior management' to make informed decisions about launch risk, while still recognising that riding in, or more precisely on a rocket for space exploration is always an inherently risky business.

What appears to have been done is to fix the known problem of insulation breakaway and impact damage in great detail to reduce the probability, including the adoption of potential repair techniques. This is a patch on an existing design, with all the attendant protections, procedures and quality measures. Hence, this particular problem is unlikely to 'ever happen again' but the basic Shuttle design is unaltered. In the NASA report, explicitly mentioned as tools, goals, judgements, evaluations and approaches are the terms 'risk assessment', 'risk management', 'design for minimum risk', 'risk review', 'probabilistic risk assessment', 'risk posture', 'acceptable residual risk', 'informed risk trade', 'risk/benefit trade', 'risk-risk trade', 'overall risk', 'risk criteria', 'continuous risk evaluation', 'risk mitigation', 'least risk', 'avoiding unnecessary risk', 'risk tolerance', 'risk profile' and 'risk reduction'. Since 'accepting risk is not taken lightly', there is a careful analysis of remaining risk and an implicit but clear recognition that it is not zero.

Despite this heavy emphasis on managing risk through improvements in both design, engineering and management processes, there did not seem to be, and we did not find, a *numerical* target or goal explicitly stated in the report for the overall probability of a Space Shuttle loss. The goal for loss due to impact is stated explicitly (on p. 109 [6]) as: for impact damage, there will be no more than a 1 in 200 risk for loss of vehicle for any single mission, or a risk of about ½%. There is also the risk to the public stated of less than one in a thousand years.

Given this past history of the two spectacular and tragic losses, NASA has a simple question to answer:

*What is the probability of the very next mission failing?*

Of course, by the time this book is published we will already know the answer to that recurring question[1] for the next mission! But as an exercise in prediction, and since it is relevant for all subsequent missions, we can and should estimate that risk using the data on prior outcomes from the observational interval.

For the Space Shuttle case, we have the number of non-outcomes given by the total of non-outcome missions, $m = (113 - 2) = 111$, and also the prior outcome or Shuttle loss probability value, $p(\varepsilon) = 0.018$. So the corresponding probability of a non-event, or of no loss, numerically is $(1 - p(\varepsilon)) = 0.982$, and would be called the Reliability in engineering terminology. The losses are rare events, so non-outcomes far exceed outcomes. Given this prior information about drawing from the Jar of Life, the number of losses, $n = 2$, being prior outcomes is small compared to the number of recorded non-outcomes, $m = 111$, so $n \ll m$.

Using the Jar of Life analogy, the theory for determining the outcome probability by sampling outcomes and non-outcomes is given in Appendix F. The full sampling model gives the probability of observing $n$ losses appearing *in any order* together with $m$ non-outcomes out of a total of $N$ losses in $(M + N)$ possible missions as the factorial expression:

$$P(n) = \frac{\binom{N}{n}\binom{M}{m}}{\binom{M+N}{m+n}}$$

where, for example, $\binom{N}{n} = \left(\frac{N!}{n!(N-n)!}\right)$

We have had two losses already and want to estimate the risk (chance) of a third on the next mission. We do not know when the next outcome (loss) actually will occur, but we assume for probability purposes that if it did, it could be on the very next one. That would make the total of the outcome losses become three in all. Then, hypothetically, since $n = 1$, we have $N = n + 2 = 3$ in total, including the next one, so $M = m + 1 = 112$. For the very next outcome, inserting the numbers and expanding out the factorials in the expression for $P(n)$ gives:

$$P(n+1) = P(\text{next}) = (3/113) \sim 0.0265,$$

---

[1]On 26 July 2005 and on 4 July 2006 the shuttle *Discovery* was successfully (re)launched, some 2½ years after the loss of the *Columbia*. NASA observed more spallation and cracking of insulation and undertook detailed reviews before proceeding with launch and re-entry. These successful launches leave outcomes unchanged at $n = 2$, but the total number of missions becomes $n + m = 115$. The revised prior loss probability is then 0.0174, which is *insignificantly different* from the previous value of 0.018, and clearly leaves the risk practically unchanged. Obviously, a single additional outcome or non-outcome does not materially change the risk statistics, likelihood or inference, despite the media and public anticipation. The interested reader can readily update the following estimates for any number of additional missions.

This sampling from the Jar value per mission is exactly what would be obtained from the constant risk, $CR$, estimate just using total mission numbers as the measure of experience, which is given by:

$$p(\varepsilon) \approx CR = (n/\varepsilon) = 3/114 = 0.0263$$

Thus, the risk for the next mission failing is nearly the same, but slightly higher than that for the prior two losses, being about a 2½% chance of a loss on the next mission. So if you were betting on mission failure, you would want odds of at least 40 to 1.

It might seem simpler to adopt the sampling theory in the usual limit of large numbers of non-outcomes (see the derivation in Appendix F), so the probability of observing any $n$ outcomes is given by the binomial expression similar to that originally adopted by Bayes:

$$P(n) = \binom{n+m}{n}\{p(\varepsilon)\}^{n}\{1 - p(\varepsilon)\}^{m}$$

For the very next outcome, $n = 1$, the risk or probability of observing it is given by just substituting the numbers into the equation. With $m = 111$ previous non-outcomes, we have the factorials and multipliers for the next mission,

$$P(n+1) = P(\text{next}) = \binom{112}{1}\{0.018\}^{1}\{0.982\}^{111} = (112!/111!1!) \times 0.018 \times 0.133$$
$$= 112 \times 0.018 \times 0.133 = 0.268$$

The expression for $P(n + 1)$ is conceptually actually the probability of an outcome happening once (0.018) times the probability of a non-outcome (1 − 0.018 = 0.982) for all the other 111 times. This estimate apparently greatly overestimates the risk, being about a 1 in 3 chance of a loss on the next mission. So this limit is not a good approximation for this case, and apparently care must be taken in using the binomial limit for rare events in a finite sample. Incidentally, we can derive exactly this same result by backwards determining the number of missions needed for the next mission $(N + 1)$ to be the very next outcome $(n + 1)$, which is given by the so-called Pascal distribution,

$$P(N+1) = \binom{N-1}{n-1}\{p(\varepsilon)\}^{n}\{1 - p(\varepsilon)\}^{m}$$

Or, since for this case $N = n + m$, for the next one to fail,

$$P(N+1) = P(n+1) = P(\text{next}) = \binom{n+m-1}{n-1}\{p(\varepsilon)\}^{n}\{1 - p(\varepsilon)\}^{m}$$

For this case, since the next outcome is assumed to be on the very next mission, having had 113 missions with two already failed, we have $N - 1 = 112$ and $n = 2$, so again,

$$P(\text{next}) = 112 \times 0.018 \times 0.133 = 0.268.$$

Additionally, we can also estimate the chance or risk of a repeat event using the 'matching probability' approach. Having already had one outcome, how likely are we to see an Echo just like it? Analogous to the chance of matching birth dates among a group of people, the probability of at *least one* repeat event can be derived based on the idea that any two of the possible outcomes can be similar types or recognisably alike. As shown by the purely chance statistical analysis in Appendix H, assuming now that $n$ is the number of outcomes that are observed and $N$ is the total possible number of matching opportunities, the probability for at least one matching is simply:

$$P(\text{Echo}) \approx 1 - e^{-n/N}$$

We can estimate the chance of having at least one failure if we presume that the possibility still exists of a 'similar' subsequent Mission failure, which had not been eliminated as a result of the changes made due to the prior outcomes. So substituting the potential matching number for the next Shuttle outcome as a minimum of at least $n = 1$, and assuming that $N \approx 113$, as it could happen for any of the total number of mission opportunities, from the matching formula we find that P (Echo, $n = 1$) $\approx 0.0088$, or simply a finite risk of about 1 in 114. This Echo result is, of course, about one-third of the value of 0.0265 obtained from using $n = 3$ in the pure sampling formula, or even in the matching probability estimate. So we could expect the risk of having at least one matching outcome (an Echo) indeed to be less than the chance of just having another subsequent outcome by about this ratio of 3:1.

## Estimating a Possible Range of Likelihoods

Now we have neither a large number of outcomes (shuttle losses), nor even non-outcomes (successful missions), and limited prior experience. Let us assume now that these $P(\text{next})$ values are equivalent to the 'likelihood' $p(\text{L})$ of the next outcome, given the fact that this is a future outcome estimate, albeit based on the limited prior data. Then we can 'correct' the $P(\text{next})$ value with a posterior estimate using the Bayesian-type conditional probability analysis where we allow for the past in estimating the future:

$$\text{Posterior, } p(\text{P}) \propto \{\text{Prior, } p(\varepsilon)\} \times \{\text{Likelihood, } p(\text{L})\}$$

Now the likelihood is an estimate of the future, and is the ratio of the probability of an outcome in the next experience increment, the probability density function of PDF, $f(\varepsilon)$, to the prior probability of the total accumulated outcomes, $F(\varepsilon) = p(\varepsilon)$. Strictly, then, from Appendix A and our later Chapter 4,

$$p(\text{P}) \propto p(\varepsilon)\} \times p(\text{L}) = p(\varepsilon)\} \times \{\text{PDF/CDF}\} = f(\varepsilon)$$

For rare events, $p(\varepsilon) \ll 1$, and a working estimate for the PDF is:

$$f(\varepsilon) \sim \lambda(\varepsilon) \sim 1/\varepsilon.$$

So for 113 missions, $p(\text{P}) \sim 1/113 = 0.008$, about three times less than our earlier estimates. As an alternative, adopting $P(\text{next}) \equiv p(\text{L})$, the posterior probability becomes,

$$p(\text{P}) = p(\varepsilon) \times P(\text{next})$$

$$p(\text{P}) \approx 0.018 \times 0.268 = 0.005.$$

This is also closer to the limit for a large number of non-outcomes, which from Appendix F is given by the approximate expression

$$P(n) \approx \frac{1}{n!} \left\{ \{p(\varepsilon)\}^n \{1 - p(\varepsilon)\}^m \right\}$$

For the very next outcome, $n = 1$, and the risk or probability of observing it is given by just substituting the numbers into the equation, so,

$$P(n+1) = P(\text{next}) = (1/1!) \{0.018\}^1 \{0.982\}^{111} \approx 1 \times 0.018 \times 0.133 = 0.002.$$

This value and the Bayes-type estimate are about 10 times less than that calculated for the first two actual outcomes (~0.018), and by sampling from the Jar (~0.027), largely due to the presence of the term for the successes, or non-outcomes.

In Appendix F, we carry out the full sampling analysis from the Jar of Life, which shows that in the limits of small probability and limited numbers of non-outcomes, the probability of any number, $n$, of outcomes varies approximately as:

$$P(n) \approx \frac{1}{n!} \{p(\varepsilon)\}$$

As a result, we can expect a single outcome $P(n = 1)$ to follow exactly the MERE probability for $p(\varepsilon)$ that was derived in Chapter 1, so the past predicts the future. But the risk of observing more than one outcome ($n > 1$) is also fully some 10 times less probable or likely.

Using these differing arguments, we have thus derived a *range* of estimates of the risk for the next mission that are comparable to or lower than the prior history, with a range given roughly by, per mission:

$$0.002 < P(\text{next}) < 0.03$$

For these rare Shuttle loss events with little data, it is quite difficult to make exact estimates: the outcomes are Bayesian, with low probability.

*What should be the risk targets or goals for intervals between outcomes?*

The aim of the NASA Program is to reach a rate five launches a year. The minimum calculated interval between losses for that many launches, using the Jar result, is a mean-time to failure, TTF = $1/(5 \times 0.03)) \sim 50,000$ hours, which is comparable to normal industrial accident and injury intervals. What is truly an 'acceptable' loss interval is hard to say since acceptable risk loss rates are not defined.

So the prior Shuttle risk history implies a loss every six years at most, with a risk of loss interval to the crews similar to that for any industry. Except, of course, in those other such 'normal' industries, the risk is spread among many more, indeed 1000's or workers, and not just among the small numbers in astronaut crews. Just like when ships sink, aircraft crash or trains collide with passengers on-board, how many people are hurt or killed depends on how many happened to be around or on-board at the time: but only *one* outcome happened. As we shall discuss later in Chapter 8, if just the number of outcomes happening dominates our perception of risk, then the rate of or actual numbers being killed or injured by outcomes are not as significant as a measure of perceived risk (to the public and ourselves) as just the outcome happening anyway!

We know that NASA has made and is making the same types of risk and loss estimates, based on the prior history of losses and using probabilistic risk analyses (Fragola et al., 2005) [7]. It is worth noting that knowing the number of non-outcomes is critical to this calculation for rare events, and accounts for a risk reduction factor of nearly a factor of 10. So the relative number of outcomes to non-outcomes really matters, but does depend on the prior probability being unchanged for future missions. If learning were to occur, and the risk management process works so the probability $p(\varepsilon)$ decreased with experience, presumably the risk would fall even faster and further. But we have not seen a reliable numerical estimate beyond that stated for a loss of vehicle by [7] 2005 of about 1 in 483 ($2 \times 10^{-3}$): so we must rely on the prior experience. Hence, Fragola et al. [7] give a range from between one in about a hundred ($\sim 10^{-2}$) to about one in a thousand ($\sim 10^{-3}$) based on the average of the ratio, $\langle n/L \rangle$, of the number of losses, $n$, to the total number of launches, $L$, for different rocket types and histories.

## Learning from Experience: Maturity Models for Future Space Mission Risk

For space travel, we must inevitably use new and risky technology like rockets and take risks of failure and death. The major paradox is that in order to reduce risk and improve designs, we must rely on those very same unfortunate and expensive prior outcomes that we have tried so hard to avoid (Hsu and Duffey, 2006) [1].

Given the NASA plans to revisit the Moon and also land on Mars sometime in the near future, a massive study has been undertaken to quantify and reduce the risk of loss of mission (LOM) and loss of crew (LOC) in unmanned and manned missions, respectively (NASA, 2005) [8]. The idea is to have less risk than with the Shuttle. By breaking down the risk into discrete mission phases, and studying alternate rocket configurations and types, a relative risk ranking was determined based on the calculated probabilities of LOM and/or LOC. The results also provide useful risk insights and design guidance for the Crew Exploration Vehicle (CEV) that can also function as a 'crew survival module' in case of a problem, an escape feature for astronauts that was not in the Space Shuttle designs. The implied design aim was about a one order of magnitude reduction from the Space Shuttle risk for LOC, from about $10^{-2}$ to about $10^{-3}$ per launch or mission.

As in any risk assessment, the probabilities for the risk of loss ($p(\text{LOM})$ and $p(\text{LOC})$) can be derived from summing (written as symbol $\Sigma$) all the products (written as symbol $\Pi$) of all the conditional success probabilities, $p$, such that:

$$p(\text{failure}) = 1 - \sum \Pi p(\text{success})$$

or, for all causes and missions of form, and all possible initiating and outcome events, then:

P(LOM, LOC) = 1 − {Sum over all mission phases of multiplications such as
$\qquad$ [$p$(mission occurring) $\times p$(launch success per mission) $\times p$(mission
$\qquad$ phase success) $\times p$(systems and controls not failing)
$\qquad$ $\times p$(survival of CEV)......]}

Results were derived by NASA for many missions with differing loss probabilities, and in particular, the study concluded: 'It is recommended that the CEV incorporate a separate Crew Module (CM), Survival Module (SM), and Launch Abort System (LAS) arrangement similar to that of Apollo[2], and that these modules be capable of multiple functions to save costs. The CEV design was sized for lunar missions carrying a crew of four'.

---

[2]Apollo was the system used for the successful series of NASA Moon landings.

Table 3.1 gives the published summary of all the NASA analyses, and can be seen to be both comprehensive and very detailed, even down to how many missions of which type are to be undertaken.

Learning is actually included in these probability estimates using an explicit assumed reduction in risk of loss with increasing number of launches and/or missions. This proposed 'maturity model' adopted by NASA (see the entries of Table 3.1) is remarkable in and by itself. This is a very appealing way to treat the gains from experience and we should expect it to be an analogy with the Learning Hypothesis where risk reduces with experience.

The trial formula used by NASA for the 'maturity model' is actually published elsewhere and was brought to our attention by some of the leading ESAS risk analysts (Putney and Fragola, 2007) [9]. The trial expression for the assumed risk reduction with experience is actually an arbitrary power law variation of decreasing probability with increasing number of launches. The risk reduction, using the present notation and assuming we learn from the few outcomes, $n$, and also the many non-outcomes, $m$, can be written as:

$$p_{n+m} = p_\infty + (p_0 - p_\infty) \times \{1 - (n+m)/n_\infty\}^k$$

where, $p_{n+m}$ is the failure probability after $(n + m)$ missions; $p_\infty$ is the 'mature' or lowest failure probability achievable; $p_0$ is the initial or novice failure probability; $n_\infty$ the number of missions until maturity; and $k$ is some decay rate constant (~2). By this definition, when the number of launches, $L$, reaches the fully mature number $(n + m = n_\infty)$ then the probability, $p_{n=m}$, also reaches its fully mature and lowest value, $p_\infty$.

It is not clear how this maturity model expression is actually applied in the details of the ESAS risk models, and to what systems and elements of the analysis. But the implication is that there is some learning happening that follows an elementary power law function, very similar to the simple psychological and economic examples that we come across later. In fact, the Putney and Fragola paper concludes: '... *it is hoped that this example spurs researchers to investigate improvements in the maturity models and the data to support them*'.

We would argue we have already undertaken and published this investigation and task using the Learning Hypothesis result from the MERE (Duffey and Saull, 2004) [10], where the influence of experience on learning is explicitly treated and derived from data. With the MERE, we would assume that the number of missions represents a relevant measure of the accumulated experience, which is then taken as somehow proportional to the accumulated number of prior like missions. Hence, in our learning theory, we are in effect also assuming that the mission number ratio is proportional to the experience ratio, so $(n + m)/n_\infty \propto \varepsilon/\varepsilon_\infty$, where $\varepsilon_\infty$ is the experience needed to attain a minimum probability.

Therefore, we can write this same NASA 'maturity model' in learning-from-experience terminology, $\varepsilon$, as we progress from being novice to expert. Substituting the equivalent relative probability change ratio into the same empirical power law we obtain the maturity law as a probability or risk ratio given by:

$$\{p(\varepsilon) - p(\varepsilon_\infty)\}/\{p(\varepsilon_0) - p(\varepsilon_\infty)\} = \left\{1 - (\varepsilon/\varepsilon_\infty)^k\right\}$$

Clearly, $p(\varepsilon)$ becomes $p(\varepsilon_\infty)$ as experience increases towards the optimum expert value, $\varepsilon_\infty$.

**Table 3.1.** Campaign results

**Missions Flight Rates**

| Missions | 2005 | 2006 | 2007 | 2008 | 2009 | 2010 | 2011 | 2012 | 2013 | 2014 | 2015 | 2016 | 2017 | 2018 |
|---|---|---|---|---|---|---|---|---|---|---|---|---|---|---|
| **Maturity Model** | | | | | | | | | | | | | | |
| SM_Orbit_Ajust (LOXCH4)/CEV ISS | 20.0% | 20.0% | 20.0% | 20.0% | 20.0% | 20.0% | 20.0% | 12.7% | 5.9% | 1.2% | 0.3% | 0.3% | 0.3% | 0.3% |
| Launcher (13.1) | 30.0% | 30.0% | 30.0% | 30.0% | 30.0% | 30.0% | 30.0% | 1.5% | 0.2% | 0.2% | 0.2% | 0.2% | 0.2% | 0.2% |
| Docking_Auto_ station | 10.0% | 10.0% | 10.0% | 10.0% | 10.0% | 10.0% | 10.0% | 7.2% | 2.3% | 2.0% | 2.0% | 2.0% | 2.0% | 2.0% |
| **Loss of Mission Risk** | | | | | | | | | | | | | | |
| Shuttle | 0.01 | 0.03 | 0.05 | 0.05 | 0.03 | 0.03 | – | – | – | – | – | – | – | – |
| HTV (H2) | – | – | – | – | 0.29 | 0.27 | 0.26 | 0.25 | 0.24 | 0.23 | 0.22 | 0.21 | – | – |
| ATV (Ariane) | – | 0.06 | 0.05 | 0.05 | 0.04 | 0.03 | 0.03 | 0.03 | 0.02 | 0.02 | 0.02 | – | – | – |
| Soyuz | – | 0.01 | 0.01 | 0.02 | 0.02 | 0.02 | 0.03 | 0.03 | – | – | – | – | – | – |
| Progress | – | – | – | 0.12 | 0.12 | 0.16 | 0.20 | – | – | – | – | – | – | – |
| CEV_DEV_SO | – | – | – | – | 0.01 | 0.19 | 0.21 | – | – | – | – | – | – | – |
| CEV_DEV_ORB | – | – | – | – | – | – | 0.44 | – | – | – | – | – | – | – |
| ISS_UnPress | – | – | – | – | – | – | 0.33 | – | 0.08 | 0.03 | 0.02 | 0.02 | – | – |
| CEV_ISS | – | – | – | – | – | – | 0.19 | 0.22 | 0.08 | 0.02 | 0.01 | 0.01 | – | – |

| | | | | | | | | | | | | | | |
|---|---|---|---|---|---|---|---|---|---|---|---|---|---|---|
| ISS_Pres | – | – | – | – | – | – | – | 0.37 | 0.14 | 0.08 | 0.07 | 0.07 | – | – |
| Con-1 | – | – | – | – | – | – | – | – | – | – | – | – | 0.03 | – |
| Con-2 | – | – | – | – | – | – | – | – | – | – | – | – | 0.03 | – |
| Con-3 | – | – | – | – | – | – | – | – | – | – | – | – | – | 0.05 |
| Con-4 | – | – | – | – | – | – | – | – | – | – | – | – | – | 0.06 |
| **Total Incidents** | **0.01** | **0.11** | **0.22** | **0.46** | **0.96** | **1.68** | **3.35** | **4.21** | **4.78** | **5.16** | **5.51** | **5.83** | **5.88** | **5.99** |

**Loss of Crew Risk**

| | | | | | | | | | | | | | | |
|---|---|---|---|---|---|---|---|---|---|---|---|---|---|---|
| Shuttle | 1.0% | 3.0% | 5.0% | 5.0% | 3.0% | 3.0% | 0.0% | 0.0% | 0.0% | 0.0% | 0.0% | 0.0% | 0.0% | 0.0% |
| Soyuz | 0.0% | 0.3% | 0.3% | 0.5% | 0.5% | 0.5% | 0.3% | 0.0% | 0.0% | 0.0% | 0.0% | 0.0% | 0.0% | 0.0% |
| CEV_ISS | 0.0% | 0.0% | 0.0% | 0.0% | 0.0% | 0.0% | 1.9% | 2.2% | 0.8% | 0.2% | 0.1% | 0.1% | 0.0% | 0.6% |
| Con-3 | 0.0% | 0.0% | 0.0% | 0.0% | 0.0% | 0.0% | 0.0% | 0.0% | 0.0% | 0.0% | 0.0% | 0.0% | 0.0% | 0.6% |
| Con-4 | 0.0% | 0.0% | 0.0% | 0.0% | 0.0% | 0.0% | 0.0% | 0.0% | 0.0% | 0.0% | 0.0% | 0.0% | 0.0% | 1.5% |
| **Total Success** | **99.0%** | **95.8%** | **90.8%** | **85.8%** | **82.8%** | **79.9%** | **78.2%** | **76.5%** | **75.9%** | **75.7%** | **75.6%** | **75.5%** | **75.5%** | **75.5%** |
| **Probability_LOC** | **1.0%** | **4.2%** | **9.2%** | **14.2%** | **17.2%** | **20.1%** | **21.8%** | **23.5%** | **24.1%** | **24.3%** | **24.4%** | **24.5%** | **24.5%** | **24.5%** |

With kind permission of NASA TM-2005-214062, November 2005 [8].

However, the MERE probability result actually shows that the probability of an outcome varies naturally with increasing experience, $\varepsilon$, as a 'bathtub' shaped curve (see Appendix A), first falling and then rising according to:

$$p(\varepsilon) = 1 - \exp\{(\lambda - \lambda_m)/k - \lambda(\varepsilon_0 - \varepsilon)\}$$

where, the homo-technological system failure rate is

$$\lambda(\varepsilon) = \lambda_m + (\lambda_0 - \lambda_m)\exp - k(\varepsilon - \varepsilon_0)$$

with $k \sim 3$ based on the world's outcome data. In fact, at infinite or large experience, $\varepsilon \to \infty$, $\lambda \to \lambda_m$ and $p(\varepsilon_\infty) \to 1$, so having an outcome is ultimately inevitable after passing through the bathtub curve. Similarly, at small experience, $\varepsilon \to 0$, and $p(\varepsilon_0) \to 1 - 1/e$ and indeed we have some constant value for an initial probability.

The Learning Hypothesis form of the NASA maturity model is the ratio of the difference between the actual probability at any experience from that finally achievable relative to the difference between the initial (novice) and final (mature or expert) values. From the Learning Hypothesis, the equivalent MERE 'maturity model' with a NASA-type relative probability variation with experience, or increasing number of missions, is the risk ratio:

$$\{p(\varepsilon) - p(\varepsilon_\infty)\}/\{p(\varepsilon_0) - p(\varepsilon_\infty)\} = \{\exp\{(\lambda(\varepsilon) - \lambda_m)/k - \lambda(\varepsilon)(\varepsilon_0 - \varepsilon)\}\}/\{1 - p(\varepsilon_0)\}$$

To evaluate this expression, we must still ascertain the failure *rate* at any future experience, $\lambda$, or the equivalent launch number. We can then determine whether the NASA assumption of a power law reduction is consistent or not with that derivable from actual data. In Appendix K, we have made comparisons with the NASA data for rocket launch failures over some 20 years that actually confirm the form for the probability expression. These data also allow a suitable choice for the experience measure, which is then directly proportional to the fractional 'burn' or ignition time multiplied by the fractional launch count.

We are faced with a conundrum in the comparison between the 'maturity model' power law and reality. In the real world, an outcome is inevitable at sufficiently large experience because the minimum failure rate attained is never zero. So say all the world's data! At large experience, we always have an event and the probability is unity, $p = 1$ – an outcome is assured if we try long and often enough (that is, if we have undertaken many, many space missions). This is not just being pessimistic, this is the reality. Using the asymptotic $p = 1$ value in the maturity models gives little risk variation, of course. But since we do reach a minimum probability at the very bottom of the bathtub, we can use the lowest probability attained at any experience as the desired NASA maturity asymptote adopted for design purposes.

So to make a valid comparison, we take the minimum probability on the bathtub ($\sim 10^{-3}$) as the definition of the attainable 'mature' value, $p(\varepsilon_\infty)$. Numerical evaluation of the NASA power law ratio relation translated to experience form and comparison to the data-based MERE formulation is shown in Figure 3.3. There is an initial factor of over 10 numerical difference between these two 'maturity' formulations, and after the bathtub minimum is reached the power law risk ratio 'blows up' and increases rapidly without bound because of the choice of experience for the 'mature' or minimum probability. The learning hypothesis retains a sensible value of the risk ratio throughout. The implication is either that the assumed

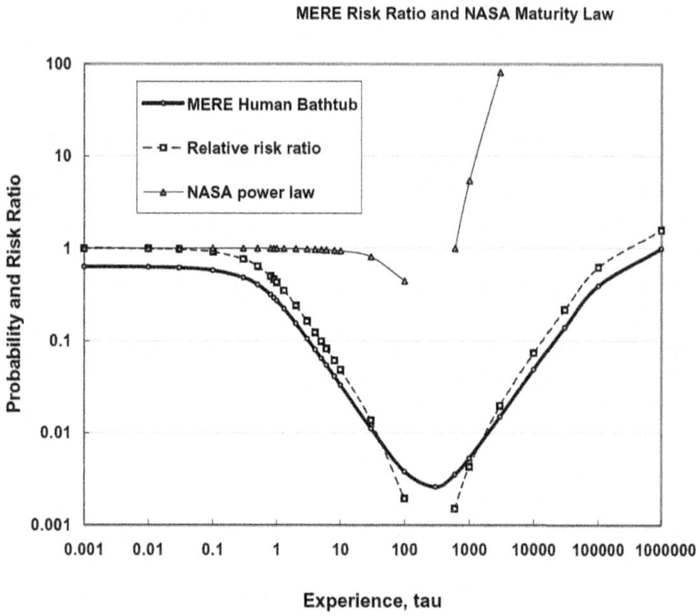

MERE Risk Ratio and NASA Maturity Law

**Figure 3.3.**  Comparison of Learning Hypothesis and NASA Maturity Model risk ratio values

NASA power law variation is indeed too simplistic; or that a factor of 10 in probability is not significant; or that the 'maturity' power-law formulation may itself be in error; or gaining experience is not directly proportional to the accumulated number of missions, as we have assumed. The only reason we, or anyone else, has for believing more in the Learning Hypothesis risk ratio result (as we obviously do) is that the MERE failure rate is based on the ULC and on outcome data from many, many diverse sources and is in accord with the observed world outcome failure rates and probabilities.

The predicted estimated risk reduction or gain is large for the Learning Hypothesis, and the implication is that the risk reduction potentially can be up to a factor of about 100 times before the inevitable happens. Apparently, we obtain this large risk ratio because the dynamic failure rate is changing non-linearly (in fact, exponentially decreasing) with increasing experience. The important point is the potentially huge reduction in future risk that is possible from learning. After all this work, the other key observation here is that making arbitrary *assumptions* about risk reduction, or the probability variation with experience and/or with repeated trials, can give wrong *predictions* of the actual numerical risk.

We illustrate this further in the detailed case study in Appendix K, where we examine the rich history of prior launch failures, based on NASA data for RL-10 type rockets between 1962–2005, which are one of the types being considered for new space exploration vehicle 'architectures'. The data are shown to follow the classic MERE ULC and also follow the bathtub risk curves we developed in Chapter 1. The failure rate declines with increased experience, and the detailed statistical analysis shows that the predicted probability of failure depends on both launch numbers and burn times, being the relevant experience measures of the learning opportunity. In addition, it is shown that traditional statistical sampling formulae although giving sensible trend results, are inadequate and extremely limited predictors when they do not account for the influence of learning.

## Technology versus Technology

We now examine another interesting risk topic: how well can we protect ourselves from attack by one technology using another technology? This was evident in the near miss and mid-air collision, where airplanes are being protected by collision avoidance technology. We have two HTS operating together as one, but not always in unison.

Imagine if the two technological systems were hurtling at each other, just as in a mid-air collision, but this time on purpose. In today's world, we face the threat of guided missiles, designed to explode or spread contamination, rendering areas uninhabitable and the population dead or frightened. The precision targeting of the 'incoming' is now exceptional. Using laser or global positioning system (GPS) guidance, the so-called 'collateral damage' (a euphemism for non-combatant, bystander or innocent deaths) from strikes against military targets can be minimised. But unlike armies, terrorists do not care about precision, or about those civilians on the sidelines: in fact, the innocent and the undefended *are* the targets. Poor targeting and random impacts themselves can be the weapons of terror.

The recent suggestion for defence against such attacks is to establish a 'missile shield'. This is an anti-missile system that has its roots and origins in the Cold War between Russia and the USA. Both sides for many years threatened to annihilate each other, with overkill potential (Mutually Assured Destruction) using intercontinental ballistic nuclear weapons. Nowadays, with that threat reduced, the intent of smaller states is to develop their own independent rockets and missiles (Iraq's SCUD system comes to mind), which can leverage wars at a much smaller scale than global warfare. If this attack technology falls into the hands of despots, dictators or terrorists, it is argued and feared they will be misused, and innocent nations threatened or targeted. The only defence, other than externally enforced 'regime change', is to be able to shoot the incoming missiles down before they hit their civilian targets in a deliberate mid-air collision.

That means having a reliable 'interceptor' missile, usually ground-based, or some other means to destroy incoming devices. The effectiveness of the 'shield' can be established by testing, using some sample of the proposed deployable devices.

*US Missile Shield Suffers Major Setback* ran the headline in December 16th's 2004 Ottawa Citizen newspaper. A test failure had occurred in the US National Missile Defense program because of a launch problem. Previous tests had also had problems, and some were known to be pre-scripted in the treatment of decoys, or to have a pre-arranged homing device to help assure interception. The report in the newspapers also quoted the past US Department of Defence's Pentagon's chief weapons evaluator as saying: *'he could not be sure that the shield would work'; and that: 'he had calculated the shield might . . . hit its targets about 20% of the time'*.

This quote was from the well-known weapons systems analyst Phillip E. Coyle, who also said in a published interview with PBS's Newshour:

> The thing that failed was supposed to be the easy part. Something that we felt we knew how to do. And, so, it actually prevented a test of the harder part that was demonstrating another intercept . . .

*The first thing that will happen is that the contractor will go through a failure matrix; try to figure out what the root cause of that failure was. They are in the process of doing that now. Once they believe that they understand the failure, obviously, it will have to be fixed so that it can't happen again. And then we'll need to do a new test perhaps not identical to the last one but very similar . . .*

*We've shown, for example, in the first intercept test that we can hit a bullet with a bullet, something that some people were skeptical we could do. We've shown we can do that. What we haven't shown yet is that we can do that in realistic, operational situations without warning and in the presence of likely counter measures.*

An outcome is a successful or unsuccessful interception. So how do we undertake realistic tests? How can we make good estimates of the risk of non-interception, of penetration of our defences? Can we use our learning model in some way to help?

To assess system effectiveness, we have the actual lessons of recent history to show us what happened in missile defence, and also how reliably we can launch missiles and intercept attacks. Assume that the risk of a launch failure is independent of risk of intercept failures even for a successful launch, which they are physically. Therefore, we can multiply the two failure rates to obtain the overall probability of failing to intercept for a given launch.

Knowing that in principle we can reduce the risk of non-interception by providing sufficient rockets to overcome launch and intercept failures and decoys – at least, that is the risk reduction idea.

## Missiles Risks over London: The German Doodlebug

In 1944, in the sky over London and the south of England, above the bombed streets and houses, and the troops gathering to join in the invasion of Europe, could often be heard a low throbbing, pulsing noise. It was the ramjet sound of Hitler's revenge weapon, the V1 unguided missile. Looking up, it could be seen, a small sleek, stubby-winged shape. When the noise of the engine stopped, people paused, waiting for the sound and fire that marked where the explosive-laden V1 blindly fell and plummeted to earth. (See Figure 3.4.)

Launched from secret sites in Germany, this advanced forerunner of today's guided weapons was the first missile to travel so far. Called the 'doodlebug' from its sound, the V1 was simply aimed to terrify and to kill civilians, to attack their morale like the early blitzkrieg of the World War II. Infuriated at the Allies successes, from 16 June 1944, the first Nazi V1s entered unscathed and untouched to London. Only anti-aircraft guns could try by chance to bring them down. A rain of terror literally descended on England, the very idea being that precision targeting was not even a concern. This was tactical bombing for the waging of 'total war', not the selection and surgical destruction of military installations and equipment.

Against the V1, initially there was no defence other than the half-buried Anderson shelter or a lucky gunshot. To counter the weapon, the UK Royal Air Force, battle-hardened from the war, developed hunting skills. They tried to shoot the V1 down by cannon and machine gun fire from their Hurricane and Spitfire aircraft, intercepting the weapons using their radar tracks. They developed new and unique skills, flying alongside to gently touch the wings of the V1s with their own wings, rolling the V1 off-course or into the ground. They intercepted and destroyed them well ahead before reaching England, over the English Channel and the

**Figure 3.4.**  The stubby-winged V1 lumbered unguided to its target in WW II


Dover Straights as much as possible, to avoid them still falling or crashing into towns and people. These were truly the very, very first anti-missile defence systems.

Deep beneath the bowels of London today is the original record of whether this effort succeeded those 60 years ago. Just how well the Air Force and anti-missile defence measures worked is listed on sheets of original and aged column-ruled, hand ink-titled and numbered paper. The sheets are placed in a glass-windowed cupboard on the painted wall of the concrete corridor in the once top-secret Cabinet War Rooms.

Here, in the subterranean cloisters used by Winston Churchill and his colleagues and staff, in the heart of London and the very heart of Europe's liberation, the daily launch and success rate was tracked, day-by-day. In those desperate times, we can imagine each latest daily record being eagerly awaited to see how well the defences were doing and the scale of the attacks.

This is probably the only large-scale track record *under real combat conditions* of the performance of any surface-to-surface anti-missile system until the 1990's Gulf War with the use of the Patriot system against incoming Iraqi SCUD missiles. These data were a totally unexpected and amazing find, discovered by accident on a visit to this truly historic site, so we patiently transcribed the listing and analysed these historic numbers.

How well did they learn to destroy the V1 in flight? How much was the risk of bombing actually reduced? How much was propaganda? How well could they have done? Did we manage the risk?

Between 16 June 16 and 2 September 1944, the complete paper lists record 7,970 missiles launched, with some 3,859 destroyed by anti-missile systems. That left some 4,111 penetrating or undamaged, and hence, potentially still able to explode on landing. The average 'kill rate' or missile intercept fraction was 48%, or just slightly less than half.

To determine if there was evidence of learning by the defence forces and anti-missile systems, the number missed or the fraction penetrating the defences to reach their targets is given in Figure 3.5 as a function of accumulated experience.

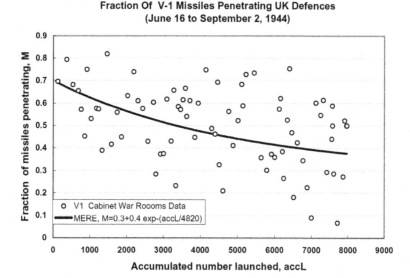

**Figure 3.5.**  The fraction of V1 missiles breaching UK anti-missile defences in 1944

The measure we took for experience was not calendar time, but was the accumulated total number launched, $\varepsilon \equiv \tau = L$. This also represents the measure of the depth of experience. The rationale behind this choice is that the learning (practicing anti-missile warfare) was on and by the total system, and how many overall chances there were to destroy the incoming missiles. As can be seen, initially from 50 to 80% penetrated, this fraction slowly reduced to a range of 10 to 50%, so clearly learning was occurring. The MERE fit, albeit with large scatter, for the 'missed missile kill', anti-missile system failure or still penetrating fraction, $M$, of the total launched, $L$, is given by:

$$M = 0.3 + 0.4\exp - (L/4820)$$

with a 95% confidence of circa ±0.1, or 10%, where the MERE fit implies a predicted asymptotic rate of 30% penetration of the defences.

So, despite evidence of learning, and considerable success and improvement, the kill rate was never enough to really stop the V1 threat. At least 30% got through, no matter how brave the defenders or loud the propaganda. In fact, the V1s and their successor and more successful V2 rockets were actually stopped from attacking by the launch sites being physically overrun and captured on the ground by the Allied Forces' invasion troops after D-day.

How well we can do today in managing the risk from incoming missiles, with more elaborate systems, detection gear and sophisticated interceptors, is still a matter of active debate. This is the desired function of ABM systems and missile shields, and of local 'theater' defence. The evidence of effectiveness to date is mixed, and apocryphical and anecdotal stories circulate of how peacetime tests and demonstration 'kills' are not really proof and may even be rigged, suggests we would be wise to deploy in-depth or layered anti-missile defences. Until we have a true, live battle scenario, it is unlikely we will really know if and how well we have learned to manage this risk.

There are more recent data for the US Patriot anti-missile system, which was deployed in Israel and Saudi Arabia to destroy incoming SCUD missiles from Iraq in the 1991 Gulf War. Although the exact intercept numbers continue to be in some dispute, one report by Alexander Simon in 1996 [11] has stated:

> *The U.S. Army which was in charge of the Patriots claimed an initial success rate of 80% in Saudi Arabia and 50% in Israel. These claims were scaled back to 70 and 40 %. Part of the reason the success rate was ... higher in Saudi Arabia than in Israel is that in Saudi Arabia the Patriots merely had to push the incoming Scud missiles away from military targets in the desert or disable the Scud's warhead in order to avoid casualties, while in Israel the Scuds were aimed directly at cities and civilian populations.*

These results and the intercept range agree remarkably well with the range of data from the V1 intercepts, the mean being between 30 and 60%. This agreement is surprising, despite being 50 years later and the interception techniques and technology being *completely* differ-ent, and hence suggests again a common and very human basis exists for the failure rate[3].

Unless this numerical range is a pure coincidence, we can argue that missile defence is just another HTS that humans must learn how to handle, with the common element of human involvement in its design and use. So we should be able to analyse it as technological system with learning.

## Launching Missile Risk

Missiles are hard to launch, as well as hard to shoot down in flight. Even in today's modern era, failures on launch are quite common, as exemplified by the space shuttle accidents, and the recent explosion of the Brazilian rocket on its launch pad. The rockets are large, expensive and symbols of national pride and technological success, but they are very complicated.

In the book 'Know the Risk', we gave the illustration of the recent launch failure of a rocket in Australia. In this case, faulty modifications to the fins, and potential debris, had contributed to a spectacular and expensive death spiral for the rocket. The idea was to show that quite unexpected items could cause failure in even high-technology operations.

It might be expected that the early launches will fail more often. Some modern data for the world's rocket launches have been recently analysed by Paté-Cornell and Guikema [12]. They looked at the first five launches of the world's rockets, there being 41 different types. Because the total experience base, the total number of launches, $N$, is limited to fewer than 300, the number of failures, $n$, are relatively few.

So the predictions of risk are hard and were estimated on a Bayesian basis, using a condi-tional estimate dependent on prior successes or failures. This means using the previous fail-ures to estimate the prior probability, $p(\varepsilon)$ from the past, so the future failure probability or risk, the so-called posterior probability $p(P)$, can be given by, as before:

---

[3]The latest success rate of 'about 60–65%' was quoted for the 'Standard Missile history for air defense weapons', by Rear Admiral Alan B. Hicks, Program Director, Aegis Ballistic Missile Defense, USN, in the transcripts of 'Aegis Ballistic Missile Defense – System Status and Upgrades' from the George C. Marshall Institute's Washington Roundtable on Science and Public Policy, November 2007 (extracted by permission from: http://www.marshall.org/pdf/materials/573.pdf).

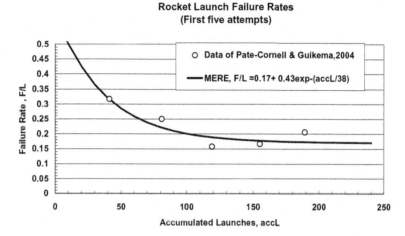

**Figure 3.6.** The failure rate of global rocket launches (data from Paté-Cornell et al [12])

$$p(\mathrm{P}) \propto p(\varepsilon) \times p(\mathrm{L})$$

The prior estimate $p(\varepsilon) = n/N$, and the likelihood of the next launch being a failure is then based on an assumption, which Paté-Cornell and Guikema took as the prior also. Here, once again, $p(\mathrm{L})$ is the likelihood that given knowing this prior knowledge, success will happen in the future.

Paté-Cornell and Guikema found that the failure rate was order 30% for the first launch, falling away to about 20% for the third, and that the uncertainty in the data was higher for the subsequent launches. The mean failure frequency for all launches was 22% based on all the data.

What do the data say? Can we estimate the failure risk using experience? The averaged data are shown plotted in Figure 3.6, where we have adopted the accumulated number of launches worldwide as a relevant measure of experience.

The learning effect is evident. In fact, the MERE curve shown was indeed the preferred fit with 83% confidence, and given by:

Failure rate fraction per launch, $F/L = 0.17 + 0.43 \exp - (L/38)$

with a 95% confidence interval or ~0.1 or ±10%. Choosing an arbitrary polynomial fit will have a higher confidence level, but of course can make ridiculous estimates outside its range, unlike the MERE learning exponential[4]. This is clearly shown below in Figure 3.7, where an example cubic fits all the few data points well, but is a useless predictor given by:

$$F/L = 0.73 - 167/L + 14{,}750/(L)^2 - 352{,}200/(L)^3$$

---

[4]In Appendix K, we further demonstrate this point and the power of the method by showing that this MERE curve agrees with independent data supplied by Professor Joseph Fragola, including the extrapolation out to the nearly 800 launches of the Russian Soyuz rockets and failures for all other major rocket type launched from 1980–2005.

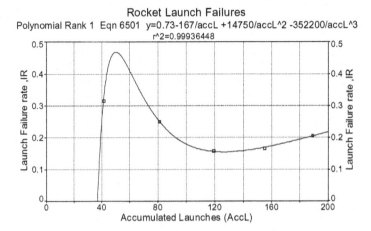

**Figure 3.7.**   The poorness of a good polynomial fit

In fact, straight-line fits have exactly the same problem of course, predicting zero failures with high confidence after about 375 launches! Such is the error of assuming the possibility of attaining zero defects.

The MERE suggests a minimum attainable failure-on-launch fraction of 17%, close to the prior mean value of 22%, and well within the MERE 95% uncertainty bands and also the straight-line 95% uncertainty of ~15%.

So the MERE result is comparable to that obtained from the Bayesian approach for rare events.

In this high-technology arena, mistakes (failures) are very expensive and having a good prediction is really desirable, even for the Space Shuttle with its exemplary low rate of failures. Only the experience of more launches and failures will show if we can beat the 1-in-5 odds of launch failures, but the MERE prediction is certainly based on a learning theory, which in principle, allows for such a reduction (see also Appendix K for the future predictions for a particular rocket type).

## The Number of Tests Required

We would obviously like to test the missile system first to make sure it will work. This is to determine what the in-action reliability actually is and that there are no design or unanticipated operational problems.

For the missile shield, the Pentagon's advisor [13] has this to say:

*A point I have made in testimony a while back is that I believe it will take on the order of 20 or 30 tests for each of the phases, each of the segments of a layered system. So that's like a hundred tests altogether. The National Missile Defence (NMD) mid-course program already has laid out those tests, and the boost phases and the terminal phase will have to do the same. But it will turn out to be I would bet 20 or 30 for each segment, or 100 total. Like the test last July, but each one different. Let's take the mid-course segment. If you've got 20 or 30 tests – and by that I mean development tests, before you get to realistic operational testing, where you do the test with no warning, in the middle of the night, maybe when the weather is bad, when the soldiers and airmen are tired, when you don't know quite what the trajectory is, you don't know quite where its coming from, you don't know what the target looks like, the composition of the target cluster.*

*All of this prior information that we've had in tests so far, you don't have all of that in operational tests. So I'm saying it's going to take 20 or 30 tests before we even get to realistic operational tests. Patriot Advanced Capability-3 (PAC-3), which is a site defense, point defense system . . . still have a couple of years of work to do before they'll be ready to do it the way you would have to do it in battle.*

*Let's take the mid-course section . . . you've got 20–30 tests and they are each going to take a year, which is the way its been going, then obviously, that's going to take 20–30 years, and perhaps those 20–30 tests can be in parallel – 20 or 30 years for the boost phase, and 20 or 30 years for the terminal phases, but if you can only do them at the rate of 1 year, its going to take 20–30 years. The administration has said they are going to increase the test rate, so that for each segment you'll get a test every three months or so. And for NMD as a total layered system, you'll have a test every month. So in August maybe you get a boost phase test and in September, you get a mid-course test you'd have a test every month, and if you can test at that rate, you can do the 20 or 30 tests required for each segment in maybe five years.*

*Maybe in four years if you really keep it up. But that's going to be the challenge whether they can really sustain that kind of an effort.*

The 20–30 tests suggested here by this eminent expert implies an uncertainty of $\sim 1/\sqrt{30}$, or about 20%, comparable to the claimed interception accuracy. Conducting fewer tests than this number would not support the claimed interception efficiency.

We also have some reported data for the improved army system, the US Army's Patriot anti-missile system (PAC-3). Flight-testing for the PAC-3 from 1997 to 2002 included 11 developmental flight tests; with four flight intercept tests with two or three incoming targets at once. It is stated that most of these tests were successful, but in two of the tests, one of the targets was not intercepted. In initial operational testing, using soldiers, three tests have been conducted, all with multiple targets, and in each test one of the targets had been missed or one of the interceptors had failed. That is an overall success rate of about 50% or less. With 11 flights, we expect an uncertainty in the results of $\sim\sqrt{11} = \pm 3$ tests or 30%, and for three tests of $\sim\sqrt{3} = 1.7$ or 60%, which puts the observed failure outcomes within the statistical uncertainties of our expected rates.

The difficulty of such testing and the evaluation of the detection methods has led to considerable and sometimes fairly acrimonious debate about how effective an NMD or theater missile system might be. In fact, the sampling approach taken in the tests to incoming detection has been described by Postol [14] as:

*These procedures are like rolling a pair of dice and throwing away all outcomes that do not give snake eyes, and then claiming that there is scientific evidence that makes it possible to reliably predict when a roll of the dice will be a snake eyes.*

The comparison to the drawing of balls from a jar is obvious, especially if and when we do not count all the outcomes. Needless to say, Postol's perhaps slightly critical views are not kindly or readily accepted by those actually designing, building and testing the systems, and he has been roundly criticised.

## Estimating the Risk of a Successful Attack and How Many Missiles We Must Fire

As an illustration of the Duffey–Saull Method (DSM) risk method, let us now assume that these historic data for launch and intercept failures are typical even for today's technology. We simply use the sample data that we have.

We know this is a gross approximation and that it does not reflect the large technological changes since it is basically assuming that we have the same methods, propulsion and interception that existed 50 years before, with the same human failings. We could certainly expect to be doing better, so the following analysis is meant as an illustration only. Even though more modern systems should have better results, surprises are possible as we shall see. Think of it as an unbiased inter-comparison of modern technology with older, more primitive ones. Thus, we can use this simple prior knowledge of the history of failure rates of launching and of interception with real full-scale systems. We can now provide a method and estimate how many defending rockets or devices we must launch to destroy just one incoming threat.

The conditional probability of interception is just the fraction that we destroy successfully with successful launches or the Bayesian-type expression:

Posterior probability of interception, $p(I) \propto$ Prior probability of successful launch, $p(\varepsilon) \times$ Likelihood of incoming destruction, $p(\mathrm{L})$

Actually, this expression is now a conditional probability based on the prior failure frequency, where destruction by interception is conditional on there being a successful launch in the first place. Using our independent failure fractions, from the purely historical data we have the dependent probability of successful interception, $p_i(I)$ per successful launch given by:

$$p_i(I) = \text{Fraction launched} \times \text{Fraction destroyed}$$

$$p_i(I) = (1 - (\text{Fraction failed to launch}, F)) \times (1 - (\text{Fraction of incoming not destroyed}, M))$$

From our analysis of the old V1 interceptions and new rocket launch data; in our happy state of ignorance based only on this prior information, we can now substitute the numbers from the observed learning curves:

$$p_i(I) = [1 - (0.17 + 0.43 \exp - (L/38))] \times [1 - (0.3 + 0.4 \exp - (L/4820))]$$
$$= [0.83 - 0.43 \exp - (L/38)] \times [(0.7 - 0.4 \exp - (L/4820))]$$

Because of the increasing reliability of launch and of destruction with launches, the resulting fraction destroyed has a slightly strange, wavy shape on a logarithmic plot.

Evaluating the numbers, it is as shown in Figure 3.8.

Starting off, for less than about 10 launches, the interception fraction (or frequency) is about $0.43 \times 0.3 \sim 0.13$, so the fraction destroyed is only just over a tenth, and is largely set by the inexperience of interception. After many launches (say >10,000), this interception fraction tends to grow to be simply $0.83 \times 0.7 \sim 0.58$, or just over a half, and is dominated by the continuing launch failures.

## Uncertainty in the Risk of Failing to Intercept

The overall uncertainty estimate is given by simply combining the uncertainties of the two independent failures, of launching and of interception. So we have the usual combination of

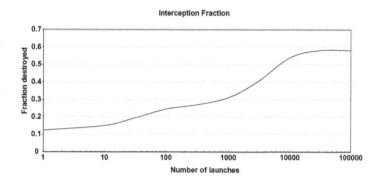

**Figure 3.8.** Example of the probability/fraction of destroying incoming missiles as we gain launch and intercept experience

the square root of the sum of the squares of the uncertainties, at the one standard deviation confidence level:

$$\text{Uncertainty, } \Delta \approx \pm\sqrt{\left\{(\text{Uncertainty in launch})^2 + (\text{Uncertainty in interception})^2\right\}}$$
$$= \pm\sqrt{\left\{(0.15)^2 + (0.1)^2\right\}}$$
$$= \pm 0.18,$$

which is about a 20% variation overall, exactly as implied by Coyle.

If all the launches were independent, we can estimate the number of interceptors, $n$, needed to attain a given intercept fraction and the confidence level. This estimate is obtained from just adding up the independent probabilities of interception success for the $L$ successive launches, given or conditional on the knowledge that we have failed before:

$$P_L(I) = \sum_L p_i (1 - p_i)^{L-1}$$

So for just one interceptor launched, the probability of an interception success with no prior misses:

$$p_1 \approx 0.13 \text{ with uncertainty, } \Delta = \pm 0.18$$

For two launched, since the probability of the previous miss is $(1 - p)$, the chance of one success next out of the two is the sum, $\Sigma p_i$:

$$p_2 = 0.13 + 0.13 \times (1 - 0.13) \sim 0.24 \text{ with uncertainty, } \Delta = \sqrt{\left\{(0.18)^2 / 2\right\}} \sim \pm 0.12$$

and so on as progressively we try more launches. For five launches, we have the chance of one success out of the five attempts as:

$$p_5 = 0.13 + 0.11 + 0.098 + 0.074 + 0.13 \times (0.87 \times 0.87 \times 0.87 \times 0.87) \sim 0.57$$

or nearly 60% with a small uncertainty, $\Delta = \pm 0.003$.

Derived from conventional probabilistic thinking, this wrong result is totally different from that derived from the learning model. The numerical calculation of the intercept rate is shown in Figure 3.6, and for five launches is still close to the initial value of ~0.14, or some two times larger!!

Now let us return to comparison of the *predictions* to the actual data from the development and testing of missile interception defence systems. The latest public report (as given in the Ottawa Citizen of 2 September 2006, p. A8) said the Pentagon's army contractor (Boeing of commercial aircraft fame) had 6 intercepts ($n = 6$) out of the total of 13 tests ($\Sigma L = N_j = 13$) conducted in the observation interval from 1999 to 2006. Assuming the complete validity and prototypicality of these tests, the prior test anti-missile success probability or intercept fraction achieved is

$$p(\varepsilon) = n/N_j = 6/13 \sim 0.46,$$

with an uncertainty or standard error of about $\sqrt{13}$, or ±0.28 for this estimate.

So solely using the testing experience suggests achievement of an intercept success probability that ranges between $0.16 < p(\varepsilon) < 0.74$, comparable to the independent prediction range of $0.13 < p(\varepsilon) < 0.58$ that we derived above. Hence, the modern test data are indeed within the predictive accuracy, especially given the potential for and the accusations of adopting atypical or questionable guidance programming to ensure or aid interceptions in some of the tests. The observed and the predicted unsuccessful or non-interception fraction of incomings penetrating, $M = 1 - p(\varepsilon)$, therefore range from

$$0.26 < M < 0.84.$$

Perhaps not coincidentally, this spread of non-interception probabilities encompasses the range that actually occurred during the now historic Doodlebug V1 intercepts, as shown in Figure 3.9. We are faced with large uncertainty that reflects the real probability of a failure to intercept.

Evidently, to have almost certain assurance of interception failure of less than a percent (or a chance lower than one in a hundred), at first we must fire at least about 5 to 10 times the number of incoming devices to be relatively sure of their destruction, and not less than about two times. There is still no certainty and the risk is not zero or completely eliminated, and the launches are *not* independent. Each learns from the prior one. This potential learning trend complements the philosophy of the rather aptly named Kill Assessment Program of the US Army Space and Missile Defense Command, which seeks to reduce the number of missiles needed in the 'salvo' or 'ripple firing' doctrines which dictate using multiple interceptors. Very brief and top-level descriptions of the objectives of the US DoD Missile Defense Agency and KA Program are available (see, for example, www.smdc.army.mil). Of course, with unknown terrorist attacks as opposed to formally declared war, we must assume random (surprise) missile attacks. So we cannot expect to have much field experience or learning opportunity, beyond that available from any pre-deployment testing.

This 'overkill' launch need eventually falls to about twice, but only as we gain much larger experience and improved launch reliability. Without knowing the full basis, these interception numbers we have derived here are not far removed from, and surprisingly as we noted, actually encompass the 20% effectiveness number estimated publicly by Phillip Coyle for a modern 'missile shield'. Independent of learning, this fraction implies again needing to launch at least five times the number of missiles to be sure of an incoming kill, even with the presence of potential decoys or diversionary threats.

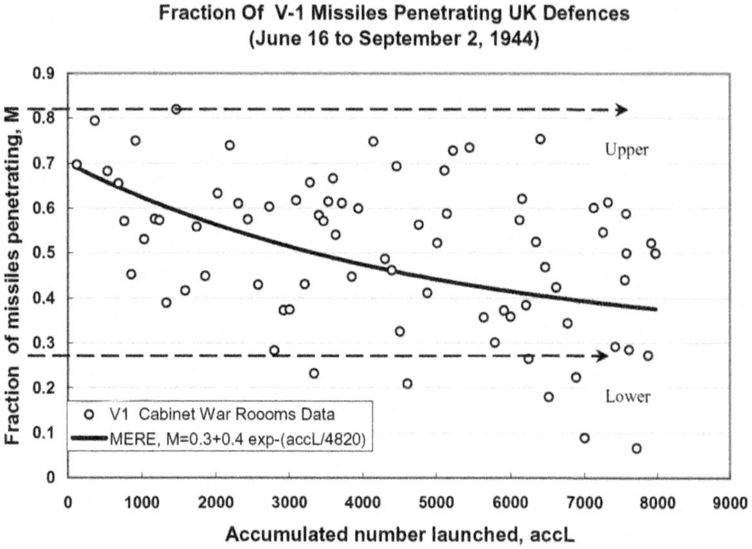

**Fraction Of V-1 Missiles Penetrating UK Defences
(June 16 to September 2, 1944)**

**Figure 3.9.** The predicted modern range of non-interception compared to the V1 data from Figure 3.5, where the arrows indicate the upper and lower estimates derived from recent anti-missile tests and the present analysis

Another estimate can be made by assuming that the prior information is correct, so that $p(I) \sim 0.13$ failure per launch at the beginning. The next launch is either successful or not according to a so-called binomial distribution (see Appendix F), so for the $L$th launch, the probability of $r$ successes is then:

$$p(r) = \left( L!/(r!(L-r)!) \times p^r(1-p)^{L-r} \right)$$

where, for learning,

$$p = [0.83 - 0.43\exp - (L/38)] \times [(0.7 - 0.4\exp - (L/4820))]$$

Again, for, say, the first five launch attempts made one at a time, $L = 5$, and for only one success, $r = 1$,

$$p(1) \approx 5 \times (0.13) \times (0.87)^4 = 5 \times 0.13 \times 0.57 = 0.37$$

which is three times higher than the learning value. These analyses are illustrative of the variations and uncertainties we can obtain in our risk estimates.

## What Risk Is There of a Missile Getting Through: Missing the Missile

This simple illustration, using real data, gives us a sense of what risks we face and can predict in designing, testing and using actual anti-missile systems. It shows how we can apply our DSM model to describe learning data and to estimate future hypothetical risks. Examining the entire prior and historic data shows interception probabilities that consistently range between 0.2 and 0.8, or hit rates varying from one in five to four out of five launches or trials. Perhaps, modern defences, missile reliabilities and designs are really much more effective, reliable and efficient than the older ones. Having survived the V1 attacks, we can but hope so.

To be reasonably sure of an incoming missile 'kill', apparently initially we must launch about five times the number of interceptors, as there are incoming missiles.

Although we have used historical intercept and missile launch failure data that may not be directly relevant to predict modern failure rates, the indirect link is we have an HTS, just as in all our other studies. The historical data show evidence of learning. From the DSM analysis, the assumption is that the error rate is dominated by the human component in the mechanical machine unreliability, even for a highly automated system. It then exhibits a strong dependency on learning and experience.

## Predicting the Risk of Industrial Accidents: The Texas City Refinery Explosion

Industrial accidents, particularly explosions and fires, occur many times not just in warfare and space travel. The US Chemical Safety Board has an excellent set of reports describing incidents due to chemicals in a wide range of plants, refineries, pipelines, processing and manufacturing equipment (see www.csb.gov). The risk of such an event is just what we need to establish, so that instead of being reactive and describing the causes of disaster that already happened, we can be proactive in establishing and managing the risk of a future outcome.

As a typical problem and a famous recent example, consider the major explosion and fire at the BP Texas City refinery in 2005. This fatal explosion was physically caused by the ignition of a vapor cloud from the leak of a large quantity of volatile liquid from the venting of an overfilled process tank. (See Figure 3.10.) The underlying and contributing causes are well described by the CSB, 2007 [15] and include, of course, the usual outcome contributors: of not following procedures; inadequate instrumentation and control information; perpetually lax safety attitudes; and an ineffective management structure that encouraged product manufacture over process safety. These issues are referred to collectively as due to a lack of 'safety culture', meaning a general malaise of not ensuring effective process safety and risk management. The warning signals were ignored, as cost-cutting measures and budget controls took precedence over expenditures on safety and maintenance.

What is the risk of such a major event, meaning the chance of such an outcome? We need to know the prior knowledge. According to the CSB report, previous events, like leaks, overfillings and fires, had all occurred at the same facility and other equipment at the site before, so we should be able to *predict*, and hence, to manage the risk based on the prior data for those outcomes. As clearly found by the owner and operator, analysing and learning from prior events is key (underlining emphasis added):

> *The fact is that Texas City was a preventable accident but that our lessons could help prevent others from falling into the same traps. The event was clearly preventable. The lessons learned are almost endless. But at the facility level seven stand out:*

**Figure 3.10.** The scene of destruction after the explosion at the Texas City refinery: the liquid over-filling occurred in the blackened column on the lower right, causing vapor venting from the adjacent smaller 'chimney' (With kind permission of US CSB Final Report, 2007)

- *The need to ensure plant leadership teams have the time to focus on day-to-day operations and aren't distracted by too many competing demands. Managers need to know what's happening in their control rooms and on the plant.*
- *The need to <u>capture the right metrics that indicate process safety trends</u>; do not get seduced by personal accident measures, they have their place but do not warn of incidents such as this one.*
- *Procedures are ineffective if they are not up-to-date and routinely followed*
- *The importance of two-way communication. If people believe leaders aren't listening or don't appear to be taking team members' concerns seriously, then soon they stop raising them. <u>We must keep our promises to each other.</u> It's the first step in rebuilding trust and the only way to earn the respect and obtain the commitment of the workforce. This is about staying in touch, being aware, being responsible and listening.*
- *The importance of investigating process incidents and loss of containment incidents the same way serious injuries are investigated. Document all incidents thoroughly. <u>Share what you learn.</u>*
- *The value of having an effective feedback loop to capture and incorporate into operating procedures and training programs <u>lessons learned from earlier incidents and process upsets</u>*
- *And lastly, keep non-essential personnel out of process areas. Take a hard look at any potential blast impact zones. And if you must have temporary structures near process areas make sure they are blast resistant. The safest way to protect your people is to move them outside of blast zones.*

Source: *John Mogford, BP, Texas City Refinery Explosion:*
*The Lessons Learned, www.bp.com, 2006, by permission*

We propose quantifying exactly this kind of deep, detailed and determined learning process, where we determine what the past is telling us about the possible future based on the (often painfully) accumulated past experience. Classical safety analysis methods, such as Probabilistic Safety Analysis, would analyse the failure rates for all the possible event sequences that might occur, and use the resulting probability of any given outcome (say, an explosion) to estimate the chance of any particular accident or event sequence. Our approach here is entirely different: we use solely the prior information on past events (the lagging indicators) to project and predict forward (the leading indicators), as suggested by the CSB [15]. We do not pretend that we can actually understand, disentangle, model or know all the possible outcomes that might occur; or know how the HTS will actually 'behave' in any detail. This inherent uncertainty of *not* knowing the precise behaviour is the essence or driver behind the risk approach (called ROAAM) advocated by Theofanous, 1996 [16] of ensuring that the possibility of catastrophic failure is 'physically unreasonable'. We take a somewhat different, but entirely complementary attack: if we can at least estimate and *predict* the chance of an outcome, and hence the *uncertainty*, we should be able to take informed risk management decisions.

We wish to make a prediction. The challenge is to use all we can extract from past data, or so-called 'lagging indicators'. The past performance or outcomes allow an informed estimate of the 'posterior' or future probability or risk, based on any learning patterns that may or may not exist. *Thus, the presence or absence of proactive safety culture, positive management actions and changing system response are intertwined via the presence or absence of a Learning Environment.*

The lagging indicators, or prior data about the past contain hidden, apparently unrelated key pieces of prior outcome information. These are the numbers we or any operator would need to make an estimate of the probability of a potential explosion for any given *future* facility start-up. In this sense, the start-up process and analysis is an exact analogy to estimating the risk of the next rocket or shuttle launch.

To our knowledge, the analysis that follows is both obvious and entirely new for this outcome.

## From Lagging to Leading: Safety Analysis and Safety Culture

We are asking a fundamental question. Based on learning from the available or known prior knowledge, what is the operational and safety risk faced by the Managers, operators and staff on 22 March 2005 of a potentially flammable and explosive release incident (which is a known hazard) during the planned start the next day? Presumably, management and all the stakeholders would and should consult and reflect on the experience gained from past events, particularly as the whole refinery was known to have a history of serious safety concerns and issues [15]. As pointed out by the CSB report, just emphasising and tracking the usual industrial personal injury 'statistics' (e.g., trips, falls, back strains, lost time events) as was the standard refinery practice, entirely missed analysing the very operational data that would indicate the cause, likelihood and uncertainty of having such a serious incident.

The CSB report contains a key statement. In six previous incidents at the same facility 'the blowdown system released flammable hydrocarbon vapors that resulted in a vapor cloud at or near ground level that could have resulted in explosions and fires if the vapor cloud had found a source of ignition' (CSB report, Section 4 [15]). These six leaks did not explode, but were 'near misses' of the chemical factory not aircraft kind, and establish a leak as a conditional precursor for an actual explosive accident sequence like the one that eventually occurred. Whether or not there is then a fire or an explosion depends on a number of imponderable and not entirely predictable possibilities: the presence of some extraneous or available ignition source; whether the vapor is in the right mix and concentration to detonate; whether wind and weather conditions allow a cloud to form or it is harmlessly blown away; or if the fire department is able to disperse or spray in time.

So, all we assume is that physically there must be an overfill for the vent or leak needed to produce the vapor required for an explosion, and hence, give the necessary conditions that are conducive to a *potentially explosive* situation. For the moment, we use the prior incidents and data as typical of what has happened already, and hence, relevant to what might occur during the next start-up. The usual problem is that prior data are missing, incomplete or unknown: importantly, their analysis may also lag the present. The CSB found that, by digging into the BP Texas City operating, firefighting and safety records for the *same* facility (CSB report Appendices I and Q [15]), there was indeed prior evidence existing of:

a) two (2) fires in the blowdown stack in 1998 and 2000;
b) six (6) facility 'blowdown incidents' between 1994 and 2004 with vapor cloud release; and
c) fifteen (15) out of nineteen (19) previous start-ups had resulted in out-of-range overfilling, between April 2000 and June 2003.

We make two plausible simple but key assumptions to make an order-of-magnitude risk estimate. Firstly, we assume there is no evidence of learning being present in the prior data, which is true at least as far as the CSB report indicates. Hence, secondly, the rates of these past incidents are assumed to be typical for that facility, staff, management, site and company, presuming that the operating 'culture', practices, regime and procedures are unchanging.

We want a *leading* indicator, so we estimate the probabilities of an event from the lagging data as follows, noting that the numbers can be refined or (re)adjusted based on any further information. Sufficient for the present purpose for establishing the order of magnitude we start with these prior data in the CSB report (a)–(c), and then use these to make an estimate of the *predicted* likelihood of an explosion on the very next start-up, $p$(next).

The probability of an explosive potential, $p(E)$, per start-up (i.e., an overfill followed by a blowdown incident) is dependent on there being vapor release. The maximum value for the probability of potentially explosive vapor release, $p(E)$, per start-up is derived from the conditional probability of having an overfill followed by or leading to a blowdown incident, or:

Probability of Explosive Release, $p(E)$ = Probability of an Overfill, $p(O) \times$ Probability
of a Blow Down Incident, $p(BDI)$

or,

$$p(E) = p(O) \times p(BDI)$$

From the data given by the CSB, the probability of an overfill, $p(O)$, in any start-up is then the fraction of reported start-ups with overfills:

$$p(O) \equiv n/N = 15/19 \sim 0.8 \text{ per start-up}$$

Now we need to know that given this probability of an overfill if that causes a subsequent problem. There were six blowdown incidents during start-up in 10 operating years, but the CSB report does not give the total number of start-ups in all of those years. The CSB report indicates 19 start-ups in 1,150 operating days between March 2000 and June 2003, and hence, there was *on average* about one start every 76 days. Assuming this interval between start-ups to be fairly typical[5], applying this same start-up interval to the 10-year span, there were perhaps about 48 start-ups in total.

The probability of a blowdown incident, $p(\text{BDI})$ per start-up over the prior 10 years is then given by the fraction of the number of start-ups with and without recorded incidents that formed a vapor cloud:

$$p(\text{BDI}) \equiv n/N = 6/48 \sim 0.125 \text{ per start-up.}$$

The maximum value for the probability of potentially explosive vapor release, $p(E)$, per start-up is derived from the conditional probability of having an overfill followed by or leading to a blowdown incident. After inserting the numbers just derived, this gives a risk of potentially explosive conditions as:

$$p(E) = p(O) \times p(\text{BDI})$$

$p(E) \sim 0.8 \times 0.125 = 0.1$, which is a chance of about one in every 10 start-ups.

This high number alone is sufficient to give pause as being a significant risk, *if* only it had been estimated at the time. As before, the probability of just having the explosive potential anyway during the next, $n$, start-ups out of, $m$, total start-ups, is approximately given by the binomial estimate:

$$P(n) = \binom{n+m}{n} \{p(E)\}^n \{1 - p(E)\}^m$$

For the very next outcome, or potentially explosive event, $n = 1$, and the risk or probability of observing such an explosive potential is given by just substituting the numbers into the above equation, taking $p(E) \sim 0.1$. With roughly, $m = 48$, prior non-outcomes, or previous start-ups without actual explosions, we evaluate the factorials and multipliers to give the probability of having a potentially explosive incident during the very next start-up, $p(\text{next})$, as follows:

$$p(\text{next}) = \binom{48}{1} \{0.1\}^1 \{0.9\}^{48}$$
$$= (48!/47!1!) \times 0.1 \times 0.0063 = 48 \times 0.1 \times 0.0063 = 0.03$$

So we find that past outcomes indicate a risk that the probability is ~0.03 of the next potentially explosive incident occurring on the very next start-up or *a chance of about 1 in 30 start-ups*. With an interval of about 76 days between start-ups, this is an explosive potential possibility once in every six years, an interval not inconsistent with having already observing the two fires.

---

[5]Other numbers can be inserted if and when there are differing data on start-up numbers and intervals.

## Missing Near Misses

We can also evaluate the claim of credit for *not* having any major explosions during many prior start-ups, despite having overfills, leaks and fires, since we were either lucky or that actually having an explosion is still unlikely (e.g., the ignition source needed to explode the vapor cloud was absent). These are the 'near misses' that are the chemical industry equivalent of the aircraft 'near mid-air collisions' or NMACs that we deliberately introduced at the very beginning of this Chapter. Now from the prior data, the probability of an ignition source, $p(IS)$, is perhaps two fires out of eight total events, or $p(IS) \sim 0.25$, implying that an ignition source was present perhaps about a quarter of the time. So the *maximum* interval for an actual explosion perhaps could be four times longer, or once in about 120 start-ups, representing an actual explosion risk of about every 25 years, say about once in the facility lifetime. This order of magnitude estimate is comparable to what has now actually occurred.

So from the very scarce *lagging* indicators in past operational and incident reporting, we have derived a useful *leading* indicator: the risk of explosion during the very next start-up. Practical and effective risk management would then direct resources and attention to significantly reducing both the probabilities of overfilling and of vapor release, and to the elimination of ignition sources *before* the next start-up. Not afterwards.

## What These Risk Estimates Tell Us: The Common Sense Echo

Note the probability (risk) estimates derived for losing a Space Shuttle, of about 1 in every 40 launches, to that of an explosive potential for the Texas City refinery equipment, from about 1 in 30 to 100 start-ups. Perhaps coincidentally, the rocket and refinery risk of a large outcome are indeed similar in magnitude, in terms of HTS experience (number of launches and start-ups) once we have stripped away the apparent differences of facility type, mission, industry and technology.

In some sense, indeed, the Texas City refinery explosion was for the petroleum industry as the loss of *Columbia* was for the NASA space exploration program – a truly catastrophic event with a too high and not effectively managed risk.

The Echo that is the common factor between these apparently disparate events in these two independent industries is not just all the inquiries and reports, and the serious and fatal nature of the incidents. It is the Common Sense Echo that these are simply HTSs containing *the human element*.

Once again, there is not a trivial or a vanishingly small risk and the 'safety culture-line management-lost production' conflict is illustrated clearly. The absence of such simple risk estimates itself is illustrative of loss of awareness and effective risk management (see CSB report; CAIB Challenger report). The preliminary results in this Chapter clearly point to the need for more complex risk analyses, and for actually implementing the additional safety measures that are obviously possible.

Presuming that such order of magnitude risk calculations could have been done, had been done and were considered, they perhaps could and should have made a major difference to the management of the operational, human, financial and system risk. The issue we all face is that the necessary data and prior information usually only surface after the event, in the incident post-mortem, massive inquiries and reports, whereas we absolutely need them collected and analysed *before* the event.

In this Chapter, we have provided some real examples of risk analysis, using the tools related to learning and the actual data, such as it is. The approaches are discussed as to quantifying risk using statistical arguments. The risk of an outcome is clearly related to the probability, and hence, apparently (at least, according to the NASA Columbia and CSB Texas City reports) links to the degree of presence or absence of 'safety culture', a relationship that we will actually quantify later in this book. How this risk management can be generalised for use in a learning environment we now show next, using the learning curve as a tool.

# References

[1] Hsu, F. and Duffey, R.B., 2006, 'Managing Risks on the Space Frontier', Chapter 30, Beyond Earth: The Future of Humans in Space, Edited by Bob Krone, Apogee Books, Burlington, Canada.

[2] Feynman, R.P. and Leighton, R., 1988, 'What Do You Care What Other People Think?: Further Adventures of a Curious Character', W.W. Norton, Appendix F.

[3] Paté-Cornell, E. and Dillon, R., 2000, 'Probabilistic Risk Analysis for the NASA Space Shuttle: A Brief History and Current Work', Submitted for Publication in Reliability Engineering and System Safety, April.

[4] Fragola, J.R. and Maggio, D., 1995, 'Probabilistic Risk Assessment of the Space Shuttle', Science Applications International Corporation, 1995, SAICNY-95-02-25, Washington, DC, Center for Aerospace Information.

[5] Dalal, S.R. Fowlkes, E.B. and Hoadley, B., 1989, 'Risk Analysis of the Space Shuttle: Pre-Challenger Prediction of Failure', Journal American Statistical Association, Vol. 84, No. 408, pp. 945–957)

[6] National Aeronautics and Space Administration (NASA), 'Implementation Plan for Return to Flight', National Aeronautics and Space Administration (Available: http://www1.nasa.gov).

[7] Fragola, J. et al., 2005, 'Reliability and Crew Safety Assessment for Solid Rocket Booster/J-2S Based Launch Vehicle', Science Applications International Corp., SAICNY-05-04-1F, April.

[8] National Aeronautics and Space Administration (NASA), 2005, 'NASA's Exploration Systems Architecture Study (ESAS)', Final Report, NASA-TM-2005-214062, November, (Available: www.sti.nasa.gov).

[9] Putney, B.F. and Fragola, J.R., 2007, 'Application of risk assessment for the NASA vision for space exploration', Proc. ESREL 2007, Stavanger, Norway, Taylor and Francis, London, ISBN 978-0-415-44786-7, Vol. 3, pp. 2129–2134.

[10] Duffey, R.B. and Saull, J.W., 2004, 'Reliability and Failures of Engineering Systems Due to Human Errors', CMES'-04, Proceedings First Cappadocia International Mechanical Symposium, Cappadocia, Turkey, 14–16 July.

[11] Simon, A., 1996, 'The Patriot Missile: Performance in the Gulf War Reviewed', (Available: http://www.cdi.org/issues/bmd/Patriot.html)

[12] Paté-Cornell, M.E. and Guikema, S.D., 2004, 'A Probabilistic Analysis of the "Infancy Problem" of Space Launch Vehicles', Proceedings PSAM 07, 2004, Berlin, Paper #042.

[13] Coyle, P.E., 2001, Senior Adviser at the Center for Defense Information, Center for Arms Control & Non-Proliferation, quoted from Press Conference on Missile Defense, 6 September, Willard Intercontinental Hotel.

[14] Postol, T.A., Professor of Science, Technology and National Security Policy, Massachusetts Institute of Technology, 'Technical Discussion of the Misinterpreted Results of the IFT-1A Experiment due to tampering with the Data and Analysis and Errors in the Interpretation of the Data'.

[15] US Chemical Safety and Hazard Investigation Board (CSB), 2007, Investigation Report No. 2005-04-I-TX, Refinery Explosion and Fire, March (Available: www.csb.gov); see also the CSB safety video/DVD 'Anatomy of a Disaster: Explosion at BP Texas City Refinery', March 2008.

[16] Theofanous, T., 1996, 'On the Proper Formulation of Safety Goals and Assessment of Safety Margins for Rare and High Consequence Hazards', Reliability Engineering and System Safety, 54, pp. 243–257.

# 4

# The Probability of Human Error: Learning in Technological Systems[1]

*'Rationality will not save you – it's a matter of luck and human fallibility.'*
*Robert S. McNamara, 'The Fog of War', 2003*

## What We Must Predict

We have shown how outcomes develop in phases from a string or confluence of factors too complex to predict but always avoidable. The bright feature is that we now know that a universal learning curve (ULC) exists and we can utilise that to predict outcome rates and track our progress as we improve. We can therefore start to manage the risk, but only if we include the human element.

Using the learning hypothesis, analysis of the human rate of learning allows a new determination of the dynamic probability and human failure (error) rate in technological systems. The result is consistent with and derived from the available world data for modern technological systems. Since the approach is based on the Learning Hypothesis, the resulting probability of outcome or error can be shown to agree with available data. We also provide comparisons to empirical parameter fitting using conventional reliability engineering methods. Hence, we relate and contrast the techniques used for component failures and show they do not work when applied to human reliability estimates.

We need to make it entirely clear what we do not propose. We will not use the existing idea of analysing human reliability and errors on a task-by-task, item-by-item, situation-by-situation basis. In that approach, which is commonly adopted as part of probabilistic safety

---

[1] This Chapter builds in part on the paper R.B. Duffey and J.W. Saull, 'The Probability and Management of Human Error', Proc., 12th International Conference on Nuclear Engineering (ICONE 12), #49287, Crystal City, MD, 25–29 April 2004.

analysis using event sequence 'trees', the probability of a correct or incorrect action is assigned at each significant step or branch point in the hypothesised evolution of an accident sequence. The probability of any action is represented and weighted or adjusted by situational multipliers, representing stress, environment and time pressures. We suggest, at least for the present, that it is practically *impossible* to try to describe all the nuances, permutations and possibilities behind human decision making[2]. Instead, we treat the homo-technological system (HTS) as an integral system. We base our analysis on the Learning Hypothesis, invoking the inseparability of the human and the technological system. Using the data, we invoke and use experience as the correct measure of integrated learning and decision-making opportunity; and we demonstrate that the HTS reliability and outcome probabilities are dynamic, simply because of learning. To quote Joseph Fragola's insightful observation[3] on modelling human error and reliability:

> Just as the physics of failure of a particular device need not be quantified in order to use a representative failure rate to determine the likelihood (within a given uncertainty) of a component failure event; so too it is not necessary to have a human performance model of a particular class of human actions (also within a given uncertainty), as long as the representative error rate can be supported by appropriate stochastic models.

The basic and sole assumption that we make every time and everywhere is the 'learning hypothesis' as a physical model for human behaviour when *coupled* to any system. Simply and directly, we postulate that humans learn from their mistakes (outcomes) as experience is gained. So, the rate of reduction of outcomes (observed in the technology or activity as accidents, errors and events) is proportional to the number of outcomes that are occurring.

For learning by skill acquisition and error reduction, the human is completely embedded in the system: the so-called 'human error' is inseparable from and equivalent to a 'system failure', and vice versa.

That learning occurs is implicitly obvious and the reduction in risk must affect the outcome rate directly. As Allison, 1984 [1] remarks in the field of sociology:

> *Intuitively, what happens is that individuals with high hazard rates experience events early and are then eliminated from the risk set. As time goes on, this selection process yields risk sets that contain individuals with predominantly low risks.*

---

[2]For the many, many possible causations, types, factors and influences on human, managerial and organisational error see, for example, the listings in G.A. Peters and B.J. Peters, 'Human Error: Causes and Control', Taylor and Francis, Boca Raton, FL, USA, 2006, Chapters 5, 9 and 10.

[3]We are indebted to Professor Fragola for an extensive exchange of information and dialogue on design risk: excellent summaries of the status and issues for modern approaches are in his tutorial 'Human Reliability Analysis', presented at the ESREL 2001 Conference, Torino, Italy, 16–20 September 2001, and paper 'Focus, Strengths, and Weaknesses of HRA', presented at the 18th ESReDA Seminar on Risk Management and Human Reliability in Social Context, Karstad, Sweden, 15–16 June 2000. A compendium and comparison of the many traditional HRA methods used in the nuclear industry is also given in the report NUREG-1842, 'Evaluation of Human Reliability Analysis Methods Against Good Practices', US Nuclear Regulatory Commission, Office of Nuclear Regulatory Research, Washington, DC 20555-0001, 2006.

In effect, Darwinian selection has occurred and conversely those who do not learn are history. Those who survive have a greater depth of experience.

To set the scene, let us make it clear that the probability of error due to the human element is quite universal, and can affect anyone and everyone in a HTS. The example cases given in the Appendices D and E illustrate clear examples of highly skilled well-trained operators, fully equipped with warning and automated systems. Both examples are taken from the airline industry, which pays great attention to safety because of the highly visible (and literal) impact of the outcomes. So all the people involved (from maintenance, ground control, management, airline operator and the pilots) are working in an almost completely safe industry (ACSI).

The two examples in Appendices D and E are very basic to safety: loss of fuel while in flight and mid-air collision. Given all the systems put in place to avoid these very obvious and fundamental risks, the outcomes still occurred. But despite all the effort, procedures and warnings, there is loss of control through loss of understanding, communication and information in the most modern of aircraft which were maintained to the highest standards. We need to estimate their chance of occurrence of the outcomes and define the risk by finding the probability of the outcomes due to the human element embedded in the HTS.

Once again, let us start with the learning hypothesis applied and applicable to any integrated (total) HTS. Thus, the human error or technological system failure or outcome rate, $\lambda$, is equivalent to a dynamic hazard function, $h(\varepsilon)$, which varies with experience, $\varepsilon$, as given by the Minimum Error Rate Equation (MERE):

$$d\lambda/d\varepsilon = -k(\lambda - \lambda_m)$$

where $k$ is the learning rate constant, and $\lambda_m$ the minimum obtainable rate. The MERE failure or outcome rate as a function of experience, $\lambda(\varepsilon)$, is then obtained by straightforward integration as

$$\lambda(\varepsilon) = \lambda_m + (\lambda_0 - \lambda_m)\exp{-k(\varepsilon - \varepsilon_0)}$$

where the outcome or failure rate $\lambda \equiv h(\varepsilon)$, the hazard function; $\lambda_m$ is the minimum obtainable rate at large experience; and $\lambda_0$ is the initial rate at some initial experience, $\varepsilon_0$.

Here, it will be remembered that the failure or outcome rate is the summation of all the $i^{th}$ rates in the technological system, so that effectively:

$$\lambda(\varepsilon) - \lambda_m = \sum_i (\lambda_i - \lambda_m)$$

Since the MERE result describes and agrees with a wide range of actual data, we hypothesise that this is indeed the correct form for the human error or outcome rate in an HTS with learning. This form has been used to derive the ULC, validated by obtaining failure rates from the world accident, injury and event data.

We have found the value of the learning rate constant, $k \equiv K^* \approx 3$, as determined from all the available data. The value for $1/\lambda_m$ also determined from observation and failure rate data is in the range 1 in 100,000 to 200,000 hours. This minimum failure rate corresponds to the maximum time between human failures when coupled to, with or in a technological system (so that MaxTTF $\equiv (1/\lambda_m) \sim 2 \times 10^5$ hours of experience).

In terms of the number of failures, errors or observed outcomes, $N_j$, then we have when sampling the $j^{th}$ observation interval the hazard function or failure rate:

$$\lambda(\varepsilon) = \left\{ \left( 1/(N - N_j) \right) \left( dN_j/d\varepsilon \right) \right\}$$

where $N$ is the total number of outcomes and $A \equiv dN_j/d\varepsilon$, the instantaneous outcome rate, $IR$, and the number of outcomes we have observed over all prior intervals is just the summation, $n \equiv \Sigma_j N_j$.

## The Probability Linked to the Rate of Errors

Given the outcome rate, now we need to determine the outcome (error) probability or the chance of failure. Conventionally, reliability engineering is associated with the failure rate of components, or systems, or mechanisms, not of human beings in and interacting with a technological system. However, as noted clearly by Jaynes, 2003 [2], the probability of failure requires a prior knowledge of the total number of outcomes, $N$, which for any predictive purposes, we do not know or have.

Fortunately, the two useful concepts are of the probability of failure (error), $p(\varepsilon)$ or *cumulative distribution function* (CDF) before or in less than any interval, $\varepsilon$; and the *probability density function* (PDF) as the differential probability of failure, $f(\varepsilon)$, in any small interval of experience, $d\varepsilon$. Usually or conventionally, elapsed calendar or component operating time, $t$, is taken as the independent variable, not the experience, $\varepsilon$, which is adopted here on the basis of world outcome data.

Recall the reliability relationships and definitions in our new experience terminology discussed in the Introduction. The symbols are also listed with each item and in the Nomenclature at the back of the book, and have the following meanings:

a) the hazard function is equivalent to the *failure or outcome rate* at any experience, $\lambda(\varepsilon)$, being the relative rate of change in the reliability with experience, $1/R(\varepsilon)$ $(dR(\varepsilon)/d\varepsilon)$;

b) the *CDF or outcome fraction*, $F(\varepsilon)$, is just the observed frequency of prior outcomes, the ratio $n/N$, where we have recorded $n$, out of a total possible of $N$ outcomes;

c) the *frequency of prior outcomes* is identical to the observed *cumulative prior probability*, $p(\varepsilon)$, and hence is the CDF, so $F(\varepsilon) = p(\varepsilon) = (n/N) = 1 - R(\varepsilon)$;

d) here $R(\varepsilon)$ is the *reliability*, $1 - n/N$, a probability measure of how many outcomes or failures did *not* occur out of the total;

e) the *future (or Posterior) probability*, $p(P)$ is proportional to the Prior probability, $p(\varepsilon)$ times the Likelihood, $p(L)$, of future outcomes;

f) the chance of an outcome in any small observation interval is the PDF $f(\varepsilon)$, which is just the rate of change of the failure or outcome fraction with experience, $dp(\varepsilon)/d\varepsilon$;

g) the *Likelihood*, $p(L)$ is the ratio, $f(\varepsilon)/F(\varepsilon)$, being the probability that an outcome will occur in some interval of experience, the PDF, to the total probability of occurrence, the CDF; and

h) we can write the PDF as related to the failure rate integrated between limits from the beginning with no experience up to any experience, $\varepsilon$,

$$f(\varepsilon) = dF/d\varepsilon = \lambda(\varepsilon)\exp - \int_0^\varepsilon \lambda(\varepsilon)d\varepsilon.$$

So, the probability of the outcome or error occurring in or taking less than $\varepsilon$, is just the CDF, $p(\varepsilon) = n/N$, conventionally written as $F(\varepsilon)$. Relating this to the failure rate, via (a) through (d) above, gives:

$$p(\varepsilon) \equiv F(\varepsilon) = 1 - e^{-\int \lambda \, \mathrm{d}\varepsilon}$$

Hence, the probability is a *double exponential* due to the exponential form of the MERE failure rate itself imposed on the probability expression. This form is related to or may be considered as an 'extreme value distribution' function that has arisen quite naturally from the learning hypothesis[4].

Substituting for the MERE hazard or failure rate and carrying out the integration from an initial experience, $\tau_0$, to any interval, $\varepsilon$, we obtain the probability as the double exponential:

$$p(\varepsilon) = 1 - \exp\{(\lambda - \lambda_{\mathrm{m}})/k - \lambda(\varepsilon_0 - \varepsilon)\}$$

where, of course from the MERE,

$$\lambda(\varepsilon) = \lambda_{\mathrm{m}} + (\lambda_0 - \lambda_{\mathrm{m}})\exp - k(\varepsilon - \varepsilon_0)$$

and $\lambda(\varepsilon_0) = \lambda_0$ at the initial experience, $\varepsilon_0$, accumulated up to or at the initial outcome(s). The corresponding PDF $f(\varepsilon)$ is the probability that the error or outcome occurs in the interval $\mathrm{d}\varepsilon$, derived from the change in the CDF failure fraction with experience, or from (f), (h) and (g) above:

$$
\begin{aligned}
f(\varepsilon) &= \mathrm{d}F(\varepsilon)/\mathrm{d}\varepsilon = \mathrm{d}p(\varepsilon)/\mathrm{d}\varepsilon \\
&= \lambda e^{-\int \lambda \, \mathrm{d}\varepsilon} \\
&= \lambda(\varepsilon) \times (1 - p(\varepsilon)), \\
&= \{(\lambda_m + (\lambda_0 - \lambda_m)\exp(-k(\varepsilon - \varepsilon_0))\} \times \{\exp((\lambda(\varepsilon) - \lambda_0)/k - \lambda_m(\varepsilon_0 - \varepsilon))\}
\end{aligned}
$$

The limits are clear: as experience becomes large, $\varepsilon \to \infty$, or the minimum rate is small, $\lambda_{\mathrm{m}} \ll \lambda_0$, or the value of $k$ varies, etc.

So, we have bypassed the problem of not knowing the total number of outcomes, $N$, by using an observation interval based on experience and a known prior variation for the outcome rates due to learning. This is equivalent to von Mises' definition of a 'collective', which is a sample for which probability can be determined (R. von Mises, 1981) [3]. We show in Appendix F how sampling theory, using the Jar of Life, can be combined with the MERE outcome probability expression to estimate the probability of any number of outcomes as a function of experience. We also show that the uniform probability assumption for *observing* outcomes is consistent with the systematic variation of the outcome probability with experience due to *learning*.

We can also determine the maximum and minimum risk likelihoods, which are useful to know, by differentiating the probability expression, the details being given in Appendix B.

---

[4]In passing, we note that this expression is also of the same mathematical form as all 'support' or 'belief' functions used in the Theory of Evidence, a topic we will return to in Chapter 8 and Appendix H.

The result shows how the risk rate systematically varies with experience and that the most likely trend is indeed given by the learning curve.

## The Definition of Risk Exposure and the Level of Attainable Perfection

We can now return to quantifying our classical risk definition, which is: *the chance of an error causing you harm, where chance is an undesigned or fortuitous occurrence or cause.*

Thus, risk is actually the uncertainty represented by the probability of the outcomes, $p(\varepsilon) = n/N$, which is the chance of any number of outcomes, $n$, in any chosen or given, voluntary or involuntary experience interval, $\varepsilon_j$. This probability is the objective measure of the subjective risk for any given risk exposure up until now: it represents the historical, known or prior uncertainty.

As we have seen, we can evaluate the probability, $p(\varepsilon)$, as (see also the derivations in Appendix A):

$$p(\varepsilon) = 1 - \exp\{(\lambda - \lambda_{\mathrm{m}})/k - \lambda(\varepsilon_0 - \varepsilon)\}$$

where the failure rate at any experience is now known to be the general MERE result

$$\lambda(\varepsilon) = \lambda_{\mathrm{m}} + (\lambda_0 - \lambda_{\mathrm{m}})\exp{-k(\varepsilon - \varepsilon_0)}$$

In relation to any number of outcomes, $n$, actually observed out of a total possible number, $N$:

$$\lambda(\varepsilon) = \{(1/(N-n))(\mathrm{d}n/\mathrm{d}\varepsilon)\}$$

The number of outcomes we will observe, $n(\varepsilon)$, in any observation or experience interval, $\varepsilon_j$, is then simply given by just the sum, or mathematically by the integral, of all those that have happened. From the above definition of the varying outcome or failure rate, from any initial up to the present experience, we rearrange the above failure rate expression and define the 'risk integral' for any infinitesimal fraction of experience as:

$$n(\varepsilon) = \int \mathrm{d}n = \int (N-n)\lambda(\varepsilon)\mathrm{d}\varepsilon$$

The risk integral term is on the right-hand side of this expression, but as written here this equation is called an implicit equation, because the number of outcomes, $n$, appears on both the right- and the left-hand sides. In addition, the total number, $N$, is in general not known.

To illustrate the risk behaviour and exposure expressions more easily, we can simplify the right-hand side because often we may expect to observe a small number, $n$, of outcomes compared to the total number possible, $N$. For this case $n \ll N$, and indeed also for rare or unknown events $n \sim 1$, so we have the approximation that since $N$ is constant even though it is unknown:

$$n(\varepsilon) \sim \int N\lambda(\varepsilon)\mathrm{d}\varepsilon = N\int \lambda(\varepsilon)\mathrm{d}\varepsilon$$

For these special limiting cases of observing relatively small numbers of outcomes, it is then easy to evaluate the risk integral from any initial experience, $\varepsilon_0$. The risk exposure integral expression simply becomes the probability or fraction, $n(\varepsilon)/N$, of outcomes in the $j$th experience or exposure interval. The risk exposure is then expresses by the probability obtained from when we divide both sides by $N$:

$$p(\varepsilon_j)_{n \ll N} = n(\varepsilon_j)/N = N_j/N = \int_j dn/N = \int_j \lambda(\varepsilon) d\varepsilon$$
$$\approx \{\lambda_m(\varepsilon_0 - \varepsilon_j) + (\lambda_0 - \lambda_m)/k\} - \{(\lambda_0 - \lambda_m)/k\} \exp - k(\varepsilon_0 - \varepsilon_j)$$

There are clearly two parts to this quantitative risk measure for a small number of outcomes. The first is the first term on the right-hand side due to the inevitable exposure contribution from the omnipresent finite minimum rate, $\lambda_m$, and from the initial rate, $\lambda_0$; whereas the second term is the decrease due to learning with increasing experience.

So explaining these findings in words, we can say rather neatly that,

[Risk exposure] is due to [Minimum plus Initial risk exposure] less [Managing risk by learning]

If we choose or measure our experience or risk exposure interval, we can then know and hence can manage our risk. Simply using the values for $k$, $\lambda_0$ and of $\lambda_m$ from prior data or estimates, we can evaluate the risk for any real, hypothetical or chosen future or actual risk exposure interval, $\varepsilon_j$, by calculating the probability or chance, $p(\varepsilon_j)$, of observing $n(\varepsilon_j)$ possible outcomes.

Numerically and practically, according to all the data that we have collected from over 200 years of technology, it appears to be difficult to achieve in actual practice a risk of much below a chance of one in a thousand for any given relevant, applicable or chosen experience unit. As we shall see, this result arises because $\lambda_m$ is about $10^{-5}$ per unit of experience or risk exposure, and $p(\varepsilon_j)$ is usually greater than about $10^{-3}$, and the inevitability of an outcome eventually offsets the reduction achieved by learning. The lowest risk attained is perhaps not coincidentally almost exactly the level of perfection achieved by the show jumper, who was quoted in the Introduction as failing only once in a thousand times for jumping a given hurdle! Note that in this particular case, the relevant risk exposure measure is taking a jump at a particular hurdle; and each and every case risk has its own unique relevant measure of risk exposure, and the relevant learning experience measure has to be carefully determined.

## Comparison to Conventional Social Science and Engineering Failure and Outcome Rate Formulations

Traditionally, in the entire Reliability, Biological, Sociological and Demographical literatures, totally empirical and even arbitrary 'models' for the outcome rates are used to describe the data obtained in a test or some observed sample. The models are actually empirical polynomial or functional fits to outcome datasets, usually for a restricted observational sample. They are thus using the prior information but are not making predictions and none of the so-called models are mechanistic. We can show that these models cannot describe the outcomes for HTS where learning is present.

In the social sciences, for example, large and small populations are studied for outcomes that exhibit potential demographic and significant change trends. The data usually appear or are analysed as time series, as naturally societies evolve and change with time passing. The events or outcomes are items like the variation of job changes with age and time; or the number of illnesses or diseases in a certain group; or the rate of graduation and dropouts from school.

The hazard function, $h(t)$, is then approximated by adopting some chosen empirical 'model', which is basically a curve fit to the observed data using a set of variable parameters or multiplication constants. A typical multi-parameter form for a time-varying hazard function is chosen (in Allison, 1984 [1]):

$$\log_e h(t) \equiv \log_e \lambda(t) = a + b(t)\varepsilon + c(t)\varepsilon^2 + \text{higher order and cross terms} \ldots$$

For our purposes here, the experience, $\varepsilon$, is taken as the so-called explanatory variable as we transform to 'experience space'; and the input parameters $a$, $b$ and $c$ are variable coefficients fitted to the outcome data. Since the hazard function $h(t) \equiv \lambda(\varepsilon)$, this logarithmic form is required to be equivalent to the MERE analytical solution for the outcome rate, which is, in our notation,

$$\log_e h(\varepsilon) = \log_e(\lambda(\varepsilon) - \lambda_m)$$
$$= \log_e(\lambda_0 - \lambda_m) - k(\varepsilon - \varepsilon_0)$$

Comparing the two expressions for the hazard function, it is clear that any such arbitrarily chosen $(a, b, c \ldots)$ parametric form for $h(t,\varepsilon)$ is inadequate to represent learning and event outcome data, unless only fitted over some very restricted range. The conventional hazard function approach is equivalent to using polynomial fitting with arbitrary multipliers. This must explain in part the difficulties of prediction faced by socio-economic studies that use such data correlations and models when learning is occurring, or when natural selection and data censoring is happening.

The expression used for species extinction, of interest to biologists and sociologists, is also based on a constant hazard (death rate) without learning. Thus, it is of the form $f(\varepsilon) = dF/d\varepsilon = \lambda e^{-\lambda\varepsilon}$, where the failure rate is a suitably averaged value and the experience is usually measured as geologic or hereditary elapsed time.

In the engineering disciplines, equipment and components are studied for failure and reliability trends. The standard works on statistical analysis and engineering reliability contain many empirical failure rate 'distributions', which are fitted to the failure data. These include the constant or averaged failure rate approximation; and the more general so-called Weibull polynomial forms, which are written as follows, translating $t \to \varepsilon$:

$$\lambda(\varepsilon) = \left(\frac{m}{\theta}\right)\left(\frac{\varepsilon}{\theta}\right)^{m-1}$$

$$f(\varepsilon) = \left(\frac{m}{\theta}\right)\left(\frac{\varepsilon}{\theta}\right)^{m-1} \exp\left(\frac{\varepsilon}{\theta}\right)^m$$

The input parameters $m$, called the 'shape', and $\theta$, called the 'characteristic life', are obtained by fitting to failure rate data. In order for the failure rate, $\lambda(\varepsilon)$, to decrease with increasing experience, $\varepsilon$, then $m \leq 1$ of necessity.

We can easily compare the MERE and Weibull failure or outcome rate analytically and numerically, and again can show that arbitrary unique choices of the Weibull parameters are not possible to describe, fit or fully approximate the MERE failure rate. This is most easily

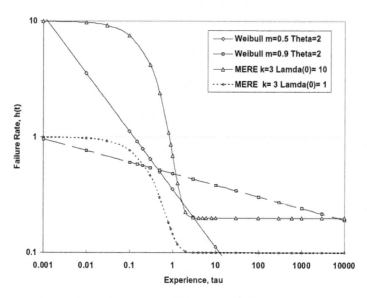

**Figure 4.1.** Comparison of Weibull and MERE failure rates

seen as we may write the MERE exponential hazard function as a power series, so the failure or outcome rate becomes:

$$\lambda(\varepsilon) = \lambda_m + (\lambda_0 - \lambda_m)\left\{\left(1 - k(\varepsilon - \varepsilon_0) + k^2(\varepsilon - \varepsilon_0)^2\big/2 - \ldots\ldots\right)\right\}$$

By inspection, it cannot be readily represented by a Weibull form without fitting or choosing values for $m$ and $\theta$ as arbitrary functions of experience.

As an example, in Figure 4.1, we compare the MERE and Weibull failure or outcome rates, $h(\varepsilon) \equiv \lambda(\varepsilon)$. The numbers are derived by substituting typical values for $m$ and $\theta$ that give the same assumed initial rates (taken here to be $h(\varepsilon) = 1$ and 10), and adopting the $k = 3$ value derived for the MERE from the world data. The experience, $\varepsilon$, is measured in arbitrary but common units, tau.

As can be seen, and it is clear on either a log–log or linear–linear plot, the rates for a given experience evolve differently between the MERE and the Weibull's, which latter are straight lines on a log–log plot. The difference is between a double exponential or a simple power law, respectively. The two cannot be made identical by shifts in the two available Weibull parameters, $m$ and $\theta$, except by making these arbitrary functions of experience, $\varepsilon$. The Weibull can be made to fit at best perhaps part of the curve, but clearly not all of it. Adding more fitting parameters just compounds the problem and does not solve it.

The fundamental differences between the MERE and the empirical Weibull fits can be further shown by comparing the estimated outcome or failure probabilities. These risks are derived from the failure rates, and we now turn to discussing that approach and how well it can be used to predict system failures.

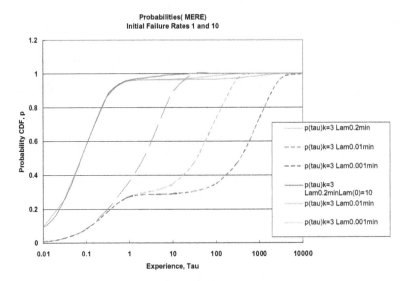

**Figure 4.2.**   The MERE cumulative distribution function, CDF

## The Learning Probabilities and the PDFs

The MERE failure or outcome rate is a well-behaved and interesting function. We illustrate the two probability parameters, $p(\varepsilon)$ and $f(\varepsilon)$ for the MERE in Figures 4.2 and 4.3, using the standard learning rate constant value, $k = 3$, with an illustrative range of the minimum or asymptotic error rates, $\lambda_m$. The initial failure rates taken for $\lambda_0$ are again completely arbitrary (1 and 10), so that the curves in Figure 4.3 can be scaled to or for any initial value.

It is evident in Figures 4.2 and 4.3 that the double exponential form for the human component plays a key role. It also shows that the initial steep decline caused by learning can be followed by a 'plateau' or 'knee', caused by the constant and finite minimum.

In other words, we learn as we gain experience and then reach a region of essentially no decrease, in rate or in probability, and hence in likelihood. It is easy to obtain the first decrease in rates or probabilities but harder to proceed any lower. This is exactly what is observed in transport, manufacturing, medical, industrial and other accident, death and injury data (Duffey and Saull, 2002) [4].

## The Initial Failure Rate and Its Variation with Experience

Having established the learning trend, we need to determine the actual parameters and values using data and insight. Now, in reality, the initial rate, $\lambda_0$, is *not* a constant as assumed so far since the outcomes are stochastic in experience 'state space'. Hence, $\lambda_0 = \lambda(\varepsilon_0)$, and it is not known when exactly in our experience we may have an error initially observed (and we might be lucky or not), and the initial value we ascribe to the initial rate observe is an arbitrary value.

This is a subtle and not easily understood point. For example, typically for industrial injuries the *average* rate for outcomes is a maximum of about 1 per 20,000 hours, whereas for

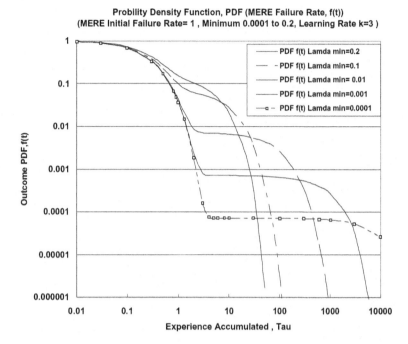

**Figure 4.3.** The MERE PDF, f($\varepsilon$) for various values of the minimum rate

extremely safe industries and technologies it can be a *minimum* of about 1 per 200,000 hours, or 10 times less. But even then, since the outcomes are 'rare events', some industries may not yet have had an outcome, or the initial rate is unknown or not recorded. We could take the range $0.000005 < \lambda_0 < 0.00005$, but only as bounding estimates.

To establish the initial rate, key data are available from commercial aircraft outcomes (fatal crashes) throughout the world. The major contributor is the human element not equipment failure, although these latter can also be ascribed to the root cause of human failings. Fatal crashes and accidents for the 30 years between 1970 and 2000 are known (e.g., from Airsafe, 2000) [5], for 114 major airlines with ~725 million hours (Mh) of total flying experience. For each airline with its own experience, $\varepsilon$, the fatal accident rate per flying hour, $\lambda(\varepsilon)$, can be plotted as an open circular symbol in Figure 4.4 versus the accumulated experience in flying hours (adopting the FAA value of ~$3\frac{1}{3}$ hours as an average flight time).

An airline may fly for many millions of hours without having a fatal crash, or for much less, because the crashes are quite random. The major influence of when and whether one occurs is actually human errors *within the system* coinciding with or surfacing throughout the technological system (in design, manufacture, operation, maintenance, regulation or flying). In addition to airlines with both large and small experience, and to cover *six orders of magnitude* of experience, we also show the data points for two other key events, which might have been expected to be different both in rate and technology but in fact are not.

These are:

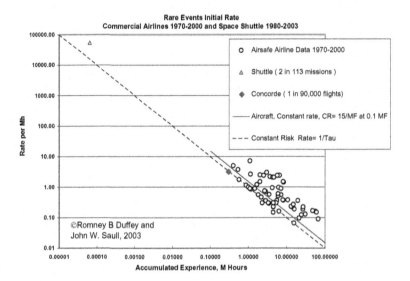

**Figure 4.4.** The initial rate based on world airline and US space shuttle accident data

a) the crash of the supersonic *Concorde* with a rate, $\lambda_0$, of one in about 90,000 flights shown as a lozenge symbol; and

b) the explosion and disintegration of the space shuttles, *Challenger* and *Columbia*, with a rate, $\lambda_0$, of 2 out of 113 total missions, plotted using the triangular symbol. The typical 'flight time' for the shuttle was taken as the 30–40 minutes for re-entry as reported by the NASA, 2003 [6] timelines, although this plot is quite insensitive to the actual value taken.

For all these data and experience, there is a remarkable constancy of risk, as shown by the straight line of slope −1, which is given by the equation:

$$\lambda\varepsilon = \text{constant}, n,$$

where the observed rate is strictly a function of whatever experience it happened to occur at, any value being possible. Thus, in the limit for *rare events*, the initial rate should be the purely Bayesian estimate from the prior experience at whenever the initial outcome occurred, which gives, with $n = N_j = 1$ for the initial outcome (see also Appendix A):

$$\lambda_0 \approx (1/\varepsilon)$$

This result can be inserted into the MERE solution and is both the simplest and a statement of common sense, in that *the initial rate is whatever it may be at the beginning*. The extreme importance of adopting the correct measure for the experience means that at very small experience, the rate of error(s) or failures can appear to be large, giving an ample and unlucky opportunity for reduction! This can appear as a 'start-up' transient of high initial rates.

This rate varying as $(1/\varepsilon)$ also corresponds *exactly* to the risk rate that is attainable on the basis of the minimum likelihood determined from the outcome probability (see Appendix B).

*There is no further <u>rate</u> reduction possible except by increasing experience*, which is exactly what the airline data show. The airlines with the greatest experience have the lowest fatal crash rates but the greater number of such crashes (outcomes) than those with the least experience, who have the highest rate but fewer outcomes. But the risk of death is the same for them all, as far as a passenger is concerned: it is one in an interval of about ~200,000 hours of actual flying time.

What the data are telling us is that the limiting initial rate is exactly what it is for the experience at which the first outcome occurs, no more and no less.

## The 'Best' MERE Risk Values

From the analysis of many millions of data points that include the human element in the outcomes, we have been able to derive the key quantities that dominate current technological systems. These now include commercial air, road, ship and rail transport accidents; near misses and events; chemical, nuclear and industrial injuries; mining injuries and manufacturing defects; general aviation events; medical misadministration and misdiagnoses; pressure vessel and piping component failures; and office paperwork and quality management systems (Duffey and Saull, 2002) [4].

From all these data, and many more, we have estimated the minimum failure rate or error interval, the typical initial error interval, and the learning rate constant for the ULC as follows:

a) minimum attainable rate, $\lambda_m$, at large experience, $\varepsilon$, of about 1 per 100,000 to 200,000 hours ($\lambda_m \sim 5 \times 10^{-6}$ per hour of experience);
b) initial rate, $\lambda_0$, of $1/\varepsilon$, at small experience (being about 1 per 20,000 to 30,000 hours or $\lambda_0 \sim 5 \times 10^{-5}$ per hour of experience); and
c) learning rate constant, $k \sim 3$, from the ULC fit of a mass of available data worldwide for accidents, injuries, events, near misses and misadministration.

Therefore, the following numerical dynamic form for the MERE human error or outcome rate is our 'best' available estimate (Duffey and Saull, 2002) [4]:

$$\lambda(\varepsilon) = \lambda_m + (\lambda_0 - \lambda_m) e^{-k\varepsilon},$$

which becomes, for $\lambda_0 = (n/\varepsilon)$, with $n = 1$ for the initial outcome,

$$\lambda = 5.10^{-6} + (1/\varepsilon - 5 \times 10^{-6}) e^{-3\varepsilon}$$

The rate, $\lambda$, can be evaluated numerically, as well as the probability, $p(\varepsilon)$, and the differential PDF, $f(\varepsilon)$. The result of these calculations is shown in Figure 4.5, where $\varepsilon \equiv \tau$ units in order to represent the accumulated experience scale.

It is evident that for $k > 0$, the probability is a classic 'bathtub' shape, being just under near unity at the start (Figure 4.6), and then falling with the lowering of error rates with increasing experience. After falling to a low of about one in a hundred 'chance' due to learning, it rises when the experience is $\varepsilon > 1,000$ tau units, and becomes a near certainty again by a million tau units of experience as failures re-accumulate, since $\lambda_m \sim 5 \times 10^{-6}$ per

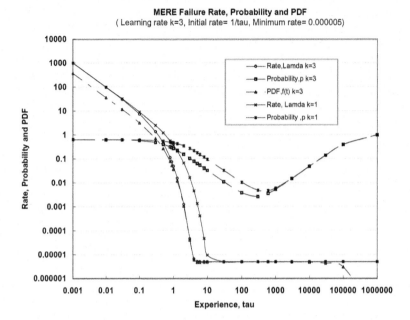

**Figure 4.5.**   The best MERE values

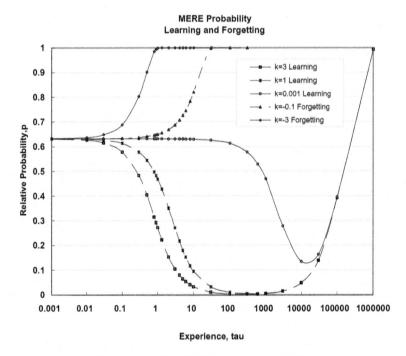

**Figure 4.6.**   The MERE outcome probability

experience tau unit. The importance of learning is evident since for $k < 0$, forgetting causes a rapid increase to unity probability with no minimum.

## Maximum and Minimum Likely Outcome Rates

By analogy to conventional statistics, we can derive the maximum and minimum likelihoods for the outcome rate. This analysis is given in detail in Appendix B, and, using typical values, illustrates the trends of decreasing likelihood with increasing experience.

Extremely useful approximations to the full expressions are derived on this basis of maximum or minimum likelihood in the Appendix B. The results are shown to be in good accord with the best learning (MERE) and the constant rate (CR) approximations.

The condition for a maximum or minimum likelihood is that the variation of the outcome probability with experience should be zero. The result of applying this condition is a first order differential equation, which can be analytically solved for the two roots.

The solution for the *maximum* likelihood for the outcome rate is exponential, falling with increasing experience as given by:

$$\lambda_{\max} = \lambda_0 \exp - \{k(\varepsilon - \varepsilon_0)/(1 + k\varepsilon_0)\} \text{ Rate for Maximum Likelihood}$$

However, the expression that gives the *minimum* likelihood indicates that the *minimum risk* rate is bounded by:

$$\lambda_{\min} \ll \{\lambda_{\mathrm{m}}\}/\{1 + k(\varepsilon - \varepsilon_0)\} \text{ Rate for Minimum Likelihood}$$

We find that the maximum likelihood expression echoes and tracks the MERE IR, and shows learning.

## Standard Engineering Reliability Models Compared to the MERE Result

Again for comparison with standard 'engineering reliability' models, we show the MERE result Equation also as a Weibull chart or 'probability plot' form in Figure 4.7.

Here, the natural logarithm $\ln(1/(1 - p(\varepsilon)))$ is shown plotted versus the accumulated experience, $\varepsilon$, measured in tau units for two learning rates, $k = 1$ and $k = 3$. The plot demonstrates that the influence of learning is to produce a distinct 'kink' in otherwise straight (or conventional) Weibull log–log lines. For comparison only, we show an example with an assumed low constant initial rate of 0.000005, consistent with our minimum value derived from data.

The dramatic changes in slope explain and emphasise why a single value for the Weibull slope or 'shape' parameter, $m$, *cannot* uniquely fit these human error/reliability information or theories. In addition, the learning rate constant would need to be known or assumed as the error rate decreases by two orders of magnitude due to learning.

Using the conventional engineering failure rate approach for the Weibull distribution shape and life parameters (Lewis, 1994; Tobias and Trindade, 1986) [7,8], the required value of $m$ can be back-calculated from the slope of the MERE best estimates of Figure 4.6, as shown in Table 4.1.

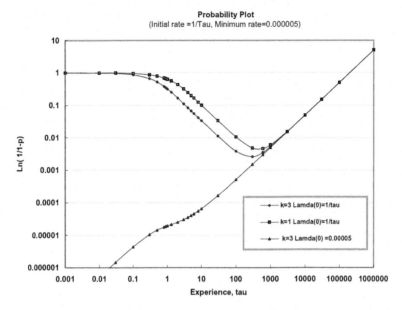

**Figure 4.7.**   Human error probability shown in a Weibull form of plot

As can be seen from the results, the Weibull fitted slope or 'shape' is generally given by a value of order $m < 0$ during learning. The exponent finally reaches $m \sim 1$ for the experience interval between $\varepsilon > 3,000$ tau units, depending on the learning rate. Basically, using Weibull parameters is an exercise in piecewise fitting of constant exponents to the actual double exponential curves.

The contrast and comparisons between the approaches can be further illustrated by evaluation of the distribution parameters, $m$ and $\theta$. Using the parameter value of $m \sim 1$, we have trivially the outcome rate:

$$\lambda(\varepsilon) = 1/\theta$$

and the PDF,

$$f(\varepsilon) = (1/\theta)\exp(\varepsilon/\theta)$$

which to have the correct asymptote for $\lambda_m$ of 0.000005 would have a value for the characteristic life of $\theta \sim 200,000$, the maximum interval.

The difference can be further illustrated by direct comparison of Weibull-type fits with the MERE 'human bathtub'. (See Figure 4.8.)

The figure compares a range of Weibull parameters (estimates for the input parameters, $m$, called the 'shape', and $\theta$, called the 'characteristic life'). The former gives the general slope and the latter used to normalise the initial probability, in this case to unity. We also show two values for the MERE learning rate constant, so $3 < k < 10$. It is clear that the idea of a bathtub shape is reclaimed using a Weibull, but the Weibull curves *cannot* be arbitrarily manipulated to agree with the MERE result over the whole range. So we would expect

**Table 4.1.**  Fitted Weibull slope parameter, $m$

| Experience, $\varepsilon$ | Weibull shape, $m$ | Weibull shape, $m$ |
|---|---|---|
| (tau) | k = 3 | k = 1 |
| 0.01 | −0.006 | −0.002 |
| 0.03 | −0.027 | −0.009 |
| 0.1 | −0.084 | −0.029 |
| 0.3 | −0.246 | −0.088 |
| 0.5 | −0.473 | −0.183 |
| 0.8 | −0.665 | −0.285 |
| 0.9 | −0.783 | −0.365 |
| 1 | −0.824 | −0.401 |
| 1.3 | −0.883 | −0.465 |
| 2 | −0.958 | −0.599 |
| 3 | −0.994 | −0.767 |
| 4 | −0.999 | −0.887 |
| 5 | −0.999 | −0.947 |
| 6 | −0.999 | −0.976 |
| 8 | −0.999 | −0.992 |
| 10 | −0.998 | −0.998 |
| 30 | −0.989 | −0.996 |
| 100 | −0.895 | −0.963 |
| 300 | −0.350 | −0.707 |
| 600 | 0.446 | −0.051 |
| 1,000 | 0.794 | 0.492 |
| 3,000 | 0.948 | 0.855 |
| 10,000 | 0.994 | 0.984 |
| 30,000 | 0.999 | 0.998 |
| 100,000 | 1.000 | 1.000 |
| 1,000,000 | 1.000 | 1.000 |

Weibull parametric fits to be successful in matching data over limited ranges, but not very useful for risk *prediction* purposes.

## Future Event Estimates: The Past Predicts the Future

The probability of human error, and its associated failure or error rate, we expect to be unchanged unless dramatic technology shifts occur. We can also estimate the likelihood of another event, and whether the MERE human error rate frequency gives sensible and consistent *predictions*. Using Bayesian reasoning, the posterior or future probability, $p(P)$, of an error when we are at experience, $\varepsilon$, is,

$$\text{Posterior, } p(P) \propto \{\text{Prior, } p(\varepsilon)\} \times \{\text{Likelihood, } p(L)\}$$

where $p(\varepsilon)$ is the prior probability, and by definition both $|P,L| > \varepsilon$, our present accumulated experience.

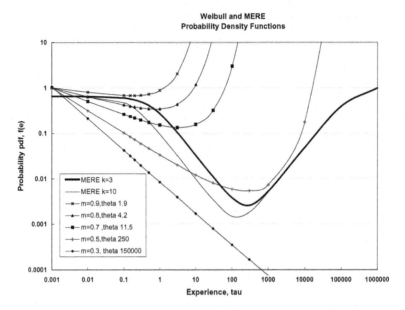

**Figure 4.8.**   Comparison of MERE and Weibull probabilities

## Statistical Bayesian-Type Estimates: The Impact of Learning

The likelihood, $p(L)$, is also a statistical estimate, and we must make an assumption, based on our prior knowledge, and often is taken as a uniform distribution. We can show that the likelihood is formally related to the number of outcomes for a given variation of the mean. Either:

a)  the future likelihood is of the same form as experienced up to now; and/or
b)  the future is an unknown statistical sample for the next increment of experience based on the differential probability, the PDF $f(\varepsilon)$.

In the first case (a), we have that the future likelihood probability $p(L)$ is the fraction or ratio of events remaining to occur out of the total possible number that is left.

In Social Science, the likelihood is defined by Allison, 1984 [1] as the probability of many, i, such outcomes (events) occurring, i.e.:

$$p(\mathrm{L}) = \prod_i f_i(\varepsilon)$$

where $i = 1, 2, 3 \ldots n$, and $p(L)$ is actually related in form to a partition function. As before, for each $i$th outcome, the PDF (now termed the 'extinction rate') is,

$$f_i(\varepsilon) = \lambda_i e^{-\int \lambda d\varepsilon} = \lambda_i(\varepsilon) \times (1 - p_i(\varepsilon))$$

In Appendix A, we derive some actual estimates using the hypothesis that we can extrapolate the past learning curve into the future if the HTS is unchanged. That enables an estimate of the ratios of the numbers of past and future expected outcomes for case (a), from which it is evident we must have that future events will occur. Hence, the future probability is unchanged from the estimate of the prior probability, $p(\varepsilon)$, for any future experience.

For the second case (b), the future is an unknown statistical sample for the next increment of experience based on the PDF, $f(\varepsilon)$. This is called a 'conditional probability', where the probability of the next outcome depends on the prior ones occurring, which was Bayes' original premise.

The so-called generalised *conditional* probability or Likelihood, $p(L)$, can be defined utilising the CDF and PDF expressions. Described by Sveshnikov, 1968 [9] as the 'generalised Bayes formula', the expression given is based on the prior outcome having already occurred with the prior probability, $p(\varepsilon)$. This prior probability then gives the probability or Likelihood of the next outcome, $p(L)$, in our present experience-based notation, as:

$$
\begin{aligned}
p(L) &= \frac{(f(\varepsilon), \text{probability that the outcome occurs in the interval } d\varepsilon)}{(p(\varepsilon), \text{probability that the outcome occurred in or less than } \varepsilon)} \\
&\equiv \{\text{PDF}/\text{CDF}\} \equiv p(P)/p(\varepsilon) \\
&= f(\varepsilon)/p(\varepsilon) \\
&= 1/p(\varepsilon)\{dp(\varepsilon)/d\varepsilon\} \\
&= \lambda e^{-\int \lambda d\varepsilon} \Big/ \left(1 - e^{-\int \lambda d\varepsilon}\right) \\
&= \lambda\{(1 - p(\varepsilon))/p(\varepsilon)\}
\end{aligned}
$$

In mathematical notation (Sveshnikov, pp. 48–49) [9], the PDF is a differential function, $f(\varepsilon) = dp(\varepsilon)/d\varepsilon$, being the probability of an outcome in any experience increment; and the CDF is an integral function for the observed outcome (failure) fraction, $F(\varepsilon)$, being the probability of the outcomes for all experience. Both functions can be evaluated using the (continuous random variable) MERE exponential solution for the outcome (failure) rate as we now show. In Bayes' original paper, the example functions taken for the PDF and CDF corresponded to those for the binomial probability, so the generalisation simply extends the functional form.

So, in the second case, for the next increment of experience, we may take the likelihood, $p(L)$ as related to the PDF, $f(\varepsilon)$, and the CDF, $p(\varepsilon)$ by the expressions for the posterior probability:

$$
p(P) = p(\varepsilon) \times (\text{PDF}, f(\varepsilon))/(\text{CDF}, p(\varepsilon)) = f(\varepsilon)
$$

As derived above and in Appendix A, this implies that the likelihood is as we stated above:

$$
p(L) \equiv \{\lambda(\varepsilon)\}\{(1 - p(\varepsilon))/p(\varepsilon)\}.
$$

We can evaluate this Bayesian likelihood and posterior expressions using our 'best' MERE values of a learning rate constant of $k = 3$ and a minimum failure rate of $\lambda_m = 5.10^{-6}$, obtaining the results shown in Figure 4.9.

It is clear from Figure 4.9 that the 'human bathtub' prior probability, $p(\varepsilon)$, causes the likelihood to fluctuate up and down with increasing experience. The likelihood tracks the learning curve, then transitions via a bump or secondary peak to the lowest values as we approach

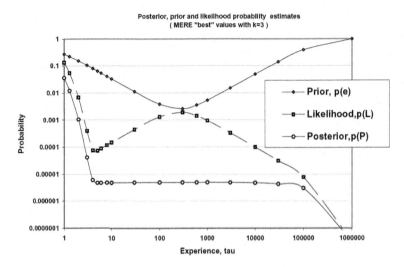

**Figure 4.9.** The estimate of the likelihood and posterior probabilities when learning

certainty ($p \to 1$) at large experience. However, the posterior probability, $p(P)$, just mirrors and follows the MERE failure rate, as we predicted, decreasing to a minimum value of $\sim 5.10^{-6}$, our ubiquitous minimum outcome rate, before finally falling away.

Hence, since the future probability estimate, the posterior $p(P)$, is once again derivable from its (unchanged) prior value, $f(\varepsilon) = dp(\varepsilon)/d\varepsilon \sim \lambda(\varepsilon)$, derived from learning from experience, and thus *the past predicts the future*.

This purely deterministic view is predicated by assuming an unchanging HTS and learning rate, thus reflecting reality, and that the prior 'collective' of outcomes is a true sample of the posterior ones. Therefore, as usual, the uncertainty is determined by the prior probability.

For *rare events*, $\lambda(\varepsilon) \sim n/\varepsilon$, and $p(\varepsilon) \ll 1$, so a sensible working estimate for the PDF is $f(\varepsilon) \sim \lambda(\varepsilon) \sim n/\varepsilon$, where $n \sim 1$.

We show in Appendix A how this estimate for the likelihood indeed corresponds to that derived from the learning theory with negligible learning (a low rate constant $k \sim 10^3$), thus showing a consistent result.

For the special case of 'perfect learning' when we learn from all the non-outcomes as well as the outcomes (derived in detail in Appendix F), the Poisson-type triple exponential form applies for low probabilities and small numbers of outcomes ($n \ll m$). Of course, the limit of 'perfect learning' is when we have an outcome, so here $p(\tau) = 1/\tau$, and is the rare event case for $n = 1$. The Perfect Learning limit fails as soon as we have an event, as it should. But there is also a useful simple physical interpretation, which is that:

a) we learn from non-outcomes the same way we learn from outcomes, as we have assumed;
b) the perfect learning ends as soon as we have just a single (rare) outcome; and
c) the influence of the finite minimum rate is then lost.

## Maximum and Minimum Likelihood

We would still like to know what the most likely path is that we will follow when learning or not.

In Appendix B, we have carried out the analysis to determine the maximum and minimum likelihoods for the outcome rate, $\lambda(\varepsilon)$, based on the MERE solution using the learning hypothesis. The forms obtained for the likelihood are different from the conventional result of the mean and the results show that the dependence on experience is strong. The result enables an answer to the two key questions:

When are the events most likely?
What rates will they occur at?

In Appendix B, we show how to derive the most and least likely probability for outcomes at any experience by using the classical mathematical search for a maximum or a minimum value. We find that the *maximum likelihood* for the risk rate is given by an exponential decline of outcome rate with experience,

$$\lambda_{\max} = \lambda_0 \exp - \{k(\varepsilon - \varepsilon_0)/(1 + k\varepsilon_0)\}$$

The result follows common sense. Our maximum risk is dominated by our inexperience at first, and then by lack of learning, and decreasing our risk rate largely depends on attaining experience. Our most likely risk rate is extremely sensitive to our learning rate, or $k$ value, for a given experience.

So, as might be logically expected, the *maximum likelihood for outcomes occurs at or near the initial event rate when we are least experienced.* This is also a common-sense check on our results: *we are most at risk at the very beginning.* Therefore, as could have been expected, the most likely and the least risks are reduced only by attaining increasing experience and with increased learning rates. In a real sense, we have now also physically ranged or 'bracketed' the possible limits on the rate and probability based on learning and not learning, which is also a judgement on the likelihood or our degree of belief.

This approach to reduce and manage risk should come as no surprise to those in the education community, and in executive and line management positions. *A learning environment has the least risk.*

## Comparison to Data: The Probability of Failure and Human Error

We may now compare the above learning theory with the available data, where we are looking for the major impact of the human element on the outcome rate. Fortunately or unfortunately, 'human error' has an overriding (typically >60%) contribution to almost all HTS outcomes and events. This is true worldwide for the whole spectrum, all the way from transportation crashes, social system and medical errors, to large administrative failures and the whole gamut of industrial accidents. Such outcome rates generally follow the ULC (Duffey and Saull, 2002) [4], where a learning pattern is clearly evident, and well over 1,000 data sources formed the basis for the estimated value of $k \sim 3$ for the learning rate 'constant' taken above.

However, to compare the failure rates to outcome data for the probability of human error now requires a further analysis step that we outline here. There are three datasets for catastrophic events with defined large human element contributions that are worth re-examining further:

a) the crash rate for global commercial airlines, noting most occur during manoeuvering and approach for take-off and landing but as we have seen can also occur in flight;
b) the loss of the space shuttles, *Challenger* and *Columbia*, also on take-off and during the approach for landing; and
c) the probability of non-detection by plant operators of so-called latent (hidden) faults in the control of nuclear system transients.

Apparently disparate, these three all share the *common element of human involvement* in the management, design, safety 'culture', control and operation of a large technological system; all are subject to intense media and public interest; and the costs of failure are extremely expensive and unacceptable in many ways.

For the first two cases, we calculate the outcome (fatal crash) probability for all and each *i*th airline, where the probability, $p_i(\varepsilon)$ is given by $n_i(\varepsilon)/N$, where $N$ is the total number of outcomes (~276 in the 30-year observation interval). To normalise the data over the observation interval of experience, we must adopt a measure for the maximum experience, which in the case of commercial airlines and *Concorde* is taken as the 720 Mh accumulated ($\tau_{max}$) of actual flying from 1970–2000 (i.e., 1 tau ≡ 1 Mh flying).

For the Shuttle, as a test we take for the experience normalisation either:

1. the maximum Mh aircraft value, thus assuming the shuttle is just another type of commercial-type flying machine with the same human elements but independent causes; or
2. just the total launch and re-entry amount for all the 113 shuttle missions, hence assuming that the failure rate and human error mechanisms are completely unrelated to that for commercial aircraft.

The comparison of the data to theory is shown in Figure 4.10 where the lines are the MERE calculated probability, $p(\varepsilon)$ using the 'best' values. The three lines use three bounding values for the minimum error rate to illustrate the sensitivity. Despite the scatter, a minimum rate of order ~$5 \times 10^{-6}$ is indeed an upper-bound value, as we estimated before.

The Shuttle data point sensitivity to the four orders of magnitude variation in choice of maximum experience shows that the outcome probability is well matched with the aircraft data when only shuttle flights are considered, demonstrating that the minimum rate is independent but indeed is about the same magnitude (~$5 \times 10^{-6}$). We note two points: the probability is now increasing with experience, as the minimum has been attained and passed; and the chance (probability) of a fatal crash for any airline is typically a maximum of between 1 and 10%. Thus, 90 to 99% of the airlines are the lucky ones and do not have one: no black ball is drawn from the Jar of Life.

For the other human element case, we have the results of the probability of non-detection (i.e., human error) of latent faults for nuclear plant transients, which are also fairly regular events. The data and the MERE error rate were normalised to fitting the curves using a maximum experience of ~100,000 h (1 tau ≡ 1 transient hour) for the specific transients, close

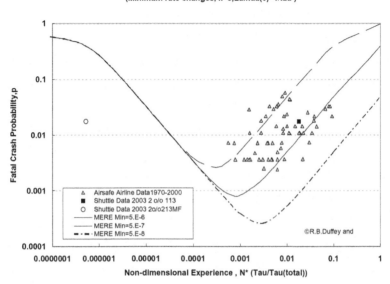

**Figure 4.10.**   The probability of failure: MERE comparison to airline and shuttle data

to the MERE minimum error interval. The initial probability was taken as unity, that is $p(\varepsilon_0) = 1$, for comparison purposes. (See Figure 4.11.)

Initially, the operators had little or no chance of detection – the latent fault remained undetected. As experience was gained and the event unfolded, the chance of finding the hidden fault increased dramatically. The data and the theory are in reasonable accord, despite the necessity of having to be renormalised. Perhaps the key two observations here are that: the shape of the data curve is indeed following the MERE failure rate prediction and that the operators were indeed on the steepest (downward) or learning part.

This probability trend is also entirely consistent with what happened in the aircraft loss of fuel event (Appendix D) discussed at the beginning of this Chapter. The latent fault was the hidden fuel-line leak, and it took about an hour, or ~$10^{-5}$ tau on this same figure scale, for the crew to make the wrong diagnosis. Assuming the same human element forces are at work between the two industries, the probability of non-detection of this latent fault we would estimate at ~90%, consistent with the actual outcome.

All the outcomes we observe are the outcomes we should have expected, given the involvement of the human element and the probability of human error.

Thus, the human error probability (HEP) is indeed *dynamic* and evolves with experience. In this difficult arena of coupled human and technological system behaviour, these new results show a very reasonable level of concordance between the MERE theory and the data, using the typical minimum error interval (100,000 to 200,000 hours). The method and approach we have validated here also allows for predictions to be made.

How can we compare these human operator probabilities to the Shuttle and aircraft outcome probabilities? We simply need to translate the experience basis to an equivalent total observation interval instead of just the transient time. The transient events examined by

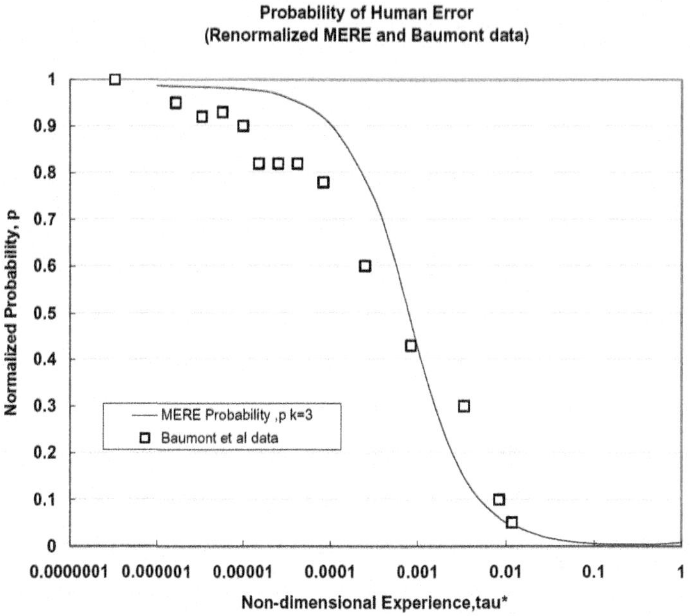

**Probability of Human Error**
**(Renormalized MERE and Baumont data)**

**Figure 4.11.**   Comparison of MERE to human error probability data of Baumont et al.

Baumont et al., 2000 [10] were derived for a total reactor 'fleet' of 58 units, which reported 900 outcomes spread over two years. The learning opportunity is the experience per outcome for all the fleet, which is then given by:

$$\text{Experience per outcome} = (58 \times 2 \text{ years} \times 365 \text{ days} \times 24 \text{ hours} \times 60)/900$$
$$\equiv \tau_M = 68{,}000 \text{ minutes per event.}$$

We now convert this latent error data from a transient time to a non-dimensional 'bathtub' plot based on the non-dimensional experience per outcome, $N^* = \tau/\tau_M$, while retaining the previous normalisation and probability estimates.

The result is shown in Figure 4.12. As can be seen, we have a reasonable fit and the trends at least seem convincing enough to continue with this new probability analysis. We are slowly filling in the bathtub!

## Comparison of the MERE Result to Human Reliability Analysis

We have been asked by several interested colleagues and readers as to how to reconcile the conundrum of the MERE view of the human element and risk taking appearing as outcomes as an integral part of the trends for an entire HTS, with the actions, decisions and errors of the actual individuals or humans within it. In effect, the MERE describes the emergent system learning and trends exhibited by the experience of the collective whole, reflecting how all the individuals within it are also learning, on-the-job and in real time, according to their own experience. Basically, the issue is how to reconcile 'human reliability' as reflecting 'system reliability', and vice versa, in terms of learning effects and outcomes, despite the drastic

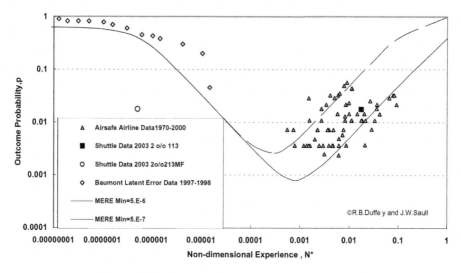

**Figure 4.12.** An outcome probability data comparison

apparent differences in system and sub-system timeframes and scope. In Appendix J, we show conclusively that results for skill acquisition and pattern recognition for individuals, known in Psychology as the Laws of Practice, follow exactly the ULC for entire systems. The experience measure is, as usual, the number of trials or tests. Hence, individual decisions and learning occurring within and by the individuals are indeed precisely reflected in and by the system outcome trends.

As we shall, the outcomes (and non-outcomes) we observe represent our experience too. According to the data, and the MERE result, the Learning Hypothesis can be applied at any level in a system, from the individual workers to the organisational whole, by simply adopting the appropriate measure for the differing *experience intervals*. The emergent system outcomes then indeed naturally reflect the collective learning of the individual(s) learning within the chosen system or sub-system.

We can illustrate this effect using data that examine decision making by system operators as they learn or not during the evolution and unfolding of an event. Here, the outcomes and behaviour of a large and complex technological machine are affected by the actions actually taken by a trained crew of skilled individuals. In probabilistic safety assessments, human reliability analysis (HRA) is used to assess the probability of successful or conversely unsuccessful human actions during transient and stressful decision making. For nuclear power plants, which are another well-known HTS where operator and human actions are required, there is even an ASME engineering standard for risk assessment (ASME RA-S-2002). This includes the explicit treatment of human error in so-called 'dependency analysis' during postulated reactor accident sequences.

The probability of human non-response (error) in a transient is handled in probabilistic safety analysis (PSA) in a number of ways, including static and dynamic terms and multipliers to include the effects and influence of cognition (understanding), implementation (action) and decision-making response (timing), as well as the human's state or basis for action (skill, rule or knowledge). The various empirical forms of the HEP functions have been summarised by G.W. Hannaman, 2005 [11]. In general, the form taken is a summation of different error components:

$$p(t) = \sum_i P_i$$

where $P_1$ is the error in detection and diagnosis, $P_2(t)$ is due to planning or non-response error, $P_3(t)$ the action error, etc., and these are also distinguished for skill, $S$, rule, $R$, and knowledge, $K$, based behaviour. The effective timescale, $t$, is based on some median decision or diagnosis time, and it is stated and clear that there are not much statistical data to support the different model elements. So appeal must be made to simulator observations, where operating staffs are put through simulated transients and their actions observed. Typical values for the probability of errors for individual tasks range from ~0.1–0.3 for non-routine or high-stress conditions, to just ~0.001 for routine tasks.

All the data and fits for the HEP values have been adjusted or normalised to some choice for the median decision or action timescale ($T_{1/2}$) based on observation of simulated events. Data on operator errors have been collected by Hannaman [11] and others for a range of some 200 simulator tests, and fitted with exponential and lognormal functions. The data and models reported show that the HEP estimates for the three classes of action are such that at any given instance the hierarchy is $p(\text{Skill}) < p(\text{Rule}) < p(\text{Knowledge})$, particularly for $P_2$, the non-response probability. So we asked Hannaman and the sponsors for access to the original data behind these unpublished functional fit curves. Although unable to release the actual data, Hannaman [12] kindly supplied us with an Excel (xls.) file containing the separate tabulations for the Skill, Rule and Knowledge probability functional fits.

To choose the needed units, $\tau$, for the experience interval to calculate the MERE failure rate and probability *during the transient*, we adopt a simple multiplier, $\xi$, making the units for the experience interval, $\xi\tau$, which then cover the possible range of timescales for Skill-, Rule- and Knowledge-based actions. The necessary assumption is that the behaviour can indeed be grouped into these three classifications.

For comparison with the MERE result for the probability of non-response error (outcome) rates for any HTS in effect, we have shifted the usual bathtub experience, $\varepsilon$, using the simple adjusted accumulated experience parameter, $\xi\varepsilon$:

$$p(\varepsilon) = 1 - \exp\{(\lambda - \lambda_m)/k - \lambda(\varepsilon_0 - \xi\varepsilon)\}$$

We adopted without any adjustment the previously determined 'best' values of $k = 3$ and $\lambda_m = 5 \times 10^{-6}$, as derived from the comparisons to the world outcome data. Recall that the minimum in the bathtub arises naturally from the intersection of the learning portion with this finite minimum, $\lambda_m\varepsilon$, at large experience.

We initially found that the lognormal functions originally used and supplied by Hannaman did not have a finite minimum probability. Hannaman, 2006 [12] then included an arbitrary constant lowest value for each of the $S$, $R$ and $K$ cases; which contrasts with the MERE minimum determined naturally by the intersection of the falling learning and rising finite minimum failure rate portions to form the bathtub. The final comparisons obtained from these choices of experience measure and minima are shown in Figure 4.13, which contains the

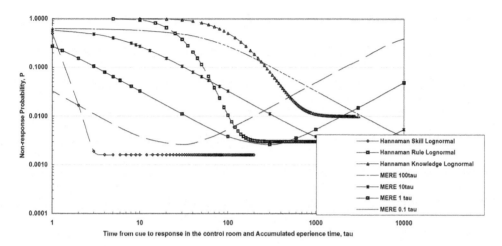

**Figure 4.13.** The Human Error Probability Comparison

MERE probability prediction and the modified lognormal functions, $p(S,K,R)$ [6]. The four MERE 'human bathtub' curves cover the range of trends exhibited by the HEP functions, using arbitrarily chosen constant experience multiplier values of $\xi = 0.1, 1, 10$ and $100$ on the experience units, $t$. The comparisons obtained from this simple choice of experience measure are shown in Figure 4.13, which contains the original Hannaman lognormal functions, $p(S,K,R)$, and the MERE probability prediction. The three MERE 'human bathtub' curves cover the range of the HEP functions, using arbitrarily chosen constant experience multiplier values of $\xi$ on the experience units, $\tau$.

Rather amazingly, the Skill, Rule and Knowledge curves generally agree with the MERE results using just these simple experience/timescale adjustments. Although it is not perfect, the agreement between the trends and magnitudes are now very encouraging given: (a) the approximations necessarily adopted in order to make the comparisons possible in the absence of the original data; and (b) the fact that the original curves are based on arbitrary (and not theoretically based) lognormal fits anyway. There is even some controversy over whether the human reliability data are even properly separable in this manner, but for our comparison purposes, we just accept the fits at their face value.

The agreement between these older data with the new MERE result is extremely encouraging given the simple shift choice made for experience, and constitutes an independent validation of the Learning Hypothesis. Hence, it clearly shows that we may use the Learning Hypothesis to determine the dynamic HEP in actual transients and events, as well as the outcomes in entire HTS.

Therefore, for estimating the HEP in PSA analysis, we recommend adopting the theoretically derived MERE 'bathtub' expression,

$$p(\tau) = 1 - \exp\{(\lambda - \lambda_{\mathrm{m}})/k - \lambda(\tau_0 - \xi\tau)\},$$

where

$$\lambda = \lambda_{\mathrm{m}} + (\lambda_0 - \lambda_{\mathrm{m}})\exp{-k(\xi\tau - \tau_0)}, \text{ and } 10 < \xi < 1,000.$$

Apparently, by shifting the experience parameter, $\tau$, we can estimate $p$(Skill) using $\xi = 10$; for $p$(Rule ), $\xi = 100$; and for $p$(Knowledge), $\xi = 1,000$, thus underlining and emphasising the performance premium obtained from having skill.

## Implications for Generalised Risk Prediction

The implications of using this new approach for estimating HEP in HRA are profound. From this comparison and analysis, we may conclude that within the uncertainties of such an analysis, the required standard HRA HEP models used in PSA can be fitted to the MERE form derived from the Learning Hypothesis. Conversely, the MERE probability (the human bathtub) properly represents all the data trends, such as they are, and hence, can be used in PRA HEP estimation provided the correct measure is taken for experience.

This new probability estimate is based on the failure rate describing the ULC, which is derived from the Learning Hypothesis, and utilises the validation from the outcome data of the world's HTSs. Thus, we have seamlessly linked all the way from individual human actions to the observed outcomes in entire systems. We have unified the approach to managing risk and error reduction using the Learning Hypothesis with the same values everywhere for the learning rate constant, $k$, and the minimum error rate, $\lambda_m$.

For the first time, we are also able to make predictions of the probability of errors and outcomes for any assumed experience interval in any HTS.

The way to do this prediction is illustrated in Figure 4.14, in which we generalise the HEP from the MERE by non-dimensionalising the experience timeframe, $\xi\tau$, available for decision making and action in any transient. We show the result of non-dimensionalising the experience interval used in the MERE to re-normalise and bracket the Skill, Rule and Knowledge data, which have also been normalised to their maximum timeframes, $t$. So for *any* transient situation provided we know or can judge the timeframe available for action, we can estimate from Figure 4.14 the probability of error at any moment or fraction within that interval of

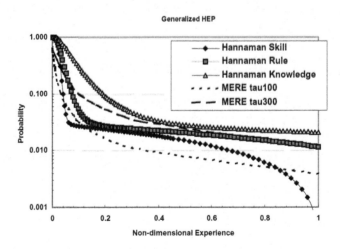

**Figure 4.14.** Generalised prediction of human error probability

risk exposure (to within an uncertainty of a factor of 10) depending on the selected, actual or desired behaviour classification.

Another implication is also that the non-response error at the HTS level, as represented by the time-adjusted MERE result, automatically and implicitly already includes the cognitive (diagnosis) and implementation (action) error probabilities. The reason is that the observed outcomes on which the analysis is based *already include* these inherent factors, as an integral part of the overall HTS. Therefore, these additional error components do not have to be distinguished or included separately in the error probability summation, as is usually the case in PSA studies.

In addition, the MERE results imply a finite lower-bound probability of $p(\varepsilon) > 10^{-3}$, based on the best values derived from all the available data. The initial (novice or starting) probability of ~0.6 decreases with accumulated experience and decision making to a finite minimum of ~$3 \times 10^{-3}$ before the effect of the learning is inevitably offset by the inexorably increasing risk exposure, which occurs with large accumulated experience.

Typically, the probabilities for error are ~$10^{-2}$, or one in a hundred, for any act of volition beyond the first 10% or so of the risk interval; whereas in that first increment or initial phase, the risk is much higher. Interestingly, this reduction in probability in the initial interval echoes, parallels and is consistent with the maze study results of Fang, discussed and displayed in Chapter 1 Figure 1.2. Fang's results showed a rapid (factor of five or so) reduction in the first 10% or so of the moves needed for success by the 'treasure hunt' players. Clearly, the same fundamental learning factors and success motivation are at work, and are reflected in the rapid decrease in errors down the learning curve.

Initially, we thought that it was perhaps also possible that these HEP data also include one hitherto unknown example of perfect learning. But actually the plunge in the fit is now known not to be believed and is invalid, thus nicely illustrating the issue of using such empirical fits. As shown in Figure 4.15, we can see the HEP suddenly decreases dramatically according to the original Hannaman Skill lognormal fit. This is precisely in accord with the perfect learning result we have derived in Appendix F, where it is shown that as soon as just one outcome ($n = 1$) occurs, none further are ever observed and the probability plummets to zero. The 'perfect learning' curve from the theory is also shown in the Figure 4.15, and reflects

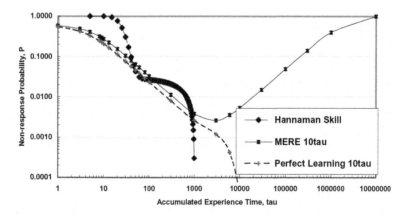

**Figure 4.15.**   Perfect Learning: a mistaken fit to an extrapolated and invalid curve

exactly the same trend. We now know that this is just a coincidence since Hannaman then updated the curve to eliminate the plunge when we informed him about this trend. As far as we know, this purely predicted theoretical 'perfect learning' limit has never been actually observed. But the implication is that an error can and has been made, by using a fit that is invalid when extrapolated since it had no clearly stated limits. Once again, we argue this is clear evidence that the use of arbitrary fitted functions is to be avoided, especially when dealing with the probability of HTS outcomes that is fundamentally non-linear.

Not surprisingly, the required cognitive corrections (the $P_1$ values) are largest for the skill behaviour, smaller for rule-based, and the lowest for knowledge-based responses. They range by a factor of 5 from 1 in 10 (0.10) to 1 in 50 (0.02). In addition, the original lognormal and Weibull functions, as apparently derived by Hannaman, obviously do not have the correct shape or asymptote at large experience without applying a finite minimum bound.

From this comparison and analysis, we may conclude that within the uncertainties of such an analysis, the standard HRA HEP models used in PSA can be fitted to the MERE form derived from the Learning Hypothesis. Conversely, the MERE probability (the human bathtub) properly represents the data trends, such as they are, and hence, can be used in PRA HEP estimation provided the correct measure is taken for experience.

In a addition, the MERE results imply a finite lower-bound probability of $p(\varepsilon) > 10^{-3}$, based on the best calculations and all the available data.

## Conclusions: The Probable Human Risk

Analysis of failure rates due to the human element and the rate of learning allow a new determination of the dynamic human error rate in technological systems, consistent with and derived from the available world data. The basis for the analysis is the 'learning hypothesis' that humans learn from experience, and consequently, the accumulated experience defines the failure rate. The exponential failure rate solution of the MERE defines the probability of human error as a function of experience.

The initial rate is given simply in the limit of rare events by the Bayesian estimate, and is proportional to the inverse of the experience accumulated up to the initial or early outcome(s). A new 'best' equation is given for the human error, outcome or failure rate, $\lambda$, which allows for calculation and prediction of the probability of human error, which is:

$$\lambda = 5.10^{-6} + \left\{ (1/\varepsilon) - 5.10^{-6} \right\} e^{-3\varepsilon}$$

We also provide comparisons to the empirical Weibull parameter fitting used in and by conventional reliability engineering and probabilistic safety analysis methods. Hence, we relate and contrast the techniques used for component failures and sociological trends with that needed for human reliability estimates. These new analyses show that Weibull fitting parameters and empirical hazard function techniques *cannot* be used to predict the human error rates and outcome probabilities, which is the dominant and major contribution to *all* accidents.

In reality, after the initial failure rate given by the purely Bayesian estimate, the subsequent failure rate is of a double exponential form, where the probability naturally follows a classic bathtub curve. The future failure rate is entirely determined by the experience; thus, the past defines the future.

Comparisons of the MERE to data from the world's commercial airlines, from the two shuttle failures, and from the nuclear plant operator transient control behaviour, show a reasonable level of accord. The results demonstrate that the error probability is dynamic and that it may be predicted using the MERE learning hypothesis and the minimum failure rate, and can be utilised for probabilistic risk analysis purposes.

## References

[1] Allison, P.D., 1984, 'Event History Analysis', Sage Publications, Thousand Oaks, CA, p. 32.
[2] Jaynes, E.T., 2003, 'Probability Theory: The Logic of Science', First Edition, Cambridge University Press, Cambridge, UK, Edited by G.L. Bretthorst.
[3] R. von Mises, 1981, 'Probability, Statistics and Truth', Dover, New York.
[4] Duffey, R.B. and Saull, J.W., 2002, 'Know the Risk', First Edition, Butterworth and Heinemann, Boston, MA.
[5] Airsafe, 2000, http://www.airsafe.com., 'Fatal Events and Fatal Event Rates from 1970–2000', September.
[6] National Aeronautics and Space Administration (NASA), 'Implementation Plan for Return to Flight', National Aeronautics and Space Administration (Available: http://www1.nasa.gov).
[7] Lewis, E.E., 1994, 'Introduction to Reliability Engineering', Second Edition, John Wiley and Sons, New York, pp. 61, 112 and 141.
[8] Tobias, P.A. and Trindade, D.C., 1986, 'Applied Reliability', First Edition, Van Nostrand Reinhold, New York, pp. 64, 70 and 117.
[9] Sveshnikov, A.A., 1968, 'Problems in Probability Theory, Mathematical Statistics and the Theory of Random Functions', Dover, New York, pp. 48, 49 and 80.
[10] Baumont, G., Bardou, S., and Matahri, N., 2000, 'Indicators of Plant Performance During Events Identified by Recuperare Method', Paper presented at Specialist Meeting on Safety Performance Indicators, Madrid, Spain, 17–19 October.
[11] Hannaman, G.W., 2005, 'Selecting Probability Models for HRA', Proceedings PSA Conference, ANS, San Francisco.
[12] Hannaman, G.W., 2006, private communications.

# 5

# Eliminating Mistakes: The Concept of Error States[1]

*'The truth belongs to everyone, but error is ours alone'*

Ken Alder *'The Measure of All Things'*

## A General Accident Theory: Error States and Safety Management

We want to reduce our risk, so we need to apply a method. We use an analogy and derive a new *emergent theory* for accident rate and occurrence prediction. We explain the observed outcomes (which appear as errors, accidents and events) as the average behaviour of a complex human-technological system (HTS), whose instantaneous microscopic or detailed behaviour cannot be described. To resolve this apparent paradox, we adopt and utilise the well-known concepts and methods of statistical physics. The hypothesis and results can explain the stochastic occurrence of failures in technological systems, coupled with the systematic key role of the human element and learning through experience. The method also potentially quantifies the impact of safety management schemes, and explains why the impact of learning changes the predictions we want to make.

What we do here is established and familiar in its basic approach, but the result themselves are novel. Also new are the use and extension of statistical physics to the concepts of learning, experience and risk.

In statistical physics, the very impossibility of predicting the instantaneous behaviour of complex physical systems led to Boltzmann's successful invention of deriving the average observed behaviour from the distribution of unobserved statistical fluctuations. The method is available in standard physics textbooks (Sommerfeld, 1956 [1]; Sherwin, 1961 [2]) and is the foundation of thermodynamics. Using this same idea translated to experience space,

---

[1] Some of the original equations were partly given in the conference paper by R.B. Duffey and J.W. Saull, 'Reliability and Failures of Engineering Systems Due to Human Errors', CMES'-04, Proceedings First Cappadocia International Mechanical Symposium, Cappadocia, Turkey, 14–16 July 2004.

we derive a physically based theory based on the distribution of *observed outcomes* (error states) for a system, where the error states define one distribution (or macrostate) out of many possible ones. Using this physical model, *we can therefore reconcile the apparently stochastic occurrence of accidents and errors with the observed systematic trend from having a learning environment.* It is further shown that learning rates depend on experience and that a formal 'experience shaping factor' emerges naturally during the total experience. We address the key question of whether and how they are indeed preventable using safety management systems (SMS).

The use of statistical techniques in modelling the physical world is well established, and quite conventional in physics and chemistry at the atomic and molecular level. We are seeking a general theory that follows the approach pioneered in the physical sciences of stating a hypothesis, modelling the phenomena while allowing for statistical behaviour, developing the working equations and testing the resulting predictions against actual data[2]. As pointed out by Bernstein, 1996 [3], the approach also satisfies Ockham's Razor, the 14th century edict adopted in science and philosophy that nothing should be more complicated than is necessary.

## The Physics of Errors

In the world and society in which we live, errors and accidents occur. As we have seen in our everyday lives, they and the opportunity for error and risk surround us. Events occur all the time, in all technologies and processes that humans have invented and use. When they are really bad, we can read about them in the newspapers, or on the web, on the TV news, or recounted in evermore detail in documentaries and historic reconstructions. They appear randomly, not only as news items but also seemingly without any obvious pattern. We do not know when they will happen.

The errors are recorded as outcomes (deaths, events, injuries, stock market crashes, losses and the like) and are the subject of investigation by humans for the assignment of cause and blame. They can also themselves be the cause of expensive inquiries, regulations and litigation.

Almost invariably, the major contribution to the cause is found to be from the human element. But like everything we observe, the occurrence of outcomes is statistical, and predictable only from the average observed behaviour. We have already shown that the rate of outcomes or events depends on the accumulated experience, as we learn from our mistakes

---

[2]Here we depart radically from the views and polemic expressed by the social scientists B. Wallace and A. Ross in 'Beyond Human Error: Taxonomies and Safety Science', Taylor and Francis, 2006, Chapter 1 et seq. of accepting statistical analysis while rejecting deterministic physical modelling methods. They do in fact adopt specific learning techniques – in their case a systematic event taxonomy – for the bottoms-up emergence of 'self-organisation', which is precisely what we term as learning from experience. Our statistical analysis results in deterministic and physically based equations that actually describe the externally observed learning curves, failure and success rates, plus the systematic outcome probabilities and error distributions emerging from the internal interactions within the overall system. The emergence of order and structure and the measurement of complexity are derived from the Information Entropy, a physical concept that is apparently not widely known or applied in the social sciences.

and errors (Duffey and Saull, 2002) [4]. But we cannot predict exactly *when and where* a given event will occur, only try to reduce its probability, or the risk, based on what we know went wrong last time. We and all society even strive to eliminate the accidents and errors we observe from 'ever happening again', using expensive enquiries which result in impressive lists of recommendations for improvement, and their implementation using empirical safety schemes. Inevitably, this results in reactive and qualitative safety management, when we would really prefer to be predictive and quantify the effect of corrective measures.

How can we reconcile the apparent randomly observed outcomes with the systematic effect of learning? How can we describe the inherent unpredictability (and inevitability) of accidents and the large contribution due to unforeseen human errors and interactions?

We present here the details of a new exercise in the adoption and adaptation of the principles and methods of statistical physics to the observation and prediction of risk, accidents and the contribution of the human element. The idea here is to find the simplest physical theory and systematically obtain the most useful results, validated against data.

The use of such physical concepts as statistical mechanics in the arena of risk and human error may at first seem an unlikely avenue of theoretical development. The field of human reliability analysis is dominated by studies of human psychology and behavioural traits in decision making, and resulting management systems concepts, not by physics. The field of statistical physics is dominated by analysis of the behaviour of atomic and molecular systems, which cannot behave like human decision makers. But by applying physics methods to the enigmas of human behaviour, we can hypothesise and use analogies that are very powerful, and show how it is possible to explain and gain insights into what we observe. The extensive work of Edwin Jaynes, 2003 [5] on the physics of statistical analysis, for example, illustrates this very well.

The use of hypotheses in theoretical analysis is the very basis of the scientific method, adopting a theory and testing it against data. This old but new physical model, in outline and results, agrees with and confirms the macroscopic Universal Learning Curve behaviour observed for technological systems, and the large contribution from the human element. The theory provides a consistent interpretation between learning models and the statistical behaviour of error occurrence, the impact of context and 'performance shaping' on learning.

All events (accidents, errors and mistakes) are manifested as *observed outcomes* that may have multiple root causes, event sequences, initiators, system interactions or contributory factors. Striking examples of these random confluences are legion in so-called accident sequences with multiple human-based causes, resulting in the risk of death in the crash of the Space Shuttle 'Columbia' being comparable to that for industrial injuries and deaths. The reason is the stochastic and pervasive contribution of the human element somewhere in the sequence of what occurred. Thus, human errors in design and operation (or failures) cause injury, accident, death and occurrence rates that for a given technological system decrease with experience. The outcomes are manifested daily as aircraft crashes, industrial injuries and accidents, auto crashes, rail derailments, near misses, ships sinking, medical mis-administrations, dam failures, etc., etc.

We explained this new learning hypothesis and statistical model idea to Professor Yuri Kirillov, of the Institute of Power Plant Engineering (IPPE) in Obninsk, Russia. Well known for his original and extensive work on fluid flow and heat transfer, he occupied a large office overlooking a tree-lined river valley, with a large desk and table and many books. With deep insight, he listened carefully, and then said something simple but very profound in its under-standing: *'It's the physics!'*.

## The Learning Hypothesis and the General Accident Theory

Based on physics and physical reasoning, we now seek a *general accident theory* that should be able to provide real predictions and be validated by and explain actual risk data. It should be testable.

Firstly, again we invoke the *Learning Hypothesis*. We have already shown that generally humans learn from their mistakes, and as a result, the error rates in a learning environment follow an exponential curve that is decreasing towards a minimum with increasing accumu-lated experience [4]. The hypothesis satisfies Ockham's Razor, in being the simplest of all hypotheses. The Learning Hypothesis is also entirely consistent with Ohlsson's psychological 'error correction' theory developed to describe individual human learning (Ohlsson, 1996) [6]. Thus, we invoke the same model and interpretation as applicable all the way from the micro-individual learning process and behaviours to the observed macro-system outcomes. In this sense, HTSs 'behave' just like a collective of *Homo sapiens* when learning and making errors. The model hypothesis is also an emergent one, which does not attempt to describe the inner unobserved myriad details behind human decision making and actions. The concept is entirely consistent with the ideas of complexity as the *'the amount of information that is discarded during the process that brings a physical object into being'* (Tor Norretranders, 1998) [7].

To recapitulate the theoretical derivation, we use the learning model for an observed error, event or accident rate, $A$. This rate is itself proportional to the failure rate, $\lambda(\varepsilon)$. The basic hypothesis is that humans learn from their mistakes as experience is gained, so the proportionality for the rate of change of the accident rate with experience is proportional to the number that are occurring (the accident rate, $A$). Thus, the *learning hypothesis* requires:

$$dA/d\varepsilon \propto A$$

or,

$$dA/d\varepsilon = -k(A - A_m)$$

where $k$ is the average 'learning rate constant' and $A_m$ the minimum possible rate. The solu-tion is derived by straightforward integration of this equation between the limits of the initial state of zero experience, $\varepsilon = 0$, when $A = A_0$, and the final condition of the minimum rate, $A_M$, at some accumulated experience, $\varepsilon = \Sigma_j \varepsilon_j$.

The equation derived from this learning hypothesis [4] that is used to correlate the data is:

$$E^* = \exp - KN^*$$

or

$$N^* = (1/K) \ln E^*$$

where $E^*$ is the non-dimensional measure of the error rate, and for correlating data, $N^*$, a non-dimensional measure or ratio of the accumulated experience, and ln is the natural logarithm. To a reasonable first approximation, when the final (minimum) rate, $A_m$, is much smaller than the initial rate, $A_0$, and/or the initial experience is negligible, we have:

$$A = A_m + A_0 e^{-k.\varepsilon}$$

Since accidents are failures, which are outcomes, the analogous expression for the general outcome or failure rate is found by simply back-substituting the outcome or failure rate, $\lambda(\varepsilon)$, for the accident rate symbol, $A$, according to:

$$\lambda(\varepsilon) \equiv \left\{ A/(N - N_j) \right\}$$

Retaining the minimum rate, the MERE expression is:

$$d\lambda/d\varepsilon = -k(\lambda - \lambda_m)$$

with the equivalent solution, taking the initial experience, $\varepsilon_0$, as small:

$$\lambda(\varepsilon) = \lambda_m + (\lambda_0 - \lambda_m)e^{-k\varepsilon}$$

Contributors to variations in the learning rate could include stress, fatigue, training, inattention, safety systems, mental models, management emphasis or the corporate culture, all overlaid on the basic way humans behave, interact and function with technological systems and machines, and with other humans. *This is all too complicated to describe easily when we do not know or cannot write equations for the workings and failings of the human mind*, especially when coupled to the system in which the humans are functioning. The impossibility of obtaining a complete physical understanding of the human (let alone the animal) learning and forgetting processes is reinforced by the massive extent of the qualitative models, terminology and ideas available in the psychological literature.

So what can we do? The major hint here is that the form of the learning result and the data is an exponential curve, so that the experience and the rate of events are linked in a physical and mathematical way. So for the second step, we invoke the concept of *error states* applicable to the observation of events as occurring stochastically within the overall learning trend, where the distribution of outcomes depends on the depth of experience. As we shall see, the resulting distribution of error states then conveys *quantitative information* that can be assimilated and utilised.

So to sidestep excessive complexity, we make a key analogy. We adopt the statistical approach of defining a distributions of errors (which are the observed outcomes), arguing that we do not and cannot know all the errors states of the system, and only observe the outcomes based on the statistically most likely behaviours.

We then do not have to know or understand all the 'rules' that may describe human and machine reliability, organisational culture and psychological reasoning, only that we must attempt to describe the actual *emergent or observed distribution* of the real outcomes (accidents, events and errors). This is known to be an exponential in the form of a learning curve. Thus, our new quantitative and general theory of errors examines and predicts the average observed behaviour of a complex system of error states (as the observed outcomes). We cannot and do not describe the detailed behaviour of the human or the machine with which it is interacting, only *the average and most likely distribution of accident outcomes* that are observed as a result of the random occurrence and existence of outcomes and interactions (errors) which contribute to the risk.

## Observing Outcomes

As we know, we observe a particular observation interval with some experience base. It is a snapshot of a moment in the world, a sample of what is happening. If you drive down the road, you or someone else may or may not have an accident in that interval, and we just record that outcome, a black or a white ball drawn from the Jar of Life. We analysed the problem of predicting the number of outcomes in Appendix F, where we show the probability of observing one outcome is exactly that given by the 'human bathtub' solution based on the Learning Hypothesis. To make this clear and help our thinking progress, let us first look at some real working examples.

Now from the Australian Traffic Safety Bureau (ATSB) we were kindly given on-line web access to their complete database for auto fatalities from 1989 to 2002 (see http://www.atsb.gov.au). We queried the database by State, driver-age, and highway speed limit. The outcomes (observed as fatalities) were distributed as shown by Table 5.1, where the numbers 0, 1, 2, ... are the number of outcomes (blackballs) observed in the experience interval shown. We took driver-age above 17 years as the surrogate measure of the depth of experience, being the licensed driver years, Dy. This is not exact, as all drivers are not licensed at the same age or time, but it is a reference that can be used as a start since actual Dy-experience is not reported. We summed up the fatalities, $n_j$, over all speed limits to estimate the total accumulated deaths,

$$N_T = \sum_I n_i(\varepsilon) = 11,538$$

And summed up the Dy's to estimate the total accumulated experience is:

$$\varepsilon = \sum_{Dy} (n_i(\varepsilon) \times Dy) = 271,264 \text{ accDy}$$

We have a matrix of error states with some 71,000 possible cells, of which 11,000 are occupied by outcomes (nearly 15%). To determine whether there is a stochastic (normal or binomial) distribution of outcomes, Figure 5.1 shows the normalised fraction of the fatalities with the normalised depth of experience, and the corresponding fitted normal distribution:

$$\text{Fatality fraction, } F = \exp 0.5 \left( \varepsilon_{Dy} / 0.2 \right)^2$$

It is evident that some 50% of the fatalities occur with less than some 10% of the depth of experience (in fact within the first 10 years of driving, or for driver-ages less than 30 years), whereas there are less than 5% for the highest experience (older) drivers. This indicates a possible fundamental influence of driver experience, and not just of age. We checked that observation, by systematically plotting the number of observed fatalities, $N_j = D$, versus the depth of experience, $\varepsilon$, in our observation interval, as in Figure 5.2.

The distribution of the number of fatalities are given by the exponential model shown as a function of the depth of experience, $\varepsilon$, in accDy:

**Table 5.1.** Error state illustrative example from traffic accidents, where observed outcomes are fatal accidents grouped by depth of experience for one speed limit in the arbitrary observation interval shown

| 1989 | 1993 | 1995 | 1996 | 1999 | 2000 | 2001 | 2002 | AccDy, $\varepsilon$ | AccDeaths, N |
|---|---|---|---|---|---|---|---|---|---|
| 0 | 0 | 0 | 0 | 0 | 0 | 2 | 2 | 4 | 4 |
| 0 | 0 | 0 | 0 | 0 | 0 | 0 | 1 | 0 | 0 |
| 0 | 0 | 0 | 0 | 0 | 0 | 0 | 0 | 0 | 0 |
| 0 | 0 | 0 | 0 | 0 | 0 | 0 | 0 | 0 | 0 |
| 0 | 0 | 0 | 0 | 0 | 0 | 0 | 0 | 0 | 0 |
| 0 | 0 | 0 | 0 | 0 | 0 | 0 | 0 | 0 | 0 |
| 0 | 0 | 0 | 0 | 0 | 0 | 0 | 0 | 0 | 0 |
| 0 | 0 | 0 | 0 | 0 | 0 | 0 | 0 | 0 | 0 |
| 0 | 0 | 0 | 0 | 0 | 0 | 0 | 0 | 0 | 0 |
| 0 | 0 | 0 | 0 | 0 | 0 | 0 | 0 | 0 | 0 |
| 0 | 0 | 0 | 0 | 0 | 1 | 0 | 0 | 2 | 1 |
| 0 | 0 | 0 | 0 | 0 | 0 | 0 | 0 | 0 | 0 |
| 0 | 0 | 0 | 0 | 0 | 0 | 0 | 0 | 0 | 0 |
| 0 | 0 | 0 | 0 | 0 | 0 | 0 | 0 | 0 | 0 |
| 0 | 0 | 0 | 0 | 0 | 0 | 0 | 0 | 0 | 0 |
| 0 | 0 | 0 | 0 | 0 | 0 | 0 | 0 | 0 | 0 |
| 0 | 0 | 0 | 0 | 0 | 0 | 0 | 3 | 9 | 3 |
| 0 | 0 | 0 | 0 | 0 | 0 | 1 | 0 | 0 | 0 |
| 0 | 0 | 0 | 0 | 0 | 0 | 0 | 0 | 3 | 1 |
| 0 | 0 | 0 | 0 | 0 | 0 | 0 | 0 | 0 | 0 |
| 0 | 0 | 0 | 0 | 0 | 0 | 0 | 0 | 0 | 0 |
| 0 | 0 | 0 | 0 | 0 | 0 | 0 | 0 | 0 | 0 |
| 0 | 0 | 0 | 0 | 0 | 0 | 0 | 0 | 0 | 0 |
| 0 | 0 | 0 | 0 | 0 | 0 | 0 | 0 | 0 | 0 |
| 0 | 0 | 0 | 0 | 0 | 0 | 1 | 0 | 4 | 1 |
| 0 | 0 | 0 | 0 | 0 | 0 | 0 | 0 | 0 | 0 |
| 0 | 0 | 0 | 0 | 0 | 0 | 0 | 0 | 0 | 0 |
| 0 | 0 | 0 | 0 | 0 | 0 | 0 | 0 | 0 | 0 |
| 0 | 0 | 0 | 0 | 0 | 0 | 0 | 0 | 0 | 0 |
| 0 | 0 | 0 | 0 | 0 | 0 | 0 | 0 | 0 | 0 |
| 0 | 0 | 0 | 0 | 0 | 0 | 0 | 0 | 0 | 0 |
| 0 | 0 | 0 | 0 | 0 | 0 | 0 | 0 | 0 | 0 |
| 0 | 0 | 0 | 0 | 0 | 0 | 0 | 0 | 0 | 0 |
| 0 | 0 | 0 | 0 | 0 | 0 | 0 | 0 | 0 | 0 |
| 0 | 0 | 0 | 0 | 0 | 0 | 0 | 0 | 0 | 0 |
| 0 | 0 | 0 | 0 | 0 | 0 | 0 | 0 | 0 | 0 |
| 0 | 0 | 0 | 0 | 0 | 0 | 0 | 0 | 0 | 0 |
| 0 | 0 | 0 | 0 | 0 | 0 | 0 | 0 | 0 | 0 |
| 0 | 0 | 0 | 0 | 0 | 0 | 0 | 0 | 0 | 0 |
| 0 | 0 | 0 | 0 | 0 | 0 | 0 | 0 | 0 | 0 |
| 0 | 0 | 0 | 0 | 0 | 1 | 1 | 0 | 12 | 2 |

Increasing Experience Depth

Observation Interval

(With kind permission of ATSB, 2002)

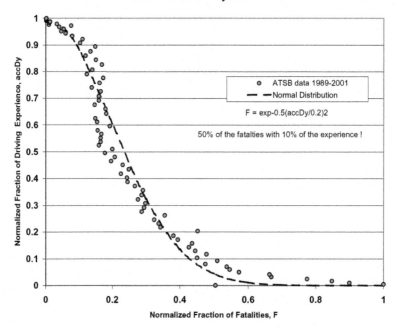

**Figure 5.1.**   Auto data

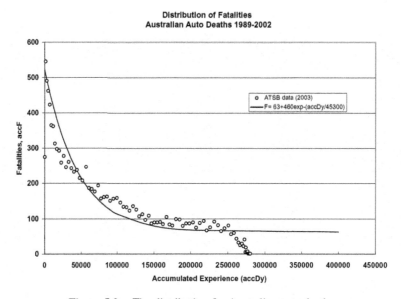

**Figure 5.2.**   The distribution for Australian auto deaths

$$\text{Number of Deaths, } D = 63 + 460 \exp - (\varepsilon/45,300)$$

with a cut-off at $\varepsilon \sim 28,000$ accDy, since there are by then no drivers active beyond age 85 years, all having died or no longer driving. This exponential is the first hint that the distribution of outcomes (deaths) in our observation interval, although apparently randomly distributed, has a systematic learning effect embedded within the data. The ratio of the initial number of 460 to the final asymptotic number of 63 is a reduction of order a factor of seven (7), very similar to the factor of five (5) reductions we observed with aircraft near midair collisions, NMACs, in Chapter 3. We do not believe that this closeness of reduction ratios is a coincidence, as we show later, although it might have seemed so superficially.

The residual or minimum number of 63 fatalities ($\pm 12$ at 95%) at the tail is also interesting: it is small and due to the irreducible influence of the human element on the HTS. This residual number corresponds to an average minimum *fatal* number of outcomes rate of:

$$\langle F \rangle = (63/270,000 \times 365 \times 24) \approx 0.00000003 = 3 \times 10^{-8} \text{ per driver-hour}$$

Now, *non-fatal* accidents or errors occur some 250 times more often than fatal ones (from the USA NHTSA estimate). So we have about $\sim 3 \times 10^{-8} \times 250 \sim 7.5 \ 10^{-6}$ non-fatal accidents per driver-hour, or circa 1 in 130,000 hours.

This error interval is almost exactly (and certainly within the precision of these estimates and calculations) the same order as the minimum error interval of $\sim 200,000$ hours that our investigations have calculated in all other human-technology interactions. It is embedded beneath the much greater number of fatal accidents caused by sheer inexperience and learning, so it is impossible to discern from average rates. Thus, when we have finally learnt, we still have a residual set of error states. However, we can eliminate error states above the minimum and reduce the risk.

Data are always key to our understanding. The results shown here, for the Australian example, provoke a key observation and insight: the distributions we have observed are not unique. They just happen to be what has been recorded in our observation interval or window on the world. The data could have been arranged (occurred) in many different ways, while conserving both experience and the number of fatal events. We just happen to have observed one macrostate (the matrix) of an arrangement of microstates, or how the fatal events are distributed. The fatalities have an exponentially decreasing form with increasing depth of experience, which seems obvious. After all, we must learn. But why do the data have that specific trend, and can we really *predict* the risk?

## A Homage to Boltzmann: Information from the Grave

So perhaps we should not try to describe all the details, but step back and ask *how to determine the distribution of the outcomes*, if we can. The clue on how to proceed comes from the field known as statistical mechanics, the art of analysing the fluctuations of the world, and averaging them to determine the behaviour, without pretending or trying to predict the actual fluctuations themselves.

We were lead in this direction by the pioneering work of Ludwig Boltzmann (1844–1906), the great mathematician and physicist. We visited his grave in Vienna in a personal homage (Figure 5.3). Just a few tram stops out of the city, the Central Cemetery is a baroque

**Figure 5.3.** The authors pay homage at Boltzmann's grave (Photo © RB Duffey, private archive)

masterpiece, full of the rich and famous families of the 18th and 19th centuries. Boltzmann's tombstone lies just across the way from those fantastic monuments of the great Brahms, Liszt and Beethoven, who made such magnificent acoustic music. (see Figure 5.3.)

Who could have predicted the power of Boltzmann's silent physical and mathematical music? The famous Boltzmann Constant, $k_B$, is a number that relates the ratio of energy to the temperature of all material. Inscribed in the stone slab above his bust is the result of his theoretical work as a silent and simple epitaph:

$$S = k_B \ln W$$

No explanation is given or indeed is needed for those who know. This result is one of the most famous theoretical achievements of the modern technological age, and in the scientific world as important as the more well-known Einstein's $E = mc^2$. In fact, the adaptation of Boltzmann's ideas to the discrete energy world of quantum mechanics did indeed presage and make possible Einstein's later atomic understandings.

Now in the above gravestone equation, $S$ is the thermodynamic entropy, a finite measure of the disorder in the universe, or of any system. It is derived from the fluctuations in state (energy) of the particles or entities that occupy the ($j^{th}$) system that we observe. The right hand side has the term, $W$, being the combination or simple measure of the number of different ways ($n_j$) outcomes can appear from among the ($N_j$) total, being the total number of possible *microstates* of a system. This term, $W$, is the link in our case to our randomly observed outcomes: *it is a measure of the order or disorder in the outcomes of our HTS and, as we shall see, in the very way that we correct errors.*

The quantity, $W$, is referred to in statistical physics as the 'degeneracy' or 'spectral multiplicity', which are elegant names for the number of possible system states. In thermodynamics, Fermi called it the 'probability' of a state, while recognising that it was really a measure of the number of possible states. In chemistry, it is known as the 'thermodynamic weight', and was termed the 'permutability' by Boltzmann himself. Physically and mathematically, $W$, is the number of possible sequences of outcomes that correspond to a particular distribution, or the number of different ways it can be realised[3]. The constant of proportionality called Boltzmann's Constant, $k_B$, is now recognised by science as a universal parameter in our description of the physical world.

It turns out that the entropy, $S$, of the Universe is forever increasing as we extract useful work from the available energy. The disorder *always* increases. The thermodynamic Entropy, $S$, is Time's Arrow, a definite and irreversible direction that the world pursues, and that all the heavens and we follow. Conversely, we cannot create order out of disorder, since we would have to run the clock backwards and reverse the processes in time.

This simple idea, both obvious and perplexing at the same time, leads directly to the arena of thermodynamics where we extract useful work, to fire up the engines of the Industrial Age. We use the order to create energy, leaving disorder behind as the residue of the process.

Boltzmann's analysis condemned us to the inevitable 'heat death of the universe', a cold state when we have extracted all that is useful, and we are left with unusable disorder. The extension to quantum theory, with the exclusion of certain states, and the knowledge that we cannot position anything beyond a certain inaccuracy, are a direct result of how we must describe our physical world at the smallest nuclear scale.

All we have to do now is to apply these ideas and concepts to the analysis or outcomes and the prediction of risk in the macroscopic world involving human interactions and experience. This task is made conceptually easier by the pre-existing basis, knowledge and techniques of statistical methods. But the development is also somewhat harder, because the application is in a totally new and unfamiliar context, and drags along all the baggage of traditional thermodynamic nomenclature, which must be discarded while the fundamental thinking must be used. It turns out that this approach also neatly encompasses the complexities of human learning and decision making in a unified manner.

---

[3]We have recently come across the use of entropy in the highly complex and mathematical field of machine or computational learning, where the concept is applied to the number of possible functions at or for a given numerical error value (see, e.g., 'Rigorous Learning Curve Bounds from Statistical Mechanics', D. Haussler, M. Kearns, H.S. Seung and N. Tishby, Machine Learning, 1996, 25, pp. 195–236, and the analysis in Appendix I).

By analogy, we simply redefine the entropy as the uncertainty or probability in what is actually observed and learned as deduced from the number of possible ways it could occur, without trying to establish the detailed, instantaneous behaviour of all the possible occurrences. In this way, the entropy turns out to be a useful measure of both: (a) complexity in decision making and skill acquisition, at the individual level; and (b) safety culture and risk perception at the collective homo-technological and social system level.

Initially unknown to us, the logical approach that we follow in dealing with the uncertainty in observed outcome information is consistent with the concepts used in the mature but apparently completely unrelated field of Information Theory. The connection between entropy as adopted in statistical mechanics has been used previously to define the probability of the number of possible inferences as a measure of the 'missing information' (Baierlein, 1971) [8]. As elegantly summarised in the text by Pierce (1980) [9], the theory was originally concerned with the encoding and transmission of signals. The use of entropy was adopted as a means to distinguish, optimise and measure the received or transmitted signal, in whatever form it is presented, from the noise, however that is measured. The applications and principals are not restricted to classical radio waves and digital data encryption, but also apply to the receipt, interpretation and observation of knowledge, words, language, symbols and information by humans (see [9]). The observation, interpretation, content and error potential in such signals are precisely the problem that we are tackling here.

So, apparently for the first time, we now are linking together the three disparate scientific fields of Thermodynamics, Communications and Psychology. This link is achieved using the unifying and powerful concept of entropy as a unique measure of the uncertainty, complexity and information content in learning. In fact, in the highly mathematical analysis of computational 'learning machines', the entropy has also been adopted as a measure of falsification.

## The Concept of Depth of Experience and the Theory of Error States

Like the Australian traffic deaths, we see errors manifested as macroscopic sets of discrete or separate outcomes that cover a whole spectrum. The gamut includes accidental deaths, ships sinking, planes or autos crashing, mis-administrations occurring, near misses happening, financial losses, stock price increases, right and wrong actions being taken, and so on.

When recorded as the time passes, each set of event data, $n$, for the time interval is usually known as an 'event history'. We are usually only sampling the full spectrum of reality, since we observe for a finite interval one of many possible distributions of outcomes that may exist or happen (say with a given interval of time, date, place, age, speed, industry, occupation ...). We have to translate our coordinates or frame of reference to one relevant to our experience. Now think of '*experience space*' as equivalent to, but instead of our usual time-passing space that we normally travel through everyday. When we observe some time interval, we have accumulated some experience up to then: and what we observe has also a depth of experience. The period during which we happen to observe and/or count the outcomes defines our range or Observation Interval, $j$. The selection of an interval arbitrarily censors the data since events or outcomes may or may not occur outside when we happen or are able to observe. The distribution of observed outcomes in experience space is one of many possible

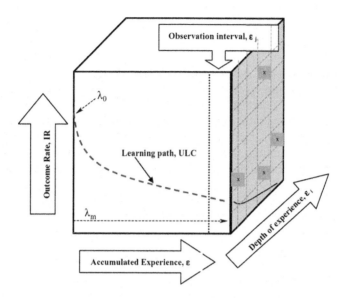

**Figure 5.4.** The cube representation of Experience Space

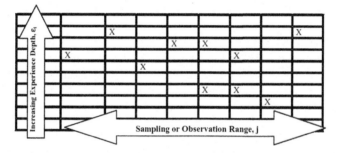

**Figure 5.5.** The Error State Matrix as a 2D slice $\varepsilon(i, j)$ of experience space for the $j$th observation interval, with outcomes distributed as the microstate pattern of $X$s, where each $X$ is a discrete outcome (accident, event, error or recorded measure)

but unique distributions. We have accumulated experience, $\varepsilon_j$, up to this interval, and have experience depth, $\varepsilon_i$, for the outcomes that occur within it.

As with statistical mechanics, we divide the outcome state (phase) space into distinct cells, defined by the existence of a possible outcome versus the level or increment of experience at which it occurs. Thus, we define an $(i, j)$ Matrix or block of cells to describe the distribution of observed error states as the pattern of the discrete outcomes, or event history data. Figure 5.4 shows a sketch in full 3D coordinates, and Figure 5.5, the 2D subset, where the $X$s are the outcomes in an arbitrarily selected interval of accumulated experience. All outcomes are assigned unique coordinates, $\varepsilon_{ij}$, according to their accumulated and depth of experience.

Therefore, we translate our world of observed outcomes to a 3D cube of 'experience space', with the three dimensions shown in our sketch in Figure 5.4. As shown here, accumulated experience increases in the horizontal $x$-direction; depth of experience increases in the $z$-direction; with the rate or number of outcomes defining the vertical or $y$-direction on the face and rear, respectively.

The ULC, representing the change in the rate of outcomes (the vertical axis) with increasing accumulated experience, is traced out on our horizontal accumulated experience axis. On the face of the cube, it starts with some initial rate, $\lambda_0$, and trends asymptotically or ultimately down towards the minimum attainable rate, $\lambda_m$, at large experience. This exponential learning curve is extremely simple in shape, and is the 'learning path' shown in Figure 5.4. In that diagram, we sketch the ULC as a dotted line on the front 2D face of 'experience space', as defined by the accumulated experience, $\varepsilon$, and the decreasing rate of outcomes, IR.

Now consider any such $j^{th}$ Observation Range, or slice of the Jar of Life. We could have observed or chosen any such range. Conventionally or usually, this Range is a time interval measured in years, hours or days, whereas we take a measure ($\tau$, tau) that is a surrogate for the learning opportunity. To visualise this in 2D space, in Figure 5.5, we rotate the $j$th observational slice from the 3D diagram, which we can do as our axes are not in physical space. For the outcomes that occur in our observation interval (the $X$s), we now allocate *experience depth* increments, $\varepsilon_i$, on one or vertical $y$-axis (denoted by, say, hours worked, driver-years, actions taken, items produced, or shipping-years at sea for the outcome in that interval). We allocate the accumulated experience, $\varepsilon_j$, that we have attained for up to the selected sampling interval, to the other horizontal $x$-axis, thus defining all experience state space, $\varepsilon(i, j)$.

In this manner, we define this $j^{th}$ range as an observational slice of accumulated experience, $\varepsilon_j$, from the entire outcome history as experience is accumulated. We observe, and will enter the total number of the observed outcomes, $n_j$, as an $X$ in a cell if it happens during the Observation Range. These $X$s represent the black balls we have drawn from the Jar of Life. Each outcome, $X$, that occurs has its own depth of experience. The presence or not of an $X$ simply indicates whether a cell or an error state, $\varepsilon_{ij}$, in the $(i, j)$ Matrix is 'occupied' by an outcome having been recorded or not.

The $i$–$j$ Matrix (which is a *macrostate*) describes then one entire distribution of the observed or unobserved error states (outcomes occurring or not) of the system. Any one of the many possible distributions of outcomes is an arrangement of *microstates, $n_i$*, by analogy to statistical mechanics. But only some microstates (forming or occupying a particular arrangement or distribution of the $X$s) have emerged or happen to have been observed as a pattern or *distribution* of outcomes or errors. It is obvious that as we observe the system we could record many different macrostates, and the pattern or arrangement is equivalent to an incomplete block of experimental data in biological assays (Finney, 1952) [10]. The increments of experience that define each 'cell' or error state can be infinitesimal to approximate a continuum, or finite as based on limited observations.

Note that, conventionally, for time-history event data recording, we would simply add up the number of $X$s in each vertical column or depth sub-interval of the $j^{th}$ Observation Range, irrespective of the experience level. *Ab initio*, we do not know the location or number of the errors in all the $n_i$ microstates that may exist since they simply occur as depth of experience and accumulated observation occurs. Summing the events or outcomes in the rows for each (level of) experience interval, $\varepsilon_i$, gives the number of $X$s as experience depth accumulates.

*The physical quantity, $\varepsilon_i$ denotes the experience level for the depth of experience.* The vertical experience depth or $y$-axis can be viewed as a continuum of levels, using an appropriate measure of experience that is relevant for learning with the given technological system we are observing. It is *not* right to adopt the usual measure of calendar time passing for our experience interval, though it may be related. Thus, the measure of experience depth for the $j^{th}$ interval can be the interval afloat for manned and crewed ships; the distance traveled by humans operating a machine; the years since obtaining a driving licence; the span or production rate working in a mine or a factory; the number of patients treated by a medical system; the number of forms and items processed or produced by a bureaucracy or a factory; or lines of coding entered in a software routine [4]. We designate these generally as measuring experience in practical 'tau' units, $\tau$, for whatever and whichever surrogate is adopted. In the psychological literature, this depth corresponds to 'consciousness', the placing into context of our experience, so we may propose that a parallel meaning or physical analogy here between these ideas.

There are many, many hypothetical macrostates (occupancy distributions) of the same number, $N_j$, of $X$s (outcomes) with the same total experience, $\varepsilon_j$. We note that any number of error outcomes, the black balls shown by the $X$s, can be distributed many different ways in the experience $\varepsilon(i, j)$ 'space' or range which we happen to be observing. In the above example, we have arbitrarily taken 10 outcomes, and randomly allocated them as subsystem 'error states' in the macrostate of 90 possible experience states, $F(\varepsilon_{ij})$, that we are observing.

So each possible different pattern of $X$s, those drawn from the Jar of Life, defines one of the distributions of outcomes or microstate occupation, $n_i$ $(\varepsilon)$, is a function of the chosen measure of experience, $\varepsilon$. Thus, we have now observed that the outcomes are distributed around in some microstate pattern that is not known beforehand. Different outcomes and hence patterns of $X$s representing many microstates, would and could have occurred for the same system over any other Interval or Range, whether we observed or recorded it or not. We just happen to have observed and illustrated one of them. Even for just the very simple case shown in Figure 5.5 there are a staggering number of more than $10^{12}$ (one million million, or a trillion) different possible ways to distribute the 10 $X$s or number of distinguishable outcomes, $N_j$, among the 90 error states.

We now make a postulate that although we just happened to observe the outcome distribution, it is not unique (see Appendix F). It is one of many possible distributions, sequences or patterns of outcomes[4]. For the same system, we could have observed another completely different macrostate, or microstate distribution of outcomes, but now while still conserving both the:

1. constant total number of outcomes, $N_j = \Sigma\ n_i$, and
2. constant total experience, $\varepsilon_j = \Sigma\ n_i\ \varepsilon_i$.

---

[4]Without the constraint of conserving the total experience, the number of random possible combinations of $N_j$ outcomes distributed among $F_{ij}$ experience states is, as usual,

$$^F C_N = \binom{F_{ij}}{N_j} \equiv \left( \frac{F_{ij}!}{N_j!(F_{ij} - N_j)!} \right).$$

**Figure 5.6.** The outcomes may appear arranged in one of many sequences, patterns or order with the non-outcomes, like this single black ball in one possible location among the white ones on the table (Photo © RB Duffey, private archive)

In our chosen $j^{th}$ observation range, the $N_j$ errors exist (just 10 are shown in our Figure 5.5 as $X$s), and by observing we do not change them or their existence. The distribution of outcomes changes stochastically, but the number of errors, $N_j$, observed as outcomes are 'conserved' for a given experience. Thus, although the macrostate number is unaltered by observation, the microstate distribution may change, while the allowable distributions are now constrained by the conservation criteria of fixed total outcomes and experience.

*All microstates (distributions or arrangements) of outcomes are equally likely.*

Interestingly, this statement for error state arrangements is an exact mirror of Laplace's, 1814 [11] 'equally probable' requirement for outcomes in the classical definition of probability, $p = n/N$. The outcomes have an equally probable, uniform but random chance of appearing, or of being observed, in some pattern or sequence out of many such possible arrangements, even though their probability varies systematically in some manner with experience. Thus, the statistical mechanics of distributions is entirely consistent with the classical statistics of observing outcomes. (See Figure 5.6.)

We do not yet know the overall or average arrangement or distribution of errors, or the total, but physics can now provide the tools. We are sampling the outcomes in two-dimensional 'experience' space, $\varepsilon(i, j)$. Hence, it is important to describe theoretically the number of distributions of outcomes (microstates) in this two-dimensional 'experience' space.

## The Fundamental Postulates of Error State Theory

We now lay the theoretical foundation, and to do that we make some basic postulates that we must justify and prove later. We simply translate the concepts used in and by statistical mechanics to 'experience space', which is analogous to the translation of static thermodynamics to collision theory. By our analogy, the fundamental postulates needed for developing Statistical Error State Theory (SEST) are adapted from the statistical physics for a closed system with an $\varepsilon(i, j)$ state space of experience:

a) all error configurations or distributions of outcomes occupy or describe a microstate, $n_i$, of the system;

b) all microstates are equally likely, and hence can occur in any $j$th interval as a distribution of outcomes with total accumulated experience, $\varepsilon_j$;

c) the outcome microstates are observed stochastically but the distribution is a systematic function of experience depth, $\varepsilon_i$;

d) the total number of outcomes (errors and failures) that exist, $N_j = \Sigma_i n_i$, distributed among the error states are conserved for the $j^{th}$ observation range;

e) total accumulated experience, $\varepsilon_j = \Sigma_i \, n_i \, \varepsilon_i$, in the $j^{th}$ observation range is finite and conserved for the observed outcomes;

f) the distribution with depth of experience that exists of the microstates is, on average, the most likely; and

g) the most likely macrostate distribution is that which gives a maximum or minimum number of microstates for a given number of outcomes for a fixed total experience.

These are postulates at this stage, not necessarily facts. We must examine the result against data and predictions. For example, as we shall see, theory not only predicts that the errors are indeed normally distributed within the observation interval, but also that the resulting distributions are of exponential shape with increasing experience.

## The Information in Error States: Establishing the Risk Distribution

Now for the above discussion to be useful, and most of all quantitative and testable, we utilise the proffered physical description to discover the mathematical relations. For simplicity, we adapt the approach of statistical mechanics in the introductory physics text by Sherwin, 1961 [2]. As before, we distribute the total observed errors or outcomes, $N_j$ (shown as an arbitrary 10 capital $X$s in our Figure 5.5) of fixed total experience, $\varepsilon_j$, in many different ways as $\Sigma_i n_i$ microstates in the $j^{th}$ observation interval. The $j$-subsystems and '$ij$-error states' matrix are only weakly interacting, so changes in one do not drastically affect others. They are independent outcomes, just like the drawing of the balls from the Jar of Life.

We now want to know how probable things like outcomes are, and how the arrangements that we might have and the number of outcomes vary with experience. For each $i$th microstate, $n_i$, the probability, $p_i$, of an outcome microstate at any depth for a total number of $N_j$ outcomes is given by the Laplace, 1814 [11] relation:

$$p_i \sim \left( n_i / N_j \right)$$

Now all microstates are equally likely: any one can occur. There are many, many combinations or distribution of the outcomes, $N_j$, that are possible among the many different microstates, $n_i$. The number of possible combinations, $W_j$, is given by:

$$W_j \Rightarrow N_j! / \Pi n_i !$$

where conventionally, the product $\Pi\, n_i\,! = n_1\,!\,n_2\,!\,n_3\,!\,\dots\,n_i\,!$. The measure of the overall State of Order (or Disorder), $H$, in the system is described by the usual definition, being the probability of the $n_i$ distributions (Greiner et al., 1997) [12]:

$$H_j = N_j! \prod (p_i/n_i\,!)$$

Following Jaynes, [5] and Pierce [9], we have distinguished the 'information entropy' by using a different symbol, H, from the usual one in thermodynamic use, $S$. As defined here, $H$ has nothing to do with thermodynamics: we have simply used the same model assumptions to derive the distributions and the probabilities. In Jaynes [5] (p. 353) terminology, $H$ is here the most likely measure of the uniformity of a probability distribution, or the 'amount of uncertainty'. It is a direct measure of the unobserved complexity of the observed system outcomes. In Information Theory, the common usage of the entropy, $H$ is as a measure of the amount of choice in the rate of the number of possible binary combinations or ways that any message, signal or symbol can be encoded, encrypted, transmitted, or presented to a receiver/ observer (see Pierce [9] pp. 78–105). Conversely, it is a measure of the uncertainty as to what will actually be received or, as we shall see later, how it may be actually perceived. In our interpretation, this uncertainty is a measure of the probability of error, recalling that this is the converse of the probability of success, which we can now call 'certainty'. With our intent and interest in managing risk and safety, the entropy, $H$, then simply reflects how we observe, interpret or perceive the distribution of HTS outcomes occurring in our experience interval.

Jaynes also made a prophetic remark, which inspired us to pursue this analysis for the case of human error, risk and accidents, when he wrote:

> If we do accept the expression for entropy, as the correct expression for the 'amount of uncertainty' represented by a probability distribution, this will lead us to a much more unified picture of probability theory in general. It will enable us to see that the ... many frequency connections are special cases of a single principle, and that statistical mechanics, communication theory, and a mass of other applications are all instances of a single method of reasoning.
>
> Quoted from E.T Jaynes, 'Probability Theory', pp. 353–354

Interestingly, the entropy, $H$, has also been proposed as a natural measure of knowledge, or a 'scoring rule' or calibration in the elicitation of expert judgement (Woo, 1999) [13]. Differences between experts are adjusted by weighting the value of H assigned to the each expert's judgement of the probability of assumed or presumed outcomes.

We are adapting this method of reasoning to human behaviour and risk. Now only specific distributions of the microstates can satisfy the physical and hence mathematical restraints. The conditions we seek for the risk case are here given in mathematical form:

1. finding a maximum or a minimum number of microstates, as a condition for learning, ($dn/d\varepsilon = 0$), so that the observed distribution is the most likely;
2. conserving the total experience ($\Sigma\, n_i\,\varepsilon_i$ = constant, $\varepsilon_j$), since we have a closed system and an arbitrary but fixed amount of knowledge and learning; and
3. conserving the number of outcomes ($\Sigma n_i$ = constant, $N_j$) as we only have a fixed number of actual outcomes, and hence, being invariant for small changes.

Note that the outcomes themselves may be either *distinguishable* or *indistinguishable*, as for quantum statistics, in the sense that the outcomes may be unique or may be a repeat event. They are independent. This distinction has the effect of changing the number of allowed/ observed microstates (or distributions) as the population of outcomes as a function of experience, $n_i(\varepsilon_i)$, changes.

Now, as before the number of possible arrangements are,

$$W_j = N_j! / \prod n_i!$$

where, from Stirling's formula for large numbers,

$$N_j! \approx (N_j/e)^{N_j} \quad \text{and} \quad n_i! \approx (n_i/e)^{n_i}$$

Using the exact same derivation as used in statistical mechanics by Sommerfeld [1] and Sherwin [2], for example, substituting the above estimate leads to the number of possible combinations,

$$\ln W_j \approx N_j \ln N_j - \sum n_i \ln n_i$$

where the summation with depth is given conventionally by

$$\sum n_i \ln n_i = n_1 \ln n_1 + n_2 \ln n_2 + \ldots \ldots + n_i \ln n_i$$

This simple-looking expression for the possible combinations leads directly to the measure of disorder, the *information entropy, $H_j$*, per observation interval.

In terms of probabilities based on the frequency of microstate occupation, $n_i = p_i N_j$ and using Stirling's approximation, we find the classic result for the information entropy [8, 9]:

$$H_j = -\sum p_i \ln p_i$$

and the *maximum value occurs for a uniform distribution of outcomes*. Interestingly, this is of course also the Laplace–Bayes result, when $p(P) \sim 1/N$ for a uniform risk.

These two classic results for $W_j$ and $H_j$ are literally full of potential information, and are also in terms of parameters we may actually might know, or at least be able to estimate.

The above result for the Information Entropy, $H$, thus corresponds to the famous thermodynamic formula on Boltzmann's grave $S = k_B \ln W$, where, $k_B$, corresponded to the physical proportionality between energy and temperature in atomic and molecular systems. But there the similarity but not the analogy ends: the formulae both look the same, but refer in our case to probability distributions in HTS, not in thermodynamic systems. In our case, for the first time, we are *predicting* the distribution of risk, errors, accidents, events, and decisions and how they vary with depth of experience and learning, in a completely new application. In fact, since $H$ is a measure of Uncertainty, we can now define the Certainty, $C$, as now given by, say, $C = 1 - H$, which is parallel to the definition of Exergy as the converse of Entropy in the analysis of thermal systems.

Provided we can now find the probability distribution of the outcomes, we can measure the entropy. In the special case of the outcomes being described by a continuous random variable, as for a learning curve, we can replace the summation over discrete intervals with an integral function:

$$H_j = -\int p_i \ln p_i \, dp$$
$$= p_i^2 \left( \frac{1}{4} - \frac{1}{2} \ln p_i \right)$$

Now we are observing an accumulated experience interval with a fixed and finite number of outcomes, in a macrostate arrangement that is one of many possible ones. We hypothesise that the most likely distribution is the one we happen to have observed! This is equivalent to the maximisation or minimisation of (information) entropy principle, which is discussed at length by Jaynes [5]. From the separate conditions of constancy of experience and outcomes, for any small change in the distribution, total experience and number of outcomes are insensitive or invariant so:

$d\left(\ln W_j\right) = 0$, for no change in the probability of a given microstate distribution

$d\left(\sum n_i \varepsilon_i\right) = \sum_i \varepsilon_i dn_i = 0$, for no change in total experience with invariant $i^{th}$ increments

$\sum dn_i = 0$, for no change in the total number of outcomes, $N_j$, and hence, in the total microstate distribution

Thus, we seek the most likely outcome distribution for the events and experience that we happen to have observed.

## The Exponential Distribution of Outcomes, Risk and Error States

With the preceding conditions, we can now solve the entire problem, thanks to the pioneers who analysed random distributions at the atomic level. By analogy to known and traditional statistical physics, the fundamental distribution of microstates as a function of experience that satisfies these three conditions is given by a classic Boltzmann–Gibbs–Maxwell exponential equation (cf. Sherwin's [2] derivation for statistical thermodynamics). The distribution of microstates with experience is then given by the formula:

$$d\left(\ln W\right) = \sum dn_i \ln\left(n_i + \alpha - \beta \varepsilon_i\right) = 0$$

or solving,

$$n_i = n_0 \exp(\alpha - \beta \varepsilon_i)$$

where $\alpha$ and $\beta$ are constants which are unknown at this stage, and $n_0$ the number of microstates or distributions at the initial or zeroth level ($i = 0$) of experience, $\varepsilon_0$. The microstate occupancy number, $n_i$, is now defined as a function of the depth of experience, and is an exponential. This exponential form is exactly what we observed with the Australian auto deaths: *it is the distribution of risk for a given experience interval*.

   As measured by the occupancy of states, *risk decreases as we gain depth of experience*, and this decrease is exactly the trend we found buried in the Australian traffic fatality data (see Figure 5.2).

This form of exponential occupancy distribution relation is called the Gibbs function or the Boltzmann distribution in the scientific fields of thermodynamics, statistical physics and quantum mechanics. The relation was used with great success when first derived in the 19th century to describe thermodynamic systems, (Sommerfeld) [1], and later adapted in the 20th century to the probability of states in quantum systems (Sherwin et al.,) [2]. All we have done is extend the use and application of statistical models from the microscopic world of energy flow to the treatment of macroscopic outcomes, as Jaynes [5] had suggested it might.

Any microstate distribution is governed by this expression for the exponential distribution: it is itself universal, although the chosen parameters may vary.

As we saw, the equivalent probability of this or any $i$th microstate is just the same as Laplace's definition, being the ratio of the microstate distribution occupancy to the total outcomes:

$$p_i = n_i \Big/ \sum n_i = n_i \big/ N_j$$

The expression for the probability of any $i$th microstate that follows is then, with the usually adopted exponential model for a given total, $N_j$,

$$p_i = p_0 \exp(\alpha - \beta \varepsilon_i)$$

*The probability of risk also decreases with increasing depth of experience.* The form of the distribution is similar to that adopted for the fractional population change during species extinction (Gott, 1993) [14], where in that case, the parameter $\beta$ is a constant extinction rate rather than a learning constant.

We note that since we have observed the outcomes, the usual normalisation condition for all the $N$ outcomes to exist is, summing the probabilities over all, $j$, observation ranges,

$$\sum_j p_i = 1$$

This normalisation, says simply that whatever happened or happens must occur. *The risk always exists, somewhere in observational space.* The summation leads to a set of so-called 'partition functions', $\Phi$, obtained by summing over our chosen observation intervals, or over all the observation space. Thus,

$$p_i = p_0 \exp(\alpha - \beta \varepsilon_i) \Big/ \sum_j p_0 \exp(\alpha - \beta \varepsilon_i)$$

or,

$$p_i = \exp(\alpha - \beta \varepsilon_i)/\Phi, \quad \text{where} \quad \Phi = \sum_j \exp(\alpha - \beta \varepsilon_i)$$

So we have the opportunity to estimate the distributions for all observation space, even into the future $(j + 1, j + 2, \text{etc.})$, if we know how the depth and accumulated experience will evolve. We can now make predictions!

## The Total Number of Outcomes

We know that we observe outcomes in any interval, that the rate and number (should) have followed a learning curve, and that the probability of observing more than one outcome decreases rapidly at any experience. For the moment, we restrict ourselves to the outcomes we observed the $j^{th}$ range of observation, and think of the larger sample including the future as some number $j + 1, j + 2$, etc., of similar intervals stacked together side-by-side to the $j$th interval. Now the total number of outcomes or errors observed in the entire $j^{th}$ range in the closed system are conserved, and equal to the total occupancy number of microstates, so that:

$$N_j = \sum_i n_i(\varepsilon)$$

So to determine $n_j$, we must sum the populations of all the possible microstates (represented by the distributions of outcomes) together over all the experience intervals to determine the total number of outcomes.

Assume for the moment infinitesimally discrete intervals of experience depth, $\varepsilon_i = 0, \varepsilon, 2\varepsilon,$ $3\varepsilon \dots$ representing the 'levels' of experience $i = 0, 1, 2 \dots$ for the $j^{th}$ interval.

At the level $\varepsilon_0$ with no experience, $\varepsilon = 0$, and there are $n_0$ microstates;
At level $\varepsilon_1$ there are $n_1 = n_0 \exp(\alpha - \beta\varepsilon)$ microstates;
At $\varepsilon_2$ we have $n_2 = n_0 \exp(\alpha - 2\beta\varepsilon)$ microstates, and so on for all the $i^{th}$ increments of experience, and as $\varepsilon_i \to \infty$,

$$n_i \to n_0 e^\alpha$$

We may regard these intervals of experience as just those that happen to exist when we observe the outcome distributions for any particular macrostate.

The total number of errors or outcomes, $N_j$, appearing in the experience interval, $\varepsilon_j$, is then given by summing or integrating the distribution of $n_i$ microstates over all the discrete experience depth level or increments, for all the microstates, for all experience levels $i = 0, 1, 2 \dots$ $n$, so:

$$N_j = \sum_i n_i(\varepsilon) = n_0 + n_1 + n_2 + \dots + n_i$$
$$= n_0 + n_0 \exp(\alpha - \beta\varepsilon) + n_0 \exp(\alpha - 2\beta\varepsilon) + \dots$$

Writing the usual symbol, e, for the exponential function, we have the distribution,

$$N_j = n_0 + n_0 e^{(\alpha-\beta\varepsilon)} + n_0 e^{(\alpha-2\beta\varepsilon)} + \dots$$
$$= \{n_0 / (1 - e^{\alpha-\beta\varepsilon})\}$$

Provided that $e^{\alpha-\beta\varepsilon} \ll 1$, (i.e., large experience and learning rate, $\beta\varepsilon \ll 1$) to first order the equilibrium outcome rate per observation interval is the distribution of number of microstates (outcomes) with experience,

$$N_j \approx n_0 + n_0^* e^{-\beta\varepsilon} - \dots$$

where $\beta$ is now the (effective learning) constant, and $n_0^* = n_0 e^\alpha$ is a constant related to the so-called partition function.

*Thus, the total number of outcomes or errors is distributed to first order as decreasing exponentially with increasing depth of experience, $\varepsilon$, in any given observation interval.* As required, the distribution of $n_j$ with incremental experience is invariant with small changes

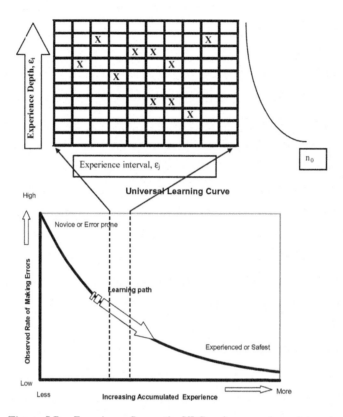

**Figure 5.7.** Experience Space, the ULC and an experience interval

in the number of outcomes, and is the so-called equilibrium distribution. Thus, at small experience, $\varepsilon_i \to 0$, the number of outcomes $N_j \to n_0 e^{\alpha}$, and at large experience, $\varepsilon_i \to \infty$, $N_j \to n_0$. So the reduction ratio is $\sim e^{\alpha}$, a constant.

The 2D diagram that describes an observational slice of experience space is shown schematically in the Figure 5.7 as a segmentation of the ULC for any arbitrary chosen experience interval. Here, the observation interval at a certain accumulated experience, $\varepsilon_j$, has embedded within it the distribution of microstates, $n_i$, that decreases exponentially with depth of experience, $\varepsilon_i$. The outcomes appear in the $j^{th}$ interval as the $X$s representing the variation of occupation with depth of experience within that interval.

## The Observed Rate and the Minimum Number of Outcomes

We can check that this new result satisfies the constraint of a minimum or a maximum observed outcome number, while conserving errors and experience, as follows. For a minimum or maximum, recall that:

$$\left(\mathrm{d}N_j / \mathrm{d}\varepsilon\right) = 0,$$

now, we have,

$$\left(\mathrm{d}N_j/\mathrm{d}\varepsilon\right) = -\beta n_0^* e^{-\beta \varepsilon}$$

which requires that

$$N_j \ (\text{max or min}) \rightarrow n_0.$$

This is the base and irreducible value of the constant number of outcomes for the initial or zeroth microstate, with probability $p_0 = n_0/N_j$. Thus, we have an invariant zeroth order number of error states (outcomes).

The required second differentiation condition gives

$$\left(\mathrm{d}^2 N_j/\mathrm{d}^2\varepsilon\right) = \beta^2\left(N_j - n_0\right),$$

and is clearly positive since in general $N_j > n_0$. Hence the exponential result represents a *minimum*, which was and is the desired ultimately attainable number of error state outcomes.

*The total number of microstates or outcomes,* $\mathrm{N}_j$, *is and must be related to the accident, error or event rate that we observe.*

Now, we need to relate the usual statistics on accident, event or injury rates, $A$. Out of a total possible number of outcomes of $N = \Sigma N_j$, we have the rate of observed outcomes with changing experience given by:

$$\lambda(\varepsilon) = \left\{\left(1/\left(N - N_j\right)\right)\left(\mathrm{d}N_j/\mathrm{d}\varepsilon\right)\right\}$$

where in terms of an observed or recorded accident or outcome rate,

$$A = \mathrm{d}N_j/\mathrm{d}\varepsilon \equiv \mathrm{d}n/\mathrm{d}\varepsilon$$

Now, we have the distribution given by

$$N_j = n_0 + n_0 e^{(\alpha - \beta\varepsilon)} + n_0 e^{(\alpha - 2\beta\varepsilon)} + \ldots$$
$$= \left\{n_0/\left(1 - e^{\alpha - \beta\varepsilon}\right)\right\}$$

To first order,

$$\left(\mathrm{d}N_j/\mathrm{d}\varepsilon\right) = -\beta n_0^* e^{-\beta\varepsilon} + \ldots$$
$$= -\left(N_j - n_0\right)\beta,$$

where $n_0^* = n_0 e^{\alpha}$ and is *not* a function of experience.

We obtain the outcome (accident or event) rate for the $j^{\text{th}}$ interval as,

$$A = \beta\left(N_j - n_0\right)$$
$$= \beta n_0 \left\{1 + e^{(\alpha - \beta\varepsilon)} + e^{(\alpha - \beta\varepsilon)} + \ldots\right\}$$

Recall that the usual normalisation condition for all the $N$ errors to exist is, summing over all, $j$, observation ranges,

$$\sum\nolimits_j p_i = 1$$

Alternatively, to find the rate at which the errors or outcomes vary per interval of experience, we could divide the expression for the total number of outcomes on both sides by the total experience in the observation interval, $\varepsilon_j$. Thus,

$$A = dN_j/d\varepsilon \equiv \left(N_j/\varepsilon_j\right) \approx \left(n_0/\varepsilon_j\right) + \left(n_0^*/\varepsilon_j\right)e^{-\beta\varepsilon}$$

We may then equate the total number of error microstates per unit experience, given by $(n/\varepsilon)$ or $(\beta n)$ from the microscopic statistical theory for any $j^{th}$ observation or experience interval as equivalent to the observed error, event or outcome rate per unit experience.

In terms given by the outcome rates, the $IR$ or $A$ in the macroscopic learning model we have, assuming the bases for the Accumulated and Depth of experience to use the same measure,

$$\lambda(\varepsilon) = \left\{\left(1/\left(N - N_j\right)\right)\left(dN_j/d\varepsilon\right)\right\},$$

where $A \equiv dN_j/d\varepsilon$, and the equivalences are:

$$\left(N_j/\varepsilon_j\right) \text{ or } \left(\beta N_j\right) \equiv A, \text{ the event or outcome rate in any interval}$$
$$\left(n_0/\varepsilon_j\right) \text{ or } (\beta n_0) \equiv A_m, \text{ the minimum attainable rate, and also}$$
$$\left(n_0^*/\varepsilon_j\right) \text{ or } \left(\beta n_0^*\right) \equiv A_0, \text{ the initial rate.}$$

*The statistical theory result is now just like the ULC.*

These equivalences also imply that the ratio between the initial and minimum rates and is simply $(A_m/A_0) = e^\alpha$, a constant, as well as for the number of outcomes. This is a new result and is consistent with the empirical observation of a typical reduction in error interval, $(A_m/A_0)$, of roughly one order of magnitude (a factor of 10). Recall that the NMACs in Chapter 3 show a reduction ratio with increasing depth of experience of a factor of five; and the Australian auto deaths in this Chapter a factor of seven. Since $\alpha = -\ln$ (reduction ratio), this parameter has the observationally determined value of $\sim -1.6$ to $-1.9$.

It is surely no coincidence that Safety Management Systems also claim to achieve this order of magnitude reduction, and in that particular case, the value of $\alpha \approx \ln 0.1$, or $\sim -2.3$. We also know from the ULC fit to world data that $\beta \sim 3$, which confirms that in practice, $\beta\varepsilon \ll \alpha$, for finite experience.

From the expressions for the outcome occurrence rate, we can now write as an observed accident or error rate, per unit experience to first order:

$$A \approx A_m + A_0 e^{-\beta\varepsilon}$$

where $A_m$ and $A_0$ are the minimum and the initial rates, respectively. This expression is exactly the same form as that obtained from the 'learning hypothesis', and we will return to this result a little later.

Thus, we are saying physically that for a nominal experience, the observed macroscopic outcomes from a system are the summation of the different distributions of the microscopic error states within the system. *For any Observation Range, the total number of microstates, $N_j$, observed per interval of experience is indeed proportional to the accident, error or event rate that we record as outcomes.*

## Accumulated Experience Measures and Learning Rates

We happen to have observed the $n_i$ microstates of a closed system in a given observation interval, which has a total accumulated experience, $\varepsilon_j$ ($\equiv$the acc$\varepsilon$). Within this $j^{th}$ observation range, this is given by the sum of all the experience depths in all microstates, i.e.,

$$\varepsilon_j = \sum_i (\varepsilon_i n_i)$$

To evaluate this summation, we make an assumption that the levels of experience are equal discrete increments, $\varepsilon$, so that the experience levels are $\varepsilon_i = 0, \varepsilon, 2\varepsilon, 3\varepsilon \ldots$ for $i = 0, 1, 2 \ldots n$.

Now the number of microstates at any experience depth $\varepsilon_i$ is given by the distribution function,

$$n_i = n_0 \exp(\alpha - \beta \varepsilon_i)$$

There is nominally no experience at first, so at $i = 0$, $\varepsilon_0 = 0$, and the total accumulated experience is given by the summation for each increment in experience depth:

$$\varepsilon_j = (0) \times (n_0 e^{\alpha}) + (\varepsilon) \times (n_0 e^{\alpha - \beta \varepsilon}) + (2\varepsilon) \times (n_0 e^{\alpha - 2\beta \varepsilon}) + (3\varepsilon) \times (n_0 e^{\alpha - 3\beta \varepsilon}) + \ldots$$

So,

$$\varepsilon_j = \varepsilon n_0 e^{\alpha - \beta \varepsilon} (1 + 2e^{-\beta \varepsilon} + 3e^{-2\beta \varepsilon +} \ldots)$$

$$\varepsilon_j = \varepsilon n_0 e^{(\alpha - \beta \varepsilon)} / (1 - e^{-\beta \varepsilon})^2$$

or, since $N_j \sim n_0/(1 - e^{\alpha - \beta \varepsilon})$, we may write this as:

$$\varepsilon_j \approx \varepsilon N_j \left\{ (e^{\alpha - \beta \varepsilon}) / (1 - e^{-\beta \varepsilon})^2 \right\}$$

Grouping the terms in the curly brackets and denoting this parameter as $\Psi$, for the $j^{th}$ interval,

$$\varepsilon_j = \varepsilon N_j \Psi$$

Hence, the total experience, $\varepsilon_j$, is simply related by this 'shape' term, $\Psi$, to the incremental experience, $\varepsilon$, via the average experience, $\langle \varepsilon \rangle$, in the $j^{th}$ interval. Hence,

$$\langle \varepsilon \rangle = \varepsilon_j / N_j = \Psi \varepsilon.$$

Evaluating this relation numerically, and assuming from data $\alpha \sim -\beta \sim 0(3)$, we find that for $\varepsilon = \tau$ units, for all $\tau \geq 1$, we have both $\Psi \lll 1$ and $|\varepsilon| \lll 1$ also. Therefore, since $e^{\alpha - \beta \varepsilon} \lll 1$, the experience in the $j^{th}$ interval tends to $\varepsilon_j \rightarrow \varepsilon N_j$, the sum of the observed depth of the outcomes actually experienced, as to be expected. This implies that the unit increment of experience naturally must be $\varepsilon \rightarrow 0$ ($\varepsilon_j/N_j$), being the experience depth increment divided by the number of outcomes in the observation interval.

The function $\Psi = \Psi(\beta, \varepsilon)$ we call the *experience-shaping parameter* (ESP), that is derived directly from the observed distribution of outcomes with depth of experience as learning occurs. We can see immediately that, provided $|\alpha| \ll |\beta \varepsilon|$, $n_j$ decreases as experience

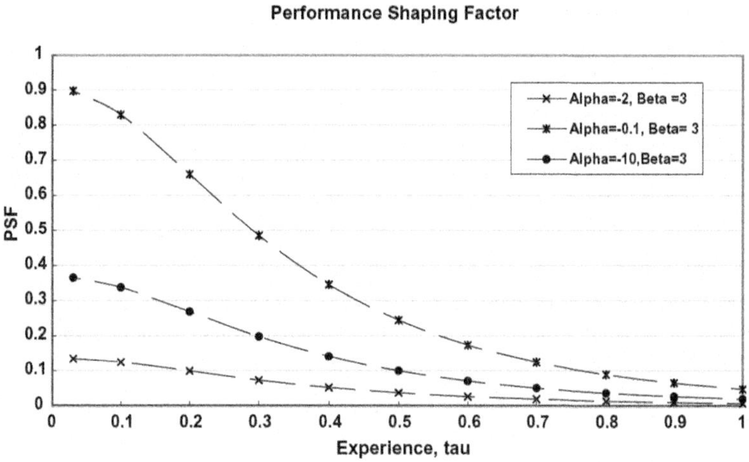

**Performance Shaping Factor**

**Figure 5.8.** The value of the Experience-Shaping Parameter, $\Psi$, with relative depth of experience

increases, which is the formal *condition for the existence of learning*. Note this is consistent with the previously estimated values of $\alpha \sim -2$ and $\beta \sim 3$ for the world outcome data.

Having no ESP is clearly undesirable. To evaluate the expression for the ESP numerically, we use the typical observed value for $\beta$ and a range of values for $\alpha$, since we must infer them. This calculation gives the curves shown in the Figure 5.8 of the ESP varying with depth of experience in tau units. Basically, the early inexperience causes different results, but as experience is gained the averages become similar. The reduction of a factor of several in the average, due to the decreasing ESP with increased learning, agrees very well with the trends shown by data.

Equivalently, we can say that by learning, we have reduced the total number of outcome microstates. For this learning environment limit of $\alpha \ll \beta\varepsilon$, then $\Psi \to (e^{\beta\varepsilon} - 1)^{-1}$ and

$$\varepsilon_j = \varepsilon N_j \big/ \left(e^{\beta\varepsilon} - 1\right)$$

This would give a very much more rapid decline in the average, particularly if it were possible to gain experience quickly!

From our analysis, the interval of experience $\varepsilon = \varepsilon_j/N_j \, \Psi$, and we can write the outcome (accident) rate equation as:

$$A = A_{\mathrm{m}} + A_0 e^{-\varepsilon/k}$$

where

$$k = \left(N_j \Psi \big/ \beta\right).$$

This result is also exactly the same (exponential) form as that derived from the Learning Hypothesis.

*Thus, the SEST has given physical meaning to the learning rate constant, K, in terms of the microstate distribution with experience.*

The influence of learning environment (conventionally the 'context') is naturally accounted for by the ESP, $\Psi$. Empirical factors that would basically do the same thing (i.e., change the error rate) are called 'performance-shaping functions' (PSF) in the disciplines known as Human Factors and Probabilistic Safety Analysis. This ESP function, $\Psi$, also explains formally the influence of variability in learning behaviour on the observed error rate as experience changes. The systematic learning patterns (outcome distributions) that arise with experience do so as a direct result of the uncertainty and randomness inherent in the human element.

Thus, we have made a key advance after all this algebra. The result is in line with what we would expect. The theory has indeed reconciled conceptually and mathematically the random occurrences of outcomes (as microstate distributions) that are observed as a result of errors from a confluence of circumstances, with the systematic trend simultaneously imposed by learning with increasing depth and accumulated experience.

## The Average Rate

It is usual common practice for many government agencies, safety authorities, industries and event databases to report and track the average rate of errors, accidents or events. The interval basis is taken conventionally as the rate of outcomes per calendar year, or in industrial injury and event data as the number of events per 100,000 equivalent workers.

From the above SEST analysis, the average rate for the $j^{\text{th}}$ interval is actually given by the term within the $\langle \ \rangle$ as the number of events per unit experience:

$$\langle N/\varepsilon \rangle = \sum_{1} n_{i}(\varepsilon) \Big/ \sum_{i} (\varepsilon_{i} n_{i}(\varepsilon))$$

or

$$\langle N/\varepsilon \rangle = N_{j}/\varepsilon_{j}$$
$$= 1/\varepsilon \Psi$$

Thus, the average rate is determined only by the experience increment and the ESP. The average over all intervals is similarly:

$$\langle N/\varepsilon \rangle = \sum_{j} \Big\{ \sum_{1} n_{i}(\varepsilon) \Big/ \sum_{i} (\varepsilon_{i} n_{i}(\varepsilon)) \Big\}$$

This explains something else. Statistical treatments of data usually rely on determining some average, like the number of people killed by road accidents per year, or the average trend in the Dow Jones index or its component stocks. Our result shows the key influence of experience in determining the average as well as the trend since we have,

$$\langle N/\varepsilon \rangle = N_{j}/\varepsilon_{j} = 1/\varepsilon \Psi$$

Usually, there is no equivalent relation for these parameters in any purely statistical analysis of data since there is no physical model of what is happening. In our case, we have invoked the learning hypothesis, plus the most likely distribution of outcomes. The result derives the trend that results from changing experience and learning behaviour.

No wonder that today accident occurrence and stock market prediction are so hard, and so empirically based. No learning is accounted for, if it exists, and the ESP is not considered or modelled.

## Analogy and Predictions: Statistical Error Theory and Learning Model Equivalence

We now invoke the Equivalence Principle or theorem, namely that the observed error or outcome rate as learning occurs is given by the total number of notional distributions of outcomes (errors) for a given experience.

The exponential form derived above for the outcomes used the classical statistical distribution of errors. This result agrees with the exponential form obtained using a macroscopic model of human learning. Thus, we note that a tantalisingly similar result for the error rate per unit accumulated experience follows totally independently from either:

a) Minimum Error Rate Theory, MERE, where the error rate reduction (learning) is proportional to the rate of errors being made; or

b) SEST, where the error rate is derived from the total number of possible distributions of errors as a function of experience.

From the equivalent statements (a) and (b), we infer that error rate reduction (learning) is proportional to the rate of errors being made, which is derived from the total number of distributions of errors. Both Learning and Forgetting are also naturally included via the ESP and/or learning rate constant. This analysis brings closure to the theory, as the microscopic distributions of error states now appear manifested as the observed macroscopic ULC.

Thus, we can now assert by physical analogy that the results from the two theories, (a) the learning hypothesis MERE and (b) the outcome distribution SEST, are equivalent and interchangeable. They represent two views (the 'top-down' average macroscopic and the 'bottoms-up' stochastic microscopic) which are essentially identical interpretations of the same error outcomes, but differently observed and averaged with the accumulated and depth of experience. The past learning and the present decision making are physically and mathematically intertwined, and order emerges from and due to disorder.

In other words, *the statistical distribution of errors among the microstates (the confluence of events or factors) determines the observed macroscopic outcomes*. From this equivalence hypothesis, we can derive that the ratio of the minimum and initially observed rates is a constant dependent on the value taken for $\alpha$ because we now have that:

$$(A_m / A_0) = (\lambda_m / \lambda_0) = e^{\alpha}$$

Empirically, we note that in large error datasets, this ratio is indeed apparently a constant of order about a factor of one-tenth, as given by dividing one in ~200,000 hours as the minimum attainable error rate by the typically observed initial rate of one in ~20,000 hours.

We have justified *a posteori* the condition for the approximation that was originally adopted, namely that $e^{\alpha - \beta \varepsilon} \ll 1$, always, when learning occurs.

## The Influence of Safety Management and Regulations: Imposing Order on Disorder

*The implications of the equivalence are very profound.* The SEST argues that the outcomes cannot be known for certain, but are random distributions and combinations of errors in the system microstates during the Observation Range for a given amount of accumulated experience. These microstates include all the different confluence of circumstances, errors of commission or omission, the latent errors, event sequences, plus the myriad of interactions, human decision making and hidden dependencies. The error distribution with depth of experience is such that the errors decrease to define a learning curve. Learning cannot eliminate the lowest or zeroth error rate: there are no 'zero defects', simply a trend towards the minimum state. The zeroth microstate now represents the 'built in' contribution from the human element.

In a sense, we have cheated: we have used the average statistical behaviour and the Learning Hypothesis as a way to avoid describing the details of what is actually happening. It is all too complex and too variable to model the entire HTS in detail, but despite that we can predict the observed behaviour.

We cannot distinguish among the many error states from observation as they have random behaviour: they simply follow a learning curve distribution. One error state distribution is not identical to another, and never will be statistically because the distribution of states with depth of experience is always different. This simple fact explains why (different) errors still occur while we try to eliminate known or previously observed causes (or microstates).

As errors occur, Managers, Society and Regulators introduce new measures (Rules) to attempt to eliminate their reoccurrence. Investigators evaluate in detail the 'event sequences' to determine the apparent causes. Measures are taken to try to control the errors caused by the role of humans themselves. New Laws or Procedures are passed that may require different safety measures. Process changes are implemented in design manufacturing or operation, or using other management means (such as safety programs, retraining and/or the reassignment of staff). Fines may be levied as a means of punishment for allowing something to even happen. The inclusion of these Rules is an example of learning, which should change the observed distribution of outcomes with experience, and hence, explains the effects of safety management or intervention in the system.

In a statistical physics sense, these Rules act like physical 'Exclusion Principles', serving to avoid certain combinations and distributions of error microstates. Thus, we may arbitrarily decide that all ships of over 30 years experience afloat cannot be used, or that anyone under the age of 30 in Australia should not drive, or that certain combinations of microstates are nearly excluded by design. We may declare that certain Rules, Regulations and Requirements will exclude an observed event from 'ever happening again', despite knowing that the probability of a similar 'matching' outcome is quite high (as discussed in Appendix H). We may even try to distinguish between microstates, by labelling system outcomes differently, so that the errors are not interchangeable between microstates. Indeed, we can show that the adoption of exclusion rules for microstate existence or occupation simply alters the error or outcome distribution, just as quantum mechanical exclusion principles precisely alter the distributions for allowed and excluded microstates.

Thus, we have practical cases that are equivalent to different statistical distributions, with both distinguishable and indistinguishable error states and/or exclusion principles and rules. We argue by analogy that we might expect the general form of the distribution of microstates to be given by similar expressions to statistical physics. These are equivalent to the use of Fermi–Dirac and Bose–Einstein statistics in quantum mechanics, which invoke and obey certain rules for the occupancy of a given error state, as well as depending on having indistinguishable outcomes. An example calculation quickly shows that the distributions do indeed change significantly with changes in these types of Rules.

We note that imposing such Rules arbitrarily can clearly be a piecemeal approach, which is trying to eliminate the observed outcomes microstate-by-microstate, case-by-case, accident-by-accident. The Rules should be optimised so as to address the multitude of other possible distributions and Observations made to determine their effect on the distribution. In fact, by changing the outcome probability for any state by a small amount, $\delta p$, there is a definite change in the information entropy, $\Delta H$, or the degree of randomness (see also Appendix I).

*To put it another way, management, laws, inquiries, regulations and safety systems try to impose order on disorder.* Implicitly, they try to reach a minimum state of disorder, or a maximum state of order, as effectively as possible using Goals and incentives (both rewards and punishments).

Management and safety specialists often track the average accident or event rate, $\langle N/\varepsilon \rangle$, as a measure of safety performance. For any accumulation of observed experience, $\varepsilon$, the average is actually and formally given by:

$$\langle N/\varepsilon \rangle = 1/\varepsilon \, \Psi$$

Plainly, the average will be sensitive to and appear to fall inversely with the experience *interval,* $\varepsilon$ and the ESP, $\Psi$, if learning is occurring. This new theory is testable, and offers the promise of determining the influence of management and other decisions on the observed rates of events and learning from experience.

In the interest of space and so as not to distract from our main purpose here, the fuller implications and derivations behind this argument will be given later in Chapter 7.

We can also show that these postulates are indeed confirmed to be the case for data from typical systems where we have available (by luck!) the relevant observational and accumulated experience. These data are namely:

a) Berman's records for shipping losses occurring over two centuries for the USA for known age of ship,
b) the P & I Club analysis of major claims (losses) for modern shipping, and
c) fifteen years of aircraft fatal accident data for Australia, divided up by pilot experience for given aircraft type.

## The Risk of Losing a Ship

Theory is all very well, but the real test is against data. Using available records, we can now validate the new theory.

We need and use data from a technological system with human involvement that is observed and includes both outcomes and a measure of experience. Shipping losses are one such system and data source, as insurers and mariners tracked sinkings; and the human element is the main cause of ship loss, rather than structural defects in the ships themselves.

Fortunately, a large dataset exists for ship losses in the USA, being Berman's epic compilation (Berman, 1972) [15]. We analysed these extraordinary data files, which cover some

10,000 losses (outcomes) over an Observation Range of nearly 200 years from 1800 to 1971. We excluded Acts of War so as to avoid uncontrolled external influences and non-human errors. It is not known how many ships were afloat in total, only which ones sank, and thus became recorded outcomes.

A ship is built in a given year, sails for a while accumulating experience in ship-years afloat, Sy, and may or may not sink. From some 10,000 ships that were lost, we took a sample of the data only for ships over 500 tons, chosen so that we can compare with modern large commercial losses. In our sample of the data there were a total (N) of 510 losses of the ships. We entered this dataset of outcomes into an $i$–$j$ Experience Matrix.

From the entire set, we show one sample Observation Range for 1850 to 1860, selected arbitrarily from the entire Matrix. (See Figure 5.9.) It is one macrostate, $n_i$, being the loss (outcome) data for 1850 to 1860, over which time 17 ships were lost which had accumulated 265 shipping-years (accSy) of depth of experience before being lost. The losses, $N_i = 17$, are sparsely distributed about the Matrix block as shown by the numbers, where we use an experience range, $E$, for all ships of up to 40 years.

In fact, the entire observation set of 1800 to 1971 can be formed by stacking these macro-states of incremental blocks or ranges together. The blocks when connected edge-to-edge form the one large Matrix for all the observed range and number of outcomes, giving $171 \times 40 = 6,840$ states of which 510 were occupied. But this again is only one subset of an array that could stretch over all recorded history, and all human experience – we just happen to not have all that data!!

The usual time history is given by the sum of the losses as shown on the bottom, labelled 'total' of the Matrix for any given year. Thus, for any year, $y$, there is a loss rate given by summing over all the experience range of losses for that particular observation, $j$th range year,

$$N_y = \sum_{\varepsilon} n_i(\varepsilon)$$

Meanwhile, for a given experience, $\varepsilon$, the total number of losses, $N$, is given by summing all the losses over the Range at a particular experience, as in the column on the right labelled '# Losses':

$$n_i = \sum_y n_i(\varepsilon)$$

The sum of the number of Sy at any experience interval is simply also shown in the column on the right labelled 'Sy' as given by adding up outcomes in each of the horizontal rows:

$$Sy(\varepsilon) = \sum_y (Sy\, n_i(\varepsilon))$$

Hence, the accumulated experience in accSys is as shown from adding the Sys vertically for all losses:

$$accSy = \sum_{\varepsilon} (Sy\, n_i(\varepsilon))$$

Now we can calculate the outcomes for all the $n^{th}$ microstates in the entire Observation Range for 1800–1971 if we stack together all the $j$-macrostates. We find the total losses of >500 tons are now of course summed as all outcomes over all microstates:

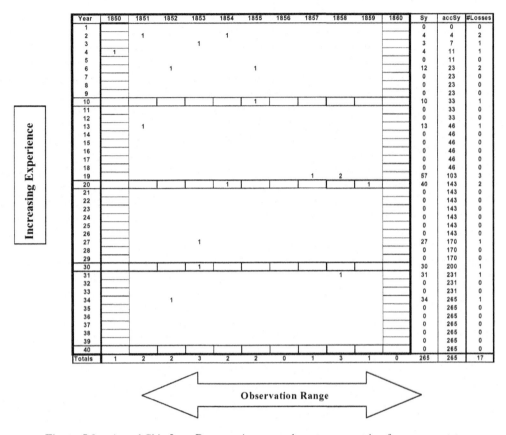

Increasing Experience

| Year | 1850 | 1851 | 1852 | 1853 | 1854 | 1855 | 1856 | 1857 | 1858 | 1859 | 1860 | Sy | accSy | #Losses |
|---|---|---|---|---|---|---|---|---|---|---|---|---|---|---|
| 1 | | | | | | | | | | | | 0 | 0 | 0 |
| 2 | | 1 | | | 1 | | | | | | | 4 | 4 | 2 |
| 3 | | | | 1 | | | | | | | | 3 | 7 | 1 |
| 4 | 1 | | | | | | | | | | | 4 | 11 | 1 |
| 5 | | | | | | | | | | | | 0 | 11 | 0 |
| 6 | | | 1 | | | | 1 | | | | | 12 | 23 | 2 |
| 7 | | | | | | | | | | | | 0 | 23 | 0 |
| 8 | | | | | | | | | | | | 0 | 23 | 0 |
| 9 | | | | | | | | | | | | 0 | 23 | 0 |
| 10 | | | | | | 1 | | | | | | 10 | 33 | 1 |
| 11 | | | | | | | | | | | | 0 | 33 | 0 |
| 12 | | | | | | | | | | | | 0 | 33 | 0 |
| 13 | | 1 | | | | | | | | | | 13 | 46 | 1 |
| 14 | | | | | | | | | | | | 0 | 46 | 0 |
| 15 | | | | | | | | | | | | 0 | 46 | 0 |
| 16 | | | | | | | | | | | | 0 | 46 | 0 |
| 17 | | | | | | | | | | | | 0 | 46 | 0 |
| 18 | | | | | | | | | | | | 0 | 46 | 0 |
| 19 | | | | | | | | 1 | 2 | | | 57 | 103 | 3 |
| 20 | | | | | 1 | | | | | 1 | | 40 | 143 | 2 |
| 21 | | | | | | | | | | | | 0 | 143 | 0 |
| 22 | | | | | | | | | | | | 0 | 143 | 0 |
| 23 | | | | | | | | | | | | 0 | 143 | 0 |
| 24 | | | | | | | | | | | | 0 | 143 | 0 |
| 25 | | | | | | | | | | | | 0 | 143 | 0 |
| 26 | | | | | | | | | | | | 0 | 143 | 0 |
| 27 | | | 1 | | | | | | | | | 27 | 170 | 1 |
| 28 | | | | | | | | | | | | 0 | 170 | 0 |
| 29 | | | | | | | | | | | | 0 | 170 | 0 |
| 30 | | | | 1 | | | | | | | | 30 | 200 | 1 |
| 31 | | | | | | | | | 1 | | | 31 | 231 | 1 |
| 32 | | | | | | | | | | | | 0 | 231 | 0 |
| 33 | | | | | | | | | | | | 0 | 231 | 0 |
| 34 | | | 1 | | | | | | | | | 34 | 265 | 1 |
| 35 | | | | | | | | | | | | 0 | 265 | 0 |
| 36 | | | | | | | | | | | | 0 | 265 | 0 |
| 37 | | | | | | | | | | | | 0 | 265 | 0 |
| 38 | | | | | | | | | | | | 0 | 265 | 0 |
| 39 | | | | | | | | | | | | 0 | 265 | 0 |
| 40 | | | | | | | | | | | | 0 | 265 | 0 |
| Totals | 1 | 2 | 2 | 3 | 2 | 2 | 0 | 1 | 3 | 1 | 0 | 265 | 265 | 17 |

Observation Range

**Figure 5.9.** Actual Ship Loss Data matrix: a sample outcome matrix of one macrostate

$$N_j = \sum_1 n_i(\varepsilon) = 510$$

and the accumulated experience is summed over the depth of experience

$$\text{accE} = \varepsilon = \sum_j (n_i(\varepsilon)\,\text{Sy}) = 11,706\ \text{accSy}$$

So we have confirmed the postulate that we may represent outcomes by a distribution of error states in a macrostate as a function of experience, and where all microstates are equally likely.

## Distribution Functions

If the losses were truly random in time, then on average, the chance is equal that a ship would be lost either side of the middle of the Observation Range, or centered on the date

$$1800 + (1971 - 1800)/2 = 1885,$$

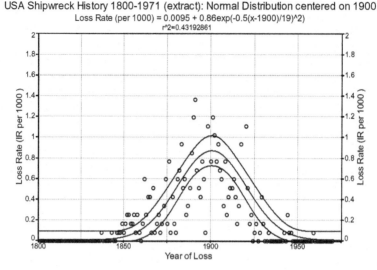

**Figure 5.10.** Loss rate fitted with a normal distribution

and the loss rate distribution should follow a binomial (normal) distribution. The actual distribution of the loss rate data does just that, and data for *the entire Observation Range* are shown in Figure 5.10, including the 95% confidence bounds.

The fitted loss rate distribution actually centres on 1900, and is given by,

$$IR(\text{per kSy}) = 0.0095 + 0.86 \exp 0.5 ((Y - 1900)/19)^2$$

where $1\,\text{kSy} = 1{,}000\,\text{Sy}$.

Since the data have a normal distribution, the outcomes are indeed randomly distributed throughout the entire 1800–1971 Range. The standard deviation of 19 Sy and the 95% confidence limits do actually encompass the predicted date of 1885, within the errors of the data sampling and fitting. The most probable loss (outcome) rate is ~0.86 per 1,000 Sy, which is close to that observed today (~1 per kSy) by major loss insurers. The most probable rate has not changed for over 200 years, and the range at 95% confidence is 0.7 – 1 per kSy.

As to the systematic effects of ship-age, it has been characteristic practice to have higher insurance for older ships, implying there risk of loss is greater, and that the outcomes (vessel sinkings, groundings, collisions, etc.) are not random. Older vessels are then *classified* as higher or greater risk. The actual data are shown in Figure 5.11 for losses in excess of 500 tons for two outcome sets spread over two centuries. Clearly, there is little difference between them; and the outcomes are almost normally distributed over the life of the ships with about 40–50 years maximum. The maximum loss fraction peak is at about 15–20 years of ship-life.

So we may state that we have confirmed the postulates in the theory that:

a) there is a random pattern of outcomes in the equally probable microstates, which is manifested as a distribution of loss rates; and

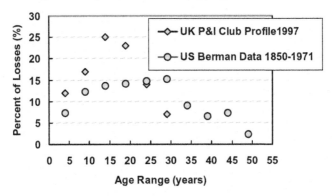

**Figure 5.11.** Comparison of ship losses as a function of age

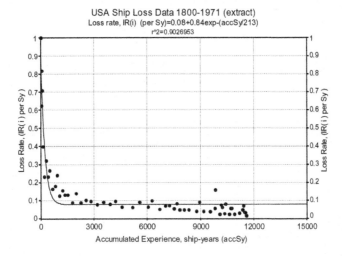

**Figure 5.12.** The learning curve for shipping

b) more importantly, the loss rate is uniform over the entire Range, even as the technology has undergone major changes from sail to steam engines and from wood to steel hulls.

These statements also show the key role of (random human) errors in determining the distributions, and not easily showing trends. Also observing for an arbitrary Range in calendar time (as is usually done) can lead to event data being distributed normally and the apparent rates being highly affected by the recorded error states and experience.

Now in terms of the influence of accumulated experience, we may plot the loss rate per ship-year versus the accumulated experience in accSy as shown in Figure 5.12.

The loss rate as a function of the accumulated experience in accSy is then given by a best-fit line of the exponential form derived for the distribution of the total number of microstates:

$$A \approx A_{\mathrm{m}} + A_0 e^{-\varepsilon/k}$$

or

$$A(\text{losses per Sy}) = 0.08 + 0.84 \exp-(\text{accSy})/213))$$

This result implies an initial loss rate many times higher than the equilibrium value, and a minimum rate of ~0.08 per Sy for those that sank. This is of course telling us that on average, the ships that sank lasted for a depth of experience afloat of about (1/0.08) or ~13 Sy, starting off lasting some 10 times less (~1 Sy). It does NOT tell us how long the average ship lasted, including those that were not lost, and indeed this is irrelevant for the moment. We just want to predict the relation between sinking rates and ship lifetimes. On an accumulated rate basis the predicted loss rate is now ~1 per 1,000 Sy, illustrating the importance of the data sample size (Observation Range) for apparently random events.

Thus, we have confirmed the postulates in the theory that:

a) a systematic learning curve exists superimposed on the apparently random losses which we observe as outcomes;
b) a relevant measure for accumulated experience and depth of experience can be found (in this case years-afloat);
c) a minimum asymptotic rate does exist, and is derivable from the learning curve; and
d) there is indeed an equivalence between observed microstates and actual outcomes.

## The Most Probable and Minimum Error Rate

We have also confirmed the results by testing the analysis against other data for modern fleets, where losses for all ships over 500 tons were tracked. These include data for modern vessels from the Institute of London Underwriters [16] for losses greater than 500 tons for 1972–1998, and for the latest UK P&I Club Major Claims data from 1976 to 1999 [17].

In these modern datasets, we also know how many ships were afloat, but the years afloat for each ship were not known (the converse to the Berman dataset). The Observation Ranges were smaller (~25 years), but covered the worldwide total losses, which are comparable in number.

The data are shown in Figure 5.13, where we have the loss rate for the ILU dataset for 1972–1998 worldwide is given by, for some 30,000 ships afloat in any Sy, accumulating nearly a million Sy in total, and some 3,000 outcomes (losses) over the 26-year Range:

$$A \approx A_{\mathrm{m}} + A_0 e^{-\varepsilon/k}$$

or,

$$A(\text{losses per kSy}) = 0.95 + 7 \exp -(\text{acckSy}/600)$$

This result shows an asymptotic or minimum loss rate of ~0.95 per kS/y for losses > 500 tons in 1972–1998 (despite observing nearly 2/kSy now). We have a similar estimate for the Major Loss data, that is greatest in terms of financial cost, which shows a loss rate of ~1/kSy (Pomeroy, 2001) [18], which is a value consistent with the above analyses.

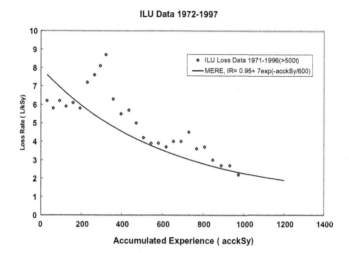

**Figure 5.13.** Modern ship losses

This lowest predicted minimum rate of ~0.95/kSy is consistent with the most probable rate independently derived from the data for losses only (i.e., $0.86 \pm 0.1$ per kSy) for 1800–1971. Since the two datasets do not overlap, meeting in 1970, and one is for losses only in the USA and one is for all ships afloat worldwide, we have shown that:

a) the minimum error rate predicted for modern ships is close or equivalent to the most probable loss rate for the last 200 years, which if correct also confirms the postulate of the most probable distribution used in deriving the microstates distribution formula;
b) the distribution of microstates (manifested as an outcome rate) is apparently independent of technology or date, and is due to the dominant contribution of the human element; and
c) the learning curve approach is consistent with the statistical distribution of error states.

## Learning Rates and Experience Intervals: The Universal Learning Curve

The two datasets we have studied are, at first sight, quite distinct, even though both are observed and recorded only for losses greater than 500 tons. The observational intervals, the accumulated experience and the number of outcomes are drastically different.

One set (set A) is from 1800 to 1971, and gives a distribution of microstates for only losses for the USA with an experience base of about 10 kSy. The other (set B) extends that set A from 1971 to 1996, but is for the distribution of microstates for losses of all ships worldwide with an experience base of nearly 1,000 kSy. Therefore, the depth of experience is quite different. The accumulated experience, $\Sigma n_i \varepsilon_i$, is then quite different for each set, by the same factor of 100. Above, we have shown that the learning curve rate constants are also different, being ~200 Sy for set A, and ~600 kSy for set B, which is a factor of ~3,000.

We would expect from the theory that the rate constants would be related by:

$$k_{A,B} = \left(n_j \Psi / \beta\right) = \beta_A \, \varepsilon_A / \beta_B \varepsilon_B$$

So since $k_A/k_B \sim 3,000$, and $(\varepsilon_A/\varepsilon_B) \cong 1,000\,\text{kSy}/10\,\text{kSy} \sim 100$, then we might expect the ratio of the learning rate constants for the sets A and B to be:

$$(k/\varepsilon)_{A,B} \sim 3,000/100 = 30$$

which is the ratio of the (unknown) value of the (learning rate $\times$ experience interval) products, $\beta\varepsilon_{A,B}$.

So, for these Ranges, the predicted 'learning rate ratio' between experience intervals for the losses only in the USA and for the whole world fleet afloat is:

$$\beta_A \varepsilon_A / \beta_B \varepsilon_B \sim 30$$

Recall again that dataset $A$ was for all ships afloat worldwide, while dataset $B$ was just for those that sank in the USA. The ratio above suggests that the experience interval ratio of the USA losses to the world fleet afloat is $(\varepsilon_A/\varepsilon_B) \sim 1/30$ (i.e., 3%), particularly if $\beta_A \sim \beta_B$.

To test that ratio prediction, recall also that for the ILU data in ~25 years, we had 3,000 losses of ~30,000 ships afloat at any time. That is a loss rate percentage for the whole fleet of order $(3,000/25) \times (100/30,000) = 0.4\%$ worldwide. But only a fraction of the world fleet actually sailed and sank near the USA. To determine that fraction, we sought another random sample Observation Range of losses and found an excellent one in the 'Atlas of Ship Wrecks and Treasure' (Pickford, 1994) [19]. Now the Atlas lists about 184 ships sunk off the East, West and Caribbean coasts of the USA between 1540 and 1956 out of a listed sample world-wide of 1,400 losses. That is only a fraction of $(184/1400) \times 100 = 13\%$ of the world's ship losses were in the waters off the USA. We assume that fraction holds for the much later ILU dataset, which was for all ships >500 tons.

So if just 13% of the ships worldwide sank off the coasts of the USA, and only 0.4% of the fleet sank in total around the world, we would have $0.4\%/0.13 \sim 3\%$ as the experience interval ratio of only the USA losses to the total world total fleet afloat. Therefore, we have near-perfect agreement versus the predicted ratio from the theory of 3% (or a factor of 30).

Given the uncertainties in the calculations, and the vast differences in the datasets, this degree of agreement with the prediction almost seems fortuitous and better than might be expected. But the comparison does confirm the general approach and indicate how to compare datasets that possess very different experience bases.

Let us try to test another prediction: if the theory, postulates and analogies are correct, the two datasets should both follow the trend predicted by the ULC. We can directly compare the two learning rates for set (A) and set (B) with their very different experience bases by using the non-dimensional formulation of the ULC for correlating data, i.e.,

$$E^* = \exp - KN^*$$

We correct the learning rate constant for the USA losses only for the ratio of ~30 derived above. The actual learning curves give all the needed estimates from the data for $A_0$ and $A_m$, which is sufficient to calculate $E^*$ for each microstate. We also have the total experience, $\varepsilon$, necessary to derive the non-dimensional value of $N^*$. Strictly speaking, $N^*$ should be taken

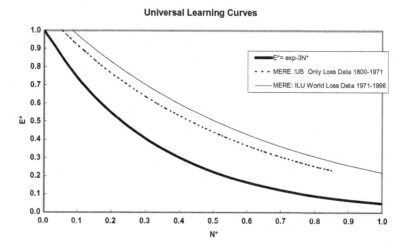

**Figure 5.14.** Comparison of trends with the ULC

as the ratio of experience, $\varepsilon$, to the experience, $\varepsilon_M$, needed or observed to reach the minimum error rate, $\lambda_m$, or at least the maximum experience already achieved with the system.

The comparisons of the ULCs suggested by the theory are shown in Figure 5.14. We have also shown the best-fit correlation to world data, i.e., with $K \sim 3$,

$$E^* = \exp - 3N^*$$

The value of $K \sim 3$ was derived from analysing vast datasets covering millions of error states that included [4] among other things (see Figure 1.7 in Chapter 1): USA data for deaths in recreational boating 1960–1998; automobile crashes 1966–1998; railway accidents 1975–1999; coal mining for 1938–1998; plus South African gold and coal mining injuries 1969–1999; UK cardiac surgeries 1984–1999; US oil spills 1969–2001; French latent error data 1998–1999; US commercial aircraft near misses 1987–1997; and also world pulmonary deaths for 1840–1970.

The two other lines, for the US (Berman) losses only and ILU world shipping datasets, are given by the MERE predictions calculated from:

$$E^* = \exp - KN^* = ((1 - A/A_m)/(1 - A_0/A_m))$$

whence

$$A = A_m + (A_o - A_m)e^{-\varepsilon/k}$$

and the values for $k$, $A_m$ and $A_0$ are derived directly from those given by the theory and the data. The 213 Sy in the exponent is adjusted for the observational experience interval ratio and becomes $k = 213 \times 30 = 6{,}390\,\mathrm{Sy} = 6.4\,\mathrm{kSy}$.

Hence, the only adjustment we have made or needed was correcting the learning rate constant for the differing depths of experience. We justify the factor of ~30 simply to bring the experience interval for the losses in the USA only data consistently into line with the world experience interval. The remaining differences between the predictions are well within the overall data scatter.

This method thus allows apparently quite disparate datasets to be renormalised and inter-compared. The universal learning trends are essentially the same and we have validated the overall theoretically predicted trend.

Thus, we have succeeded in not only getting the two very different datasets on the same plot, but in obtaining agreement with the world trend derived from a wide range of totally independent data. Using the non-dimensional variables derived from theory, we have shown that the trends are correct. This agreement is despite the numerical changes being very large, by a factor of ~100 in the learning rate ratio and a factor of 1,000 in the accumulated experience, as we have discussed above.

## Reducing the Risk of a Fatal Aircraft Accident: The Influence of Skill and Experience

The acquisition and learning of human skills involves undergoing experiences (Norretranders, p. 364 [7]). Using the error state ideas, we should also be able to predict the reduced risk, if any, due to having an increasing *depth* of experience for the human(s) operating any HTS. This decreasing shift in risk with experience and learning has many implications. For example, whether the premiums for insurance or the needed training should be greater for less-experienced operators who potentially have higher risk than those with more experience. The individual risk or chance of breaking a leg when skiing should perhaps be less for an experienced skier than for an inexperienced one for the same speed and slope. So, as a final check on our work, we examine a totally different example to see how applicable and useful the SEST results are for interpreting actual outcomes and how we might predict and manage them.

We need an explicit measure of depth of experience. As one test case, we found the relative risk of a fatal aircraft accident for commercial pilots as they gained flying experience. The information given was how much flying experience pilots have had before dying in accidents; and was buried in an otherwise annual analysis of Australian fatal accident data, for ATSB, 2006 [20]. The observed outcomes, $n_i$, as a function of flying experience, $\varepsilon_i$, reported were a subset of all the commercial pilots who are flying, whose prior total flying experience is not known or recorded. That study was conducted nominally to show how deaths were (linearly) reducing with our old friend *calendar time* or year.

Of course, we already know that the true variation is not linear with year but follows an exponential curve with experience, and should really be examined using an experience measure. But by sheer good luck, the deaths of a total number of pilots, $N_i = \Sigma n_i = 247$ were also sorted by the prior time they had spent flying the type of aircraft in which their accident occurred. The number of pilots killed, $n_i$, were binned into 100-flying-hour experience intervals, where the intervals were up to 100 flying hours, then to 200 flying hours, 300 flying hours, etc ... all the way up to 1,000 flying hours. These experience 100-hour 'bins' represents the levels of the depth of experience in the chosen 15-year observation interval, with mean experience levels of 50, 150, 250 ... etc., flying hours, up to the maximum of 1,000 flying hours.

This prior flying experience in flying hours is called 'time on type', and is *exactly* a relevant measure of the depth of experience from learning, risk exposure and skill acquisition. In this

15-year or $j^{th}$ observation interval, it can be clearly seen from the data plot that the number killed, $n_i$, decreases rapidly as the i-levels of depth or 'time-on-type' experience increase.

The total number of errors or outcomes, $N_i$, distributed over the experience levels, $\varepsilon_j$, is then given by summing or integrating the distribution of $n_i$ microstates over all the discrete experience depth level or increments, where the mean experience levels corresponding to the adjacent 100-hour intervals are $\varepsilon_1 = 50$ flying hours, $\varepsilon_2 = 150$ flying hours ... etc. So the total number of outcomes or deaths, $N_j$, observed in the entire $j^{th}$ range in commercial aircraft is equal to the total occupancy number of microstates in the closed HTS of pilot fatalities. Summing overall the experience levels, of course:

$$N_j = \sum_i n_i(\varepsilon) = 247$$

The number killed is a small fraction of the total number flying, so the non-outcomes vastly outnumber the outcomes. Within this 15-year $j^{th}$ interval, from the SEST that the equivalent probability of observing any $i^{th}$ microstate is just the same as Laplace's definition, being the ratio of the microstate distribution occupancy to the total outcomes. The cumulative probability, $p(\varepsilon_i)$, of a pilot having the fatal accident with the given flying depth of experience, $\varepsilon_i$, whenever it occurred is then estimated, as usual, from the fraction killed at that experience level out of the total killed:

$$p(\varepsilon_i) = n_i \Big/ \sum n_i = n_i/N_i \, ,$$

where $N_i$ is the total experience in pilot-hours of all the pilots killed up to that experience interval, $\varepsilon_i$.

We note that since we have observed just the fatal outcomes, the usual normalisation condition for all the $N_i$ outcomes to exist is, summing the probabilities over all the 15 years of the observation range,

$$\sum_j p(\varepsilon_i) = 1$$

To first order the equilibrium outcome number of microstates (deaths) in the observation interval (outcomes) is expected to be distributed as a function of experience, $\varepsilon$, and from the SEST is approximately,

$$N_j(\varepsilon) \approx n_0 + n_0^* e^{-\beta \varepsilon}$$

The exponential-like decrease in the number with increasing 'time on type' experience, $\varepsilon$, is precisely what is observed in the actual pilot data. We can express the distribution of the number of fatalities as a function of each of the $i^{th}$ 100 flying hours experience depth intervals as a normalised fractional probability of death. To do that, we just divide both sides by the total number of fatalities, $N_j = 247$ observed in all the experience levels during the 15-year interval, giving the probability distribution as

$$p(\varepsilon) \approx p_0 + p_0^* e^{-\beta \varepsilon}$$

In Figure 5.15, we show the extremely good prediction made by this new error state formulation, when used to describe the ATSB fatal accident data on pilot deaths. Here, the depth of

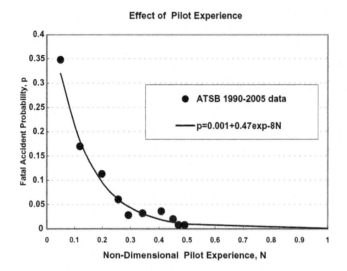

**Figure 5.15.** The exponential distribution with depth of experience of the probability of death for commercial pilots

experience in any 100-hour interval has been conveniently normalised to the total experience $\varepsilon_T = \Sigma_i n_i \varepsilon_i = 43{,}600$ pilot flying hours. This total experience is simply the sum of the nqumber of deaths in each of the 100-hour experience levels times their mean 'time on type' flying hours, over the entire 15-year interval. The non-dimensional depth of experience at any of the $i$th levels is then written as $N^* = \varepsilon_i/\varepsilon_T$.

The theoretically based exponential fit for the distribution of these commercial pilot fatality data is also shown as the fatal accident probability:

$$p = 0.001 + 0.47e^{-8N}$$

The exponential trend in the data with depth of experience is clearly in total accord with the distribution predicted by the new error state theory. This simple fit also implies not only that experienced pilots fly more before dying, but that inexperienced pilots with 100 pilot-hours or so (less than 10% of the total experience) have a large probability of death of all those who die (since $p > 0.35$ as $N^* < 0.1$). Similar to the automobile accident data that motivated and began this Chapter, and as beautifully mirrored in Figure 5.2, it is clear that depth of experience is absolutely key. Plainly, learning from experience is highly effective in reducing risk in all such HTSs.

We have now transformed these pilot death data to experience space, and thus, we can make our general statement specific to this typical practical example. *The total number of pilot deaths observed, and hence, the probability of when the death occurs among all the deaths, is distributed to first order as decreasing exponentially with increasing depth of experience, ε, as measured by pilot time-on-type in any given observation interval (such as for these 15 years).*

Not only do the data clearly show this trend, being expected human experience, they also confirm our new theory of learning using the statistical analysis of error states. As we might have expected from the very beginning, we have proved the obvious: *lack of experience represents the greatest risk!*

## Conclusions: A New Approach

This Chapter has been long and hard going, with sometimes-dense mathematics and some tricky concepts and reasoning about microstates, experience space and outcome distributions. We hope and believe it is worth both the journey and the effort. The results represent a new way to describe risk, how to measure and report outcomes, and how to analyse outcome data to make predictions. At last, we have a general and consistent theoretical model, however simplified it may be, which describes the outcome distributions in HTS and is based on stated assumptions and classic concepts. The theory is quantifiable and testable versus the existing data and potentially able to make predictions, which was and is our key objective.

To sidestep excessive complexity, we made a key analogy. We have described how to adapt the statistical approach of defining distributions of error states. We argue that we do not and cannot know all the error states of the system, and only observe the outcomes based on the average behaviour as a function of depth of experience. We then do not have to know all the 'rules' that may describe human and machine reliability, but only describe the emergent distribution of the outcomes (accidents, events and errors). The measure for learning is the experience, which is introduced as the relevant physical parameter. The distribution of outcomes with depth of experience is constituted from microstates, which are all equally probable, but what we actually observe is the most likely.

We have described and explored the novel adoption and adaptation of the principles and methods of statistical physics to the measurement of risk, the prediction of accidents and the contribution of the human element. In particular, utilising concepts from statistical mechanics, the observed properties of macroscopic systems are predicted by the microscopic distributions of outcomes among error states. This approach and analysis is entirely consistent with the methods and assumptions in classical sampling statistics and in information theory. We have incidentally unified risk management and prediction with information technology, reflecting how humans operating within HTS deduce the signal from the noise, and hence, take actions and decisions. The Information Entropy, $H$, is a powerful and universally applicable concept that provides a precise measure of the distribution of errors and reflects that judgements and decisions occur in HTS as knowledge and learning occurs. We will see in later Chapters that this model has important ramifications for both safety management systems and for risk perception.

Using this physical model, we can therefore reconcile the apparently random occurrence of outcomes (accidents and errors) with the observed systematic trend from having a learning environment. The entire outcome distribution depends on the depth of experience. It is further shown that learning rates depend on the experience, and that a formal 'experience-shaping factor' emerges naturally during and from the total experience.

We can now explain and predict these outcomes and the apparently random occurrences. We show why the human element component is persistent and large in risk analysis.

The result of applying this physical theory to the enigmas of human behaviour provides new analogies that are very powerful. The resulting equations have been derived that define the equilibrium distribution of outcomes (observed as accidents, errors or events) the total number of errors and the accumulated experience. The total microstate distribution with experience is consistent with the learning curve derived from the macroscopic hypothesis that humans learn from their mistakes.

We infer that *risk reduction (learning) is proportional to the rate of errors being made, which is derived from the total number of distributions of errors.* Both Learning and Forgetting are also naturally included via the experience-shaping function and/or learning rate constant. The theory provides a consistent interpretation between learning models and the statistical behaviour of error occurrence, and explains why zero defects do not occur in a technological system.

This analysis brings closure to the theory since the microscopic distributions of error states now appear manifested as the observed macroscopic ULC for entire systems, which in turn reflects the individual human's learning process and skills acquisition.

We validate the new theory using data from a technological system with human involvement that includes both outcomes and a measure of experience. We analysed shipping losses over the last 200 years, which are an example of one such system and a rich data source because insurers and mariners tracked sinkings. Human error is and was the pervasive and main cause of ship loss, rather than structural defects in the ships themselves. We have analysed independent datasets for ship losses from 1800 to 1997. The lowest predicted minimum rate is consistent with the most probable loss rate for the last 200 years. If correct, this result also confirms the postulate of the most probable distribution adopted in deriving the microstates distribution formulae.

The distribution of microstates (manifested as outcomes) with accumulated experience is apparently independent of technology or date, and is due to the dominant contribution of the human element through the accumulated experience. The learning curve approach is consistent with the statistical distribution of error states and highlights the importance of the depth of experience interval. The validation results support the basic postulates and confirm the macroscopic ULC behaviour observed for technological systems.

Further work is needed, both on understanding the fundamental universal learning rates and the impact of exclusion rules derived from applying the techniques to safety management. In addition to bringing all available data together on a common basis and understanding, our new theory offers the prediction and the promise of determining and quantifying the influence of management, regulatory, liability, legal and other decisions.

## References

[1] Sommerfeld, A., 1956, 'Thermodynamics and Statistical Mechanics: Lectures on Theoretical Physics', Academic Press, New York.

[2] Sherwin, C.W., 1961, 'Basic Concepts of Physics', First Edition, Holt, Rinehart and Winston, New York, pp. 308–338.

[3] Bernstein, P.L., 1996, 'Against the Gods', John Wiley and Sons, New York, p. 8.

[4] Duffey, R.B. and Saull, J.W., 2002, 'Know the Risk', First Edition, Butterworth and Heinemann, Boston, MA.

[5] Jaynes, E.T., 2003, 'Probability Theory: The Logic of Science', First Edition, Cambridge University Press, Cambridge, UK, Edited by G.L. Bretthorst.

[6] Ohlsson, S., 1996, 'Learning from Performance Errors', Psychological Review, Vol. 103, No. 2, 241–262.

[7] Tor Norretranders, 1991, 'The User Illusion: Cutting consciousness Down to Size', Penguin Books, London, UK, p. 290.

[8] Baierlein, R., 1971, 'Atoms and Information Theory', W.H. Freeman and Co., San Francisco.

[9] Pierce, J.R., 1980, 'An Introduction to Information Theory', Dover, New York.

[10] Finney, D.J., 1952, 'Statistical Method in Biological Assay', Hafner Publishing Company, New York, Second Edition, 1964.

[11] Laplace, P.S., 1814, 'Essai philosophique sur les probabilités', extracted as 'Concerning Probability' in J.R. Newman's 'The World of Mathematics' Vol. 2, p 1327, 1956

[12] Greiner, W., Neise, L. and Stocker, H., 1997, 'Thermodynamics and Statistical Mechanics', Springer, New York, pp. 150–151.

[13] Woo, G., 1999, 'The Mathematics of Natural Catastrophes', Imperial College Press, London, UK, Chapter 6, p. 161 et seq.

[14] Gott III, J. Richard, 1993, 'Implications of the Copernican principle for our future prospects', Nature, Vol. 363, pp. 315–319, 27 May.

[15] Berman, B.D., 1972, 'Encyclopaedia of American Shipwrecks', Mariners Press, Boston.

[16] Institute of London Underwriters (ILU), 1988 et seq., 'Hull Casualty Statistics', data for 1987–1997, International Union of Marine Insurance Conferences (Available: http://www.iua.co.uk).

[17] UK Protection and Indemnity Mutual Insurance Club, 2000, 'Analysis of Major Claims', London (Available: http://www.ukpandi.com).

[18] Pomeroy, V., 2001, 'Classification – Adapting and Evolving to Meet Challenges in the New Safety Culture', Safety of Modern Technical Systems, TUV, Saarland Foundation, Germany, p. 281.

[19] Pickford, N., 1994, 'The Atlas of Ship Wrecks & Treasure', Dorling Kindersheg Publishing, New York.

[20] Australian Transportation Safety Board (ATSB), 2006, 'Analysis of Fatality Trends Involving Civil Aviation Aircraft in Australian Airspace between 1990 and 2005', Aviation Research Paper B2005/0388, March, pp. 22–23.

# 6

# Risk Assessment: Dynamic Events and Financial Risks[1]

*'If there is no price to be paid, it is also not of value.'*

*Albert Einstein, 1927*

We have developed a means to estimate the failure probability of *any* homo-technological system (HTS). How can we use this new knowledge?

It is a recognised, established and thriving business to insure against such failures when they cause or are liable for direct or indirect financial losses. We need to also estimate the return on an investment given a probability that the system might fail. Basically, the insurers and the investors gamble on the success of the venture or the likelihood of accidents. To offset the inherent risk in such activities, insurers ask for a premium that is sufficient to pay for the maximum probable loss plus some margin; and investors ask for a premium on the rate of return on the investment sufficient to hedge against failure.

In fact, investors will and must judge the risk based on the failure probability. This estimate is either based on prior knowledge of previous losses due to failures or accidents, being the risk 'history', or on the estimate of the future risk 'exposure'. This is completely outside the normal fiscal fields of accounting and auditing, which aim at ensuring a low risk of improper financial reporting[2]. This is achieved through independent assurance of due

---

[1]The learning curves for price reduction in this Chapter were first discussed in part in the paper by R.B. Duffey, 'Innovation in Technology for the Least Product Price and Cost – A New Minimum Cost Relation for Reductions During Technological Learning', Int. J. Energy Technology and Policy, Vol. 2, Nos. 1/2, 2004.

[2]An investment Echo in the finance industry is evidenced by the 2007 near failure and 'run' on the Northern Rock bank, the first in the UK for nearly 140 years. In order to save the possible effects of the potentially serious consequences for the investors and the UK financial reputation, the bank had to be taken into Government ownership for an undetermined period. The Four Phases of an Echo are clearly becoming evident, i.e., 1) Precursers: high–risk strategy, lack of proper control and auditing by the regulatory organisations, i.e., FSA (Financial Services Authority), the Bank of England and the

---

diligence, ethical behaviour; and by the professional and strict application and adherence to formal rules for how the corporate ledgers are to be kept and how executive management should behave.

We need to provide an independent predictive estimate of *dynamic* loss rates, based on experience, to use as an aid to setting investment and insurance premium magnitudes, thus assisting the management of loss ratios and reducing the potential risk exposure.

To estimate premiums or investment returns, the expected loss rate must be based on historical loss data and a reasonable expectation of future losses. The assigned risk is then based on a suitable estimate of uncertainties and margins. The actual premium is then based on this analysis, competitive rates, the company's actual loss ratio and the expected profit margin given the competitive market.

The usual or most popular formula used in financial 'risk' is based on future investor choices and expectations, given the assumption that the market behaviour is essentially purely random with some superimposed general upwards or downwards trend. On that assumption, we may use simple normal distributions for the uncertainties as a measure of the stock price 'volatility'. These assumptions are embodied in the famous Black–Scholes formula [1], the original mathematical derivation of which gives even some financial analysts pause. The risk model is based on a stock portfolio where the investor can choose deterministically from an assumed variable proportion of shares that at any time are at risk, while the rest of the portfolio money will be invested in the money market account, with a risk free rate of return, $r$. The stock market price or cost, $C$, is assumed to follow a combination of geometric noise or purely random Brownian motion with a steady 'drift' (profit or loss) with time. The variation of price with time, $dC/dt$, can then be written as a proportionality varying as:

$$dC/dt = \mu C + \sigma C dW/dt$$

Here $C(t)$ is the selling price (or buying cost) at any time, $\mu$ is a constant, and $W$ is some random variable with standard deviation, $\sigma$, which is assumed to be a (constant) measure of the price volatility. The standard deviation, $\sigma$, is the usual statistical estimate of the assumed normal spread at 65% confidence in the price distribution. Hence, the 'noise' in the price variation is a measure of the financially defined risk, which is due to uncertainty (see the Introduction). We would perhaps also interpret this noisy variation as a manifestion of information entropy existing in the marketplace, as we shall see later. We shall also show later how we can directly adapt and extend this Black–Scholes functional form to predict the impact of learning on product cost and price in the competitive marketplace.

The dependency of the *value, V*, with time to any selling price, $C$, after some algebra we need not give here, turn out to be related by a second-order differential equation of the form,

$$dV/dt = rV - \{(\sigma^2 C^2/2)d^2V/dC^2 + rP dV/dC\}$$

Treasury; 2) Confluence of events: mortgage concerns (US Sub-Prime effect) increasing world economic concerns; 3) Escalation: the 'Run' with private investors withdrawing millions of pounds deposits due to lack of confidence; 4) Denial: all parties involved blaming each other in Parliamentary investigations. The Bank of England is now resigned to implementing tougher procedures.

Hidden behind the deteministic and random assumptions, there is actually implied learning which is not immediately apparent in this form of equation. The practical evaluation of the random quantities is inherently on a portfolio or stock–by-stock basis. The rate of change of the value is proportional to the return due to the fixed interest rate plus or minus any random fluctuations or earned changes of the value with price. Although there seems to be no learning apparent in present-day gambling or investing in stock market *values*, we shall see later the effect of learning and competition on the *price* variation is actually implicitly included and assumed in the Black–Scholes type of model. This new extension includes application to the prediction of the impact of innovation on cost and price trends in manufacturing.

There have even been empirical relations proposed for stock market 'crashes' where the rate of change of the time-varying hazard function or potential failure rate of the market is assumed to be proportional to the hazard rate, *h*. This hazard function represents somehow the effects of the multitudinous trader-to-trader interactions (Woo, 1999) [2]. Thus, it is assumed that

$$\mathrm{d}h/\mathrm{d}t \propto h^{\delta},$$

where the assumed power exponent, $\delta > 2$, clearly must be fitted to data. After integrating, this 'power law' variation gives a non-linear time dependence of the hazard function between or before crashes. According to Woo [2], the same variation has apparently been proposed for volcano eruption prediction using prior historical data to estimate, $\delta$.

The analysis that has been developed here includes a semi-theoretical analysis of loss rates based on prior history and a future prediction based on the projected uncertainty or assigned risk. The premium prediction can be based on failure rate analysis. We have tested this method for loss rate prediction using comparisons to shipping losses, and to airline, railway, and road (traffic) accidents, as well as with industrial accident rate data for the last 10–20 years.

## Future Loss Rate Prediction: Ships and Tsunamis

Actuaries and others have studied mortality and loss statistics for centuries, so the odds for any one of us dying on or by a certain age are well known. For industrial and product insurance, against injury or death, the insurers must charge a premium that takes into account the risk of the individual loss, plus some margin of profit. For large natural catastrophes, like earthquakes and tsunamis [2], providing loss coverage and reimbursement examines the risk exposure for the insurer as well as the insured. Just like a stock portfolio, the risk is assessed as being of two types or parts due to:

a) the random factors of when, where and what outcome might occur (the so-called random aleatory or process risk); and
b) the uncertainty in the potential loss of how much damage might occur (the so-called lack of knowledge epistemic or parameter risk).

These uncertainties are fundamentally probability estimates, which include the uncertainties in occurrence of such natural outcomes, their magnitude and their location. The parallels to predicting probability of particular outcomes for HTS are obvious, particularly for the prediction of rare events, where the prior knowledge of outcomes is sparse. The difference is that for HTS the outcomes are essentially due to human contributions; whereas for natural catastrophes while the consequences are due to human contributions, the probability of occurrence is not.

Because insurers are businesses, they work largely on a yearly basis, with current premiums covering current losses with a lag, and the fixed assets and investments covering the total risk exposure. To minimise that loss potential, re-insurance is used. So if there is a particularly valuable cargo on a train, plane or boat, or an inventory of great flammability, or a history of losses, an excess charge or premium may also be applied, just as it is for household insurance and personal jewelry. If the hazard or risk is too great or catastrophic, it will be excluded. This is the process of 'underwriting', which assigns a premium cost to cover the risk of loss.

After the great Asian tsunami of 2004, killing over 200,000 people and leaving untold numbers destitute, one interview that ran on the media was not on the effect on the displaced people and the injured victims, but on potential losses for insurance companies. It was noted that the loss due to a tsunami was regarded as due to a flood and/or an Act of God: under the normal rules and contract clauses, these causes are usually excluded from any liability for payment. Floods are so destructive, and homes near coasts so vulnerable, insurers will not insure them. There is a message here for personal and investment risk management: if an insurer will not insure the risk, it is probably a significant one. Building near water is a known risk.

Just like sailing on it.

To provide another route to loss estimation and insurance, when learning is present, we have developed the following guidance. We then apply it to shipping losses as an example. The approach that is suggested to establish loss rate estimates:

1. Establish the historical loss rate.
2. Compare and correlate with theoretical loss rate equation.
3. Establish uncertainties and statistical variation.
4. Estimate the risk exposure interval and insured or capital value.
5. Add additional margin for risk.
6. Add margin for profit and premium value.
7. Compare to conventional rate(s) and adjust.
8. Predict rates for premium 'futures'.
9. Compare predicted and actual loss rates.
10. Adjust premium or company loss ratio data, needs and history.

As an example, and to set the order of magnitude, it is estimated that a hypothetical worldwide fleet of 30,000 vessels of >500 tons each with an average cargo value of ~$10M per vessel would be covered by a premium of between $120–360M per year (or $10–36M per month), dependent on the assigned risk. This is without profit margin, or correcting for the specific company loss ratio history, which is an average of order one loss per 1,000 ship-years, or an average of 30 such total losses each and every year.

Compare this HTS loss to a 'natural disaster' like the great 2004 Asian tsunami from an Indian Ocean earthquake. On Boxing Day, a giant wave destroyed the homes and livelihoods of about 5,000,000 or so people living and vacationing near the shores in many countries.

With average value or 'utility' of somewhere between $1,000 and $100,000 per capita, we are faced with total losses of between $5B to $500B. The purely 'economic' loss due to loss of tourism, jobs and manufacturing could be of similar magnitude, together with the loss of over 150,000 lives. These are seemingly staggering one-time, once-in-a-lifetime losses. But with a rate of about one such large tsunami event per 100 years or so, the loss per year is only a maximum risk of $5B to $10B per year, or a premium of only just over 10 to 20 times that of the losses in the world's shipping. But since a tsunami is hopefully a massive one-time event, and the maximum premium per capita is from $50 up to $1,000 per month, neither can the loss be covered on a yearly basis (the hypothetical insurance companies as well as the people are wiped out every 100 years), nor can the premium be afforded by those living near the ocean who really need the insurance coverage. Fundraising for relief efforts then help solve the immediate issues of food, essential supplies, temporary housing, medical attention, clean-up and urgent repairs. But clearly charitable and voluntary donations are inadequate for the longer term and are only a small part (a few %) of the total loss.

Interestingly, around the world, many people still live near volcanoes, mudslide areas or flood zones. Major cities with millions of people, like Mexico City and Naples, are in the literal shadow of still occasionally rumbling and active volcanoes. The roman cities of Herculaneum and Pompeii bear mute and literally petrified witness to the awesome destruction; as do some of the bodies of their citizens caught in the pyroclastic burst, hot ash and gas cloud, and the final lava and mud flows.

Earthquake insurance is expensive, with large deductibles before any money is paid out for a loss. The world's fifth largest economy, California, is built over a vast and active network of earthquake faults, but the probability of damaging events is still largely unknown (Woo, Chapter 5) [2]. Damaging seismic events are so common that the demolishing of freeways has occurred, and the oldest buildings from the 19th century that still exist have already been rebuilt or repaired many times. In Japan, earthquakes are also common, as is the loss of life. Building standards in Japan and California now require earthquake-resistant structures, and the larger facilities, like nuclear power plants and office skyscrapers, are made robust to survive the worst expected acceleration from the 'design basis earthquake'.

But the risks are generally ignored as we go on with our lives. What is the use of worrying about them anyway? Natural disasters are an accepted hazard, as we sprawl like ants over the face of the Planet. The pleasure of living today far outweighs the fear of death tomorrow. There is a subconscious and fatalistic cost-benefit decision, and the passive decision is to take the risk, along with your fellow humans. It is still only a one in a million chance that you personally will be killed, on average. The relative probability varies with your personal choices, just like your risk of death in an auto crash can only occur if you are actually in a vehicle. But of course, if you actually live very near a natural hazard (the sea, a volcano, a cliff edge, a flood plain, a seismic fault) the risk is higher, and so are your insurance costs.

There is really no point in developing insurance against risks unless there is a learning history, which decreases or contains future losses and minimises the risk exposure. Otherwise the losses would either be constant or increase as the population increases, which is good for a purely premium-taking or volume-based insurance business. We do have technological fixes available to reduce natural risks; like having flood barriers, or not building and living near the shoreline or a volcano, designating flood zones, and providing advanced warning systems, that at least could demonstrate that we are indeed learning something.

## Predicted Insurance Rates for Shipping Losses: Historical Losses

The historical loss record for shipping greater than 500 tons is shown in Figure 6.1. Clearly the loss rate in Mt/y is slowly decreasing as experience increases, as measured in 1,000s of shipping-years afloat.

The rate of losses is better given as the loss rate per 1,000 ship-years (kSy) as shown in Figure 6.2. The loss rate is represented by the MERE semi-theoretical equation. Similar relations can be developed for the total loss rate per thousands of ship-years, kSy, and is given by:

$$(L/\text{kSy}) = 0.38 + 9\exp(-\text{kSy}/60)$$

Therefore, the asymptotic minimum total loss rate is ~0.38 per 1,000 ship-years and shows evidence of learning. The fractional loss rate, the ones we need to insure against, is the number sinking versus the total that is afloat at any given time. This fraction is shown in Figure 6.2, as a typical example for the observational interval covering ~5 Bty afloat for the 10 years from 1987–1997.

A reasonable fit is again given by a learning curve, that suggests we lose about ~0.38 Mt for every Mty afloat. This is a risk of ~$4 \times 10^{-5}$ per hour afloat for a 1 Mt loss, or expressing the risk another way, a loss of 1 Mt every 23,000 hours interval, or about every three years.

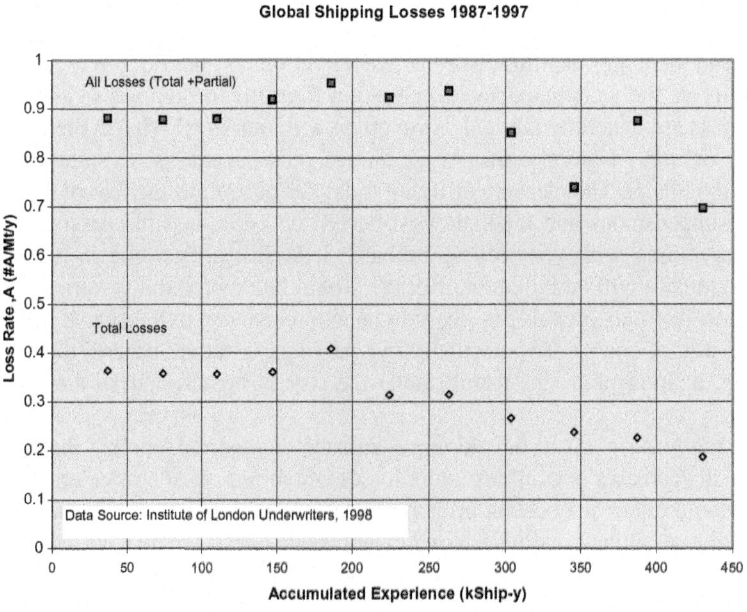

**Global Shipping Losses 1987-1997**

**Figure 6.1.** The shipping loss history

**Figure 6.2.**  Typical shipping loss rate correlation

## The Premium Equations

The estimated premium is based on predicting the loss rate and covering that with a premium payment. Thus, for a ship with a cargo value of $V$ \$/t and $N_T$ tons, then the premium $P(L)$ in \$ to cover a loss is:

$$P(L) = R(L) \times V \times N_T$$

where the probable rate of loss $R(L)$ is given by:

$$R(L) = (L/kSy) \times N_{kSy}$$

where $N_{kSy}$ is the number of kSy the cargo is afloat and is hence given by:

$N_{kSy} = N_{kS} N_y$, the product of the number of ships in the fleet and the years afloat.

The final premium equation is therefore:

$$P(L) = R(L) \times V \times N_T \times N_{kS} \times N_y$$

which for the asymptotic value for large experience (kSy's) the premium for the cargo is:

$$P(L) = 0.38 \times V \times N_T \times N_{kS} \times N_y$$

The total premium, $P$, is then the cargo plus the ship value, so for a ship of value $V_S$ is:

$$P = 0.38 \times ((V \times N_T) + V_S) \times N_{kS} \times N_y$$

Partial looses are then covered by simple fractionation, noting that the data indicate about a three times higher loss rate.

## Financial Risk: Dynamic Loss and Premium Investments

In any investment decision, the return should be greater than that from a 'risk-free' option. Since the basis for these options is usually bonds, or so-called gilt-edged Government stock with a guaranteed percent return rate, $G$.

In his book 'The Business of Risk', Moore, 1983 [3] makes the points that the investor's return must be greater than this $G$-value, otherwise there is no point in making the investment itself; and there has to be a safeguard against the risk factor, or the probability of failure, $p(L)$, of the investment target (such as projects, businesses, futures, stocks, etc.).

Considering only these two factors and ignoring for the moment tax breaks or penalties which are specific, the investor rate of return, $I$, must be given by the Moore formula:

$$I = G(1+\delta)/(1 - p(L))$$

where $\delta$ is the uplift fraction of the investment above the basic.

So the value over the base of Gilt-edged returns is the investment premium that the project or investment vehicle must make to be acceptable and is, obviously,

$$I/I_0 = (1+\delta)/(1 - p(L))$$

We know now that the probability of failure for any technological system is given by the double exponential of the Human Bathtub curve. So the expression for $p(L)$ is simply the probability as the double exponential:

$$P(L) = p(\varepsilon) = 1 - \exp\{(\lambda - \lambda_m)/k - \lambda(\varepsilon_0 - \varepsilon)\}$$

where, the failure rate is,

$$\lambda(\varepsilon) = \lambda_m + (\lambda_0 - \lambda_m)\exp - k(\varepsilon - \varepsilon_0)$$

and $\lambda(\varepsilon_0) = \lambda_0 = n/\varepsilon$, at the initial experience, $\varepsilon_0$, accumulated up to or at the initial $n$-outcome(s) where $n \sim 1$.

So now the risk premium must be a function of experience, however that is measured. We can calculate the *dynamic* risk premium ratio from the typical values we have estimated for $k \sim 3$ and $\lambda_m \sim 5.10^{-6}$. The result shown in Figure 6.3 on a logarithmic plot to encompass the large variation.

What is immediately evident is that the risk is high (the most) near the beginning, falls away to a few percent as experience is gained, and again sharply rises near the end. If we simply slapped on or imposed a minimum margin, say to cover the $\delta$-factor, administrative costs, overhead and a nominal profit markup in total of, say, 20% (any other number can be taken) then we have the curve changing as shown in Figure 6.4, with the ratio never falling below 20%.

So the biggest returns on the investment gamble are when the risk is highest: at the beginning and at the end.

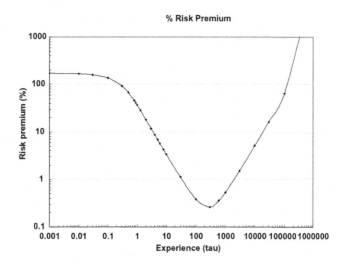

**Figure 6.3.**  The dynamic risk premium ratio without margin

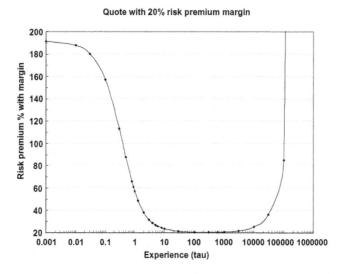

**Figure 6.4.**  The effect of including a margin

## Numerical Example

To provide an example, for one ship ($N_{kS} \sim 0.001\,kS$) of zero value ($V_S = 0$) afloat for one month ($N_y \sim 0.1$ year) with $N_T = 10,000$ tons of cargo, with a value $V$ of \$1,000/ton, the loss policy face value, before margin and risk, is given by:

$$P(L) = A \times 1,000 \times 10,000 \times 0.001 \times 0.1$$
$$= 1,000\,A\$/\text{month afloat}$$

## Overall Estimates of Shipping Loss Fraction and Insurance Inspections

Shipping losses are well-behaved and have very little variation with increased accumulated time or shipping years. The average loss rate is about ~1.3 per kSy (see Figure 6.5) and has been at that rate for centuries based on the Institute of London Underwriters (ILU) and Berman's US data. We can show the losses in insurance-style format by focusing on the fraction of ships are lost as a function of ship-age. This is a parallel to varying insurance premiums for cars with driver-age!

Knowing the prior shipping loss history, the insurers can apply varying premiums to a varying future risk, and also determine the inspection interval for seaworthiness that might be desirable before renewing a policy or for adjusting a premium.

We analysed the loss fraction for ships of different age, for two very disparate data samples for ships of over 500 tons displacement. One set is for the UK P&I Club data for losses of modern shipping worldwide; and the other set is for Berman's data for losses from 1800 onwards just for the USA. We plotted this as a fraction (%) lost as a function of ship-age, and binned the losses into five-year intervals as shown in Figure 6.6. This is really a plot of relative loss probability versus depth of experience, if the ship-age is taken as the experience measure. Crews of varying experience man-the-ship and change-over very often during a ship's life, which might obscure any expected exponential trend with experience, even if it existed.

The trend for the two data samples is extremely similar and very compelling, peaking in the interval of a ship-age (life) of about 15–20 years. The two observations from the graph, which are somewhat surprising, are:

1. There is little difference between the loss fractions with age of ship over the last 200 years, although modern ships tend to sink about 5% more often somewhat sooner in their life. Therefore it is possible to make future predictions of loss fraction with some confidence,

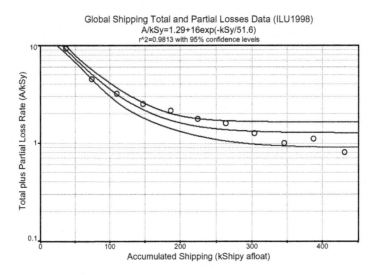

**Figure 6.5.** Overall shipping loss rate as a function of experience

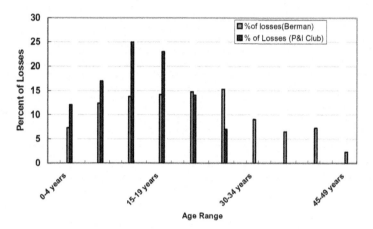

**Figure 6.6.**  Overall trend in loss fraction for ships of varying age (5-year bins)

and hence premium values, suitably adjusting for market conditions and current actual loss ratios.

2. The older ships (>30 years old) are less of a relative risk compared to the newer ones (<20 years of age). The (re)inspection interval for the insurance of ships is now about every three years, based on ancient historical practices for sailing vessels' average trade voyage duration and hence absence from port. There seems no rational reason for that inspection interval today, and every 5–10 years appears to be sufficient *on average*, with more inspections needed for the ships of ages 10–20 years old which dominate the risk. (See Figure 6.6.)

## The Loss Ratio: Deriving the Industrial Damage Curves

Accidents and losses are observed all the time, and if we are insuring against them, we would like to know how often they occur and how big the damages might be. In industrial accidents, for example, it turns out that the value of damage incurred is a function of the frequency of the event or loss. Large damage (or losses) is less likely, and there exists a distinct 'damage curve' (Hanayasu and Sekine, 2004) [4]. In this way we know that the severity or magnitude of the risk is related to the frequency or failure rate.

The probability density function of an accident is assumed to vary according to a well-known empirical power law (cf. power blackouts, stock market risks and price reductions) of the form:

$$f(\varepsilon) = K/\mathrm{h}(\varepsilon)^{q+1}$$

where, $K$, is a constant, and, $q$, is the fitted exponent to the data, with a value of $2 < q < 3$ for the outcome studies given, where in this case the measure of experience, $\varepsilon$, is actually a function of the loss, $h(\varepsilon)$. The actual failure rate, $\lambda(\varepsilon)$, is related to this probability density, $f(\varepsilon)$, and the rate of the number, $n$, occurring by the usual expression,

$$\lambda(\varepsilon) = f(\varepsilon)/R(\varepsilon) = \{1/(1 - F(\varepsilon))\} \, \mathrm{d}F(\varepsilon)/\mathrm{d}\varepsilon$$
$$= \{(1/(N - n))(\mathrm{d}n/\mathrm{d}\varepsilon)\}$$

The probability of an outcome with damage of at least $h$ is then given by integration of $f(\varepsilon)$ as:

$$p(\varepsilon) = K/q \, h^q$$

so that the probability is less the greater the damage. Assuming that the initial (prior) losses, $h_0$, are known for some initial (prior) probability, $p(\varepsilon_0)$, then we can non-dimensionalise the subsequent risk of damage (losses) relative to that known initial loss, i.e.,

$$(h/h_0) = \{p(\varepsilon_0)/p(\varepsilon)\}^{1/q}$$

But we already know that if we are learning from these losses and the damage, the probability of a loss (the risk) for any and all HTS is given by the MERE result:

$$p(\varepsilon) = 1 - \exp\{(\lambda - \lambda_m)/k - \lambda(\varepsilon_0 - \varepsilon)\}$$

So we can combine these two results to obtain the damage or loss ratio, $(h/h_0)$, as a function of experience. Assuming that our usual $\tau$ tau units are a suitable measure of experience, shown in Figure 6.7 are the calculations for a range of several plausible values for $q$ of 1.5, 2 and 3.

The remarkable observation is that the damage ratio rises as experience is gained right up until the minimum is reached in the HTS 'Human bathtub' failure probability curve. We may also derive this trend mathematically, and as such, it represents a totally new result. What has happened is that the loss probability has not decreased fast enough at first to offset the

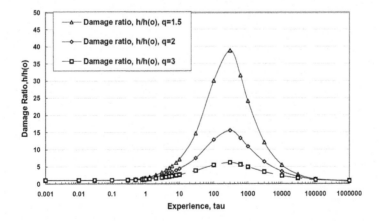

**Figure 6.7.**   The damage ratio for industrial outcomes

simultaneous increases in damage, so increasing damages occur until enough experience is gained. Thus, the insurance or set-aside 'cash reserves' must be built up substantially at first in order to cover adequately the initially increasing actual damages, and to offset the actual losses incurred during learning.

The above damage ratio function can also be well approximated by a log-normal, or a two exponential fit for any given $q$-value, adequate for risk estimation purposes. This exercise in risk and loss estimation is clearly indicting how sometimes apparently counter intuitive trends may be obtained once learning is included (via the failure rates varying with experience). In the results and analysis shown by Hanayasu, for example, a constant failure or outcome rate was assumed, resulting in only a single exponential form for the damage ratio curves.

## Making Investment Decisions: Information Drawing from the Jar of Life

Given all the uncertainty and risk in investment choices, how can we proceed? How do the professionals try to beat the odds? What premium should we seek, and what return should we expect for our risk exposure?

It turns out to be largely subjective, a gut feel, and that all the data and trend analysis break down when the prior knowledge is incomplete, and the future uncertain....

Various formal approaches to 'decision analysis' have been defined. It is another means by which we try to rationalise our often wrong choices. The methods provide a formal way of ranking and judging alternate risks. Available techniques are many and all rely on prior information.

We may weigh outcomes against each other in terms of their *utility*, being their perceived value to us. This ubiquitous phrase was introduced by Bernoulli, 1713 [5] into economics theory in order to 'explain' the irrational behaviour when we are making a subjective choice over an objective prediction. Various ideas have been put forward to quantify the utility, from the inverse of the wealth already possessed, to functional forms and curves, to the relative change any gain might make. If we knew what it was, we could even predict consumer choice and preference.

Since there is uncertainty and financial risk, we are not all billionaires. The prudent investor can spread his risk, just like laying off the exposure of insurance companies by adopting 're-insurance' against huge or unacceptable (not directly underwritten) losses. The total amount at risk is shared among many for an agreed share of the profits. This obviously leads to the question of whether there is an optimum spread, or risk-lowering strategy also. By balancing off the risk of one loss against the chance of another gain, we have also 'covered' our bet. This is the gamblers dilemma: of staking all on one risk, one winner, or of spreading the odds around and still hope to come out ahead.

Since there is no single indicator of how well any given investment will perform in the future, we are actually choosing probabilities and taking a hopefully educated risk. The concept of a 'loss function' has even been introduced to account for guessing the wrong outcome, where the function can have some assumed algebraic form.

Rarely are the odds known as, say, they are in roulette or a lottery with one winning number out of many equally possible ones. In those cases, the winners are out of our control, drawn at random by others, and we only make the decisions of how many gambles to make or entries to buy in a random pick. Not so in card hands, where we know the total number of cards, their suites and their face values (five of spades, Queen, Ace). As we voluntarily draw or are dealt cards from the deck, just as balls drawn from the Jar of Life, we can estimate accurately our chance, our probability of a specific card, and even of matching it in some way with our existing hand for a flush, a pair, a run. The risk of winning or losing depends on what has been drawn before by others, as well as by yourself, and what are the winning-hand combinations.

Whether we are picking out a winning investment, or not, the prior data (Bernstein, 1996 'Against the Gods') [6] shows that stock market price variations and average fluctuations follow a normal or 'bell-shaped' curve and that, in Bernstein's words, 'the stock market is unpredictable'. The outcomes we observe are simply those that we are most likely to see and variations from the average are not only just randomly plus and minus, about some mean value, but will follow a pattern or well-defined distribution *if* learning is present.

## Information Entropy and Minimum Risk

How to characterise a distribution of unpredictable outcomes is exactly the problem we have been tackling all along. It has been analysed mathematically in detail by Jaynes, 2003 [7], who proposed that:

> *This suggests that ... entropy might have an important place in guiding the strategy of a business-man or stock market investor.*

Using the prior information, as derived in Chapter 5 from Statistical Error State Theory (SEST), we found that a measure of the degree of order in a system, or of the uniformity of the probability distribution was given by the information entropy, designated by $H$. We could expect a similar argument to hold for the pattern of gains and losses that we observe in the market. Recall this quantity, H, was a reflection of how many different ways the outcomes could be arranged, so we may explore the algebra to see what it tells us.

For the given $j^{th}$ observation interval, as a measure of the uncertainty for a uniform distribution:

$$H_j = -\sum p_i \ln p_i$$

where the probability of an outcome for any $i^{th}$ depth of experience is,

$$p_i = p_0 \exp(\alpha - \beta\varepsilon_i)$$

So the maximum gain or minimum loss (min–max) occurs when,

$$dp_i/d\varepsilon_i = 0$$
$$= -\beta p_i = -\beta(n_i/N_j), \text{ of course, giving,}$$
$$= -\beta(n_0/N_j)\exp(\alpha - \beta\varepsilon_i)$$

This result gives a min–max and goes to zero when $\beta$ or $n_0 \rightarrow 0$, being for no learning or no ground state, respectively; $N_j \rightarrow \infty$, for a large number of outcomes; or for large learning when $\alpha \ll \beta\varepsilon_i$. The first two conditions are not applicable, according to the world's error data, so we are left with the latter two conditions.

With an infinite sample or number of outcomes, $N_j \to \infty$, and even if it were possible we would have no uncertainty, so that result is trivial and unachievable. The last condition on $\beta$ is only possible if we have learning evident in the prior data, something we have already noted is lacking in the market!

The implication is that there is no risk minimisation present in the market; and that maximum gain or minimum loss is not possible, at least theoretically, unless there is learning.

If learning were present, then the information entropy is given by,

$$H_j = -\sum p_i \ln p_i$$
$$= -\sum p_0 \{\exp(\alpha - \beta \varepsilon_i)\} \times \ln \{(p_0 \exp(\alpha - \beta \varepsilon_i))\}$$
$$= -\sum p_0 \{\exp(\alpha - \beta \varepsilon_i)\} \times \{\ln p_0 + (\alpha - \beta \varepsilon_i)\}$$

For learning, the necessary condition is $1 < \alpha \ll \beta \varepsilon_i$, so

$$H_j \approx p_0 \sum \{\beta \varepsilon_i \exp - \beta \varepsilon_i\}$$

Hence, for this learning limit, the information is only a function of the learning rate and the depth of experience. The lack of learning must be why traditionally and historically, analysts and ourselves discern no pattern in the outcome distributions.


## Progress and Learning in Manufacturing

As we developed the ideas and concepts implied by the Learning Hypothesis, we became aware of the extensive work and study done in the past on improving workers output in manufacturing. Not surprisingly, during the early 20th century, there was great interest in reducing or at least optimising labour costs, and hence, on the influence of acquired skill on increasing output, particularly for mass production or assembly lines. In the fields of industrial engineering, economics and process management, the potential increase in output and the associated reduction in cost acquired its own name of 'productivity'. The progress of the whole organisation (or HTS as we call it) could be measured, as it strove towards sharpening the company's manufacturing skills, increasing production and enhancing competitive advantage.

Learning is everywhere, and not surprisingly it is hard at work in the competitive marketplace. In fact, 'learning curves' for product price decreases have been known and been around for some time, apparently since 1936 in manufacturing (Jordan, 1972) [8] and even earlier in the psychological literature (Buck, 2006) [9]. In industry, the learning curve or relationship between increasing accumulated output and decreasing specific cost became known by the title 'Progress Functions'. Not surprisingly, the main interest was in measuring and reducing the time it took to make or produce anything, hence reducing costs.

The empirical forms for the progress functions varied by the type, nature and size of process under study, which covered all the way from individual workers to the entire factory. The functions adopted also varied by author, and by field of field, with simple power laws, modified exponentials, and polynomial-type expressions being adopted to fit the data. It was often hard to collect and disentangle the data since it is not always clear how one cost or

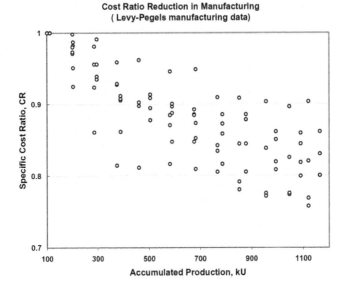

**Figure 6.8.**   Typical Manufacturing Cost Reduction Data

time component affected or influenced another, which is a feature common of systems with human involvement. The simplest power law is a function of amount produced, and was criticised as giving unreasonable extrapolations (with which we agree and return to later), so alternative functions were created and proliferated. It was a battle to see which empirical form was 'best', just as can be seen in the psychological literature over the fitting of curves to human response times as learning occurs. In fact, it should be no surprise that industrial manufacturing and psychology have much in common with the study of human skill acquisition.

So, since we expect the reduction in manufacturing time to be a direct result of error correction and learning, we would also expect the MERE result and the Learning Hypothesis to extend and apply here too. The outcomes from learning can be enhancement in productivity, but can also appear as improved products (See Figure 6.8).

## Innovation in Technology for the Least Product Price and Cost: Reductions During Technological Learning

The classic power law relationship between price and quantity is the locus that describes the matching of supply and demand, and the exponent is called an 'elasticity' by the economics profession. Much research has been undertaken to determine empirically the 'elasticity' of goods, services, products, minerals and even money, which means finding the exponent that best fits the rate of decline that has been observed to occur. Obviously, if the cost or price of an item goes down as we get better at making, marketing or selling it so we can sell more, that is good for sales, profits and the future of both the item maker and of the economy.

We show and introduce a new method, based on the Learning Hypothesis, to obtain least product cost and price that includes the effect of innovation and technological learning in manufacturing and production. This key result is a new paradigm instead of the usual economic 'power law' formulation. The new analysis is based on extensive analysis of many technological systems, and is directly related to the presence of learning as experience is accumulated. The results agree with the observed data. By using a consistent basis, the method replaces previous empirical 'power law' descriptions of the technological learning curve with a new 'marginal minimum cost equation' (MCE).

Thus, we are also able to unify apparently quite disparate fields of technology improvement. The same learning MCE formulation and theory links the diverse influence of economics in the (technological and economic) marketplace with the error reduction due to accidents and errors in social, transportation and industrial processes.

Such a universal learning trend has been observed over the entire course of the modern Industrial Revolution and is due to the fundamental ability of humans to learn, as experience is accumulated with technological systems (Duffey and Saull, 1999; 2000; 2001; 2002) [10,11,12,13].

## Cost Reduction in Manufacturing and Production: Empirical Elasticity 'Power Laws' and Learning Rates

Historically, as we noted above, the observed and desirable decrease in cost of any manufactured item with increases in production is well known (Wright, 1936) [14] and (McDonald and Schrattenholzer, 2001) [15]. The decrease parallels the classical economics price/demand relation with increases in quantity produced, and these references contain sufficient background that we need not repeat the historical basis here. This decrease is obviously due to a combination of technological and market factors such as:

a) economy of scale with numbers made, repeat orders and standardised processes;
b) streamlined and bulk ordering of supplies, parts and equipment;
c) increasing experience of the labour force and its management;
d) product, process and production improvements;
e) market forces and price pressures; and
f) innovation and technology shifts

McDonald and Schrattenholzer (2001, 2002) [15,16], Andress, 1954 [17] and others point out, because experience accumulates with time, unit costs decrease for a given technology where the important variable is the 'accumulated experience', not time passing. So the measure of experience – or its surrogate – is key, exactly as observed in modern technological systems exhibiting error, accident, event, injury and incident reduction. This basic fact is shown by the theory and data in Chapter 1 and Duffey and Saull (2002) [13]. The decrease is non-linear.

The economic formulae (or 'model') proposed and used to date are empirical and describe a cost reduction rate or trajectory with experience. The simplest are of the form of a power law relating the cost reduction rates to a production parameter, for example, material and/or labour cost. Thus, Wright's (1936) [14] original formula is an empirical power law of the form:

$$\text{Cost Reduction Factor, } F = (\text{Quantity, } N)^x$$

where $x$ is an unknown or observed power 'law' factor. Since the cost reduction factor is related to the cost of the first unit, $C_0$, then $F \equiv (C/C_0)$ and the accumulated production quantity can be written as, $\varepsilon$, this relation is then of decreasing cost or price with increasing production/experience:

$$C = C_0(\varepsilon)^{-b} \text{ Power Law}$$

where the power law parameter, $x = -b$, is derived from experience, and accN = $\Sigma N$, the accumulated experience or total number or quantity of relevant units produced, accN. Equation (1) we will refer to as the $b$-power law. A slightly more general form that has been used since is, for the $i$th interval, the 'General equation' (see, e.g., Rubin, 2002) [18]:

$$y_i = ax_i^{-b}$$

where,

$y_i$ = time or cost to produce $i$th unit ($C$ in our notation)
$x_i$ = cumulative production thru period $i$ ($\varepsilon$ in our notation)
$b$ = learning rate exponent (or elasticity)
$a$ = coefficient (a constant)

The actual observed price or cost or time decrease is then 'piecewise' fitted by a series of values of, $b$, which vary with production/experience (i.e., $b = f(\varepsilon)$). The percent cost reduction for a doubling of cumulative output is often used as a measure of the learning rate, $LR$, where,

$$LR = (1 - 2^b) \times 100\%$$

McDonald and Schrattenholzer's (2002) [16] expression for the 'concept of technological learning' in the capital cost of energy systems is of the similar power law form:

$$\text{Specific cost, } C = (\text{Initial cost, } C_0) \times (\text{Installed capacity, Ccap})^b$$

where $b$ (like the power law factor, $X$) is termed in economic jargon a 'learning elasticity' and Ccap is equivalant to $\varepsilon$. The same formulation can hold for Price, if market forces are active.

They showed how many energy systems can be fitted with $b$-values. It is actually observed that the cost curves are not of constant slope (i.e., $b$ varies with accumulated experience too) as shown in Figure 6.9. Thus, continuous learning or experience curves are approximated by a series of piecewise fits, varying, $b$, so that it is a non-unique function with accumulated production. This must also be able to correct for the wrong asymptote with the implication is that the price, $C$, tends to zero at large experience ($\varepsilon \to \infty$), whereas in reality, there is always minimum price/cost for a product in the commercial market – unless it is a loss maker. This has lead analysts to introduce so-called 'kinked' power law models or variants, with an arbitrary change of slope or $b$-value at some experience, quantity produced or date.

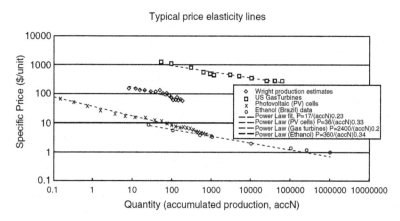

**Figure 6.9.** Typical empirical 'learning curves' and 'rates' for energy-related technologies fitted to the elasticity b-power law (See also Rubin, 2002 [18])

In their earlier paper, McDonald and Schrattenholzer (2001) [15] derived learning rates (that is values for, $b$) using both cost and price data for nearly 30 technologies. They found $b$-values of order −0.03 to −0.3 (implied learning 'rates' of between 2 and 20%) using both cumulative production and installed capacity where appropriate as the measure of accumulated experience. McDonald and Schrattenholzer (2001, 2002) [15,16] discuss the limitations and hidden factors that can affect apparently good fits of data with $b$-values, including the inclusion of a 'learning floor' given by a finite price at large experience, the influence of both forgetting and of 'learning depreciation' acting to decrease the slope.

As shown by Figure 6.9, the value of, $b$, can vary and the choice of the accumulated experience, $\varepsilon$, in this case was predicated by the accumulated sales for each technology. This measure for the experience was and is relevant to these energy technologies competing in the power market. The technologies are price-takers dependent on the local market price of power sold to consumers and/or wholesalers or marketeers, where the incentive is to reduce unit investment cost (measured in $/unit installed, sold or made) as quickly as possible to the value needed for market penetration and sales.

Such empirical 'power laws' are similar to those so-called 'economy of scale' relations, where a reduction in cost of, say, 10% follows from an increase in, say, unit size by 20%, if following a square root power 'scaling law' (i.e., $b = 0.5$). The empirical 'power laws' or fits for the arbitrary parameters for different technologies are now the subject of study by international bodies such as the IEA and IIASA, using this to actually predict future rates and/or costs for energy systems and technologies.

# A New General Formulation for Unit Cost Reduction in Competitive Markets: The Minimum Cost According to a Black–Scholes Formulation

*We can now develop a more complete analysis, which shows the inherent non-linearity and the (exponentially) decreasing trend with increasing technological and unit experience/ production down to a constant cost.*

Using our newly learned knowledge, we can now therefore correct the problems arising from the:

a) empirical basis of the elasticity curve or '$b$-power law';
b) wrong limit of zero price/cost at large production/experience/sales;
c) fact that the elasticity exponent, $b$, is not constant, but varies such that $b = f(\text{experience}, \varepsilon)$;
d) implied learning rate is independent of the market cost/price target; and
e) inconsistency of the elasticity model with modern financial risk analysis.

The basic set of economic assumptions we now make is that *the overall rate of production cost or market price reduction (learning) in a technology or market is proportional to the competitive pressure* (as measured by the unit market price or cost). Market forces and competitive pressures both drive the price down, either to a profitable or market-determined value, using both innovation and experience.

As we gain experience and learn, the rate of decrease in cost (or price) is proportional to the instantaneous cost (or price) above the ultimate market value. This assumption (or hypothesis at this stage) is justified a posteriori by data and model comparisons.

Recall the Black–Scholes formula adopted for the valuation of stock portfolios at the start of this Chapter. We can now show that this formula for the price variation implicitly includes a hidden feedback due to market competition since the price was assumed to vary as,

$$dC/dt = \mu C + \sigma C dW/dt$$

For the present purposes, let us ignore or neglect the purely random and statistical variations represented by the last term on the right-hand side and focus solely on the *systematic* trend of the rate of change of the item or unit specific price corresponding to the first term. We can now translate the Black–Scholes formulation directly to learning in the competitive market place by adopting accumulated experience units, $\tau$, as the independent variable instead of time, $t$. This experience measure then corresponds precisely to the effective 'exposure' interval of the portfolio owner or of the manufacturer to the relevant market forces.

The new market competition theory is then an emergent theory that avoids describing the details behind the observed behaviour. The competitive market, labour force, social, policy and tax structure are, ceteris paribus, all interwoven into one composite learning rate. Thus, at any moment in experience, $\tau$, the rate of reduction of price (or cost) is in mathematical terms the Black–Scholes formula reduced to:

$$dC/d\tau \propto C$$

or, given what we now know from the Learning Hypothesis, we write

$$dC/d\tau = -k(C - C_m)$$

where, $C$ is the unit cost or price (we return to the matter of profit margin later), $k$ is the learning rate characteristic (time) constant equivalent to the Black–Scholes $\mu$-term, and $\tau$ is the accumulated experience (measured in some surrogate units of production or quantity) with the specific technology. The minimum cost, $C_m$, corresponds to the 'learning floor', market-driven, base production or target value. The learning rate constant, $k$, is particularly interesting since a positive value ($k > 1$) implies a learning curve of decreasing cost with increasing experience. On the other hand, a negative value ($k < 1$) implies forgetting, with increasing cost: and we can write the constant to include this effect as, $k \equiv k(1 - f/k)$, where $f$ is the forgetting rate.

The resulting differential Minimum Cost Equation (MCE) is directly soluble, and the solution form corresponds to the so-called 'exponential model' for the marginal cost. The costs decline to a minimum as market and manufacturing experience is gained, such that:

$$C^* = \exp - k(\varepsilon),$$

Here, $C^*$, is the non-dimensional cost or price, relative to the initial entry or development value, $C_0$, and the minimum achieved production cost or market price, $C_m$, and is written:

$$C^* = (1 - C/C_m)/(1 - C_0/C_m)$$

Now, $\varepsilon$ is a measure of the accumulated experience, but it is $k$, the learning rate constant, that determines how fast the price falls or rises. The deceptively simple and incredibly convenient exponential model gives the cost/price relation for the marginal cost variation with experience:

$$C = C_m + (C_0 - C_m)\exp - k(\varepsilon) \quad \text{Minimum Marginal Cost}$$

In words, the cost, $C$, at any accumulated production or experience, accN, is equal to the sum of the minimum attainable cost, $C_m$, that occurs at large accumulated experience, and which is only achieved via an exponentially declining rate from the initial cost, $(C_0 - C_m)$. This is the fundamentally new and useful result of the analysis that we will refer to as the *minimum (or least) marginal cost equation* (MCE) and is the so-called *exponential model* for the learning rate. All production, process and management actions are determined by the in-built, explicit or implicit need to follow the curve. We use this MCE form repeatedly for data analysis: in fact, we find all data that have learning do agree with this model and the learning hypothesis. So, the cost reduction factor is simply given by:

$$F = (C/C_0) = (C_m/C_0) + (1 - C_m/C_0)\exp - (k\varepsilon)$$

The equivalent elasticity is represented by the marginal variation of quantity with price, or by the inverse of ($dC/d\varepsilon$), and is by:

$$b_{eq} \equiv (d\varepsilon/dC) = -k/(C - C_m)$$

and is the inverse of the variation of the cost margin above the minimum, varying naturally from being infinitely elastic when $C \to C_m$, and also varying with the value of the learning rate, $k$, and as $C = f(\varepsilon)$. Conversely, the learning rate constant, $k = -(C - C_m)b_{eq}$.

The total amount of recorded or accumulated experience, accN, in modern settings and when recorded, is typically measured by items such as the system operating time, items manufactured or shipped, units sold, number of vehicles made, industrial production hours, etc. Hence, as $\varepsilon \to \infty$ then $C \to C_m$, the *asymptotic minimum cost*, which is also nearly a constant cost at large production/experience.

We have already shown the wide use of this simple exponential learning model formulation in fitting and predicting technological 'learning curve' data (Duffey and Saull, 2002) [13]. Beyond the inherent simplicity, the advantages of using this learning curve or exponential form are that it is:

a) theoretically based and therefore plausible;
b) enabling *predictions* and the associated confidence limits to be estimated;
c) not an entirely arbitrary choice, being dictated by the extension of reliability theory to economic learning rates; and
d) provides a framework that is consistent with economic price/cost/market theory.

To analyse the data, *the accumulated experience* can and should be used as the explanatory variable. Thus, this new approach provides a very different view of the data using the accumulated experience, and providing a ready comparison to the constant rate.

Thus, the MCE provides:

a) comparison to the inherent expectation of the power law;
b) prediction of future costs;
c) determination if the cost data are following a learning curve;
d) quantification of the minimum cost/price has been attained; and
e) theoretical basis and underpinning for the above prognostications.

Obviously, the cost, $C$, is made up of many components – the costs of labour, raw materials, manufacturing, construction, and installation and licensing. Presumably, these components of the total unit cost all follow their own 'learning curves' and hence, $k$, is an effective overall learning rate constant, such that $k = \Sigma_i k_i$, for all the $i$th technologies.

## Universal Learning Curve: Comparison to the Usual Economic Power Laws

How does this new general MCE formulation compare to the expected trends with increasing experience/production, and with the more traditional exponential $b$-power laws of the conventional elasticity form? We show this comparison in Figure 6.10, where the cost factor is plotted versus the experience for more than a single unit.

A plot of the instantaneous observed cost, $C$, normalised by the initial cost, $C_0$, versus the accumulated experience or units produced/sold, $\varepsilon \equiv$ accN, should therefore exhibit a simple exponential decline with increasing accumulated experience. We call this the ULC, and *ceteris paribus* would be followed for any technological system exhibiting learning and which is well behaved in its asymptotic limit as production, product and market experience is accumulated. Figure 6.10 indicates this to be of order by 10–1,000 units, and it is clear that the MCE and the power law models have different shapes, but can lie close to each other depending on the values of the learning rate, k, and the initial (developmental) to final (minimum market) price ratio, MPR, given by $(C_0/C_m)$.

It is very clear from the Figure 6.10 that 'average' values of, $b$, can be chosen that approximates the MCE (i.e., $b \sim 10k$, say), but that the fundamental fact and difference that the final

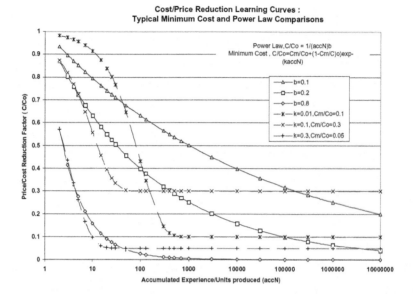

**Figure 6.10.** Comparison of learning curves

price/cost is finite has an important effect. The whole trajectory is determined by the minimum cost actual or target value of MCR for the MCE; but *not* for the power law, which always declines to zero price. Whether this minimum cost/price is ascribed to the presence or not of a 'learning floor', 'technology depreciation' or 'forgetting' is immaterial.

For the initial start-up, when $10 < accN < 100$, say, we can see that for reasonable learning rates ($0.1 < b < 0.2$, or $0.01 < k < 0.1$) that the factor $F(= C/C_0)$ declines to typically 20–70% of the initial cost.

Thus, as a cost-management tool, we may use the MCE to define targets for the learning rate given the need to attain a certain cost reduction by a given production quantity.

In the examination of the Price and Cost relations for a new product, (which is one measure of profit!) the developmental and market entry, and mature product phases have been distinguished (McDonald and Schrattenholzer, 2002) [16]. A price/cost curve is hypothesised that decreases from the near purely Cost-determined phase during innovation in the development and market entry, to the Price-determined stable phase in the long run, as units of production increase. This has the form shown in Figure 6.11, and here on a log-log scale the constant cost–price lines have slopes of −1.

This curve shape and trend is exactly the same (in fact identical in form) as the MCE, and is the ULC previously derived (Duffey and Saull, 2002) [13], which has its basis in the learning hypothesis. This form has been shown to hold for many technologies, over the 200 years of the industrial age, and it is relatively independent of the country, nation or world region.

The 'shake-out' rate is now determined by the learning rate constant, $k$. So the new theory is consistent with existing economic observations. To a first approximation, in a mature market, the unit profit, $P$, may be given by the difference, $P = \Sigma(C - MC_m)$, depending on whether a 'normal' ($M = 1$) or 'economic' profit ($M > 1$) margin is being made.

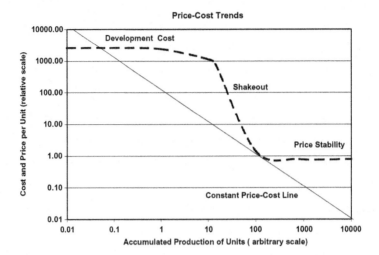

**Figure 6.11.** Typical Universal Learning Curve or classic cost reduction learning curve (derived from McDonald and Schrattenholzer (2002) after the IEA and BCG, and from Duffey and Saull (2002) failure rate data and the MCE). The MCE theory line is dashed, and the constant decline rate is the solid line

From the MCE, we can also expect any new system to have an initially higher cost, $C_0$, called a start-up cost. In the presence and enforcement of suitable management and other production and sales systems, the cost will then trend exponentially steadily downwards as production and market experience is accumulated. Thus, we can construct and use such a curve (the MCE) to determine if the data or system is well-behaved, and is tending towards or has attained its minimum price. The latter effect of tending to a finite fixed cost is also called 'experience depreciation' in the learning-curve economics literature.

## The Learning Rate $b$-Value 'Elasticity' Exponent Evaluated

Recall the empirical power law form quoted at the beginning and the exponential expression for the marginal cost was the MCE. Equating these two for any given marginal cost reduction factor, $(C/C_0)$, we have the result that the marginal cost elasticity, $b_{MC}$, is a function both of price target, MCR, and the learning rate, $k$:

$$b_{MC} = -\ln(C_m/C_0) + (1 - C_m/C_0)e^{-k\varepsilon})/\ln(\varepsilon) \qquad b\text{-value}$$

where the Specific Cost, $C = C_0(\varepsilon)^{-b}$. From the early economic traditions, we term this equation the $b$-value. For the limit of large experience, accN $\rightarrow \infty$,

$$b_\infty = \ln(C_m/C_0)/\ln(\varepsilon) \qquad b\text{-value limit}$$

Some numerical estimates for the $b$-value as a function of accumulated experience/production/sales, $\varepsilon \equiv$ accN, for varied learning rates and final price/cost targets are shown in Figures 6.12 and 6.13.

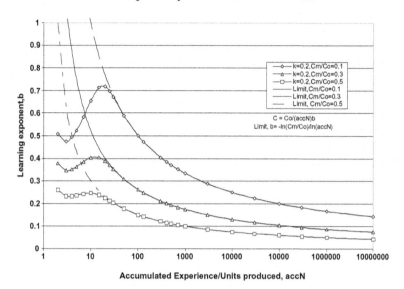

**Figure 6.12.**   Estimated learning exponent $b$-values

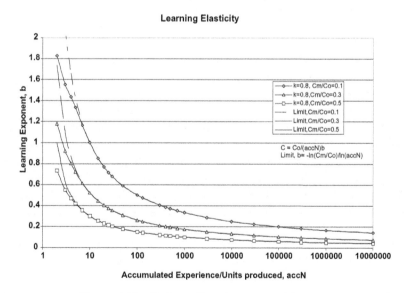

**Figure 6.13.**   Estimated learning exponent $b$-values

The typical values calculated for, $b$, lie between $0.1 < b < 1$, in accord with the observations of Learning Rates, LR, from 7–50%. The asymptotic limit equation does a good job of predicting the values for accN > 10 units of production. During start-up, some variations occur in the fitted $b$-value.

For the special *constant cost* case, a useful form is to write the cost as the identity:

$$CC(\text{accN}) = C_0(N_0/\text{accN})$$

Here $N_0$ is the initial experience (unit production) and $CC(\text{accN})$ the expected cost based on the accumulated experience, accN, up to that point, and on a log–log plot of price versus accN is a straight line of slope −1.

Ideally, one would like an invariant system of measuring and reporting, spread over a large history to acquire sufficient trend information. In reality, this is the exception, as the apparently never-ending quest for modernisation, improvement and change continues in production, development and marketing.

## Equivalent Average Total Cost $b$-Value Elasticity

The MCE implies a cost change relative to an *always* finite (non-zero) final cost, which the empirical elasticity or power law relation does not predict or encompass. The latter implies that $C \to 0$ at large unit production or experience, as $\varepsilon \to \infty$ whereas the learning theory gives $C \to C_m$. Therefore, it also gives a false lower cost limit at high production: nothing is produced at zero cost or can be sold at zero price (except as a 'loss leader' or as part of a total packaged deal). *This is not a trivial difference*, particularly if we try to project or extrapolate wrongly into the far future cost estimates, either in markets, costs, production or technology expectation. Such a situation is common, for example, in economic and energy models for the 21st century, which may then embody many false assumptions about future prices and/or technological learning.

For the two models, we can also make linear approximations to the full learning theory. For the two approximate forms to be equivalent, $k\varepsilon \cong b$, for the $i$th units, which is what we would expect to first order. The empirical elasticity, $b$, can now be seen to actually be the learning constant with an in-built dependency on the total number of items or units produced. So as postulated, the empirical relation is indeed only really a (solely first-order) piecewise curve fit to the more complete relation as given by the MCE.

A second useful approach makes use of the fact that usually we have the average total cost, ATC, spread or estimated over many units and production, $\varepsilon \equiv \text{accN}$, not the instantaneous marginal values for single units produced. In some systems, we may have a constant work force or manufacturing capability, within which observations are made at regular and unchanging intervals, or averaged over the same time frame. The price/cost rate may be trending down, up or be nearly constant: we need the equivalent average cost (EAC).

The total cost or sales, for a given production/sales, accN, is then given by the sum:

$$\text{Total sales, } S = \sum_1 C_i = \int_0^{\text{accN}} C\,dN$$

Hence, the ATC or average total cost/sales per unit, $\langle S_u \rangle$ through accN units is then given by:

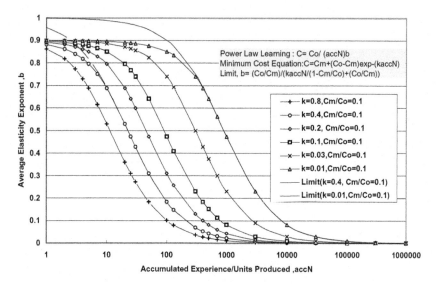

**Figure 6.14.**   Equivalent average total cost elasticity $b$-values, $b_{ATC}$

$$<S_u> = S/accN$$

We proceed by carrying out the integration for the total cost separately to any experience/ production accN. Equating the two expressions for the ATCs, per unit from these integrations of the elasticity-based Power Law and the learning-based MCE, in effect assumes the average total cost/sales to be identical. Hence, we obtain the expression for the equivalent average total cost elasticity as,

$$b_{ATC} = (1-(C_m/C_0))(1-e^{-k\varepsilon})/((C_m/C_0)k\varepsilon+(1-(C_m/C_0)(1-e^{-k\varepsilon}))$$

with the limits, as $\varepsilon \to \infty$:

$$b_\infty = (C_m/C_0)/((k\varepsilon)/(1-(C_m/C_0)+(C_m/C_0)) \qquad \text{Average value limit}$$

and, as $\varepsilon \to 0$,

$$b_0 = (1-(C_m/C_0)) \qquad\qquad\qquad \text{Lower limit}$$

We can see that the value of $b_{ATC}$ is dependent both on the experience and the final target MCR. Typical numerical results for the b-average elasticity, $b_{ATC}$, from the equivalent total cost equation are plotted in Figure 6.14, together with the limit equation.

Note that the Limit approximation is very good for the range of, $b$, of interest, and that the curve again depends on the value of the learning constant, $k$. We can directly compare the two estimates (for the instantaneous marginal and the average total cost) for the $b$-values numerically as shown in Figure 6.15 for typical ranges.

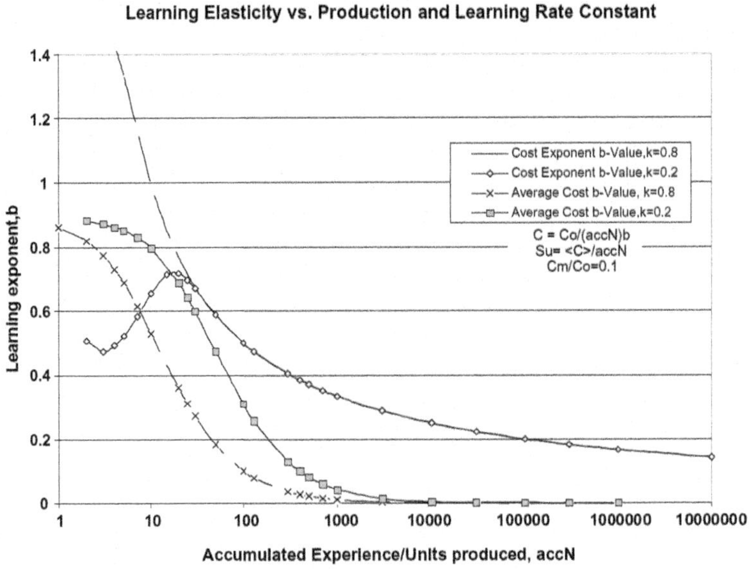

Learning Elasticity vs. Production and Learning Rate Constant

**Figure 6.15.**   Comparison estimates

In this example case, the average learning rate falls to near zero by ~1,000, whereas the instantaneous rate is still ~0.2. For the practical ranges of units initially produced $3 < \text{accN} < 100$, the value of, $b$, is ~0.2 to ~0.8, or an $LR$ of 10–40%, typical of that observed.

In fact, variations in $b$-values or equivalent $LR$s are common, and have been ascribed to many causes and policy changes. The suggestion here is to let the market forces and technology innovation proceed naturally through to production maturation. The cost decline cannot be forced, except by management changing the $k$-value or the market cost target.

## Profit Optimisation to Exceed Development Cost

The purpose of business is to make money, and a measure of that is the Profit, $P$, per unit or total units sold. Using the MCE formulation, we assume the final price, $C_m$, is the fixed or mature cost plus a percent or fractional profit margin, $M$. To a first approximation, in a mature market, the total profit may be given by the difference at any accumulated production and/or sales of accN:

Hence, $P =$ (Sales Revenue) $-$ (Production plus Manufacturing Costs)

Assuming that the MCR value is actually attainable and that the economic profit margin is a fraction, $M$, of the minimum price, we have:

$$P = \sum_i (C_i - MC_m) = \int_0^{\text{accN}} (C - MC_m)\,dN$$

giving,

$$P = C_m(1-M)\text{accN} + (C-C_0)/k.$$

The average marginal profit per unit is then,

$$<P_u> = (P/\text{accN}) = C_m(1-M) + (C-C_0)/k\text{accN}$$

Now, at the beginning innovation or learning, in order not to sell at a loss, $C > C_m$, always until the total development costs, $D$, are reclaimed such that:

$$P > D$$

Given the importance again of a wise choice for the MCR, a production quantity or experience amount, accN, to make a profit is required such that:

$$\text{accN} > D/C_m(1-M) + (C_0-C)/kC_m(1-M)$$

## The Data Validate the Learning Theory

We have now developed a new cost reduction relation, the MCE. Now, theory is all very well, but we need to compare this new learning-based MCE to some established data to validate and test it. We deliberately choose a challenging range of significant historical and independent information to show the power of the MCE. There are many cases of learning or experience curves we can choose from given in and by McDonald and Schrattenholzer (2001, 2002) [15,16] for energy technologies, appliances and manufacturing.

### a) Aircraft Manufacturing Costs Estimate Case

Wright (1936) [14] pioneered cost estimating with the first elasticity Power Law, used because he was interested in competitive markets in what was then completely new technology, namely transportation and commercial aircraft manufacture. The competitive market pressure was (back then) to have air travel compete with the cost of the available alternate of motor vehicle *road*-transport. The technology issue was how to scale up both the size and the production of aircraft and keep them cheap.

Using experience-based costs as a function of size, Wright estimated the cost of producing a new four-seater plane, based on some 10 years of prior manufacturing experience and using a materials and labour base largely from previous wire-and-string technology. The data he estimated and derived showed a decrease with increased quantity made as the measure of experience (i.e., where accN is equivalent to the number made or sold). The cost estimates are compared to the MCE in Figure 6.16, where we show the cost reduction from Wright versus the accumulated production in number of airplanes produced, accA.

We see immediately that the data show a decline in specific unit cost to a non-zero cost as mass production reduces costs, another new effect of the 20th century. The MCE correctly captures this key trend and predicts the uncertainty band for future potential cost reduction.

Wright estimated the elasticity, $b$, separately for these data, using $b \sim 0.3$ for labour, and $b \sim -0.1$ for materials, or *LR*s of between 7 and 20%, and projected a minimum cost ratio (MCR) of $(C_m/C_0) \sim 0.05$ for a million units produced.

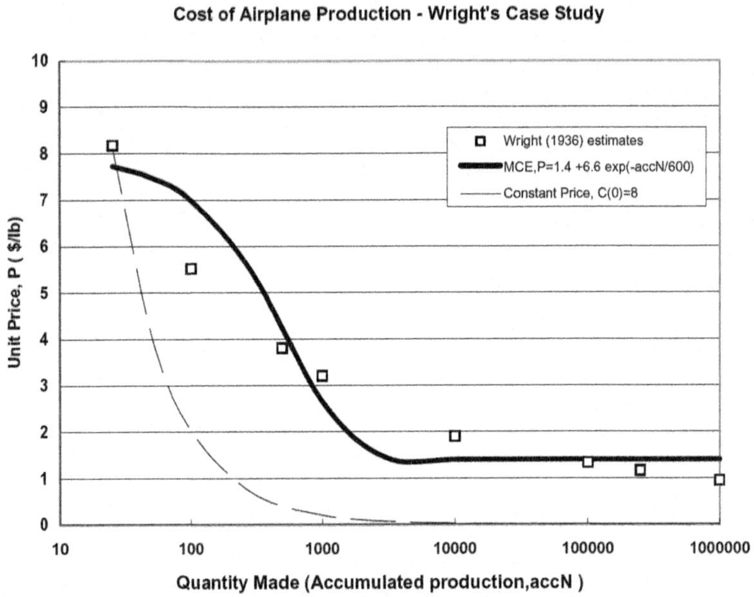

**Cost of Airplane Production - Wright's Case Study**

**Figure 6.16**  Comparison of the MCE to production cost estimates

The MCE fit to these estimates is given by:

Specific production cost ($/lb), $P = 1.4 + 6.6 \exp -(\text{accN}/600)$

where accN is the accumulated quantity made.

We see that the MCR is indeed ~0.2, the e-folding production learning rate constant is $k \sim 600 \, \text{accN}$ (aircraft made), and the minimum cost has an uncertainty of about $\pm \$1/\text{lb}$.

The goodness of the 'fit' is >93%, and is statistically comparable to the best-fit $b$-power law with $b \sim 0.23$ or:

$$P = 17 (\text{accN})^{-0.23}$$

The power law thus implies a factor of two higher initial cost than given by the MCE (17 versus $8/lb), and of course a lower cost beyond a production quantity of ~10,000 units. The $b$-value implies an $LR$ of ~15%.

So the MCE gives a different view of these estimates. This first example using the MCE was sufficiently encouraging in trends, goodness of fit, uncertainties and predictions, to warrant the further tests that follow.

## b) Photovoltaic Case

Later in the 20th century, the invention of the light-sensitive $p$–$n$ junction lead to the manu-facture of so-called PV or 'solar cells'. The competitive market pressure was and is to lower the cost of power generation to sell PVs into the distributed and central power generation

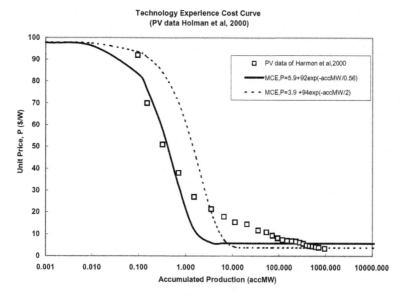

**Figure 6.17.** Comparison of the MCE to photovoltaic production data

markets, and to establish niches for small uses. The technology issue was how to reduce the cost of production of both large and small cells, by increasing the cell light-to-power output conversion efficiency and by reducing the defects or rejected items that can arise in manufacture.

The data for the costs of manufacture have been collected by Harmon (2000) [19] and show a marked reduction in specific unit cost (in this case per watt output) with increased experience, over the 30-year interval 1968–1997, in this case using the total or integrated power output of units sold (so accN ≡ accMW(e)).

The comparison with the MCE is shown in Figure 6.17, where we see a non-linear fall to a finite minimum cost asymptote, which has not quite yet been reached.

The MC equation we derive is:

$$\text{Specific price, } P\,(\$/\text{W}) = 5.9 + 92\exp - (\text{accMW}/0.56)$$

implying a final finite MCR of ~0.07, and a learning rate constant, k, of order 500 kW. The goodness of fit to the data is >95%. The MCE gives a reasonable but not exact fit to the data, but does enable an estimate of the minimum cost today for the future production at ~$6/W with an uncertainty of about 50% of ±$3/W. This has important ramifications, implying that PVs may remain above $3,000/kw installed. Indeed the data show some clear evidence of perhaps already having markedly flattened out from about 10,000 accMW(e).

There are clearly some variations in the lower cost 'tail' of the data. To cover uncertainty, and give a range of possible fits we also show the MCE variant of:

$$\text{Specific price, } P\,(\$/\text{W}) = 3.9 + 94\exp - (\text{accMW}/2),$$

which implies a smaller MCR but with slightly slower learning.

Comparisons to these data, using the conventional elasticity Power Law, have been given by Harmon (2000) [19] and McDonald and Schrattenholzer (2001) [15]. They show a significant variation of, $b$, with date (year) when expressed as a '% learning rate', $LR$, exactly what we would expect. The typical value range observed for the $LR$ is between 10–40%, or elasticity range $0.2 < b < 0.8$, with a ratio of $(C_m/C_0) < 0.1$, which then corresponds to the MCE learning rate constant of $k \sim 0.2$.

The best fit *single* $b$-power law is also >95%, and is:

$$\text{Specific cost, } P(\$/W) = 34(\text{accMW})^{-0.4}$$

implying an *average* overall learning rate, $LR$, of c 24%, but with an initial cost of \$34/W.

## c) Air Conditioners Case

The sales and production of modern appliances also lend themselves to learning curves and MCE analysis. The unpublished data of Akisawa (2001) for heat-pump type air conditioner unit prices in Japan was reported by McDonald and Schrattenholzer (2002) [16] along with other information. The competitive market pressure is to reduce costs to compete with refrigerant-type units, in both cost and performance, as well as perfecting the technology.

The MCR attained was ~0.5 for some 60 million AC units sold, accM, in Japan. Although these are price rather than cost data, they are a comprehensive set of actual market data, so are worth analysing with the MCE.

We compare to these data reported of Akisawa in Figure 6.18, and the MCE is given by a reasonable fit of:

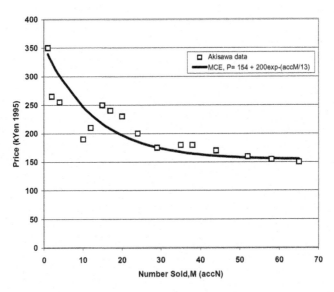

**Figure 6.18.** Comparison to air conditioner sales data of Akisawa (as reported by McDonald and Schrattenholzer, 2002)

$$\text{Unit Price, } P(\text{kYen}) = 154 + 200 \exp -(\text{accM}/13)$$

Hence, an asymptotic market price of ~150,000 Yen is predicted, for a production out to 100 million units, with an uncertainty of ±25,000 Yen, and the estimated MCR is exact.

In comparison, the *single-value b*-power law used by McDonald and Schrattenholzer (2002) [16] is given by:

$$\text{Price, } P(\text{kYen}) = 313(\text{accM})^{-0.16}$$

which exponent implies a *LR* of ~10% and a price at 100 accM units that is within the uncertainties the same as the MCE. Once again, the MCE is again a reasonable 'fit' to the data and gives a testable prediction on market price.

## d) Ethanol Prices Case

As a final test, we examined the case of prices in ethanol production, as reported by McDonald and Schrattenholzer (2002) [16] for the data for Brazil for 1979–1995. The competitive market pressure is the costs versus alternate fuels (e.g., imported oil) and the technology challenge to reduce the costs of manufacture. The result is shown in Figure 6.19.

The accumulated experience was the volume production (in millions of cubic meters, $\text{Mm}^3$). The MCE shown is given in this case by:

$$\text{Price (US\$/bbl), } P = 43 + 118 \exp -(\text{accMm3}/77)$$

which 'fit' was the preferred equation at ~95%, and predicts a MCR of 0.36, with an asymptotic price of ~$40/bbl. for ethanol, at ±$15/bbl. This result compares to the 'b-power law' fit of:

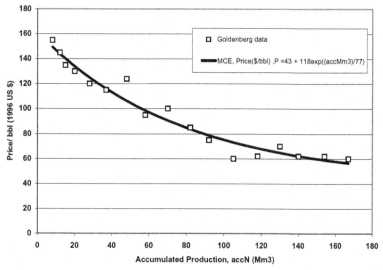

**Figure 6.19.** Comparison to the data for ethanol production prices in Brazil

$$\text{Price}, P(\$/\text{bbl}) = 311(\text{accMm}^3)^{-0.3}$$

This power law not only has a slightly worse overall fit, but implies an initial price that is too high, and an asymptote by $200\,\text{Mm}^3$ production of about \$60/bbl, systematically higher than the MCE prediction of ~\$50/bbl. at that production level.

Those markets, dealers and/or producers who are betting on ethanol's future should perhaps take this variation in the uncertainty into account.

### e) Windpower Case

There has been a surge in building windmills for power production, mainly with vertical towers with rotating blades. It is conventional technology, but the new application is to mount the generators, space the units optimally, and develop large and efficient blades. The development has proceeded utilising windy sites and developing turbines of increasing size, capacity factor and power output. Because the windmills (turbines) must compete to sell power into the electricity market, there is an incentive to reduce costs. Early (FOAK) introduction costs have been partially offset by government and/or generator required subsidies, portfolios or tax/investment credits. Nevertheless, the desire to reduce capital and generating costs is great, and the need to make future estimates pay is also considerable.

The recent study by Junginger, 2005 [20] compares the cost history for the UK and Spanish installed units. We asked Junginger for tabulations of the original data from the paper, but received no reply. So we transcribed the data from the graphs given, with a slight accuracy reduction, but with a clear trend. There is a slight difference in the data, with the UK installed costs being quoted as slightly higher than those in Spain. To normalise for this effect, and show the learning trend, we calculated the cost reduction ratio.

The result of our analysis for these data is shown in Figure 6.20, as a plot of the cost reduction ratio versus the amount of installed power (in MW(e)) as taken from the original paper. The best MCE fit to these data is given by:

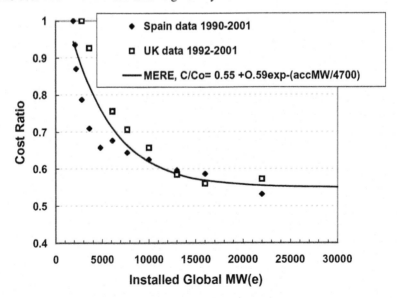

**Figure 6.20.** The wind price reduction

$$C/C_0 = 0.55 + 0.58 \exp - (\text{accMW}/4700)$$

This implies a final cost of some 55% of the original at the start of building, and a reduction has occurred for about every ~5GW(e) installed. Since modern wind turbines are on average about ~1 MW(e) each, this reduction has been for every 5,000 units installed, a not unreasonable estimate. However, we would not expect any further significant cost reduction based on these data, unless there is a technology shift, say to even larger units or different materials.

## f) Gas Turbine Power Case

The final example, from the data reported in Figure 6.9, is for the capital cost of gas turbines for power generation in the USA. This is a case that is different, in that it requires very large capital expenditures (several $100M per unit). The significant market competitive pressures were to compete with the generating costs using alternate fuels for power generation (e.g., indigenous coal), and the technology challenge was to translate the technology from large aircraft turbine engines into multi-purpose high-efficiency units for the power industry. The data in Figure 6.9 given by IIASA/NEA are shown replotted in Figure 6.21, where the specific capital cost is the key indicator of competitiveness for investment.

The accumulated experience is the MW($e$) installed, and at greater than 95%, the MCE derived for this case is given by:

$$\text{Capital cost } (1990\,\$/\text{kW}), C = 290 + 1,000 \exp - (\text{accMW}/470)$$

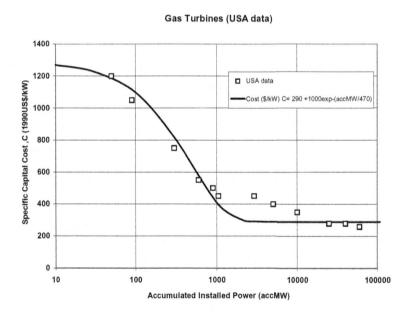

**Gas Turbines (USA data)**

**Figure 6.21.**   Comparison to gas turbine costs (Data source: Figure 6.9)

The minimum cost is then estimated at $290 \pm \$50/\text{kW}$ (1990), close to the values most recently attained, with an MCR of ~0.3. There is some evidence in these data that the minimum cost asymptote has already been almost reached.

The data have also been fitted by the '$b$-power law' as shown in Figure 6.9, where it was apparently found necessary to use a 'kinked' fit, with two slopes because of distinguishing the development phase from the lower slope due to more deployment at higher installed capacities. This also avoids a key problem with the power law where the cost is inexorably decreasing to zero.

The power-law *single* fit is also greater than 95% and is given by:

$$C(\$/\text{kW}) = 2,900(\text{accMW})^{-0.23}$$

An important and interesting difference still occurs in the predictions when extrapolating to the future market cost. At an installed capacity of 1,000,000 MW(e), the MCE predicts a minimum cost of ~$290/kW, whereas the power law gives ~$100/kW, and the 'kinked' fit in Figure 6.9, gives a value of ~$200/kW, all in 1990 values. Clearly, the power law cannot make predictions without arbitrarily adjusting the $b$-exponent.

Thus, we have shown by these six diverse examples (A) through (F) the overall power of the MCE, and its ability to correlate diverse technological systems and cost and price data. Learning has been clearly exhibited, and the price 'floors' projected.

## g)  The Progress Curve for Manufacturing

Even if we had no innovation and were just repetitively making the same items or products, time after time, we should expect performance to improve just by skill acquisition. That is after all why apprenticeships and training are used, and why 'experienced' or licensed operators are in demand. They know what to do, produce more and can work without extensive supervision, We would expect the ideas on learning to extend to the individual tasks that are part of the entire HTS, or manufacturing process.

To test that idea, and just as a representative example, we analysed one simple and early case which includes the data on the output of skilled crafts operating offset presses, which were presumably used for printing (C.C. Pegels, 1969) [21]. The data were actually used to try to distinguish what 'best' empirical curve fit should be used, so an extensive statistical fitting analysis was performed. The specific data were for the cost (task time) reduction for two operators, on different work shifts, as a function of accumulated output, which in this case was for a total of some 8 million units, obtained about a million at a time. The results are shown as a meta-analysis (all the data are lumped together) in Figure 6.22, as the cost reduction ratio from the start (CR) versus accumulated output in thousands of units (kU) from each operator for different work shifts.

For the data expressed as the cost reduction ratio, we show three types of 'progress curve' fit: the simple $b$-power law, a more sophisticated exponential, and finally the present MCE form. What is evident is that statistically, and just looking at the fits by eye, it does not make a lot of difference what curve is chosen! In fact, all the fits have nearly the same statistically significant fitting values to this particular dataset.

Naturally, we are biased, and modestly prefer the present MCE formulation over the other alternatives; and so says the TableCurve routine as it is also preferentially chooses the MCE

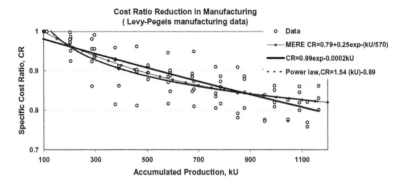

**Figure 6.22.**   Comparison of progress curves for manufacturing data

as the best or first fit. To be fair to the other curves, we now know better, and we have learned since they were introduced. In addition, not only is the MCE theoretically based of course it also fits the world's other data. By now, we expect it to also be more truly representative of the hidden psychological aspects of learning and skill acquisition process, and hence, clearly superior over some arbitrarily chosen curve.

For all these reasons, in the spirit of the manufacturing literature, the MCE result for the offset press data on outcomes is proposed, and is given by the 'progress function':

$$CR\,(\text{cost reduction ratio}) = C/C_0 = 0.79 + 0.25\exp - (\text{kU}/570)$$

We would therefore also have more confidence in the MCE *prediction* of the future cost reduction potential than in any of the others. Apparently, the risk in managing this offset press technology in 1965 is, in fact, that the maximum achievable reduction is not likely to be less than ~79% of the initial value, and was nearly at that level already. The minimum cost/time has been nearly reached with whatever machine and management system was then in place. A savings or productivity increase of perhaps another ~5% is potentially possible for all shifts, but not for all operators, based on the reductions that have been achieved to that date with that technology. Bringing in new workers would just put them through exactly the same learning and skill acquisition process, and we could use these prior results as a benchmark for the trainees and apprentices. We also note that the reduction in specific costs due solely to skill enhancement is much less than that attainable by introducing technological innovation.

The benefit of learning from technological innovating and having new ideas is clear over just doing the same old things faster and faster. The risk is of not having innovation while we improve existing processes!

We could analyse more industrial data, or spend more time on more fits, and even on more fitting models. But our major point is that the very *same learning process is hard at work here* in the manufacturing and market learning places, just as it is in all the other industrial safety settings. Rather than just show more fits, it is much more interesting now to reflect on the impact of technology advances and innovations as major influences on further productivity, risk and learning improvements that radically increase market share.

## Non-Dimensional UPC and Market Share

It is convenient to also compare technological and manufacturing changes on a common basis. We can now show how these disparate technological curves can be plotted and compared using the MCE theoretical formulation: that this is even possible has not been established before. We use the non-dimensional form of the MCE equation for the price, $P$, or cost, $C$:

$$C^* = (1 - C/C_m)/(1 - C_0/C_m) = \exp - k(\varepsilon)$$

or,

$$C^* = \exp - K^* N^* \qquad \text{Universal Marginal Price Curve, UPC}$$

where, $N^*$ is the non-dimensional accumulated experience, $\varepsilon/N_T$, and $K^* \sim kN_T$. We may plot the values of $C^*$ versus the non-dimensional quantities, $n^*$, for the Cases we have examined.

In some of the data, the asymptotic least cost has already been attained, or nearly so, and further decreases are small. For those systems still on the learning curve, as an initial example of how this might work, we chose the two Brazil ethanol and Japan air conditioners cases, adopting the values for the MCR as the relevant non-dimensional parameters.

Since we have dealt largely with prices we plot, the price, $P^*$, as fitted by the Universal Marginal Price Curve, UPC:

$$P^* = \exp - 1.5 N^* \qquad \text{Fitted Marginal Price Curve, UPC}$$

The result is shown in Figure 6.23, where the fit is shown for $K^* \sim 1.5$, implying in this case $kN_T \sim 0.7$. We also show the curve for:

$$P^* = \exp - 3 N^*, \qquad \text{Universal Learning Curve, ULC}$$

which is the ULC fit given by Duffey and Saull (2002) [13] for a large range of technological and human error learning data. Comparing the slopes via the rate of decrease, the implication is that we learn how to correct errors a little faster than we learn how to reduce prices, at least for the two cases shown. The rates are comparable overall, implying the same mechanisms of human actions and goal setting.

There is a fundamental reason why the resulting cost reduction is important: having a competitive advantage increases market share. Assuming that the basic reason for wanting to produce products cheaper is to sell more, what impact will a given price reduction have on the resulting market share?

It turns out that, at least in competitive energy markets, which our detailed case studies examine and presumably in others, the market share for given technology is observed to be non-linear. In fact, in a truly freely competitive market a reasonable hypothesis is that the *fractional change in market share, $\Delta S/S$, is proportional to the competitive (price) advantage, $\Delta C$*, over the nearest competitor.

Thus, at any instant, assuming for the moment no time lags and a perfect market, the fractional change in market share is given by,

$$(\Delta S/S) \propto \Delta C$$

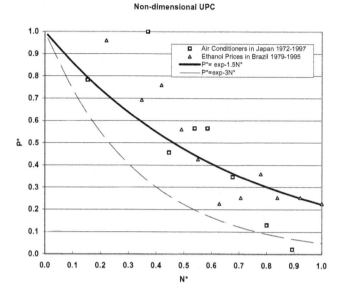

**Figure 6.23**   The Universal Price Curve – an example and comparison to the technological error learning rate

Rearranging this equation and turning the delta increments, $\Delta$, into the limit of truly small differential terms, we then have,

$$dS/dC = BS$$

where $B$ is a market-specific constant. Solving this differential equation for any given change in market share from some initial or reference value, $S_0$, we find that, of course,

$$S = S_0 \exp B(C - C_0)$$

Therefore, *the market share rises exponentially with increases in the competitive advantage.* We could call this the 'Wal-mart Trend', reflecting that company's rapid rise to be the world's largest retailer. Clearly, the market behaves and responds to price advantage in a highly non-linear and unexpected manner. Needless to say, this is a highly commercial and very sensitive area, where the future of products and companies are both at stake. So data to analyse and confirm the theory are not easily or readily available, though we do know that companies will go out of business as the market share goes to zero!

A typical example where some price and market share data are available is for the electricity markets in various countries. These markets are all locally regulated and nationally politicised to some extent, so as a result of these external interference and time lags the market shares are not likely to fully attain the instantaneous values they would with a totally 'free market' constraint. The energy market data are available country-by-country from the International Atomic Energy Agency IAEA in Vienna (http://www.iaea.org), as a fraction of the terawatt-hours (TWh) generated by various fuel sources. The generating costs for the various power plant and fuel options are available from the OECD in Paris

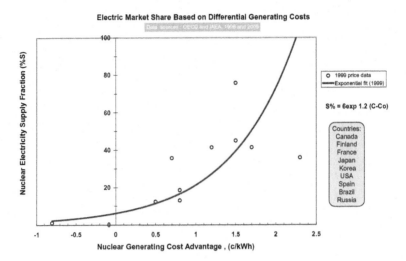

**Figure 6.24**   The electricity market share for nuclear energy

(http://www.oecd.org), for various assumed discount rates for capital, and currently assumed power plant designs.

Since the competitive advantage varies by country, as do the costs and market share fractions, it is imperative to have reliable information. As an instructive test case, the results obtained for 1999 after a period in which energy prices and markets were relatively stable, are shown in the Figure 6.24. The data were calculated for just the nuclear power generating fraction achieved in the various national electricity markets as a function of the competitive (generating price) advantage. This competitive advantage was derived from the published price data per kilowatt-hour (in US $c$/kWh) relative to other possible sources, being coal and gas generation, and using whichever was the closest competitor for any given country market.

The theoretical best fit shown in the Figure 6.24 for the percent market share, %$S$, is given by our predicted form,

$$\%S = 6\exp 1.2\,(C - C_0)$$

This new analysis implies that the nuclear market share $S_0$ is only ~6% if there is zero competitive advantage, but then rises quickly. With a negative advantage (more expensive) only a very small market share is probable; but with a positive advantage (cheaper), the market share potential is very large. Obviously, in this energy case, the influences of national preferences, nuclear policy, historical events and political nuances are all present: but despite all those, the predicted general trend exists. Whether they know it or not, Nations apparently roughly follow what makes economic sense, minimising the financial and social risk exposure to excessive costs and maximisng the economic and social benefit of cheap power.

Of course, lags exist because fluctuations in energy prices on timescales shorter than the timescales over which capacity addition or generating changes can be made. The market cannot behave perfectly. Nevertheless, the fractional or percentage difference between the instantaneous and the expected values, multiplied by the known total market size or expected demand gives a straightforward estimate of the actual or expected 'Market Potential'.

The impact of learning on price reduction on market share can also be significant, via the Marginal Cost Equation:

$$C = C_m + (C_0 - C_m)\exp-(k\varepsilon)$$

Combining this learning curve for cost as a function of experience with the market share as a function of competitive advantage, we have the general prediction that the market share is given by,

$$S = S_0 \exp[B\{(C_m - C_0) + (C_0 - C_m)\exp-(k\varepsilon)\}]$$

This result for the fractional market share is again of double exponential form, $e^e$. It is clearly important not only to have a competitive advantage but also to attain that advantage as quickly as experience will allow. Whoever brings the first and most competitive product to the market wins the most shares, as any economist and business owner will confirm.

## Conclusions: Learning to Improve and Turning Risks into Profits

The risk in and to any investment is of a loss, where the future price or profit does not follow what we want or wish. To predict future price and cost trends in competitive markets we must have theory or model that contains the forces that are at work, and this is even more acute for investing in and the introduction of new technology developments. This is the arena where venture capital operates, and where fortunes (and careers) can be made or lost depending on the trends and achievements in product cost and competitive advantage in our rapidly evolving technological and global society. The cost or price of a new technology declines as experience is accumulated and the product moves from development to full market deployment. The driving forces for innovation and cost reduction are those of the competitive market. The minimum cost equation is based on the postulate that learning to reduce cost is directly dependent on market price differentials and target costs.

The rate of cost reduction is proportional to the excess price above the attainable minimum, and results in a new MCE, with a finite final product cost. The rate of learning (price/cost reduction) is dependent on the accumulated production quantity and the market target price. This theory is consistent with the learning rates exhibited by multiple technological systems, and is a direct adaptation of the basic Black–Scholes model for the systematic variation of price with learning in modern stock portfolios.

This learning postulate replaces the previously used 'power law' estimates of price reductions, which require arbitrary exponents and incorrectly predict a steady declining and ultimately zero final cost. By analysis of the average total cost to any production and the rate of cost reduction, we state and derive equivalence expressions for the power law exponent to the MCE.

Comparisons of the MCE are shown to a wide range of specific technological and product cost and/or data (for photovoltaic cells, air conditioners, ethanol production, airplane production and gas turbines). The equivalent power law comparisons are also shown, which also indicate clearly that the MCE can be used for prediction and uncertainty estimates, whereas the power law cannot.

We may conclude that the new MCE is a useful tool and not only represents a basic feature of competitive markets, but also demonstrates the role of innovation in product price reduction. For the first time, predictions are also possible for the market share potential from the resulting competitive advantage, including learning effects. We have unified the ideas behind learning to reduce price and cost in the competitive marketplace with learning to reduce outcomes in industrial HTSs, and with trying to maximise profits from buying and selling stocks. The risks of not learning are now very clear. Which after all, is simply what modern technological societies and systems are all about: learning to improve and manage risk.

# References

[1] Available: www.Wikipedia.com

[2] Woo, G., 1999, 'The Mathematics of Natural Catastrophes', Imperial College Press, London, UK, p. 242.

[3] Moore, P.G., 1983, 'The Business of Risk', Cambridge University Press, Cambridge, UK, p. 152.

[4] Hanayasu, S. and Sekine, K., 2004, 'Damage Assessment of Industrial Accidents by Frequency-Magnitude Curve', Proceedings of PSAM 07, Paper # 0229.

[5] Bernoulli, Jacob, 1713, 'Ars conjectandi (The Art of Conjecture)', Basel, Switzerland.

[6] Bernstein, P.L., 1996, 'Against the Gods', John Wiley and Sons, New York, p. 8.

[7] Jaynes, E.T., 2003, 'Probability Theory: The Logic of Science', First Edition, Cambridge University Press, Cambridge, UK, Edited by G.L. Bretthorst, pp. 343–371.

[8] Jordan, R.B., 1972, 'How to Use the Learning Curve', Third Edition, Cahners Books, Boston, MA.

[9] Buck, J.R., 2006, 'Learning and Forgetting', International Encyclopaedia of Ergonomics and Human Factors, Ed. W. Karwowski, Vol. 1, pp. 767–774, Taylor and Francis, New York.

[10] Duffey, R.B. and Saull, J.W., 1999, 'On a Minimum Error Rate in Complex Technological Systems', Proceedings of the 52nd Annual International Air Safety Seminar on Enhancing Safety in the 21st Century, Rio de Janeiro, Brazil, pp. 289–305.

[11] Duffey, R.B. and Saull, J.W., 2000, 'Aviation Events Analysis', Proceedings, Joint Meeting of the Flight Safety Foundation (FSF) 53rd Annual International Air Safety Seminar IASS, International Federation of Airworthiness (IFA) 30th International Conference and International Air Transport Association (IATA), Improving Safety in a Changing Environment, New Orleans, LA, 29 October-1 November.

[12] Duffey, R.B. and Saull, J.W., 2001, 'Errors in Technological Systems', Proceedings, World Congress, Safety of Modern Technical Systems, Saarbrucken, Germany.

[13] Duffey, R.B. and Saull, J.W., 2002, 'Know the Risk', First Edition, Butterworth and Heinemann, Boston, MA.

[14] Wright, T.P., 1936, 'Factors Affecting the Cost of Airplanes', Institute of the Aeronautical Sciences, Journal of Aeronautical Sciences, Vol. 3, pp. 122–128.

[15] McDonald, A. and Schrattenholzer, L., 2001, 'Learning Rates for Energy Technologies', Energy Policy, Vol. 29, pp. 255–261.

[16] McDonald, A. and Schrattenholzer, L., 2002, 'Learning Curves and Technology Assessment', Int. J. Technology Management, Vol. 23, Nos. 7/8, pp. 718–745.

[17] Andress, F.J., 1954, 'The Learning Curve as a Production Tool', Harvard Business Review, Vol. 32, pp. 87–97.

LII. *An Effay towards folving a Problem in the Doctrine of Chances.* By the late Rev. Mr. Bayes, F. R. S. *communicated by* Mr. Price, *in a Letter to* John Canton; *A. M. F. R. S.*

Dear Sir,

Read Dec. 23, 1763.
I Now fend you an effay which I have found among the papers of our deceafed friend Mr. Bayes, and which, in my opinion, has great merit, and well deferves to be preferved.

Thomas Bayes 1701?–1761, FRS: the concept of conditional probability published in his 'Essay' in 1763 (Even the probable authenticity of this only known likeness is in dispute)

# THÉORIE

### ANALYTIQUE

## DES PROBABILITES;

#### Par M. LE COMTE LAPLACE,

Chancelier du Sénat-Conservateur, Grand-Officier de la Légion d'Honneur; Membre de l'Institut impérial et du Bureau des Longitudes de France; des Sociétés royales de Londres et de Gottingue; des Académies des Sciences de Russie, de Danemarck, de Suède, de Prusse, de Hollande, d'Italie, etc.

#### PARIS,

M.ᵐᵉ Vᵉ COURCIER, Imprimeur-Libraire pour les Mathématiques, quai des Augustins, n° 57.

1812.

Pierre-Simon Laplace 1749–1827, MAS: the definition of outcome probability published in the book 'Analytical Theory of Probabilities' in 1812

## JACOBI BERNOULLI,

Profeff. Bafil. & utriufque Societ. Reg. Scientiar Gall. & Pruff. Sodal.
MATHEMATICI CELEBERRIMI,

## ARS CONJECTANDI,

OPUS POSTHUMUM.

*Accedit*

### TRACTATUS
## DE SERIEBUS INFINITIS,

Et Epiſtola Gallicé ſcripta

### DE LUDO PILÆ
#### RETICULARIS.

#### BASILEÆ,
Impenſis THURNISIORUM, Fratrum.
cIɔ Iɔcc xiii.

Jacob Bernoulli 1654–1705: the sampling of outcomes from an urn published in the book 'Art of Conjecture' in 1713

**Plate 1**: The foundations of modern probability theory to determine risk were laid, starting some 300 years ago, by the famous pioneers who developed the key concepts in our thinking about the ideas of chance, probability and the prediction of the future based on past observed successes and failures (With kind permission of St. Andrews University, Scotland, Historical Biographical Archive at http://www-history.mcs.st-andrews.ac.uk)

This interstate roof collapsed onto a vehicle: the root cause was the inadequate strength of the glue used for the retaining bolts set into the concrete tunnel itself, which also had not been properly inspected (With kind permission from Ceiling Collapse in the Interstate 90 Connector Tunnel Boston, Massachusetts, 10 July 2006, Report NTSB/HAR-07/02, available at http://www.ntsb.gov).

This highway overpass collapsed onto several vehicles: the root cause was the inadequate strength due to corrosion of the reinforced concrete in the bridge itself, which also had not been properly inspected (With kind permission from Report of the Commission of Inquiry, October 2007, Quebec, available at http://www.cevc.gouv.qc.ca/UserFiles/File/Rapport/report_eng.pdf)

**Plate 2**: Tunnel and bridge collapses are Echoes of major infrastructure failing due to inadequate risk management practices: the common symptoms between these two highly publicised events are of inadequate design margins and lack of effective inspections, resulting in undetected weakening in service.

Boltzmann's grave is carefully tended in the Vienna Central Cemetary . . .

. . . and his bust almost fiercely stands under the S = k log W formula inscribed above

**Plate 3**: Ludwig von Boltzmann (1844–1906), the Father of statistical mechanics and the concept of entropy as a measure of disorder

. . . as illustrated by explosion of the Challenger on lift-off . . .

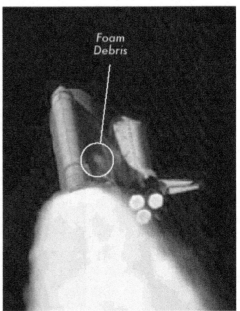

Foam
Debris

Shuttles are complex homo-technological systems . . .

and . . . impact of debris lead to disintegration of Columbia on re-entry

**Plate 4**: Outcomes can be observed as echoes in the failure of homo-technological systems as discussed in Chapter 2 (With kind permission from Columbia Accident Investigation Board, Report, CAIB Report, Volume 1, August, 2003)

Kean Canyon explosives facility overview (before) with Booster Room location arrowed

The mixing equipment in Booster Room 2, room (before) showing the mixing pots in the background

Booster Room 2 levelled by the explosion (after)

**Plate 5**: The Kean Canyon explosives mixing accident described in Chapter 7 (Photos with kind permission from U.S. Chemical Safety and Hazard Investigation Board Report, Report No. 98-001-I-NV)

The points lever device used for changing train tracks fractured and move (arrow) . . .

. . . where inadequate installation, maintenance and inspection practices had also allowed simple nuts to loosen and undo

Travelling at normal speed, train derailed at the points, with debris damaging automobiles on the road below, and also causing one carriage/coach to spectacularly fly, slide and roll across the station platforms into where more passengers were waiting (note: the stabilizing props were erected post-crash)

**Plate 6**: Train derailments can and do still happen for many simple reasons, as in this famous UK example at Potters Bar which killed 7 and injured over 70 people, which is discussed further in the context of other major train events in Chapter 8. (With kind permission from UK HSE Report Train Derailment at Potters Bar, 10 May 2002, A Progress Report by the HSE Investigation Board, May 2003. Photographs reproduced by permission of the Hertfordshire Constabulary and by UK Government License.)

This gasoline pipeline rupture lead to a fire . . . so about 240,000 gallons leaked from the hole in the 16-inch pipe

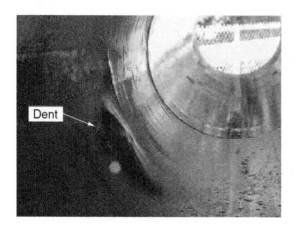

This pipe had been previously damaged and gouged by digging equipment . . .

. . . in addition, during testing the relief valve (arrowed) setting had been altered

**Plate 7**: Spills from pipelines, like this one and those discussed in Chapter 8, can have wide implications and often arise because of simple installation, inspection and maintenance errors (Photo with kind permission from 'Pipeline Rupture and Subsequent Fire in Bellingham, Washington, June 10, 1999', NTSB Report NTSB/PAR-02/02 PB2002-916502, October, 2002)

Heating of caramel mixture by this steam pipe coil . . . in a similar then standing tank to this one, which was blown over . . .

. . . by the explosion, which destroyed the facility . . .

. . . also toppling a chlorine tank, which then leaked gas.

The explosion was caused in part by having a blocked vent line and no pressure relief valves

**Plate 8**: Explosions of tanks containing heated and pressurised fluids is common even today and due to simple causes as discussed in Chapter 7 (With kind permission from CSB Investigation Report No. 2003-11-I-KY, March 2004, 'Catastrophic Vessel Failure: D.D. Williamson & Co., Inc., Louisville, Kentucky', 11 April 2003, NTIS number PB2004-103035) (See Appendix G)

[18] Rubin, E.S., 2002, 'Environmental Technology, Innovation and its Implications for Carbon Management', EXCETP5 Workshop, Washington, DC, 11 March.

[19] Harmon, C., 2000, 'Experience Curves of Photovoltaic Technology', IIASA Interim Report, IR-00-014.

[20] Junginger et al., 2005, 'Global Experience Curves for Wind Farms', J. Energy Policy, 33, pp. 133–150.

[21] Pegels, C.C., 1969, 'On startup or learning curves: an expanded view', AIIE Transactions, Vol. 1, No. 3, pp. 216–222.

# 7

# Safety and Risk Management Systems: The Fifth Echoes[1]

*'Can you measure it? Can you express it in figures? Can you make a model of it? If not, your theory is apt to be based more upon imagination than upon knowledge.'*

*Lord Kelvin*

## Safety Management Systems: Creating Order Out of Disorder

As we mentioned in the Introduction, creating order is exactly also the intent and function of 'Safety Management Systems' (SMS), which are so popular today. In fact, it is a requirement in many corporations and industries to have an SMS, whatever that means. After all, it sounds good: it must be good to have. So in many places, to remain current and keep up with the latest trends, traditional quality organisations, safety specialists and managers often simply transform themselves into an SMS, with a whole new set of organisational structures, rules, procedures and reporting. It is somewhat harder to quantify the actual risk reduction. It is vital that chief executives and senior management are dedicated to the application and control of safety management policies; and know the actual attitudes to risk and safety that pervade their organisation.

Our goal now is to provide a *quantifiable* means and method to track, and hence, manage and predict risk in actual operation. This means understanding and *measuring* the benefits and effectiveness of so-called 'organisational safety', 'safety management' or 'safety indicators' systems, including the application of quasi-statistical approaches to quality assurance and control, including 'six-sigma' methodologies. To reduce and manage outcomes, the emphasis of such systems is often on the creation of a 'safety culture', coupled to an organisational structure, which places unending emphasis on safety at every level. We propose and

---

[1] The concept of measuring safety management given in this Chapter was first established in R.B. Duffey and J.W. Saull, 'Measuring and Predicting Organizational Learning and Safety Culture', Proc. The Eighth International Conference on Probabilistic Safety Assessment and Management (PSAM 8), New Orleans, USA, 14–19 May 2006.

*Managing Risk: The Human Element*   Romney B. Duffey and John W. Saull
Copyright © 2005 and 2008 Romney B. Duffey and John W. Saull, Published by John Wiley & Sons, Ltd

prefer the use of the term and the objective of sustaining a 'Learning Environment', where mistakes, outcomes and errors are used as learning vehicles to improve. We explain here why that is true and support the argument by examining a wide range of actual event data.

The function of management is to provide structure, order and some discipline in the conduct of their operations. In a very real sense, the job of managers is to create order from disorder; and hence, to provide structure, dignity and purpose to the natural chaos of everyday human happenings.

It is well known that in the structured chaos of modern industrial life (everyday factory work, manufacturing jobs, production lines, plant operation, construction and maintenance) many humans are involved. All responsible industries strive to provide safe working conditions. But over 70% of the accidents, injuries, events, loss time and lost production, safety violations and fines can be traced to unsafe *acts*, not to unsafe conditions. Being the Human Element, this fraction of even up to 80% or more is observed in almost all homo-technological systems (HTSs), from aircraft crashes to ship losses, from auto accidents to train collisions, from manufacturing defects to operational errors.

## Workplace Safety: The Four Rights, Four Wrongs and Four Musts

These are truths, which are obvious once stated, but should never be taken for granted in establishing the basis for effective risk management. In the workplace, all employees and workers have legal rights, which often form the basis for so-called Labor Codes and for complex Environmental Safety and Health legislation and rules.

The Four Rights:

The Right to Know about hazards
The Right to Participate in how things are to be safely done
The Right to Complain about safety issues and concerns
The Right to Refuse to perform anything unsafe

There are also the Four Wrongs, which we have seen contribute repeatedly to major events in our everyday life:

Failure to Document what is, has or will be safely done
Failure to Train (= no learning environment)
Failure to Report, both outcomes and non-outcomes
Failure to be Aware or know what is safe or not to do

Finally, for managers, supervisors and corporate owners, there are the Four Musts:

To Train all staff, unendingly in needed skills and task readiness
To Supervise and instruct staff in what is actually done
To Qualify and ensure safety competence in all their staff
To Observe and coach, continually improving safety

These Rights, Wrongs and Musts are the necessary but *not* sufficient conditions for safe working. They are the conventional Principles of good risk and safety management, forming a foundation of good practices at the individual working level. But even if all these good things are done, outcomes will still occur: no matter how much legislation or rules we have, unsafe acts will still occur. What matters is whether and how we learn from them, thus determining where we are on the ULC and how fast we are descending it. It is what we learn and how we learn from our mistakes that is key to the prediction of future risk management.

## Acceptable Risk: Designing for Failure and Managing for Success

It is important to note that we are *not* simply discussing here the traditional view of safety management as applied to obviating or minimising the mechanical failure probability of modern engineering structures (e.g., bridges, pipelines, oil platforms, buildings, tunnels, aircraft and ships). In safety terms, there is some acceptable risk of failure included in design methods.

That *design* approach is focused on applying standard rules, inspection requirements, operating procedures and maintenance practices based on providing sufficient 'safety margin', 'fault tolerance' or 'Accidental Collapse Limit State' (ALS) criteria in the as-built structure against expected or hypothetical deterministic loads and events. The enforcement of these rules and codes of good practice is by classic Quality Assurance and Quality Control (QA/QC) schemes, which require planning, procedures, qualification, auditing, reporting and correction of deviations and findings. These methods are based on centuries of engineering practice. The safety, risk, structural and engineering analyses include allowing for known material property variations, unknown faults, likely or unlikely earthquakes, possible large fires, potential collisions, and material fatigue and corrosion during life. In a real sense, we are designing for failures, not against them, since the fundamental idea is to set a failure probability for total loss that is typically about 1 in 100,000 years of life or operation (or $10^{-5}$ per year) for the structure, so it is unlikely to fail during its lifetime (see, for example, Moan, 2004) [1].

But failures of major structures still occur: all these standard design methods are highly necessary but absolutely *not* sufficient because of the underlying and remaining human element. We know that major outcomes (failures) in any HTS occur at no less than about 1 in 200,000 hours, or once every 30 years or so, which is much more often than the engineering design goal. As clearly pointed out and recognised by Moan [1] in his review of major oil industry failures and engineering practices:

> But the main causes of actual structural failures are the abnormal resistance and accidental loads due to human errors and omissions. . . . Gross errors dominate as the cause of accidents . . . and cause 80–90% of the failures of buildings, bridges and other engineering structures. . . . Different safety measures are required to control error-induced risks. . . . The nature of human errors differs from that of natural phenomena and 'normal' man-made variability and uncertainty.

These error effects are precisely what are found for the risk of all accidents in all our modern systems. Therefore, for managing such human-induced risks, we need a new and different approach. Some 10 existing occupational health and safety management 'models' (i.e., non-quantitative schemes) for safety management have been examined for their common features and recommended practices (Makin and Winder, 2007) [2]. Nearly 60 common items were found and listed, that covered all the mechanical and managerial aspects from workplace and personal safety to corporate policy, from training to reporting and auditing. It is clearly important to cover and be conscious of all these ideal and theoretical aspects, but the key is how to effectively manage risk and to define risk acceptability in practical terms out 'in the field' where the real safety issues exist.

It has also been proposed for large engineering structures like offshore oil and gas plat-forms (e.g., by Moan [1] and as summarised by Trbojekic, 2006 [3]; Wang and Trbojekic, 2007 [4]; and many others) that there is some boundary definable between 'acceptable' and 'unacceptable' risk in terms of the consequences, in this case, the numbers of deaths caused. This risk concept is intended to give designers, managers and regulators some known numeri-cal target to achieve in terms of overall system safety and the consequences, and has its roots in the idea that risk is definable as some combination or accident probability (or frequency) and the consequences (or damage). This type of boundary exactly echoes that originally proposed nearly 40 years earlier by Farmer, 1967 [5] in a paper that launched the concept of a boundary line for use in the probabilistic safety assessment for nuclear power plants. Farmer also clipped off the upper end of the line to reduce the allowable frequency of having too many nuisance low-consequence events. This boundary-line idea has been much used since and is referred to as an '$F$–$N$ curve'.[2] The assumed boundary line or region between socially acceptable and unacceptable risk (or between tolerable and intolerable) for major structures is given by the relation between the annual rate of outcomes, $F$, causing more than a certain number of deaths and the total number of deaths caused, $N_D$, so that:

$$\mathrm{d}n/\mathrm{d}y = F = \Omega N_D^{-\alpha}$$

Here $\Omega$ is a constant that sets some base or hinge point for an 'acceptable' risk or perhaps a 'tolerable' occurrence frequency, and is apparently often taken by regulators and designers as about 100 deaths per 10,000 facility operating-years or so (~1 death in 100 years). The parameter $\alpha$ sets the slope of the boundary, and is taken as $\alpha = 1$ for a constant risk boundary so the simple multiplication of $(N \times F)$ is always $\Omega$, or a constant value. To account for any presumed societal *risk aversion* to outcomes with very large numbers of deaths, then the slope magnitude may be chosen such that the magnitude of $\alpha > 1$, making them less 'likely'.

The values of $\Omega$ and $\alpha$ chosen for the Moan line are such that very nearly:

Frequency of Allowable, Acceptable or Tolerale Outcomes per year,
$$\mathrm{d}n/\mathrm{d}y \sim 0.02 N_D^{-2/3}$$

The lines shown in Figure 7.1 are for this and various other limits proposed or assumed by different authorities, articles and authors (Trbojekic) [3] for aiding the decision-making pro-cesses for the design and licensing of large-scale facilities.

It is not precisely clear why the lines lie exactly where they do or have the assumed slope, other than on the basis of plausibility, acceptability, achievability and feasibility reasoning. Generally, the idea is to make the added risk of death from failure negligible compared to some normal or implicitly 'socially accepted' rate. For nuclear plants, the equivalent risk boundary originally proposed by Farmer is about 100 times lower (less frequent and/or

---

[2] This boundary has been proposed again recently as a 'frequency-consequence' (F-C) curve for risk-informed nuclear plant licensing (See U.S. NRC Report NUREG 1860, 2007).

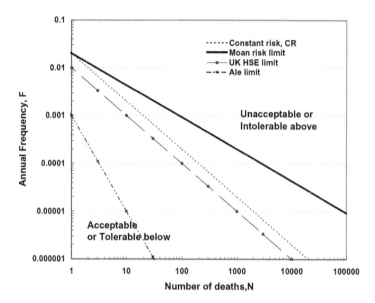

**Figure 7.1.** The graphical definition of an 'acceptable risk' boundary

smaller consequences) than Moan's offshore facility line, but with $\alpha = 3/2$ slope to more steeply decrease the subjective risk boundary for large but infrequent outcomes (or risk aversion), hinged from a point of also a smaller risk of death of $\sim 10^{-3}$ per person at a frequency of $\sim 10^{-2}$ per year. The design and management intent would then to be always below the 'acceptable' line, by a judicious combination of safety features, design margins and mitigating measures. The drawbacks are obvious of having such a large spread of semi-empirical and arbitrary boundaries for determining relative, absolute, acceptable or tolerable risk regions. There is also the unacknowledged presence of, and any needed incentive or allowance for, human learning and error correction in designing, managing and operating such large HTSs. Only deaths count in $F$–$N$ plots, but as we also now know, 'expected deaths' is not the sole or real measure of risk; it is the *uncertainty* that is key. Importantly, to support this view, the actual outcome data that we have from modern society clearly indicate that – as far as we can tell – we are in no way actually meeting these desired risk levels. The actual outcomes have greater uncertainty and hence higher risk.

We can show this fact by analysing the prior data. In Figure 7.2, we plot the simple apparent $F$–$N$ values for the Four Echoes and for other recent echoes and major outcomes that caused accidental deaths during their actual operating life, all costing billions of dollars ($B) in direct damage and indirect losses. Rounding off the numbers, since we do not need high accuracy, these are: the *Concorde* aircraft crash (over 100 passengers and crew killed in some 27 years of operation); *Columbia* and *Challenger* Shuttle losses (14 crew killed over an interval of 17 years between the flights); Texas City refinery explosion (15 workers killed in about 30 years operation); Toulouse fertilizer plant explosion (30 workers killed in say 100 years of manufacturing); and the Chernobyl reactor explosion (some 30 firemen and workers killed in an average 30 years of plant life). Just for comparison purposes, we also show the 500 or so deaths from driving cars in and around Australia, recorded over an interval of some

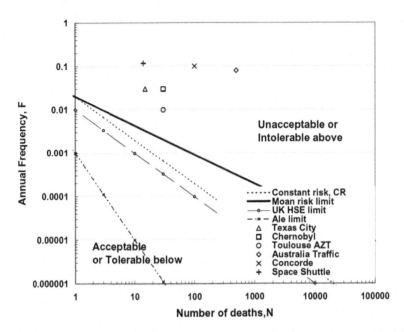

**Figure 7.2.**  Data from some recent major outcomes compared to proposed acceptable risk lines

12 years but treated here as a single once-in-a few-years occurrence rate. All these now known risk outcomes lie well above the proposed 'tolerable-acceptable' risk regions, despite being officially licensed or approved for operation before the outcomes actually occurred. Basically, the *unexpected* reality of the *uncertain* human element accounts for the increase above any expected, desired or as-designed risk goals. These known outcomes would still be far too frequent even if we adopted or allowed an order of magnitude lower frequency estimate by claiming credit for the operating experience of all other similar facilities without outcomes.

These known events all apparently represent socially acceptable risks, or uncertainty, despite the brief protestations and bold headlines, and the reactive inquiries occurring *after* the tragic events to declaim just how intolerable they are. *They are and were acceptable risks until they actually happened.* We are apparently not actually meeting these postulated *F–N* standards for acceptability: but we are presumably learning why not as we continue to experiment on ourselves.

As far as we are aware, there is no common standard for relative or acceptable risk, except what is actually practiced until something fails or goes wrong. The acceptable risk for any outcome defined or adopted on a society-wide basis is that used today by the many and varied governmental bodies responsible for licensing the construction and operation of individual technologies. For example, recalling the First Echo (Figure 2.1 in Chapter 2), the risk to any population (us) of a large power blackout intriguingly has exactly same −2/3 slope as structures and power plants, which is probably not purely a coincidence. But the *relative* risks are very different. The chance of a major blackout happening to some number of people (including you or me) is supposedly about 100,000,000 times ($10^8 \times$) more likely than the risk of being killed by an engineered structure failing, or about $10^{10}$ times more likely than the risk of death from radiation accidentally released from any nuclear power plant. The national bodies governing these incredibly disparate numerical risks (which in these cases are electricity reliability commissions, building inspectorates, and nuclear safety regulators, respectively) not only frame the laws and regulations, but are themselves both the judges and the juries for defining their own 'acceptable' risks.

In addition to ensuring safe design, it is an obligation of every management system and every manager within it to ensure that their specific operation for which they are responsible, whatever it may be, is conducted and operated in a safe manner. This is not a trivial responsibility: it is a vital imperative. In industry, this means determining the safe operating boundaries or envelop within which their HTS must remain and should be performing (Howlett, 1995) [6]. Therefore, management is personally and professionally accountable, which also means potentially legally liable, for leading, instilling, enabling and promoting safety, and the reduction of errors through learning. Howlett also invoked a principle, or what he termed the 'cardinal rule of operation', which is a simple and obvious statement:

> *Humans must remain in control of their machinery at all times. Any time the machinery operates without the knowledge, understanding and assent of its human controllers, the machine is out of control.*

So outcomes actually reflect loss of control of the HTS, and basically, loss of control reflects exactly what happened in all the Four Echoes, and all the many other events with which we are now all too familiar. An objective measure of and for 'control' is what we now seek.

## Managing and Risk Matrices

The best SMS are layered and fully interacting at all levels. All the people affected know where they are in the system, what they are responsible for, what procedures to follow, what training to have and how they are meant to behave. As the US Navy has found in maintaining and operating warships, it is important to report problems, and to make it a duty to do so, without fear of punishment or reprimand. Hence, we must help those doing the work to get on with it, and to discover and correct the problems using learning. Those in management (corporate officers included) must get out of the way of those actually doing it. Thus, the inherent disorder is not replaced but is used to ensure reporting; the chaos to provide guidance; and the outcomes to introduce learning and new habits. Notice that outcomes, undesirable as they may be, are to be expected and represent a real-world learning opportunity.

This learning view of SMS is important, as it is also consistent with the models and theories for individual learning and human psychological behaviour within systems. Specifically, learning is based on error correction and unlearning; and decision making on unconsciously distinguishing order among the information entropy. In our model of experience space, the outcomes could be distributed in many possible ways, but the most likely is that which we observe or discern among all the many based on our accumulated experience, and our learning depends on the outcome rate.

Detailed 'guidance' and even requirements on SMS has been issued in the commercial aircraft industry for what operators should do in the UK, Australia, Canada, the USA and elsewhere (UK Civil Aviation Authority, 2001; Transport Canada, 2002; Australian Civil Aviation Safety Authority, 1998) [7,8,9]. There are specific items in these documents to be followed: on what is an SMS; what is it expected to achieve; and how do we go about implementing and maintaining such an SMS. There are a plethora of formal specific accountabilities, responsibilities, plans, audits, reviews, organisation (an 'organogram' as it is called), safety training, event reporting, management oversight, risk analysis, corrective actions, tools and monitoring. Human Factors play a major role in SMS with such issues as human fatigue and decision making becoming a critical issue.

Given the myriad of possible, potential and actual safety issues, problems, occurrences and laws that face managers and any HTS operator, we obviously cannot solve everything at once, let alone eliminate them all. We must somehow discern the signal among the noise, the significant from the unimportant, the systematic from the random. Some means or method to prioritise both management decisions, operator actions and safety programmes must be available, and common use is made or a 'risk matrix' to determine risk management priorities. Utilising the classic industrial and probabilistic safety assumption definition that *relative* (not absolute) risk is assumed to be 'probability times consequence', the resulting risk prioritisation matrix is basically a plot defined in terms of increasing probability versus increasing 'severity' or the magnitude of the consequences. On the basis of that specific risk definition, the risk matrix ends up looking something like this sketch:

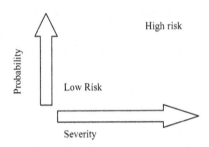

This tool of a 'risk analysis matrix' means we must determine the measures of both 'Severity' and 'Probability', and one has to enter minimum, moderate, and high-risk levels using a numerical scale based on *judgement*. The idea is to find some relative ranking and prioritisation of issue importance and/or urgency, and the need is obvious for quantification and numbers. Hence, there is a caution because of this qualitative and relative nature:

> *Risk Analysis is the first element in the risk management process. It encompasses risk identification and risk estimation. . . . To use the risk assessment matrix effectively it is important that everyone has the same understanding of the terminology used for probability and severity. For this reason definitions for each level of these components should be provided.*
>
> Source: *Transport Canada*

A typical and practical risk matrix is shown in Table 7.1, where in this particular and specific working example the highest risks are at the top left and have been assigned a numerical value or ranking of 0 through 5. In ranking, each outcome or risk is assigned to a box in the

**Table 7.1.** Typical Risk Assessment Matrix

| | Potential Consequence of the Incident | | | | Increasing Probability | | | | |
|---|---|---|---|---|---|---|---|---|---|
| Rating | People | Environment | Assets | Reputation | A Unknown but possible in the industry | B Known in the industry | C Happened in this company | D Happened >3× in this company | E Happened >3× in this location |
| 0 | No injury | Zero effect | Zero damage | No impact | | | | | |
| 1 | Slight injury | Slight effect | Slight damage <US$50K | Slight impact | | | | | |
| 2 | Minor injury | Minor effect | Minor damage <US$50K | Local impact | | | | | |
| 3 | Serious injury | Localised effect | Local damage <US$250K | Industry impact | | | | | |
| 4 | Single fatality | Major effect | Major damage <US$1M | National impact | | | | | |
| 5 | Multiple fatality | Massive effect | Extensive damage >US$1M | International impact | | | | | |

matrix depending on the magnitude of its damage or impacts, and on the relative (not absolute) probability of prior outcomes. Each HTS has 'generic' risks and probable event outcomes: these should be made available to all industry companies within each HTS via association-type bodies.

As an assessment tool, the matrix approach forces a classification and ordering in order to assist managing risks. There have even been suggestions to make the matrix three-dimensional with an additional axis or dimension to reflect a hierarchy of corrective actions and processes.

There is also an SMS requirement for a Safety Case that is a fully documented account, to show that hazards have been identified, assessed for severity and frequency, and that measures are in place to reduce the risks to 'As Low As Reasonably Practicable' (ALARP).

This whole field of SMS study has been dignified with the title of 'organisational culture and organisational factors', and become the subject of long and wordy multinational studies just to define it (Baumont et al., 2002) [10]. Our efforts and request to attend the workshop where this EU-funded work was to be discussed were apparently ignored or fell on death cyberspace! Like many such activities, it is really just another 'project' or 'study'. These organisational factors have been defined and described as all the admirable features, desirable attributes, and understood behavioural norms and values that lead to some perfection or end state in an organisation's structure and working.

In a simplified manner, attempts have been made (for example, by Papazoglou et al., 1999) [11] to adjust the likelihood of outcomes by adjusting the prior probability or frequency by the influence of 'organisational and management factors'. These adjustments are intended to quantitatively reflect the qualitative effectiveness of an SMS. Remembering our definition of the conditional future, in any experience interval chosen:

Future failure (Posterior) probability, $p \propto$ Past (Prior) probability, $p(P) \times$ Chance of future failure (Likelihood), $p(L)$.

To simplify the logic, this expression can be written as the logarithm, so

$$\text{Log } p = \log p(\varepsilon) + \sum\nolimits_i \log p_i(L)$$

Here, $p_i(L)$ is now assumed to be dependent on some subjective weighting for the $i^{th}$ safety area that is under review, based on an assigned categorisation of the effectiveness or impact using physical audits of improved human performance, inspection techniques and SMS applicability.

For any outcome, we can seek out 'root causes', assign and partition responsibility, define corrective actions, and apply audits and reviews, all to give us the experience we need to improve. We *must* measure where we are on the learning curve, using this experience, and how much we are improving by recording the outcomes in an open and honest manner.

## Organisational Factors and Learning

Since any one and everyone works and operates within some corporation, company, building, union or environment, the safety performance is obviously related to the environment and culture in which it occurs. We, as individuals, make and take decisions, learn and acquire skill, as part of the norms and practices that naturally envelop and surround us, whatever the job, task or responsibility. We have emphasised repeatedly that the human being cannot be separated from the technological system in which it exists, the entire homo-technological system. In human reliability jargon, this is part of the organisational 'context' in which actions are taken.

The other related field is called 'organisational learning', which has a whole gamut of qualitative models and a whole distinct lexicon of learning terminology. The formal processes, individual models and social behaviours all can contribute to the creation of knowledge and its use (see Bethan Jones, 2002) [12]. But the overall guiding theory is the obvious one: organisational learning is key, a major tool, and a focus on learning encourages greater safety, better error reporting and correction, and the development of more effective coping strategies. Just as practicing effective group communication enhances safety and understanding. We are still faced with how to quantify what all this means in terms of risk prediction and reduction, other than we know if we do not learn we have more risk. It is like we will know a 'learning organisation' if and when we see one, and understand and can list all the necessary and desirable attributes, but we cannot actually measure what that means. Other than not having them is a bad thing, just as practicing group communication enhances safety and understanding (Reason, 1997) [13].

The issue is how to communicate effectively, and adopt a learning environment throughout an organisation. The individual skill acquisition is an integral part of the collective learning, and vice versa. Typical large corporations and organisations have pieces of themselves structured functionally, so that they do not fit together well. From finance and accounting, to corporate planning, to R&D facilities, to business and sales, to design, manufacturing and maintenance, to human resources, each and all have their own goals, methods, norms and styles. Like it or not, that is the reality.

We illustrate the problem and its solution conceptually in Figure 7.3. The different functional sub-organisations, and sub-cultures within the larger organisation and culture are shown as *not* fitting quite deliberately, as opposed to the usual Venn diagram model of overlapping circles. The stakeholders are both within and outside the learning circle.

The SMS is meant to *create order out of this disorder*, to reduce the 'information entropy', to make all these different pieces fit, to interlock and interact in some way for the common purpose of improved safety. By learning from our experience, both good and bad, and by forming a true 'learning circle,' hopefully we will have achieved our goal. We at least want everyone to be conscious of his or her role and *know* where he or she is on the learning curve, both individually and collectively.

It is crucial to success that the SMS is driven from the top management and that there are appropriately staffed safety committees including independent members with external and/or independent members to continually review its progression. This helps avoid becoming incestuous and complacent. The major factor under consideration is the Human Element and its failings that are directly responsible for making over 75% of errors.

## A Practical 'Safety Culture' Example: The Fifth Echo

We have seen before the common threads, phases and human involvement in major events and disasters, as well as in everyday outcomes. In Chapter 4 on the Four Echoes, we analysed

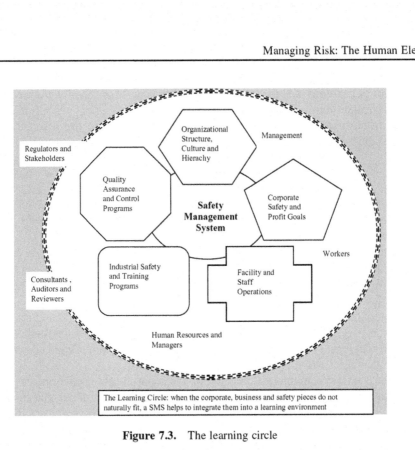

The Learning Circle: when the corporate, business and safety pieces do not naturally fit, a SMS helps to integrate them into a learning environment

**Figure 7.3.** The learning circle

in detail the Space Shuttle losses, the Concorde aircraft crash, the Great North East Electrical Blackout and the Chernobyl reactor accident. But just as we might predict, yet another Echo of major importance happened. The event also had major industrial and political consequences with a profound focus on 'safety culture' expectations, and on managing the risk of operating large industrial enterprises and facilities.

The 23$^{rd}$ of March 2005 was just another usual day at one of the largest gasoline refineries at Texas City in the USA. But the events there shook the oil and gas industry with consequent potential damage and financial liabilities of billions of dollars, altering many personal and professional lives forever. On that fateful day, 15 people were killed and over 170 harmed as the result of a fire and explosion on the isomerisation plant (ISOM) at the BP Products North America owned and operated refinery. The incident has been thoroughly documented by BP, who have undertaken extensive reviews and self-appraisal (BP, 2005) [14].

The event happened during routine processing, with the physical sequence and cause as described in full detail in the comprehensive Mogford Report:

*There was an explosion caused by heavier-than-air hydrocarbon vapors combusting after coming into contact with an ignition source, probably a running vehicle engine. The hydrocarbons originated from liquid overflow from the F-20 blowdown stack following the operation of the raffinate splitter overpressure protection system caused by overfilling and overheating of the tower contents.*

*The failure to institute liquid rundown from the tower, and the failure to take effective emergency action, resulted in the loss of containment that preceded the explosion. These were indicative of the failure to follow many established policies and procedures. Supervisors assigned to the unit were not present to ensure conformance with established procedures, which had become custom and practice on what was viewed as a routine operation.*

*The severity of the incident was increased by the presence of many people congregated in and around temporary trailers which were inappropriately sited too close to the source of relief. Many of those injured could have been warned and left the area safely had warning been provided by those who were aware of events. It is not clear why those aware of the process upset failed to sound a warning. The likelihood of this incident could have been reduced by discontinuing the use of the blowdown stack for light-end hydrocarbon service and installing inherently safer options when they were available.*

*The team found no evidence of anyone consciously or intentionally taking actions or decisions that put others at risk. While the site management had introduced improvement programs, such as the 1000-day program, had completed a site-wide Major Accident Risk assessment exercise (MAR) and, following previous incidents, had begun to introduce many improvements in the areas of training, audit, and culture, the team found many areas where procedures, policies, and expected behaviors were not met.*

Source: *BP Mogford Report, by permission [14]*

In this 'Mogford Report', all the physical causes and the detailed events are extremely well documented so need not be repeated here, and were stated as due to:

- loss of containment;
- raffinate splitter start-up procedures and application of knowledge and skills;
- control of work and trailer siting; and
- design and engineering of the blowdown stack.

But the underlying causes were more complex and were comprehensively discovered by critical self-examination and learning, and were fully described by the owner and operator as follows:

- *Over the years, the working environment had eroded to one characterized by resistance to change, and lacking of trust, motivation, and a sense of purpose. Coupled with unclear expectations around supervisory and management behaviors this meant that rules were not consistently followed, rigor was lacking and individuals felt disempowered from suggesting or initiating improvements.*
- *Process safety, operations performance and systematic risk reduction priorities had not been set and consistently reinforced by management.*
- *Many changes in a complex organization had led to the lack of clear accountabilities and poor communication, which together resulted in confusion in the workforce over roles and responsibilities.*
- *A poor level of hazard awareness and understanding of process safety on the site resulted in people accepting levels of risk that are considerably higher than comparable installations.*
- *Given the poor vertical communication and performance management process, there was neither adequate early warning system of problems, nor any independent means of understanding the deteriorating standards in the plant.*

Source: *BP Mogford Report, by permission [14]*

The risk management issues are clear. Once again, we can see here the classic features of major human involvement and contribution to this HTS outcome. There had been prior incidents at this facility and, what is more, this Echo was also apparently an echo of incidents at the company's Grangemouth facility in the UK. So, as for all the other Echoes, the prior knowledge and experience was not fully incorporated or learned from. *We have Echoes, within echoes, within echoes*[3]. Since we do not know where we are on the learning curve, we also do not know the probability of such an event, and we have no objective measure of the 'safety culture'.

But the emphasis on finding a so-called 'lack of safety culture' has resulted in an extensive and detailed study of the safety management and process safety of all of the company's US operations (BP, 2007) [15].

One simple worldview is that at least 90% of events (outcomes) are really due to management causes and issues, which we regard here as simply categorised as insufficient learning at the HTS level. To solve that problem, the attributes of a desired organisational 'safety culture' have been defined and investigated in a number of ways, primarily based on structured surveys, interviews and questionnaires. The idea is to provide a qualitative measure or idea of how staff and management really feel and act about safety, which we regard here as some implied elimination of the error states. There are no equations and no theory: it is social science and psychometrics applied to safety[4].

The 'Baker Panel' study duly surveyed the staff and management throughout the company at all levels for attitudes and approaches to safety and risk management. The Panel's questioning found many problems in internal communication, corporate direction and lack of safety emphasis, with highly variable attitudes to safe operation. The Panel proposed many solutions and 10 major recommendations emphasised improving the safety management of the process plants and their staff, which can be summarised as follows:

- Corporate management must provide effective leadership on and establish appropriate goals for process safety.

---

[3] As an echo-within-an-echo, never-happening-again example, on 14 January 2008 at the same BP refinery in Texas City, Texas, an employee was killed by a process-related accident in an ultracracker unit due to an overpressure event, the third fatality at the refinery since the March 2005 explosion. An investigative team was deployed from the US Chemical Safety Board (CSB), and it was stated: 'In deciding to proceed with this investigation, we weighed a number of factors. These factors included the severity of the accident, the likelihood that hazardous chemicals were involved, and the learning potential for BP and other refiners that operate similar hazardous processes. Consistent with the CSB's procedures, we also considered the serious history of accidents at the Texas City refinery. Over the past 32 years, a total of 41 people have died in workplace accidents at this site'. (Source: Statements of CSB Board Member William Wark and CSB Lead Investigator Don Holmstrom 'Updating the Public on the Fatal Accident at the BP Texas City Refinery on January 14, 2008', League City, Texas, 7 February 2008).

[4] A standard set of questions and checklists for a 'methodology for the inspection of safety culture' was even developed for use by railway inspectors in the UK covering 'a limited number of indicators that are known to influence safety culture (namely, leadership, communication, employee involvement, learning, and attitude towards blame). . . . The toolkit outlines a consistent and effective method by which the characteristics of a positive safety culture can be measured. . . . Safety culture should be measured against assessment criteria, which are key behaviours or company practices that are relevant to each of the five indicators' (quoted in part from 'Development and Validation of the HMRI Safety Culture Inspection Toolkit', UK Health and Safety Executive, 2005, Research Report 365, www.rail-reg.gov.uk, by PSI License).

- Establish an integrated and comprehensive process safety management system;
- Develop and implement a system to ensure that all management and all US managers, supervisors, workers and contractors possess an appropriate level of process safety knowledge and expertise.
- Develop a positive, trusting and open process safety culture within each US refinery.
- Clearly define expectations and strengthen accountability for process safety performance at all levels.
- Provide more effective and better-coordinated process safety support for the US refining line organization.
- Develop, implement, maintain and periodically update an integrated set of leading and lagging performance indicators for more effectively monitoring the process safety performance.
- Establish and implement an effective system to audit process safety performance;
- The Companies' Board should monitor the implementation of the recommendations of the Panel and the ongoing process safety performance.
- Use the lessons learned from the tragedy and from the Panel's report to transform the company into a recognised industry leader in process safety management.

Based on the survey and interview approach adopted by the Panel, these are indeed fine goals, excellent standards and great advice: they are all good things to do. In fact, Management generally wants to do what is right, so even without any special knowledge or incidents, many corporations and management systems will utilise what is fashionable, prudent, sensible, available or accepted by their industrial peers, especially when they help to make the pain go away. Regulators particularly seem to like this type of 'safety survey' approach, as it attacks management failings of licensees and facility operators in a hopefully non-threatening and constructive way. The surveys are aimed at the attitudes, beliefs, practices and norms that hopefully characterise a proactive approach to improving safety. Actually, as one of us knows from experience, when such a survey system is first applied, it can strike real fear particularly into those managers uncomfortable with the negative potential (retribution and firing!) of bad survey results, especially in a creative working environment. So management must not misuse or misapply the results. They must also maintain and refresh the momentum behind the application, before the newly created enthusiasm and commitment fades.

Safety culture was also discussed by the US Chemical Safety Board, which analysed the incident in detail. A sign of 'safety culture deficiencies' according to the CSB BP Report, 2007 [16] is the presence of both prior and subsequent accidents and events, and is as important as the immediate physical cause of the outcome. Thus, concludes the CSB report, serious so-called 'organisational failures' existed, spreading throughout the management fabric of the company, in addition to the measured outcomes that were simple personal or industrial injury rates usually presented.

These accident rates, or lost work time data are regurgitated and often required, recorded, reported and republished as accident 'statistics' or occurrences, on a routine annual or fiscal year basis. Many companies even have goals and management requirements to keep the rates below target levels, and failure to achieve the goals can be reflected in individual pay raises and performance reviews. This practice raises the pressure at all levels in the entire organisation to under-report, to minimise outcomes and to avoid recrimination.

But we know and will show that the measured outcomes, if analysed carefully and correctly, provide a key objective and non-threatening insight into safety, and in creating and sustaining a learning environment. The data we so expensively collect must be used with care to support, not threaten; used to inspire, not create fear; used to instill learning, not suppress innovation.

What we propose and develop in this Chapter are the validated means, tools and methods for management to use to: understand the trends; manage risks; prioritise work and recommendations; objectively measure and report the state of learning and the 'culture'; and also provide the company a rational approach to try to actively *predict* outcomes. In that sense, what we propose is to move away from reliance on qualitative surveys of culture to special emphasis on the quantitative measurement of learning using the acquisition of the knowledge and skills gained from experience.

## Safety Culture and Safety Surveys: The Learning Paradox

Regulators apparently now want 'safety culture' as a desirable even essential attribute, but what is it? The US CSB quotes the UK Health and Safety Executive as describing safety culture as: 'the product of individual and group values, attitudes, competencies and patterns of behaviour that determine the commitment to, and the style and proficiency of, an organisation's health and safety programs'. Clearly then, we will know it when we see it, and it is indeed 'the way things are done'. But how can we actually *measure and predict* such an elusive and qualitative quality?

The application by the Baker Panel of attitudinal pseudo-psychological survey or audit approaches to evaluating 'safety culture' in HTS is quite common in the nuclear and other industries. One other recent real-life example examined the human, management and non-mechanical factors contributing to the circumstances that lead to undetected severe pressure vessel corrosion in a nuclear power plant (Haber, et al., 2005) [17]. The incident was clearly avoidable, but apparently happened due to management emphasis on production rather than safety, and gaps in the regulated inspection requirements. Hence, there was a clear desire by the regulator to 'fix' the management system; and by the owner/operator to also correct any perceived and actual problems that caused safety priorities to be neglected.

The descriptive analysis methodology is formally well developed. The 'cultural' surveys focus on determining the relevant aspects, so the factors considered important include the organisation's so-called 'artifacts' (executive statements, behaviour, mission statement, etc.), claimed values (zero defects, safety first, etc.), and basic assumptions (the beliefs and attitudes etc.) of the staff. The descriptive desirable or desired attributes of such an ideal 'safety culture' concept in an organisation include (Haber et al., 2005) [17]:

a) safety as an intrinsically recognised value, effectively communicated;
b) clear accountability for and ownership of safety in all the organisation;
c) integration of safety into all organisational activities and behaviours;
d) leadership process(es) that successfully align the organisation with the safety goals;
e) development and recognition of a learning-driven organisation; and
f) totally implemented and sustained safety 'conscious' environment.

These are all fine words: they echo nicely the problems identified in the Four Echoes back in Chapter 2. Subsidiary factors in implementation are trust and communication, plus predictive and leading safety indicators, backed by model behaviours. Lacking are any quantitative measures or predictions: it is simply a description of what exists compared to the apparent ideal or belief. After all, such attributes surely are a necessary even if not a sufficient condition. The recommendations for action that flow from falling short of the ideal are based on what is perceived to be missing, hence needing improvement. In this approach, learning and measures are simply one small part of achieving an overall desired state of safety well-being. The surveys or analyses purport to establish the prerequisites that determine the level of risk propensity in an organisation, and hence, what should be changed or receive management attention.

Interestingly, there is no implied priority between (a)–(f): all are necessary and interwoven. *In our view, and so say the actual outcome data, a 'learning environment' is the very foundation of all these needed partial attributes* of and improvements to a safety culture in any HTS. This argument makes item (e) the needed priority Objective Goal that underpins everything, and all the others should support. But the whole conceptual structure desperately needs quantification and indicators based on actual data and correctly chosen performance measures. Otherwise, these fine but illusive attributes (a)–(f) only represent a desired view of a 'we will know one when we see it' condition; or a preferred, idealised and relative 'state of being'. These model or desired attributes actually require measurement and quantification, as Lord Kelvin has forcefully pointed out so well. There is no assurance that this structure of organisational safety 'mores' is complete or unique, so we must test it or assume that it is incomplete, which we indeed now do and demonstrate. Deep criticisms of this qualitative analysis of the attitudinal aspects of safety culture and organisational learning are clear, and are expressed here as questions.

How can we actually measure safety culture using such methods? After all, a snapshot of attitudes is just that, and no more. The fact that these attitudes may or may not have changed since the last snapshot recalls the issue of pre-selecting an observation interval without any measure of accumulated experience. Censoring of non-observed and unrecorded outcomes, and using rating systems are clearly arbitrary. By not containing measures that allow quantified prediction, there is just a sense or a feeling, rightly or wrongly, that things are or are not what they should be, whatever that is. We have shown that we must manage based on measures and trends, not just our sense of comfort in the perceived state relative to some desire.

What is the probability and risk of the next outcome? The danger of cultivating 'looking-good' or 'me too' image polishing, or misdirected management systems, is that they will be and are used to give all the appearance of adopting the right approach, but without the needed and necessary predictive substance. We must select proactive indicators of progress to support such cultural analyses and change, and make *numerical predictions* of the next outcome probability based on data. We must heed and answer the questions asked by Bernoulli and Bayes so long ago: Knowing what we know has already happened, how can we predict what will happen next?

What is the desired end state and how will we recognise it? The implication that one type of culture or organisational state of being *de facto* is more desired or desirable than another is akin to ignoring the virtues of diversity, of innovation and of learning itself. After all, we can *only* reduce risk likelihood by having outcome probabilities and distributions that are reduced to less than their prior values, whatever they may be and however it is achieved. Otherwise, it is change for the sake of change, becoming simply a spurt of refreshing staff personal goals and safety consciousness. The danger is of becoming just another (potentially failed) management initiative along with others, so we need to find ways to instill and sustain change by permanent learning.

How can we reach the relative ideal anyway? Scaling or assigning numerical values to the spread or span of the ascribed attributes may quantify the surveys in some relative sense, using ratings or checklists. However, the implication is unfounded and unsupported by any data that achieving any such hypothetical, well-attributed but immeasurable organisational learning condition will eliminate *all* mistakes or outcomes. We know and have shown that the organisations that have best approached this ideal (the almost completely safe industries (ACSI)) still have errors and accidents, and may not be progressing on the learning curve, even if implementing massive SMS.

What happens if we have limited prior knowledge? *The fundamental paradox is that we cannot learn other than by making those very errors, which we seek to avoid.* Thus, being in or attaining the hypothetical state of a perfect 'Safety Culture' is probably undesirable, as our 'perfect learning' limit in Appendix F demonstrates. We still must follow the learning curve, even if we have no outcomes!

Where are we on the learning curve? As we have shown throughout our text, it is *entirely* self-evident that these stylised organisational attributes or desired end-state attributes do represent risk reduction potential. We must descend a learning curve, whether we like it or not, and do so as fast as we can. We illustrate this point again here.

## Never Happening Again: Perfect Learning

After a serious observed outcome, almost inevitably, as inevitable as the events themselves, inquiries and retribution are invoked to discover what happened, and what went wrong. The phrase invariably used is: 'So we can be sure that it will *never happen again*'.

That ideal goal is the complete elimination of an error state and the implied reduction of the risk to zero for the causes of the prior observed or similar outcomes. The learning process from the outcome is, in our terminology, called 'perfect learning'. Interestingly enough, this limit of ideal risk reduction has a theoretical result that can be derived simply by assuming that we learn from all the prior non-outcomes, hence reducing the future likelihood.

The two key cases of the MERE human bathtub curve and of the perfect learning limit are shown in Figure 7.4. The one labeled as 'perfect learning' is the result of learning from all non-outcomes, or so-called 'near misses', as well as from outcomes (see the derivation in Appendix F). We follow the usual MERE learning hypothesis path, that is the human bathtub, until the divergence caused by the catastrophe of single outcome. Since we now learn everything, the subsequent probability is essentially zero. The rapid decline is caused mathematically by a triple exponential term, which physically arises due to superimposing or compounding the prior double exponential bathtub with another exponential sampling likelihood probability.

*No data in the world follow such a perfect learning path*, unless of course, the HTS is destroyed as a direct result of this first and only outcome. Effectively, such was the case for the *Concorde* aircraft, where it was withdrawn from service before a second catastrophic event could occur.

Therefore, we assert that the contrary and testable Learning Hypothesis, which is also shown, is supported and quantified by world data, and contains and requires real and explicit measures based on outcomes and non-outcomes, being the:

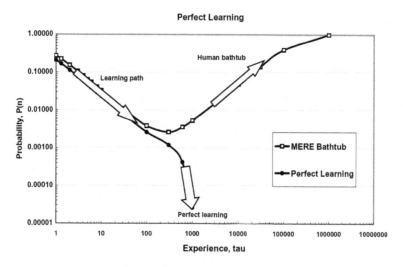

**Figure 7.4.** The learning paths

1. experience measure,
2. outcome rate,
3. outcome numbers,
4. distributions with experience,
5. information entropy, and
6. learning curve location.

To answer and examine these important questions in some more depth, let us now look at some recent case reports of outcomes that illustrate what happens in the real world, as opposed to some hypothetical one. We can then emphasise these key points about attributes, learning, measures and prior knowledge. Using that basis, we can proceed to quantify these desirable 'safety culture' attributes and measures utilising the SEST, MERE and $H$-factor tools.

## Half a World Apart: Copying the Same Factors

Haunting similarities emerge as we study outcomes, as eerily the same types of mistakes and common errors appear. Industrial accidents, explosions and fires have a depressingly familiar habit of re-occurring, with similar if not identical causes. Thus, worldwide, there is a continual stream of major losses due to poor operating and management practices, as in recent examples of sometimes billion-dollar damage and losses at offshore oil rigs (see the P-36 platform www.petrobras.com.br), inland oil storage facilities (see www.buncefieldinvestigation.gov.uk), railway lines (see www.ntsb.gov and www.atsb.gov.au), and operating chemical plants (see www.csb.gov, and the Texas City refinery and Toulouse fertilizer explosions). This has extreme significance in risk management and great importance in the development of safety management systems, not to mention the large impact on insurance costs and corporate losses.

This outcome similarity appears in the apparently obscure but highly relevant recent example of a study of loss of power in twin-engine aircrafts in Australia from 1993 to 2002 (ATSB, 2005) [18]. Some 35 out of the 58 reported two-engine plane accidents (being 60% or $n/N_j \sim 0.6$) were found to be *essentially similar in cause*, that is due to one engine causing an asymmetric and hard to control power loss. This percentage is eerily close to the purely statistical prediction in Appendix H of a repeat probability of ~63%, which is based on purely random outcome matching, and close to the usually observed fractional contribution of the human element with small experience. Since we know that similar or 'matching' events are actually quite likely, in the statistical probabilistic sense discussed in Appendix H, if you have already had one outcome, do look out for another.

It is like *we are doomed to repeat our mistakes*, over and over, simply confirming the known psychological observation that task knowledge is actually hard to transfer.

The parallels for events around the world show that even in an industry and between industries, there is no effective feedback from learning. There is excessive reliance on people doing the right thing when they, all too often, have neither the knowledge, tools and training, nor the experience to do so. Complacency sets in, with an acceptance of poor practices, and a marked cessation in any self-questioning. The ways things were always done before becomes the way they continue to be done, even if they are wrong. New things are then also done wrongly according to the old established practices and norms.

A recent and powerful example is the explosion that occurred at the AZF fertilizer factory or 'l'Usine Grande Paroisse' in Toulouse, France, on 21 September 2004 [19]. This major hazard caused 30 deaths and thousands of injuries (about the same as the Chernobyl accident), damaging 26,000 homes and costing two billion euros (~$3B), from a blast estimated at 20 to 40 tons of high explosive (TNT equivalent). This industrial manufacturing and storage facility was operating within the norms and limits of existing practices, laws, inspection and reporting, and the applicable safety analysis and safety management requirements. This terrible event has caused serious rethinking in relation to the hazards of siting new facilities throughout Europe as well as in France, including the aspects of co-location of major hazard operations, and the degree of urbanisation (housing) that is built in the surrounding areas of such plants.

There had been over 100 previous incidents at such fertilizer plants over the last century, so the explosive hazard of ammonium nitrate fertilizers was both already known and the risk established. Resulting changes to the laws (and the so-called EU Seveso Directives) and vastly increased inspections are designed to adopt best practices and reduce the probability of this type of event 'ever occurring again' at similar high hazard operations. In particular, it is stated [19]:

*'les Plans prevention des Risques Technologiques (PPRT) sont un des nouveaux introduits par la loi relative a la prevention des risques technologiques 'with the intent' pour effet de limiter l'exposion de la population aux consequence des accidents. Ils permittront . . . d'eviter qu'une situation se renouvelle dans l'avenir'.*

This can be simply interpreted as the new laws avoiding the re-occurrence of such situations in the future. The entire focus of the plans and reports are on the politically necessary aspects of 'prevention des risques industriels' (prevention of industrial risks) through legal measures, not on establishing a learning environment [20].

With Western Europe currently making about 8 tons a year of ammonium nitrate, we may expect one such event every 10 years or so (or 87,000 hours). This risk was apparently considered acceptable before the event occurred, but totally unacceptable afterwards, although it is close to the minimum interval attained by modern industrial HTSs. We might expect a risk reduction of perhaps a factor of two to be ultimately possible, to say ~200,000 hours, depending on changes made in the manufacturing, transport and storage process technology.

Now, partly because of the nature of the destruction and the facility, there is not much known about the actual sequence of events and cause at the AZT Toulouse factory, other than the temporary storage mode used for special or 'reject' material was unsafe. The number of deaths is not a good risk measure, being a function of happenstance as to how many unfortunate injuries or collateral damage occurs.

Here we look at deaths at two other dissimilar chemical mixing facilities as a telling global example. The first is taken directly from our previous book, where we looked at the presence or absence of learning. The second one is new, but although only a year apart just fell outside our first observational interval. The two case studies do not share all the same features, not in their physical location of half a world apart, nor in their processes or cultures which are a whole world apart. But from the JCO factory in urban Japan, to the Kean Canyon plant in the western desert of the USA, the confluence of events is strikingly similar in both type and timing. There was no way one organisation could know about the other, even though they are almost identical copies in terms of causes. The lack of learning, management, knowledge, training, understanding and adequate regulation that were shared was and is quite universal.

These outcomes occurred within our observation interval. In both cases, there are extensive reports and analysis by the relevant safety authorities and their advisors that we use here to extract the salient factors underlying the HTS errors. They also exhibit exactly the same Four Phases that the more visible catastrophes we have already examined possess, namely:

*Phase 1:* the Unfolding, of the precursors, the initiators and the preliminaries.
*Phase 2:* the Confluence of events, circumstances and bases of errors.
*Phase 3:* the Escalation where the unrecognised unknowingly causes the event.
*Phase 4:* the Denial caused by lack of comprehension, followed finally by acceptance.

The reader is encouraged to identify these in passing, so we will give a clue by adding asterisks near the end of each phase in the salient places.

## Using a Bucket: Errors in Mixing at the JCO Plant

The JCO plant in Japan manufactured custom nuclear fuel used in commercial power plants, which needed differing but highly specified amounts of uranium [20]. Limiting the amounts of uranium in any solution or part of the manufacturing process was also necessary simply to avoid attaining an accidental 'critical mass', that would cause a harmful, runaway uncontrolled nuclear reaction. So, the JCO plant and the process were regulated and licensed in Japan as a nuclear facility, mixing amounts correctly since 1981, or nearly 20 years without a serious incident.

A new batch of fuel was ordered with higher-than-normal uranium, which hence was easier to make critical. So the mixing process and procedures for the solution had been changed, and agreed by the company safety committee. The plant operation and procedures were all designed so that having a critical mass could not happen*.

Near the end of their shift on Friday, 30 September 1999, while mixing this batch of chemicals used to make the fuel, three workers wanted to finish on the planned schedule that day, and to be ready to train others the next week. The mixing process usually used some 100 hand operations, cross-mixing the liquids between many small bottles to ensure that all eventually contained about the same mix of liquid. The plant and procedures were all designed to avoid having too much liquid in any one bottle. But with the new procedure, they could use a bigger tank to mix them together and use a bucket to fill the tank, which was faster and easier than using many smaller bottles. But the workers had not been trained on the dangers, physics and importance of critical masses. Since the new mixing procedures using a larger vessel were quicker, it became the usual practice, even though unwittingly violating both the criticality rules and the licence**.

The workers took the solution in the bucket and tipped it into an even larger available process vessel, not the usual one, to speed up the mixing even more. The workers and their supervisor thought it was safe as it had been done like this before, although never for the new mix***. The solution mass in the larger vessel exceeded the critical mass, so a brief uncontrolled nuclear reaction occurred which fatally irradiated two of the workers, who then died in hospital. The subsequent search for the guilty included public castigation, removal and prosecution of the responsible plant management****.

As also discussed in detail by (Kohda et al., 2000) [21] in this JCO incident we have:

a) inadequate safety planning, procedures, training and regulation;
b) violation of operational rules related to critical mass*;
c) wrong decision making in taking a short cut**;
d) inattention due to time pressures**;
e) unawareness of risk and/or danger***;
f) criticality accidents not being a consideration****.

So the JCO mixing event is and was a classic example of the compounding of errors, multiple unintentional mistakes, coupled with failed safety management.

## Using a Bucket: Errors in Mixing at the Kean Canyon Explosives Plant

The faraway echo was early in the morning, 7:54 a.m. on 7 January 1998, when two explosions in rapid succession destroyed the Sierra Chemical Company (Sierra) Kean Canyon plant near Mustang, Nevada, USA, killing four workers and injuring six others. Like JCO, the plant had been operating for over 20 years without event, so the maximum interval achieved was ~175,000 hours, about what we expect.

The Kean Canyon plant manufactured explosive boosters for the mining industry. The plant and process were regulated and licensed in the USA. Boosters are initiated by a blasting cap or detonation cord, and provide the added energy necessary to detonate less-sensitive blasting agents or other high explosive. The boosters manufactured at the Kean Canyon plant consisted of a base mix and a second explosive mix, called Pentolite, both of which were poured into cardboard cylinders. The pre-mixing was done by hand. The workers put explosives into steam-heated pots (buckets) that utilised electric motor-driven mixer blades to stir the constituents to produce a uniform product that could be poured into the cylinders.

The day before the incident, one melt/pour operator working in Booster Room 2 needed to leave work early. So at 3:00 p.m. on 6 January, this operator from Booster Room 2 pressed on and left work early, leaving some melted explosive base mix in a pot. He mentioned this part mix, and offered it for use, to the other operator in the room, who later checked and saw the residual explosives in the pot. He estimated it to be about one bucket full, or some four inches deep, weighing about 50 lbs; but he did not use it.

The mix partly covered the mixer blade, about two inches into the mix. The mix solidified overnight as it was cold, and the steam was not left on to trace heat it, like it was in the other mixing room (Booster Room 1) where the operator had been trained and had worked before.

Unknown to the workers and the regulator, this mixing procedure violated the rules and its licence since it could allow an unknown and unstable explosive mixture to be left unattended. But this was done regularly*.

Batches of unknown exact mix from military surplus explosives were often used with different (higher) amounts of explosive. Sometimes, to further speed up the mixing process, the workers added 'flakes' of other explosive (TNT) to the solution in the bucket; or physically hammered and broke pieces of explosive from larger blocks so they would fit and heat faster in the buckets. Clogged lines and valves were manually scraped out and picked open with improvised tools. The workers had not been told by the supervisor if it was not safe to do this: since it had been done rather like this before, the response was to carry on doing such things.

The training of the facility personnel was inadequate. The Managers believed that, short of using a blasting cap, it was almost impossible to detonate the explosive materials they used or produced. Worker training was conducted primarily in an ineffective, informal manner that over-relied on use of on-the-job training and verbal translation into Spanish of English instructions. Poor management knowledge and worker training led to a lack of appreciation of the hazards involved in manufacturing explosives**.

The following morning, 7 January, the shift workers arrived, and explosives manufacturing operations began shortly after 6:00 a.m. in Booster Room 1. Two teams of two workers each had finished mixing operations for the first batch of the day and were beginning to pour, and a fifth worker was also working, packing the finished boosters from the previous day.

The operator for the west side of Booster Room 2 arrived at work and at about 7:30 a.m. visited Booster Room 1 to greet his fellow workers who were already pouring boosters. He talked briefly about a pouring pitcher he had returned to that worker's locker in the change room and then left at about 7:35 a.m. The supervisor arrived at approximately 7:40 to 7:45 a.m., stopped in Booster Room 1 for about 5 minutes, then went to another facility nearby.

Seemingly unaware that the explosives had not remained heated and fluid, the same operator turned on the steam heat and the motor to the mixing pot in which the mix had stratified and solidified overnight. The bottom part of the mixer blade, which was embedded in the solidified explosives in the pot, tried to rotate and doing so detonated the explosives. Besides the operator assigned to the west side of Booster Room 2, there were three other workers in or near Booster Room 2 who were all found dead afterwards.

The explosive shock wave from the pot detonated several thousand pounds of explosives in the room that then destroyed the building. Debris from this explosion fell into and through the roof of a second explosive building, initiating a second (and larger) explosion a few seconds later***. (See Plate 5)

Generally speaking, people do not take an action leading to bad results if they know them. Workers do not deliberately intend to blow themselves up at work; and explosive manufacture is known to be hazardous. Nevertheless, to get the job done on time and on schedule, unsafe work practices were regularly used and the workers and the management did not know or understand the dangers. The US CSB Report, 1998 [22] on Kean Canyon, from which all the above details are taken, is very thorough and states among other items:

> The Kean Canyon Plant is covered under the Occupational Safety and Health Administration's (OSHA) Process Safety Management (PSM) Standard (29 CFR 1910.119). The PSM standard requires that companies using highly hazardous materials have in place an integrated safety management system. The investigation of this incident revealed that many essential elements of process safety management were missing or deficient.
>
> The Uniform Fire Code (UFC) contains explosive safety requirements in Article 77, 'Explosives'. The CSB investigation team determined that (local fire) inspectors were not trained or qualified to do an explosive safety evaluation; their inspections, therefore, tended to focus on fire prevention.
>
> The Federal Bureau of Alcohol, Tobacco and Firearms (BATF) licensed the Kean Canyon plant to manufacture and import explosives. The BATF inspects licensed facilities to ensure the safe and secure storage of explosives, that explosives are properly inventoried and controlled, and that all records are kept accurately. The last BATF inspection of the Kean Canyon plant was conducted in 1995. Although the BATF licenses manufacturers of explosives, it does not inspect the manufacturing process.

After the events, the inspection rules were changed by a Nevada Governor's Executive Order to require safety inspection of explosives manufacturing facilities at least twice per year****.

## The Prediction and Management of Major Hazards: Learning from SMS Failures

Can we actually predict when such explosions will occur?

Assuming that we are smarter and learning from our mistakes, can we reduce their probability?

Are we actually able to effectively manage the risk of 'major hazard' facilities?

Large explosions and fires at chemical and industrial facilities have occurred before, many times over the last century, some with loss of life and mass evacuation of neighbourhoods. Based on past outcomes and events, and the lessons learned, improved storage techniques and requirements for 'Safety Management Systems' (SMS) have been implemented in some countries. In the EU, the so-called Seveso Directive 1996 (named after an infamous earlier chemical release) legally requires large complexes and facilities, numbering some 65,000, to have specific inventory, safety analysis and risk assessment measures, plus local warning and evacuation plans. Other similar safety management measures for such major hazard facilities exist in many other countries, enforced by national standards and bodies (see, e.g., Filippin and Dreher, 2004) [23]. In particular, Filippin and Dreher call for 'a properly constructed risk management database to demonstrate effective management and control of the risk associated with their operation'. Since this idea is data-orientated, we are very much in favour of such a practical step if it enables us to *predict* the probability and uncertainty in the risk of outcomes.

We need to manage the risk of operating facilities that make potentially dangerous materials, which means predicting the risk of an outcome, just as we have been stressing all along.

Consider again the major explosion that occurred at the chemical manufacturing AZF Facility in the city of Toulouse, France, in September 2001. The facility was covered by the Seveso Directive, so is a good test of how this SMS approach failed and what was learned. The explosion and its extremely broad implications are well documented in the formal French government inquiry reports [20,24]. The plant made and handled fertilizer with ammonium nitrate (AN), a well-known and potentially explosive substance if ignited in the right (or wrong) way, but AN is not considered an explosive when made for fertilizers. Mixed with fuel oil (diesel), it can be a terrorist's bomb, but that was not the case here. The explosion of the stored AN was equivalent to detonating some 20–40 tons of TNT, and blew the factory and surroundings apart, killing 30 people, injuring and hospitalising some 3,000, and damaging over 11,000 homes. The French reports state that the explosion occurred in a 'downgraded ammonium nitrates' store, which was authorised for 500 tons and contained between 300 and 400 tons of AN product on the day of the explosion. The 'downgraded' products came principally from the ammonium nitrate production and packaging workshops for producing fertilizers or industrial ammonium nitrate; the downgrading could be linked to irregularities in the particle size and also to the (varying) composition of the products. These products were stored temporarily, bagged and then sent to other factories for re-use in the manufacture of complex fertilizers.

Just as in our other case studies, an explosion was not expected or thought possible; there were no fire or other alarms on the storage and handling facility; and so there was no warning and no evacuation. In the AZF facility, the out-of-specification, reject and/or unsatisfactory AN product was temporarily stored in a converted building. Because it did not house actual AN product, and because it was not classified as an explosive, the safety analysis in the SMS did not consider an explosive event at this storage building. In addition, there were large quantities of highly poisonous gases also being manufactured nearby, namely chlorine, ammonia and phosgene, so co-location of hazards is also an issue even though no 'domino' or magnification effect occurred in this case.

By learning from this outcome, these unintentional loopholes in the safety laws, SMS system and EU Directives have since been closed; inspections have increased and safety analysis enhanced. New rules for the co-location of hazardous facilities, complexes and people are being promulgated, evaluated and implemented throughout Europe. However, measures for what constitutes an 'acceptable risk' are still missing.

Apart from what can be deduced from the damage evidence, the exact sequence and cause of the explosion will never be exactly known because of the widespread destruction and deaths. Having put these added safety and social measures in place, and with uncertainty in the actual cause, can we actually predict if and when explosions at major hazard facilities will occur?

What *is* known is the prior knowledge: fires and explosions with AN have occurred occasionally before in the world, usually through inadequate storage techniques or accidents in transport. One important result of the Toulouse AZF outcome is that more data have surfaced on ammonium nitrate (AN) major events. So we can actually make a prediction of the probability or chance of having another one. This prior knowledge is the lists of previous major and infrequent AN explosions and fires (Heather, 2002) [25].

As a relevant measure of overall manufacturing, handling and storage experience in this industry, being the learning opportunity, the data for the world use of nitrogen nutrient fertilizer are also available (International Fertilizer Association, 2007, www.fertilizer.org/ifa/statistics) [26]. There were 12 major outcomes (fires or explosions) reported between 1970 and 2006, during which time about 2.5 billion (2,500,000,000) tons of fertilizer were used. We adopt the usual DSM approach of determining the failure (hazard) rate, $R$, per million tons used, Mt, as a function of accumulated fertilizer used, accMt. We find the rate follows the flattened-out, almost asymptotic learning curve shown in Figure 7.5, where the MERE expression is given by:

$$R = 0.014 + 0.69 \exp - (\text{accMt}/36)$$

The Toulouse AZF data point is shown on the graph as the '$X$' to distinguish it from all the others. This major outcome falls exactly on the same minimum rate of $R \sim 0.014$ per million tons of AN used, as deduced from all the prior data. This is not an unexpected coincidence.

With an average of 70 million tons of nitrate used worldwide each year between 1970–2005, apparently we could expect, on average, about one major accident per year *worldwide* at such a major hazard facility. Since the EU is about 10% of the world AN production and use, this translates into one major fire or explosion outcome about every 10 years for Europe. Because of the small number of major fire or explosion events, the uncertainty at 95% confidence is about 60%. Based on the reports, the chance of a fire versus an explosion is about 50/50. So explosions should not be an unexpected, un-analysed and unforeseen risk unless the cause is eliminated, and will occur *in the EU* perhaps about once every 20 to 30 years, based on these prior data. This is a pragmatic prediction, which is entirely consistent with

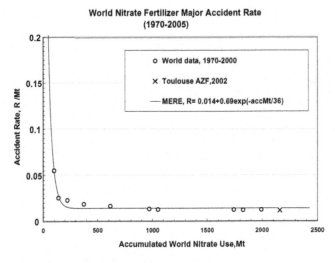

**Figure 7.5.** The ammonium nitrate explosion rate: world data

the maximum error interval of 100,000 to 200,000 hours observed in other HTS. Having a working but failed SMS clearly does not obviate the risk.

## Learning Environments and Safety Cultures: The Desiderata of Desires

Uncannily similar, in these events chosen by chance within our observation interval, so we have just two examples where the litany of the same causative factors was literally at work. In addition, the Toulouse explosion simply highlights how often these may occur, despite having a then state-of-the-art SMS in place.

Amazingly, in 2003, an explosion occurred at a USA chemical (food) plant, again due to errors in the safety design, procedures and management processes (see Appendix G). There is no way the managers, regulators and staff of that facility could have known about the JCO, Kean Canyon and AZF Toulouse events: they were in very different industries, in completely different locations, with very different regulators, and entirely different processes. But they shared major common features. Just like the recent two major fires and explosions at the huge gasoline/oil refineries and storage facilities in Texas City (BP, 2007) [16] and Buncefield (UK HSE, 2005) [27], they are all, as were all HTS, with humans going about their usual 'mixing and making chemicals' jobs the way they have always done, not knowing the risks they were exposed to or could create.

The contributory factors to the observed outcome 'error states' were essentially the same, and we can list some of them just from these accounts as:

a) lack of a learning environment;
b) absence of training and knowledge;
c) ignorance of danger and risk;
d) complacency of management;
e) ineffectiveness of regulation and inspection; and
f) reliance on the human to 'do the right thing'.

What will work here? What is the 'fix' we can use? How can the risks be avoided? How can we integrate the different parts of the organisation, so all learn together and from each other? How can we create a 'learning environment' where it is OK to ask the hard question to learn about what is needed, and to improve on the way things have 'always' been done?

We need a model of the Goals and the approach for an SMS, which includes the elements of success. We can paraphrase an existing SMS familiar to one of us, which is again based on the attributes of a learning environment. In combination with effective performance management at the management unit and individual worker levels, the culture must be shifted from:

- Blaming the worker to *focusing on root causes*
- Shooting the messenger to *leadership roles and coaching*
- Non-problem reporting to *finding problems ourselves, and learning from them*
- Externally driven problem identification to 'self-assessment' and improvement
- Firefighting reactive mode to *a proactive learning environment*

Interestingly, exactly this approach was adopted by the US Navy for its nuclear ship and submarine programmes. The highest standards of manufacture, operation and training were needed for this new and costly venture of using nuclear reactors as the motive power for aircraft carriers and submarines. In a presentation entitled 'Nuclear Safety Culture: the Nimitz Precomm Model' [28], Charles Jones said it all. In that successful Navy endeavor, which may only be possible in a militarily controlled environment where rank, discipline and obeying orders are paramount, the major elements were the means to identify and resolve outcomes and errors. In a listing of desiderata for the everyday behaviours we have:

- No fault problem management
- No filtering of problems
- Daily self-training
- Weekly formal training
- Progress reports to commander from each manager and worker
- Reports containing problems, obstacles, support needs and plans
- Stop testing and fix it
- Factory and maintenance presence
- Verbatim procedure compliance
- Focus on 'red flags'
- Stop, correct, approve and proceed

Most startling yet obvious of all, as a result the management structure was literally turned on its head. It was an Upside-Down organisational philosophy, with the *managers supporting the workers*, who were the most important personnel. It was a reverse of the traditional organisational tree; the most compelling that has never been seen in a Boardroom.

As the old saying goes: 'Those managing the work should get out of the way of those actually doing it'. This new paradigm is very threatening to both Managers, who are giving away their authority, rank and privilege, and to Workers, who are now assuming greater responsibility for their own actions.

Jones also gave the following definition of a good safety culture:

*The integrated body of specific characteristics and personal attitudes, which together ensure that problems are aggressively sought out, and that all concerns and issues raised are promptly addressed in a way that maximizes worker . . . (and) public safety.*

We totally agree with this approach, and our work reinforces it. In our work, we have echoed these matters as quantifiable and measurable attributes that follow the laws of physics, as exemplified by the learning hypothesis. We have emphasised and expressed the need for a Learning Environment, with the measurement and tracking of events and errors, and the quantification of learning rates, goals and probabilities feeding back into improvement. We have opposed the:

- setting of arbitrary management goals;
- setting up of bureaucratic safety systems and procedures;
- generally poor or inadequate reporting of data;
- lack of experience measures;
- arbitrary assignment of blame; and
- fruitless quest for zero defects.

Of course, what happens in practice is a much more rigid and regulated structure is invoked that addresses the high-level corporate issues (growing the finances, enhancing the cash flow, strategic marketing and improving return on investment), legal responsibility for safety (the possible suing of corporate officers for liability and assigning responsibilities), and plain management prudence (ensuring that accountability and responsibility are defined). In Canada recently, in a very public hearing on a large political and fiscal scandal, the definitions were hotly debated of the different nuances between the words 'accountability', 'responsibility' and 'answerability', which, of course, may also then endow the attribute of deniability.

Everything must be defined otherwise there is no definition.

## Safety Performance Measures: Indicators and Balanced Scorecards

We have seen the progressive nature of events, how they were all preventable, and how a confluence of circumstances contributed to the outcomes. Given that major events always have precursors (prior knowledge) that we ignored or did not realise their importance, how can we predict how well we are doing?

How can we best track performance and measure improvement?
How good is good?

We need a new way to track and measure safety and performance using learning curves derived on a mathematical basis. When unusual or abnormal events occur in plants and equipment, the regulator and good management practice requires they be reported, investigated, understood and rectified. In addition to reporting so-called 'significant events', both management and the regulator often set targets for individual and collective performance, which are used for both reward and criticism.

For almost completely safe systems (in ACSI) like nuclear power plants, commercial aircraft and chemical facilities, many parameters are tracked and measured. Continuous improvement has to be demonstrated, as well as meeting reduced occurrence rates, which are set as management goals or targets. This process usually takes the form of statistics for availability of plant and equipment, forced or unplanned maintenance outage, loss of safety function, safety or procedural violations, etc. These are often rolled up into a set of so-called 'Performance Indicators' as measures of how well safety and operation is being managed at a given facility. The overall operating standards of an industry are also measured. A whole discipline is formed of tracking, measuring, reporting, managing and understanding the plethora of indicators and data. Decreasing occurrence rates and meeting or exceeding goals are seen and rewarded as virtues.

None of the Indicators can yet tell us if we are about to have an accident. These are due to unforeseen combinations or confluences of circumstances.

Amalberti, 2001 [29] has written about the pitfalls that exist in 'ACSI', where excessive attention to the wrong items can distract from focusing on the right ones when we are at the limits of accident prevention, and really important events are rare. In the airline industry as in others, no single set of 'safety indices', or a 'risk indicator', or 'operational performance indicators' have been found that represent the true safety status in terms of the probability of an actual accident. So *in the absence of theory*, we must fall back on what is considered good management practice and judgements.

For the three ACSI, being the Nuclear, Chemical and Commercial airlines, the consequences of large accidents are perceived or deemed very undesirable and must be of low probability. We have already shown that the macroscopic indicators of safety performance – the industrial injury rate – are comparable and demonstrate clear learning curve behaviour, and the industrial accident rate is about one in every 200,000 hours. The ACSI are already doing a very good safety and performance job. But even further improvement is proving difficult because of the large contribution of unexpected human errors and confluence of factors to rare events.

Managers and operators need to know how good is their safety management system that has been adopted and used (and paid for), and whether it can itself be improved. We show the importance of accumulated experience in correctly measuring and tracking the decreasing event and error rates. We show that the rate of improvement constitutes a measurable 'learning curve', and the attainment of the goals and targets can be affected by the adopted measures. We examine some of the available data on significant events, reportable occurrences and of loss of availability. We suggest the use of learning curves as a means of accurately tracking progress and stress the importance of a sustained *learning environment* in performance improvement.

## Safety and Performance Indicators: Measuring the Good

We have analysed the performance of humans in designing, constructing, operating managing and measuring complex technological systems. We have analysed over 200 years of data from multiple industries in the areas of safety and performance, including the key role of the human element.

We have developed an analysis and theory (the DSM MERE) to explain and predict event and accident rates in the chemical, nuclear, transport, manufacturing, industrial and human living environments.

We now apply this insight and approach to Events and Performance Indicators in the nuclear power industry.

The industry generally believes that a safe workplace is not only good for the employees and those who work there, but is also good business. A safe workplace is more productive, there are less lost hours due to injuries and outages, the plant tends to operate smoothly; there is pride in the workplace, and maintenance supports safe operation. In addition the training and support provided often avoids unnecessary accidents. All these measures promote a 'safety culture' which emanates throughout executive management, line management and staff attitudes, and echoes in improved worker performance and expectations. We shall return to some of these topics later, but key questions are, even if we do all this:

a) What is our error rate?
b) How safe are we in the workplace?
c) Can we expect accidents, events and injuries not to happen?
d) What can be done to improve?
e) Can we measure safety performance?

Many government agencies report and study the so-called industrial accident data and reporting of this is quite extensive. Employers and trade Associations also track such data, for their own plant or industry. If the industry is perceived as a 'high risk' one, then more attention is often paid to it. Some industries have their own regulator, so that specialists can review and license the details of the equipment and plant design and operations. We authors are specialists from two such industries, aircraft and nuclear, where the regulators have a large say in what is done, how it is done and by whom. The monitoring of the management, safety and performance of nuclear power plants has now reached a high level. The US Nuclear Regulatory Commission Reactor Oversite Program (US NRC ROP) is underway, and like a set of traffic lights (red, amber, green), attempts to indicate whether it is safe to proceed.

A well-run facility is a safer facility, so good performance goes along with management attention to safety performance. At a plant, managers and operators need to know how good is their safety management system that has been adopted and used (and paid for), and whether it can itself be improved.

When unusual or abnormal events occur in plants and equipment, the regulator and good management practice requires they be reported, investigated, understood and rectified. In addition to reporting the so-called 'significant events', both management and the regulator often set targets for individual and collective performance, which are used for both reward and criticism.

There is a trend to collect more and more information about less and less events. But having a plethora of tracking or performance statistics can be counterproductive, with the plant wrongly focusing on the minutiae of data collection and managing to keep within the 'green zone'.

We really need to know the trends – where we are on the learning curve?

## Human Error Rates Passing Red Lights, Runway Incursions and Near Misses

Beneath the macroscopic are the detailed operational and safety performance measures which can be measured and tracked. What does the experience of other industries tell us? Generally, they confirm what is our common sense, that we can improve but not eliminate errors and hence accidents.

We all want to follow the 'rules', and hence, adhere and follow procedures: nevertheless, procedures are not complete since they represent only what we know and expect, and can reduce but not eliminate human error even with extensive training. The green, yellow, red light analogy to traffic works well here too: we should all stop before or when the light turns red. But it is well known that operators of equipment often pass signal lights at danger (in cars and trains) despite many automatic devices, visual cues, warnings and training. It happens about once in 20,000 operator hours on the UK trains. It is not usually malicious, but simply human error and/or risk taking. The presence of a yellow 'caution' light followed by a signal at danger or red light will and should raise both regulator and operator awareness and action, but does not of itself indicate that an accident will or might happen or that it can be prevented.

Quite often, it is the experienced members of staff who take risks – they have done the tasks many times before and work up short cuts, not following procedures, which leads to complacency. It is not the technology that let us down – it is usually the simple procedural errors that lead to a combination of circumstances leading to an event.

Air travel is also an ACSI, and Runway incursions and Near Misses in the USA are similar examples of significant events that should not occur, but do. The air- and ground-spaces are crowded, and the number of movements has been steadily increasing. Much has been done to improve (decrease) the rates, but the chance of being in the wrong place at the wrong time remains. We have already published our analysis of airline event data, showing the existence of common learning curves and a finite (non-zero) minimum error rates for near misses of about one in every 200,000 flying hours. But there is no apparent relationship between the number and rates of these significant Events, and the rate of fatal aircraft accidents, even though the rate per operating hour is about the same and is largely due to the human element. The JCO criticality event demonstrates the confluence of factors that can lead to an accident in an ACSI, when errors in procedures, training, design management and licensing all combine.

We have shown that *all* industries and human activities in modern HTS produce errors and accidents that include a high level of human error, that all follow a universal learning or forgetting curve. This finding is true for the last 200 years of the Industrial Age where we have data, records and statistics (including transportation modes and industrial accidents and injuries) and for both active and passive errors.

## Risk Informed Regulation and Degrees of Goodness: How Green Is Green?

Today there is no magic 'Safety Indicator', a single scale or thermometer against which we know our state of risk at any instant for a technology. The idea that 'accident precursors' exist is also irrelevant in this context, unless we know precisely what is a significant precursor. We can manage to minimise the chance of a repeat event, but we can never eliminate completely a similar but perhaps not identical event. We must do the best we can and dynamically track our progress as we continuously learn and improve.

The real Goal is Continuous Performance Safety, and Quality Improvement (CPSQI) to reduce the chance of accidents and loss to their absolute attainable minimum, as quickly and efficiently as possible. This has happened in the ACSI. Everyone would like to know: How do we measure the improvements? How safe are we? How much are we or can we improve? The current reporting and tracking systems, excellent and exhaustive though they are, do not yet do this tracking of the learning and improving rate in a quantitative manner. Simply stating that the events and errors are below thresholds is not sufficient.

In the limit if we have zero or de minimus events we have nothing to report or to measure. So are zero events the right place to be? Are we still learning and improving? We all wish to be seen and to be excellent: how is that to be measured?

The NRC has the most complete Indicators system, embellished with the titles 'Cornerstones'. It is both thorough and comprehensive, and tries to integrate safety, performance, risk and inspection efforts. Available over the Internet, the NRC records and tracks 27 parameters, some a legacy of a past schemes. (See Figure 7.6 and Table 7.2.)

This is a comprehensive list of systems and measures: some groups or items clearly overlap, others do not. The WANO set focuses squarely on excellence in managing plant operational and safety performance. All of these Indicators should have values within goal, prescribed or regulated limits, and the outages and unavailabilities and failures should be within 'acceptable' limits. Each and every plant, and each and every one of these parameters for each plant are tracked, plus the industry averages for each Quarter.

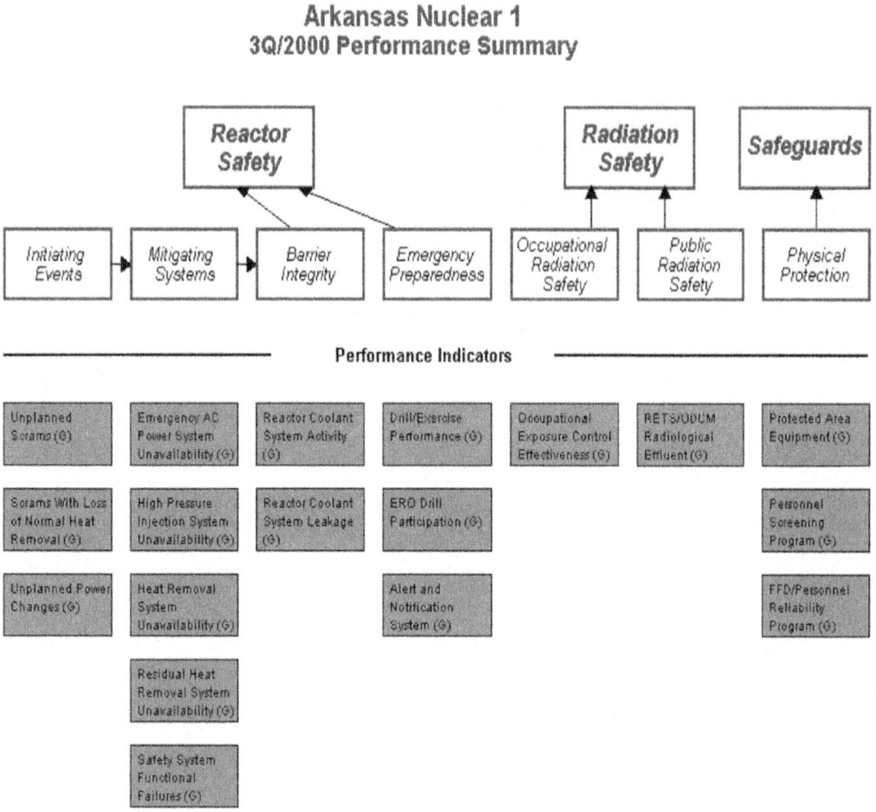

## Arkansas Nuclear 1
### 3Q/2000 Performance Summary

**Figure 7.6.** A typical example of a set of ROP Indicators shown by the 'green' boxes (tinted in this diagram), with the so-called Cornerstones above (With kind permission of US NRC)

At the individual plant level, there is more detail on Quarterly inspections and reports, giving the regulator and operator a common set of performance parameters to report, inspect, manage and measure against as follows (italics added):

The new inspection program will include baseline inspections common to all nuclear plants. *Inspections beyond the baseline will be performed at plants with performance below a specified threshold, based on performance indicators inspection findings.*

*Additional inspections may also be performed in response to a specific event or problem at a plant.* The baseline inspection program will be based on the 'cornerstone' areas important to safety. It will focus on activities and systems that are 'risk significant,' that is those activities and systems that have a potential to initiate an accident, mitigate the effects of an accident, or increase the consequences of a possible accident. The inspection program will also review how the utilities find and fix problems. The inspections will be performed by NRC resident inspectors stationed at each nuclear power plant, and by inspectors based in one of the four NRC regional offices or in NRC Headquarters in Rockville, Maryland.

*The redesigned inspection program was developed using a 'risk-informed' approach to select* areas to inspect within each cornerstone. The inspection areas were selected because of their importance from the point of view of potential risk, past operational experience, and regulatory

**Table 7.2.** US NRC and WANO Indicators

| NRC AEOD Performance Indicators | NRC ROP Performance Indicators | NRC Accident Sequence Precursor (ASP) | WANO Performance Indicators |
|---|---|---|---|
| • Automatic Reactor Scrams (IE) | • Unplanned Scrams (BI) | • Precursor Occurrence Rate (IE&MS) | • Unit Capability Factor |
| • Safety System Actuations (MS) | • Unplanned Scrams with Loss of Normal Heat Removal (BI) | • Conditional Core Damage Probability (IE&MS) | • **Unplanned Capability Loss Factor** |
| • Significant Events (MS) | • **Unplanned Power Changes (BI)** | | • Unplanned Automatic Scrams |
| • Safety System Failures (MS) | • Unavailability, Emergency AC Power (MS) | | • Safety System Performance |
| • **Forced Outage Rate (MS)** | • Unavailability, High Pressure Injection – HPCI (MS) | | • Fuel Reliability |
| • Equipment Forced Outage Rate (MS) | • Unavailability, High Pressure Injection – HPCS (MS) | | • Chemistry Performance |
| • Radiation Exposure (OR) | • Unavailability, Heat Removal System – RCIC (MS) | | • Industrial Safety Accident Rate |
| | • Unavailability, Heat Removal System – AFW (MS) | | • Collective Radiation Exposure |
| | • Unavailability, Residual Heat Removal – PWR (MS) | | • Thermal Performance |
| | • Unavailability, Residual Heat Removal – BWR (MS) | | • Volume of Radioactive Waste |
| | • Safety System Functional Failures – PWR (MS) | | |
| | • Safety System Functional Failures – BWR (MS) | | |
| | • Reactor Coolant System Activity (BI) | | |
| | • Reactor Coolant System Leakage (BI) | | |
| | • Drill/Exercise Performance (EP) | | |
| | • ERO Drill Participation (EP) | | |
| | • Alert & Notification System Reliability (EP) | | |
| | • Occupational Exposure Control Effectiveness (OR) | | |
| | • RETS/ODCM Radiological Effluent Occurrences (PR) | | |
| | • Protected Area Security Equipment Performance (PP) | | |
| | • Personnel Screening Program Performance (PP) | | |

Category 'Green' – Performance only calling for NRC 'baseline' oversight.
Category 'White' – Performance calling for increased regulatory response.
Category 'Yellow' – Performance calling for required regulatory response.
Category 'Red' – Unacceptable performance.

requirements. *Within each inspection area, the scope of the inspection will be set using the same assessment of risk significance. The degree to which the area is measured by a performance indicator also affects the scope.* Each performance indicator is designed to determine acceptable levels of operation within adequate safety margins. The performance indicators will be monitored by the NRC staff and reported quarterly by the utilities. Significant problems identified by performance indicators or by NRC inspectors will be dealt with promptly.

Source: New NRC Reactor Inspection and Oversight Program, http://www.nrc.gov, 1999

It would be useful and cost beneficial to determine which of these Indicators are the most useful or instructive, and have a Baseline determined such that it may shift with increasing experience. Already WANO has deleted two marked * on the grounds that they 'are no longer needed because of significant performance improvements in these areas'.

The NRC ROP Indicators were examined carefully as reported from the start in 1998 up to October 2001 (http://www.nrc.gov/NRR/OVERSIGHT/ROP/trends.html). Most were in the 'green zone': nothing anywhere was in the 'red zone'. The trends showed that of the 18 ROP items, for the industry average most showed apparently random ups and downs. For 1998 to 2001, *four classes showed significant and pronounced downward trends* (evidence of learning curves): ERO Drill Participation, Reactor Coolant System Activity, BWR and PWR Safety System Functional Failures, and Protected Area Security Equipment Performance. The other 13 are either invariant, scattered or show no apparent overall trend: from the WANO argument, should these 13 be discarded also? Or are they relevant at the plant level? How, if at all, should the reporting, inspection and maintenance regimes be modified if there is no discernible trend?

This entire carefully constructed scheme also fell flat on its face, when a large corrosion area was found nearly all the way through on a reactor pressure vessel head (at the Davis Besse plant). Not only had this plant been 'in the green' and was a good performer from an indicator's perspective, the lack of inspections that would have found the corrosion was acceptable to both the regulator and the industry. There was prior knowledge of the corrosion potential, and for the need for more rigorous inspections. After the usual flurry of activity, and much public penance, the head was replaced, the owners castigated, and the plant is now back at power. Why then have Indicators at all?

We asked three other key questions:

What do the trends, if any, mean?
Can the past trends be predicted?
What is the future expected trend?

To answer we all need a theory (not just a 'model') that will and can be proven to analyse errors and events, be tested on the data, and can make sensible predictions based on past observations. We now show how that can be done using the DSM. We try to explain the mathematics carefully in words, observing that the application of physical theory is generally unknown in this largely management and regulatory field.

## Modelling and Predicting Event Rates and Learning Curves Using Accumulated Experience

It is important to provide a theoretical basis for these trends, so to inter-compare these apparently disparate data. We treat events given as Indicators (such as functional failures, unavailabilities, unplanned outage, etc.) as a failure rate, just like other errors, injuries and accidents.

*The general hypothesis is that humans learn from the events that occur as a result of mistakes and errors, and we can take the rate of learning (event or error rate reduction) as proportional to the instantaneous event or error rate.* The exponential model form follows from that hypothesis, and is obtained using the analogous classic formulation from failure rate modelling but using the accumulated experience and allowing for a finite asymptotic (minimum) rate.

We construct the non-dimensional event rate equation simply by redefining the event or error rate, $A$, as relative to and normalised by the minimum or asymptotic observed rate, $A_M$. We define a non-dimensional rate, $E^*$, normalised by the rate $A_0^*$ of the initially observed events or errors when the technology began or at the start of reporting. Thus, solving the Minimum Error Rate Equation (MERE), we have the non-dimensional event or error rate, $E^*$, given by the *Universal Learning Curve (ULC)*:

$$E^* = A^*/A_0^* = \exp - KN^*$$

where $A_0^* = (1 - A_m/A_0)$ and $A^* = (1 - A_m/A)$, $N^*$ being a measure of the accumulated experience, and $k$, is the learning rate constant of proportionality. By renormalising to the physically based parameters of the initial and asymptotic minimum accident rates, we have derived a workable inter-comparison basis using accumulated experience as a measure of the technological system maturation.

Often, as we learn and successfully apply corrective strategies, the high initial event rate falls away quickly. In this case, it can be that $A_M \ll A_0$, so an approximate result very useful for correlating data trends and for predictive purposes is:

$$A = A_m + A_0 \exp - kN$$

The resulting *exponential model* is a simple and useful form for correlating data trends, determining the learning rate, estimating the minimum rate and making predictions (with confidence levels) about future errors. In addition, for the first time, data from many disparate sources can now be directly inter-compared and used to determine the correct measure for the accumulated experience. In statistical terminology, by using the accumulated experience, the problems of time-varying explanatory variables, time-variance and data censoring are all avoided. We call this the DSM (Duffey–Saull Method) approach and as a direct result of the theoretical analysis, we have developed a set of rules, which we call the DSM Rules, for analysing error (e.g., event, accident, injury or loss) data. Particularly important is determining, finding and adopting the correct measure for the accumulated experience.

To compare data, we u se the following DSM Rules:

a) Report and plot the event data as *Instantaneous Rates* (*IR*) versus the accumulated experience which we define as:

  $IR = $ (Total number of events in an interval of experience)/(Experience in the same interval)

b) Use the *Accumulated Rate* (*AR*) defined as:

> $AR$ = (Total number of events in a given interval of experience)/(Experience
> accumulated up to that interval)

When both the *IR* and the *AR* are plotted versus the accumulated experience, we find typical trends. Basically the *IR* can wander around, and may follow a learning curve or not, exhibiting insufficient learning. On the other hand, the *AR* may be indicating a declining trend: note however, that this apparently declining hazard rate is partly due to having a nearly constant hazard (Allison, 1984) [30].

c) Thus, the *Constant Rate* (*CR*) for comparison purposes is given by:

> $CR$ = (Initial Observed or expected Event rate)/(Accumulated Experience from each
> succeeding interval).

Also key is comparing the *IR* to the exponential model theory and the *AR* to the expectation of the constant rate (*CR*). In this way, using the DSM Rules, the past and future trends can be determined to see if there is the start of an upward trend due to forgetting and/or insufficient learning. It is thus possible to quantify where the technology or system or plant is placed on the learning curve, if the minimum error rate has been attained or not, and how the value of the error rate compares to other technologies.

We define the measure of accumulated experience *NOT* using calendar time (hours or years) which are the usually adopted arbitrary cosmological or human fiscal scale. This is because the fleet size, management, operating performance and production experience will all vary with time. We need to determine the 'correct' measure for the learning opportunity, whatever that may be.

To show that the MERE explains some of the observed trends in the indicators, we must compare to the data.

Recall that by comparing to past trends we can find the Learning and Forgetting rates, and make statistically significant predictions about future event rates. We do not state or claim that we are predicting an accident or event, simply what the likelihood of the events are in the future based on the accumulated experience and what has been learned to the present.

## Using the Past to Predict the Future: How Good is Good?

We need to determine where we may be on the ULC and whether there is a trend or not. In effect, we are often analysing event data over different-sized samples (being differing plants around the country with differing accumulated experience bases), covering many disciplines and technologies. The observed rates reflect both the sample size and the rate of learning for that snapshot of time, but with differing accumulated experience in each plant or country and vastly different 'cultures, standards and styles'. But we have shown before that there really is a common learning curve trend, where the correct measure of the experience can be different for each event type or Indicator.

The exact shape of the expected learning curve is given by the exponential model from solving the MERE in our analysis. Basically, the learning model gives a rational reason and defensible reason or basis for choosing one 'fit' over another since the form is given by theory. The only alternative is to fit the data with arbitrary polynomials, series or exponentials, which would not have the correct basis for extrapolation and can never be accurate for prediction purposes with large fluctuations in the basic datasets and historical trends. The obvious linear trend is simply not a valid basis for analysis purposes.

We show here two typical cases of interest: reportable events and reactor shutdown scrams, for the USA and for Japan. We seek:

a) common trends in the *data* with increasing accumulated experience;
b) insights on the fundamental and underlying human error rates;
c) clear indications (or not) of a universal learning curve, or of insufficient learning;
d) the presence or absence of an attainable, discernible or observable minimum rate;
e) evidence of any influence on error rates of the effect of technological change;
f) predictive techniques for estimating *future* error rates; and
g) suitable goals and management approaches to error minimisation.

## Reportable Events

These data were given by Kansler (2001) [31] for all events reported to the US NRC from 1989–2000: there is a dramatic decline due to excellent performance. Figure 7.7 shows that based on the usual standard calendar time plot, we would expect with high confidence that there be no events reported in 2001. But the total plant electricity output rose by 42% from 1989 to 2000, and may change in the future. If we use the accumulated production as a measure of the experience, we see that the curve can now take the predicted exponential shape:

$$IR\,(\text{events}/\text{BMWy}) = 0.33 + 3.8\exp-(\text{accBMWy}/206)$$

The DSM 95% confidence *prediction* for 2001 is then ~0.36/BMWy, plus or minus 0.3, or up to about 35 reportable events in total. The data for Japan, for very different plants, reporting and production show a similar trend. The magnitudes and learning rates are quite differ-

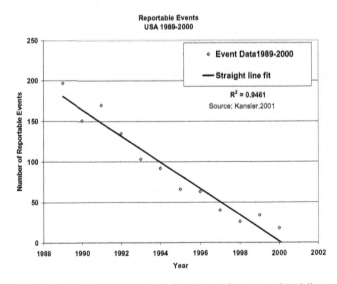

**Figure 7.7.** Reportable events in calendar time and a conventional linear trend

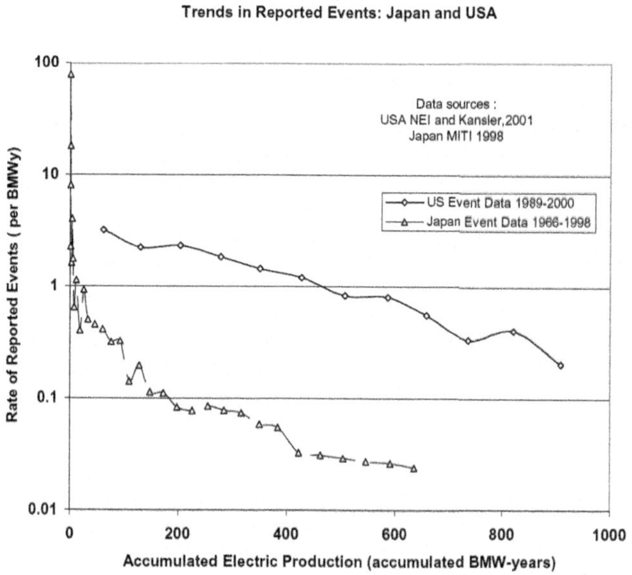

**Trends in Reported Events: Japan and USA**

**Figure 7.8.**   Reportable events plotted against accumulated production

ent, by a factor of 10, presumably due to different regulatory and operating and reporting standards. (See Figures 7.8 and 7.9.)

## Scrams and Unplanned Shutdowns

Plants are provided with automatic and manual shutdown systems. Trips mean lost production, actuation of safety and shutdown equipment, and usually a lengthy examination of the 'root cause'. The data for scrams and shutdowns are also collected. (See Figure 7.10.)

The two curves are similar on the conventional per unit per year basis and the accumulated production.

The MERE is given by:

$$IR(\text{shutdowns per BMWy}) = 1.75 + 4.9\exp - (\text{accBMWy}/32)$$

The fitted learning curve suggests a minimum rate of about ~2 per accBMy. In Figure 7.11, we show the data according to the theory and compare it to the mean theoretical ULC curve derived from all industrial data given by $E^* = \exp - 3N^*$.

Thus, we may conclude that certain overall performance parameters ('Indicators') show trends that follow clear learning curves (the five parameters from the ROP) as well as reportable events. They are in accord with the general learning trends of other industries and human activities. The other Indicators do not follow such trends so it is less clear what to do, and how to track the trends and cost-effectively conduct the inspection and maintenance regimes.

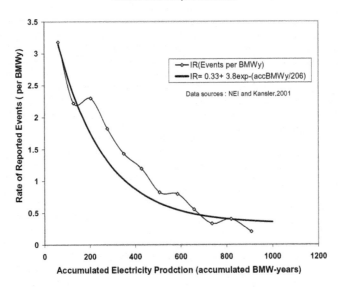

**Figure 7.9.** Comparison of trends in reportable events from the USA and Japan

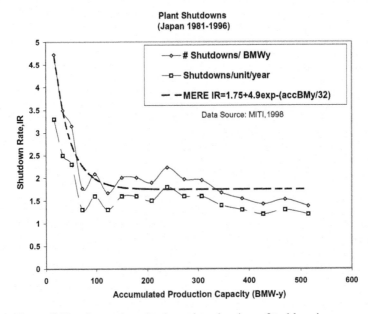

**Figure 7.10.** Japan plant shutdown data showing a fitted learning curve

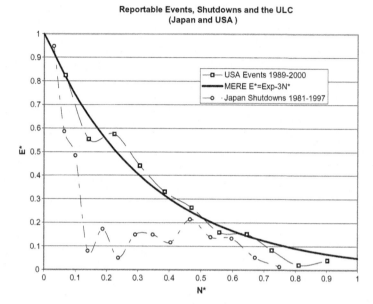

**Figure 7.11.** Non-dimensional Universal Learning Curves

## Common-Cause Events and Latent Errors

Two of the more difficult but important parameters to measure safety performance against are the incidence of so-called latent errors, which remain hidden during the event, and common-cause events. We have already shown from the analyses of EdF data carried out by Baumont et al. [10] that the detection of latent errors follows a learning curve. The rate of *non-detection* of latent errors is consistent with the error rate for other human activities, namely of order one in 200,000 hours.

Errors can also be inadvertently embodied in the design, so multiple redundant and diverse trains are included in control and safety systems to avoid 'common-cause' events, where similar equipment can or may malfunction due to similar faults or initiators. A database of such failures is available (apparently to participating regulators only) via the International Common Cause Data Exchange (ICDE) project of the OECD/NEA as summarised by Hessel (2001) [32]. Redundancy is defined as double (CC), triple (CCC), quadruple (CCCC) or more levels, such as having several different types of safety and/or relief valves, multiple trains of ECC, or redundant shutdown voting systems. Since 1994, some 200 reactors have been tracked (i.e., over 1,000 years of operating experience) and nearly 500 events reported and classified.

In Figure 7.12, we show the fraction of events in each category, by level of defense, and also show a fitted learning curve. The data also are plotted as separated according whether human error was stated as the cause (shown as the open symbols) or not: it can be seen that this cause dominates.

By 10 or more levels of defense, there have been no events, which does not mean there will not be, but certainly that the rate is extremely low (<1 in 1,000 ROYs). For each increase

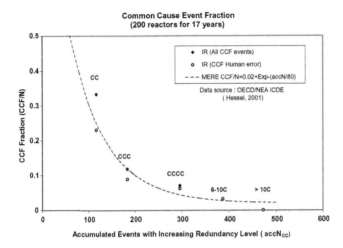

**Figure 7.12.** Common-Cause Events for 1994–2001 for 200 plants

in the number of levels (degree of redundancy/diversity), the fraction of events fall as the number of levels increase, as we might have expected.

Thus, the multiple levels of defense adopted in design against common-cause failures is the correct approach and can reduce common-cause events by a factor of 10 or more, but adding six or more levels does not give a large or proportionate decrease. Thus, we can argue that designers have learned in the design process, and have successfully applied and validated the principles of redundancy and diversity. The designs should apparently adopt no more than four levels based on these data, and inspection and maintenance regimes should focus on the role of the human element, and not just on mechanical, component or system failure.

It would seem that maintenance and inspections should take cognizance of the decreased rates, and adopt decreased inspection requirements for such systems if a learning curve can be demonstrated.

## Performance Improvement: Case-by-Case

We have analysed the background and the detail behind Safety and Quality 'Performance Indicators'. We have shown that some of these follow well-defined learning curves, and have trends consistent with those found in other industries and activities. The theory and mathematics show that the ULC is directly relevant and applicable.

The data we have analysed are from North America, Europe, Australia, Africa and Asia, and cover human equipment and design errors in medical practice, injuries and accidents to industrial workers, deaths and near misses in aircraft, automobiles and the operation of ships and trains, plus failures in millions of components and tires, and details of a century of coal and diamond mining, and incidents in both chemical and nuclear plants and facilities (criticality and SERs, etc.)

We have analysed typical examples of plant parameters and events for diverse operating plants, countries and industries. We have sought the existence or not of learning trends *in the data*. For plant shutdowns and latent errors, we have shown the existence of learning curves when measured against increasing accumulated experience and electricity production. For common-cause events, there is also a learning curve that follows increasing levels of diversity and redundancy. For those Indicators or Measures that do not show a well-defined trend or demonstrate a learning curve, or are not related to meaningful estimates of increasing experience, and there are many, it is not possible to justify tracking these on a continuous basis.

It is key to sustain a learning environment, in order to have continuous improvement and to learn from errors and mistakes. It is also important to establish a performance indicator system that measures parameters and trends from which meaningful information and predictions can be extracted. Inspections and reporting can then better focus on what is important as well as measurable.

The DSM analysis and the examples described here provide such an SMS approach.

## Lack of Risk Reduction: Medical Adverse Events and Deaths

Medical science, and indeed all of science, relies on the application and use of statistical techniques, as emphasised clearly and eloquently by Senn, 2003 [33]. The benefit of any treatment, vaccination, surgery, preventative care, lifestyle change, precautionary measures, and new technology and drugs have to be founded on how much they reduce the chance of illness, sickness, disease or death. As we advance the technology and the treatments, we should learn from the past mistakes and inadequacies. Obviously, patients are treated and only get better if the procedure, medication or remedy has a sufficient and measurable probability of success; but at the same time there is always a real and finite chance of failure, or of adverse consequences, including death.

Patient safety is now a big issue in medical circles. We had already analysed the available data on medical 'errors' before in 'Know the Risk', which was largely based on the US Institute of Medicine review [34]. The data found about a 5-to-10% chance that a real risk, a so-called 'adverse event', could kill you. This is not really just likelihood: it is a prior certainty.

There has been an important role for statistical analysis in the medical profession regarding the prediction of the odds of patient death, using the so-called 'biostatistics', [33]. The fundamental idea is to plan and use the results of clinical trials on a selected or volunteer group of patients in a consistent and defensible manner, while demonstrating some significant advantage or gain occurs in health or survival rates. The human tests usually happen after some tests on animal substitutes, but eventually a demonstration or trial use has to take place. This approach is necessary for the approvals for new drugs, novel treatments and new procedures in a consistent manner. The risk or benefit is based on the observed comparative rate of outcomes versus non-outcomes for the test groups or clinical populations under study. The relative probability of improvement or survival is derived, meaning the decreased chance of an outcome, since there is a probability of dying anyway whether treated or not. Thus, showing a statistical significant effect in the data using human subjects is key, based on some hopefully representative sample that establishes – within some uncertainty – the degree of efficacy of the treatment or drugs being used.

Errors can and do rarely occur in such trials, as well as during regular treatments, where the wrong trial dose is given or used, or the treatment has some undesirable side effects. In essence, these 'human trials' are actually a clear and practical manifestation of determining risk using learning opportunities. Paradoxically, here again without mistakes, and using trials and experiments, we cannot advance the application of medical science and save more lives. But even after extensive testing, problems may still occur, as the risk is never zero.

Now doctors, physicians, specialists, clinicians, surgeons and nurses until recently have not been in the business of reporting mistakes. They are in the business of saving lives and treating ailments, sicknesses, syndromes and phobias. But they can advise a patient about the risk of a procedure, say for cancer, or of heart surgery, or of a hip replacement. After all, there are data, even if just from clinical trials on a few instead of millions of patients, so there is prior knowledge.

In the UK, there is now a strong and new emphasis on learning from past mistakes and in constructing a learning environment (safety culture) that encourages open reporting. In fact, the latest National Health Service (NHS) Expert Group study, 2000 [35] gave some harrowing and startling information on the scale of the problem. The Expert Group study stated that NHS reporting and information systems provided a 'patchy and incomplete picture of the scale and nature of the problem of serious failures in health care'. They found that *every year:*

- 400 people die or are seriously injured in adverse events involving medical devices;
- nearly 10,000 people are reported to have experienced serious adverse reactions to drugs;
- around 1,150 people who have been in recent contact with mental health services commit suicide;
- nearly 28,000 written complaints are made about aspects of clinical treatment in hospitals;
- NHS pays out around £400 million a year settlement of clinical negligence claims;
- has a potential liability of around £2.4 billion for existing and expected claims;
- hospital acquired infections – around 15% of which may be avoidable – are estimated to cost the NHS nearly £1 billion;
- adverse events in which harm is caused to patients occur in around 10% of admissions – or at a rate in excess of 850,000 a year; and
- adverse events cost the service an estimated £2 billion a year in additional hospital stays alone, without taking any account of human or wider economic costs.

With actually about 10 million patients treated as admissions to UK hospitals every year, this error rate probability estimate is $<p(\varepsilon)> \sim 850,000/10,000,000 = 0.085$, or 8½%, which is really a large, not a rare outcome rate. The report goes on to propose addressing the problem of organisational failures by improved organisational learning, and by introducing a uniform error reporting system. Partly as a result, the UK formed the National Patient Safety Agency (NPSA) that is specifically charged with the reporting and reduction of medical errors. The NPSA had focused mainly on procedures to correct 'mismatches' between wrongly identified patients who then receive incorrect treatments.

In fact, we found even more data available from the independent accrediting body in the USA, which was formerly called the Joint Commission on Accreditation of Health Care Organizations. The Joint Commission (formerly the JCHAO) examines the very grandly termed 'sentinel events' and states the definition:

*In support of its mission to continuously improve the safety and quality of health care provided to the public, The Joint Commission reviews organizations' activities in response to sentinel events in its accreditation process, including all full accreditation surveys and random unannounced surveys and, as appropriate, for-cause surveys.*

*A sentinel event is an unexpected occurrence involving death or serious physical or psychological injury, or the risk thereof. Serious injury specifically includes loss of limb or function. The phrase 'or the risk thereof' includes any process variation for which a recurrence would carry a significant chance of a serious adverse outcome.*

*Such events are called 'sentinel' because they signal the need for immediate investigation and response. The terms 'sentinel event' and 'medical error' are not synonymous; not all sentinel events occur because of an error and not all errors result in sentinel events.*

*© The Joint Commission, 2008. Reprinted with permission.*

The Joint Commission defines the events that are subject to formal Review by the Joint Commission under their Sentinel Event Policy which meet specific criteria:

*The definition of a reviewable sentinel event takes into account a wide array of occurrences applicable to a wide variety of health care organizations. Any or all occurrences may apply to a particular type of hospital. Thus, not all of the following occurrences may apply to your particular hospital. The subset of sentinel events that is subject to review by the Joint Commission includes any occurrence that meets any of the following criteria:*

* *The event has resulted in an unanticipated death or major permanent loss of function, not related to the natural course of the patient's illness or underlying condition*

*Or*

* *The event is one of the following (even if the outcome was not death or major permanent loss of function unrelated to the natural course of the patient's illness or underlying condition):*
* *Suicide of any patient receiving care, treatment and services in a staffed around-the-clock care setting or within 72 hours of discharge*
* *Unanticipated death of a full-term infant*
* *Abduction of any patient receiving care, treatment, and services*
* *Discharge of an infant to the wrong family*
* *Rape*
* *Hemolytic transfusion reaction involving administration of blood or blood products having major blood group incompatibilities*
* *Surgery on the wrong patient or wrong body part*
* *Unintended retention of a foreign object in a patient after surgery or other procedure*
* *Severe neonatal hyperbilirubinemia (bilirubin >30 milligrams/deciliter)*
* *Prolonged fluoroscopy with cumulative dose >1,500 rads to a single field or any delivery of radiotherapy to the wrong body region or >25% above the planned radiotherapy dose.'*

*Source: © The Joint Commission, 2008. Reprinted with permission*
*(see* http://www.jointcommission.org/SentinelEvents/
PolicyandProcedures/se_pp.htm)

## New Data: Sentinel Events, Deaths and Blood Work

We had examined information from the former JCHAO website on rates and numbers for these so-called sentinel events for the interval 1995 to 2004. Throughout the USA, the 'reviewed' event rate varied state-by-state and had a low to high range of between 6 and 23 per million population, and we can ascribe an average rate of about 15 per million based on simply averaging this range. For 1995–2007, the newly named Joint Commission reported that it had reviewed 4,817 of nearly 4,945 events, of which some 70% (about 3,478) caused patient death. As of December 2007, the following causes and percentages were listed, where the number of actual cases are shown in the brackets ( ):

*Patient suicide (596) 12.4%*
*Operation/post-operation complication (568) 11.8%*
*Wrong-site surgery (625) 13%*
*Medication error (446) 9.3%*
*Delay in treatment (360) 7.5%*
*Patient death/injury in restraints (176) 3.7%*
*Patient fall (281) 5.8%*
*Assault/rape/homicide (177) 3.7%*
*Transfusion error (113) 2.3%*
*Perinatal death/loss of function (143) 3%*
*Unintended foreign body (141) 2.9%*
*Patient elopement (76) 1.6%*
*Fire (72) 1.5%*
*Ventilator death/injury (50) 1%*
*Anesthesia-related event (81) 1.7%*
*Infection-related event (100) 2.1%*
*Medical equipment-related (82) 1.7%*
*Maternal death (70) 1.5%*
*Abduction (28) 0.6%*
*Utility systems-related (24) 0.5%*
*Infant discharge to wrong family (7) 0.1%*
*Other less frequent events (610) 12.5%*

Source: © *The Joint Commission, 2008. Reprinted with permission.*
(*See* http://www.jointcommission.org/NR/rdonlyres/D7836542-A372-4F93-8BD7-
DDD11D43E484/0/SE_Stats_12_07.pdf)

In the last few years, there have also been more international data appearing. The studies of medical error have been expanded and now include data from Canada, Italy, France and New Zealand. We wanted to see what the risk also was in these countries, if there was any improvement occurring, and determine the relative safety and risk variations for patients in different countries. We communicated with the corresponding or lead authors of each study in Canada and New Zealand. We pointed out our results, and as before and apparently as seemingly usual for the medical profession, *we again received absolutely no reply or comments.*

The data collection methods used in the studies were invariably impeccable. There was careful record selection, with professional scanning and re-reading of the medical records of patients, looking for signs of misdiagnosis, misadministration of drugs and/or treatments, incompetent or wrong treatment, and just bad luck. We have no reason to doubt the database or results reported.

As we recalculated the data, we found a small numerical error in some of *our* previous estimates as reported in 'Know the Risk' for the USA rates. This proves that we are not error-free either, so we corrected those points for that mistake, although no readers have reported it. All the data we reviewed and analysed are shown in the Table 7.3, and includes media reported information for comparison. The technique of data pooling from different studies is apparently known as a 'meta analysis' in the medical community [33].

We used the patient sample size as a measure of the experience, knowing this was an approximation, or the total population for the large samples from Phillips et al. and the Joint Commission, which then gave rates of order 10–30 per million.

What is evident is how much the death rates *apparently* do depend on the chosen sample (experience) used in each study. But this difference is usual for outcome analyses. To illustrate

**Table 7.3.**    Internationally reported data for medical adverse events

| Study or Source | Date | Number of Errors | Events/Million |
|---|---|---|---|
| Phillips et al., 1998 (IOM) | 1983 | 2,800 | 12 |
|  | 1984 | 3,400 | 14 |
|  | 1985 | 3,700 | 15 |
|  | 1986 | 4,200 | 17 |
|  | 1987 | 4,000 | 16 |
|  | 1988 | 4,900 | 20 |
|  | 1989 | 5,100 | 21 |
|  | 1990 | 4,500 | 18 |
|  | 1991 | 5,300 | 21 |
|  | 1992 | 6,000 | 24 |
|  | 1993 | 7,300 | 29 |
| Cohen et al., 1986 (IOM) | 1975–78 | 2,634 | 91,980 |
|  | 1979–83 | 3,383 | 98,460 |
| Brennan et al., 1991 (IOM) |  | 98,609 | 36,906 |
| CMA, 1977 (IOM) | 1977 | 870 | 41,699 |
| Barker and McConnell 1961(IOM) | 1961 | 93 | 162,587 |
| Barker et al., 1966 (IOM) | 1966 | 2,920 | 265,093 |
|  |  | 393 | 129,149 |
|  |  | 1,461 | 149,249 |
| Shultz et al., 1973 (IOM) | 1973 | 196 | 53,290 |
|  |  | 22 | 6,382 |
| Ottawa Citizen (Adverse Events) | 2004 | 187,500 | 75,000 |
| Ottawa Citizen (Deaths) | 2004 | 24,000 | 9,600 |
| Davis et al., 2001 (New Zealand) | 2001 | 123 | 16,488 |
| Terra and Verbano, 2007 (Cineas, Italy) | 2002 | 320,000 | 40,000 |
| Baker et al., 2004 (Canada) | 2004 | 401 | 107,076 |
| JCHAO, 2004 (US Sentinel events) | 1995–2004 | 2,966 | 12 |
| Michel et al., 2005 (France) | 2005 | 191 | 39,400 |

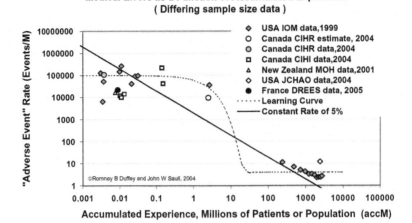

**Figure 7.13.**  Comparison of medical outcome data

this effect more clearly, we plotted the rate data as shown in Figure 7.13, where we can see a cluster of points for less than 100,000 in the sample size with the addition of the new data from Canada (Baker et al., 2004) [36], France (Michel et al., 2005) [37], and New Zealand (Davis et al., 2001) [38]. The new data from France were subdivided into types of medical and surgical 'serious undesirable events' (EIGs), and measured according to days of hospitalisation, rather than by the deaths due to adverse events. For the present purpose of comparing these event data with all the other studies, we took just the total result of 3.94% as being equivalent to the outcomes in the other studies.

We show a possible MERE learning curve fit, which winds its way through the data. But far more interesting is the line labeled *CR* 5%, meaning a risk of about 1 in 20 of having a problem. It is quite a good fit to the data. The data actually follow the theoretical line trend given by the minimum likelihood rate, $\lambda \sim n/\varepsilon$, or a constant rate, *CR*. Hopefully, there will be a significant increase in medical error datasets available over the coming years as governmental and public pressure is applied.

From this graph, it is quite apparent that there is no real learning, and that a *CR* of about 5% (no matter where you are) is a reasonably good global assumption. Over the last five years, adverse event (death) rates have not reduced. The uncertainty (scatter) is large, of up to a factor of 10. But certainly no one country can claim to be lower or better, yet or, worse still, to have learned much. Medical practice and the patient risk worldwide are about the same everywhere it would seem. There is not an overwhelming evidence of learning from or in the medical adverse events or outcomes from or in the studies completed to date throughout the world.

We can compare this plot to our desired learning trends in the Introduction. The lack of evidence of reduction or learning in these data and studies is despite massive efforts, publicity, focus and new confidential reporting systems. Within the HTS medical community, the culture of reticence to admit to error apparently must persist, and/or the medical system continues to have practices that make it prone to error.

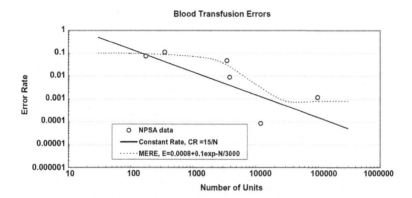

**Figure 7.14.** The collected data for blood transfusion errors (With kind permission of UK NPSA report, 2004)

The above results are all for 'top–level' studies of the overall errors and deaths due to many types of errors, and does not explain or address if this trend also holds for individual treatments and patients. Luckily, we also found data to confirm that fact. The UK NPSA has published work aimed at the patient 'mismatching' issue, which reported the collected summary of prior studies on errors occurring in blood transfusions (Sujan et al., 2004) [39]. The studies analysed giving the wrong blood units to the wrong patient, including mistakes in blood typing and transfusion amounts, as well as errors in patient identification. These 'blood work' errors did not all result in death, fortunately for both the patients and for our analysis purposes; so we are not dealing solely with fatalities but with simple but common mistakes. Six of the separate studies had actual data summaries, in which the clinical and study populations ranged in size from a few hundred to many thousands of units. So, just like we did for the overall data, we have to separate out that size effect by showing all the blood transfusion error data for the six studies in Figure 7.14 as an error rate per unit on a log–log plot versus the study size.

The rate data show the characteristic decline with increased study sample size, despite the scatter or spread. The comparative risk seems larger, in the sense it is more likely for patients to have a blood work error (and live) than some other medical error (and die). Once again, it is not clear that there is much learning present at this individual treatment level for transfusions, one of the most commonly used medical procedures. The straight solid line through the data of slope −1 in Figure 7.14 is the best *CR* constant rate ($E = 15/N$). The best learning curve MERE fit (with $r^2 = 0.9$) is also shown as the dotted line in Figure 7.14 given by:

$$\text{Errors per unit, } E = 0.0008 + 0.1\exp{-N/3{,}000}$$

The risk *prediction* and implication from the MERE fit is the lowest blood work rate that likely can be eventually achieved is of order one error in a thousand units, which is suitable as a management and risk goal.

Reinforcing the apparent lack of learning, in our search we came across data on adverse medical drug events (ADEs) reported by the US Food and Drug administration (FDA) who stated:

**Figure 7.15.** Reported number of adverse events due to drugs, 1990–2000 (With kind permission of US FDA, 2008, http://www.fda.gov/ope/fy02plan/adevent.html)

*Approximately 1.3 million people are accidentally injured by medical therapy in the U.S. annually. Many errors are associated with the misuse of drugs and medical devices regulated by FDA. Costs from these medical errors range from $20 to $75 billion annually . . . 'We believe there is serious under-reporting of adverse events.'*
Source: *U.S. Food and Drug Administration Performance Plan and Summary, 2002, Section 1.2.1,* http://www.fda.gov/ope/fy02plan/default.htm

The reported FDA data for drug events internationally are shown in Figure 7.15, and clearly show no learning. The variation with depth of experience is an increasing and not a decreasing trend for the observation interval of 1990–2000 shown. The reports and data are now collected electronically under the FDA National Electronic Injury Surveillance System (NEIS).

In addition to these published data, the FDA Center for Devices and Radiological Health (CDRH) has an extensive adverse event database for medical devices called MAUDE (**man**ufacturer and **u**ser facility **d**evice **e**xperience database).

In the MAUDE information file that we downloaded and examined, there were over 400,000 records of reported events from the use of medical devices up to 2002, with nearly 50,000 more added for 2003 alone. These data consist of all voluntary reports since June 1993, user facility reports since 1991, distributor reports since 1993, and manufacturer reports since August 1996. 'Devices' include the whole gamut of tools, instruments and machines for the administration of diagnostic, emergency, remedial, surgical, post operative, monitoring, radiological and therapeutic care. Since this is a highly proprietary area, where sales, profits, lives, liability, and both patients and patents are at risk, the data files are highly impersonalised. The data files defied our analysis capabilities by not being in a form easily transferable to xls. format: but it is clear that the number of events is not decreasing significantly and does *not* exhibit learning.

## Medication Errors in Health Care

It should be easy, and is obviously important, to give the right patient the right drug in the right amount at the right times, based on the correct diagnosis of symptoms and monitoring of the patient's reaction. However, errors can and do occur in labelling, dosage, injection and administration; in confusion or mix-ups between drugs, and from illegible or wrongly read prescriptions; and even in the reconciliation of patients and their medications during extended treatment and between multiple facilities and stages of care.

An outstanding and somewhat frightening collection of examples is given by Cohen, 1999 [40] of such medication problems, and of major confusions in both labelling and doses. By including many remedial actions, in fact the entire book by Cohen is an excellent example of empirically and retroactively learning from mistakes. Typically, the data show medication administration errors decreasing by a significant factor following the adoption of corrective actions and independent checking processes.

Notably, Cohen reported medication error rates for over 40 independent studies in North America from 1962 to 1995 (his Table 6-1). The error rates were stated as a function of the number of 'medication opportunities', TOE, which were for a total sample of $\Sigma N_j = 103,290$, with $n = 7,430$ outcomes, giving an average outcome probability of $p(\varepsilon) = n/N = 0.072$. In addition, the results of trials were given for both before and after improvements in the medication system for both medication dosage and distribution procedures. The entire dataset from Cohen, excluding only the wrong-timing errors, are shown in Figure 7.16, taking the TOE for each study as the measure of experience, or the learning opportunity. The data have never been plotted in this DSM manner before now, which as can be seen readily and naturally accounts for the different sample and study sizes. The separate comparisons include both the 'before' and 'after' datasets, as well as the constant rate line, $CR$. The *average* of the 'before' rates is some 9% and the 'after' about 5%, or a one-time one-shot decrease of a factor of nearly two (2), showing how much improvement is possible. But as usual, there is no evidence of learning with experience and there exists significant scatter.

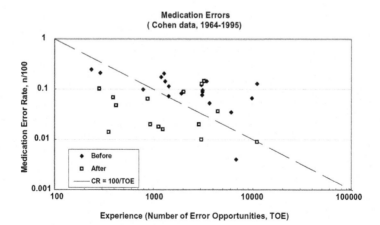

**Figure 7.16.** Historical medication error rates

By comparing Figures 7.13 and 7.14, we see that medication errors are 10 times more likely than transfusion errors on a per procedure basis for any given number of patients, and has basically remained unaltered for over 30 years. Because such errors are so common, special attention has recently been paid to measuring 'patient safety' for the case of medications, which is really a euphemism for 'patient danger'. In fact, in the USA, there is a National Coordinating Council for Medication Error Reporting and Prevention (see http://www. nccmerp.org), consisting of members from all the leading medical organisations, health agencies and professional associations. Their stated purpose is to assist better and standardised reporting and to develop improved strategies. But the situation is actually so poor that in 2002 it was recommended *not* to use error rates for inter-comparison purposes, but only for internal tracking, as follows.

*Use of medication error rates to compare health care organizations is of no value (because):*

*Differences in culture among health care organizations can lead to significant differences in the level of reporting of medication errors.*

*Differences in the definition of a medication error among health care organizations can lead to significant differences in the reporting and classification of medication errors.*

*Differences in the patient populations served by various health care organizations can lead to significant differences in the number and severity of medication errors occurring among organizations.*

*Differences in the type(s) of reporting and detection systems for medication errors among health care organizations can lead to significant differences in the number of medication errors recorded.*

*The Council believes that there are no acceptable incidence rates for medication errors. The goal of every health care organization should be to continually improve systems to prevent harm to patients due to medication errors. Health care organizations should monitor actual and potential medication errors that occur within their organization, and investigate the root cause of errors with the goal of identifying ways to improve the medication- use system to prevent future errors and potential patient harm. The value of medication error reporting and other data gathering strategies is to provide the information that allows an organization to identify weaknesses in its medication-use system and to apply lessons learned to improve the system. The sheer number of error reports is less important than the quality of the information collected in the reports, the health care organization's analysis of the information, and its actions to improve the system to prevent harm to patients.'*

*The Council's recommendations support the concept that, at this time in the patient safety journey,' said John R. Combes, M.D., Council chairperson and senior medical advisor at The Hospital and Health System Association of Pennsylvania and the American Hospital Association, 'it is more important to create the open environment that encourages the reporting of errors and near-errors than to develop less meaningful comparative error rates. The goal for an organization's medication safety programs,' he continued, 'is to learn as much as possible about active and latent error and through that understanding prevent harm to patients'.*

Source: ©2002 National Coordinating Council for Medication Reporting and Prevention.

The goals here are very clear and worthwhile, discouraging the reporting of just numbers while emphasising both analysis and improvement. But the error reporting system is apparently in a very discouraging state of affairs, as we would emphasise and suggest that comparing error rates is needed just to know where each system resides on the universal learning curve. Both feedback and benchmarking on *comparative learning rates* are essential for determining the existence, or not of successful learning. Hence, not performing comparative rate analysis runs directly counter to the:

a) available best practices on reporting;
b) world outcome data trends;
c) verified Learning Hypothesis model;
d) DSM analysis of Cohen's error rate results (in Figure 7.16); and, lastly,
e) every recommendation stemming from the present risk work.

We have repeatedly stressed the need for tracking both outcome rates and numbers (the prior data) to determine the learning trends, the influence of corrective actions and the effectiveness of risk management systems. Only by tracking, measuring, reporting and using prior information can improvement and learning occur. In the absence of a unified and scrutable reporting and tracking system as adopted in, say, the aircraft, nuclear, chemical and industrial safety arenas, in the medical system the patient, the nurse and the physician are very much left alone in the frontline of managing risk themselves.

Recognising the institutional problem, recently efforts have been made to address the needed training, guidelines, measurement and reporting for actual individual health-care providers, like doctors and nurses (R. Newhouse and S. Poe, 2005) [41].

Other relevant data exist, but are really difficult to derive or analyse for learning or forgetting trends. Significantly, the National Canada Health Agency maintains a Canadian Adverse Drug Reaction Information System (CADRIS) database (see http://www.hc-sc.gc.ca/hpfb-dgpsa/tpd-dpt/fact_cadris_e.html) as part of Health Canada's Canadian Adverse Drug Reaction Monitoring Program (CADRMP). Adverse reaction reports are submitted by health professionals and lay persons on a voluntary basis, related to outcomes from using marketed health products, such as pharmaceuticals, blood products, therapeutic and diagnostic vaccines, natural health products, and radio-pharmaceuticals. The website reports that by 2004, CADRIS contained over 160,000 suspected reports that had occurred since 1965, including relevant patient characteristics, the adverse reaction, the suspected health product(s), concomitant health products, medical history and laboratory data, treatment, and last but not least the 'patient outcome'. No trends are given anywhere that we could find, but with an average *reported* rate of about 4,000 adverse reactions a year, this is clearly a serious medical and patient risk.

We would modestly suggest that, in the absence of published data showing the risk trends and learning rates, any patient should undertake self-protection and risk reduction by adopting a truly Personal Safety Management System (PSMS©). Ask about all possible side effects, health risk factors, error rates, learning trends, and of known or possible adverse and prior outcomes, for all prescribed or administered drugs *before* taking them.

It may be that the risks inherent in the HTS of modern medical practice mean that a 5% adverse event rate, or risk of death, is about as good as we can get. Safety Management and confidential reporting systems have not yet reduced the event rates. But it would be a very illuminating exercise in medicine and safety management generally to set a goal of, say, 1%, and track to see if and how it can be achieved. And if not, why not?

## Organisational Learning and Safety Culture: the '$H$-Factor'

Having examined the data and methodologies used to establish SMS, let us now return to the definition of 'safety culture', which is where we started this Chapter.

Recall that the desiderata for the creation of a 'safety culture', coupled to an organisational structure, places unending emphasis on safety at every level. We propose and prefer the use of the term and the objective of *sustaining a 'Learning Environment'*, where mistakes, outcomes and errors are used as learning vehicles to improve, and we can now define why that is true. Therefore, we can *manage and quantify* safety, effectively tracking and analysing outcomes, using the trends to guide our needed organisational behaviours.

Recall that in the Statistical Error State Theory (SEST) in Chapter 8, we found the variation in outcomes varied exponentially with depth of experience. Also, the degree of order attained in a HTS was defined by 'information entropy', H, the summation of a function of the probabilities of error state occupation.

The $H$-factor is well known in statistical mechanics where it is called the 'uncertainty function' (see, e.g., W. Greiner et al., 1997) [42]. It has some key properties, namely: 'as a fundamental measure of the predictability of a random event, which also enables inter-comparison between different kinds of events'. This property is exactly what we would require to assess a Safety Management System's effectiveness in reducing outcomes as they emerge from the Jar of Life.

In addition, the $H$-factor has the useful and necessary properties that for equally possible outcomes, the Laplace–Bernoulli condition of a uniform prior presents the largest uncertainty, as we would expect. For a 'sure thing', the $H$-factor is independent of the probability and also satisfies the condition of additive probabilities for independent events. Its obvious application to safety management *measurement* is however totally new as presented here and arises quite naturally from the need for management to create order from disorder.

In terms of probabilities based on the frequency of microstate occupation, $n_i = p_i N_j$ and using Stirling's approximation, we have the classic result for the Information Entropy:

$$H_j = -\sum p_i \ln p_i$$

and the *maximum value occurs for a uniform distribution of outcomes*. Interestingly, this is also equivalent to the Bayes-LaPlace result, when $p(P) \sim 1/N$ for a uniform risk.

The occupancy number was given by:

$$n_i = n_0 \exp(\alpha - \beta \varepsilon_i)$$

which gives the corresponding probability of occupation:

$$p_i = p_0 \exp(\alpha - \beta \varepsilon_i)$$

We note that since we have observed the outcomes, the usual normalisation condition for all the $N_j$ outcomes to exist is, summing the probabilities over all the $j$ observation ranges,

$$\sum_j p_i = 1$$

For the probability distribution of a continuous random variable, we can transform the sum to an integral:

$$\int_0^\infty p_i \mathrm{d}p = 1$$

This normalisation says simply that whatever outcomes happened must occur. *The risk always exists, somewhere in observational space.*

In practice, the probability of occupation according to the SEST is approximated by a fit to the available outcome data given by (see Chapter 8):

$$p_i = p_0 \exp - aN^*,$$

where, $a$ is a constant, and $N^*$, the non-dimensional measure of the depth of experience, $\varepsilon/\varepsilon_M$. Thus, for our continuous probability function, we can evaluate the (so-called grand) partition function, $\Phi$, and write the probability of error state occupancy as:

$$p_i = p_0 \exp(-aN^*)\Big/ \int_0^\infty p_0 \exp(-aN^*)$$

or,

$$p_i = (a/\varepsilon_M)\exp(-aN^*),$$

and hence, the probability decreases as the learning rate and experience depth increases. Since the outcomes are represented by a continuous random variable learning curve, the information entropy in any $j$th observation interval is also given by the integral:

$$H_j = -\int p_i \ln p_i \mathrm{d}p$$
$$= p_i^2\left(\frac{1}{4} - \frac{1}{2}\ln p_i\right)$$

So, substituting in the expression for the information entropy, H, which we term the 'H-*factor*':

$$H_j = \frac{1}{2}\{p_0 e^{-aN^*}\}^2\left\{aN^* + \frac{1}{2}\right\}$$

where, on a relative basis, $p_0 = 1$, and then $H \to 0.25$ as experience decreases as $N^* \to 0$.

This parameter, $H_j$, is an objective measure of the uncertainty, and hence, of the *risk for any system*. Expanding the exponential term, we have the series:

$$H_j \approx \frac{1}{4}p_0^2(1 + aN^* - 2a^2N^{*2} + 4a^3N^{*3} - \ldots)$$

As either the learning rate or depth of experience increases ($N^* \uparrow$ or $a\uparrow$), or the zeroth order occupancy decreases ($p_0 \downarrow$), so does the value of the $H$-factor decline, meaning a more uniform distribution and increased order. We illustrate the variation in the relative information entropy, $H$, with non-dimensional experience depth, $N^*$, in Figure 7.17, taking the zeroth probability as unity ($p_0 = 1$) for a range of learning rates. The range chosen varies around the 'best' value of $a = 3.5$, which is as derived in Chapter 8 from the aircraft near miss and auto death data so that:

$$P_i = p_0 e^{-3.5N^*}$$

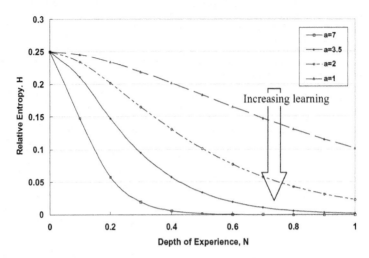

**Figure 7.17.**  Organisational learning and depth of experience: the *H*-factor


Clearly, the relative value of the information entropy *H*-factor at any experience depth is a direct measure of the aspect of modern technologies called '*organisational learning*'. This terminology is meant to describe the attributes of an HTS and its ability to respond effectively to the demands for continuous improvement, as reflected in internal organisational and communication aspects.

The faster decline and decrease in the *H*-factor with increasing depth of experience and increasing learning constant is a reflection of increasing HTS organisational order. This is to be expected, and makes sense: it is exactly what safety management intends. This relational effect is also exactly what *we* mean by maintaining a Learning Environment and has been derived from the new SEST analysis.

Before this discovery, all one could conduct were semi-empirical, qualitative and highly subjective comparative surveys of 'organisational attitudes and beliefs'. These would review opinions and attitudes to management, training and personnel systems without having a truly objective measure.

Clearly, the relative value of the information entropy, *H*, at any experience depth is also a direct measure of the cultural aspect of modern technologies called 'organisational learning' since it reflects the degree of learning and the extent of management 'order' or effectiveness. The so-called organisational learning and safety culture attributes of an HTS and its management's ability to respond effectively to the demands for continuous safety improvement. The resulting structure and probability of observed outcomes are a direct reflection of the internal organisational and skill acquisition caused by the innumerable human learning and unlearning interactions occurring within.

As eloquently suggested by Ilya Prigogine, a non-equilibrium and statistically fluctuating system can evolve towards an ordered state, where the measure of order adopted in physical systems is also entropy, and the stability condition simply represents how a molecular system responds dynamically to thermodynamic entropy changes. We postulate a direct analogy with the risk outcomes and measures for any HTS to define an Organizational Risk Stability Criterion such that $dH/dp \leq 0$ (see Appendix I). As a major bonus, this criterion naturally provides an objective measure of what has been called the 'resilience' of an entire system or organisation to mishaps, events and outcomes.

## Risk Indicator Data Analysis: A Case Study[5]

The Petroleum Safety Authority Norway (PSA) has a major programme on 'Risk Indicators', with key measures that track *relative* safety improvements in specific areas and also defines an *overall* risk level, with the objective 'to create a reliable decision making platform for industry and authorities' (PSA, 2003) [43]. The yearly trends of the quantitative data are analysed as to whether these show change (increase, decrease or not) of both the numbers and rates of indicator outcomes; and whether there is any relation to more qualitative measures based on attitudinal surveys.

A reasonable objective is to show we are learning from our past mistakes and what is the *predicted* risk for the future. The recent report [43] above states: 'On the basis of the data and indicators used in this project, no clear positive or negative trends can be observed in risk level. Most major accident indicators show an improvement in 2003 in relation to 2002. Serious injuries to personnel also show a decrease in 2003. The position is now on a level with the average for the previous 10 years. Cooperation and trust between the parties are seen as good'.

Using our experience-based statistical analysis, we can now discern the learning trends and determine the learning rates for construction, maintenance, operation and drilling activities in the North Sea oil and gas industry. This provides a basis to determine, prioritise and compare the learning rates and injury trends between different key work phases. This analysis approach also allows risk predictions, and provides guidance for workers, management and safety authorities to focus on the most meaningful trends and high-risk activities.

The procedure we use is to first determine the rates and numbers of risk outcomes, and their *distribution* with experience. The basic prior data for Norway for 1996–2005 are reported by the PSA, 2006 [44] in both graphical and tabular form. All the data are typically given and are analysed by calendar year, such as the numbers of injuries to workers, broken down by different sub-categories of severity (e.g., major or total), and work location and/or activity-type (e.g., fixed or mobile facility, drilling or maintenance).

To convert to a learning basis for analysis, we use the relevant *measure of experience as the accumulated worker-hours*, summing the year-by-year numbers reported. A typical xls. spreadsheet tabulation and analysis of the rates is shown in Table 7.4 for a subset of the observational interval. In this case, the data are for injuries in drilling at fixed facilities for Norway, and similar tables were made for all the various sets where numbers were available.

---

[5]This North Sea case study was suggested by Dr. Ann Britt Skjerve, to whom we are most grateful: a full co-authored paper on the analysis was presented to the ESREL Conference, Valencia, Spain, 2008 [45].

**Table 7.4.**  Typical data subset – Norway well-drilling injuries 1996–2005

| Well drilling (hours) | Injuries, $n$ | AccMh | $N^*$ | Entropy, $H$ | Injury Rate/Mh | Year |
|---|---|---|---|---|---|---|
| 4,670,117 | 145 | 4.670118 | 0.088633 | 0.27047 | 31.04847 | 1996 |
| 4,913,477 | 141 | 9.583595 | 0.181884 | 0.266685 | 28.69658 | 1997 |
| 4,967,799 | 133 | 14.55139 | 0.276167 | 0.258794 | 26.77242 | 1998 |
| 4,418,068 | 117 | 18.96946 | 0.360016 | 0.241637 | 26.48216 | 1999 |
| 4,696,224 | 121 | 23.66569 | 0.449144 | 0.246107 | 25.76538 | 2000 |
| 5,168,486 | 110 | 28.83417 | 0.547236 | 0.233505 | 21.28283 | 2001 |
| 5,506,589 | 103 | 34.34076 | 0.651744 | 0.224957 | 18.70486 | 2002 |
| 5,827,360 | 90 | 40.16812 | 0.762339 | 0.207881 | 15.44438 | 2003 |
| 6,248,973 | 54 | 46.4171 | 0.880937 | 0.150437 | 8.64142 | 2004 |
| 6,273,504 | 59 | 52.6906 | 1 | 0.159497 | 9.404633 | 2005 |

Table 7.4 is, in general, for the $j^{th}$ observation interval, with the sub-intervals within it. Such a tabulation is not by itself very informative, apart from illustrating the manipulations and steps in the necessary arithmetic for each experience increment:

a) adding up prior worker-hours to obtain the running total of the accumulated millions of hours of experience, $\varepsilon$(AccMh) for each $i$th sub-interval;
b) turning the injury numbers, $n_i$, into risk Rates per Mh by straightforward division;
c) calculating the non-dimensional experience $N^*$ by dividing each AccMh interval, $\varepsilon_i$, by the total accumulated experience, $\varepsilon_T(\varepsilon_T = \Sigma Mh = 53\,Mh)$; and
d) calculating the entropy ($H_i = p_i \ln p_i$) in each $i$th sub-interval from the probability, where $p_i = n_i/N_j$, where $N_j$ is the total number of injuries ($N_j = \Sigma n_i = 1,073$).

To simplify, the data are normalised to the initial probability at the initial or lowest experience, where we take $p_0 = 1$, by definition. Figure 7.18 shows the Norway North Sea injury data compared to the theory (SEST) prediction, but adopting a value of $a = 1$ for the shape or slope parameter in the entropy distribution.

Rather satisfyingly, the theory and data easily appear side-by-side on the same graph, lending major credence to this analysis. The other data shown for comparison purposes are the commercial aircraft near misses (NMACs), because of the significant and traditional airline emphasis on safety. The NMAC line up rather better with the theoretical prediction, but there are clearly some key differences between the oil and gas dataset trends. Despite the scatter, we note for this data subset that the:

a) entropy distribution with experience lies above the theory line;
b) slope trend is less than the theory, indicating insufficient attainment of order;
c) data lie above the best aircraft practices (aircraft near misses); and
d) best (but still far from perfect) fit to all the injury data is a straight line, not an exponential as we should expect.

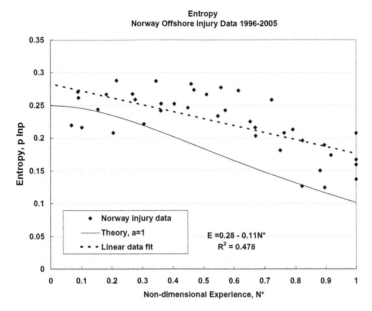

**Figure 7.18.**   Comparison of theory to North Sea risk data

The approximate straight-line 'fit' shown is $H = 0.28 - 1.11N^*$, which actually corresponds to the first two terms of the series expansion of the rather slowly decaying exponential. Therefore, the implied first-order approximate value is $a \approx 1.11$ for the distribution exponent.

All these trends and comparisons suggest not only 'cultural', but also actually *real* symptoms of potentially insufficient learning, giving inadequate reduction in risk compared both to the expected ideal, and with other industries. This adverse trend was confirmed by plotting the rates against the Universal Learning Curve, and finding a similar value of $k \sim 1$ for the learning rate constant.

We can now argue that this apparently purely theoretical concept of degree of order, the H-*factor*, is actually a true quantitative measure of the elusive quality termed 'safety culture' by sociologists, human-factor experts and industrial psychologists. Safety culture is therefore a reflection of the degree of order attained in and by any HTS; and creating order is equivalent to reducing the probability of outcomes.

## Meeting the Need to *Measure* Safety Culture: The Hard and the Soft Elements

The essential qualities of what constitutes a desirable safety culture have been summarised by the Federal Aviation Administration (FAA) (Loague, J.W. 2007) [46]. The concern and context was over 'runway incursions' due to an aircraft or vehicle on the ground causing a near or actual collision with another one at airports. The NMAC trends analysed above are for near-collision events while in flight, whereas collisions and near misses are also possible and do also occur while aircraft are on the ground. The major past outcome was the infamous collision in fog in Tenerife in 1977 of two large commercial jumbo jets, one on takeoff colliding with one on the ground, killing 582 and traumatising the world. The lessons learned are startlingly simple, according to one of the pilots (Bragg, R.L., 2007) [47]:

- Anyone – no matter how qualified – can make serious mistakes.
- Communication must be effective and readily understood.
- When in doubt, don't.
- Check, double-check, and re-check.
- Constant emphasis on . . . resource management.

Even before Tenerife, and the FAA re-focusing in the 2000s, runway incursions were 'known knowns'. The FAA concern at their Forum in 2007 was the lack of decline in the rate and numbers of incursion occurrences, even after extensive publicity, procedures, training and awareness efforts over several years, and stated public a commitment to reduce their occurrence. Needless to say, the latest FAA data did not show a reduction in numbers, rate or severity of incursions as shown in Figure 7.19.

Here, the plot is the rate of incursions per millions of movements managed by control towers at USA airports, taking as the accumulated number of movements as the learning opportunity or experience since new awareness and procedural measures were adopted. The reported incursion rate is about 5 per million operations, MFO, and the serious incursions rate (so-called Types A and B) when actual collisions were imminent or avoidance actions needed is about 10% of the total (~0.5/MFO). Although a learning curve is implied, it is not separable in the data, but we can estimate if learning is happening, and whether an improvement might be expected from the new measures or what may be necessary to manage the rate.

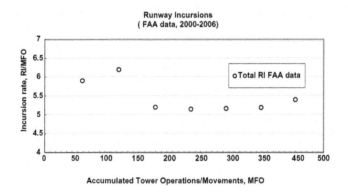

**Figure 7.19.**  Runway incursion data (With kind permission of US FAA, 2007)

We can analyse the available data to compare with other outcomes and errors worldwide, with just one assumption of the average time involved in a movement. Since we do not have the actual time-on-runway data, we assume about a 10-minute interval is the average for elapsed runway residence times for any given 'movement', (covering one of the author's experience at major US airports). We can then readily convert the incursion rate to an outcome interval and could of course adjust the result for any other value if and when available:

$$5 \text{ incursions per MFO} \sim 5 \text{ per 10 million minutes}$$
$$= 5 \text{ per } 170,000 \text{ runway hours} = \text{one incursion per } 34,000 \text{ hours.}$$

This outcome interval is typical for similar operational errors in homo-technological systems, like train derailments or passing signals at danger (SPADS), and almost exactly the same order as that derived by us for *almost any non-fatal industrial injury* in the USA (Duffey and Saull, 2002) [48]. Where humans are involved with a complex system we obtain the same intervals. The largest interval, for serious Type *A* and *B* incursions, is then 10 times larger, or one per 340,000 runway hours, and already corresponds to the *lower limit* order of magnitude for the minimum error rate attainable in any and all homo-technological systems.

So, the FAA runway incursion data imply not only that ineffective SMS measures were being taken, but the analysis also highlights the need for a radical re-look at the risk management strategies and priorities. Without a major shift in technology to reduce their possibility and probability, then incursions will undoubtedly continue.

The safety culture factors listed by the FAA included were listed as follows, in the order given:

1. Personal dedication and accountability √
2. Individual attitudes and behaviours √
3. Shared vision with structures to attain it √
4. Organisational processes, methods and metrics √√
5. Commitment to improve (resist complacency) √√
6. Beyond simple adherence to procedures √√
7. Learning and continuous improvement √√
8. Pervasive safety thinking √√
9. Commitment to excellence √√
10. Integration of safety into all activities √√
11. Climate in which news is quickly and easily communicated √
12. Committed to investing the time and resources √√

The elements addressed directly by adopting a quantitative and measurable '*H*' factor measure are those marked with a double tick mark (√√). These are the *essential 'hard' safety management commitments: to measure, to learn, and to improve*. Effectively communicated, funded and implemented throughout the organisation or homo-technological system, the *H*-factor then *addresses indirectly all those other 'soft' attributes*, marked by a single mark (√), which are the more personal skills and the contextual commitments. We would re-order, re-prioritise and re-emphasise establishing the hard elements with a double mark as the first priorities, and the soft as the essential attributes that follow both with, and from the effective implementation of the hard ones.

## Creating Order from Disorder

As we stated in the very beginning of this Chapter, it is management's expressed aim and intent in any HTS to create order from disorder, which it can *only* achieve by decreasing the information entropy. Unfortunately, most safety managers who are trained in traditional industrial safety methods, and corporate officers familiar to the world of business and accounting decisions and risks, would not recognise the concept of entropy, let alone information entropy, if they saw it. However, it is so simple to communicate the *concept of the learning hypothesis* and the impact on organisational learning, that it should be possible to obtain the management buy-in needed to adopt this approach to assess risk and safety.

Equally important to this quantification is the realisation that this *H*-factor uses the actual *outcomes* as an explicit function of organisational learning, system 'resilience' and management effectiveness. We manage what we can measure. This is simply common sense.

## References

[1] Moan, T., 2004, 'Safety of Offshore Structures', Second Keppel Offshore and Marine Lecture, National University of Singapore, CORE Report No. 2005-04.
[2] Makin, A-M. and Winder, C., 2007, 'Emergent trends in safety management systems: an analysis of established international systems', Proc. ESREL 2007, Stavanger, Norway, June 2007, Vol.2, p. 1237, Taylor and Francis, London, ISBN 978-0-415-44786-7.
[3] Trbojekic, V.M., 2006, 'Another look at risk and structural reliability criteria', Proc. ESREL 2006, 'Safety and Reliability for Managing Risk', Estoril Portugal, Taylor and Francis, London, pp. 1547–1551.
[4] Wang, J. and Trbojekic, V.M., 2007 'Design and Safety of Marine and Offshore Systems', MarEST, London, Chapter 5, pp.140–143.
[5] Farmer, F.R., 1967, 'Siting Criteria- A New Approach', IAEA Conference on Containment and Siting, Vienna, Austria, Paper SM-89/34.
[6] Howlett II, H.C., 1995, 'The Industrial Operator's Handbook', Techstar/Gary Jensen, Pocatello, ID, p. 74.
[7] CAA (UK Civil Aviation Authority), 2001, 'Safety Management Systems for Commercial Air Transport Operation: A Guide to Implementation', Report # CAP 712, Air Transport Operations Safety Management Group, London.
[8] Transport Canada, 2002, 'Safety Management Systems For Flight Operations And Aircraft Maintenance Organizations Safety Management Systems: A Guide to Implementation', Commercial and Business Aviation Branch and the Aircraft Maintenance and Manufacturing Branch, Ottawa, Canada.
[9] Australian Civil Aviation Safety Authority (CASA), 1998, 'Aviation Safety Management: An Operator's Guide to Building a Safety Program'.

[10] Baumont, G. et al, 2002, 'Organizational Factors: Their definition and influence on Nuclear Safety', Final Report, VTT Tiedotteita – Meddelanden – Research Notes, 1235-0605 (soft back edition) 1455-0865 (Available: http//www.inf.vtt.fi/pdf/).

[11] Papazoglou, L.A. and Aneziris, O., 1999, 'On the Quantification of the Effects of Organizational and Management Factors in Chemical', in Reliability Engineering and System Safety (15): 545–554.

[12] Jones, B., 2002, 'Theoretical Approaches to Organizational Learning', Learning Organizations for Nuclear Safety, EU contract n° fiks-ct-2001-00162.

[13] Reason, J., 1997, 'Managing the Risks of Organizational Accidents', Ashgate Publishng Limited, Aldershot, Hampshire, UK.

[14] BP, 2005, 'Fatal Accident Investigation Report: Isomerization Unit Explosion', Final Report, Texas City, TX, 9 December (known as The 'Mogford Report') plus 26 Appendices (Available: www.bp.com).

[15] BP, 2007, 'The Report of the BP U.S. Refineries Independent Safety Review Panel', (the 'Baker Panel') January 2007 (Available: www.bp.com).

[16] U.S. Chemical Safety and Hazard Investigation Board (CSB), 2007, 'Refinery Explosion and Fire, BP, Texas City, March 23, 2005', Investigation Report No. 2005-04-I-TX.

[17] Haber, S.B. et al., 2005, 'Independent Assessment of the Davis Besse Organizational Safety Culture, Including Safety Conscious Work Environment', Assessment Number 2004-0104, NRC Docket number 50-346, License number NPF-3, First Energy Operating Company, Ohio, USA.

[18] Australian Transportation Safety Bureau (ATSB), 2005, 'Power Loss Related Accidents Involving Twin-Engine Aircraft', Research Report, B2005/0085, June.

[19] Republique de France, 2004, Ministere de l'Ecologie et du Developpement Durable, 'AZF, Trois Ans Apres l'Explosion', September, (Available: www.ecologie.gouv.fr).

[20] Republique de France, 2002, Assemblée Nationale Constitution du 4 octobre 1958, Onzième Legislature, Enregistré à la Présidence de l'Assemblée Nationale le 29 Janvier 2002, N° 3559, Rapport fait Au Nom de la Commission d'Enquête sur la Sûreté des Installations Industrielles et des Centres de Recherche et sur la Protection des Personnes et de l'Environnement en Cas d'Accident Industriel Majeur (1), Président M. François Loos, Rapporteur M. Jean-Yves Le Deault, Députes, Tome I, 182 pp.

[21] Kohda, T. et al, 2000, 'Root Cause Analysis of JCO Accident Based on Decision-Making Model', Proceedings (PSAM 5) International Conference on Probabilistic Safety Assessment and Management, Osaka, Japan, 27 November.

[22] US Chemical Safety and Hazard Investigation Board (CSB), 'Investigation Report: Explosives Manufacturing Incident, Sierra Chemical Company, Mustang, Nevada, 7 January, 1998', Report 98-001-I-NV.

[23] Filippin, K. and Dreher, L., 2004, 'Major hazard risk assessment for existing and new facilities', A.I.Ch.E., Process Safety Progress, 23, No. 4, pp. 237–243.

[24] Barthelemy, 2001, Report of the General Inspectorate for the Environment, Affair No. IGE/01/034. 'Accident on the 21st of September 2001 at a factory belonging to the Grande Paroisse Company in Toulouse, produced jointly with the Explosives Inspectorate and with help from the INERIS', 24 October, Inspection Générale de l'Environnement, Paris, France.

[25] Heather, D., 2002, 'A review of past ammonium nitrate accidents & lessons learned', Presented at Workshop on Ammonium Nitrate Safety, JRC Ispra, Italy, January.

[26] International Fertilizer Association (IFA), 2007, www.fertilizer.org/ifa/statistics.

[27] Buncefield Major Incident Investigation Board, 2005, 'Initial Report to the Health and Safety Commission and the Environment Agency of the investigation into the explosions and fires at the Buncefield oil storage and transfer depot, Hemel Hempstead, on 11 December', Health and Safety Executive (HSE), London, UK.

[28] Jones, C., 2003, 'Nuclear Safety Culture: the Nimitz Precomm Model', Proceedings 2003 American Nuclear Society Annual Meeting, San Diego, CA.

[29] Amalberti, R., 2001, 'The paradoxes of almost totally safe transportation systems', Safety Science 37, 109–126.

[30] Allison, P.D., 1984, 'Event History Analysis', USA: Sage Publications, p. 32.

[31] Kansler, M., 2001, Presentation at Ninth International Conference on Nuclear Engineering (ICONE 9), Nice, France, 8–12 April.

[32] Hessel, P., 2001, 'Modelling CCFs in CANDU PSA', Proceedings IAEA/AECL PSA Workshop on Probabilistic Safety Assessments for Pressurized Heavy Water Reactors, Mississauga, Toronto, Canada, 1–4 October.

[33] Senn, S., 2003, 'Dicing with Death: Chance, Risk and Health', Cambridge University Press, UK, ISBN 0 521 54023 2, Chapter 11.

[34] US Institute of Medicine (IOM), 2000, 'To Err is Human: Building a Safer Health System', Editors, L.T. Kohn, J.M. Corrigan and M.S. Donaldson, Committee on Quality of Health Care in America, US National Academy's Institute of Medicine, National Academy Press, Washington, DC (also http://www.Aetnaushc.com 'Aetna US Health Care Announces New Initiatives to Help Reduce Medical Errors'; and British Medical Journal, March 18, 320(7237)).

[35] UK Department of Health (DoH), 'An Organisation with a Memory', 2000, Report of National Health Service Expert Group on Learning from Adverse Events, London.

[36] Baker, G.R., Norton, P.G., Flintoft, V., Blais, R., Brown, A., Cox, J., Etchells, E., Ghali, W.A., Hébert, P., Majumdar, S.R., O'Beirne, M., Palacios-Derflingher, L., Reid, R.J., Sheps, S., and Tamblyn-Baker, R., 'The Canadian Adverse Events Study: The Incidence of Adverse Events among Hospital Patients in Canada', Canadian Medical Assoc. J. (CMAJ), 2004, 170(11), pp. 1678–1686.

[37] Michel, P., Quenon, J.L., Djihoud, A., Sarasqueta, A.M., Domecq, S. et al, 2005, 'Les evenenments indesirables graves lies aux soins observes dans les establissement de sante', Etudes et Resultats, DREES, No 398, May.

[38] Davis, P., Lay-Yee, R., Briant, R., Schug, S., Scott, A., Johnson, S., Bingley, W., 2001, 'Adverse Events in New Zealand Public Hospitals: Principal Findings from a National Survey', New Zealand Ministry Of Health, Occasional paper No 3, December (Available: http://www.moh.govt.nz/moh.nsf/).

[39] Sujan, M.A., Henderson, J., and Embrey, D., 2004, 'Mismatching between Planned and Actual Treatments in Medicine-Manual Checking Approaches to Prevention', Human Reliability Associates Report for National Patient Safety Agency (NPSA), UK, pp. 16–18 (also NPSA at http://81.144.177.110/).

[40] Cohen, M.R., 1999, 'Medication Errors', American Pharmaceutical Association, Washington, DC.

[41] Newhouse, R. and S. Poe, (Editors), 2005, 'Measuring Patient Safety', Jones and Nartlett, Sudbury, MA, 2005.

[42] Greiner, W., Neise, L., and Stocker, H., 1997, 'Thermodynamics and Statistical Mechanics', Springer, New York, pp. 150–151.

[43] Petroleum Safety Authority Norway (PSA), 2003, 'Trends in risk levels- Norwegian Continental Shelf, Summary Report, Phase 4 – 2003', Ptil-04-04, p. 11, Petroleum Safety Authority, Norway.

[44] Petroleum Safety Authority Norway (PSA), Annual Report 2006, 'Supervision and Facts', Stavanger, 26 April 2007, Petroleum Safety Authority, Norway, (Available: www.ptil.no).

[45] Duffey, R.B. and Skjerve, A.B. , 2008, 'Risk Trends, Indicators and Learning Rates: A New Case Study of North Sea Oil and Gas', Proc. ESREL 2008 and 17th SRA – Europe Annual Conference, Valencia, Spain, 22–25 September.

[46] Jeffrey W. Loague, 2007, 'Reducing the Risk', FAA, Office of Runway Safety, Safety Services, Air Traffic Organization, presented at NTSB, Runway Incursion Forum, Washington, DC, March.

[47] Bragg, R.L., 2007, 'Revisiting the Past', Presentation at National Transport Safety Board (NTSB), Runway Incursion Forum, Washington, DC, March.

[48] Duffey, R.B. and Saull, J.W., 2002, 'Know the Risk', First Edition, Butterworth and Heinemann, Boston, MA.

# 8

# Risk Perception: Searching for the Truth Among All the Numbers[1]

*'All our knowledge has its origins in our perceptions.'*

*Leonardo da Vinci, 1452–1518*

## Perceptions and Predicting the Future: Risk Acceptance and Risk Avoidance

Based on the progress and success with our learning and statistical models, we now examine risk perception. Our modest but also ambitious aim is how, if at all, we may be able to *quantify and predict* this highly debated, psychologically contentious, socially sensitive and traditionally subjective human aspect.

Many decisions on risk taking, and other things in life, are coloured by our perception. Our perception of risk is dominated by unknown factors that determine what risk we consider acceptable and what is to be avoided. Perception, some say, is reality. That view is coloured by our own experience, by our expectations, by our own needs, and by the media and the information we are exposed to. After all, the media are in the business of reporting newsworthy events, *not* risk comparisons. Whether and how we expose ourselves personally to risk, and how much, is a matter of *choice*. As Bernoulli understood, it may depend on the 'utility' or the perceived benefit of the risk to the individual. Our perception of risk is a highly intuitive recognition or action in which the mind senses and decides, coloured or affected by many subjective factors. These include the degree to which the risk is known or unknown,

[1] The notion of measuring and replacing arbitrary risk perception was expounded in R.B. Duffey, 'The Prediction of Risk: Replacing Paranoia with Probability', Proc. 29th ESReDA Seminar on Systems Analysis for a More Secure World, Ispra, Italy, 25–26 October 2005; and of experience depth was described in R.B. Duffey and J.W. Saull, 'The Probability of System and Organizational Failure: Human Error and the Influence of Depth of Experience', Proc. International Topical Meeting on Probabilistic Safety Analysis (PSA'05), San Francisco, CA, 11–15 September 2005.

voluntary or involuntary, acceptable or avoidable, threatening or attractive, controlled or uncontrolled.

This is not a risk versus benefit decision, although safety experts, accountants, lawyers and investors use that approach. Some decision analysts even define the 'value' of a human life to trade against the potential loss, or try to quantify or judge the 'downside' versus the 'upside' risk. To determine our risk, the least we can or should do is *know* where we have come from in the past, *measure* how well we are doing in the present, and *predict* what might happen next or in the future. Short-term considerations and pressures like a high fiscal rate of return, stock price trends, selling short or transient leveraging opportunities all combine to make long-term analysis more difficult. Our instantaneous risk decisions are affected both by our past experience and by our present knowledge.

Where the subjective mind rules over the objective data, can we quantify risk perception? What factors determine it? Can we determine a measure of the difference between the perceived versus the real risk? Can we determine the balance between the objective versus the subjective risks?

In the sciences of Psychology and Biology, the physiological and mental processes of learning have been much studied. The research has particularly focused on the neural pattern and pathway changes that might occur as we attain skill. Humans, or indeed any animal, respond using the neural net and central nervous system to filter inputs, sensing the pleasant versus the unpleasant options, and utilising reinforcement in the establishment of a learned behaviour. But as noted by Robert Josephson, 1968 [1] long ago, and still true today:

> *But at any level, the goal of completely explaining the behaviour of an animal is in most cases unrealistic. The complexity of the behavior of most animals precludes the possibility of complete analysis. ...*

We need to address how the behaviour of the individual humans within the system affects the outcomes that we actually observe from the system, whatever it may be, and the risks that we perceive. Our emergent learning theory is applied at the 'systems level', that of the homo-technological system (HTS), where the integrated behaviour of the human and the machine is observed as outcomes. We deliberately avoid describing any details of the complexity of the human learning responses, of the neural and central nervous system function and its interaction with a technological machine. In a sense, this model approach is consistent with the 'systems theory'. Using this approach, we already have shown two key results for any HTS based on the Learning Hypothesis:

*Firstly*, we should know where we are on the Universal Learning Curve (ULC). We can find out by collecting and plotting the data for the rate and distribution (number) of outcomes against chosen experience coordinates, along with any goals. Just quoting event and outcome numbers will not do: we must generate a baseline trend so we have some 'feel' or a measure of where we are.

*Secondly*, we must assume that the future probability, rate and number is the prior trend based solely on the past experience if we make no changes to our HTS. Without any other knowledge, we must assume that our future learning rate and distribution will depend on, or be exactly like our past rate. The MERE past or prior probability we have shown formally predicts the future outcome probability and number. Future rate and number reductions will

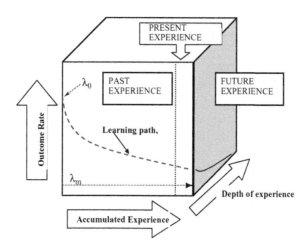

**Figure 8.1.**  The Past, the Present and the Future

depend on our sustaining a true learning environment. Only then we can 'sense' and test if we are making any difference when and if we change anything in the HTS.

We can see this clearly using the concept in Experience Space. In Figure 8.1, we again show the cube of experience, but add the simple words of Past, Present and Future. All that has happened in the Past, including how we have learned (the $k$-value), the past outcome rate ($IR$) and number ($n$) of outcomes in our experience, $\varepsilon$, determine where we are on the ULC. We should know where we are, or be able to reconstruct it, unless we have a completely new system or absolutely no past data on outcomes, or no idea of our previous experience. Somewhere in the future are the unknowns, those outcomes that we can only guess about, or form a judgement as to whether, where and when it may happen, harm or help us.

The Future is of course strictly unknown, in the sense we do not have the experience yet. But if we know, or can extrapolate what we might have planned or intended, then we can use the Past learning curve (MERE) form to make a projection. Using Bayesian–Jaynes reasoning, the Past (the prior data) determines the conditional Future (the posterior) unless we have a possibility (a likelihood) of a significant change to our HTS and/or invoke exclusion rules that eliminate error states systematically. Now we know that, in words, the future is a mix of the Past and of the likely expectation in a conditional Future:

[Posterior probability] is proportional to [Prior probability] times [Likelihood]

or, symbolically, and clearly,

$$\text{Future, } p(\mathrm{P}) \propto \text{Past, } p(\varepsilon) \times \text{Likelihood, } p(\mathrm{L})$$

So somehow, sometimes, our past experience can be overwhelmed by a bias on the likelihood. Why do we physically or mentally 'close our eyes', and consciously or subconsciously sometimes apparently ignore or accept the future risk, despite the past learning? What influences the choices involved?

**Table 8.1.**   Likelihood Ratings

| Likelihood rating | Description |
|---|---|
| Almost Certain | Will undoubtedly recur, possibly frequently |
| Likely | Will probably, but it is not a persistent issue |
| Possible | May recur occasionally |
| Unlikely | Do not expect it to happen again but it is possible |
| Rare | Can't be believe that this will ever happen again |

(With kind permission of UK NPSA, reproduced by permission)

The UK National Patient Safety Agency (NPSA) has even published and defined 'likelihood ratings' for assessing the chance of recurrence of an incident, which is used for medical risk assessment purposes (see Table 8.1 available at http://www.npsa.nhs. uk/).

Note that this rating or risk ranking uses words like 'may', 'possibly', 'will probably', 'do not expect' and 'can't believe'. These terms and usage are vague and require purely subjective judgements, being very speculative and highly qualitative: there is no real formal probability or mathematical analysis. They represent risk perceptions for repeat events, but are now given from the perspective of the professional medical provider. They represent, to some degree, what are often called 'belief statements'.

We also expect to observe outcomes that determine our risk no more than one at a time, with observing multiple events being unlikely. However, that is exactly what the media report, using outcomes from all over the world, and that also impacts our perception.

We do not usually think of links between errors and risk perception.

Risk perception is a purely human trait, which can span between imaginary and real, subconscious or conscious, but something which is not generally speaking natural. Hence, the likelihood of human error is always present, as a result of inadequate or possibly complete lack of consideration for a given possible event or combination of contributing events. In HTSs, professional in-depth operational risk analysis is carried out to defined criteria to determine correct actions to aid decision making. However, it requires perception and understanding of the factors involved and situational awareness. At the most critical level, as evidenced by serious incident and accident investigation reports, the real challenge is due to the complexity of the combination of circumstances and the sequence of human errors. This is the challenge that is faced here – if only we could better predict the likely combination of human errors and their effect(s) on events, we could see how better to prevent them happening.

With regard to the link between risk perception and training, the combination of knowledge and experience, which equates to understanding, are the two major factors involved. Perception by an individual that a task(s) can be continuously carried out to a satisfactory level is a result of training, formal or informal, and level of experience. However, there may be certain situations that have not been envisaged, which demand on-the-spot decisions: even more so, experience is a most valuable factor, including the understanding of situational awareness.

## Fear of the Unknown: The Success Journey into What We Do or Do Not Accept

So we must try to relate our perception of risk with our knowledge, experience and training. We can simplify risk perception by categorising it a rational or irrational fear of the 'unknown'. The risk or trepidation is about the black ball that is still inside the Jar of Life that we do not know will happen or not and when. We may or may not have seen other similar or identical outcomes already; we may have been trained to expect or deal with them or we may not; we may have some experience that lets us know that such black balls are 'bad' or 'evil', 'dangerous' or 'risky'. We apparently do not perform any probability calculation in some rational way, but form a judgement based both on what we know and what we do not know, and decide what risk to accept or not.

By using the Human Bathtub, we can perceive this as a 'success' journey, so that our risk perception becomes easier and clearer to describe and hopefully to understand. We have noted before that in probability terms:

$$P(\text{Success}) = 1 - P(\text{Failure}).$$

So for convenience, we cut the curve into three broad categories or trends to try to explain what is the nature or type of risk that we perceive as we learn, and why.

*Risky*: When we start out as a Novice, we are at the highest risk (the beginning of the curve is labelled 'Risky' in the Figure 8.2). We must observe both outcomes and non-outcomes, and we must learn quickly from the initially unknown mistakes and errors, whatever they are, as and if they occur. We fear these unknown outcomes, we are not accepting of them,

**Figure 8.2.**    A perceived risk perception curve

and we shun them and try to avoid them happening. These unknowns are like the terrorist attacks or the accidents that have not happened yet, since even if we have observed only a few, we are not sufficiently experienced or familiar with them.

*Improving*: If we survive our early mistakes and the unknown outcomes, and learn from them, we are hopefully 'Improving', as the curve is labelled. The chance of success, or not failing, or not having an unknown outcome becomes less, both from our successful experience and what we already know about the unknown outcomes. This experience implicitly gives us some knowledge or training, and hence, hopefully some greater comfort level or familiarity about the risk, even if it is not negligible. We will continue to sail in ships, work in large factories and go to the doctor or hospital, having done so before, but we hope that things will get better somehow.

*Inevitable*: Ultimately, we descend the success curve again, as we become Experts who are even more knowledgeable, comfortable and accepting of the known and perhaps more likely risks. We have had a lot of experience of outcomes by then, and we now regard outcomes as acceptable since they are in fact 'Inevitable' as the final part of the curve is labelled. Even if outcomes happen, or have occurred, we have so much experience that we are not necessarily surprised by them or afraid of the risk anymore. Because the outcome probability is now rising at the end, perversely and paradoxically it seems we are actually at greater risk but have much less concern. These inevitable outcomes are also the everyday risks that we accept, like crossing the street, driving a car, living near a nuclear plant, or flying in an airplane.

Note that the real risk may be different from the perception, and will vary from person to person, culture-to-culture and society-to-society. In a sense, figuratively speaking, we all travel this success path, both individually and collectively, as victims, students, novices and experts; all knowledgeable to differing degrees about different risks depending on our experience and the path we each have followed. So both qualitatively and quantitatively, this perceived Risk Perception curve gives us a consistent and useful sketch, or some mental or perhaps even physical 'model' behind our learning experience and our feelings about risk. We do not have to pretend or claim that this model curve or description is perfect. Even if idealised and simplified, we can carry this curve with us as a guide, keeping it in our mind's eye as we journey forward even further into the murky world of *quantifying* risk perception.

## A Possible Explanation of Risk Perception: Comparisons of Road and Rail Transport

We have already seen in our prior work the influence of perception. The recent case of train derailments in the UK showed how the fear caused many commuters and travellers to use automobiles as an alternate mode of transport even though it has a higher risk. The perception was that trains were dangerous, more so than being in a car. Why?

The data may show a possible reason, so let us look at it in more detail. In Figure 8.3, we plot the derailment number, $D$, for the given accumulated experience in billions of passenger rail – kilometres travelled as reported by the UK DETR for 1988 to 1999[2].

---

[2] The rich history of derailments in the UK goes back far into the 19th century (see the amazing website, reports and data available at www.railwaysarchive.co.uk).

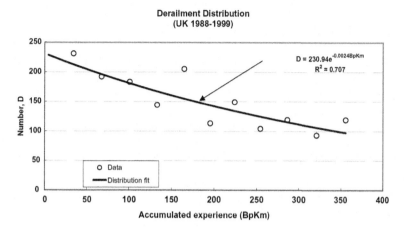

**Figure 8.3.**   Distribution of train derailments in the UK

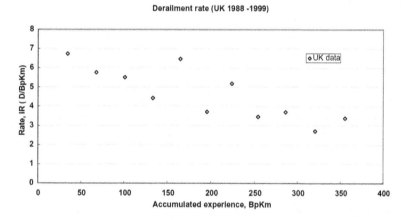

**Figure 8.4.**   Rate of derailments in the UK

The distribution seems to follow an exponential, as we might expect, for learning. The rate of derailments, IR, is shown in Figure 8.4.

The fluctuation in the rate is now clearer than just in the number and the minimum rate is ~3 per BpKm. For an average train speed of about 50 km/h, this is an interval of about $10^9/(3 \times 50)$ ~ 6 million passenger-hours.

This is very large interval: the derailment risk on railways in the UK is entirely negligible compared to the chance of being in an auto accident and to other industrial injuries. The interval for auto accidents is about one collision (dings included) every 6,000 auto-hours. For fatalities, the risk interval is about ~200 times more, because of all the extensive mitigating measures included in autos to protect the occupants (bumpers, seat belts, air bags, crushable material, compartment design, frame protection, etc.). This becomes an interval of about every 1,200,000 hours for an auto accident fatality based on the individual exposure. Turning this auto interval into a distance travelled in 1,200,000 hours at an assumed 50 km/h average speed, the risk is ~17 deaths per Bkm of road travel. With a reported overall fatality rate on UK railways of ~0.5 per BpKm travelled, the risk of derailment (~3/BpKm) is about six times more than the risk of death for rail passengers (~0.5/BpKm) for the same distance travelled, and about one-sixth of the risk of death on the road (~17/BpKm).

Comparatively, we have ~0.5 passenger deaths/BpKm on the railway and ~17 deaths/km in autos. So the road is *~35 times more risk* than rail based on individual death risk per unit interval of travel distance (experience) accumulated; and also road is ~6 times more risk than the chance of derailments at 3/BpKm. But the public (you and I) completely ignore this huge difference, and take so much fright at the reported outcomes of derailments on the railways to switch to driving on the roads. We do not think at all of risk in terms of the rate of outcomes for the passenger kilometres travelled by everyone else, or even of the risk as being of the 'probability times the consequences', let alone as any 'cost versus benefit'. We still drive, even when we could take a train.

If we think we have to take a risk, we do. We think of our risk *only* in terms of our personal experience, what we know and have learned, and not about the experience of everyone else.

But we have about three (3) derailments every BpKm, or about 100 per year, compared to many more auto collisions. We must expect a few derailments unless we make trains that physically cannot derail! So derailments are relatively common, just like auto accidents. But the more spectacular derailments, which can injure many people, are reported in the media, just like multiple auto crashes. Comparatively much safer for any individual traveller, trains suffer from having too many derailments with little prospect of a large reduction. Unless of course, Brunel's technology shift in the 19th century of the wide gauge is re-adopted to reduce derailment risk. But we have already largely rejected that solution in the interest of fiscal economy. So say the data.

Similarly, after the terrorist attacks of 11 September in the USA, airline travel plummeted. This was despite the fact that based on prior data, the risk of a hijack was only ~1 in a million flights, or only about one every ~3 MFh of flying experience, which is a totally negligible risk. With about 100 passengers per plane travelling at ~500 km/h, this is a risk of circa one hijack every ~3,000,000 × 100 × 500 ~ 1 in a 150 BpKm travelled, more than a hundred times less than the rail and auto death risks. But fear and irrational risk avoidance dominated. The perception we had observed on the media was that somehow deadly hijacks would be more common, and avoidance dominated all of the thinking. Airports and airlines were quiet for almost a year, although the events were quite rare. In addition, governments now dutifully and routinely warn their citizens about all the possible terrorist threats and dangers when travelling and vacationing in apparently exotic locations. At www.state.gov, www.fco.gov. uk, and www.smarttraveller.gov.au lists of risks also include kidnappings, rebel activity and drug running, even when the actual individual risk of bodily harm is usually less than one in a million visits (see, for example, Conde Nast Traveler, October, 2006, pp. 84–96). Despite these perceived worldly threats and increased levels of diplomatic concern, the most dangerous part of any trip still remains voluntarily driving to and from the airport!

In Moore's book [2], the well-known comparison of risk rankings is reproduced for actual risk of selected activities (like swimming, smoking, or being in the police) in terms of annual deaths. This 'real risk' ranking is compared to the subjective ranking by the League of Woman Voters, College Students and Business people. Needless to say, they do not agree with the ranking of real risks, or often with each other! Low risks (like death from nuclear power) are ranked high, but truly high risks (like death from electric power) are ranked low.

## How Do We Judge the Risk?

So obviously, humans are absolutely hopeless at making considered, rational comparative risk judgements at these levels of everyday, common occurrence, and of comparing to outcomes with little probability of happening. Or are they? Perhaps we are just accounting for past happenings, trends, fears and misinformation in our judgements. Perhaps we simply reinforce our biases and preconceptions with selected information.

This lack of objectivity in risk choices implies a postulated risk–reward strategy:

a) We judge and perceive risk by the latest number of outcomes, not by the rate, by what we have seen and experienced ourselves that increase or reduce the apparent number, not using any comparative, relative or numerical risk. This then corresponds to the quantity or the *amount* of 'pain' or 'gain' we experience or perceive.

b) We learn based on the rate of outcomes, not by the number of them, but by what we have seen and experienced ourselves that reduce the rate. Hopefully, if we have a goal (a 'target risk'), we sense how close we might be to our goal. This then corresponds to reducing the rate or the *feeling* at which 'pain' or 'gain' is experienced or perceived.

Whether physiologically and psychologically this is true might be shown by experiment. The usual approach with tests is the rate of learning when subjected to, say, risk aversion reinforcement like electric stimuli of varying number and rate. Since we expect to observe outcomes one at a time based on our prior experience, with multiple events less unlike, observing or 'experiencing' increasing numbers might cause risk aversion.

What about the ULC? What does that tell us? We show this in Figure 8.5, where the IR data for the UK derailments are compared to the ULC curve of $E^* = \exp - 3N^*$. The

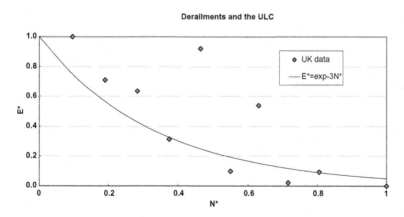

**Figure 8.5.**  Comparison to the ULC rate of outcomes

normalisation for $E^*$ is to the observed initial (highest) and final (lowest) rates. The data show scatter around the line: learning is present but apparently inconsistently and at a slower rate than the average world data fit.

We may even construct a hypothetical model of how mental processes might function to arrive at judgements and perceptions, using the insights from the latest theories of how humans make conscious and unconscious decisions (e.g., Tor Norretrander, 'The User Illusion') [3]. The basic idea is that the shear complexity of all the information and stimuli that have to be processed are simplified and made manageable for decision making by unconsciously eliminating the unnecessary information. By analogy, the information about the many possible unseen combinations of potential error states occupation is ignored, by being processed unconsciously into just the meaningful information of the number of outcomes ordered according to the depth of experience. We eliminate unconsciously most distributions of the mistakes, represented here by the information entropy. The rate of outcomes directly affects the observed outcomes as a direct result of this *unobserved* ordering due to error correction and complexity reduction. Thus, learning occurs by feedback and appears as the emergent outcomes systematically varying with experience. This conceptual model is simply the Learning Hypothesis stated in psychological terms and corresponds to classic 'pattern recognition', but now in a statistical sense.

## Linking Complexity, Order, Information Entropy and Human Actions

We know that humans, within an HTS distill knowledge, make decisions and take actions based on what is known, observed or perceived on the basis of the individual and collective experience, and that error correction and learning occurs. Hence, the outcomes at the collective HTS level reflect in some unknown but integrated manner the actions, outcomes and decisions taken at the individual level.

Let us postulate and develop a working model where we use the entropy analogy as a measure of the uncertainty in predicting risk behaviour. We know from Information Theory that we receive the transmitted knowledge as bits or patterns. The measure of choice of the uncertainty as to how the information in this noisy signal is received or perceived is the Information Entropy, and is also related in psychology to the field of language recognition and use (Pierce, 1980) [4]. The outcome information (the signal) is sifted unconsciously from among the many possible observations (the outcome noise) in the given experience interval (the past and the present), to somehow make conscious rational or irrational choices and decisions based on learning, rule revision and correcting errors. The past or prior outcomes constitute a part of the entire learnt knowledge base from which we might make such decisions and choices. So we observe outcomes (risks) in which there is a subconscious degree of order or distribution of error states, as we make and take conscious decisions. The decisions are based on the perceived or actual degree of order resulting from what is happening all around in the HTS, in which and at some past experience level and present experience interval we happen to be. The outcome probability depends directly on the experience, and the inseparable degree of 'situational awareness' is formally known or labeled in human reliability analysis as the 'context' in which the actual behaviour occurs.

To examine how we perceive and judge risk as we descend the ULC, we now recall the results of the Statistical Error State Theory (SEST). We have noted before in Chapter 5 that the objective measure of disorder or uncertainty is the *information entropy*, $H_j$, for the outcome distribution observed in the *j*th observation interval. This quantity reflects the information that any observer will see and somehow must understand and utilise in order to create learning. In terms of probabilities based on the frequency of error state occupation, $n_i = p_i N_j$ the classic result is:

$$H_j = -\sum p_i \ln p_i$$

For an effectively continuous distribution of outcomes based on the Learning Hypothesis, this result becomes the *H-factor*,

$$H_j = -\int p_i \ln p_i \mathrm{d}p = p_i^2\left(\frac{1}{4} - \frac{1}{2}\ln p_i\right)$$

Thus, the information entropy we observe is directly related to the probability distribution of the outcomes. In psychologically based models of skill acquisition and human performance, as summarised for example in R.W. Proctor and A. Dutta, 1995 [5], the information entropy is related to their probabilities, $p_i$, of the stimuli causing the observed reaction. In our case, *these stimuli correspond to the observed error state outcomes that are causing learning.*

In typical learning experiments on skill acquisition and tasks learned by sequential repetition, the individual's response time, *RT*, or time to correctly complete a given task or achieve some desired objective is recorded as a function of the number of trials or attempts, or as we would say, of increasing experience (see the discussion in Chapter 1 and Proctor and Dutta [5]). Generally, if and as learning is occurring, the *RT* to given stimuli for an individual decreases with repeated trials.

The well-known empirical Hick–Hyman law relates the observed *RT* to the information content of the stimuli as being a linear function of the information entropy, *H*. The *RT* increases simply as and because the information 'noise' adversely affects and delays, or increases the experience needed to find the right response or signal. Hence, assuming that $a_j$ and $b_j$ are fitted constants for the *j*th observation interval, the Hick–Hyman law implies for the *j*th observation interval:

$$RT_j = a_j + b_j H_j$$

or, using our result,

$$RT_j = a_j + b_j p_i^2\left(\frac{1}{4} - \frac{1}{2}\ln p_i\right)$$

Therefore, with this new expression we have now related the observed human behaviour, as measured by the observed action or *RT* to the actual risk probability of an outcome, p, as measured by counting (observing) the distribution of outcomes. In effect, the human filters out the useful patterns or knowledge embedded in the distribution of the probability of the error states that have been observed, improving with increased experience, and learning from the mistakes that occur.

*The individual human performance is intrinsically and inextricably coupled to the system outcomes,* thus uniquely defining what is meant by an HTS.

Clearly, the risk is perceptually and measurably greater, as implied by the larger *RT*, when there is a larger degree of disorder $(H_j)$. Thus, the *RT* is higher for larger probabilities of error, and vice versa *as we learn*, or as we transition from being a 'novice' to being an 'expert'.

Conversely, this new result suggests that measuring $RT$ is really quite a poor means or measure to determine error or outcome probability: it is a highly non-linear function that depends on the number of errors and the error state distribution. Even studies of skill acquisition using additive or differential subtractive responses would be difficult to interpret as a probability or risk shift. We can see this easily, since again, from Chapter 5, we may write the probability distribution with *depth* of experience as,

$$p_i \cong p_0 + p_0^* e^{-\beta \varepsilon}$$

Substituting this probability distribution into the expression for the $RT$ gives the trends we can now expect. The $RT$ now represents the observed human action as a result of the complex cognitive processes, and is a highly non-linear function of experience and the number of outcomes.

The difference in $RT$ between a novice (with little practice or experience, $\varepsilon \to 0$) and an expert (with infinite practice and much experience, $\varepsilon \to \infty$) is now clear, and potentially large. In fact, the difference can be written symbolically as an increase, $\Delta RT$, given by:

$$\Delta RT = RT_{\varepsilon \to 0}\{\text{novice}\} - RT_{\varepsilon \to \infty}\{\text{expert}\}$$
$$= \frac{1}{2} b \left\{ (p_0^2 \ln p_0^* + (p_0^*/p_0)^2 \left( \frac{1}{2} - \ln(p_0 + p_0^*) \right) \right\}$$

So it is clear that the difference observed between a 'learner' and an 'expert' as skill is acquired depends on the outcome probability distribution and its variation with the *depth* of experience. The different result also explains why it is convenient in $RT$ experiments in psychological testing to subtract from the observed $RT$, the asymptotic expert or lowest achieved minimum time, $RT$ {expert}; and why the resulting difference still depends on many contextual and experience factors. We can numerically calculate the sensitivity of the $RT$ as a function of values for all the many variables and shape constants that can affect it, including experience, namely:

$$RT_j = RT\left( a_j, b_j, p_0, \beta, \varepsilon \right)$$

The knowledge and skill acquisition, error correction and risk reduction at the individual level is then influenced directly by the outcome probability distributions. Just as an illustrative example, in Figure 8.6 we show the results of two arbitrary calculations for a final 50 and 10% chance ($p_0 = 0.5$ and 0.1), adopting a typical error state distribution parameter, $\beta$, of 3. It can be seen that the theoretical $RT$ learning curves follow a well-behaved and typical falling exponential form, according to the Learning Hypothesis. For just these examples, it takes almost 1,000 arbitrarily chosen trials to learn from experience, before the probability of an outcome decreases to reach its asymptotic (lowest) value. But even then, the $RT$ has only varied by just 10% as a result of the five times variation in probability. No wonder it is hard to design and perform definitive experiments using $RT$ as an outcome measure of the error probability.

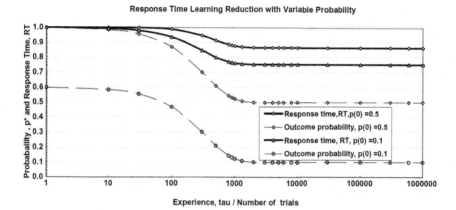

**Figure 8.6.** Theoretical response time variation for arbitrary final outcome probabilities using the Hick–Hyman law

## Response Times, Learning Data and the Universal Laws of Practice

As a further test against real experiments, an analysis was conducted for Ohlsson's $RT$ data [6], the results of which are shown in Figure 8.6. In that figure, the data points are shown, plus the line derived from the theory based on the information entropy, $H$, repeating the derivation for convenience and emphasis:

$$RT_j = a_j + b_j H_j$$

where $H_j = -\int p_i \ln p_i dp = p_i^2 \left( \frac{1}{4} - \frac{1}{2} \ln p_i \right)$

and hence,

$$RT(\varepsilon) = a + bp^2 \left( \frac{1}{4} - \frac{1}{2} \ln p \right)$$

Hence, we know that the response time varies explicitly as,

$$RT_j = a_j + b_j (p_0 + p_0^* e^{-\beta\varepsilon})^2 \left( \frac{1}{4} - \frac{1}{2} \ln\{p_0 + p_0^* e^{-\beta\varepsilon}\} \right)$$

For purposes of comparison since we do not know the prior knowledge, the $RT$, as a function of the number of trials were normalised to the initial value at the first trial, $RT(0)$. Thus, the ratio of the novice to expert response times is a constant, which is a strong function of the probability distribution parameters, $p_0$ and $p_0^*$.

The relevant experience parameter units was chosen as the amount of practice given by the number of trials and adjusted to correspond in scale ($\varepsilon = 1,000\tau \equiv n$). The following constants were also arbitrarily selected for the comparison: $a = 0.0001$, $b = 6$, $\beta = 3$, and $p_0 = 0.006$, corresponding to a relatively small probability of initial success but a normal rate of learning for this specific task.

The values may be fairly typical since the resulting fit shown depends most sensitively on the initial probability distribution parameters. These numerical values all might be expected to vary from subject-to-subject, specific test or experiment. The only general statement we make is that we have shown in principle that the entropy model can and does fit these individual learning data.

Simple (inverse) power laws are usually fitted to the trends used by psychological experimentalists (cf. the variable 'elasticity' parameter adopted in economics for unit costing as a function of demand or sales.). From our comparisons and those in [7], simple power laws are inferior in the degree of statistical fit attainable, and these Ohlsson *RT* data do follow almost exactly an exponential curve, as does the distribution. (See Figure 8.7.) We have made no effort to further optimise or refine the fit, as has been done elsewhere (see [7] and Appendix J).

Using these initial parameter values, the trend in the data is then nearly exactly reproduced by the information entropy model. Considering the entirely different origins of the theory (based on the distribution of system outcomes), and the data (derived from measuring individual timed responses), the fact that a reasonable fit can be obtained at all is remarkable. It cannot yet be determined if the agreement and values of the coefficients have greater psychological or system significance, and for the moment, this must be left as a topic for future work and research. *But the key point is that we are able to utilise the same learning model at both the individual and the collective levels when linked by the uncertainty as measured by the entropy concept.*

It turns out that in the vast psychological literature on learning and skill acquisition, a similar power law fits have been used to describe learning trends with repeated trials where it is known as the 'law of practice'. The trend is of decreasing errors and/or response times with increasing practice. Recently, it has been confirmed by comparison to thousands of data that empirical exponential fits to such *RT* data are better overall (Heathcote *et al.*, 2000) [7]. Moreover, the form of the preferred empirical fit or 'rule' is identical to the one that we have derived using the statistical analysis and entropy theory. The detailed mathematical and numerical comparisons are shown in Appendix J, where we compare the trends in the conventional and historical *RT* and error data to the present ULC and *RT* entropy theoretical results. The theory is almost uncannily accurate in predicting the learning trends, considering that we are comparing and validating the ideas developed from entire system outcomes to the totally independent data obtained for individual subjects.

As a result, in Appendix J, we have derived the theoretical basis for fitting *any* RT data, using the approximate simplified expression as a new correlating and consistent ABC Law of Practice:

$$RT_j = A_j + B_j e^{-\beta t} + C_j e^{-2\beta t}$$

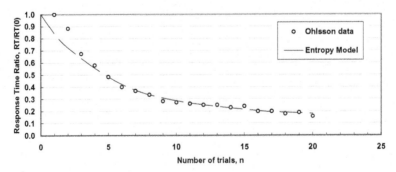

**Figure 8.7.**  Comparison of the learning model to response time data of Ohlsson, 2006

where $A_j$, $B_j$ and $C_j$ are constants determined from comparison to repeated trial, $t$, data. In Appendix J, we also derive a new error rate expression with *exactly* the same form as the ULC, namely:

$$E^* = \exp - 3t^*$$

where $E^*$ is the non-dimensional error rate and $t^*$ is the non-dimensional number of trials. These new expressions for $RT$ and $E^*$ are *Universal Laws of Practice* since they fit all the system outcomes as well as the individual learning trend data with increasing experience. Moreover, they share a common basis that supports the overarching concept of observing and producing order (systematic learning patterns, distributions and trends) by obtaining knowledge and rules from the very unobserved disorder (random outcomes, noise and error correction processes) that exists. This new general theory also distinguishes nicely between, and offers a new explanation for: (a) the influence of accumulated experience for learning repetitive tasks on the overall learning trend, as given by $E^*$; and (b) the influence of entropy and depth of experience of discerning patterns (order from disorder) for instantaneous decision making, as reflected by $RT$.

The risk is judged higher until the $RT$ decreases with more experience; and is higher the more information we have, or that is perceived. Perhaps this also explains why the continual (and often noisy!) media reporting affect and distort our risk perception and judgement. The multitudinous and unfiltered media reporting of trivia act as stimuli and signals (i.e., information entropy) that often imply or convey impressions of uncertainty in perceived high risk when actually there is none or little. Simply reporting multitudinous numbers of events as newsworthy without learning repetition or evaluation drastically increases the difficulty of comprehension and skill acquisition, as in any learning situation. Simply put, having a multitude of headlines causes confusion and difficulty in acquiring the real message and eliminating mistakes. One thing that the media does not report is their uncertainty or entropy generation.

We just cannot discern or judge the real risk signal for all the noise. There is just too much ado about nothing.

## The Number and Distribution of Outcomes: Comparison to Data

We have already shown how the probability of observing one outcome, which is what we might expect, follows the MERE probability (the human bathtub). We can also expect observing more than one outcome to be some 10 times less likely. What we have also now proved using the SEST is rather obvious and perhaps really self-evident: the number of outcomes in any observation interval also decreases with increasing depth of experience, as does the rate of outcomes we observe, if and when we have learning. The rate and the number of outcomes (events, accidents, and errors) are connected via the experience we have accumulated in our observation interval.

Roughly then, the rate of outcomes is just the number of outcomes divided by the experience that we have, so the $IR$ is $A \sim (N_j/\varepsilon_j)$. We have already determined from our statistical reasoning that the number of outcomes is distributed exponentially, as

$$N_j = n_0 + n_0 e^{(\alpha - \beta \varepsilon)} + n_0 e^{(\alpha - 2\beta \varepsilon)} + \ldots$$
$$= \{n_0 / (1 - e^{\alpha - \beta \varepsilon})\}$$

Provided that $e^{\alpha - \beta \varepsilon} \ll 1$, (i.e., large experience and learning rate, $\beta \varepsilon \gg 1$) to first order the equilibrium outcome rate per observation interval is the total number of microstates (outcomes) divided by the experience in the interval, or:

$$IR \equiv <N_j / \varepsilon_j> \approx 1 / \varepsilon_j \{n_0 + n_0^* e^{-\beta \varepsilon} - \ldots \ldots\}$$

where $\beta$ is now the (effective learning) constant, and $n_0^* = n_0 e^{\alpha}$ is a constant related to the so-called partition function.

Now the distribution of microstate occupation with outcomes is:

$$n_i = n_0 \exp(\alpha - \beta \varepsilon_i)$$

So, the probability of occupation of the $i$th level, relative to the zeroth experience level is the ratio of the outcome microstate occupancies of the levels,

$$p_i = (n_i / n_0) = \exp \alpha \times \exp - \beta \varepsilon_i$$
$$= \text{constant} \times \exp - \beta \varepsilon_I$$

So we expect the number of outcomes to decrease exponentially with experience for the $j$th observation interval. That this form fits the available data reasonably well is shown in Figure 8.8, where we have the outcomes for two very distinct and diverse datasets in two HTS that have clear evidence of learning, one for aircraft and one for automobiles.

In this plot, we have shown the relative probability for two comprehensive datasets. The US FAA data are air carrier near misses (NMACs) for the observation interval of 1987 to

**Nondimensional Outcome Distribution**

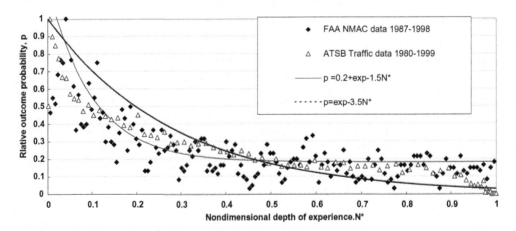

**Figure 8.8.** The distribution of outcomes with depth of experience

1998, with a total number of outcomes of 2,245. The ATSB auto deaths are for the interval 1980 to 1999, with a total number of outcomes of 11,538. The occupancy number, $n_i$, for each experience increment, $\varepsilon_i$, is calculated as a probability, $p_i$, relative to that at the zeroth observed level, $n_0$. To enable us to compare these sets directly on the same plot, the data are also independently normalised to a depth scale based on the maximum depth of experience level in the observation interval for each dataset.

The exponential fit shown is the simple SEST relative occupation probability, taking $p = p_i/p_0$ where $p_0 = 1$ as an arbitrary normalisation,

$$p_i = \exp - 3.5N^*,$$

where $N^*$ is the non-dimensional experience level, $N^* = \varepsilon_i/\varepsilon_j$. The agreement is not perfect: this equation type over predicts slightly at lower experience levels, and then under predicts at the higher ones. A somewhat better fit can be derived, based on the MERE form, which is also shown in Figure 8.8.

$$p_i = 0.2 + \exp - 1.5N^*$$

This result implies that there is never a risk of less than 20% probability of outcomes at any experience depth. The implication is that over the (large) observation interval chosen to derive the datasets, learning and forgetting occurred as experience was accumulated, which we have already shown before. So the SEST theory is not exact because of this varying influence.

To illustrate the generality of this analysis, we simply note and add that the commercial pilot fatality distribution of the probability of death as a function of pilot 'years-on-type' (discussed in Chapter 5) also follows this exponential trend. So do all data that exhibit learning trends.

## Risk Perception: Railways

Let us now return to the derailments in the UK, which were *perceived* as more dangerous than road travel. Comparison of the derailment data to the distribution predicted by the SEST now also shows an important point.

The data are compared in Figure 8.9 to the probability of occupation predicted by fitting the NMAC and ATSB auto deaths, namely $p_i = \exp - 3.5N^*$. It is clear that the derailment data, shown as the points, fall well above this line fitted to the NMAC data for aircraft and the ATSB auto deaths. There is evidence of *insufficient learning* compared to these other world outcome data.

Did we subconsciously perceive this lower learning rate, and did this affect our risk aversion and avoidance behaviour? Strictly speaking, this is purely speculation, and we do not know, and must be confirmed by more analysis and better data. So we have re-analysed the data that we have, looking for trends in risk perception.

As we learn from our mistakes, we adjust our systems and their overall management as a natural part of learning from experience. But for entire socially connected systems, the agents of change are often politically and legally motivated as well as being technically and managerially desirable. In addition, there is a legal trend to assign responsibility and liability. In

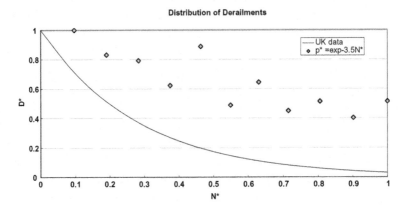

**Figure 8.9.** Comparison of derailments to other industries using the fitted SEST distribution

the UK, this has lead to 'The Corporate Manslaughter and Corporate Homicide Act 2007' which: *'introduces a new offence for prosecuting companies and other organisations where there has been a gross failing, throughout the organisation, in the management of health and safety with fatal consequences'(see http://www.justice.gov.uk/guidance/manslaughteract-guidance.htm).* The emphasis is now on *'Managing risks – not risk aversion . . . where a gross failure in the way activities were managed or organised results in a person's death.'*

An example of fatal accidents driving fundamental changes in regulation and safety management thinking is in the UK railway infrastructure, where we have already discussed derailments and their relatively low risk. Following privatisation of the previously publicly owned entire rail system in the UK in the early 1990s, the railway HTS suffered four pivotal fatal accidents. These were:

1. a collision between a high-speed passenger train and a freight train at Southall (September, 1997) with 7 fatalities and 139 injuries;
2. the collision at Ladbroke Grove (October 1999) of a high-speed and a commuter train with 31 fatalities and 400 injuries;
3. derailment of a high-speed train at Hatfield (October 2000) with four fatalities and over 70 injuries, and fines subsequently levied of over $20M; and
4. derailment at Potters Bar (May, 2002) of a commuter train with seven fatalities and again more than 70 injuries[3] (see Plate 6).

There was considerable national, political and media attention, leading to the public *perception* of inadequate railway safety standards. The prior knowledge was all there for everyone to see, was not placed in any risk context, so passengers transferred to other forms of transport, including vehicles that we have already shown have a higher risk. Following the accidents, at Southall and Ladbroke Grove, the UK Health and Safety Commission (HSC)

---

[3] The detailed investigation reports, Inquiry documents and updates on recommendation status for these accidents, and for many others, are available ©HMSO in full at the UK Office of Rail Regulation, www.rail-reg.gov.uk. The most recent echo is the 23 February 2007 derailment at Grayrigg in Cumbria, with one fatality and injuries to 28 passengers and two train crewmembers.

set up four major Public Inquiries, and since then have been tracking progress on the implementation of recommendations. So after significant loss of life and public embarrassment, we have a recognised need for learning:

> *The Government agreed that the 295 recommendations from the four Public Inquiry reports set a convincing, necessary and challenging agenda for change. The scope of the Inquiry recommendations ranged from specific detailed technical issues to underlying conditions of culture and management practice. Some are fundamental to achieving overall improvements in the state of the industry's safety management, whilst others are less wide ranging. ... In reviewing progress it would be misleading to focus on only a count of recommendations closed. This is a simplistic view of what the industry has achieved but the agenda set by Public Inquiries is more about change and improvements in attitudes, leading to better management of risk across the railway system. By accepting that certain recommendations have been completed we are not becoming complacent about safety and we know that the industry agrees with this.*
>
> Source: *The UK Office of Rail Regulation*

The national rail network infrastructure (track, signalling, bridges, tunnels and stations) is, as of 2004, owned and operated by Network Rail under a network licence issued from the UK government. Since there was also a recommendation to track the recommendations (!), the latest status report shows that the recommendations continue to deliver some results, such as Network Rail and the train-operating companies completing the fitting of the train protection and warning system (TPWS). But that is not all: the entire system is under continued scrutiny, review and some stress as related to the operation of this entire infrastructure.

A new strategy was published by the UK Department for Transport (DfT) in July 2004 [8] on the developments in the railway infrastructure after privatisation. Being a component part of a major HTS, we have a specific interest in the control of engineering and maintenance standards being promulgated and enforced. The pertinent paragraphs of Chapter 4 state:

> *4.1 Successive governments have failed to ensure that sufficient investment has been made in the rail network on a consistent basis. And where major projects have been taken forward, they have often been subject to false economies - for example the electrification of the East Coast Main Line, where lightweight structures have proved vulnerable to high winds. The 10-Year Plan has provided substantially increased funding for the industry, but a legacy of under-investment remains, which will take time to address.*

> *4.2 The privatisation of the rail industry in the early 1990's assumed that private sector innovation and discipline would drive down the railway's subsidy requirement and drive up the quality of service. In part this has been borne out – demand for both passenger and freight services has risen since privatisation. But it proved entirely incorrect in relation to the operation of the infrastructure. Railtrack's engineering work was outsourced to maintenance companies that were given responsibility not only for maintenance and renewals, but also for specification and inspection of their own work. This led to Railtrack's knowledge of the state of its assets diminishing and to a maintenance strategy that saw the condition of the track deteriorate rapidly.*

> *4.3 The accident at Hatfield in October 2000 exposed the extent of this deterioration. And the widespread speed restrictions that followed caused a steep decline in reliability. The reaction to Hatfield also undermined public perceptions of safety on the network.*

> *4.4 In response, Railtrack increased the level of maintenance and renewal work, but this generated a steep increase in costs. This, combined with the separate loss of cost control on the West Coast*

*Main Line project, contributed to a worsening financial situation which led, eventually, to the company's entry into administration. Network Rail, a company limited by guarantee which operates in the wider interest and which is accountable to the railway industry through its members, has now taken over responsibility for the rail network and has made some progress in addressing the problems of the past.*

*4.5 Rail is now carrying record numbers of passengers, its safety levels are improving, its customer focus has got better, and, in the aftermath of the accident at Hatfield, reliability is slowly recovering.*

                                 *Source:* 'The Future of Transport', UK Department of Transport

The engineering- and maintenance-related accidents at Hatfield and Potters Bar also highlighted deficiencies in the outsourcing of rail network maintenance to companies given responsibility not only for maintenance renewals but also the specification and inspection of their own work. The Hatfield derailment accident was caused by a defective (broken) rail, and the Potters Bar derailment accident was a result of a defective set of points (used for track changeover), both due to inadequate maintenance practices and procedures. Several major recommendations were made, reflecting Howlett's 'loss of control' in this case of maintenance contractors, track condition, and maintenance quality and of the costs.

In the last few years, a myriad of significant changes were made in legislation and regulation following the spate of fatal railway accidents. They reflect the complex situation of transitional arrangements of legislation and organisational changes, several stemming directly from the Public Inquiry recommendations. Some of the major changes we identified are establishment of:

a)  the Rail Safety & Standard Board;
b)  the Office of Rail Regulation (ORR); and
c)  the Railway Accident Investigation Branch (RAIB), consistent with the Maritime and Air Accidents Branches (AAIB and MAIB). In addition, in HTS management Railtrack was replaced by Network Rail, who are responsible for operating the rail network and for its performance; and HM Railways Inspectorate (HMRI) has been transferred to the Office of Rail Regulation (ORR).

So what we have is a complex and comprehensive attempt to create order and structure, via rules, regulations, legislation and standards, in response to public perception of the consequences of the human element. Somewhat depressingly, the latest available data from the UK shows that about the same *number* of derailments are still occurring each year[4].

## Risk Perception: Coal Mining

We note in passing that a similar trend is seen in coal mining outcomes (deaths and injuries) in the USA. Coal mining is *perceived* as a dangerous occupation. However, there is a clear

---

[4]The numbers of derailments for 2004, 2005 and 2006 are 59, 63 and 47, respectively, according to the UK Office of Rail Regulation (ORR) 'Railway Safety Statistical Report, 2006', Table E.1 on p. 21 (available at http://www.rail-reg.gov.uk/upload/pdf/rss_report_06.pdf), which is nearly the same number as in previous years.

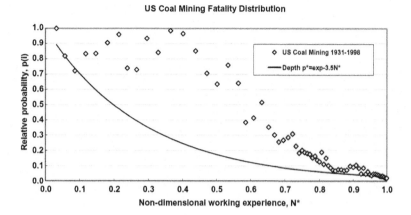

**Figure 8.10.** The variation of coal mining deaths with depth of experience

reduction in the rate of outcomes per unit production of coal as production experience increases (Duffey and Saull, 2002) [9]. But the number of outcomes (deaths) decreased more slowly in this century than the exponential expected from pure learning of $p^* = \exp - 3.5N^*$, as derived from the Australian auto fatalities and US aircraft near-miss data.

For the coal mining experience measure, we adopted the millions of working hours [10]. Overall for the observation interval of 1931 to 1998 the USA had an accumulated experience, $\varepsilon$, of ~23 Billion ($2.3 \times 10^{10}$) mining hours worked, and a death total of $N_j = \Sigma n_i = 31,770$ outcomes. We show the analysis result in the Figure 8.10, as the relative probability versus the depth, and it clearly shows little evidence of learning compared to these other cases until about 40% of the total experience, or about 30 years ago.

The perception of coal mining is that it is a dangerous occupation and industry, when in fact the outcome *rate* is similar to that for other industries. However, the persistence of the number of outcomes lagging learning, with the associated media reports showing bodies being recovered from underground and grieving relatives waiting for information, continues to give a perception of a highly hazardous and risky industry despite what the data imply.

## Risk Perception: Nuclear Power in Japan

In Japan, nuclear energy is widely deployed and continues to be controversial. Caught without fossil fuel reserves and possessing an industrial economy, from necessity, Japan uses nuclear power for electricity production and is a major plant builder and developer.

Several incidents have highlighted the latent fears of the Japanese, who after all were subjected to two nuclear weapon attacks in WWII. These recent events are scandalous in Japan: (a) the JCO fuel plant criticality event (see Chapter 7) which is analysed in 'Know the Risk'; (b) the sodium fire at the Monju demonstration nuclear reactor; and (c) the suppression or non-reporting of reactor inspection data that showed pipe cracking on TEPCO's reactor fleet. In the last case, the effect was to shut the plants down in order to resolve the matter, leaving metropolitan Tokyo with minimal electric power supply. All of these incidents caused a public loss of confidence; and nuclear energy was *perceived* as risky and dangerous.

The data do not support this: after all these outcomes did not kill any members of the public, and caused inconvenience and fear, not death. Events and incidents are reportable in Japan, and the data on outcome (reportable event) rates were discussed in Chapter 7 as part of Safety Management.

The data shown there before indicate a reduction in reported events as electrical capacity was added, using the MW(e)-y installed as the measure of the experience. The relative probability versus the depth is shown in Figure 8.11.

The fitted curve shown indicates a much higher number with depth of experience than we might expect from the theory, about 100 times more. So there were just too many events. But what if we correct for the early small amount of installed capacity: after all we have more staff and operators for more plants. So when we calculate the events per installed gigawatt ($1\,\mathrm{BMWy} = \mathrm{GW(e)} - \mathrm{y}$), the result is strikingly different (Figure 8.12).

The many events when the installation started lead to a decided learning curve. This can be dramatically shown by plotting the result non-dimensionally, and comparing to the base relative occupation probability of $p^* = \exp - 3.5N^*$ from autos and airline near misses (Figure 8.13).

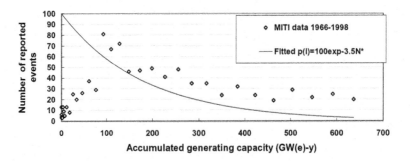

**Figure 8.11.** Nuclear power plant events reported in Japan

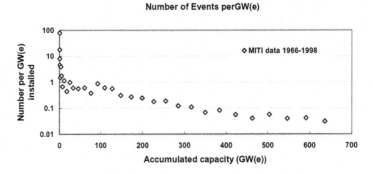

**Figure 8.12.** Nuclear events on a capacity basis

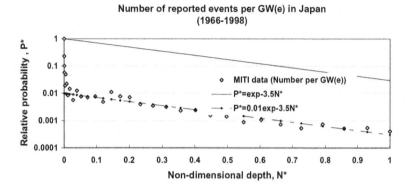

**Figure 8.13.** The comparison between industries: auto deaths, airline near misses and nuclear events

The data fall well below this accepted risk curve as derived from near misses in the air and auto deaths in Australia. Ignoring the events from early start-up transient, the best fit to the nuclear event data after the first few plants is $p^* = 0.01 \exp - 3.5N^*$, about *100 times less* than we would have expected. The agreement in the slope over the whole range with that derived from the other data is very remarkable, and the learning constant is given by the value of ~3.5. *The learning constant is essentially identical for three very disparate but safety conscious activities.* That is the clear trend from these data.

So clearly, in Japan, the complex interaction of an HTS with society as a whole has led to a misperception. Because nuclear energy is perceived as a risk, reporting errors and events simply reinforce that learning. The public pay more attention to the number of events, which are mandated and legislated to be reportable and are decreasing slowly, than to their rate of occurrence per unit generated power which is decreasing much more dramatically. This experience from Japan suggests another complicating and perhaps fundamental cultural factor that is lurking in these data, which may partly explain the comparatively low number compared to other industries shown in Figure 8.13. Perhaps because of the extreme sensitivity to admitting error, there is the distinct possibility of the under-reporting of events. It is known that a number of events/incidents have *not* been reported, in particular: (a) cracks detected in metal components during inspections mandated by licensing requirements; and (b) unintended power excursions (so-called inadvertent criticality events) due to rod ejection during scheduled maintenance while shutdown. Major management, public and regulatory upheavals occurred as a result. We can argue that plotting the data as shown in Figure 8.13 is also a clear indicator of a possible under-reporting problem, despite the consistency of the overall learning rate or decrease with depth of experience. Using such apparently simple comparisons and ideas, fundamental 'safety culture' lessons potentially surface after previously being hidden beneath the conventional data.

The event rate, if correct, is 100 times less than what we might expect due to learning, but the high-risk perception remains. Also, there is clear evidence in these data of a higher rate at the beginning, due to lack of experience: the initial outcome rate, $A \sim n/\varepsilon$, is large as a result.

## Risk Perception: Rare Events and Risk Rankings

For the special case of *rare events*, we know the rate is $\sim n/\varepsilon$, where $n \sim 1$, and we are surprised by the outcome occurrence, and often have no or little prior information or data. The reaction to these rare events is different: we seem to pay them more attention than the everyday occurrences. Since rare events also have little or no learning opportunity, perhaps we sense they are special and deserve our attention, as they do not follow the ULC. Experience increases reduce the rate, but not the number of outcomes.

There is an implication in our analyses presented here that humans today are not as dumb at making arbitrary risk avoidance decisions as we may seem! If there is a hint of insufficient learning, perhaps we perceive that somehow from the media coverage that report events *not* rates. It is evident that we do not avoid air travel due to NMACs, or driving autos. And the UK has returned to taking trains. So the risk avoidance is temporary, and dependent on the information on learning that we are exposed to and learn from *in our observation interval.*

Turning again to the numerically ordered risk ranking survey given by Moore [2], Table 8.2 compares the actual relative and perceived risk for the five HTS cases where we have experience-based data analyses. The 'real' and 'perceived' risk rankings are taken from the data given by Moore. We have to group the trends in the rail outcome data (deaths, derailments and SPADS) for the rail travel case and similarly use the rare event data (fatal crashes and near misses) for the air travel case. We also changed the risk ranking to be a broader one using the thirds of High, Medium and Low out of all the selected examples to avoid the impression of excessive accuracy for this qualitative exercise.

In every case, the outcome rate with experience was falling as a learning curve, but the number trends with experience depth were different, having flattened out or decreased more slowly than apparently possible with learning. For this limited set of outcome data, the perception of relatively 'high risk' occurs both as agreements and disagreements with the 'real' risk when the outcome number with experience depth is changing more slowly than the expectation of learning. Hence, we do not judge risk based on rate trends alone, since all cases exhibit falling rates with learning. Although this is too small a sample to be definitive or conclusive, there is a hint of some connection of number trends with perception. This could also be a potentially misleading example because of the original risk case selections.

Since the outcomes are a continuous random variable learning curve, the information entropy is given by the H-*factor*,

**Table 8.2.** Comparison of subjective risk perception and real risk ranking

| Risk | 'Real' rank | Rate versus Experience | Number versus Depth | 'Perceived' rank |
|------|-------------|------------------------|---------------------|------------------|
| Autos | High | Falling | Constant | High |
| Rail travel | High | Falling | Constant | High |
| Air travel | Medium | Falling | Falling/Constant | Medium |
| Medical | High | Falling | Constant | High |
| Nuclear events | Low | Falling | Falling | High |

Rank: High = top third; Low = bottom third; Medium = central third.

$$H_j = -\int p_i \ln p_i dp$$
$$= p_i^2 \left( \frac{1}{4} - \frac{1}{2} \ln p_i \right)$$

In general, the probability of occupation according to the SEST is,

$$p_i = p_0 \exp - aN,$$

so, the information entropy is:.

$$H_j = \frac{1}{2} \{ p_0 e^{-aN} \}^2 \left\{ aN + \frac{1}{2} \right\}$$

where, on a relative basis, $p_0 = 1$. As either the learning rate or depth of experience increases ($N\uparrow$ or $a\uparrow$), or the zeroth order occupancy decreases ($p_0 \downarrow$), so does the value of $H$ decline, meaning a more uniform distribution and increased order.

In non-dimensional experience form, $N^*$, for convenience we can adopt:

$$H = \frac{1}{2} \{ p_0 e^{-aN^*} \}^2 \left\{ aN^* + \frac{1}{2} \right\}$$

The evaluation of this single parameter, the $H$-factor, using this formula is shown in Figure 8.14. The data are for aircraft near misses, traffic deaths, train derailments, nuclear events and coal mining. The typical values for the exponential factor, a, are taken from fitting the data plots previously shown. The evaluation of the experience is taken as the non-dimensional values, $N^*$, and the probability multiplier as the best-fit value, recalling that our 'base' value was for the commercial NMACs.

Using the $H$-factor as the single measure, the relative risk ranking is clearly, in order of apparently decreasing risk:

- Train derailments
- Coal mining
- Airline near misses
- Nuclear events

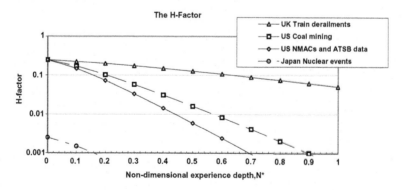

**Figure 8.14.** The $H$-factor evaluation examples

So the *H*-factor idea we propose here is not in conflict, or at best is not rejected by these example cases and our risk perception. *We can suggest that humans can and do somehow quantify the basis for our relative risk perceptions based on our expectation of learning due to the number of outcomes.* Other factors, like fear, risk aversion or risk taking behaviour, and personal risk exposure obviously may have an influence, and be stronger in some cases than others.

## Predicting the Future Number of Outcomes

Hence, what we can argue is that we have *demonstrated the principle of a dependence of the distribution of the number of observed outcomes on the depth of experience,* and that this trend is possibly reflected in our perception of risk.

Perhaps of most importance to the present discussion is that the SEST modelling provides the basis for analysing trends, and also provides a theoretical basis for both the data-fit and predictions. This result will be of interest to those analysts and scientists who already use (arbitrary) exponentials for fitting curves to the distribution of risk data, such as in the social sciences, since it justifies the adoption of that particular 'model' choice.

The key result is this one: given the number of outcomes at any experience *we can predict the future number* at a yet to be attained experience, including the uncertainty. This result is formally derived in Appendix F, as one approximation for sampling from the Jar of Life, where we show the probability of observing any given number of outcomes is based on our prior (MERE) experience. Observing many outcomes is much less likely than observing just one.

All this sounds obvious and should enable us to formulate a 'risk formula' for our lives. But our experience is that it is only selected industries and/or their regulators that have systematically collected the right data. Data that exist are often fragmentary, not in the right form, or have no measure of experience. This is a frustrating state of affairs for modern technological society to be in, but that is where we are today. There are no standards for data collection, assimilation, filing, reporting analysis or display, other than those required for quality control and assurance (QA and QC) purposes.

As an example, a working real case of data collection and analysis, we will now examine oil spills. The oil industry is huge, world wide and modern. Vast quantities of oil are pumped, shipped, stored and used around the globe. We were asked to examine this information in detail by an interested oil company safety specialist.

## A Worked Example: Searching Out and Analysing Data for Oil Spills

Oil transport should be a simple and easy example, representing one extreme of a large (HTS) system where we transport huge volumes of inflammable and environmentally hazardous fluid around the planet. Tankers, barges, truck and pipelines almost everywhere, everyday, carry oil as we burn it as an energy source, and use it for chemical production and transportation fuel. But we spill oil also, by accident, and each spill is an outcome.

Water and oil do not mix well, and spills into water can destroy beaches, seabirds and affect fishing communities. Spills are so bad in impact and so common in occurrence that regulations for safe transport are invoked, and the impact and clean-up of the largest spills are costly, damaging and litigious. The Exxon Valdez tanker spill in Alaska springs to everyone's mind. Double-hulled tankers are now being required to help avoid the spill of the millions of gallons being carried around.

It was suggested we look at the oil spills occurring in the petroleum industry, so we did look for data to see if learning was apparent. We provided an initial analysis of importance to the safety and environmental impact of the oil storage and transportation industry, using *publically* available USA data on oil spills, shipping losses and pipeline accidents. Despite our request, we were not given or allowed access to the oil and gas industry's privately held spill database. (Duffey, Saull and Myers, 2004) [11].

Spills and accidents can arise in many ways, e.g.:

- while filling,
- in storage,
- during transport,
- at process and transfer facilities, plus
- failure of vessels and pipelines.

We would expect significant human involvement in the design, management and operation of all these technological activities, in the piping, pumping, tanks, valves and operations. For handling and storage of (petro) chemicals, the risk of a spill or a loss is also dependent on the human error rate in the transport or storage mode and the accumulated experience with the transport or storage system. The American Petroleum Institute (API) we understand has a proprietary or private database on the events retained by and for their sponsors, but we could not gain or have access to that data. So instead we turn to the public reporting system.

A summary of major spills 'case histories' is given by the US NOAA, 1992 [12] for 1967 to 1991 for over 200 outcomes, but only for spills of more than 10,000 gallons at sea. Although interesting as a historical record of brief statements of what happened, where and when, this is not a dataset we could analyse in any further detail.

A more complete set for pipelines from 1986 to 2003, by the US DOT, 2003 [13] lists 3,246 outcomes which caused 37 deaths, and covered ~160,000 miles of pipeline. These data suggest an average failure rate of 190 per year, for a spill risk rate of ~$10^{-3}$ per pipeline operating mile-year. This sounds a reasonable risk value for piping failures in general. The resulting spills totalled nearly 3 M bbls, and cost over \$800M in property damage alone. But these summary data are not amenable to more detailed analysis.

The US Coast Guard database for oil spills was the most comprehensive we found, but is given in the usual annual format of tables of data, such as shown here in Table 8.3 for a random year. For shipping spills, in the USCG oil spill database for the observation interval from 1973 to 2000, we found information for 231,000 spill events for the USA, while transporting a total of oil of nearly 68 Btoe, of which 8,700 events were spills of more than 1,000 gallons. Assuming there is pressure from the EPA, industry, owners and others to reduce spills rates, then there is a nominally large HTS learning opportunity. We can easily extract the number of spills from such tables. But to use such data effectively, we must transform it to experience space, as otherwise it is still just a list of numbers of outcomes on a purely calendar year reporting basis.

**Table 8.3** Typical USCG data format for oil spills

| SPILL SIZE | NUMBER OF SPILLS | % OF SPILL INCIDENTS | SPILL VOLUME (GALLONS) | % OF SPILL VOLUME | AVERAGE SPILL SIZE | MEDIAN SPILL SIZE | MAXIMUM SPILL SIZE |
|---|---|---|---|---|---|---|---|
| 1 – 100 GALLONS | 7541 | 92.2% | 84,043 | 1.1% | 11 | 2 | 100 |
| 101 – 1,000 GALLONS | 447 | 5.5% | 154,858 | 2.0% | 346 | 250 | 1,000 |
| 1,001 – 3,000 GALLONS | 80 | 1.0% | 140,140 | 1.8% | 1,752 | 1,680 | 3,000 |
| 3,001 – 5,000 GALLONS | 34 | .4% | 131,861 | 1.7% | 3,878 | 3,890 | 5,000 |
| 5,001 – 10,000 GALLONS | 22 | .3% | 157,762 | 2.0% | 7,171 | 6,900 | 10,000 |
| 10,001 – 50,000 GALLONS | 34 | .4% | 717,809 | 9.1% | 21,112 | 16,065 | 50,000 |
| 50,001 – 100,000 GALLONS | 11 | .1% | 734,618 | 9.3% | 66,783 | 60,000 | 94,500 |
| 100,001 – 1,000,000 GALLONS | 7 | .1% | 1,893,916 | 23.9% | 270,559 | 250,000 | 473,000 |
| 1,000,000 – GALLONS | 1 | .0% | 3,900,000 | 49.3% | 3,900,000 | 3,900,000 | 3,900,000 |
| YEAR-END STATISTICS | 8177 | 100.0% | 7,915,007 | 100.0% | 968 | 3 | 3,900,000 |

| WATERBODY | NUMBER OF SPILLS | % OF SPILL INCIDENTS | SPILL VOLUME (GALLONS) | % OF SPILL VOLUME | AVERAGE SPILL SIZE | MEDIAN SPILL SIZE | MAXIMUM SPILL SIZE |
|---|---|---|---|---|---|---|---|
| ATLANTIC OCEAN | 92 | 1.1% | 13,400 | .2% | 146 | 10 | 5,750 |
| PACIFIC OCEAN | 480 | 5.9% | 624,494 | 7.9% | 1,301 | 5 | 397,236 |
| GULF OF MEXICO | 1834 | 22.4% | 4,115,264 | 52.0% | 2,244 | 1 | 3,900,000 |
| GREAT LAKES | 194 | 2.4% | 129,131 | 1.6% | 666 | 3 | 115,000 |
| LAKES | 11 | .1% | 383 | .0% | 35 | 15 | 200 |
| RIVERS & CANALS | 1749 | 21.4% | 1,755,142 | 22.4% | 1,105 | 5 | 473,000 |
| BAYS & SOUNDS | 988 | 12.1% | 163,436 | 3.3% | 267 | 3 | 152,000 |
| HARBORS | 940 | 11.5% | 455,108 | 5.7% | 484 | 5 | 250,000 |
| OTHER | 1889 | 23.1% | 538,649 | 6.8% | 285 | 5 | 57,162 |
| YEAR-END STATISTIS | 8177 | 100.0% | 7,915,007 | 100.0% | 968 | 3 | 3,900,000 |

(With kind permission from http://www.uscg.mil/hq/gm/nmc/response/stats/summary.htm)

We downloaded all the USCG datatables available for 1969 to 2000 as Adobe.pdf formatted files. Although the format changed slightly through the years, it was much as shown in the example in Table 8.2.

We transformed all the files into Excel (.xls) datasheets, and used that for calculations, as will be seen later. To give us a manageable task, we recorded and entered the data only for the $N_j = 8,700$ outcomes of spills greater than 1,000 gallons, as a starting pint.

Of course, this USCG data are in typical year-by-year reporting, an arbitrary but standard format. It is an impressive dataset and quite comprehensive. But is just that: data. The USCG and others use this information for yearly reporting, so that yet another year's reporting can occur. To justify the need for action, a reduction in the number of spills is one indication that some improvement is happening. How much improvement is there?

The USCG data files also show the number of spills by calendar year for 1973 to 2000, which is an interesting graph in and by itself, so it is reproduced here. (See Figure 8.15.)

Clearly, the number of spills each year is going down, particularly after 1985, when there was almost a step change to nearly a constant thereafter. But by 2000 there were still about 100 a year.

Interesting questions emerge. What is the spill rate? Why is it that number? Has the HTS changed? Is there learning occurring? Where are we on the ULC? What fraction of oil is being spilt? Are we going towards the USCG and EPA goals of zero spills?

This graph, impressive though it is, still does not tell us any of the answers, or enable us to make a prediction. Looking at the Past data (the prior information) we would just expect about 100 spills over 1,000 gallons for the next year, and every next year.

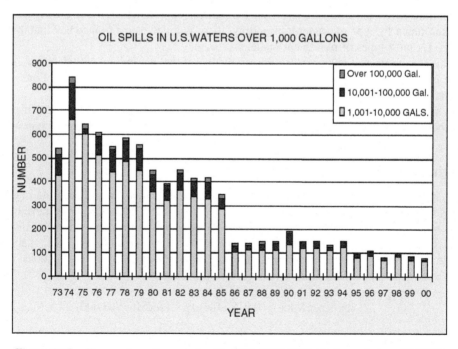

**Figure 8.15.** The number of reported spills 1973–2000 (With kind permission of USCG)

We need a measure for experience. Strictly, we would like to know the shipping-years accumulated by all the vessels carrying the oil. But the number of ships involved in the spills is not reported, nor is the total number of vessels used for oil transport. So the measure for the accumulated experience we took was the total amount of oil being shipped, which, as can be seen, is not given in or by the USGS raw datatables. But in a fine example of tacit interagency (non-) cooperation and data diffusion, we found the data elsewhere, since each different government branch or agency is interested in different things about oil use for different reasons.

The US DOE do track the oil consumption information and where it comes from for purely energy analysis purposes. The datatables for crude oil and petroleum products was given in the DOE Petroleum Overview, for 1949–2001.

## Typical Worksheet

We calculated the amount of oil shipped into and out of the USA for each year. Using the DOE data available by country, we derived the total imports and export volumes of oil shipped into and out of the USA. The tabulated data are shown below, taken from a typical xls. worksheet. (See Table 8.4)

The total number of outcomes $N_j = 8,696$, for the total experience of ~68 Btoe shipped, and average of ~1 spill per 10 Mtoe shipped.

## Plotting the Data

Replotting these spill data, the result for the number of spills is shown in the Figure 8.16. Broken down by type of vessel transporting, there is a decrease in outcomes (numbers of spills) for most types of movement mode.

This raw number of outcomes is a representation of the distribution with depth of experience for oil spills. Recall that this was the line sketched on the right-hand-edge of our observation interval in our cube of 'experience space'.

When turned into a spill rate (the IR), immediately we see that the distribution of purely numbers of spills hides a learning trend, as shown for pipelines and tankers in Figure 8.17.

## Fitting a Learning Curve

The apparent presence of a learning curve (exponential decline) in the outcome rate data leads immediately to the fitting of a learning curve expression. That is easily achieved using the commercial routine Tablecurve 2D, or any other such software, and the result includes confidence levels and goodness of fit parameters. We show that in Figure 8.18, again as a working example, where the data are for tankers and all oil spills over 1,000 gallons.

We can see that the MERE fit is very good to these data:

$$IR(\text{Spills per Mtoe}) = 0.018 + 0.4 \exp - (accMtoe/21,600)$$

What is evident is that the future projected or *predicted* minimum rate of ~0.018 spills per Mtoe has *not* yet been achieved in this observation interval, based on these prior data. It is

**Table 8.4.** Worksheet data for US oil spills

| Year | Total Shipped (Mtoe) | Experience (accMToe) | Number >1000 gals | Volume (kg) > 1000 gals | Tankship Number | Experience (accMToe) | Tankers IR/Mtoe | Spill IR/Mt |
|------|------|------|------|------|------|------|------|------|
| 1973 | 1,860 | 1,860 | 541 | 14674.74 | 694 | 1,860 | 0.373182 | 0.29091 |
| 1974 | 1,902 | 3,762 | 842 | 15018.67 | 846 | 3,762 | 0.444821 | 0.442718 |
| 1975 | 1,934 | 5,696 | 645 | 20855.55 | 595 | 5,696 | 0.307638 | 0.33349 |
| 1976 | 2,492 | 8,187 | 610 | 17931.48 | 526 | 8,187 | 0.211105 | 0.244818 |
| 1977 | 3,038 | 11,225 | 547 | 7601.812 | 533 | 11,225 | 0.175449 | 0.180058 |
| 1978 | 2,885 | 14,111 | 583 | 10228.16 | 678 | 14,111 | 0.234973 | 0.202049 |
| 1979 | 2,891 | 17,002 | 557 | 20287.71 | 647 | 17,002 | 0.22376 | 0.192635 |
| 1980 | 2,355 | 19,357 | 452 | 12067.06 | 547 | 19,357 | 0.232261 | 0.191923 |
| 1981 | 2,042 | 21,399 | 390 | 8486.002 | 419 | 21,399 | 0.205202 | 0.191 |
| 1982 | 1,715 | 23,115 | 452 | 9884.09 | 279 | 23,115 | 0.16264 | 0.263488 |
| 1983 | 1,603 | 24,717 | 413 | 7955.289 | 258 | 24,717 | 0.16098 | 0.257692 |
| 1984 | 1,736 | 26,454 | 417 | 17564.8 | 238 | 26,454 | 0.13706 | 0.240143 |
| 1985 | 1,533 | 27,986 | 345 | 8080.082 | 164 | 27,986 | 0.107013 | 0.22512 |
| 1986 | 1,987 | 29,973 | 140 | 4043.091 | 196 | 29,973 | 0.098638 | 0.070456 |
| 1987 | 2,141 | 32,115 | 143 | 3398.456 | 158 | 32,115 | 0.073782 | 0.066777 |
| 1988 | 2,342 | 34,456 | 148 | 6370.645 | 222 | 34,456 | 0.094806 | 0.063204 |
| 1989 | 2,601 | 37,058 | 151 | 13220.51 | 200 | 37,058 | 0.076881 | 0.058045 |
| 1990 | 2,589 | 39,647 | 189 | 7676.106 | 249 | 39,647 | 0.09616 | 0.072989 |
| 1991 | 2,437 | 42,084 | 150 | 1637.646 | 220 | 42,084 | 0.090293 | 0.061563 |
| 1992 | 2,487 | 44,570 | 151 | 1599.663 | 193 | 44,570 | 0.077612 | 0.060723 |
| 1993 | 2,700 | 47,271 | 132 | 1863.957 | 172 | 47,271 | 0.0637 | 0.048886 |
| 1994 | 2,753 | 50,024 | 149 | 2280.333 | 172 | 50,024 | 0.062469 | 0.054115 |
| 1995 | 2,644 | 52,668 | 100 | 2474.153 | 148 | 52,668 | 0.055974 | 0.03782 |
| 1996 | 2,788 | 55,456 | 109 | 2959.566 | 122 | 55,456 | 0.043754 | 0.039092 |
| 1997 | 2,918 | 58,374 | 82 | 821.597 | 124 | 58,374 | 0.042499 | 0.028104 |
| 1998 | 3,084 | 61,459 | 94 | 760.604 | 104 | 61,459 | 0.033718 | 0.030476 |
| 1999 | 3,154 | 64,612 | 87 | 1046.8 | 92 | 64,612 | 0.029172 | 0.027586 |
| 2000 | 3,270 | 67,882 | 77 | 1313.236 | 111 | 67,882 | 0.033947 | 0.023549 |
| Totals | 67,882 | | 8696 | | 8907 | | | |

clear that tankers are typical and that the decline in spill rate is very large as improvements in industry standards and methods have occurred. But the present and ending rates are not zero, and on our prediction never will be using the current HTS. The risk should eventually reduce to about $2.10^{-2}$ per million ton shipped (Mtoe), or about 2% per Mtoe.

For a hypothetical million ton tanker, for each shipping-year (Sy) at 100% usage, this is a >1,000 gallon spill interval of 365 days × 24 hours divided by $2.10^{-2}$, or a risk of one per 438,000 shipping-hours.

## Challenging Zero Defects

Once again, using the data, we can challenge the presumptive goal of zero outcomes, errors, defects and accidents. Now zero spills is still a regulator's goal and desire as shown

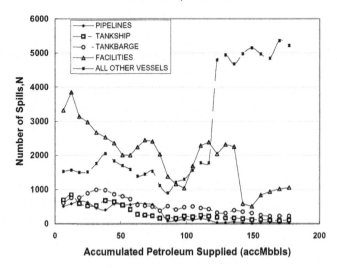

**Figure 8.16.** Number of oil spills for 1973–2000 in the USA

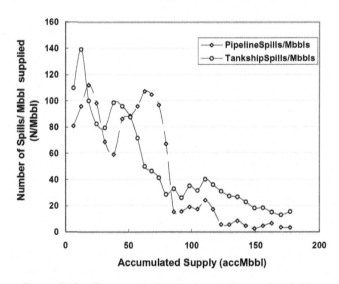

**Figure 8.17.** The rate of oil spills for pipelines and tankships

by this quote from the Report of the USCG Tank Barge Transfer Spills Quality Action Team
[14]:

> *This QAT was commissioned by the Coast Guard-AWO National Quality Steering Committee to
> discover the causes of transfer spills and develop solutions to reduce them. To achieve this end,
> the QAT used a proven methodology to outline vessel loading and discharge processes, analyze*

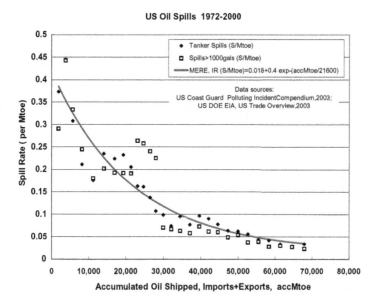

**Figure 8.18.** MERE fit to oil spill data

*available data, summarize the data, and finally, develop root cause diagrams. Through this process, the QAT identified five root causes of transfer spills, and developed comprehensive lists of solutions to address them.*

*The QAT concluded that most transfer spills can be prevented, and that the responsibility for prevention performance falls mainly on the management of marine operating companies. The QAT developed several resources to aid marine companies in reducing spills during transfer operations, including an action register for company management, consisting of comprehensive lists of recommended actions to reduce spills.*

*The QAT believes that the use of these resources will help industry manage toward zero spills.*

Although all accidents and events are preventable, available world data have no evidence to show that this USCG 'zero spill' goal is actually attainable. The learning curves show that regulations should not be focused on 'zero' since that only leads to failure to achieve the goal. Rather, the regulatory pressure should drive reductions in incidents and should force best practices on companies that can reduce their rate of incidents. However, both in fact and in reality, the US EPA was not interested in hearing our presentation on oil spills and declined us an invitation to speak made on our behalf by and for a professional industry gathering. This is typical of organisations that may have preconceived agendas based on unrealistic projections. (See Plate 7)

A far more realistic view and approach is being taken by the Norwegian oil and gas regulator, the Petroleum Safety Authority Norway (PSA), who are responsible for overseeing the safety of many of the massive deep sea platforms operating in the storm-swept North Sea, clearly a high-hazard undertaking. We have recently been made aware of the PSA's newly developed program on 'Risk Indicators', where key measures have been defined for the purposes of tracking and evaluating both *relative* safety improvements in specific areas plus defining an *overall* risk level, with the objective 'to create a reliable decision making platform for industry and authorities' (PSA, 2006) [15]. In a wide-ranging approach to 'measure risk for an entire industrial sector', 21 risk indicators define situations of hazard and accident (called DFUs), covering many known major and minor outcomes. These include:

– Leaks of hydrocarbons and from pipelines,
– Loss of well control,
– Fires and explosions,
– Occupational injuries, illnesses and diving accidents,
– Tanker and supply collisions and helicopter crashes,
– Damage to production platforms and other subsea equipment,
– Safety barrier availability/robustness, and
– Noise and chemical work environment.

Each risk indicator is analysed and assigned an increasing, decreasing, stable or no discernible trend of the observed outcome numbers and/or rates on a calendar year basis. We independently analysed the data using our experience-based DSM to discern the learning trends, and have found an apparent relatively low learning rate. The individual DFU indicators are summed by the NSA with an undisclosed 'weighting factor' to yield a total indicator, which is some perceptual indicator of the overall risk trend. Regarding all the data analysed up to 2006, the PSA conclusion is in fact inconclusive (PSA 2006 report above, section 2.2) [15]:

> All in all, it is not possible to observe any underlying positive trend for the total indicator relating to major accidents . . . the fact that the level of risk remains stable in the same period implies that we have not been able to reduce the loss of life potential in the same way.

As this major effort and the Texas City explosion clearly demonstrate, Zero risk or outcomes are not attainable in the oil and gas sector, one of the world's largest and most important industries. But how does the risk trend compare to other industries?

## Comparison of Oil Spills to Other Industries

The next and final step is to compare to other industries, and to the ULC and the distribution of outcomes. We can see already that learning curves are evident in the spill rate and transportation accident data. This is shown in the Figure 8.19.

It is clear that the oil spills do not follow the same trend as the other aircraft near miss (NMAC) and auto deaths (ATSB) trends that we previously derived in Chapter 3. Recall that this is the non-dimensional variation of outcomes, $J^*$, with depth of experience according to the exponential fit for the simple SEST relative occupation probability,

$$J^* \equiv p_i = \exp - 3.5N^*,$$

Where, $N^*$, is the non-dimensional experience level, $N^* = \varepsilon_i/\varepsilon_j$. A somewhat better fit can be derived, based on the MERE form, which is shown in Figure 8.8.

**Nondimensional Outcome Distribution**

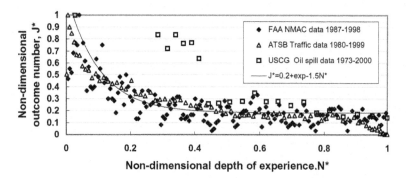

Figure 8.19.   Comparison of oil spills to other industries

**US oil spills compared to the ULC**

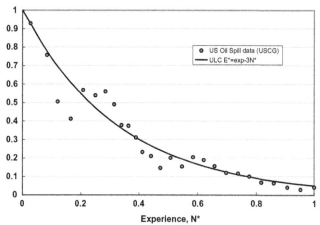

Figure 8.20.   Comparison of IR for oil spills to other data

$$p_i = 0.2 + \exp - 1.5N^*$$

Until we are about 50% of the experience, the number of outcomes is greater for oil spills for a given experience level, and then falls as the other two industries do. The *prediction* is that in the Future, oil spill numbers will continue to decrease, and oil spill risk will be reduced.

Now, the trends and rates for oil spills are also consistent with other world data (namely the ULC) when accumulated experience is considered. This is shown in Figure 8.20 compared to the usual ULC form:

$$E^* = \exp - 3N^*$$

The agreement is very close, suggesting that the rate ($IR$) is indeed of the correct magnitude given the experience, with the typical learning rate constant.

The spill risk is ~0.02 per Mtoe shipped for a nominal 1 Mtoe shipped, this is a spill interval of ~1 in 480,000 hours per ship-year afloat, Sy.

## Predicting the Future: The Probability and Number of Spills

How likely is an oil spill from a ship or tanker? What is the future trend? Can we make a prediction? Will there be less or more spills?

After all, making some predictions was one of the goals of this book, and of all our theories. The final piece of analysis is to determine the probability of a spill, and hence, where we are heading in experience space. The learning curve analysis shows how learning has been occurring, and we may expect a lower *rate* of spills in the future.

Once again, simply for convenience and severity considerations, we focus on the largest shipping spills of over 1,000 gallons in the USCG dataset for 1973–2000. Now, in this category of spills, in our total 27-year observation interval there were $N = \Sigma N_j = 97,645$ total outcomes (or spill events) while shipping, which provides the outcome probability for any $j^{th}$ observation interval. The 222 million gallons spilled while shipping, which gives an average of over 2,000 gallons per spill, similarly provides the total accumulated shipping spill experience, $\varepsilon_M$.

We non-dimensionalise both the number and spill experience to these for each reported $j^{th}$ interval in the USCG dataset to give a probability of any given spill, $p(\varepsilon) = n/N$, for any spill size experience, $\varepsilon/\varepsilon_M$. As we did for the Space shuttles and aircraft crash cases, we can compare this to the calculated MERE probability for any outcome. This probability prediction varies with experience, and for low outcome probabilities is given in Appendix F approximately as:

$$P(n) = \frac{1}{n!}\{p(\varepsilon)\}^n$$

Here $p(\varepsilon)$ is given by the MERE learning 'bathtub' result, so the result becomes:

$$P(n) \approx \frac{1}{n!}\left\{1 - (1 - p(\varepsilon_0))\exp[\{\lambda_m(\varepsilon - \varepsilon_0)\} + \{(\lambda_0 - \lambda_m)/k\}]^{e^{-k(\varepsilon - \varepsilon_0)}}\right\}^n$$

We adopt the 'best' MERE values derived from global data analysis, including the learning rate constant of $k = 3$, which already we know fits the oil spill rate data to the ULC without any adjustment. The result of the calculation mirrors the Shuttle and aircraft analysis case, and is shown in Figure 8.21, which contains the comparison of the risk prediction with the prior data.

Again, assuming and given all the approximations in the analysis, the agreement is remarkable. The comparison and the *prediction* also show that the oil spills are already close to the minimum of the bathtub that, if true, means that we can expect to start climbing out, implying an increased probability of more large spills in the future. Fortunately, the industry is now switching to the use of double-hulled tankers, which should reduce the large spill risk. The

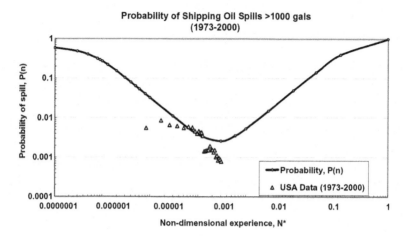

**Figure 8.21.**   The probability of a large oil spill

prediction of the future that is shown here supports such a change in the HTS as a mitigating measure. We also expect the rate to fall as we follow the learning curve.

## Observations On This Oil Spill Case

The learning rate for oil spill outcomes now seems to be comparable with other industries. However, it would be preferable to have the actual shipping-years as an experience measure, and the spill data reported to include the number of ships. It would also be useful to know how much oil was being shipped in and out of the USA, and by how many ships/tankers in total.

It would be useful if one organisation gathered this information, not two or more, and that the outcome data and experience be recorded to allow an experience-based analysis.

We suggest and ask that others look internally into their own, often private, datasets and examine their own status using this type of analysis. Hopefully, the results can eventually be made publicly available, as evidence of learning and incident prevention and reduction. The hope is this will encourage detailed analysis that will lead to more and better ways to record, track, analyse, prevent and predict such accidents and events.

In our most recent work on risk indicator data from Norway (PSA Norway reports) [15, 16, 17] and (Duffey and Skjerve, unpublished) [18], we have shown how the entropy measure can be used to discern trends between different tasks in offshore facilities, and how maintenance and drilling represent the highest risk in the North Sea oil fields.

## Knowing What We Do Not Know: Fear and Managing the Risk of the Unknown

In many instances in life, both managing and taking risks requires planning for unknown disasters and outcomes. We must understand and take into account both what we know and what we do not know about the risk. We must expect the unexpected and anticipate the unanticipated, and be able to respond. This dilemma is crystallised in decision theory and analysis, when we must determine our response, decisions and actions based on both what we do and do not expect to happen.

The need to counter the actions of terrorists and extremists is one recent example of risk caused by the unknown. After the attacks on the World Trade Center, Mayor Rudolph Guiliani of New York made it clear that collectively they did not expect to be attacked in that way: it was an unknown and unanticipated outcome. But because of 'relentless preparation', the emergency services (fire, police, ambulance, security, treatment, transport, etc.) with the direction of the Mayor, were able to stitch together an effective emergency response and command structure from the remnants or pieces of *prior* anticipated (or known) events, capabilities, planning, exercises and knowledge. This is truly what is called Emergency Preparedness in action, when nothing happens according to expectations or plans but the risks of escalation and disaster recovery are still managed. This almost ad hoc risk management strategy was a feature that was apparently absent in the unexpected recent flooding of New Orleans by (known) potential levee failure due to a (known) 'beyond design basis' magnitude Hurricane Katrina. In weather forecasting and meteorology, the accuracy in the prediction of the probability of the formation and landfall of such uncertain hurricanes based on *prior* data is termed a 'degree of skill'.

In risk management, preparedness for the unknown has important connotations for the management and mitigation of risks, all based on the prior or known experience. As pointed out by US Defense Secretary Donald Rumsfeld, 2003 [19] in discussing the potential for terrorist threats, there are actually four logical classes of knowledge about anything that is known or unknown:

1) things we know that we know (Known Knowns, KK);
2) things we know that we do not know (Known Unknowns, KU);
3) things we do not know that we know (Unknown Knowns, UK), and finally,
4) things we do not know that we do not know (Unknown Unknowns, UU).

Design basis and beyond design basis threats, plans and outcomes fall into categories (1) through (3). We either know or do not know, but some aspect of the issue is known even if it is unexpected knowledge. The data are truly 'censored' if we have no record or even knowledge. Thus, in risk terms and in logical thinking, the last category (4) is a particular problem and poses a severe threat. We instinctively fear the unknown.

How can we possibly know anything about what it is we do not know about what we do not know?

This appears to be a hopeless logical paradox of a classic nature. If we knew anything about the unknown, then it is not an unknown but a known! But there is a useful analogy to real events, outcomes and sampling, which we may use to help us out of our apparently logically dead-ended thinking. In our risk terminology, these knowledge issues are all really the probability or likely risks of outcomes and non-outcomes, as we shall see, whether we know it or not. We are entering here the world of 'decision theory' and 'fuzzy logic', where judgements on risk perception and on degree of belief are quantified by statements covering some uncertain *range* of knowledge rather than just by single numbers.

Luckily or not all prior outcomes, just like the Four Echoes, can be considered to be Unknown Unknowns, being actually not known as to their particular (unknown) development and unexpected (unknown) confluence of (unknown) factors until they actually happen. As soon as they happen or are observed they become Known Unknowns.

We actually did not know and had absolutely no idea beforehand what we did not know as to the severe consequences of: debris on the runway for the Concorde; or insulation falling off the Space Shuttle for Columbia; or having power lines near untrimmed trees in Ohio; or turning off the safety systems at Chernobyl. We simply did not know about the unknowns that we did not know were unknown.

We rationalised afterwards, using hindsight, the causes and contributors of the outcome Echoes, effectively turning the unknown into the known by the processes of formal inquiry and detailed investigation. These Unknowns had combined with other later Unknown Unknowns (such as the presence, influence and consequence of tire failure, or damaged re-entry from space, or unintended power overloads, or a rapid power increase on shutdown) on all these very different HTS that were already unknowingly damaged in prior unknown ways. So let us return to and sample the Jar of Life, to see how that analogy might help. We can show how just the same problem is embedded there, but given in and using apparently quite different terminology that we can reconcile with existing probability thinking. If we can somehow illuminate the unknown using the known, we have made an advance.

## White and Black Paradoxes: Known Knowns and Unknown Unknowns

Consider the Knowns and the Unknowns as simply being one of two possibilities: known things (expected outcomes) happen or unknown things (unexpected outcomes) happen. So as we sample the white and black balls from the Jar of Life, we observe the white non-outcomes, which we now call the Known Knowns, KK, because we have seen them. We observe the black ball outcomes, now called the Known Unknowns, KU, since as soon as they have happened, just by happening they cease to be Unknown Unknowns and become Known Unknowns. The other unknowns include the white Unknown Knowns, UK, which are still in the Jar. We do not really know if the Unknown Knowns actually exist since they have not occurred and we cannot see or count them. The others that we do not know anything about are the Unknown Unknowns, UU, which remain such that we have no knowledge about having no knowledge about their existence. We just cannot see what unknowns are still in the Jar. It is like we are in our own physical world, and have no knowledge about other physical worlds that we do not even know if they exist. But we can still speculate or propose that they do exist in what we call an Existence Postulate. (See Figure 8.22.)

As before, we can now ascribe numbers to what we have observed or now know about, and even to what we have not observed and know nothing about. Recalling our analogy to drawing from the Jar of Life, we sample or observe in our observational experience just the Known Unknown outcomes, $n$, from among the many unknown of the (unknown) Unknown ones, $N$, which we have no idea about. We also have observed the sample of Known Knowns, $m$, out of a total number of Unknown Knowns, $M$, which hopefully we may, but perhaps may not record or observe.

So, from what we have experienced so far in sampling the Jar of Life, we know that we can assign numbers to the actually observed Knowns and Unknowns:

**Figure 8.22.**   The Knowns and the Unknowns

$m$ = Known number of Known Knowns

$n$ = Known number of Known Unknowns

So, for any future, assuming only that they exist whether we know or not, for the yet unobserved knowns and unknowns:

$M$ = Unknown number of Unknown Knowns

$N$ = Unknown number of Unknown Unknowns

But as Bernoulli observed long ago, in essentially the same paradox, who can possible know, $N$, the total of the unknown number of unknown equally possible unknown outcomes, $N$? No one knows!

To further aid our thinking, we can create a logic diagram that links sampling from the Jar of Life to the full array or arrangement of possible Knowns (at the top) and Unknowns (on the side) to form a 'Knowledge Matrix'. The possible quadrants[5] or states that illustrate the types are shown as the coloured squares in Table 8.5 as follows:

## The Probability of the Unknowns: Learning from What We Know

This matrix of four options parallels the four quadrants of so-called 'conflicting evidence' (Glenn Shafer, 1976) [20] when considering alternate hypotheses about likelihood and belief.

The purpose of all of this knowledgeable discussion and definition about the known and the unknown is really to show and reiterate that we must learn from what we know. *We can only know what we know we know*, based on our prior experience, however that is defined and measured. The *probability* of an unknown can then be estimated based on that prior

---

[5]The matrix of the Knowns and Unknowns is due to and was actually drawn by Professor David Blockley during an Invited Lecture given at the 29th ESReDA Seminar, JRC, Ispra, Italy, October, 2005, at which one of us (RBD) was present. It is a classic tool for decision making in Win-Win, Win-Lose, Lose-Win, Lose-Lose analysis situations between adversaries or competing choices.

**Table 8.5.**   The Rumsfeld Knowledge Matrix

|  |  | Known | |
|---|---|---|---|
|  |  | Knowns | Unknowns |
| Unknown | Knowns | KK, m | UK, M |
| | Unknowns | KU, n | UU, N |

knowledge. The mathematical and physical relations between these Knowns and the Unknowns can be derived in just the same way as for outcomes and non-outcomes emerging to be observed from or remaining hidden in the Jar of Life. This will give an estimate of our risk of observing or having any number of Known Unknowns, $n$, among all the Known Knowns, $m$, provided the total number of knowns is much larger than the total number of unknowns. This is usually the case (i.e., numerically $m \gg n$ and $M \gg N$) since attacks and sabotage are still comparatively quite rare, at least compared to other everyday risks.

From the LaPlace–Bernoulli definition, we can write the probability of the four known and unknown possibilities formally as:

$$p(K,K) = m/(n+m)$$
$$p(U,K) = M/(M+N)$$
$$p(K,U) = n/(n+m)$$
$$p(U,U) = N/(M+N)$$

For the limit of rare unknowns, $m \gg n$ and $M \gg N$, so $p(U,K) \to M/M \to 1$, a certainty, and $p(U,U) \to N/M \to 0$, or vanishingly small of course. The probabilities are also related through the idea of reliability since the chance an unknown is normalised to happening so that:

$$p(U,U) = 1 - p(U,K)$$
$$p(K,U) = 1 - p(K,K)$$

What if we have had never observed any Unknown outcomes so far? The whole issue is that we must have some knowledge about something in order to estimate the risk, even if it is a rare event (compare to the near constant rate and risk of aircraft crashes). We really would like to know $p(U,U)$, the probability of the Unknown Unknowns so we can do that based on the fact that the first Unknown outcome will still have a probability *if we knew our accumulated experience to date*. This is because for the first Unknown outcome the probability is *always* $p(K,U) = p(U,U) \sim 1/\varepsilon$, in what is known as a 'subjective probability' choice in decision making (S.K. Campbell, 2002 [21]). So we can switch the problem from counting events, which we have not had because they are so few, to estimating a subjective lower-bound probability based on a measure of how much experience we have got away with so far without actually observing an Unknown outcome!

When we have already observed at least n of the Known Unknowns, what then is the risk of our having (observing) the very next Unknown Unknown? It is given by the classic hypergeometric distribution, discussed in Appendix F, of having a given number of sample outcomes (successes). Still given or known must be the sample size, $n + m$, and the number of outcomes, n, and the total population size, $N + M$, with a finite population, where each observation is either an outcome or a non-outcome, and where each subset of a given size is chosen with equal likelihood. The probability of the $n$th Unknown Unknown in any sequence or patterns of the numbers $n$, $m$, $N$ and $M$ of Knowns and Unknowns is then,

$$P(n) \equiv p(\mathrm{U,U}) = \frac{\binom{N}{n}\binom{M}{m}}{\binom{M+N}{m+n}}$$

Of course nice though it would be, we have not obtained something for nothing, as we still have to estimate or guess the total numbers of Unknowns $M$ and $N$, which we do not know. But for the special case of large numbers of Knowns, $M \gg N$, and small probability of Unknowns the result for $p(\mathrm{U,U})$ becomes the surprisingly simple binomial expression, but still includes the prior probability of an Unknown.

## The Existence of the Unknown: Failures in High Reliability Systems

In a sense we are frightened or apprehensive of the unknown because it is unknown, but we may know more about the unknown than we know we know! We have the paradox of a so-called 'high reliability' organisation that has in fact experienced no outcomes. The parallel here is reliability testing of highly reliable equipment, when as desired no failures have occurred so far (in tests or in the field), but an estimate of the failure rate is still needed.

How to put some bound on the unknown failure rate, and hence, on the estimate of probability of failure is an exercise in reasoning about prior knowledge (or lack of it) as well as statistical mathematics. In recent work this high reliability problem has been called 'the case of zero failures' (Coolen, 2006) [22]; (Coolen and Coolen-Schrijner, 2006) [23]. The estimate for the range of the probability of an Unknown Unknown, $p(\mathrm{U,U})$ is given using assumptions on the prior distribution, and deducing a minimum–maximum, or lower and upper bounds from binomial sampling as was used by Bayes himself. The result is obvious and the range of belief is given by:

$$N/(M+N) < p(\mathrm{U,U}) < 1$$

To make some progress we make use of an Existence Postulate. Let us assume, although strictly we do not know, that there will be at least one Unknown Unknown future rare event ($N \sim 1$). When and if it occurs $n = 1$ also, and we can approximate $p(\mathrm{U,U}$ for $n = 1) = 1/\varepsilon$. So we have for the very first Unknown Unknown the risk when and if it occurs given by:

$$P(\mathrm{U,U}) \rightarrow \{1/\varepsilon\}\left\{1-(1/\varepsilon)^{m}\right\}$$

Which is expandable if $m/\varepsilon \ll 1$, to give,

$$P(U,U) \sim \{1/\varepsilon\}\{1 - m(1/\varepsilon) - \ldots\ldots\}$$

Assuming that the number of Known Knowns, m, already observed is proportional to our experience, so $m \propto \varepsilon$, or $m = U\varepsilon$ where U is some unknown constant. So, naturally,

$$P(U,U) \sim \{1/\varepsilon\}\{1 - U - \ldots\}$$

Again, approximating the term in the brackets, for the first Unknown Unknown,

$$P(U,U) \sim (1/\varepsilon)\exp - U$$

Not surprisingly, the more experience the less is the threat of the Unknown!

It is also shown in the Appendix F that given the special case of perfect learning from observing or experiencing the Known Knowns, KK, $m$, as soon as we have just one Known Unknown, KU, $n = 1$, then the subsequent probability drops to zero.

## The Power of Experience: Facing Down the Fear of the Unknown

Having a probability expression is all very well, but still according to this analysis we must:

a) estimate the risk of how many Unknowns we might actually have or expect, assuming that we have a risk of the Unknowns, and
b) manage the risk of future Known and Unknown Unknowns by evaluating the information we have on the prior Known number(s) observed.

So the estimation of the Likelihood is crucial, which we may define and write as corresponding to the equivalent symbolic dependent probability expression:

$$
\begin{aligned}
P(\text{Posterior of an Unknown Unknown}) &= (\text{Prior of a Known Unknown}, p(K,U)) \\
&\quad \times (\text{Likelihood of an Unknown Unknown}, \\
&\quad\quad p(U,U)) \\
&= \{n/(n+m)\} \times \{(1/\varepsilon)\exp - U\}
\end{aligned}
$$

Using the previous arguments, we use the Existence Postulates and assume that:

a) the Unknown Unknowns do exist but are so rare that $N \sim n \sim 1$;
b) as far as we know Knowns exceed Unknowns so $m \gg 1$; and
c) our experience is proportional to the already observed Knowns.

We can then obtain the estimate for knowing the unknowable as

$$P(U,U) \sim (1/U\varepsilon^2)\exp - U$$

This order of magnitude estimate shows a clear trend of the probability decreasing with increasing experience as a power law, $(\varepsilon)^{-2}$. For every factor of 10 increase in experience measured in some tau units, $\tau$, the posterior probability falls by 100 times. This trend is illustrated in the Figure 8.23, where we have taken three arbitrary values for the constant, U,

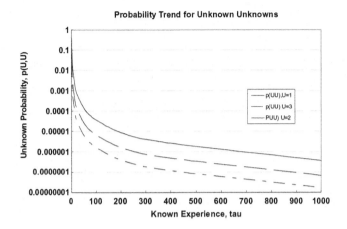

**Figure 8.23.** The power of experience

of 1, 2 and 3 and estimated the resulting magnitude of the posterior probability, $P(U,U)$. But it does not matter if we do not know the exact numbers: the trend is the key for decision making and risk taking. *The rational choice and implication is to trust experience and not to be afraid of the perceived Unknown.*

Of course this result is only an estimate based on postulating that something unknown exists in the unknown future that we do not know about. By assuming we will have an Unknown, and if and only our prior experience base of the Knowns is 'typical', then we have at least some chance of making an educated 'guesstimate' about the trends and magnitude of the posterior chance of observing an Unknown Unknown. After all, we did not expect the prior Unknowns that we have already observed either!

As another attack on this problem, and as a sanity check, we can adopt a uniform (equally possible) distribution of outcomes such that we have the Laplace prior, $p(\text{LaP})$. The logic, derivation and use are discussed extensively by Jaynes [24], who refers to this sampling case as the 'truncated uniform prior'. In that special case, applying the Rule of Succession says the probability of the very next outcome is:

$$p(\text{LaP}) \equiv (n+1)/(N+2)$$

Now we do not know precisely how many outcomes we might have, so for the Unknowns, there are negligible prior outcomes. With little to no experience of Unknowns, then all we know is a range $0 < n < 1$, with perhaps $N \sim 1$ if at most one Unknown Unknown exists or an outcome is even possible.

These estimates for the number of Unknowns and Unknown Unknowns give the potential numerical range for the unknown next outcome probability as

$$1/3 < p(\text{LaP}) < 2/3$$

In our ignorance, without any experience, surprisingly we still have a nearly equal chance of observing an Unknown outcome or not. Also, the limit for the MERE, as experience is small, has $p(\varepsilon) \rightarrow 1 - 1/e \sim 0.63$, which is very near the upper range value of 2/3; and similarly $p(U,U) \sim 0.37$, which is very near the lower range value of 1/3. These values are close enough to the LaPlace result to at least suggest a nearly consistent starting estimate; and clearly only as we gain experience can and will the unknown probability of an Unknown decrease.

If this exercise in logical thinking and paradox is thought of as a little bizarre, it clearly is. But the discussion does show that even when we think we may know nothing, we may know more than we know about the unknown.


## Terrorism, Disasters and Pandemics: Real, Acceptable and Imaginary Risks

Terrorists often practice their attacks too and these are also the non-outcomes (the Unknown Knowns) that we have not seen that contribute to their learning processes about what might actually work to damage an HTS and what might not (the Unknown Unknowns).

Given the role of perception of risk in our thinking, it is no surprise that coverage by the news media of perceived threats also make great headlines and reporting. There are no shortage of great topics with riveting, attention-getting headlines and dramatic pictures:

- Hurricanes flooding cities like New Orleans, and destroying homes;
- Terrorists bombing hotels, buses, markets, subways and tourist resorts;
- Avian ('bird flu') influenza spreading to humans in a giant pandemic;
- Rapid flooding or cooling caused by climate change;
- Meteor impact destroying the world as we know it;
- Masked gunmen assassinating helpless people . . . and so on, and so on.

Since having scary news is also potentially scare mongering, the generally non-technical media reader must be and are generally careful to always have 'experts' on hand. Thus, we have endless interviews with those who represent some related interest, have published or headed some study, lead some organisation or have written a book on some similar topic or title. These are the talking heads who are on hand to rationalise and explain why we should all be fearful, prepared and petrified, or not.

Since the threat of the risk itself is often disruptive to our normal life, and perhaps designed to be, the news and fears are worse than the reality, to you and me. Whether we are fearful, frightened or brave, what should we do? What is a real risk? What is a potential risk, what just a threat? Should we really worry?

What can be ignored is never stated. What is stated cannot be ignored.

How can we place these threats and fears in perspective, and predict and manage our risk? How can we place some context around this fear of the unknown and get on with our lives?

The risk of any of us being killed by a terrorist attack is quite negligible, unless one is in a 'high-risk' area, such as Baghdad. It is simply prudent not to be where the rates and probability of death are high. But even so, terrorists like soft targets, with maximum media exposure, and try to demoralise, panic, frighten and destroy. Thus, the Twin Towers at the World Trade Center had the twin aims of being highly visible and attacking not just soft people targets but *economic* targets (i.e., Wall Street and New York).

Governments and politicians cannot afford to be caught unawares or unprepared by such threats and events. They must show awareness, sensitivity, leadership, fearlessness and foresight. These are hardly the qualities that politicians are best known for. Contingency and Emergency Plans, vaccine production and stocks, vulnerability minimisation plus homeland security must all be put in place, and are all visible and expensive measures that are available 'just in case'. It is what Rudolph Giuliani, the Mayor of New York, known for his management of the aftermath of the 9/11 terrorist attacks on the Twin Towers, characterises as the leadership principle of 'relentless preparation'. Our approach allows the quantification and placing in perspective what has been termed this 'resilience' (see Appendix I) or the ability of an HTS (organisation), including the people within it, to manage risk, and hence, remain stable under stressful and testing times.

## Estimating Personal Risk of Death: Pandemics and Infectious Diseases

When the latest disaster has passed, say the 'deadly' hurricane has gone, it is forgotten, and is simply followed by another apparently equally threat, a new 'deadly' virus or pandemic in the offing. Time, they say, is the greatest healer.

But what is an *acceptable* risk?
How much should we spend on risk prevention versus disaster recovery?
What should we worry about?

The three greatest *voluntary* personal risks in terms of death or injury rates caused by your own actions are well known:

Being at home doing work around the house
Driving to work
Smoking or being overweight

The largest *involuntary* death risk rates caused by just living are also known:

Heart disease
Cancer
Being young

None of the favourite media topics are on the media 'hot list': these are all too mundane, simply everyday risks that we 'accept' as part of living today.

Death rates around the world are known. We like data, so in Figure 8.24 they are shown for 1994 to 1997 for both men and women as a function of the population in some 60 countries. The health data were collected by the UN World Health Organization (WHO) and the population data by the World Bank. We do not expect any bias or sensationalism in the reporting, as these international intergovernmental organisations are not competing for our attention or for advertising revenue.

We plot the death rate per 100,000 versus the country population as some indication of the total experience or sample size.

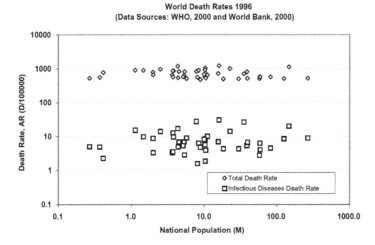

**Figure 8.24.** The world death rates for Europe, Russia and North America

Amazingly, the prior data say that from the USA to the Ukraine, and from Canada to Croatia, there is not much difference in death rates. The death rate is, on average, about 750 per 100,000 and is largely independent of population. That means you or I have, on average, a risk of death of just 0.75%, or a 99.25% chance of living. We will reach a nearly certain 100% chance of death by living to about age 75 when on average we are all dead.

The data also show the same largely invariant risk trend is true for infectious diseases such as influenza, measles, SARs (an old media favourite), malaria, tuberculosis, and West Nile virus (remember that other dreaded and real 'bird disease'? . . .). The death rate is about 8 to 20 per 100,000, or about 10% or so of the total death rate. So the chance is that at least one in 10 of this population will die from an infectious disease, which is already a huge number, whether we have another influenza pandemic or not. Extrapolating to a world population of about 5 billion, and taking a convenient average life span of, say, 50 years, then 100 million people die every year, of which about 10 million die of infectious diseases. Large flu pandemics before have killed a few million people, which is about what we would expect based on our prior experience. Based on that prior knowledge and experience, we could expect the risk of that number of deaths for a cross-species transmission of something like a 'bird flu pandemic'.

We can also compare these risks of death on the basis of what risk we are voluntarily exposed to. So, as we now show, depending on our choices in life, the risk of dying from catching some infectious disease is much more than the risk of hijacking, but of course less than our risk of dying anyway!

The hijacking rate was one in a million flights, or each $3.10^{-7}$ per risk exposure experience hour, assuming one is flying as a choice. However, in a typical lifetime of 75 years or so, you accumulate ~660,000 hours of experience or risk exposure, assuming one is living by choice. In that life interval, you have one and only one chance of dying (a certainty), or on average, one in $1.5 \times 10^{-6}$ per risk exposure hour if uniformly distributed (which is not quite exact as the chance of death is greater when young or old!). So for an infectious disease, from the WHO data, the risk rate is 10 times less or about one in $1.5 \times 10^{-7}$ per risk exposure hour.

The individual risk ratio in any such risk exposure situation is then given by how long we expose ourselves to the risk:

Hijack to Infection risk ratio $=$ (Number of personal flying hours $\times 3 \times 10^{-7}$)$/$
$$\text{(Number of personal infection exposure hours} \times 1.5 \times 10^{-7})$$

So any normal person who spends only a little of their lifetime in airplanes (less than 10 flights of three hours, say), but much of it (more than two hours a day or so) in crowded places for their working and daily life of 200 days a year for 20 years or so where other peoples' diseases are present. The risk ratio is very nearly in the ratio of the exposure times so, for this nominal case, the risk ratio for hijackings to death from infection in a lifetime would be:

$$(10 \times 3 \times 3 \times 10^{-7}/(2 \times 200 \times 20 \times 1.5 \times 10^{-7}) \sim 0.008$$

or at least about 100 times less. So we are much less likely to be hijacked than die from catching an infectious disease! Of course, we may also choose not to fly, or not to be next to others, so the number of hours of actual risk exposure is highly personal.

But this risk of societal-related causes is still 10 times less or negligible compared to the certainty of dying anyway. Now the pessimists may say this prior information does not include a recent pandemic. But it does: the HIV-AIDS pandemic has already caused and is causing many deaths.

Using Bayesian reasoning, let us use the prior information to see what it suggests. The posterior probability per exposure hour is simply our usual expression:

$P(\text{Posterior}) \propto p(\text{Prior}) \times p(\text{Likelihood})$
$= \text{Prior probability of hijacking or of infectious disease} \times \text{Likelihood}$

Even if the chance of a pandemic is a complete and utter certainty, then $p(L) = 1$, and the future risk still cannot be greater than the prior. This is both the strength and the weakness of relying on prior data and information, but what else do we have? We make such risk choices, informed or not, and like it or not every day, based on the implicit belief in the prior experience that we have already acquired. It should not be based on what the media reports as the fear or threat from today's headlines.

We drive to work, we operate electric-powered machines, we climb steps and ladders, we play sports, we cross the street, just like we have always done. We accept these voluntary risks because we and everyone else have to.

This lifestyle or approach to personal risk management is enabled because we do *not* carry risk ratios, comparative risk numbers, cost–benefit estimates, risk exposures or nominal death rates around with us in our heads. We do not consult risk tables before swimming or boating or driving or joining a crowd. Nor do the media or the experts help us to know the risk ratios, despite their best reporting of the headline-making events. These professional risk estimates are impersonal numbers, not obtained from, in or by our own personal experience.

We have no real idea about relative risks except what we have experienced, seen or heard ourselves and since accidents always happen to others, we do not have that experience to use. Those who do suffer personally from accidents may and do often change their risk exposure (behaviour or lifestyle) as a result. But not always.

## Sabotage: Vulnerabilities, Critical Systems and the Reliability of Security Systems

Terrorist attacks are generally viewed as causing unwanted outcomes (attacks and disruption) from external acts made against an HTS. On the other hand, sabotage is a malicious and deliberate attempt to cause damage to an HTS, and is usually viewed as due to an insider, or from an unwanted intruder. Sometimes we have an unexpected situation that apparently does not obey any rules. Thus, sabotage is another human action, executed against an HTS in order to intentionally disable or damage the system. Laying a rock on a railway track is a common event, always caused by trespassers and often by thrill seekers.

The systems under attack may not be hardware but also software, such as a virus infection against a software operating system (by so-called malware).

The *vulnerability* of the HTS to such attacks and damage is the major issue, and so-called *critical systems* have been defined that must be hardened or defended against malicious acts and damage.

Examples of these HTS include facilities such as airports, bridges, electricity distribution, chemical storage tanks, railways, tunnels, pipelines, transport systems and power plants. Obviously, all these cannot be made 'bullet proof' and we cannot eliminate all 'possible' events so they cannot happen. The best idea expressed is to establish the vulnerabilities and then define the recovery mechanisms, processes and actions needed for coping, mitigation and repair of the consequences. This avoids the lack of prior data issue if no attacks have occurred yet, and provides a rationale for defensive measures to be defined when the threat and risk are not estimated.

The act of attack may be premeditated or spontaneous. It may be planned or unplanned. But in any case, sabotage has a probability of an outcome, of success or failure, of drawing a black or white ball. Depending on whether you have the viewpoint of the saboteur or the sabotaged, the black and white colours may be interchanged, and the issue for security and anti-terrorist systems is this paradigm shift. What is a success from one viewpoint is a failure from another, and the learning from experience process could lead to more and more successful attacks. We thus have learning on the part of both the attacker and the attacked, and postulated or actual recovery rates.

The analogy to the MERE is now complete. The rate at which errors and outcomes occur or are detected (attacks are allowed and are successful) is dependent on the learning rate to suppress vulnerabilities, or namely the reliability, especially for rare events. Conversely, the unreliability represents the damage and rate of successful attacks and is a measure of learning by the saboteur or attacker.

Interestingly, there are data to support this somewhat pessimistic but realistic view from our prior knowledge of successful espionage during the 50 years of the Cold War. For example, in the Manhattan project developing nuclear bombs and shortly after, in both the USA and the UK, a few spies infiltrated and leaked nuclear weapons design knowledge to the Russian adversary. This was despite major security, counter-intelligence, surveillance, investigations, background checks, and other unknown detection and human processes. There were several who spied and were caught (the known unknowns). There may be still some who were not caught (the unknown unknowns). Who can say?

## What Is the Risk?

According to our analysis of HTS globally, the established prior minimum outcome rate that can be achieved in and for any known HTS today is about 1 in $5 \times 10^{-6}$ per experience or risk exposure hour. We will never therefore achieve a successful attack rate lower than this for any security or critical system vulnerability, no matter the claim, or for any HTS we have invented or use where human are actively involved

For a normal human being, a risk of $5 \times 10^{-6}$ per experience or risk exposure hour is a minimum attainable risk of an outcome of about once in 23 years of continuous exposure (24 hours/365 days) to any given risk activity. If we expose ourselves to that risk for just eight hours a day, assuming that we sleep, take breaks and eat, it is now once in 70 years, comparable to our lifetime anyway. So society has unconsciously found, purely empirically and subjectively, that an *acceptable risk is one that does not appreciably impact or reduce your individual and very human mortality.*

## The Four Quadrants: Implications of Risk for Safety Management Systems

We need to reconcile the subjective risk perceptions with the objective risk data. We now know how to measure and predict the number of outcomes (the distribution), and the rate of outcomes (the learning curve) with increasing experience. Clearly, now we have defined from our Experience Space a Past, Present and Future comprised of four possibilities. We can now characterise risk based on observed and predicted outcomes, both the Knowns and the Unknowns. This is *not* at all like a Risk Matrix, with a combined display of the probabilities of severity and consequence, but is based on the probabilities of outcome number and rate only. The risk spaces are shown in the Four Risk Quadrant diagram, where we have the rate of outcomes as the vertical (up–down) axis and the number of outcomes as the horizontal (left–right) axis, where the positive sign is increasing and the negative sign is decreasing based on the prior values. (See Figure 8.25.)

The four quadrants are defined by the obvious variations:

DD:  Decreasing rate + Decreasing number of outcomes (minus-minus), with UK
DI:  Decreasing rate + Increasing number of outcomes (minus-plus), with UU
II:   Increasing rate + Increasing number of outcomes (plus-plus), with KU
ID:  Increasing rate + Decreasing number of outcomes (plus-minus), with KK

A clear distinction exists between the DD quadrant, which shows Learning and is Low Risk, because only the Knowns are unknown, from the II quadrant, which is High Risk (see the diagram) due to Forgetting, and the Unknowns are known and occurring. The other two quadrants are now associated with risk perception, and may contain some learning. The DI quadrant is defined here as a Perceived Risk, because it contains the Unknown Unknowns

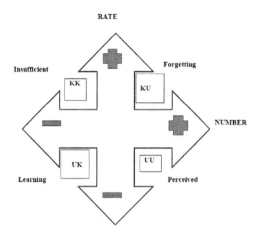

**Figure 8.25.**   The Four Risk Quadrants: perceptions and realities

we know nothing about and fear, and have not happened; and the ID quadrant which has an Insufficient Learning Risk, since we have only Known knowns and no Unknowns to learn from.

The special case of rare events or first outcomes fall in the DI quadrant and is where the Unknown Unknowns are hidden. The rare event rate is ~$n/\varepsilon$ always, and is nearly constant with the paradox of an increased number of outcomes, and a reducing rate without any apparent reduction due to learning. Rare events are then a perceived risk, perhaps precisely because we have no prior information or data, and are largely an unknown risk with no evidence of learning.

Based on all the HTS we have examined to date, we could allocate them to the Quadrants. The Risk Quadrants are a simple working classification of risks, without any appeal to anything other than learning trends.

The speculation that follows is clear: when it comes to risk perception, humans think and act more in response to the number of outcomes (How many? How much?), than to the rate of outcomes (How often? How fast?). We decide our risk based on what we have learnt from our experience, and extrapolate that past linearly into the expected future to deal and confront the unknown future. We make instantaneous judgements based on our depth of experience, and discern the 'right' patterns and order from the randomness that is characterised and measured by the information entropy. We then hopefully correct ourselves if we were or are wrong. This idea contrasts nicely with the subjective assessment of risk using the widespread 'Blink' view that our instant judgements of people and situations are usually correct. This cannot apply unless learning is occurring. Only if we have experience and prior knowledge can we trust to instinct only, and we allow learning to occur. We must filter the signals from all the noise, using past experience and present knowledge to help and hopefully make the 'right' logical choices, and suitably and continuously modifying our knowledge, judgements and actions as we go. As a result, without experience and correction, we can make snap judgements on risk – and quickly reach the wrong conclusions.

**380**
Managing Risk: The Human Element

# References

[1] Josephson, R.K., 1968, 'Functional components of systems controlling behavior in some primitive animals', p. 246 in Systems Theory and Biology, Ed. M.D. Mesarovic, Springer-Verlag, New York.

[2] Moore, P.G., 1983, 'The Business of Risk', Cambridge University Press, p. 152.

[3] Tor Norretranders, 1991, 'The User Illusion: Cutting consciousness Down to Size', Penguin Books, London, UK, p. 290.

[4] Pierce, J.R., 1980, 'An Introduction to Information Theory', Dover, New York.

[5] Proctor, R.W. and Dutta, A., 1995, 'Skill Acquisition and Human Performance', Sage Publications, Thousand Oaks, CA, Chapter 3, pp. 72–75.

[6] Stellan Ohlsson, 'Learning from Performance Errors', Psychological Review, 1996, Vol. 103, No. 2, 241–262.

[7] Heathcote, A., Brown, S. and Mewhort, D.J.K., 2000, 'The Power Law Repealed: The Case for an Exponential Law of Practice', Psychonomic Bulletin and Review, 7, 2, pp. 185–207.

[8] UK Department for Transport (DfT), 2004, 'The Future of Transport: A Network for 2030', Presented to Parliament by the Secretary of State for Transport by Command of Her Majesty, HMSO, Chapter 4 Transforming our Railways, July (Available: http://www.dft.gov.uk/about/strategy/whitepapers/fot/).

[9] Duffey, R.B. and Saull, J.W., 2002, 'Underground coal mine safety – worldwide trends and learning curves in fatal accidents and injuries', Journal of Mines, Metals & Fuels, Mining Industry Annual Review for 2002, India, December, pp. 424–429 and 438. Editor: Prof. Ajoy Kumar Ghose; Publisher: books@satyam.net.in.

[10] US Department of Labor, 2001, Mine Safety and Health Administration (MSHA), 'Statistics: Historical Data', http//www.msha.gov/STATS/PART50/WQ/1931/.

[11] Duffey, R.B., Saull, J.W. and Myers, P., 2004, 'Learning from Experience: Application to the Analysis of Pipeline and Storage Tank Safety Data and Potential Spill Reduction', Presentation given at National Institute for Storage Tank Management's 7th Annual International Conference in Orlando, Florida, 12-14 May.

[12] US National Oceanic and Atmospheric Administration (NOAA), 1992, 'Summaries of Significant US and International Oil Spills, 1967–1991', NOAA Hazardous Materials Response and Assessment Division, Report No, HMRAD 92-11, September, Washington, DC.

[13] US DOT, 2003, Office of Pipeline Safety – 'Hazardous Liquid Pipeline Operators Accident Summary Statistics by Year', 1/1/1986, 30 June (Available: http://ops.dot.gov/stats/lq_sum.htm).

[14] United States Coast Guard, 2004, data source at http://www.uscg.mil/hq/gm/nmc/ptp/awoweb/abstracts/tbts.htm http://www.uscg.mil/d14/units/msohono/spill/spill.htm#_Toc410196452.

[15] Petroleum Safety Authority Norway (PSA), 2006, 'Trends in Risk Levels: Summary Report Norwegian Continental Shelf, Phase 7 – 2006', Report Ptil-07-03, Stavanger, June, 2007, available with the reports for 2000–2005 at http://www.PSA.no/rnns).

[16] Petroleum Safety Authority Norway (PSA), 2003, 'Trends in risk levels – Norwegian Continental Shelf, Summary Report, Phase 4 – 2003' Ptil-04-04, p. 11, Norway.

[17] Petroleum Safety Authority Norway (PSA), 2007, 'Supervision and Facts', Annual Report 2006, Stavanger, Norway, 26 April (Available: www.ptil.no).

[18] Duffey, R.B. and Skjerve, A.-B., 2008, 'Risk Trends, Indicators and Learning Rates: A New Case Study of North Sea Oil and Gas,' Proc. ESREL 2008 and 17th SRA Europe Annual conference, Valencia, Spain, 22–25 September.

[19] Rumsfeld, Donald, 2003, US Defense Secretary.

[20] Shafer, G., 1976, 'The Theory of Evidence', Princeton University Press, NJ, p. 82.

[21] Campbell, S.K., 2002, 'Flaws and Fallacies in Statistical Thinking', Dover, New York.

[22] Coolen, F.P.A., 2006, 'On probabilistic safety assessment in the case of zero failures', Proceedings, Institution of Mechanical Engineers, Part O, J. Risk and Reliability, Vol. 220, No. 2, pp. 105–114.

[23] Coolen, F.P.A. and Coolen-Schrijner, P., 2006, 'On zero-failure testing for Bayesian high-reliability demonstration', Proceedings, Institution of Mechanical Engineers, Part O, J. Risk and Reliability, Vol. 220, No. 1, pp. 35–44.

[24] Jaynes, E.T., 2003, 'Probability Theory: The Logic of Science', First Edition, Cambridge University Press, Cambridge, UK, Edited by G.L. Bretthorst.

# 9

# I Must Be Learning

*'It is time to turn our thoughts to another branch of this subject: I mean, to cases where an experiment has sometimes succeeded and sometimes failed.'*

Thomas Bayes, 1763

## Where We Have Come From

The above Chapter title is also paraphrased in the lyric of the rock band Queen's 'The Show Must Go On', a haunting reflection on what it takes to continue the show that life demands, even when the stresses and strains are great.

No matter what we experience, unless we give up, we must just go on. So it is with technology, with human progress, with learning and with life itself. So it is with the work we have presented here. To address Bayes' question, how well have we succeeded or failed in our experiment of trying to make sensible risk predictions? In our studies, we have often been faced with either opposition or support, from colleagues, professionals, institutions, agencies and people. We have all experienced such mixed reactions in both our personal and professional lives.

The opposition is in the form of indifference, inertia, rejection, or worse, silence. Any objection, excuse or foot dragging is possible. These critics and naysayers are usually those with vested interests, fixed positions, faded paradigms and management controls that all inhibit learning – their minds are closed to innovative thinking. As one industrial expert remarked, why would management change their existing, well-established and expensive DINO system? (DINO being the acronym 'Data In, Nothing Out'.)

On the other, brighter side, the enlightened and the inquisitive have helped with positive critiques, and have used what we have proposed and developed in the quest to reinforce safety efforts, with no fixed or predetermined position to defend. Their learning and thinking is positive and challenging – their minds are open.

Naturally, we would like to favour and only communicate with the second group, and ignore the first. But we cannot! Those in the first or more resisting position presumably have a high probability of failure: the second or more accepting group likely has a dramatically higher probability of success.

---

*Managing Risk: The Human Element*   Romney B. Duffey and John W. Saull

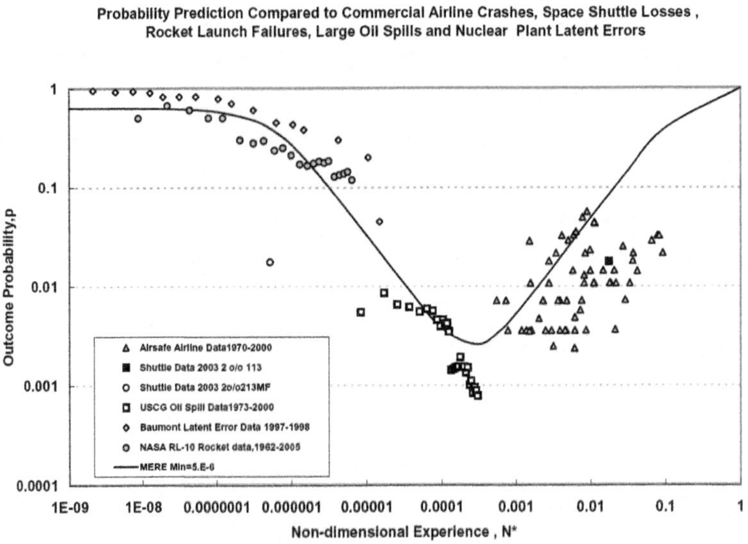

Probability Prediction Compared to Commercial Airline Crashes, Space Shuttle Losses ,
Rocket Launch Failures, Large Oil Spills and Nuclear Plant Latent Errors

**Figure 9.1.** The human bathtub as a prediction of the probability of an outcome as we gain experience

If we are truly learning from our mistakes, the first group is the one that really needs help, communication and change, not the second.

The first group is really the challenging one and is where safety management has been institutionalised to the point where it must be right, simply because we are doing it that way, always have and/or always will. Until the next change is imposed, somehow by someone, or until the next outcome occurs, sometime, as it undoubtedly will.

In this book, we have come a long way in our journey through the risky outcomes of the world, through death, destruction, accidents, tragedies, fires, floods, collisions, business risks and financial speculation. (See Figure 9.1.) But as we are reminded by a great explorer:

> *No, it is not the goal but the way there that matters, and the harder the way the more worthwhile the journey.*

> Source: *Wilfred Thesiger, 1959, in 'Arabian Sands'.*

## What We Have Learned

We do *not* have to concern ourselves with learning from the myriad of different types of errors or individual experiences; or with the details of the multitude of learning processes involved in skill acquisition and problem solving; or examine the detailed deliberations to learn about root cause and assignment of blame. Instead, we are concerned with explaining and managing the risk from the entire integrated and inseparable improvement and development of modern technological society. We have focused on the prediction of the outcomes and disasters, successes and failures, gains and losses emerging from the entire set of systems that we all use and operate within, using the existing data, examples and new ideas.

We can relate the learning behaviour of individuals in a system to the observed behaviour of the system, or collective, as a whole. Learning constitutes the creation of order from disorder, by the processes of acquiring rules, knowledge and skills from experience. The individual learning process, and the innumerable chaotic interactions between individuals, produces and results in the observed systematic trends and patterns at both the individual and the organisational levels. These external events, although apparently random in occurrence, are characterised by the unconscious behaviours and organisational culture that produce the conscious outcomes, both good and bad. We observe externally the patterns that result from the learned internal decision-making processes, where the outcomes represent the integral response of the entire system to the combination of the individual sequences, actions, errors, interactions and behaviours that occur internally, both in the system and the individual processes, whatever they may be. In that sense, the individuals and the system are inseparable – one affects the other. The fundamental premise is that the innumerable individual learning interactions are random and statistical, the distribution of which then surprisingly results in the systematic observed outcome trend, being the collective learning curve. As a result, we have shown that the individual Universal Practice Curve (UPC) for repetitive tasks exactly follows the Universal Learning Curve (ULC) form. Hence, the system learning trends reflect exactly the individual learning trends.

Therefore, at both the collective and individual levels, we can interrelate the system and individual behaviours using the mathematical concepts of probability. The number and distribution of outcomes already consciously observed (the numbering, patterns, trends and order of outcomes that we might actually observe) relate to the cognitive concepts of unconscious learning based on our prior knowledge of those very same outcomes (the patterns, beliefs, rules and interpretations that we use to actually decide). The statistical fluctuations, complexity or disorder, caused by random errors at the individual (human) level, are manifested as dynamic learning patterns, or order, in the observed outcomes at the system (technological) level. This is in accord with and analogous to the scientific idea of non-equilibrium fluctuations bringing 'order out of chaos' (Prigogine and Stengers, 1984) [1]. The analogy stated here is between the microscopic fluctuations representing disorder and complexity, and the emergent macroscopic patterns representing the resultant emergence of order and structure via the systematic distributions that are observed as a result of learning. So we have a statistical relation between the indescribable, unknown and multitudinous interactions between and among humans in a collective in their everyday existence, which manifests itself as an observed and known distribution of the overall collective organisational 'learning curve' behaviour (cf. Prigogine and Stengers' termite nest-building analogy).

The complexity of the interactions is measured by the numbers of possible combinations, which are myriad and unknown, and is characterised by the Information Entropy (or $H$-factor). The individuals posses knowledge, experience and skills that are affecting the distribution of outcomes as a function of experience. Here experience is an operator on time, providing the 'frame of reference' in which learning by interaction and from outcomes occurs. To proceed and utilise that measure of risk, we must determine the probability of the outcomes. We must measure what we manage. The measure is then the Information Entropy, $H$, the Uncertainty that is the very opposite or complement of Certainty. The uncertainty in the outcomes is a direct measure of the risk and is given by the degree of order observed as the depth of experience changes. As a result, for individuals, we have shown that the individual decision making (as measured by response time testing) follows the Hick–Hyman Information Entropy form. Hence, the system trends and distributions (that govern the 'culture') also reflect exactly the individual trends (that govern the 'responses').

For our experience in this book, we started out with the Four Echoes, which included the Space Shuttle losses, the great Northeast power blackout, the crash of the supersonic *Concorde* aircraft, and the explosion of the Chernobyl reactor. We worked our way through the risks due to the human actions and reactions embedded within all homo-technological systems (HTSs), ultimately ending with large oil spills at sea. Paying due homage to the pioneers of probability thinking, we adapted the techniques and approaches of statistics and engineering to *predict* the dynamic reliability of HTS as we gain experience.

We found out that we are only human, learning as we go. Faced on our way with the enigmas of predicting when risk would emerge from the Jar of Life, we recreated the ULC, and turned this into a dynamic risk probability curve, which we called the Human Bathtub. This analysis provides a rigorous basis for quantifying and applying the concept of organisational learning to Safety Management Systems (SMS), by determining where any organisation or technology exists on the learning curve. When we learn from all the non-outcomes, as exemplified by near misses and/or unreported non-events, the ideal case of Perfect Learning follows exactly the same learning path. The result of the 'Human Bathtub' risk curve is that we fall into it as we learn, and ultimately climb out of it again as we are eventually doomed to have an event. We have slowly filled the bathtub with data as we gained the predictive power! We have found and examined a global span of apparently disparate outcome data and reduced it to a common basis. In Figure 9.1, we show the summary comparison of data to our predictions of the probability based on learning. The actual commonalities of the causes, the importance of experience, the trend in the probability prediction, and of the fundamental need for a learning approach are all self-evident and clear.

To explain the fluctuations and uncertainties in the outcomes we observe, we invented Experience Space, and adapted the approaches used in statistical mechanics to describe the distribution of error states and outcomes with depth of experience. As a direct result, we also discovered that we had ESP, the Experience Shaping Parameter.[1]

We found out how to make predictions. We showed how to calculate the probability of the risk of any homo-technological outcome as we gain experience and how to make a *risk prediction* about the future chance of an event based on our prior history. We tried to show how to apply these probability concepts while still trying to avoid the controversies and pitfalls of statistical theory and logical inference. We used the intuitions derived from existing statistical and Bayesian ideas to establish a method to predict the likelihood of future risks, based on our prior knowledge of the frequency of the past risks.

We determined the objective measure for risk. The random and unpredictable nature of risks and outcomes we actually then were able to turn to our advantage. It turns out that a statistical Error State model approach produces results in accord with psychological theories of how humans learn and take decisions using error correction and the mental processing of complexity. In particular, we found a rational basis for the Learning Hypothesis for the entire HTS as being consistent with Ohlsson's Theory of Error Correction for individuals. The Information Entropy then provides an objective measure of complexity, and hence, also links human learning and error reduction at the individual level with the reduction of outcomes observed for the collective of total systems, and is also consistent with unconscious reduction in complexity with increasing depth of experience. We showed that the information embedded

---

[1] We can also speculate that these distributions are reflected in the actual neural connectivity in the human brain, which is of major importance in present day 'cognitive psychology' and relevant to the establishment and understanding of rule-based and learning behaviour.

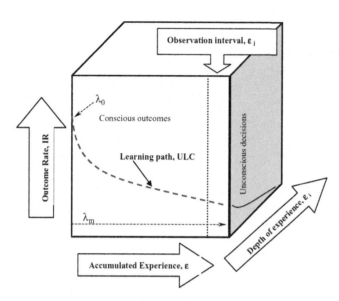

**Figure 9.2.** The concept of Experience Space, where we consciously track down the emergent learning curve as we unconsciously process information entropy to reduce complexity in order to make decisions

in the prior knowledge or observed history is, in fact, the well-known Information Entropy, the $H$-factor, that enables us also to actually *quantify* the meaning of the management concept of a Safety Culture. The function of corporate and safety management is then simply to create order from disorder, which is precisely what all humans do in decision making. The $H$-factor provides a unique measure of and for organisational learning, for safety and management systems effectiveness, as well as providing a new criterion for organisational stability.

We learned a little about how humans make a lot of decisions. Quite incidentally, we have learned that the reduction in the risk of macroscopic outcomes that are *consciously* observed for whole systems is due to the reduction of complexity that is inherent in *unconscious* human decision making. Thus, in Figure 9.2, we can illustrate this insight using the cube of Experience Space. We simply indicate 'Conscious outcomes' on the face surface as we gain experience by progressing down the learning curve; and we write 'Unconscious decisions' on the slice of the actual observational depth that contains the outcome distribution. This representation and illustration brings both pictorial and physical meaning to Tor Norretranders' rather oblique and somewhat obscure statement that for humans 'consciousness is depth experienced as surface'.

We found that systems actually, and perhaps not surprisingly, depend on the humans within them. The unexpected bonus is that apparently the risks of outcomes from modern HTS actually reflect the way in which the individuals within them behave, interact, correct their mistakes and process information. We manage risk in corporations and businesses very much like we manage ourselves, truly integrating human decision making and risk taking. We also have found out, almost coincidentally, that the very same systematic learning processes are hard at work in the apparently chaotic world of the competitive marketplace. As a result, the learning concept thus unifies the apparently disparate fields of safety, financial risk, industrial productivity and stock market portfolio management with the forces inherent in human decision making and risk taking.

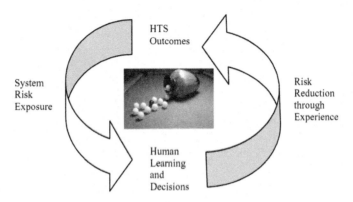

**Figure 9.3.**   Managing risk: completing the learning

The use of Experience Space is founded on explaining the trends in the risk of outcomes that we observe in our real and everyday technological world. This whole concept of Experience Space and of the Learning Path is based on the most likely distribution of the observed outcomes for entire HTS due to the learning process. Such ideas are precisely reflected in the key role of experience in the unconscious mental processing of complexity, which then causes the conscious outcomes we actually observe as the individual behaviours of learning and decision making. We have completed the endless learning circle (Figure 9.3) and found out how to manage risk, including our perception of risk.

*The system risk is the human: and the human risk is the system.*

## What We Have Shown

During this learning process and journey, we have managed to relate and show the essential unity and interrelationship of a whole range of apparently unrelated topics and ideas. In fact, previously, these have been considered almost as separate technical disciplines. Several of these are very well known concepts in the diverse fields of science, economics, government, statistics, psychology and engineering, so the linkages are fundamentally important.

The Learning Hypothesis is consistent with models of human skill acquisition in Psychology, and hence, with the Theory of Error Correction expounded by Ohlsson [see Introduction and Chapter 1].

The phases that all major events go through are essentially similar; and all involve the inextricably interwoven and inseparable involvement of humans with the modern technological system in their integrated decision making, judgement and experience [see Chapter 2].

No matter what system we examined, predictions based on the observed prior information and events inevitably have significant uncertainty, and illustrate clearly the key role of learning from experience, at both the individual and system levels [see Chapter 3].

We related the reduced probability of risk as directly resulting from learning from errors, analogous to the essential role of failure leading to success in Engineering, as pioneered by Petroski [see Chapter 4].

We established that the random nature of the outcomes could be treated by the approaches established in the classic analyses in Physics originated by Boltzman. The randomness we observe in system outcomes as we gain experience constitutes information entropy, consistent with the statistical concepts in Communication theory of Shannon [see Chapter 5].

We found that information and learning produces the systematic trends related to price and cost variations in competitive markets, as also exemplified by the well-known risk modelling in Economics of stock portfolios according to the well-known Black–Scholes relation [see Chapter 6].

The extension of these findings to the quantification of safety management is explored, and we found that the information entropy explains the trends in learning behaviour, and the emergence of patterns at both the system and the individual level, analogous to Prigogine's non-equilibrium thermodynamic analyses [see Chapter 7].

Since the human response is dependent on the information entropy, this explains the relationship in Psychology of the response-time variation for human learning in repeated trials, as embodied in the Hick–Hyman correlation. Because the probability of risk due to future or possible unknowns is related to prior outcomes, it appears in Government via the defense and terrorism considerations and risk conundrums of facing the 'unknown unknowns' posed by Rumsfeld [see Chapter 8].

The prediction of the probability of outcomes and of the future risk when learning can be evaluated using the classic ideas of Statistics, as eloquently expounded by Jaynes and others [see Chapters 1, 4, 5, 6 and 8].

In order to improve, to innovate, to profit, to gain skill, to reduce cost, to go faster, to build better, to anticipate problems, or just to correct simple or known mistakes, involves going beyond existing knowledge. At both the individual and the collective system levels, the process of learning by trial and error proceeds, in our own actions and reactions, and in our technological system designs and structures. In a reflection of human development, in order to progress, change or advance we must experiment and go beyond what we know now that does or does not work, to try or to acquire something new or better.

Paradoxically, to improve we must risk making the very mistakes we really want to avoid.

Learning is then itself a risk. Managing that risk requires the ability to predict what is likely or probable to happen as a result of our own learning, using our experience to anticipate, bound and understand what the resulting future holds.

## Legal, Professional and Corporate Implications for the Individual

We have learned that predicting outcomes, and the probability of success, failure or risk, is not just an academic or impersonal exercise. It can have very real consequences, implications and highly personal outcomes for us, the individuals within any HTS, and for its management. The risk of death, wealth or health can all be involved. The importance of our new learning concepts and ideas, and how we should be improving and learning, is that they form a logical, documented and manageable basis for demonstrating improvement and due diligence, not only personally, but also professionally and managerially. In today's legalistic and litigatious world, this approach to learning is the only sure way for corporations, managers and organisational governance to demonstrate that they are undertaking responsible actions, using due care and pursuing the relentless intention to improve. The risk must be managed.

At legal stake may not only be reputations, but also probability of cause and consequence. The balance of the probabilities must be determined to assign liability. Money (awards and legal costs) can be at stake, too, and probable allocation of damages.

We can illustrate the highly personal and important legal nature of these apparently impersonal probabilities. A patient recently brought a legal case over a delay in medical treatment (perhaps causing a greater chance of death) for a misdiagnosed cancer with originally a roughly equal chance of recovery (50:50 or 50%) as expertly derived from prior data. The questions for the law to consider included whether the facts constituted a reasonable basis for cause and damages due to: negligence on the part of the physician; unnecessary pain and suffering beyond that to be expected anyway from treatment and disease; and/or loss of life expectancy, even though the patient then still survived against the steeply declining odds. So here we have the probability of future personal survival depending and conditional on past wrong decisions resulting in a probably incomplete treatment that itself is likely to have changed both the past and future chances of risk based on the prior data. Independent of the details and outcome of this fascinating case, in the written judgement, the most senior UK Judges made the following profound observations about the legal role of predictions of the future based on the past knowledge (note: underline emphasis added):

*As to what constitutes proof, traditionally the common law has drawn a distinction between proof of past facts and proof of future prospects. A happening in the past either occurred or it did not. Whether an event happened in the past is a matter to be established in civil cases on the balance of <u>probability</u>. If an event probably happened no discount is made for the possibility it did not.*

*Proof of future possibilities is approached differently. Whether an event will happen in the future calls for an assessment of the <u>likelihood</u> of that event happening, because no one knows for certain what will happen in the future.*

*This distinction between past and future is applied also when deciding what would have happened in the past or future but for a past happening such as the defendant's negligent act. What would have happened in the past but for something which happened in the past is, at least generally, a question decided by the courts on the all-or-nothing basis of the balance of probability. On this the authorities are not altogether consistent, but this seems to be the generally accepted practice. In contrast, what would have happened in the future but for something which happened in the past calls for an assessment of likelihood . . . .*

*The role of the court in making an assessment of damages which depends upon its view as to what will be and what would have been is to be contrasted with its ordinary function in civil actions of determining what was. <u>In determining what did happen in the past a court decides on the balance of probabilities.</u> Anything that is more probable than not it treats as certain. But in assessing damages which depend upon its view as to what will happen in the future or would have happened in the future if something had not happened in the past, <u>the court must make an estimate as to what are the chances that a particular thing will or would have happened and reflect those chances,</u> whether they are more or less than even, in the amount of damages it awards.*

*This sharp distinction between past events and future possibilities is open to criticism. Whether an event occurred in the past can be every bit as uncertain as whether an event is likely to occur in the future. But by and large this established distinction works well enough. It has a comfortable simplicity which accords with everyday experience of the difference between knowing what happened in the past and forecasting what may happen in the future . . . .*

*There is no inherent uncertainty about what caused something to happen in the past or about whether something which happened in the past will cause something to happen in the future.*

*Everything is determined by causality. What we lack is knowledge and the law deals with lack of knowledge by the concept of the burden of proof.'*
Source: *House of Lords, Session 2004–05, 2005, UKHL 2, on appeal from: [2002] EWCA civ 1471, Opinions of the Lords of Appeal for Judgment in the Cause, Gregg (FC) (Appellant) v. Scott (Respondent), on Thursday, 27 January 2005, reproduced by Parliamentary License.*

All this legal argument is totally consistent with the methods and ideas developed and taken in this book. The approach to judgement fits precisely with the concepts of prior knowledge about outcomes and non-outcomes that determine the past probability; and with how to inform the estimate of the future likelihood. But it also is clear that such legal definitions, arguments and implications are not just confined simply to medical cases or potential professional negligence. This probability type of argument, and the distinction between how the past influences the future, holds for *any* activity, decision, process or action where the correct thing was not done, or was delayed in the past and then caused possible future harm or increased risk. Therefore, it is reasonable, prudent and just to estimate the likelihood of the future risk. The possibilities are based on the knowledge and the causal influences of the past events including the elements of human choice and actions. The uncertainty is translated into practical proof based on possible probability.

We believe that the recommended course of action naturally includes using the past learning opportunities; and underlines the essential role of prior experience in assessing and managing the future risk likelihood or chance. The knowledge of the probable Past is coupled to the likely unknown Future.

## Just Give Me the Facts

From when we started out, we have learned the following, which we present as a list of Facts, or in media terminology 'factoids':

*Humans and Machines*

- The human is inseparable from the technological system.
- Outcomes with human involvement share the same four phases.
- All outcomes are preventable, but only afterwards.
- Procedures, rules, laws, regulations and punishments do not stop outcomes.
- We can predict nothing unless we learn.
- Media reporting can distort our judgement and risk perception.

*Learning and Risk Reduction*

- Humans learn from their mistakes.
- There is a learning curve that we all follow, like it or not say the data.
- The learning hypothesis agrees with the data, as far as we know.
- The rate of outcomes falls off exponentially with experience, if we are learning.
- We can predict where we are on the ULC but only if we measure.
- The learning 'constant' has a universal value, but of unknown origin.
- The learning model also works in the marketplace of competition for cost reduction and sales.

*Safety Goals and Safety Management*

- The lowest achievable rate of errors is finite, so (regrettably) there are no zero defects.
- The usual data reporting by calendar year time does not uniquely reveal learning.
- The lowest achievable rate of outcomes is universal, about one every 200,000 hours, but we do not really know why
- By using a learning environment, we can manage to reduce our risk by about a factor of five with experience.
- The role of safety management is to create order out of disorder.
- The key to risk reduction is sustaining a learning environment.
- Organisational stability, and hence resilience, are predictable.
- The measure of safety culture and organisational safety is the information entropy.

*Training, Experience and Risk Reduction*

- Training is vital to substantiating sound experience.
- Everything depends on our experience and we must track that.
- Risk is determined by our rate of making mistakes and by our prior knowledge.
- Outcomes occur or are observed randomly, but follow a pattern with learning.
- Depth of experience matters and can be measured.
- We observe outcomes as just a sample of the whole world of outcomes.
- The maximum likelihood or minimum risk is when we follow the learning curve.
- Perception of risk is coupled to numbers of outcomes, not rates.
- Technological change does not necessarily obviate the outcomes due to the human element.

*Predictions and Insights*

- The human error probability is shaped like a bathtub, falling and then rising.
- Statistical theory can really help us understand outcomes we observe.
- Experience (performance) shaping parameters are real and exist.
- Non-outcomes are as important as outcomes for reducing risk.
- Perfect learning follows the same risk-reducing learning trend.
- The maximum risk is at minimum experience.
- The risk decreases with increased experience before ultimately increasing.
- The likelihood of future events is quantifiable.

## Where We are Going

Nothing will change unless we make it change.

We believe the ideas presented here should and can be used by industry, owners, workers, operators, managers, experts, investors and regulators to better manage their risk, and the risk of the other humans involved.

We need to *demonstrate* that we know where we are and that we are: (See Figure 9.4)

a) learning,
b) reducing outcomes and risk as fast as we can,

c) measuring and recording the right information, and

d) using prior experience as a guide.

Today, in all our modern HTS, this is not true.

Our new models, ideas and theories are all very well for now, and may even last a little while. Hopefully, they will cause others to pause and think, and to improve safety. The MERE, SEST and ULC are fine ideas, and are useful, lasting and provocative concepts. The concept of Information Entropy, the $H$-factor, is helpful and links outcomes to many fields and multiple uses.

But there has to be a better theory, a more refined approach, a more exact treatment out there, just waiting to be discovered. Predicting and preventing the next outcome is what it is all about. Someone, somewhere should develop that thought.

We must manage our risk today: and predict our risk tomorrow.

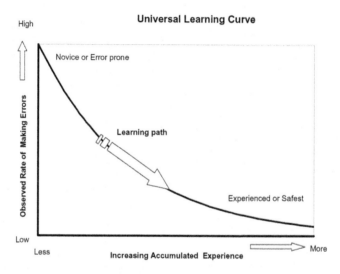

**Figure 9.4.** Universal Learning Curve

# Reference

[1] Prigogine, I. and Stengers, I., 1984, 'Order from Chaos: Man's New Dialog with Nature', Shambhala Publications, Boulder, CO, p. 287.

# Nomenclature (second or multiple usage, if any, after semicolon)

## Symbols

| | |
|---|---|
| $a$ | constant in fitted (distribution) curves |
| $A$ | outcome occurrence rate, $dn/d\varepsilon$ |
| $A,B,C$ | constants in laws of practice |
| acc | accumulated value of experience parameter |
| $b$ | elasticity exponent for cost or price, or fitting constant |
| $B$ | market share constant; |
| $c$ | exponent in law of practice |
| $C$ | specific cost |
| $CC$ | constant cost |
| $^{N}C_{n}$ | number of combinations of N total outcomes observed as n outcomes, n < N |
| $D$ | development cost |
| Dy | driver-years |
| exp | exponential function, e |
| $E^{*}$ | non-dimensional error rate |
| $f(\varepsilon)$ | probability density function, PDF , from the differential $dp(\varepsilon)/d\varepsilon$ |
| $F$ | annual rate of outcomes, $dn/dy$; or event frequency |
| $F(\varepsilon)$ | failure fraction, $n/N$, the cumulative probability distribution function, CDF, link with above line $p(\varepsilon)$ |
| $G$ | gilt-edge financial return rate |
| $h(t)$ | hazard function variation with time |
| $h(\varepsilon)$ | hazard function variation with experience, the outcome failure rate, $\lambda(\varepsilon)$ |
| $H$ | information entropy, the $H$-factor |
| h | hours; or loss ($h$) |
| $I$ | investor rate of return |
| $i,j$ | experience space matrix parameters |

*Managing Risk: The Human Element*   Romney B. Duffey and John W. Saull
Copyright © 2005 and 2008 Romney B. Duffey and John W. Saull, Published by John Wiley & Sons, Ltd

| | |
|---|---|
| $j$ | $j^{th}$ observation interval of experience |
| $k$ | learning rate constant of proportionality or exponent; or number of outcome types; |
| $k_B$ | Boltzmann's constant |
| $K$ | correlating non-dimensional learning rate constant, $k/\varepsilon_M$ |
| $L$ | number of launches |
| $LR$ | Learning rate |
| $m$ | number of observed non-outcomes; Weibull distribution shape function; or law of practice exponent |
| $M$ | total number of all possible non-outcomes; |
| MFh | millions of flying hours |
| $M_c$ | millions of customers |
| $n$ | number (integer) of observed outcomes |
| $n_i$ | microstate occupation at $i^{th}$ experience level |
| $N$ | total number of possible outcomes; components tested or units produced; or number of deaths |
| $N_j$ | number (integer) of outcomes observed in $j^{th}$ interval |
| $N^*$ | non-dimensional experience, $\varepsilon/\varepsilon_M$ |
| $P$ | probability of total possible outcomes; or profit |
| $p$ | prior outcome probability, $n/N$ |
| $p(\varepsilon)$ | probability of observed outcomes at any experience, $n(\varepsilon)/N$ |
| $p(P)$ | posterior probability |
| $p(L)$ | likelihood probability in Bayesian formulation |
| $P(LaP)$ | Laplace prior probability from the Rule of Succession,$(n + 1)/(N + 2)$ |
| $P(N)$ | probability of observing $N$ outcomes in any order |
| $P(n)$ | probability of observing $n$ (integer) outcomes in any order |
| $p(N)$ | probability of $N$ outcomes in $(N + M)$ outcomes and non-outcomes, $N/(N + M)$ |
| $p(n)$ | probability of n outcomes in $(n + m)$ outcomes and non-outcomes, $n/(n + m)$ |
| $q$ | loss ratio exponent |
| $r$ | number of successes or failures |
| $R(\varepsilon)$ | reliability fraction, $(1 - F(\varepsilon))$ |
| $s$ | belief function |
| $S$ | thermodynamic entropy; or sales number; or competitive market share |
| Sy | ship-years |
| kt | airspeed in knots |
| $t$ | time; or number of trials in law of practice |
| $t^*$ | non-dimensional practice, $t/t_T$ |
| $U$ | number of units produced |
| $w$ | weight of belief |
| $W$ | total number of permutations; or watts of power (W) |
| $x,y,z$ | axes in experience space |
| $X$ | observed outcome in experience state space |
| y | years |
| $\langle\,\rangle$ | average value |

## Greek symbols

| | |
|---|---|
| $\alpha$ | learning depth; or risk boundary exponent |
| $\beta$ | depth exponent |
| $\delta$ | uplift fraction on investment; or exponent in hazard function |
| $\varepsilon$ | experience, level or increment |
| $\varepsilon(i,j)$ | experience state space parameters |
| $\theta$ | Weibull distribution characteristic life parameter |
| $\lambda$ | outcome failure rate, $A/(N-n)$ |
| $\tau$ | practical unit (tau) of experience |
| $\xi$ | experience unit multiplier |
| $\Delta$ | uncertainty; or incremental change |
| $\Phi$ | partition function; or proportional constant in experience measure |
| $\Psi$ | experience shaping parameter, ESP |
| $\Omega$ | constant in $F\!-\!N$ risk boundary |
| $\Sigma$ | sum of terms/items/total number |
| $\Pi$ | product of terms |

## Subscripts

| | |
|---|---|
| D | deaths |
| eq | equivalent value |
| F | failures |
| i | increment in depth of experience |
| j | observation interval |
| k | outcome type |
| m | minimum value |
| M | maximum value |
| max | maximum |
| min | minimum |
| MC | marginal cost |
| 0 | initial or zeroth value |
| S | successes |
| t,T | total value |
| u | per unit |
| $\infty$ | asymptotic value |

## Prefixes on multiplied units (common usage)

| | |
|---|---|
| B | billion: 1,000,000,000 times |
| G | giga: or billion times |
| k | kilo:1,000 times |
| M | mega: million, 1,000,000 times |
| T | tera: 1,000,000,000,000 times |

## Abbreviations and Acronyms used in text (organisation names capitalised)

| | |
|---|---|
| AAR | American Association of Railroads |
| ACNP | American College of Nuclear Physicians |
| ACSI | almost completely safe industry |
| ABM | anti-ballistic missile |
| ACSI | almost completely safe industries |
| AD | airworthiness directive |
| ADE | adverse drug event |
| ALARP | as low as reasonably practical/achievable |
| AMA | American Medical Association |
| API | American Petroleum Institute |
| ASME | American Society of Mechanical Engineers |
| ATC | average total cost; or air traffic control |
| ATS | automated traffic systems |
| ATSB | Australian Transport Safety Bureau |
| AWS | automated warning systems |
| BEA | Bureau d'Enquêtes Accidents |
| BFU | Bundesstelle für Flugunfalluntersuchung |
| BLS | Bureau of Labor Statistics |
| BP | British Petroleum LLC |
| BTS | Bureau of Transportation Safety |
| CAA | Civil Aviation Authority |
| CADRIS | Canadian adverse drug reaction information system |
| CAIB | Columbia Accident Investigation Board |
| CDC | Centers for Disease Control |
| CDF | cumulative or integral probability distribution function |
| CIHI | Canadian Institute for Health Information |
| CR | constant outcome occurrence rate |
| CSB | Chemical Safety and Hazard Investigation Board |
| CVR | cockpit voice recorder |
| DETR | Department of Environment, Transport and the Regions |
| DHS | Department of Homeland Security |
| DOD | Department of Defense |
| DOE | Department of Energy |
| DoH | Department of Health |
| DoT | Department of Transportation |
| DoJ | Department of Justice |
| DSM | Duffey–Saull Method |
| EASA | European Aviation Safety Agency |
| ECCS | emergency core cooling system |
| EPA | Environmental Protection Agency |
| EPRI | Electric Power Research Institute |
| ESP | experience-shaping parameter, $\Psi$ |
| EU | European Union |

| | |
|---|---|
| FAA | Federal Aviation Administration |
| FEMA | Federal Emergency Management Agency |
| FDA | Food and Drug Administration |
| FRA | Federal Railroad Administration |
| F–N | risk boundary for frequency, $F$, of exceeding $N$ deaths |
| FO | first officer |
| FOAK | first of a kind |
| GDP | gross domestic product |
| GIHRE | Group Interaction in High Risk Environment |
| GPS | global positioning system |
| HEART | human error and reliability technique |
| HEP | human error probability |
| HRA | human reliability analysis |
| HSE | Health and Safety Executive |
| HTS | homo-technological system |
| ICAO | International Civil Aviation Organization |
| IEA | International Energy Agency |
| ILO | International Labor Organization |
| ILU | Institute of London Underwriters |
| IMO | Independent Market Operator |
| IoM | Institute of Medicine |
| IPCC | International Panel on Climate Change |
| IPSN | Institut de Protection et de Sûreté Nucléaire |
| IR | instantaneous observed outcome rate, $A$ |
| ISO | International Standards Organization; Independent System Operator |
| LR | learning rates |
| MAUDE | manufacturer and user facility device experience base |
| MAIB | Marine Accident Investigation Board |
| MCE | minimum cost equation |
| MERE | minimum error rate equation |
| MISO | Midwest Independent System Operator |
| MITI | Ministry of Trade and Industry |
| MPR | market price ratio |
| MSHA | Mine Safety and Health Administration |
| NASA | National Aeronautics and Space Administration |
| NCC MERP | National Coordinating Council for Medication Error Reporting and Prevention |
| NEI | Nuclear Energy Institute |
| NHTSA | National Highway Transport Safety Administration |
| NMAC | near midair collision |
| NMD | national missile defence |
| NPSA | National Patient Safety Agency |
| NRC | Nuclear Regulatory Commission |
| NTSB | National Transportation Safety Board |
| OECD | Organization Economique pour Cooperation et Development |
| ORR | Office of Rail Regulation |

| | |
|---|---|
| ORSC | organisational risk stability criterion |
| OSHA | Occupational Safety and Health Administration |
| PDF | differential probability density function |
| PRA | probabilistic risk assessment/analysis |
| PSA | probabilistic safety assessment/analysis |
| PSA | Petroleum Safety Authority Norway |
| PSF | performance-shaping function |
| PSM | process safety management |
| PSMS | personal safety management system |
| QA | quality assurance |
| QC | quality control |
| RI | runway incursion |
| RO | reactor operator |
| ROP | reactor oversight program |
| RT | response time |
| SARP | Standards and Recommended Practices |
| SE | sentinel event |
| SEST | statistical error state theory |
| SMS | safety management system |
| SPAD | signal passed at danger |
| STCA | Short Term Conflict Alert System |
| SUV | sports utility vehicle |
| TCAS | traffic collision avoidance system |
| TEPCO | Tokyo Electric Power Company |
| TNT | tri-nitro toluene |
| TSB | Transportation Safety Board |
| TTF | time to failure |
| UN | United Nations |
| UFC | uniform fire code |
| UK | United Kingdom |
| UKHL | UK House of Lords |
| ULC | universal learning curve |
| UPC | universal price curve; universal practice curve |
| ULP | universal law of practice |
| USA | United States of America |
| USCG | United States Coast Guard |
| USN | United States Navy |
| WANO | World Association of Nuclear Operators |
| WHO | World Health Organization |

# Appendices

'It is the mark of an instructed mind to rest satisfied with the degree of precision which the nature of the subject permits and not to seek an exactness where only an approximation of the truth is possible.'

*Aristotle*

# Appendix A

## The 'Human Bathtub': Predicting the Future Risk

The solution of the MERE equation derived from the Learning Hypothesis is:

$$\lambda(\varepsilon) = \lambda_{m} + (\lambda_{0} - \lambda_{m})\exp - k(\varepsilon - \varepsilon_{0}) \tag{A1}$$

For a novice or a new system there is often no experience at the beginning, so $\varepsilon_{0} \to 0$. The probability of the outcome or error occurring in or taking less than $\varepsilon$, is just the Cumulative Distribution Function, or CDF, conventionally written as the failure fraction $F(\varepsilon)$:

$$p(\varepsilon) \equiv F(\varepsilon) = 1 - e^{-\int \lambda d\varepsilon} \tag{A2}$$

where the probability, $p(\varepsilon) = n/N$ and the integration can be taken over any experience interval from an initial value, $\varepsilon_{0}$ to the value, $\varepsilon$, corresponding to observing the number of outcomes, n.

Hence, the probability of error is a double exponential or 'bathtub' as shown in the text due to the exponential form of the failure rate itself imposed on equation (A1).

Substituting this MERE (largely) human failure rate from equation (A1) into equation (A2) and carrying out the integration from an initial experience, $\varepsilon_{0}$, to any interval, $\varepsilon$, we obtain the probability as the double exponential[1]:

$$p(\varepsilon) = 1 - \exp\{(\lambda - \lambda_{m})/k - \lambda(\varepsilon_{0} - \varepsilon)\} \tag{A3}$$

where,

$$\lambda(\varepsilon) = \lambda_{m} + (\lambda_{0} - \lambda_{m})\exp - k(\varepsilon - \varepsilon_{0}) \tag{A4}$$

---

[1]Contrast this double exponential expression to the linearised approximation often used in PSA for estimating sensitivities, where $p(\varepsilon) \equiv \Sigma_{i} p_{i}(\varepsilon) \approx ap_{i} + b$, where $p_{i}$, is for the $i^{th}$ 'component' and $a$ and $b$ are constants.

*Managing Risk: The Human Element*   Romney B. Duffey and John W. Saull
Copyright © 2005 and 2008 Romney B. Duffey and John W. Saull, Published by John Wiley & Sons, Ltd

and $\lambda(\varepsilon_0) = \lambda_0 = n/\varepsilon$, at the initial experience, $\varepsilon_0$, accumulated for the initial $n$-outcome(s), and for the first event $n \sim 1$.

The fractional reliability, $R(\varepsilon)$, represents all those events that by chance have *not* occurred by $\varepsilon$ (and conversely the unreliability or failure fraction, $F(\varepsilon)$, all those that have). Hence the failure rate, $\lambda(\varepsilon)$, is written,

$$\lambda(\varepsilon) = f(\varepsilon)/R(\varepsilon) = \{1/(1 - F(\varepsilon))\}\,\mathrm{d}F(\varepsilon)/\mathrm{d}\varepsilon \qquad (A5)$$
$$= \{(1/(N - n))(\mathrm{d}n/\mathrm{d}\varepsilon)\}$$

where $(\mathrm{d}n/\mathrm{d}\varepsilon)$ represents the observed *rate* of outcomes, $A$, (as accidents, errors and events per unit experience). Thus, as stated before, the observed event rate usually recorded or reported is directly proportional to the failure rate, $A \propto \lambda(\varepsilon)$, being exactly so when, $n \lll N$, and we have few events observed and/or many possible ones. For the special case of the first or rare events, $\lambda(\varepsilon) = 1/\varepsilon$.

The failure rate, $\lambda \equiv h(\varepsilon)$, in conventional engineering reliability is a dynamic 'hazard function'. Now, $\lambda_m$, is the minimum obtainable at large experience and is found from the lowest observed for commercial air travel and industrial injury rates to be about $\sim 5 \times 10^{-6}$ per experience hour. That is a frequency of one event about every 20 to 30 years – at present we do not know why it has this value[2]. The initial rate at some initial experience, $\varepsilon_0$, is given by the *prior* (historical) rate, $\lambda_0 \sim n/\varepsilon_0$, where, $n$, is the number observed with past experience out of an unknown possible total, $N$.

The key influence of experience on decreasing the probability of an outcome (an event, accident, or failure) is straightforwardly evident as can be seen by examining the theoretical expressions (A2), (A3) and (A4). Consider the two limits corresponding to being a novice with very little experience, $\varepsilon \to 0$ and being an expert after attaining or achieving much experience, $\varepsilon \to \infty$.

For the first *novice* case, we have a small initial experience, $\varepsilon_0$, and few outcomes ($n \lll N$). The failure rate from (A3) and (A4) at small experience is the initial value, $\lambda_0$, which for few events gives the failure rate as $\lambda_0 \approx n/\varepsilon_0$. So the 'novice' outcome probability is, from (A2),

$$p_0(\varepsilon) \approx 1 - e^{-n} \qquad (A6)$$

Hence, for the limit of first or rare events, $n = 1$, so

$$p_0(\varepsilon) \approx 1 - e^{-1} \qquad (A7)$$

This simple limit result suggests we have about a probability of $\sim 0.63$ (the value of $1 - 1/e$) of observing an outcome when a novice[3].

For the second *expert* case, we have a large experience, $\varepsilon \to \infty$, and of course presumably many outcomes to have learnt from by then ($n \to N$). The failure rate from (A3) and (A4) at

---

[2] The possibilities include a combination of some socially acceptable risk, inter-generational forgetting, and/or premature and natural relaxation interval after a period of success or absence of failure.

[3] Implying a sound theoretical limit by comparison of $p_0(\varepsilon) = 0.63$ to the 'nominal error probability' of $\sim 0.55$ for an unfamiliar, rapidly performed task in the HEART methodology, as described in James Reason's 'Managing the Risk of Organizational Accidents', Ashgate, England, 2000.

large experience declines to the minimum attainable value, $\lambda_m$. So the 'expert' outcome probability is, from (A2),

$$p_\infty(\varepsilon) \approx 1 - \exp\{-\lambda_m(\varepsilon - \varepsilon_0)\} \tag{A8}$$

Hence, for the limit of large experience, $\varepsilon \gg \varepsilon_0$, and $\lambda_m \varepsilon \to \infty$, so

$$p_\infty(\varepsilon) \approx 1 \tag{A9}$$

This simple limit result suggests we actually have a certainty of eventually observing an outcome, when an expert if we have accumulated very large experience.

Ultimately, fate catches up and we are doomed to have an outcome, since even a very small failure rate cannot eventually offset the inexorably increasing risk exposure interval. This result may seem paradoxical at first, but in fact the only region where the probability is less than these two extreme limits of near unity probability, i.e., for when $p(\varepsilon) \ll 1$, is in the bathtub 'learning' region of experience between $\varepsilon_0 < \varepsilon < \infty$.

## The Differential Formulation for the Number of Outcomes

In terms of the probability, p, we may also derive an equivalent differential formulation, since we have the failure rate relation from (A5), simplifying with $\varepsilon \gg \varepsilon_0$,

$$\lambda(\varepsilon) = \{1/(1-p)\}\,dp(\varepsilon)/d\varepsilon = \lambda_m + (\lambda_0 - \lambda_m)e^{-k\varepsilon} \tag{A10}$$

Now, from the Learning Hypothesis, we also have:

$$d\lambda/d\varepsilon = -k(\lambda - \lambda_m) \tag{A11}$$

Combining these results, (A10) and (A11), we find that the dynamic probability, $p$, is a solution of the second-order equation:

$$\frac{d^2 p}{d\varepsilon^2} + \left(\frac{1}{1-p}\right)\frac{dp}{d\varepsilon}\left\{\frac{1}{1-p}\left(\frac{dp}{d\varepsilon}\right) - k\right\} = 0 \tag{A12}$$

This equation implies of course that the *dynamic* error probability ($p \equiv n/N$) if equated to the observed outcome count frequency is a function of the experience and the learning rate, $p(\varepsilon, k)$, i.e.,

$$\{(1 - p(\varepsilon))/(1 - p(\varepsilon_0))\} = \exp[\{\lambda_m(\varepsilon - \varepsilon_0)\} + \{\lambda_0 - \lambda_m\}/k]^{e^{-k(\varepsilon - \varepsilon_0)}} \tag{A13}$$

which is the double exponential 'human bathtub' form cf. equation (A3).

In terms of the numbers of events or observed outcome count, we may simply rewrite the learning hypothesis (A11) using the failure rate (A5) as, noting that $p \sim n/N$ for any interval with n outcomes according to the probability definition,

$$\frac{d^2n}{d\varepsilon^2} + \left(\frac{1}{N-n}\right)\frac{dn}{d\varepsilon}\left\{\left(\frac{1}{N-n}\right)\left(\frac{dn}{d\varepsilon}\right) - k\right\} = 0 \tag{A14}$$

This second-order differential equation is soluble for the number of outcomes, $n(\varepsilon)$, given a knowledge of $N$, the total number. In accord with the original hypothesis, the variation in the rate of numbers of observed outcomes clearly depends on learning, through the constant, $k$, anyway.

We can check the predictions from the limits. For the special case of *rare events*, $n \sim N \sim 0(1)$, the second term in the above differential equation dominates in magnitude compared to the first so that:

$$\left(\frac{dn}{d\varepsilon}\right) \approx k \tag{A15}$$

So the variation with experience has the number of outcomes occurring nearly as:

$$n \sim k\varepsilon \tag{A16}$$

The number increases linearly with experience, and a similar result holds as $n \to N$ for large experience. The minimum of the bathtub occurs of course when $dn/d\varepsilon = 0$, and is actually a point of inflection.

For the *very first outcome*, $n = 1$, and for $N = 1$, at experience, $\varepsilon_0$, the initial apparent learning rate is $k_0 \sim 1/\varepsilon_0$, which corresponds to the purely uniform Bayesian prior probability.

## The Future Probability

For completeness, we repeat the argument and derivations given in the main text. Once again, we may use Bayesian reasoning for conditional probability. The posterior or future probability, $p(P)$, of an error when we are at experience, $\varepsilon$, depends on the prior or as noted above,

$$\text{Posterior, } p(\text{P}) \propto \{\text{Prior, } p(\varepsilon)\} \times \{\text{Likelihood, } p(\text{L})\} \tag{A17}$$

where the prior probability $p(\varepsilon)$ is *given from minimum error rate theory*, and by definition both $B$, $L > \varepsilon$, our present accumulated experience. We can create the needed estimates for the probabilities using the derived error rate (frequency of events) as a *function of experience*, so that:

$$p(\varepsilon) \sim n(\varepsilon)/N \tag{A18}$$

The likelihood, $p(\text{L})$, is also a statistical estimate for which we must make an assumption *based on our prior knowledge*. Often it is taken as sampling from a uniform or a binomial distribution. We can show that the likelihood is formally related to the number of outcomes for a given variation of the mean. Either: (a) the future likelihood is of the same functional (learning curve) form as that experienced up to now; and/or (b) the future is an unknown statistical sample for the next increment of experience based on the PDF, $f(\varepsilon)$.

a) In the first case, we have the future likelihood probability $p(L)$ as the fraction or ratio of events left remaining to occur out of the total possible number, $N$. Now, the posterior probability,

$$p(P) \propto \{\text{Prior, } p(\varepsilon)\} \times \{\text{Likelihood, } p(L)\}$$

So the likelihood is,

$$p(L) = [p(P)/p(\varepsilon)] \tag{A19}$$

and,

$$p(L) = \left( \frac{\displaystyle\int_{\infty}^{\varepsilon} n(\varepsilon)\,d\varepsilon}{\displaystyle\int_{\infty}^{\varepsilon_0} n(\varepsilon)\,d\varepsilon - \int_{\varepsilon}^{\varepsilon_0} n(\varepsilon)\,d\varepsilon} \right) \tag{A20}$$

As a consistency check, i.e., from the initial experience, $\varepsilon_0$, out to some experience, $\varepsilon$, we observe $n(\varepsilon)$ out of the $N$ total outcomes. Then for all the foreseeable (infinite) future we have the probability of any event conditional on the next or following event:

$$p(P) = p(\varepsilon) \times \left( \frac{\displaystyle\int_{\infty}^{\varepsilon} n(\varepsilon)\,d\varepsilon}{\displaystyle\int_{\infty}^{\varepsilon_0} n(\varepsilon)\,d\varepsilon - \int_{\varepsilon}^{\varepsilon_0} n(\varepsilon)\,d\varepsilon} \right) \tag{A21}$$

Now, we know that from the theory of statistical error states that the distribution of observed outcomes, $n(\varepsilon)$, is a function of experience. For any finite experience interval where $\varepsilon > \varepsilon_0$, the distribution is very nearly given by:

$$n(\varepsilon) \approx n_0 \exp - k(\varepsilon - \varepsilon_0) \tag{A22}$$

where, $n_0$, is a measure of the residual number or 'ground state' population of errors that occur irrespective of learning. So, by inspection or using the error state exponential error rate distribution and evaluating the integrals, it is evident we must have that:

$$p(L) \rightarrow 1 \tag{A23}$$

and thus,

$$p(P) = p(\varepsilon) \tag{A24}$$

Hence, the future (posterior) probability is unchanged from the estimate of the prior probability, for any future experience, $\varepsilon (\equiv p(\varepsilon))$ where,

$$p(\varepsilon) = 1 - \exp\{(\lambda - \lambda_m)/k - \lambda(\varepsilon_0 - \varepsilon)\} \tag{A25}$$

This argument is somewhat of a circular one, in that we assume initially a likelihood form that is derivable from a learning curve distribution.

b) In the second case, for the next increment of experience, $\delta\varepsilon$, we may take the likelihood, $p(L)$ as conventionally given by the ratio of the PDF, $f(\varepsilon)$, to the CDF, $p(\varepsilon)$, so that:

$$
\begin{aligned}
p(P) &= p(\varepsilon) \times p(L) \\
&= f(\varepsilon) = \lambda(\varepsilon) \times (1 - p(\varepsilon)) \\
&= \{(\lambda_m + (\lambda_0 - \lambda_m)\exp(-k(\varepsilon - \varepsilon_0))\} \{\exp((\lambda - \lambda_0)/k - \lambda_m(\varepsilon_0 - \varepsilon))\}
\end{aligned}
\tag{A26}
$$

implying also that:

$$
p(L) \equiv \{\lambda(\varepsilon)\}\{(1 - p(\varepsilon))/p(\varepsilon)\}
\tag{A27}
$$

To a reasonable approximation when learning is occurring, numerically $f(\varepsilon) \sim \lambda(\varepsilon)$, so,

$$
p(P) \sim \lambda(\varepsilon)
\tag{A28}
$$

The future (posterior) probability estimate is once again derivable from its unchanged prior learning value, and *thus the past frequency predicts the future probability*.

## Insufficient Learning

As a numerical example for the other extreme when learning is slow to non-existent, we took a case with a learning rate constant of $k = 0.001$. We show the Posterior probability, $p(P)$, as calculated from the Likelihood, $p(L)$, and Prior probabilities, $p(\varepsilon)$, where

$$
p(L) = \text{PDF}/\text{CDF} = f(\varepsilon)/p(\varepsilon)
\tag{A29}
$$

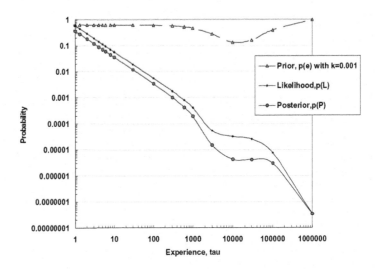

**Figure A-A1.1**    Example case of little learning

and, hence,

$$p(P) = p(\varepsilon) \times p(L) = f(\varepsilon) \tag{A30}$$

We can evaluate these expressions numerically using our 'best' MERE values. As can be seen in Figure A-A1, the Posterior probability simply decreases as $p(P) \propto 1/\varepsilon$, close to a constant risk line as might have been anticipated, until learning causes the small dip in the outcome (prior) probability.

In fact, this result is entirely consistent with the working analytical estimate derived in Chapter 4 for rare events, when the outcome rate $\lambda(\varepsilon) \sim n/\varepsilon \sim 1/\varepsilon$, and the probability of an outcome is small, $p(\varepsilon) \ll 1$.

Since the PDF, $f(\varepsilon) = \lambda(\varepsilon) \times (1 - p(\varepsilon))$, a working estimate for the PDF is then:

$$f(\varepsilon) \sim \lambda(\varepsilon) \sim 1/\varepsilon \tag{A31}$$

So we have,

$$p(P) \sim 1/\varepsilon \tag{A32}$$

almost exactly as shown by the lines drawn in Figure A-A1, until some learning eventually occurs that causes the wiggle in the curves near the minimum of the CDF probability.

# Appendix B

## The Most Risk, or Maximum Likelihood, for the Outcome (Failure or Error) Rate while Learning

*'It is truth very certain that, when it is not in our power to determine what is true, we ought to follow what is most probable.'*

*Rene Descartes, 1596–1650*

### The Most or Least Likely Outcome Rate

When are we most or least likely to have an event, an error or an outcome?

To answer that question, we need to take a brief excursion into some applied mathematics, which illustrate the determination of when (i.e., at what experience) the most likely outcome will occur. The result is a pure prediction derived from the Learning Hypothesis.

In traditional statistics, the value for the mean of a set of outcomes is often taken as that which maximises the likelihood of the outcomes (Bulmer, 1979) [1]. In our learning model, this maximum likelihood is simply equivalent to finding the maximum for the probability of an outcome in experience space. We show here that the learning curve outcome rate has the maximum likelihood, so is the most likely, and the constant risk rate is the minimum likelihood and so is the least likely. The range between these two high and low estimates constitutes a subjective judgement, or a working hypothesis, or a degree of belief, or a statement of evidence about the previously observed (prior) learning behaviour and path, and whether and how much we are actually learning.

In our learning situation, instead of some regular (normal) distribution of outcomes around the mean, we have an exponential curve of the probability of an outcome that depends on the accumulated experience and the learning rate. So we need a new analysis to determine the maximum likelihood.

*Managing Risk: The Human Element*   Romney B. Duffey and John W. Saull
Copyright © 2005 and 2008 Romney B. Duffey and John W. Saull, Published by John Wiley & Sons, Ltd

Now recall the Laplace expression for the probability of any outcome at experience, $\varepsilon$, based on observing, $n$, prior outcomes out of a total of, $N$, possible ones is,

$$p(\varepsilon) = n/N$$

This probability of an outcome (failure or error) occurring in or taking less than, $\varepsilon$, is just the cumulative distribution function, CDF, being the fraction of observed outcomes out of the total possible outcomes, conventionally written as $F(\varepsilon)$ so:

$$p(\varepsilon) \equiv F(\varepsilon) = 1 - e^{-\int \lambda d\varepsilon}$$

where, $\lambda$, is the failure rate. Hence, the probability of an outcome is a *double* exponential due to the exponential form of the outcome (failure) rate, $\lambda$, arising from the MERE solution:

$$\lambda(\varepsilon) = \lambda_m + (\lambda_0 - \lambda_m) \exp - k(\varepsilon - \varepsilon_0)$$

where the initial experience is often taken implicitly as zero, so $\varepsilon_0 = 0$. Now the formal condition for a maximum *or* a minimum in the probability of occurrence is that the differential of the probability having a value of zero identifies the peak or trough, so that mathematically the maximum or minimum occurs when:

$$dp(\varepsilon)/d\varepsilon = \lambda e^{-\int \lambda d\varepsilon} = 0$$

This procedure is simply equivalent to setting to zero the differential probability density function, PDF, i.e., $f(\varepsilon) = dp(\varepsilon)/d\varepsilon = 0$, and finding the experience and outcome rate that satisfies this required condition.

To include learning effects, we can evaluate the exponential expression $e^{-\int \lambda d\varepsilon}$ for the integrated outcome or failure rate, $\lambda$, by substituting the MERE hazard or failure rate into the probability expression. Carrying out the integration from an initial experience, $\varepsilon_0$, out to any interval, $\varepsilon$, we obtain the probability as the double exponential:

$$p(\varepsilon) = 1 - \exp\{(\lambda - \lambda_m)/k - \lambda(\varepsilon_0 - \varepsilon)\}$$

In general, the maximum likelihood expression is obtained by equating the differential of the probability with experience to zero, so:

$$dp(\varepsilon)/d\varepsilon = \{(1/k - \varepsilon_0)d\lambda/d\varepsilon + \lambda\} \exp\{(\lambda - \lambda_m)/k - \lambda(\varepsilon_0 - \varepsilon)\} = 0$$

## The Maximum and Minimum Risk: The Two Solutions

Thus, the *two* solutions or roots that give the most (maximum) or least (minimum) likely outcome rates correspond to the likelihood constraint,

$$\{(1/k - \varepsilon_0)d\lambda/d\varepsilon + \lambda\}\{\exp\{(\lambda - \lambda_m)/k - \lambda(\varepsilon_0 - \varepsilon)\} = 0$$

or, writing the two multiplying terms as the bracketed products $\{A\}$ and $\{B\}$,

$$\{A\} \times \{B\} = 0$$

So there are two solutions when the $\{A\}$ and $\{B\}$ terms are independently zero. The maximum solution $\{A\}_{max}$ is derived from determining when the differential equation equals zero so:

$$(1/k - \varepsilon_0)(d\lambda_{max}/d\varepsilon) + \lambda_{max} = 0$$

This root is the maximum likelihood, because the second differential $d^2p/d\varepsilon^2$ has a negative value, confirming that the *maximum risk* rate is given by solution $\{A\}$. We show below that this corresponds exactly to the limiting case of low outcome rates.

Integrating the equation, we find that the rate for the *maximum risk* or likelihood is:

$$\lambda_{max} = \lambda_0 \exp - \{k(\varepsilon - \varepsilon_0)/(1 + k\varepsilon_0)\}$$

which is exponentially declining with increasing experience.

The minimum solution $\{B\}_{min}$ is derived from determining when the exponential term is also equal to zero, which occurs when the magnitude of the exponent is negative and infinite. So potentially we have the asymptotic limit that the minimum rate is when,

$$\lambda_{min}\{(\varepsilon_0 - \varepsilon) - 1/k\} \gg \lambda_m/k$$

This indicates that the *minimum risk* rate or minimum likelihood is bounded by,

$$\lambda_{min} \ll \{\lambda_m\}/\{1 + k(\varepsilon - \varepsilon_0)\}$$

This is the minimum since the second differential, $d^2p/d\varepsilon^2$, has a positive value when, $k(\varepsilon - \varepsilon_0) \gg 1$, or at any finite experience.

## Low Rates and Rare Events

We often have low outcome rates or perhaps rare events, which implies that the outcome rate, $\lambda \ll 1$. So a very convenient approximation for this low outcome rate case is that the probability expression,

$$p(\varepsilon) = 1 - \exp\{(\lambda - \lambda_m)/k - \lambda(\varepsilon_0 - \varepsilon)\}$$

can be simplified by expanding the exponential term for small rates. Noting that generally $\lambda \gg \lambda_m$, and making the small rate approximation, we have

$$p(\varepsilon) \approx 1 - (1 - \lambda/k + \lambda(\varepsilon_0 - \varepsilon) - ....)$$
$$\approx \lambda(1/k + (\varepsilon - \varepsilon_0)), \text{ for } \lambda \ll 1 \text{ and neglecting the higher-order terms.}$$

Hence, at the maximum likelihood we must have, from differentiating this low rate approximation for the probability,

$$dp(\varepsilon)/d\varepsilon \approx (d\lambda/d\varepsilon)(1/k + \varepsilon_0) + \lambda = 0$$

This limiting case of low rates is *identically* the same equation given above by the first order differential equation $\{A\}_{max}$ for the maximum likelihood for the outcome (failure) rate $\lambda_{max}$.

$$d\lambda_{max}/d\varepsilon = -k\lambda_{max}/(1+k\varepsilon_0)$$

So the maximum likelihood occurs at low outcome rates.

## The Limits of Maximum and Minimum Risk: The Two Solutions

From integrating the first order differential equation, the solution from $\{A\}_{max}$ for the *maximum* likelihood of the outcome rate is exponential, falling with increasing experience as given by:

$$\lambda_{max} = \lambda_0 \exp - \{k(\varepsilon-\varepsilon_0)/(1+k\varepsilon_0)\} \quad \text{Failure Rate for Maximum Likelihood}$$

However, the solution from $\{B\}_{min}$ gives the *minimum* likelihood of the outcome rate derived from the unity exponent condition is parabolic, falling inversely with increasing experience as:

$$\lambda_{min} << \{\lambda_m/\{1+k(\varepsilon-\varepsilon_0)\} \quad \text{Failure Rate for Minimum Likelihood}$$

This is a lower bound on the rate, when we expect to be learning. Note that the maximum likelihood is *not* given by the mean or average value as in conventional time series or sampling statistics, simply due to the presence of learning with experience. The maximum and minimum likelihoods systematically change value with both experience and with learning.

These max–min rate limits have a parallel in the process of assigning or assessing upper and lower bound probabilities for the purposes of reasoning and inference (Wally, 1991) [2]. The difference from our case here is that we expect the failure rate trend to be dynamic, and bounded between these physically reasonable max-min limits that vary systematically with experience.

So, once again, we have found that the minimum likelihood of risk is not zero, but a finite value that depends on experience. We now look at the limiting cases for these two interesting solutions for the maximum or minimum likelihood as a function of experience.

## Common Sense: The Most Risk at the Least Experience, and the Least Risk as the First Outcome Decreases with Experience

At the limit of very *large* experience ($\varepsilon \to \infty$) we have, for the two cases,

$$\lambda_{max} \to \lambda_0 \exp - k\varepsilon/(1+k\varepsilon_0)\} \to 0,$$

$$\lambda_{min} \to 1/\varepsilon \to 0$$

So the most likely rate becomes zero in both cases at large experience when $\varepsilon \to \infty$. In actuality, the asymptotic rate tends to the small minimum rate of $\lambda_{max} \to \lambda_m \sim 1/\varepsilon = \lambda_{min}$ within the limits of the rare outcome approximation that we have invoked above.

The variation of rate with experience as a, $1/\varepsilon$, dependency is the common sense attainable minimum (for the very first event), and is also exactly the Bayes limit for the initial event ($n = 1$). This trend is observed in the aircraft data.

So to minimise the numerical risk rate, it is essential to accumulate lots of experience, as shown by the commercial airline data with millions of flights, and by Dupont's Lost Time rate accumulated for over 100 years of industrial production.

At the other limit of very *small* experience $(\varepsilon \to 0)$

$$\lambda_{max} \to \lambda_0 \exp\{-k\varepsilon_0)/(1+k\varepsilon_0)\} \to \text{constant}$$

$$\lambda_{min} \to \lambda_m/\{1-k\varepsilon_0\} \to \text{constant}$$

So the most and least likely rates both becomes constant at low experience when $\varepsilon \to 0$. If $k\varepsilon_0 \gg 1$, then $\lambda_{max} \to 0$, and we have no outcomes.

The experience, $\varepsilon_{max}$ and $\varepsilon_{min}$, that yields the maximum or minimum likelihood of outcomes is given by a simple inversion of these two outcome (failure) rate expressions. This straightforward manipulation yields:

$$\varepsilon_{max} - \varepsilon_0 = -(1/k + \varepsilon_0)\ln(\lambda_{max}/\lambda_0)$$

$$\varepsilon_{min} - \varepsilon_0 = (\lambda_m/k\lambda_{min})-1$$

For the *very first* or rare event, $n = 1$ and $\lambda_0 \sim 1/\varepsilon_0$, and we have that the maximum likelihood rate given by:

$$\lambda_{max,n=1} \sim (1/\varepsilon_0)\exp-\{k(\varepsilon_0 - \varepsilon_0)/(1+k\varepsilon_0)\} \to 1/\varepsilon_0$$

or, equivalently,

$$\lambda_{max,n=1} \to \lambda_0$$

So, as might be logically expected, the *maximum likelihood for outcomes occurs at or near the initial event rate when we are least experienced.* This is also a common sense check on our results: *we are most at risk at the very beginning.*

## Typical Trends in Our Most Likely Risk

Figure A-B1 illustrates the relative trends for the maximum and minimum likelihood outcome rates as a function of experience measured in arbitrary units (tau, $\tau$). The curves trace out the locus of the maxima and minima in the outcome rate as experience varies.

For the purposes of only these relative calculations, the arbitrary values taken for experience in (tau) units of per experience hour were:

(a) a minimum attainable rate of $\lambda_m \sim 5 \times 10^{-6}$;
(b) an initial outcome rate of unity, $\lambda_0 = 1$; and
(c) an initial experience interval in tau units of $\varepsilon_0 = 0.1 \ \tau$.

To illustrate the sensitivity to the learning rate, $k$, results are shown as calculated for a range of three values of $k$ of 0.1, 1 and 3.

The trends shown follow the patterns predicted by our analytical limits. Clearly, the maximum likelihood rate decreases quickly (exponentially as $\sim\lambda_0 \exp\{-k\varepsilon_0)/(1 + k\varepsilon_0)\}$) from

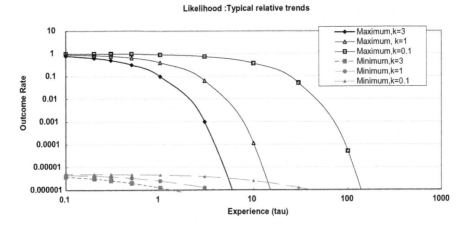

**Figure A-B1.**  Typical comparative likelihoods as a function of our experience

its initial value, $\lambda_0$, as experience is gained and learning is greater. If the learning rate is less with experience ($k$ decreases), the rate decrease is less.

The minimum likelihood rate, $\lambda_{max}$, trends downwards as the inverse of experience, $1/\varepsilon$.

Our maximum risk is dominated by our inexperience at first, and then by lack of learning, and our most likely risk rate is extremely sensitive to our learning rate for a given experience.

To complete our risk likelihood comparisons, Figure A-B2 shows the maximum likelihood for the outcome rate from the analytical limit as compared to the 'best' values for the outcome rates given by the MERE. The comparisons shown use a single value for the learning rate constant of $k = 3$.

In Figure A-B2, the MERE solution for the outcome rate, $\lambda$(IR), is calculated with the 'best' values derived in Chapter 4 as given by:

$$\lambda(\text{IR}) = 5 \times 10^{-6} + \left(1/\varepsilon - 5 \times 10^{-6}\right) e^{-3\varepsilon}$$

Also shown is the so-called 'constant rate' line, $\lambda$(CR), for the first outcome, $n = 1$, given by:

$$\lambda(CR) = 1/\varepsilon$$

It is evident that the MERE result tracks the maximum likelihood risk rate closely:

$$\lambda_{max} = \exp - \{3(\varepsilon - \varepsilon_0)/(1 + 3\varepsilon_0)\}$$

An approximate risk rate expression that follows the, $\lambda$(CR), is given by:

$$\lambda_{CR} \sim \{1 + \lambda_m/k\}/\{1/k + (\varepsilon - \varepsilon_0)\} = \{1 + 5 \times 10^{-6}/3\}/\{1/3 + (\varepsilon - \varepsilon_0)\}$$

Despite all the approximations, we have found good working methods for analysing data and determining trends. The method and values are consistent with and derived from the world's experience where the learning curve rate is the most likely.

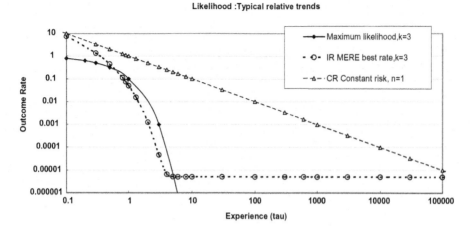

**Figure A-B2.** Comparison of the Likelihood results with the MERE learning *IR* and the constant risk *CR*

Obviously, we expect the actual data to fall somewhere between the limits of the MERE *IR* and the *CR* rates. What we find in practice is that certain industries, risks and outcomes follow one *or* the other trend. Either there is:

a) reduction with experience and learning discernable, and the MERE or maximum likelihood trend is followed; or

b) no reduction or learning with increasing experience beyond that expected from a constant risk (the outcomes will always occur).

## The Distribution with Depth of Experience

Finally, we also have a distribution of outcomes as a function of the depth of experience, where the probability of any distribution is given by an exponential curve.

Specifically, for the $i$th depth of experience the probability is:

$$p_i = p_0 \exp(\alpha - \beta \varepsilon_i)$$

and empirically, this expression fits data using the simplified form $p_i = p_0 \exp - (a\varepsilon)$.

The maximum or minimum likelihood is similarly given by setting $dp/d\varepsilon = 0$, to give:

$$-\beta p_0 \exp(\alpha - \beta \varepsilon_i) = 0,$$

and is a minimum. So the likelihood condition is that $\alpha = 1 + \beta \varepsilon_i$, or

$$\varepsilon_i = (\alpha - 1)/\beta, \text{ a constant.}$$

Back substitution of this result gives $p_i = 0$, so the probability of an outcome is zero.

# References

[1] Bulmer, M.G., 1979, 'Principles of Statistics', Dover Publications, Inc., New York, p. 170.

[2] Walley, P., 1991, 'Statistical Reasoning with Imprecise Probabilities', Monographs on Statistics and Applied Probability 42, Chapman and Hall, London, UK.

# Appendix C

## Transcripts of The Four Echoes

*'The fact is that the more we probed, the more we learned and the more we wanted to learn. Our list of questions grew and grew.'*

*John Mogford, 2006*

### Power Blackout, Columbia Space Shuttle loss, Concorde Crash and Chernobyl Accident

### The Combination of Events

If there is anything we know, it is that we do not really know anything at all. Our understanding of reality is based on approximate physical 'laws' that describe how the universe we observe behaves. The complexities of the human mind, when coupled with complex technological systems that have been created by that same mind, produce both outcomes we expect (results and/or products) and some that we do not (accidents and/or errors). Since one cannot expect to describe exactly all that happens, and since we only understand the cause(s) afterwards, reactively assigning *a posteriori frequencies,* any ability to proactively predict the probability of outcomes *a priori* must be based on a testable theory that works.

That is true for all the accidents that surround us, because of the *overwhelming contribution of human error* to accidents and events with modern technological systems. *The human failings and the failures are what cause them.* That is *the* common human element in the four echoes. But when faced with an error, major or minor, humans always first deny, then blame-shift, before accepting it as their very own. It is a natural survival instinct; it is part of living and our self-esteem. We do so as individuals, and seemingly also as part of our collective societies.

Our mistakes are embedded or intertwined as part of a larger 'system', be it a technology, a corporation, a mode of travel, a rule or regulation, or an individual action or responsibility. They arise as and from an unforeseen combination of events that we only understood afterwards.

*Managing Risk: The Human Element*   Romney B. Duffey and John W. Saull
Copyright © 2005 and 2008 Romney B. Duffey and John W. Saull, Published by John Wiley & Sons, Ltd

Their consequences (the outcomes) can be large or small, but all are part of a larger picture of which we humans are the *vital* contributor, invariably in some unforeseen way that was only obvious afterwards.

## The Four Echoes Share the Same Four Phases

The classic accidents, the unthinkable events, the shocking tragedies, and the routine injuries share common traits and phases. We shall show that the same four Phases characterise these most heavily publicised, documented and visible of recent major accidents with our best but still experimental technological systems:

*Phase 1*: The Unfolding, of the precursors, the initiators and the preliminaries.
*Phase 2*: The Confluence of events, circumstances and bases of errors.
*Phase 3*: The Escalation where the unrecognised unknowingly causes the event.
*Phase 4*: The Denial caused by lack of comprehension, followed finally by acceptance.

## Appendix. Blackout Chronology and the Dialogue from Midday 14 August 2003

The Four Phases emerge as events unfold:

*Phase 1*: The *unfolding* occurred as the power line monitoring system became inoperable, during a time of changing power demand and supply, and while seemingly small known and unknown upsets and faults are also occurring.
*Phase 2*: With an already weakened power grid, there was the *confluence* of the competing pressure to sell power and distribute to customers becoming a priority for discussion, despite uncertainty about the overall system status and its ability to handle the existing and increasing power demand.
*Phase 3*: The *escalation* of overloads on various power lines, power imbalances, and faults to ground caused by trees all lead to increasing loss-of-control problems.
*Phase 4*: The *denial* becomes evident, as it was not known at the various control centers that the repeated and numerous power line trips were escalating, eventually causing blackouts all over the East coast, until they were finally recognised from watching the television/media reports.

Information Source for dialog: Control Center Transcripts Midwest System Operator (MISO), by permission [2].

(Note: the * and bold time mark indicates a Cause identified in and by the US–Canada Report, while the italics are used for emphasis)

12:04 Low voltage alarms received at First Energy (FE).
12:05 EST AEP's Conesville Unit (376 MW) tripped carrying 245 MW. The cause of this trip is not available.
**\*12:15** MISO State Estimator turned off and reliability assessment compromised until 16:04.

12:25 Low voltage alarms received at FE from Inland, Fox and Harding.

12:46 Transmission Load Request (TLR) for Kentucky –Indiana flow monitored by MISO.

12:51 AEP's Dumont 765 kV transmission reactor bank #2 opened. This transmission voltage control equipment connects with the AEP 765 kV transmission system near the western Michigan–Indiana border.

13:00 (approximate) A Dayton Power & Light (DPL), Cinergy and AEP (collectively referred to as 'CCD') jointly-owned generating unit at the Stuart plant experienced an upset with the cause not available. This unit connects with the DPL 345 kV transmission system south of Columbus, Ohio.

13:01 MISO State Estimator corrected but not enabled by analyst, so does not update, who then goes to lunch.

13:02:53 AEP's Gavin Unit 2 (1300 MW) began its return to service. It was supplying about 50 MW at 16:00 p.m. This unit connects with the AEP 765 kV transmission system in southern Ohio.

13:03 (approximate) A flow reversal occurred at the PJM–NYISO interface. The power flow between NYISO and PJM reversed from exporting 150 MVA to PJM to importing 250 MVA to NYISO.

The Cinergy company relays and discusses the problems over the phone with MISO Control Center.

MISO: (This is) Midwest ISO.

Cinergy: This is ... Cinergy.

MISO: Yes, sir.

Cinergy: Hey, we got big problems, buddy.

MISO: We don't want no big problems.

Cinergy: No, we've got a huge problem.

MISO: What's the matter?

Cinergy: We lost the 345 (kV) line between Columbus and Bedford, and we kind of cascaded into some other outages.

MISO: That's where that Petersburg (problem) is coming from, isn't it?

Cinergy: Yeah, probably. Big unit or something down there?

MISO: I don't know. Hey, give me a ... what have you got?

13:13 MISO asks for voltage support from FE, begins telling operators that voltages are sagging 'all over'.

13:14 DTE's Greenwood Unit 1 (600 MW) was removed from service for a fuel related problem. Automatic Reserve Sharing (ARS) was not requested from within ECAR for this event. This unit connects with the International Transmission Company (ITC) 345 kV transmission system near the MECS-IMO interface.

13:30 MISO tells Cinergy that bringing on the Wheatland unit is causing grid voltage drop problems.

\*13:31:34 FE's Eastlake Unit 5 (597 MW) tripped. This trip occurred in the process of restoring the voltage regulator from manual to automatic control in order to stabilise reactive output and later resume the requested voltage schedule. This unit connects with the FE 345 kV transmission system.

13:34 Automatic Reserve Sharing (ARS) was initiated for 595 MW from within ECAR, of which FE supplied about 342 MW. FE's share of the ARS was accomplished by cutting a 300 MW sale into PJM.

13:35-54 Additional flow reversals at the PJM–NYISO interface within a range of 100 MVA importing or exporting.

13:57 DTE's Greenwood Unit 1 (600 MW) breakers closed to permit its return to service. At 16:00 the unit was supplying approximately 400 MW.

**\*14:02** DPL's Stuart (CCD)–Atlanta (CCD) 345 kV line supplying the area south of Columbus, Ohio tripped. The status of the line at the time of the event is unavailable to FE.

**\*14:04** MISO State Estimator update problem found but still does not solve as the Stuart-Atlanta line fault was unknown and out of their jurisdiction.

14:08 At MISO the various line options are discussed with Cinergy, and then at the end of the phone conversation there is, some two hours before it happens, *an amazing premonition of an Echo of the last big blackout:*

Cinergy: Well, if you look ... if you've got ... if you have a map there and it shows you, basically, we cut the state in half.

MISO: East to west.

Cinergy: Across east to west, and then straight down.

MISO: Right.

Cinergy: So we isolate ... basically, we isolated the whole southwestern corner of Indiana with one tie-line. And you've got all those units out there, so they just ... they basically ... *you know, it's a vortex-type thing. It just sucks everything in.*

MISO: Uh-huh.

Cinergy: That's the thing about it. *You never know when that happens, it can cascade and well, that's how the last big blackout happened. 500 megawatt line took out the whole east coast.*

MISO: I know. Okay. I mean, I know Wheatland is it's own control area, and they ... Wheatland. They don't have any control, don't have any ... they don't see any of it, so I don't know. Someone might want to call DEVI and see exactly where they're going to, because they're sucking down the 345 voltage.

MISO: Okay. I'm going to call them and see what's going on.

Cinergy: Okay. Well, let me know what happens.

MISO: We'll get back with you.

Cinergy: Okay. Appreciate it.

MISO: All right. Thanks.

Cinergy: Bye.

MISO: Bye.

14:19 The Wheatland Unit problem is discussed directly by phone between MISO and the company, Allegheny Energy.

Here is the transcript from MISO:

Allegheny: Allegheny.

MISO: Hey, this is (reliability coordinator) at MISO Carmel.

Allegheny: Yes?

MISO: Your Wheatland unit –

Allegheny: Yes.

MISO: – *is causing voltage problems at AMO* – they're beginning to trip out there.

Allegheny: Oh, the voltage problems.

MISO: At the AMO bus.

Allegheny: Okay.

MISO: And we need to figure out how to do something about this.

Allegheny: Okay.

MISO: So, is there anything that we can do to replace that generation with something else, to the north maybe?

Allegheny: Can you explain that again?

MISO: We're having some voltage problems – some voltage stability problems around the AMO bus in Cinergy. And, *because Wheatland generation – and turning us in there, we've lost a couple of lines inside Cinergy.* They did just lose a – we're still trying to figure out – This is (Allegheny), right?

Allegheny: Yes, I have a bunch of people around me that are going to fix it.

MISO: Okay. Okay, they did trip at Francis Creek – the 345/69 transformer there. Okay.

MISO: Let's see if we can –

Allegheny: Did you say 325?

MISO: Yes.

Allegheny: I'm showing 347.

MISO: Okay. Well, I'm going with Cinergy, and it may be going up or down, so . . .

Allegheny: Okay. Well, we'll call and increase it, but – we'll increase it to what we can, based on the design and (inaudible) of units, *but I have concerns with them saying it's 325.*

MISO: Are you increasing megawatts, or increasing VAR support?

Allegheny: VAR support.

MISO: Okay. Can they increase VAR support for Cinergy? He's talking about decreasing megawatts and increasing VARs, is what he needs. Because –

Allegheny: All right, we'll give (Wheatland) a call. Okay, well good. We'll give (Wheatland) a call and we'll call you back, how's that?

MISO: Okay.

14:22: The dialogue continues about the Wheatland plant and the incompatible voltage readings, and this is now discussed with Cinergy:

MISO: (This is) Midwest ISO.

Cinergy: Hey . . .

MISO B: You MISO A?

MISO A: Hey, . . . here again.

Cinergy: Yes.

MISO A: They are going to give Wheatland a call and see what they can do to decrease megawatts and increase VARS, but I don't think they're real sure about how they're going to do that yet. So, they're going to give me a call back here in a minute.

Cinergy: They can bump it some, just don't – I don't know what that 69 is doing. But we don't want to open the line.

MISO A: We don't want any more lines opening up.

Cinergy: No, I'm not going the line, I was just – open the Tap to their generation –

MISO: Okay. If we can.

Cinergy: I'm serious here. We're on a mandate from – big problems here from that generation.

MISO A: Are you talking to them now . . .?

Cinergy: Pardon me?

MISO A: Are you talking to them now . . .?

Cinergy: I was talking to you.

MISO A: *I'm sure not in control of it.*

Cinergy: I understand.

MISO A: Yes, so it would be kind of a voluntary thing. Now, you guys, I know you've lost a couple of lines and you're trying to figure that situation out. But, you need to purchase at all costs and that's pretty much, by NERC policy, you probably know that.

Cinergy: Yes.

MISO A: And that includes the VAR support and any reactive schedules you can set up – anything like that, just to have the support there. If you need to set up schedules to keep your system intact, then *that's what you have to do at all costs.*

Cinergy: I understand.

MISO A: You know, so I just want to make sure you guys realise that. I mean, the lines tripping is one thing, but we've got to figure out how to overcome it now, so . . .

Cinergy: Oh, absolutely.

MISO A: And voltage supports can be handled with reactor purchases, if possible. So, if Allegheny-Wheatland would like you to purchase some VAR support, would that be okay if you have to set up a megawatt schedule between, you know, north to south?

Cinergy: Well, that's possible, you know? But –

MISO A: He's going back here going crazy trying to figure things out too, so . . .

Cinergy: Do you know who Wheatland's selling to?

MISO A: *I sure don't.*


14:27:15 South Canton (AEP)-Star (FE) 345 kV interconnection line protection systems automatically tripped due to a phase-to-ground fault and reclosed at both ends successfully.

14:31 The unresolved power and voltage issues are again discussed between MISO and Allegheny, as the observed and measured voltage numbers across the grid power lines do not agree with each other.


MISO A: Hello, . . .

Allegheny: Yes, Allegheny Energy Supply.

MISO A: Hi.

Allegheny: Does it look better?

MISO A: He said he's still seeing 325 (kV). What are you showing . . .?

Allegheny: 349 (kV) on our end. We've got the VARS, we've got them maxed out.

MISO A: Where are you reading that in?

Allegheny: We're reading that at Qualitech.

MISO A: Where at, now?

Allegheny: Off the AMO line. Hold on one second . . .

MISO A: Yes, I can't hardly hear you.

Allegheny: That's the line voltage we're reading from Qualitech.

MISO A: Qualitech?

Allegheny: Off the bus there.

MISO A: Okay. MISO B's on the other line talking to Cinergy right now.

Allegheny: Hey . . .?

MISO A: What's that?

Allegheny: . . . question for you . . . *I got a call from the people at our marketing end. And they want to bring on another unit at Wheatland.*

MISO A: Oh, really? We would have to say no to that, at this point – until we can figure out that the AMO bus here, what's happening.

Allegheny: We're reading something much different. I'm not sure where you're reading the 325, but we're reading 349. And we talked to the plant and he said, prior to them coming on, it was reading at 352.

MISO A: You're reading at Qualitech though? Well, somebody's values are incorrect, here. And I'm not sure who's it is. He's reading 329 at Qualitech, so . . .

Allegheny: Aren't you selling – we're showing 349 – I can't imagine that would be down to 325. Ours is showing 349, in case you didn't hear that.

MISO A: I know you're showing 349 at Qualitech.

Allegheny: Yes.

MISO A: They're showing 329 at Qualitech, right? And 325 at AMO. So, someone needs to verify. Can you verify that your numbers are correct, or who are you getting your numbers from . . .?

Allegheny: Off our EMS.

MISO A: Off your EMS?

Allegheny: It's coming from the RTU.

MISO A: Straight from the RTU? We're trying to investigate the numbers here . . .

Allegheny: Call us back?

MISO A: I can call you back. I would appreciate it if you could hold out. *If you can't, I hate to command you to do it, but it may end up coming to that,* if we have too many problems and we're not –

Allegheny: You mean as far as starting, or sending, a third unit?

MISO A: Yes.

Allegheny: Okay.

MISO A: So, right now, I would say, *my boss is telling me to say no,* and I should go with what my boss is saying.

Allegheny: That's okay, that's fine, okay.

MISO A: But, okay?

Allegheny: Yes, sure, we'll wait to hear from you.

MISO A: All right. Thanks . . . Bye.

14:43 MISO is trying to understand and control the situation without having a State Estimator working.

Cinergy: Full contingency analysis where you run it?

MISO C: Right, right. That's our State Estimator. We're having it solve the case or having
it solve the model. Then after it solves the model, it will run off the state – or the
contingency analysis. Yeah. Those numbers I gave you before for AMO to Wheatland might have been a little low.

(Break in tape.)

Cinergy: Are you guys there?

MISO C: Yeah, I am.

Cinergy: Have you got a TLR (Transmission Line Relief) out on anything at this point? Did
you end up calling one on the 230 up at Wabash River?

MISO C: I'll check.

MISO B: Do you know what it would take to make this problem better? *What do you err on
the side of, reliability?*

MISO D: Okay ... with Cinergy, call Cinergy. Tell them to lower Gibson. We need to bring
that flow gate down to load another and try and do this pro rata with Wheatland.
We need to figure out how much we need to lower Gibson to fix this problem, how
much we need to lower it, period. And then we – you know, Roger either and then
we – you know, ... either said, 'Call Wheatland, tell them you need to shut down
or try and work something pro rata out with them'. You know, if we're bringing
Cinergy down this much, we need to come down this much.

MISO B: How much? Where is Wheatland right now? They were scheduled to (Inaudible.)

SPEAKER: I don't know.

MISO B: *We don't know the data,* but we need to be a lot worse than what we're at. I do
know one thing.

MISO C: What do you see coming out of Wheatland right now?

SPEAKER: That's it.

Cinergy: Wheatland. It looks like they're either net numbers, about 236 megawatts, and 58
mega-VAR.

MISO B: *The State Estimator has been down for an hour and a half.*

MISO D: Yeah. Do you guys know how much they need to lower the output?

MISO C: That's what we're just now talking about ...

And later in the same dialog:

Cinergy: Are they going to curtail Gibson for sales out of Wheatland? 17

MISO C: They're actually going to curtail both Gibson and Wheatland kind of pro rata.

Cinergy: Gibson is setting at 3254 (MW) gross. That is gross megawatts.

MISO C: Okay.

MISO D: That's what we need to figure out.

MISO B: Here is the State Estimator unless you want to value it.

MISO E: *The State Estimator was invalid up until two minutes ago. Everything you did off
this estimator was invalid.*

Cinergy: Have you got the State Estimator running yet?

MISO C: It's still State estimating right now. We had a little problem with it. *It's always not
there when you need it, right?*

Cinergy: Yeah. There you go.

MISO C: Wheatland output, net number is 236 megawatts, 58 VARs; Gibson gross
3250 (megawatts), 54 (VARS).

SPEAKER: Now, how much do you need to come down on –

MISO C: How much to come down on Gibson? Okay.

MISO D: (Cinergy) agrees. He's with Cinergy because we agree. He's in a meeting . . . He understands this. So he knows he needs to bring it down . . . if we could bring down Gibson in a pro rata – not Gibson – Wheatland in a pro rata manner, that's fine, but we need to know how much we have to bring it down to get within stability limits. So if we could figure out how much we need to bring Gibson down to, in fact, what we need to, then we can call and have Cinergy bring it down. And we can tell Wheatland to come down as well. So can you guys figure out how much we need to bring down Gibson?

MISO C: Yeah. The way to do that would be in STCA or pull it into the – or pull it into power flow and then tweak it that way, right? Okay. What the concern is, Gibson is – Cinergy is willing to back down Gibson, come pro rata along with Wheatland. *The question is, how much do we need to back down to get back within stability limits?*

MISO D: What are we going to need as a proxy for stability limits?

MISO C: Well –

SPEAKER: I don't know.

MISO C: What are we using as a proxy for stability limits?

SPEAKER: Well, we do have a couple of flow gates, of course, *based on the State Estimator, which isn't running well.*

MISO D: It's solved? It's running, the State Estimator?

SPEAKER: It's not.

MISO D: Okay.

MISO E: Explain to him.

14:47 MISO is still trying to fix its State Estimator analysis tool

MISO D: This is Midwest ISO. May I help you, please?

MISO A: Hey, . . . this State Estimator has got some malfunctions happening here.

MISO D: I am looking for – we are looking at it right now.

MISO A: Okay. Thanks. Bye.

15:05:41 Chamberlin (FE)–Harding (FE) 345 kV line tripped due to a phase-to-ground fault. The cause of this fault is under investigation, although under similar loading and weather conditions during June 2003, the line experienced no problem. At the same time, the Harding-Juniper (FE) 345 kV segment overtripped and successfully reclosed. Operating conditions at the time of this occurrence reflect loading at 40% of the line's rated line capability (488 MVA with a 1195 MVA maximum rating).

*15:09 MISO informed of Stuart-Atlanta line fault, but think the line is still in service so the input to the State Estimator solution *means that it does not correctly match the observed data.*

15:17 AEP's Conesville Unit supply breaker closed to permit the unit to synchronise to the transmission system and begin its ramp-up procedures for its return to service. At approximately 16:00, the unit was supplying about 150 MW.

*15:29 MISO State Estimator now corrected for Stuart-Atlanta line fault, and gives updated solution.

15:32 (approx.) FE's Sumpter Unit located in southeast Michigan experienced power and reactive fluctuations beginning at this time. System dispatchers thereafter noted higher than normal reactive flows to the south and southwest.

15:32:03 Hanna (FE)–Juniper (FE) 345 kV line tripped due to a tree contact. A forestry crew working two spans from the occurrence because of regular cycle right-of-way clearing contacted system dispatchers to remove the tree hazard condition. Operating conditions at the time of this occurrence reflect loading at 85% of the line's rated line capability (1169 MVA with a 1400 MVA maximum rating).

16:33 MISO is still working on voltage drops and power generation matching:

MISO E: Wheatland . . . we – they actually requested additional transmission service, which we refused that. So they're going to be backing down but not quite as quick.

Cinergy: Okay.

MISO E: That will be at the top of the hour. But that's 236 megawatts that we just denied. So we should see some improvements in voltages.

Cinergy: Good.

MISO E: Okay?

Cinergy: That will help some.

MISO E: Why don't you give us –

Cinergy: Do you think they will come completely off line in –

MISO E: They do not have transmission service is my understanding. So I don't know how they would continue to generate onto the Cinergy grid. Why don't you give us a call here? Can you keep an eye on what your – keep an eye on the voltages as Gibson ramps down and give us a call if you're started to get satisfied with the voltage as well? Give us a call either way.

Cinergy: Yeah, we could do that.

MISO E: Okay. We'll be monitoring it here also, obviously, but – all right?

Cinergy: Sounds good.

MISO E: Okay. Thanks.

Cinergy: Bye.

MISO E: Bye.


15:38:42 South Canton (AEP)–Star (FE) 345 kV repeatedly tripped, automatically attempted to reclose at both ends and then locked out. Operating conditions at the time of this occurrence reflect loading at 85% of the line's rated line capability (1175 MVA with a 1385 MVA maximum rating). System dispatcher communications between FE and AEP were initiated to determine the cause and to confirm the lockout of the line at both terminals. A cause has not been confirmed.

15:42:00 Operators at FE's Perry Unit reported 345 kV network voltage fluctuations and frequency spikes.

15:42:53 Cloverdale (FE)–Torrey (AEP) 138 kV line tripped and remained open as a result of loading increases in response to the Star-South Canton line trip. Operating conditions at the time of this occurrence reflect loading of 145% of the line's rated line capability (354 MVA loading with a 245 MVA maximum rating).

15:44:12 East Lima (AEP)–New Liberty (AEP) 138 kV line automatically tripped and locked due to a phase-to-ground fault. The cause of this fault is not available to FE. Operating conditions at the time of this occurrence reflect loading of 80% of the line's rated line capability (152 MVA loading with a 188 MVA maximum rating). This line is owned entirely by AEP.

15:44:40 Pleasant Valley (FE)–West Akron/West (FE) 138 kV line tripped and locked out for a phase-to-ground fault. The cause of this fault is under investigation. Operating conditions at the time of this occurrence reflect loading of approximately 114% of the line's rated capability (163 MVA loading with 143 MVA maximum rating).

15:45:00 At the Erie West (FE)–Ashtabula (FE) 345 kV line (FE-PJM interface) the power flow reversed from FE exporting 80 MW to PJM, to PJM supplying about 95 MW to FE.

15:45:51 Cloverdale (FE)–Canton Central (AEP) 138 kV line automatically tripped, reclosed and locked out. Operating conditions at the time of this occurrence reflect loading of 168% of the line's rated line capability (332 MVA loading with a 197 MVA maximum rating).

15:45:51 Canton Central (AEP)–Tidd (AEP) 345 kV line tripped due to a breaker failure protection scheme at Canton Central which opened a 345 kV motor-operated switch, isolating the 345-138 kV transformers #1 and 2 from the Canton Central-Tidd line. After this occurrence the Canton Central–Tidd line restored automatically, with an outage duration of about one minute

15:58: The numbers for the voltages and power loads on the grid lines are not looking good, but the Estimator has to be checked as it is clearly not giving reliable numbers now.IPL: Transmission operations. This is (IPL)

MISO F: Yeah. This is … MISO. I have a quick question to ask you. Are you showing a P-0 (power overload) to Hannah (line) … getting a P-0 Thompson line that is right now overloaded? In our State Estimator, we're showing an overload. *We want to make sure that's true.*

IPL: Sure. Which lines, now?

MISO F: Petersville to Hannah and Petersville to Thompson.

IPL: Petersburg you mean?

MISO F: Yes. Is it not Petersville? I'm sorry. Petersburg.

IPL/Bill: Yeah. Hold on a second.

MISO/Norris Henderson: Okay. Petersburg.

IPL: I'm showing on the Petersburg to Thompson 882 megawatts at this time (and IPL confirms a 30 MW overload).

IPL: How about Pete to Hannah (line)? We're not – that Petersburg to Hannah is not even in alarm.

MISO F: Okay, sir. So just your Petersburg to Thompson is showing 30 (MW) over its
limit?

IPL: At this time, right.

MISO F: Beautiful. Okay. Thank you, sir.

But even more checking has to happen:

IPL: This is IPL.

MISO F: Yes. This is … MISO again. The reason why we are bothering you, we've got estimations showing both the Petersburg to Hannah and the Petersburg to Thompson being overloaded. But you had called me and told me just the

Petersburg to Thompson is overloaded. Can you give me a number rating on your Petersburg to Hannah?

IPL/Paul: The current rating, the rating or the load that is on there?

MISO F: The current rating. I said our estimator. We think the rating of it is too low and that's why it's showing alarm, where you're saying that's not the case. *So we want to correct that estimator.*

IPL: Sure.

**\*16:04** MISO State Estimator restored to full auto operation.

16:06:03 The Sammis–Star 345 kV line then disconnected at which completely blocked the 345 kV path into northern Ohio from eastern Ohio. This left only three paths for power to flow into northern Ohio: 1) from northeastern Ohio and Pennsylvania around the southern shore of Lake Erie, 2) from southern Ohio (recall, however, that part of that pathway was severed following the Stuart–Atlanta line trip at 14:02), and 3) from eastern Michigan. This also substantially weakened northeast Ohio as a source of power to eastern Michigan, making the Detroit area more reliant on the west-east Michigan lines and the same southern and western Ohio transmission lines.

15:42:49–16:08:58 multiple 138 kV lines across northern Ohio disconnected themselves. This blacked out Akron and the areas west and south.

16:08:58–16:10:27 Transmission lines into northwestern Ohio disconnect, and generation trips in central Michigan.

16:09 The Control Center staff can only watch as the blackout spreads.

TRANSCO A (calling in to MISO): 'It's slowly working its way down . . . so we're going to hang in there and hope something else bad doesn't happen to us.

MISO reply: Oh, OK.

MISO B (calling in): What's happening?

MISO reply: Oh, all hell's breaking loose, good buddy.

MISO B: I heard the east coast is like dark?

MISO reply: Yes, I don't know the extent of it . . . I know we had problems, starting out, but . . . and *just freak coincidences happening*, you know? And then suddenly a couple low voltages, but I'm not sure if it was our area, or not, that triggered the full event, so . . .'

16:10:00–16:10:38 Transmission lines disconnect across Michigan and northern Ohio, generation trips off line in northern Michigan and northern Ohio, and northern Ohio separates from Pennsylvania.

16:10:40–16:10:44 Four transmission lines disconnect between Pennsylvania and New York.

16:10:41 Transmission line disconnects and generation trips in northern Ohio.

16:10:42–16:10:45 Transmission paths disconnect in northern Ontario and New Jersey, isolating the northeast portion of the Eastern Interconnection.

16:10:46–16:10:55 New York splits east-to-west. New England (except southwestern Connecticut) and the Maritimes separate from New York and remain intact.

16:10:50–16:11:57 Ontario separates from New York west of Niagara Falls and west of St. Lawrence. Southwestern Connecticut separates from New York and blacks out.

16:13 Cascading sequence essentially complete.

16:22: MISO is still trying to restore power and work out what has happened.

MISO A: Hi.

ATC: I am looking at Arnold Vinton.

MISO A: *I am looking at all kinds of things.*

ATC: Yeah, what happened here?

MISO A: Something has happened that we have lost – it looks like some load, and possibly some generation trip.

ATC: Yeah, I think you lost some load because the frequency and some generation must have tripped somewhere, because I loaded up and just bang.

MISO A: So what I am recommending is that we all control our generation here and let's get things back in order, because we are starting to go downhill quickly. *It is across the board.*

ATC: Have you been in contact with Alliant generation?

MISO A: I have not.

ATC: Okay.

MISO A: So we have multiple overloads on your system right now.

ATC: I know it.

16:26 MISO finds out that New England and Ontario are down.

MISO B: This is . . . Midwest ISO reliability coordinator. Okay. We are experiencing multiple outages, and First Energy, Cinergy, and apparently DTE, which is part of the MECS control area. First of all, we want to know if anybody else is experiencing any problems to start with?

SPEAKER: At New England, *we are falling apart.*

MISO B: New England is falling apart?

SPEAKER: Yes.

MISO B: With outages?

SPEAKER: We have outages, and we have power lines out, and we have generators tripping. And then . . .

MISO C: This is MISO . . . from St. Paul. We just got an (inaudible) from Manitoba that Ontario Hydro is in real bad shape. They didn't give us any Manitoba hydro information. They just said they are in bad shape, real bad.

16:33 Now everyone finds out what is happening from watching the television.

MISO E: Okay. Well, we'll . . . I'm going to start calling control areas and telling them to make sure they have generation running. We've got blackouts all over the place. There's power . . . *you're watching the TV?* We've got lines tripping everywhere.

Cinergy: Control center.

MISO E: . . . This is the Midwest ISO. Can I talk to somebody in charge over there, maybe . . . the manager of the operation?

Cinergy: Well, you've got me. That's the ...

MISO E: Okay.

Cinergy: Supervisor.

MISO E: Oh, you're supervisor?

Cinergy: Yeah.

MISO E: That works for me. *I don't know if you've been watching the TV,* but we have been experiencing a ton of line trips.

Cinergy: Yep.

MISO E: There are cities going black, I understand. I would make sure that you have as much generation on your transmission system running as you can possibly due to make sure that we have generation available if need be.

Cinergy: Okay. What areas are being affected most? We saw a tremendous swing on the north part of our system a while ago.

MISO E: To be honest with you, it is mass chaos right now. We know First Energy has had events. We know that there has been low voltages in Michigan. We know that there have been the events in your system. We know that there has been an event of some sort in Minnesota, we believe. We don't know exactly what in Minnesota. I mean, you know, I'm looking down the hall here, and everybody is on the phone. So I'm trying to gather information as I can.

16:39 then NERC calls in with more news and to find out what is happening:

NERC: This is NERC trying to call to get some info. We are getting all kinds of calls from Washington and what not, and maybe we can share something here as to what is going on, and what I know so far is this. That there is major outage in the Detroit area, and that there have been some outages in the New Jersey area. We had a momentary outage here, and our power is on.

## Sources

[1] ITC Analysis of Grid Collapse, 20 August 2003.

[2] Midwest System Operator (MISO) Transmission Control Center phone transcripts, by permission of Midwest ISO, Indiana, September, 2003.

[3] 'August 14, 2003 Outage Sequence of Events' U.S./Canada Power Outage Task Force, Interim Report, 12 September 2003.

[4] EPRI, 'Factors related to the Series of Outages on August 14, 2003', White Paper, 20 November 2003, www.epri.com.

[5] UCTE (Union for the Coordination of Electricity Transmission), Interim Report of the Investigation Committee on the 28 September 2003, blackout in Italy, 27 October 2003.

[6] Swiss Federal Inspectorate for Heavy Current Installations, 'On the blackout that occurred in Italy and border regions of Switzerland on September 28, 2003', 12 November 2002.

## The Second Echo: Columbia/Challenger

The four Phases are here evident again:

*Phase 1*:   The early *unfolding* precursors were insulation damage events that had caused structural damage; and the routine of launching that meant that deadlines for launch took priority as funds and time could not be made up.

*Phase 2*:   The *confluence* occurred when other events conspired to make the damage vital and irreparable, although efforts to characterise and look at the damage region were rebuffed, and instruments did not provide direct information on either the damage or potential re-entry temperatures and failure.

*Phase 3*:   The *escalation* was in the repeated and continuing emphasis and attempts to ensure the Mission remained on schedule, rather than isolation of the failure, estimating the effect on the system of the system, and mending those first, rather than pressing on with the day's seemingly routine tasks.

*Phase 4*:   The *denial* is evident in the Board report pointing out serious institutional issues, whereas subsequent NASA statements focus on a relaunch schedule for subsequent Missions (of about a year). Not only did the launch managers at the time realise the full problem, and how it happened, but clearly many still believe that the design is still robust enough for further Missions to proceed again.

## Appendix: Shuttle Dialogue and Transcripts

Recounted and interweaved is the transcripts of the NASA Johnson Control Center ('Mission Control') and the official chronology as given in the CAIB Reports.

8:48:39 a.m. A sensor on the left wing leading edge spar showed strains higher than those seen on previous Columbia re-entries which was not telemetered to ground controllers or displayed to the crew.

8:49:32 a.m. Traveling at approximately Mach 24.5,Columbia executed a pre-planned roll to the right, beginning to normally limit the rate of descent and heating.

8:50:53 a.m. Traveling at Mach 24.1 at 243,000 feet, Columbia entered the usual 10-minute period of peak heating, during which the thermal stresses were at their maximum.

8:52:00 a.m. Nearly eight minutes after entering the atmosphere and some 300 miles west of the California coastline, the wing leading-edge temperatures usually reached 2,650 degrees Fahrenheit.

8:53:46 a.m. (EI+577) Signs of debris being shed were sighted at, when the superheated air suddenly brightened, causing a noticeable streak in the luminescent trail. Observers witnessed another four similar events during the following 23 seconds.

8:54:25 a.m. to 8:58 Witnesses see a bright flash just seconds after Columbia crossed from California into Nevada airspace when the Orbiter was traveling at Mach 22.5 and 227,400 feet, and another 18 similar events in the next four minutes as Columbia streaked over Utah, Arizona, New Mexico, and Texas while back at Mission Control, re-entry appeared normal.

8:54:24 a.m. Maintenance, Mechanical, and Crew Systems (MMACS) officer informed the Flight Director that four hydraulic sensors in the left wing were indicating 'off-scale low,' a reading that falls below the minimum capability of the sensor. As the seconds passed, the Entry Team continued to discuss the four failed indicators.

Here is the dialogue:

MMACS: 'FYI, I've just lost four separate temperature transducers on the left side of the vehicle, hydraulic return temperatures. Two of them on system one and one in each of systems two and three.'

Flight: 'Four [hydraulic] return temps??'

MMACS: 'To the left outboard and left inboard elevon.'

Flight: 'Okay, is there anything common to them? DSC [discrete signal conditioner] or MDM [multiplexer-demultiplexer] or anything?? I mean, you're telling me you lost them all at exactly the same time?'

MMACS: 'No, not exactly. They were within probably four or five seconds of each other.'

Flight: 'Okay, where are those, where is that instrumentation located?'

MMACS: 'All four of them are located in the aft part of the left wing, right in front of the elevons, elevon actuators. And there is no commonality.'

Flight: 'No commonality.'

8:55:00 a.m. (EI + 651) nearly 11 minutes after Columbia had re-entered the atmosphere, wing leading edge temperatures normally reached nearly 3,000 degrees Fahrenheit.

8:56:02 a.m. The diagnosis continues:

Flight: 'MMACS, tell me again which systems they're for.'

MMACS: 'That's all three hydraulic systems. It's . . . two of them are to the left outboard elevon and two of them to the left inboard.'

Flight: 'Okay, I got you.'

Then a little later . . .:

MMACS: 'Flight – MMACS.'

Flight: 'All other indications for your hydraulic system indications are good.'

MMACS: 'They're all good. We've had good quantities all the way across.'

Flight: 'And the other temps are normal?'

MMACS: 'The other temps are normal, yes sir.'

Flight: 'And when you say you lost these, are you saying that they went to zero?'

[Time: 8:57:59 a.m., EI+830] 'Or, off-scale low?'

MMACS: 'All four of them are off-scale low. And they were all staggered. They were, like I said, within several seconds of each other.'

Flight: 'Okay.'

8:58:00 More indicators of a problem occur.

MMACS: 'Flight – MMACS.'

Flight: 'Go.'

MMACS: 'We just lost tire pressure on the left outboard and left inboard, both tires.'

8:58:20 a.m. (EI + 851) at 209,800 feet and Mach 19.5, Columbia crossed from New Mexico into Texas, and about then shed an insulating tile, which was the most westerly piece of debris found in a field in Littlefield, northwest of Lubbock, Texas.

8:59:15 a.m. (EI + 906) MMACS informed the Flight Director that pressure readings had been lost on both left main landing gear tires, who then told the Capsule Communicator

(CAPCOM) to let the crew know that Mission Control saw and was evaluating these indications. The Flight Control Team had not understood the crew's last transmission.
8:59:32 a.m. (EI + 923) the broken and last response from the Shuttle's Mission Commander was recorded: 'Roger, [cut off in mid-word] . . .'
9:00:18 a.m. (EI + 969) While ground videos revealed that the Shuttle was disintegrating, the discussion on the measurements went on.

Flight: 'MMACS – Flight . . .'
MMACS: 'Flight – MMACS . . .'
Flight: 'And there's no commonality between all these tire instrumentations and the hydraulic return instrumentations.'
MMACS: 'No sir, there's not. We've also lost the nose gear down talkback and the right main gear down talkback.' (Talkback = data transmission)
Flight: 'Nose gear and right main gear down talkbacks?'
MMACS: 'Yes sir.'

9:03:45 Still neither the Flight Team and Mission Control 'had no indications of any serious problems . . . or any way to know the cause of the failed sensor measurements (instrument readings)' says the CAIB. So the dialogue still proceeds:

MMACS: 'Flight – MMACS.'
Flight: 'MMACS?'
MMACS: 'On the tire pressures, we did see them go erratic for a little bit before they went away, *so I do believe it's instrumentation.*'
Flight: 'Okay.'

9:03 to 9:12 a.m. Communications were unable to be restored with the Shuttle – the Mission Control learns from someone via a cell phone call from outside that the Shuttle break up had been seen on television (cf. the Blackout).
9:16 a.m. Shortly after the scheduled landing time, NASA declared a 'Shuttle Contingency' and executed the Contingency Action Plan established after the Challenger accident, whereby the NASA Administrator activated the International Space Station and Space Shuttle Mishap Interagency Investigation Board at 10:30 a.m.

## Source

[1] CAIB (Columbia Accident Investigation Board), Final Report, Volume 1, and Appendices, August 2003.

## The Third Echo: Concorde Tires and SUVs

Information Source: 'Accident on 25 July 2000 at La Patte d'Oie in Gonesse (95) to the Concorde registered F-BTSC operated by Air France Ministere de l'Equipement des Transports et du Logement', Bureau d'Enquetes et d'Analyses pour la Securite de l'Aviation Civile – France, report translation f-sc000725a (see www.bea.aero) by permission

The four Phases are here evident again:

*Phase 1*:   The early *unfolding* precursors were tire failure events that had caused airframe damage; and the routine of flying meant that deadlines took priority.

*Phase 2*:   The *confluence* occurred when other events conspired to cause the tire damage by the undetected metal strip.

*Phase 3*:   The *escalation* was enabling the subsequent structural failure, fuel loss and fire to spread uncontrollably.

*Phase 4*:   The *denial* is evident in the efforts subsequently to shift the blame to the source of the metal strip, and in modifying the plane to make it more resistant to tire failure.

The common factor is the unavoidable involvement of humans in all the stages and uses of the design, manufacturing, production, and operation of technology.

## Appendix: Dialogue for the Concorde Crash

Interweaved is the chronology from the Official Report by the BEA, including the Cockpit Voice Recorder (CVR) transcripts, the Flight Data Recorder (FDR), and the analysis of eyewitness accounts.

Paris Charles de Gaulle Aerodrome had one northern runway 09/27 and two southern parallel runways 08/26 that day. Work was being carried out on the north runway, from 15 June to 17 August 2000, and its available length was reduced during this period of time from 3 600 to 2 700 metres, its width being unchanged at 45 metres.

13:58, the crew requested: 'Concorde for New York on Echo 26 we need the whole length of 26 right'.

14:07, the controller confirmed: 'Plan for 26 right . . .', the crew read back '. . . on 26 right . . .'.

14:13:13 s, Flight Engineer (FE): 'So total fuel gauge I have ninety-six four with ninety-six three for ninety-five on board'.

14:13:46 s, First Officer (FO): 'Fire protection', FE: 'Tested'.

14:14:04 s, FO: 'ZFWZFCG', FE: 'So I have ninety-one nine and fifty-two two'.

14:14:17 s, Captain: 'The reference speeds so V1 one hundred fifty, VR one hundred ninety-eight, V2 two hundred twenty, two hundred forty, two hundred eighty, it's displayed on the left'.

14:14:28 s, FO: 'Trim', Captain: 'It's thirteen degrees'.

14:14:53 s, Captain: 'Then the lever is at fourteen and you'll have an N2 of ninety-seven and a bit', FE: 'Ninety-seven'.

14:22:22 s, Captain: 'Right we're going to do one hundred eighty-five one hundred that's to say we're going to be at the . . . structural limits', 'structural . . . fifty-four per cent balance . . . see'.

14:34, the Controller said: 'Air France 45 90, good morning, taxi to holding point 26 right via Romeo' then added '. . . do you want Whisky 10 or do you want taxiway Romeo'. The crew confirmed: 'We need the whole runway'. The Controller replied: 'OK so you're taxiing for Romeo, Air France 45 90'. The crew read the information back.

14:39:04 s, Prior to takeoff, the takeoff speed, and the set procedures in case of an emergency are talked through, including possible tire failure or engine fire warnings as the takeoff speed increases. Captain: 'So the takeoff is ... at maximum takeoff weight one hundred eighty tons one hundred which means four reheats with a minimum failure N2 of ninety-eight', 'Between zero and one hundred knots I stop for any aural warning the tire flash', 'Tire flash and failure callout from you, right', 'Between one hundred knots and V1 I ignore the (speed warning) gong. I stop for an engine fire, a tire flash and the failure callout', 'After V1 we continue on the SID we just talked about: we land back on runway 26 right'.

14:40:02 s, the Controller transmitted: '45 90 line up 26 right'. The crew replied: 'We line up and hold on 26 right, 45 90'.

14:41:09 s, FE: 'Brake temperatures checked one hundred fifty ...'

14:40:11s, Captain: 'Prepare for takeoff'.

14:40:19 s, Captain: 'How much fuel have we used ?' FE: 'We've got eight hundred kilos there'.

14:42:17 s, the Controller said: '45 90 runway 26 right wind 090 8 kt cleared for takeoff. The crew replied '45 90 takeoff 26 right'.

14:42:30.4 s, The engine thrust levers are brought to their (fully open) stop for takeoff

14:42:31 s, Captain: 'Top'.

14:42:54 s, FO: 'One hundred knots'.

14:42:57 s, Confirming the engines reheat status were correct, FE: 'Four greens'.

14:43:03 s, Confirming reaching reference take off speed, FO: 'V1'. One second after the V1 speed callout, CAS: 151 knots(kt) Heading: 269°

14:43:07 s to 14:43:13 s, Changes in CVR background noise.


An intense fire has started under the left wing, in an area not provided with extinguishing equipment, while the aircraft was accelerating between the takeoff V1 (150 kt) speed and planned rotation (nose up) speed, VR (192 kt). At this point, there is no real time to abort.

The background noise was also unexpected and unknown, and the movements experienced in the cockpit were highly abnormal. The overall sensory perceptions in the cockpit at that moment were similar to those of a lateral runway excursion (a swerve), resulting in early corrective actions on the controls.

Flight simulator analysis showed that for double engine failure on takeoff, the visual sensation is that of an imminent lateral runway excursion: the aircraft has uneven thrust and is skewing sideways. The tire marks left on the runway near takeoff show a lateral swerve to the left. The actual rotation was now made at a slightly lower speed, VR, than planned because the aircraft was losing its runway heading.


14:43:13.0 s, presumably in response to the swerve, FE: '*Watch out*'.

14:43:13s FO: '*Watch out*'.

14:43:13 s the controller stated: '... *45 90 you have flames ... you have flames behind you*'.


The crew acknowledged this transmission, and the aircraft is now airborne.

CAS: 188 kt Heading: 267°

14:43:20 s, FE: '*Failure eng. . . failure engine two*'.

14:43:22 s, Engine Fire alarm, Radio altitude positive (rotation and liftoff has occurred), CAS: 201 kt Heading: 270°

14:43:24 s, FE: '*Cut engine two*'.

14:43:25 s, Captain: '*Engine fire procedure*' and one second later, end of fire alarm.

This engine had been at idle power for several seconds with the fire alarm sounding. The engine was therefore shut down following the procedure after having run for twelve seconds at low power. It is important to note that the Flight Manual requires an immediate reaction by the crew in case of a red (fire) alarm.

14:43:27 s, FO: 'Watch the airspeed, the airspeed, the airspeed'.

14:43:28 s, Transmission on the same frequency: 'It's really burning and I'm not sure it's coming from the engines'.

14:43:29.3 s, Fire extinguisher actuation handle pulled in the cockpit.

14:43:30 s, Captain: 'Gear on retract'. First Officer: 'Yes, Roger'.

Over the following eight seconds, the crew try unsuccessfully to retract the landing gear several times, CAS: 199 kt Heading: 266°, Radio altitude: 100 ft

14:43:31 s, the controller confirmed: '45 90 you have strong flames behind you' and continued, '. . . as you wish you have priority for a return to the field'. The crew acknowledged this transmission.

14:43:32.6 s, The forward toilet smoke alarm sounds; the cockpit door is open.

14:43:42 s, Fire alarm sound on CVR.

14:43:44.7 s, Sound similar to firing the extinguisher with the first shot pushbutton.

14:43:45.6 s, FO: 'I'm trying' FE: 'I'm firing it'.

14:43:46 s, Captain: '(Are you) cutting engine two there'.

14:43:48 s, FE: 'I've cut it'.

14:43:49 s, FO: 'The airspeed'.

14:43:56 s, FO: 'The gear isn't retracting'. CAS: 211 kt Heading: 271° Radio altitude: 182 ft.

14:43:58.6 s, Third fire alarm.

14:43:59 s and 14:44:03 s, Three GPWS 'Whoop, whoop – pull up, pull up' aural alarms are heard, and at the same time the FO: says 'The airspeed'.

14:44:05 s, the controller transmitted: 'Fire Service Leader ... the Concorde I don't know his intentions get into position near the southern parallel runway' then 'Fire Service Leader correction the Concorde is returning on runway 09 in the opposite direction'.

14:44:14 s, FO: 'Le Bourget, Le Bourget'. Captain: 'Too late. No time. No'. Then a few seconds later, FO: 'Negative we're trying for Le Bourget'. CAS: 208 kt, Roll: –2.57° then –4.69° Heading: 270° Radio altitude: 199 ft

14:44:27s, CAS: 136 k Roll: –95.58° then –108.17°(left) Heading: 193° Radio altitude: 459 ft [1]

14:44:31 s, The CVR stops recording as the aircraft crashes in flames some 9500 m (or about 6 miles) from the runway just one minute and 18 seconds after the fire started. The crew were all found at their takeoff positions, and the passengers in the seats assigned at boarding, which were all fragmented. All the seat belts found were fastened. The fire and the crash damage to the aircraft meant that the accident was not survivable.

14:45:10 s, the Controller told the Fire Service Leader: 'The Concorde has crashed near Le Bourget, Fire Service Leader'.

14:46:09 s, the Controller announced: 'For all aircraft listening, I will call you back shortly. We're going to get ourselves together and we're going to recommence takeoffs'.

14:55:47 s, an aircraft informed the Controller: '... there is smoke on runway 26 right, there's something burning apparently, for information ...'

14:57, a runway vehicle after inspecting told the controller: 'There's tire' then 'pieces of tire which are burning'.

## Source

[1] BEA (Bureau d'Enquêtes Accidents), 'Accident on July 25, 2000, at La Patte d'Oie in Gonesse (95) to the Concorde Registered F-BTSC Operated by Air France', Translation f-sc000725a, 2002 (see www.bea.aero)

## The Fourth Echo: TMI/Chernobyl

The four Phases are here evident again:

*Phase 1*:  The early *unfolding* precursors were the delays and lack of test procedures and training, events that were routine happenings.

*Phase 2*:  The *confluence* occurred when other events conspired to cause the plant safety systems to be disconnected and bypassed, without any limit while the plant approached unknown and unstable operating territory.

*Phase 3*:  The *escalation* was enabling and allowing the subsequent test to proceed, even though the conditions were well outside that needed or desired, and control was being performed manually.

*Phase 4*:  The *denial* is evident in the official efforts; first to deny that anything serious had even happened. Then, when the full scope was obvious (due to the uncontrolled release of radioactivity from the burning reactor), subsequently to try shift the blame to any system or operator other than understand there was a real design issue.

## Appendix: Chronology and Transcripts of the Chernobyl' Reactor Unit 4 Accident

The following chronology is interweaved, assembled and extracted from official sources of the sequence given by the Ukrainian Academy of Sciences in 1995 [1]; by key Russian and Ukrainian scientific experts, papers and witness sources at the Chernobyl Workshop, held at Dagomys, Sotchi, USSR in 1989 [2]; and from other reputable organisations and accounts [3,4]. Explanations are noted and given as to why things were done as they were, as derived from the author's own work, presence and contacts within the nuclear technical community in Russia, the Ukraine and North America. The events and times are based on actual instrumentation and data logging time records, actual written operational logs, and statements from plant staff.

This chronology and account is therefore as accurate and complete as possible, based on what is believed to have occurred, and is not therefore from second hand reportage, or taken or sourced from any of the many news reports or published books.

25 April 1986

01:00 The reactor was running at full power with normal operation. Steam power was directed to both turbines of the power generators. The reactor was scheduled to shut down for maintenance.

01:06 Preparation for low power testing commences by the Reactor Operators (RO) reducing power, using manual control as agreed with Chernobyl' Control Center.

03:47 Reactor power now at 1600 MW(t), or about 50% of normal power.

13:05 One turbine generator (left hand LHS TG) now disconnected by RO from the power grid as planned. Half of the main pumps (3 o/o 8, with the one spare not running per normal) on left hand side (LHS) and feedwater pumps (2 o/o 4) are used to feed the one remaining TG on RHS with steam, so power, feed flow and reactor water flow are matched.

14:00 With the reactor at 1600 MW(t), *the Emergency Cooling System (ECCS), needed and designed for cooling the reactor if a loss of water inventory occurred, is disconnected (valved out) by the plant operators (RO)*. The reason for doing this is that the water content (inventory) is expected to and does fluctuate during testing, and spurious injection would be undesirable and could trip (power down) the reactor. Under the normal procedures of the test the reactor would have been reduced to 30% power, but the electrical power authorities refused to allow this because of an apparent need for electricity elsewhere, so the reactor remained at 50% power for another 9 hours.

23:10 At about 23:00 hrs the grid controller agreed to a further reduction in power, and reduction recommenced down to 800 MW(t) (25%).

26 April – Shift Commander Alexander Akimov

00:05 to 00:28 The Chernobyl staff received permission to resume the reactor power reduction. Power reduced from 720 to 500 MW(t), but as the power control is switched by RO from the automatic power control to the main range controller, suitable for the power range, the power unexpectedly and quickly drops to 30 MW(t).

The operators made a mistake, forgetting to reset the controller, which caused the power to fall to a power level too low for the test. This is most likely due to the so-called and well known 'xenon poisoning', where xenon (a neutron absorbing gas) is produced from decay of the products of the fission reaction itself. Eventually, after about eight hours or more before of part- or load reduced-power operation, sufficient xenon was produced with absorption enough to reduce the reactor power.

00:04 To correct the low power, the RO started to increase power by withdrawing control rods, thus overriding the xenon effect *but without automatic control being available.*

The operator forced the reactor up to about 200 MW(t) power by removing all but six of the control rods. *This was a violation of normal operating procedures* since the reactor was not designed to operate at such low power; enough rods were meant to be in reserve and ready and now were not; and the test was supposed to occur at much higher power, at about 1,000 MW(t).

The RO now tried to *manually control the flow* of the feedwater, which is very difficult because of the time lags between changes in flow and the concomitant changes in power, level and pressure.

00:34:03 Low steam drum level (water inventory) indicates below trip, but ECCS is not on.

00:41 to 01:16 (log book entry) The remaining TG on RHS is disconnected by RO per the test requirements for determining the vibration characteristics at ~200 MW(t).

00:43:37 *Emergency protection for TG trips* are 'taken out of service', and reset occurs of steam drum level trip level.

00:52:27 to 01:00:04 The Reactor Operators (RO) raise and stabilise the reactor power, causing steam drum water level fluctuations, finally stabilised when reaching 200 MW(t).

01:03 The spare reactor pump is started by the RO, thus overcooling the reactor and causing steam void reduction, and hence low steam drum level.

01:06 Excessively high feedwater flow recorded (>1400 tonnes/hour sufficient to remove >800 MW(t)) due to having too low a steam drum level.

01:07 Additional reactor main pump restarted by the RO on the side (RHS) which as originally turned off at the beginning.

01:08: Rapid feedwater flow decrease, to 90 t/h on RHS and 180 t/h on LHS, or only 0.5% of the total reactor flow, presumably turned down by the RO

01:09:45 All eight main pumps now turned on by RO, so the reactor core is overcooled for the low power it is at, so the steam voids are reduced again, and hence the steam drum levels drops below the emergency set point.

01:15 Apparently determined to still continue to complete the test, *the operators (RO) deactivate manually the steam drum low level and reactor low pressure trip signals.* The reactor is now unprotected against sensing low levels or loss of water inventory, and only protected by the control and shut off rods against severe power excursions. The RO blocked out the automatic shutdown trips because a reactor shutdown would abort the test, and they could have to repeat it. It could even be delayed for another year until the next shutdown for regular maintenance.

01:18:52 To increase water level (inventory) and hence the water level in the steam drum, the RO increase the feedwater (FW) flow.

01:19:58 Now with feedwater (FW) flow at three times normal, finally the drum water levels rise, but the reactor is overcooled by too much flow and feedwater. The water temperature is well below normal, voids are reduced (condensed) in the core, but the automatic control rods withdraw fully to try to raise power as there is not enough steam void for the operating power level.

01:21:40 The FW flow is reduced by the RO to slow or stop the water level increase in the drums.

01:22:10 Now as a result of this decreased feedwater flow, voids (steam) forms again in the core, thus raising the power, so the automatic control rods move in to try to decrease it. Everything now is out of sync, while the RO manually work to match the level, flow and power.

01:22:30 FW flow is now at 11/2 times less than normal for the power level, so there are more voids than usual, the reactor is stable *but the power effect of this extra steam is not measurable or known to the RO.*

01:23:04 The test is attempted. The remaining turbine (TG) stop valves are shut, closing off the steam flow from the reactor, and the TG coasts down starts. The special MDBA button is pressed, reducing the FW flow to match the reduced steam flow.

01:23:10 The reactor pressure rises, because of the lack of a steam path due to the TG valve closing, and the volume of steam is compressed and hence decreased. So the automatic control rods withdraw for about ten seconds to compensate by increasing the power to increase the steam void, but hence further increases pressure, which is a controlled setpoint for steady operation.

01:23:21 As the TG runs down, the combination of sustained low FW flow, momentary higher power and pressure, means the reactor water has heated up and is closer to its boiling point. The staff hear an increasing low frequency noise. The eight main reactor pumps trip automatically, presumably due to too much steam in their inlet and resulting excessive pump vibration but, as always, it would take at least 35 seconds for them to coast down and stop rotating or pumping altogether (i.e., until at least 01:23:56).

01:23:30 The data logger (SKALA magnetic tape recorder) system is turned on by the RO for the test.

01:23:35–01:23:36 The reactor water is now nearly at its boiling point (saturation temperature for the operating pressure), so the main pumps must be cavitating, and the flow is low and reducing. Unknown to the RO, the reactor is in an unstable physical, neutronic and thermodynamic situation, and disaster is just waiting.

01:23:40 Power in the reactor began to gradually rise because of the boiling due to the reduction in water flow caused by the turbine shutdown and main pump trips.

The Senior Engineer for the reactor control, L. Toptunov had heard a strange increasing low frequency noise, and noticed that the power was increasing. He reported to A. Akimov, the Shift Chief who said to stop the reactor.

The reactor shutdown ('scram') button AZ-5 is pressed and some two seconds later the shut-down rods start to move into the reactor core. The rods are designed so that total insertion would take about 25 seconds and decrease the power, but in fact they are now too few to do that and actually caused a further increase in power from about 300 up to at least 1,000 MW(t). This was because the small designed-in increase in power on initial movement (the rods had a leading length without shut down poison) caused even more boiling than usual because of the hotter water, which caused more power, which caused yet even more boiling to occur. This self increase, or feedback in power as the rods slowly insert is enough to tip the balance to instability. What was normally safe to do had unknowingly become unsafe.

'We pushed the button,' continues Toptunov's account reported later: 'AZ-5, rods went down and then I found they had stopped. I pushed the AZ-5 button one more time, but the rods did not go into the core. Then we received signals: automatic speed protection, power protection, . . . and by all indicators of power protection, *something had happened.*'

At this same time, Velry Perevozchenko, Chief of the reactor shop shift, was entering the central hall at the refuelling level at the reactor top. He observed the blocks of shielding material that was placed on the floor (weighing about 350 kg each) begin to jump up and down: 'and the entire surface ... had come to life and it was rocking in a wild dance'. He ran from the building, hurtling down stairs and along a corridor, just as he heard an explosion.

01:23:42.5 Large and sudden increases occur in the electric current to the pumps (by at least a factor of six), indicating pump overspeed and possible circuit break. An increasing low frequency noise and sharp changes in flow rate on the (coasting down) pump were reported by Senior Engineer B. Stolyarchuk: 'We received signals of pressure in the steam drum, the main protection valve, the fast speed reduction device switch was on. Everything was suspended. There were water shocks'.

01:23:43–44 The reactor power indicators (ionisation chambers) show a rapid high power spike, off-scale on the instruments and later calculated to be ~320,000 MW(t), or about 100 times normal reactor power. This pulse is postulated to be the cause of the reactor fuel elements failing and fragmenting by excessive heating due to the overpower. This leads to the channels failing some five seconds later.

01:23:45 Pressure increases in the steam drums, and the main steam valve closes

01:23:47 The pumps now show a flow decrease of 40%, and there is an increase in steam drum pressure and level.

01:23:48 Steam drum pressures and levels still increasing, core flow 'near normal'.

01:23:49 Failure of electric-powered control rods drives indicated by voltage signals.

01:24 (Log book entry in Control Room) 'Strong shocks'.

It is postulated that this was after the lower reactor channel joints had failed (and possibly much other pipework), allowing steam into the reactor cavity or vault. The vault is only designed to safely vent the steam from one channel, not from many. The resulting unvented steam causes pressure forces that are enough to raise the concrete and steel sealing disc, and the graphite shielding blocks, and lift the entire reactor assembly up and out of its cavity. This tears more pipework apart and lifting up the whole concrete disc, tossing the fuelling machine aside, and much more.

There is another large explosion as the exposed reactor power increases uncontrollably, since the shut off rods are no longer in the core and it is dry. This second large power increase vaporises some of the fuel, and the force of this explosion fails the reactor building and tosses fuel, graphite blocks and core parts directly into the outside night.

Eye witnesses at various locations around the site (two fishermen, an administrator, and a fireman) confirm hearing first large steam discharges, then two distinct explosions, one after the other, the second seen sending incandescent pieces of debris 150 m into the night sky.

Central Control panel, Shift Chief Engineer Boris Rogozkin, who was at control panels for the entire Chernobyl' complex, reported afterwards: 'I heard a deafening shock, after 1–2 seconds system electrical accident began ... the lights went out ... there was a wild noise from the apparatus ... everything droned, wailed and blinked ... a fuel assembly (ejected from the reactor, one of many) had fallen on the bus of the Unit 4 transformer. I heard the cause of the ... shock was the collapse of the turbine hall roof'.

He continues: 'I received reports from the chiefs of the shift and RO, including Vice-Chief Engineer A.S.' Dyatlov who said: 'Boris, *I can't understand anything*. We pushed the button for AZ-5 and nothing had happened.'

(Rogozkin) asked: ' Is water going into the reactor?'

Shift Chief A. Akimov: 'Water is flowing (from the ECCS), *but we don't know where it is going.*'

## Sources

[1] Ukrainian Academy of Sciences, ISTC, 1995 'The Chernobyl' 4 Accident Sequence: Update – April 1995', Kiev, Ukraine, (edited by Edward E. Purvis III).
[2] Duffey, R.B., 1990, 'Chernobyl Reactor Integrated Accident Process and Timeline', EG&G Report EGG-EAST-8947, Idaho National Engineering Laboratory, Idaho, USA.
[3] World Nuclear Association, 2003, http://www.world-nuclear.org/info/chernobyl/, London, UK.
[4] Rhodes, R., 2007, 'Arsenals of Folly: the Making of the Nuclear Arms Race', Alfred A. Knopf, Random House, NY, First Edition, pp. 10–26.

## Conclusion and Echoes: Predicting the Unpredictable

We have analysed in detail the causes, sequences and lesson-learned from four major events, each one echoing the next. They are actually representative of the millions of everyday events that occur around and to us all.

Unique in their sequence, unpredictable in their occurrence, and major in their message, they share the errors that humans make as they experiment with technology on themselves.

These four echoes have received more attention simply and only because they were larger, highly reported and extensively documented. They were so visible and unforgettable, yet all were preventable.

They cover, a wide spectrum of technologies, deliberately chosen and carefully revealed. Thus, though all are different, in fact all are the same. They share the human element in their design, their operation and their cause, however that is assigned.

Because these events (and hence most others) show and contain the same causal factors, as a result they demonstrate the same general and logical development path. Specifically, they contain a set of four conveniently grouped 'watch out' Phases, which we should now be able to instantly recognise and which are intertwined, interdependent and overlapping:

*Phase 1*: Contains the early unfolding precursors, which were known to happen but unrecognised as to their significance and/or uncorrected satisfactorily by the humans building, using and operating the system;

*Phase 2*: Develops as the confluence occurred of failures and events where, despite the humans nominally being in control, they actually had no choice but to make the wrong decisions. Based on inadequate data, commercial or fiscal management pressure, they relied on software or instruments that did not provide up-to-date or believable control information for the actual circumstances that existed.

*Phase 3*: Results as the escalation occurs in the repeated and continuing emphasis and attempts to ensure that everything remains more or less understood, when it is not and/or far from normal. Thus, rather than isolation of the failed parts of the system, and mending those first, effort is devoted to pressing on with the day's seemingly necessary tasks which further compound the situation.

*Phase 4*:  Finally denial and blame shift is evident in the humans involved, where they do not realise their full responsibility, and how the outcome occurred. Management believes that actions taken or not could have saved the day (thus saving the investment), and others are to blame for whatever happened, while in fact all were and are an integral part of the shared problem.

We demonstrate that – in the presence of learning – the future event probability (the likelihood) is given solely by the past (the prior) frequency, as it varies systematically with experience. Thus, the stochastic events and confluence of factors in the Phases is well represented by a systematic overlay due to learning from those same mistakes. The future estimate for the probability is once again derivable from its unchanged prior value, and *thus the past frequency predicts the future probability.*

Therefore, the Four Echoes, in all their apparent complexity, are simply reminders that the Past appears time and again. The observations are the outcomes or major events, being the manifestations of human error embedded within any given technological system.

# Appendix D

## The Four Phases: Fuel Leak Leading to Gliding a Jet in to Land without Any Engine Power

Information source:

Gabinete de Prevenção e Investigação de Acidentes com Aeronaves, Government of Portugal, Ministério das Obras Públicas, Transportes e Comunicações, Aviation Accidents Prevention and Investigation Department, 'All Engines-out Landing Due to Fuel Exhaustion Air Transat Airbus A330-243 marks C-GITS Lajes, Azores, Portugal 24 August 2001', Accident Investigation Final Report 22/ACCID/GPIAA/2001.

### The Bare Facts and the Sequence

Since the early 1990s, twin turbine-engine aircraft have been allowed for use on long (e.g., trans-Atlantic) flights by safety regulators, but only providing special requirements were met. This so-called extended twin-engine operation (ETOPS) allowed reduction in fuel used, the flight crew/pilots not needing a flight engineer, increased operating flexibility, and reduced overall flight cost. However, because engine failure was much more critical, continued operation and landing with only one engine, with one failed, was required to be demonstrated and possible. Moreover special maintenance requirements precluded the same staff making the same repairs or service both engines at the same time, so the same error could not affect or disable both engines.

In brief, the replacement engine was fitted with the wrong part with the wrong paperwork when it was installed in the Airbus aircraft before the flight[1]. The wrong part used was for a

---

[1] Aircraft engines are issued with a Type Certificate (Approval) and built to a specified engine configuration standard for installation in a particular type, series and model of aircraft. Modifications (Service Bulletins) are applied following service experience that can affect safety or performance, or economics, and are classified as Mandatory or Optional depending on their function.

---

hydraulic line using a force fit which resulted in chafing and wear through of an adjacent fuel line in flight. The fuel leak was not detected by the flight crew because of inadequate indicators, despite prior leak events, and because they did not believe there was a leak. The warning signs showed a leak was happening but the crew was not trained nor used the correct diagnostic and recovery actions from the Procedures. When the flight crew found (diagnosed) the cause after about one hour, the crew wrongly transferred remaining fuel to the leak, and did not isolate it. Industry data show that *installation* mistakes account for some 70% of all human errors in aircraft maintenance.

In our terminology, this is a latent fault, and the chance of non-detection by the operating crew of 1 in about 20,000 hours, with a high probability of non-detection during the first experience intervals.

Since remaining fuel was wrongly transferred out of the leaking pipe as the flight crew pressed on, the plane ran out of fuel. Here are the facts from the Portuguese Inquiry report [1].

*On August 24, 2001, Air Transat Flight TSC236, an Airbus 330-243 aircraft, was on a scheduled flight from Toronto Lester B Pearson Airport, Ontario (CYYZ), Canada to Lisbon Airport (LPPT), Portugal with 13 crew and 293 passengers on board.*

*At 05:33, the aircraft was at 4244N/2305W when the crew noted a fuel imbalance.*

*At 05:45, the crew initiated a diversion from the flight-planned route for a landing at the Lajes Airport (LPLA), Terceira Island in the Azores.*

*At 05:48, the crew advised Santa Maria Oceanic Control that the flight was diverting due to a fuel shortage.*

*At 06:13, the crew notified air traffic control that the right engine (Rolls-Royce RB211 Trent 772B) had flamed out.*

*At 06:26, when the aircraft was about 65 nautical miles from the Lajes airport and at an altitude of about FL 345, the crew reported that the left engine had also flamed out and that a ditching at sea was possible.*

*Assisted by radar vectors from Lajes air traffic control, the crew carried out an engines-out, visual approach, at night and in good visual weather conditions.*

*At 06:45, the aircraft landed on runway 33 at the Lajes Airport.*

*After the aircraft came to a stop, small fires started in the area of the left main-gear wheels, but these fires were immediately extinguished by the crash rescue response vehicles that were in position for the landing. The Captain ordered an emergency evacuation; 16 passengers and 2 cabin-crew members received injuries during the emergency evacuation.*

*The aircraft suffered structural damage to the fuselage and to the main landing gear.*

*The post-outcome investigation determined that the double-engine flameout was caused by fuel exhaustion, which was precipitated by a fuel leak developing in the right engine as the result of the use of mismatched fuel and hydraulic lines during the installation of the hydraulic pump (on a replacement engine of the wrong type).*

*Facilitating the fuel exhaustion was the fact that the crew did not perform the FUEL LEAK procedure that was specifically designed by the manufacturer to reduce the consequences of an in-flight fuel leak.*

*Up to the point that the crew became aware of the fuel quantity anomaly, the flight was prepared and conducted in accordance with existing regulations and operational directives.*

The accident report [1] focused on why:

- the aircraft maintenance organisation *did not detect* the mismatch in engine configurations prior to starting the engine change; then
- once the configuration difference was detected during the engine change, the installation of the hydraulic pump and hydraulic and fuel lines was not completed in accordance with manufacturer's specifications; and
- a qualified flight crew trained in accordance with approved training programs, while attempting to analyse the situation and taking actions in reaction to the situation, did not take the actions prescribed by the manufacturer to mitigate the consequences of a fuel leak situation, and took action that exacerbated the situation.

## The Four Phases

*Phase (1)* of the early unfolding precursors which were known to happen but unrecognised as to their significance by the humans who built, use, insure and operate the system.

The Investigation report [1] is clear that:

*A review of aircraft manufacturer and engine manufacturer occurrence databases revealed that since 1994 there have been at least 25 in-flight fuel-leak events. Although some of these events were minor in nature, a number were significant … in that they lead to a loss of fuel that resulted in a serious incident, such as an engine fire or a loss of fuel that resulted in a diversion or emergency situation. Because the fuel leaks were clearly attributable to technical faults, few of the events were investigated and even fewer were analysed to determine operational factors that may have increased the seriousness of the event.*

*Prior to the Air Transat A330 occurrence there had not been another recorded occurrence that involved total (emphasis added) fuel exhaustion due to a fuel leak, although there had been a number of cases of significant fuel loss, some of which would have been mitigated by following the manufacturer's recommended procedures. Since this occurrence, there has been one commercial airliner occurrence involving a fuel leak that resulted in fuel exhaustion and an off-airfield forced landing, fortunately without any serious injuries to passengers or crew.*

Prior knowledge about fuel leaks and the problems of their detection existed from prior events, and the needed changes had not been made. The leak constituted a latent (hidden) fault, which the crew was unable to properly diagnose and detect in flight until too late. The precursors there were both a previous fuel leak and detectable maintenance errors.

Studies of 'fuel exhaustion and starvation' show these outcome or events to be quite predictable, and the propensity for the crew to take the wrong actions previously known. The Australian Transport Safety Body (ATSB) stated in their study:

*Experience on aircraft type has been found to influence the occurrence of fuel-related incidents in that pilots with fewer hours on type are more likely to be involved in fuel-related occurrences, and this may be a consideration for pilots in the private category. Alternatively, fatigue and high operator workload may contribute to fuel-related accidents in the agricultural category.*

*'Pre-Flight Preparation' (including incorrect assessment of fuel quantity and miscalculation of fuel required) and 'Events During Flight' (including inattention to fuel supply and continuing with flight regardless of fuel problem) are the factors most commonly contributing to fuel exhaustion accidents.*

*'Events During Flight' (including mismanagement of fuel system and inattention to fuel supply) and 'Technical Factors' (including component failure and malfunctioning fuel system) are the most common contributing factors in fuel starvation accidents.*

*One in four pilots involved in a fuel-related accident appears to have used inappropriate aircraft handling techniques after the engine failure was experienced.*

*These findings emphasise the importance of sound procedures and training. An education program focused at increasing levels of awareness of fuel-related issues within the aviation industry may be beneficial.*

*The (Australian) Civil Aviation Safety Authority (CASA) is currently reviewing the civil aviation regulations with the aim of making them simpler, clearer and generally harmonised with those of other leading aviation nations. As part of this process, a number of additional fuel management requirements have been proposed. It is hoped that these changes, along with a greater awareness of fuel-related issues within the Australian aviation industry will allow for a reduction in the number of fuel-related accidents. Aircraft owners and operators may also wish to consider the use of fuel flow management systems as an additional defence against fuel-related accidents.*

Source: Australian Aviation Accidents Involving Fuel Exhaustion and Starvation, ATSB,
Research Paper, December 2002.

Incorrect management and measurement of fuel quantity appears to be still an issue on some aircraft types/models (see e.g., [2]) where low fuel indication may not be mandatory and/or faulty. The final report [1] states:

*As demonstrated in this occurrence and other earlier fuel leak occurrences, flight crews have difficulty in assessing the seriousness of fuel leak situations due to the following:*

*– The absence of confirming data in the form of knowledge and the lack of operational exposure to similar events.*

*– The absence of physical evidence of fuel leaking from the aircraft or abnormally high fuel flow indications.*

*– The lack of a direct system warning to alert the crew to the precise critical condition.*

*– The appearance of another system indication that diverts the crew's attention to another more-easily understood situation of lower criticality.*

*– The lack of training covering conditions likely to cause fuel leaks and the procedures to be followed if a fuel leak is experienced.*

As to prior events:

*In a prior 24 August 1997 fuel leak event, an Air France (Airbus) A320 aircraft experienced a fuel leak. The crew involved in this event took similar (wrong) action to balance the fuel. The investigation into this (previous) 24 August 1997 Air France A320 occurrence resulted in a 6 September 1997 BEA (the French Air Safety Authority) recommendation (on the re-examination) of the adequacy of systems and procedures, and as an interim measure to notify all crews of the circumstances of the occurrence.*

*The FUEL LEAK checklist was improved, a FUEL IMBALANCE checklist was developed and pilot information was promulgated.*

*At the time of this Air Transat A330 occurrence, a leak warning system had not been incorporated in any A330 aircraft. Additionally, fuel leak training had not been incorporated into the Airbus A330 training program.*

*The A330 Fuel Control and Monitoring Computer (FCMC) system was not designed to consider the type of fuel leak that occurred during this flight. As a result, after the FCMC did what it could do to maintain a fuel level of 4 tons in the right tank and when it was no longer able to maintain that level, it advised the crew that there was an imbalance. Specifically, the FCMC, no longer able to deal with the fuel leak through its pre-programmed fuel balancing, shed the task to the crew. This shedding took the form of a fuel imbalance computer generated Advisory warning message (ADV.)*

*Had the Air Transat crew taken the actions required by the FUEL LEAK checklist when the fuel loss was first recognised at 05:53, the aircraft would not have run out of fuel before reaching land.*

An engine change had occurred on the plane just prior to the flight.

*When the spare engine arrived at the company's premises on 1 August 2001, it was processed in accordance with the Air Transat Maintainence Control Manual (MCM) procedures. The process only involved an inventory check and verification that the parts on the Carry Forward Items List were available. Because the engine was positioned at Mirabel (the airport in Canada), solely as a contingency measure, and there were no immediate plans to install the engine on a company aircraft, the engine remained under the control of the engine manufacturer's representative. Neither the MCM, nor Canadian regulations, require Service Bulletins (SB's) to be checked as part of this type of inventory check. This check was based on a comparison of the spare engine against the Rework Summary Sheet and the Carry Forward Items List provided by the company that had completed the last shop visit of the engine. Based on the available information and a visual inspection of the condition of the engine, it was assessed that the required parts were available if and when an engine change to one of the company's A330 became necessary.*

*Of importance to this occurrence, the engine receiving process did not identify that the configuration of the loaned engine did not match the configuration of the other A330 engines at the company.*

**Phase (2)** where the confluence occurred of developing failures and events where, despite the humans nominally being in control, they actually had no choice but to make decisions based on inadequate data, commercial or fiscal management pressures, and rely on software or instruments that did not provide up-to-date or believable control information for the actual circumstances that existed.

Note here that both the engine work crew and the flight crew activities were conducted as if processes were per usual. The information to make correct choices to correct or mitigate the faults were available to both in non-normal (indirect or obscure) ways, but not accessed or used in the pressure to continue as normal. Latent faults were undetected in both the engine type identification and in establishing the fuel line leak itself.

The wrong engine part was used with the wrong paperwork, and there was no direct means of leak detection for the crew.

*The following factors may have influenced this incorrect assessment of the engine type:*

– *Because all the A330 engines in use at the company were in the post-SB configuration and the company personnel had never been involved with pre-SB configured engines, there was no information that would have caused a heightened concern regarding the configuration of the loaned engine.*
– *The physical appearance of the pre-SB and post-SB configurations are similar and cannot be identified through a cursory inspection such as is conducted during engine receipt.*
– *The part number of the hydraulic pump, as documented in the carry-forward list, was incorrectly identified as a post-SB hydraulic pump, Part Number 974976.*
– *Hydraulic pump, Part Number 974976 was installed on other company A330 aircraft.*

*The Air Transport Association (ATA) identifies SB's as the only means for the manufacturer to notify operators of a product modification. Comparing the status of non-mandatory SB's on components of the same part number, such as an engine, is not a method generally used to assure inter-changeability, for the following reasons:*

– *there is no regulatory requirement to do so;*
– *the absence of documentation on non-mandatory SB's does not constitute a risk to safety;*
– *the number of non-mandatory SB's that may apply to a major aircraft component may be very large, and conducting the comparison would be time consuming; and*
– *the parts catalog (IPC) contains all the information regarding the applicability of SB's.*

*The Transport Canada (TC) regulator-approved MCM did not require that non-mandatory SB's be checked when planning for an engine change; consequently, a comparison of SB's was not carried out at the time of engine receipt, nor during the planning of the engine change.*

*Because the company maintenance planners were not aware of the differences in configuration between the two engines, the only work cards that were generated were those associated with a normal engine change.*

*Additional work sheets for the installation of the carry-forward items were to be completed during the course of the engine change. The fact that the differences in engine configuration were not identified during the receipt and planning phases, resulted in a situation wherein the responsibility to detect the incompatibility between the hydraulic pump and the fuel and hydraulic lines was deferred to the technicians doing the engine change.*

*During the course of the engine replacement, the interference noticed between the hydraulic pump and the fuel tube was the first indication of a problem with the changeover of the hydraulic pump to the engine that was being installed on the occurrence aircraft. Once it was realised that the difficulty with the hydraulic pump installation could be related to the differing SB status, the lead technician attempted to view the SB. However, he could not access the SB on the Rolls-Royce computer-based parts catalog (EIPC CD) from his work station due to a network problem. Not being able to access the SB through the network, the lead technician sought engineering guidance via MCC as per the MCM procedures.*

*Neither the lead technician nor the MCC considered accessing the SB through the Trent EIPC on a stand-alone computer. Had the Trent EIPC been used, access to the SB would have been achieved. Access to the SB would have revealed that there were two interrelated SB's that required replacement of the fuel tube and the hydraulic line, as well as other associated components.*

*When the lead technician contacted the Engine Controller, the Engine Controller's knowledge of the SB and its background comforted the lead technician into feeling that the Engine Controller had a good grasp of the problem at hand. Acknowledgement by the Engine Controller that the fuel tube needed to be replaced confirmed the lead technician's mental model that this was the only requirement for completion of the installation. The confirmation was reinforced by the fact that the Engine Controller was associated with the engineering department, which had the responsibility for resolving unexpected or non-routine maintenance issues.*

Quality Control (QC) issues existed, because:

*QC is limited to verifying that the documentation is complete, (which means that) the quality assurance verification of the aircraft and engine maintenance logs would likely not have detected that the installation of the hydraulic pump and fuel line was not in accordance with applicable SB's. Rather than relying on a post-maintenance review of the engine documentation, the presence of a quality control representative during the engine installation may have facilitated the research into the interference problem and the full implementation of the SB prior to the release of the aircraft.*

*The investigation determined that the engine was received in an unexpected pre-SB configuration to which the operator had not previously been exposed. Also, the identification of a component is first and foremost carried out through its part numbering. The documentation attached to the loaned engine, in using a part number for a post-SB hydraulic pump, may have masked the pre-SB engine configuration until near completion of the engine change. Typically components of different configurations are identified via a part number prefix, suffix or dash number; however, this is not practical for complex components, such as modern aircraft engines.*

*Non-mandatory SB's may not directly impact on airworthiness when embodied on their own. However, when two or more interrelated non-mandatory SB's, with interacting components, are not carried out in tandem they have the potential to degrade airworthiness, as seen in this occurrence. Although the use of SB's was the only viable method for determining the compatibility of the replacement engine with the engine being removed, the comparison of SB's is not a commonly used means of configuration control, as evidenced in this occurrence.*

*Phase (3)* results when the escalation occurs during the repeated and continuing emphasis and attempts to ensure that everything remains more or less understood, when it is not and/or far from normal. Suffering from 'pressonitis', we continue on rather than isolating the failed parts of the system, addressing those first, rather than pressing on with the day's seemingly necessary tasks that further compound the situation.

This Phase happened both during the maintenance activity of installing the wrong part on the replacement engine, but also in the subsequent actions. Difficulties in installing new (replacement) parts are not uncommon, but the significance in the mismatch of the paperwork and the lack of mechanical fit was unrecognised by the skilled maintenance staff.

*Even though aircraft configuration is affected by Service Bulletins (SB's), there is no airworthiness requirement to review all non-mandatory SB's on a component prior to its installation nor is there a system in place to facilitate the checking of SB parity. Although Transport Canada audits include the scrutiny of the implementation of SB's, the management of SB's (assessment of applicability, implementation time frame, embodiment and recording) is left to the carrier's discretion. In the absence of a requirement to conduct an SB parity check, and of an easy-to-use method of carrying this check out, there is a risk that incompatible components may be installed on aircraft and not be detected by existing maintenance planning processes.*

*There was also the time-pressure factor to complete the (engine replacement) work in time for a scheduled flight and to clear the hangar for an upcoming event. This pressure also may have played a role in reliance on direct and personal information about the SB, rather than trying to resolve the existing problem of not being able to access the SB's.*

*With the solution at hand, being behind schedule, and having spoken to the Engine Controller, the lead technician felt confident that the fuel tube replacement was the only remaining requirement to complete the hydraulic pump installation. During discussions on the estimated time for completing the engine change, the Engine Controller was made aware that the lead technician had been unable to access the SB. Although both individuals acknowledged that the unavailability of the SB's was of concern, the discussion reverted to the issue of work completion time, and no further discussion of the SB took place.*

*Effectively, the Engine Controller and the lead technician agreed to the fuel tube transfer with no further reference to the SB.*

*Exchanging the fuel tube was considered by the lead technician to be a maintenance action similar to the changing-over of other components on the Carry Forward Items List. He believed that the replacement of the fuel tube would establish the engine configuration in the post-modification status.*

*Although it was recognised that the fuel tube from the replaced engine was different from the one being removed from the engine being installed, the aircraft IPC entry was not referenced.*

*Adequate clearance between the fuel and hydraulic lines reportedly was achieved during the installation of the hydraulic pump line by applying some force to position the line and holding the line while applying torque to the 'B' nut. This clearance subsequently was verified by the lead technician.*

*Although it is not abnormal that a line be positioned to achieve clearances in this manner, if clamping is not used, the tendency is for a flexible line to straighten when pressurised. This is particularly critical when there is a 90° bend in the tube adjacent to the 'B' nut, as was the case for this installation. The risk associated with the application of force while installing mixed construction lines is not well known in the maintenance community, and is not covered in the training of maintenance technicians.*

*Although the marks on the fuel and hydraulic tubes suggest that some implement may have been used to assist in establishing clearance between the tubes, technicians denied that tools were used in this manner. The investigation could not resolve this issue. The pressurisation of the hydraulic line would have been sufficient to cause the hydraulic line to move back to its natural position and come in contact with the fuel line, which resulted in the chafing and failure of the fuel line.*

*Post-installation inspections of the engine change were done both by the lead technician and another independent inspector. However, the inspections were limited to ensuring that engine controls were properly connected and secured, and that the remaining work was complete, was within tolerances and was secured. The methods used for these inspections would not very likely detect a mismatch in components, and for the occurrence engine did not detect the incompatibility of the fuel and hydraulic lines that existed.*

*Neither the aircraft nor the engine log recorded the fuel line change because the technician forgot to make the entry. In addition the verification of the documentation associated with the engine change completed on 18 August 2001 was not done before the occurrence flight. Consequently, the opportunity for the quality assurance review of the documentation to detect the installation error was negated.*

## Flight Crew Actions

As demonstrated in this occurrence and other earlier fuel leak occurrences, flight crews have difficulty in assessing the seriousness of fuel leak situations.

### *Initial Recognition of the Fuel Loss (04:38–05:33)*

At 04:38, the Airbus Digital Flight Data Recorder (DFDR recorded an increased rate of reduction in the fuel quantity. Post-outcome analysis of this DFDR data determined that this anomaly was the start of the fuel leak in the right (#2) engine, low-pressure fuel line. The increased rate of reduction in fuel quantity would have been indicated in lower-than-anticipated fuel on board (FOB) quantity figure on the early warning display (EWD) to the crew.

At 04:44, the DFDR recorded a decrease in oil quantity on the right engine; however, because the oil parameters were within operating limits an electronic (ECAM) message was not generated.

At 04:56, the DFDR recorded the commencement of a two-minute forward transfer of fuel from the trim tank to the main wing tanks. Total transfer was about 0.3 tons. During this transfer, a green TRIM TANK XFR ECAM message would have been displayed in the memo section of the EWD. The (plane's) crew did not recall seeing this message.

The fuel leak started at 04:38, but a fuel problem was not noticed by the crew until 05:33, when the fuel ADV message was generated. During this time, there were a number of cockpit indications that there was a fuel-loss problem, as follows:

– The fuel on board was decreasing at an unusual rate; this information would have been displayed in the FOB figures on the EWD page.
– The estimated fuel on board at destination was decreasing; this information would have been displayed to the crew in the multi-purpose display unit (MCDU).
– The full forward transfer of the fuel in the trim tank was premature given the fuel load on departure from Toronto of 46,900 kg. (~47 tons).

A prolonged, 19-minute TRIM TANK XFR memo (message) between 05:11 and 05:30, and then the TRIM TANK XFRD memo between 05:30 and 05:33 would have displayed this information.

Although the fuel leak started at 04:38, the higher-than-normal rate of fuel quantity reduction was not recognised by the crew until after the Fuel page was called up at 05:34 by them as the result of the fuel imbalance ADV message. By the time the crew was able to take initial actions to the situation at 05:36, more than 7 tons of fuel had already been lost.

The suddenness and the magnitude of the indicated fuel loss were perceived (by the crew) as being incredible and not linked to any explainable cause.

The following factors probably contributed to this delayed recognition of the low fuel quantity problem:

– The only fuel check required by standard operation procedures during this timeframe was done at 04:58 as the aircraft crossed 30° West. At this time, the fuel *quantity was unremarkable, because it was within 0.2 tons or 1% of the planned fuel quantity.*

- *The crew was then involved in position reporting, recording entries on the flight log, and checking instrument indications.*
- *The unusual oil readings created a level of uncertainty in the cockpit.*
- *This uncertainty resulted in the crew becoming occupied in activities to resolve the ambiguities, including reviewing manuals and contacting the MCC.*
- *The final forward transfer of the 3.2 tons of fuel from the trim tank into the right wing tank delayed the generation of the fuel ADV message by approximately 15 minutes.*

*Although the TRIM TANK XFR memo was premature given the stage of flight, the initial appearance of the memo would have been unremarkable, because it comes on routinely during flights. Also, given the crew activities associated with resolving the unusual oil readings, it is understandable that, during this time frame, the crew did not recognise the prolonged nature of the TRIM TANK XFR memo, the presence of the TRIM TANK XFRD memo, and the subtle changing of the FOB and EFOB figures.*

*From 04:38, the time that the fuel leak started, until 05:04, the time when the unusual oil indications were recognised, cockpit activity level was normal. However, the task of resolving the oil indications raised the activity level and drew the attention of the crew away from routine monitoring of other displays.*

*All of the fuel-related information and messages were provided in the form of text-type status messages and digital counter displays, none of which conveyed a sense of urgency to cause the crew to abandon activities associated with resolving the oil reading anomalies, and none of which conveyed the critical nature of the fuel leak.*

*Of importance is that during this time, the forward transfer caused the fuel in the trim tank to be loaded into the right wing, delaying the generation of the fuel ADV message, masking the fuel leak problem from the crew.*

*By the time that the fuel imbalance advisory was generated at 05:33, fuel on board had reduced to 12.2 tons and 6.65 tons of fuel had been lost.*

*In summary, it was highly unlikely that the crew would have become aware of the fuel anomaly during this time frame, given the subtleties of the available indications. The fact that this could occur highlights the limitations of the warning and alert system in this kind of situation.*

## Crew Reaction to the Fuel Imbalance Advisory (05:33–05:45)

*At 05:33, a pulsing, white ECAM advisory ADV message was generated and displayed in the memo area of the EWD, indicating a 3,000 kg fuel imbalance between the right and left wing tanks. Under normal conditions, this ECAM advisory brings up the FUEL system page on the system display (SD) to the crew. However, the manual selection of ENGINE systems page used by the crew inhibited the display of the fuel page. A 3,000 kg fuel imbalance is an abnormal condition that does not result in a display of the corrective action required to correct the imbalance. To ascertain the required corrective action, the crew must view the fuel page, diagnose the pulsing fuel quantity indications, and then refer to the appropriate page in the Quick Reference Handbook (QRH).*

*At 05:34, the crew deselected the ENGINE page, and the FUEL page was displayed in the SD.*

*At 05:36, having noted the fuel imbalance, the crew opened the crossfeed valve and turned off the right-wing fuel pumps, establishing a crossfeed from the left wing tank to the right engine. An amber FUEL R WING PUMPS LO PR message would have appeared on the left side of the message area of the EWD and a green WING X FEED memo would have appeared on the right side. Shortly afterward, the crew also noted that the remaining fuel on board was significantly below the planned quantity. Fuel losses or leaks themselves cannot be identified as such by the ECAM system; consequently, a specific ECAM warning is not generated for these conditions, although related system messages would be generated as normal parameters were approached or exceeded.*

*After becoming aware of a fuel problem at 05:33, the crew's initial action was to cancel the display of the engine page in order to view the FUEL page. Because of the nature of the ADV, the ECAM did not display a checklist procedure and the crew was required to review the indications on the FUEL page to determine the problem.*

*Based on the flashing displays associated with the right wing tank, the crew assessed that there was a fuel imbalance situation. Then at 05:36, by memory and without reference to the QRH, the fuel balancing procedure was initiated by opening the crossfeed valve and turning off the right wing tank pumps. At this time, fuel on board had reduced to 11 tons and 7.3 tons of fuel had been lost.*

*The opening of the crossfeed valve resulted in the fuel from the left wing tanks being fed to the leak in the right engine. In doing the fuel imbalance procedure by memory, the crew overlooked the FUEL IMBALANCE Caution that, in the event that a fuel leak is suspected, the FUEL LEAK procedure should be done.*

*It was just after taking the initial actions to establish the crossfeed that the crew became aware of the following other indications that reflected a fuel loss problem:*

*– The fuel on board was 7 tons lower than predicted for the stage of the flight.*
*– The estimated fuel on board at destination had decreased significantly from the planned amount.*

*The sudden discovery of an unexplainable, lower-than-expected fuel quantity, resulted in the crew attempting to resolve the discrepancy, as follows:*

*– The fuel loading, flight planning documents and flight records were reviewed for errors; none were found.*
*– Engine and fuel system indications and displays were reviewed to determine if there were other indications of a problem with the engines, fuel flow or fuel system; none were found.*
*– There had been no prior sounds or other perceived aircraft symptoms that would suggest an aircraft structural or fuel problem.*

*When the ECAM ADV alerted the crew to the fuel imbalance, there was a large disparity between the actual fuel system state and the crew's understanding of it. Although there were other indications that the situation was more serious than a fuel imbalance, the crew initially reacted by doing the FUEL IMBALANCE procedure because that was the only anomaly that was exposed by the ECAM system. The crew did the procedure from memory because the crew was familiar with it, having been frequently required to monitor fuel balance during simulator training sessions.*

*The cockpit activity level during this 12-minute period would have been high, and the crew's attention would have been focused on the perceived ambiguity of the fuel situation and activities involved with the diversion to Lajes (the airport in the Azores). Consequently, the crew would have had little time and limited mental capacity to re-examine its mental model of the situation and to question actions already taken in response to the fuel ADV. Doing the FUEL IMBALANCE procedure fulfilled the immediate, perceived goal of managing the fuel imbalance.*

*Neither of the crewmembers had ever experienced a fuel imbalance of any magnitude during flying operations, nor been exposed to a fuel leak situation during training or operations.*

*Once the EFOB at destination reduced below minimums, the Captain made an appropriate decision to divert to the ETOPS alternate of Lajes.*

*In summary, the crew was presented with an ADV that did not require immediate action. The Flight Crew Operating Manual (FCOM) required that the crew refer to the Quick Reference Checklist (QRH) before taking action, and crew resource management (CRM) principles suggest that, before taking action in response to the Fuel ADV, the crew should have taken into account all available information about the fuel system. Such a review would have revealed that over 6 tons of fuel had been lost. The combination of the fuel-loss indications and the substance of the Caution note in the FUEL IMBALANCE procedure in the QRH should have led the crew to the FUEL LEAK procedure.*

*The FUEL LEAK, LEAK FROM ENGINE procedure requires that the leaking engine be shut down; the FUEL LEAK NOT FROM ENGINE OR LEAK NOT LOCATED requires that the crossfeed must remain closed. Either of these actions would have conserved the fuel in the left wing tanks and allowed for a landing at Lajes with the left engine operating.*

*Opening the crossfeed valve put the fuel in the left tank at risk, and initiated a worsening of the serious fuel leak situation that existed.*

## Crew Reaction to the Continued Fuel Loss (05:45–06:10)

*Distracted by everything that was happening, the crew pressed on with their actions as if there were no leak.*

*From 05:45, the time that the diversion was initiated, to 05:51, when the Flight Director-cabin services (FD) left the cockpit to do the visual inspection for signs of a fuel leak, the level of activity in the cockpit would have been very high. In particular, much of the crew's efforts would have been occupied with preparing the aircraft systems for the diversion and approach to Lajes, and crew's requirement to advise Air Traffic Control (ATC) and the FD about the decision to divert, all tasks required by the diversion.*

*At the time that the diversion (crossfeed) commenced at 05:45, fuel on board had reduced to 8.7 tons, 9.3 tons of fuel had been lost, and fuel from the left wing tank was being used to feed both engines, and the 13 tons-per-hour fuel leak.*

*During the time when the diversion was being planned, the crew stated (afterwards) that doing the FUEL LEAK procedure had been considered. However, they were still uncertain as to the validity of the fuel quantity indications and the precise nature of the problem.*

*At 05:52, the caution message ENG 2 FUEL FILTER CLOG appeared on the EWD. This message indicated an abnormal (and sometimes temporary) pressure loss across the fuel filter of the right engine. This type of message does not require action by the crew; it is only generated for crew awareness and monitoring, if necessary.*

*The crew further stated (afterwards) that they discounted doing the LEAK NOT FROM ENGINE or LEAK NOT LOCATED procedure because doing so would require a descent to a lower altitude and would further degrade an already critical situation. Notwithstanding, had this procedure been initiated before 05:54, completing the action to close the crossfeed valve would have conserved the fuel in the left wing tanks and allowed for a landing at Lajes with (only) the left engine operating.*

*At 05:54, the Captain having reconfigured the fuel pumps to establish the crossfeed from the right tanks resulted in the fuel in the right wing tank feeding the left engine, thereby isolating fuel in the left tank from the leak in the right engine and conserving the fuel in the left tank that would be normally feeding the left engine. The momentary configuration of crossfeed from the left tanks at 06:02 in reaction to a suggestion from the Maintenance Control Center (MCC) had little consequence on the fuel situation.*

*At 05:58, the FUEL R WING TK LO LVL message appeared, indicating less than 1,640 kg of fuel remaining in the right inner tank for more than 60 seconds.*

*At 06:08, the FUEL L+R WING TK LO LVL message appeared, indicating that inner tanks on both wings were now below 1,640 kg for more than 60 seconds.*

*At 06:13, the ENG 2 STALL and ENG 2 FAIL messages were displayed indicating that the right engine had flamed-out. The engine speed (RPM) decay resulted in the ENG 2 STALL message; the ENG 2 FAIL message indicated that core engine speed had decelerated to below idle with the master switch 'on' and the fire pushbutton 'in' (not pushed).*

*At 06:21, the FUEL TRIM TK PUMP LO PR message was displayed indicating that the trim tank transfer pump switch had been selected to FWD and no fuel remained in the trim tank.*

*At 06:26, the ENG 1 STALL and ENG 1 FAIL messages were generated as the left engine flamed-out.*

*As the associated generator decelerated, the aircraft would have automatically reverted to the emergency electrical configuration, with power supplied by the automatic extension of the ram air turbine. The EMER ELEC CONFIG warning may have been inhibited by the ENG ALL ENG FLAMEOUT warning; neither warning was recorded on the Post Flight Report.*

*Between 05:57, the start of radio (HF) communications with MCC, and 06:13, the time when the right engine flamed out, much of the crew's efforts were involved with communications with the MCC totalling over 10 minutes. The workload was sufficiently high that the crew did not have time to action the ECAM action items associated with the FUEL R WING TK LO LVL and the FUEL L+R WING TK LO LVL messages that appeared at 05:58 and 06:08 respectively.*

*Although not actioning these checklists did not adversely affect the flight, the crew's involvement in non-critical communication with MCC reduced the time available for them to more accurately assess the situation.*

*Notwithstanding indications that there had been a massive loss of fuel, the crew (still) did not believe that there was an actual fuel leak.*

*The following factors supported this mental model of the situation:*

– *The combination of the suddenness and the magnitude of the indicated fuel loss were such that it could not be linked to any explainable reason.*
– *The earlier problem with the oil indications had established a level of uncertainty.*
– *There was no ECAM warning or caution message indicating a severe problem.*
– *No other indication of an engine problem was discovered.*
– *Some information, like the cabin crew confirming that there were no visible signs of a leak, countered the possibility of a leak.*

*The crew, realising that the situation was continuing to deteriorate, hypothesised that a computer malfunction would account for the ambiguous indications. The lack of training for a fuel leak situation, never having experienced a fuel leak, and having no knowledge of similar events meant that the crew had no relevant information to counter the basis for their hypothesis.* The snap judgement was wrong.

## Crew Reactions to the (Two) Engine Failures

*The automatic alarm messages were now coming in quickly to the crew on their displays.*

*At 06:10, the time that the crew stated that all fuel pump switches were selected ON, the aircraft was 175 miles from Lajes, with approximately 1.0 ton of fuel in the left tank and 0.2 tons in the right tank.*
*At 06:13, the ENG 2 STALL and ENG 2 FAIL messages were displayed indicating that the right engine had flamed-out. The RPM decay resulted in the ENG 2 STALL message; the ENG 2 FAIL message indicated that core speed had decelerated to below idle with the master switch 'on' and the fire pushbutton 'in' (not pushed).*

*It was not until the right engine had flamed out that the crew began to reassess their mental model. Even at this point, they were unable to account for the flameout and were under the hypothesis that the indications still could be erroneous.*

*At 06:21, the FUEL TRIM TK PUMP LO PR message was displayed indicating that the trim tank transfer pump switch had been selected to FWD and no fuel remained in the trim tank.*
*At 06:21, the crew, attempting to ensure that all usable fuel from the trim tank was available to the remaining left engine, selected the trim tank transfer pump switch to FWD, which resulted in the display of the FUEL TRIM TK PUMP LO PR message, indicating that no fuel remained in the trim tank.*
*At 06:26, the ENG 1 STALL and ENG 1 FAIL messages were generated as the left engine flamed-out. As the associated generator decelerated, the aircraft would have automatically reverted to the emergency electrical configuration, with power supplied by the automatic*

*extension of the ram air turbine. The EMER ELEC CONFIG warning may have been inhibited by the ENG ALL ENG FLAMEOUT warning; neither warning was recorded on the Post Flight Report.*

*Based on recorder data available, the crew's reaction to the engine failures and actioning of the required checklist procedures were in accordance with procedures specified in the FCOM. The performance of cockpit duties, interface with cabin crew, and communications with air traffic were professional and highly effective.*

*For the Glide Approach and Landing, the Captain's handling of the aircraft during the engines-out descent and landing was remarkable given the facts that the situation was stressful, it was night time, there were few instruments available, pitch control was limited, and he had never received training for this type of flight.*

*The Captain's decision to apply and maintain maximum braking on the second touchdown was justified based on the facts that the aircraft speed was well above the recommended speed when crossing the threshold, and that, following the initial bounce, the aircraft touched down significantly beyond the normal touchdown zone.*

*The First Officer provided full and effective support to the Captain during the engines-out glide and successful landing.*

**Phase (4)** finally denial is evident from all the humans involved, where they do not realise their full responsibility and contribution, and how it happened. Also management and society believes that actions taken or not, could have saved the day (thus saving the investment), and others are to blame for whatever happened, while in fact all were and are an integral part of the shared problem.

In this dangerous risk case, we have the wrong engine refit, the wrong crew diagnosis, reliance on automatic systems, inadequate auto warning messaging, plus the lack of procedural training, and lack of regulations which all contributed. The report [1] simply spreads the blame around between these factors as follows.

*A significant fuel imbalance during normal operations is a rare and unlikely event. The only time a fuel imbalance would be expected to occur is if there is a significant difference in fuel consumption between the left and right engines, such as when an engine failure occurs. Even in such an emergency situation, the imbalance would remain low unless the time to landing was long. In such a situation, the reason for the imbalance would be easily understood.*

*A fuel imbalance in the range of the 3.0-ton magnitude required to generate a FUEL ADV would only likely occur if there were a significant fuel leak. Without training on fuel leaks or on other conditions that would lead to such a suddenness of such a change in fuel, flight crews have had difficulty in determining the reason for the change, in particular if other supportive, easily understood, (fuel use) rate-type information was not available.*

*Although lessons learned from previous fuel-imbalance occurrences resulted in fuel leak checklists and system software changes being established, training on factors that may create a fuel imbalance, and the conditions under which the FUEL IMBALANCE procedure should not be used was never incorporated into training programs.*

*The perception that a fuel imbalance is a low-risk situation* is evidenced by the following:

– *the situation is not announced by a caution or a warning or alert;*
– *the Caution note in the FUEL IMBALANCE checklist that the checklist should not be used if a fuel leak is suspected is not prominent;*

- *the conditions that should be used to assess if a fuel leak exists are not located on the FUEL IMBALANCE checklist; and*
- *the exposure of A330 crews to fuel imbalance situations is limited to situations that only require a monitoring of fuel balance, and not to situations that require an active response to a FUEL IMBALANCE advisory.*

*Although two green TRIM TANK XFR ECAM advisory messages would have been displayed in the memo section of the E/WD during the flight, these two memos would have been unremarkable, first because this type of message comes on routinely during flights, and second because the message is a status type text message that neither conveys urgency or requires immediate action.*

*In addition, the subtle addition of one text letter 'D' from the TRIM TANK XFR to the TRIM TANK XFRD message is not a high-salience change and did not draw this crew's Attention. Even the last TRIM TANK XFR message that lasted 19 minutes and the TRIM TANK XFRD message for remainder of the flight did not alert the crew to an urgent situation, in part because they were occupied in higher priority cockpit tasks such as completing flight documentation, communicating, analysing the unusual engine oil parameter anomalies, and then attempting to resolve the fuel imbalance and ambiguity of the fuel quantity.*

*Of importance is that the forward transfer caused the fuel in the trim tank to be loaded into the right wing, feeding the leak in the right engine and masking the fuel leak problem from the crew.*

*This masking contributed to an unnoticed loss of 3.5 tons of fuel.*

*During training and actual operations, the crews are taught to place trust in the ECAM (A330 automatic warning system) that the system will provide the needed information for significant, abnormal or emergency situations.*

*For this occurrence, the only alerting provided to the crew was the white ADV message only requiring system parameter monitoring, even though by this time the aircraft had actually lost 6.5 tons of fuel. This low level of alerting created an atmosphere of little or no urgency associated with the situation that was being conveyed.*

*The current design approach of the automated system not monitoring and analysing available aircraft information that would be characteristic of a fuel leak situation implies that a FUEL LEAK is very low probability event and a low-risk event. This A330 occurrence and the 1997 A320 occurrence indicate, however, that a FUEL LEAK is not only a high-risk situation that can be misidentified by qualified and trained crews, but also requires clear, unambiguous alerting of the crew and guidance as to the handling of the situation to mitigate the risk.*

*Other than FUEL IMBALANCE and FUEL LEAK procedures, there is no mention in any manufacturer or company documentation that provides information, guidance or direction on these two issues. In particular, other than in the QRH procedures and indirectly in SOPs, there is no information or training as to how to interpret symptoms to conclude that actioning of the FUEL LEAK procedure would be appropriate. As a consequence, crews are neither trained in fuel leak procedures nor on fuel imbalance situations caused by fuel leaks. This crew was inadequately prepared to deal with the type of emergency that was encountered on this flight. This situation is not unique to this A330 operator or to operators operating other Airbus aircraft having similar fuel and flight management systems.*

*Had the crew consulted the caution in the FUEL IMBALANCE procedure according to their SOP's, there would have been sufficient information to guide them to follow the FUEL LEAK procedure to mitigate the consequences of the fuel leak. Notwithstanding, in a situation of surprise, heightened activity, and stress, and the lack of direct training and clear annunciation of a critical situation, can result in crews resorting to other well rehearsed routines that may not be appropriate for the actual situation, in this case a fuel balancing procedure done by memory.*

*Some regulatory agencies (e.g., FAA and DGAC – France) already require that aircraft flight manual include procedures that will enable flight crews to identify fuel system leaks, and procedures for crews to follow to prevent further fuel loss. However, there are a number of commercial aircraft that do not have identification procedures or fuel leak checklists.*

*There are also no specific regulatory requirements for training on fuel leak scenarios, and prior to this occurrence little if any training on this type of aircraft malfunction was conducted by any airline.*

*Had this particular crew been trained in the symptoms of fuel leak situations and strategies to identify and counter such a situation, they would have been better prepared to take appropriate actions.*

*So the recommendations finally blame others as if poor maintenance practices, fuel leak risk and crew errors had not been thought about before or were not even subject to prior safety regulation. In part, they say:*

*Therefore, it is recommended that Transport Canada, and Direction Genérale de l'Aviation Civile of France, and the Civil Aviation Authority of the United Kingdom, as well as the EASA and civil aviation authorities of other states responsible for the manufacture of aircraft and major components:*

*Review applicable airworthiness regulations and standards, as well as aircraft, engines and* component maintenance manuals, to ensure that adequate defences exist in the pre-installation, maintenance planning process to detect major configuration differences and *to establish the required support resources for technicians responsible for the work.*

*Therefore, it is recommended that Direction Genérale de l'Aviation Civile of France, in consultation with Airbus:*

*Review the automated, fuel-transfer systems on Airbus aircraft to ensure that the systems are able to detect abnormal fuel transfers, that systems exist and procedures are in place to inhibit abnormal transfers, and that the crews are notified, at an appropriate warning level, of abnormal fuel transfers.*

*It is also recommended that the civil aviation authorities of other aircraft manufacturing states, such as Canada, United States of America, and United Kingdom, as well as the European Aviation Safety Authority:*

*'Review the adequacy of the fuel indications and warning systems, as well as procedures associated with fuel imbalance situations to ensure that the possibility of a fuel leak is adequately considered.'*

Typical from such a thorough and lengthy incident report, and the recommendations made [1], we can estimate that another twin-engine Air Transat Airbus plane should not land out of fuel for perhaps another 100,000 hours of accumulated flight, and certainly not in the Azores.

# References

[1] Gabinete de Prevenção e Investigação de Acidentes com Aeronaves, Government of Portugal, Ministério das Obras Públicas, Transportes e Comunicações, Aviation Accidents Prevention and Investigation Department, 2001, 'All Engines-out Landing Due to Fuel Exhaustion Air Transat

Airbus A330-243 marks C-GITS Lajes, Azores, Portugal 24 August 2001', Accident Investigation Final Report 22/ACCID/GPIAA/2001.

[2] ATSB, 2008, Transport Safety Investigation Report, 'Fuel starvation Jundee Airstrip, WA – 26 June 2007 VH-XUE Empresa Brasileira de Aeronáutica S.A., EMB-120ER', Aviation Occurrence Investigation AO-2007-017, Interim Factual Report.

# Appendix E

## The Four Phases of a Midair Collision

Information Source:

Investigation Report, AX001-2/02, Bundesstelle für Flugunfalluntersuchung (BFU), German Federal Bureau of Aircraft Accident Investigation, May 2004 (extracts by permission of BFU, available at http://www.bfu-web.de).

### The Bare Facts

> *On July 1, 2002, at 21:31:32 hour (9:31 pm), a collision between a Tupolev TU154M, which was on a flight from Moscow, Russia to Barcelona, Spain, and a Boeing 757-200, on a flight from Bergamo, Italy to Brussels, Belgium, occurred north of the city of Ueberlingen (Lake Constance). Both aircraft flew according to Instrument Flight Rules (IFR) and were under control of ACC, Zurich, Switzerland. After the collision both aircraft crashed . . . . There were 71 people on board . . . none of which survived the crash.*

So here we have two very modern aircraft from two experienced countries, flown by experienced crews, colliding at over 700 mph in the skies over Europe. In full view of the controllers on the ground, both aircraft using modern collision avoidance equipment, and clearly sighting each other when miles apart, they still collided. The pictures of the debris graphically show almost complete disintegration of the aircraft on impact: what a harrowing short descent and almost instant death it must have been.

### The Four Phases

*Phase (1)* of the early unfolding precursors which were known to happen but unrecognised as to their significance by the humans who built, use, insure and operate the system.

Midair collisions between commercial or any other aircraft are not meant to happen, but they do. Because of their severity, long ago rules were introduced to enforce separation distances between aircraft in flight. Monitored from the ground via Air Traffic Controllers (ATC), both vertical and horizontal minimum clearances are *always* required.

Despite these requirements, as we have so often found, the rules by themselves do not stop events from happening. In fact Near Mid-Air Collisions (NMACs) are not uncommon. In the USA, the NMACs now occur at an interval of about 1 in 200,000 hours, consistent with the minimum achievable rate of $\lambda_m \sim 5.10^{-6}$ per flying hour (Duffey and Saull, 2002) [1]. In countries such as Canada and the UK with less experience, the rate is somewhat higher as they descend their own but entirely similar learning curve.

In fact, another potential 'loss of separation' NMAC event has occurred on 19 June 2004 between two Boeing 767 Australian commercial flights in Indonesian air space.

Because of this continuing issue, aircraft were equipped or back fitted with a new automatic system known as TCAS (Traffic Collision Avoidance System). Using radar based information processing; the crew could be given advice and warnings of loss of separation or rule violation. The system covers an airspace of $40 \times 15 \times 20$ miles, and about 9,000 feet up and down vertically and has a preset array of warnings (lights, messages and sounds) depending on angle and speed of approach. TCAS was installed and working both on the TU and the B757, and the pilots could see each other.

The International Rules of the Air state the pilot in charge (PIC) retains and has full responsibility at all times for collision avoidance, despite whatever advise any system gives. In fact, all the Rules, Guidance and National regulatory requirements all try to steer this fine line between telling the pilot what to do by following the TCAS and other ATC warning and advice, without trying to remove from the PIC authority for decision making in actually flying the aircraft.

At Zurich, the usual confluence of events occurred. There was only a single controller on active duty, due to known insufficient night staffing. This controller was covering other air movements and shuttling between multiple workstations (control screens). Distracted by other aircraft, the controller divided in his attention. These are all known problems, and had existed before for some time without correction. The immediate causes for the collision are given by the BFU report as simply:

a)  that ATC Zurich did not notice the loss of separation, and instructed the TU154 to descend when the separation with the B757 could not be ensured, and

b)  the TU crew followed the ATC instruction to descend even after the TCAS advised them to climb.

*Phase (2)* where the confluence occurred of developing failures and events where, despite the humans nominally being in control, they actually had no choice but to make decisions based on inadequate data, commercial or fiscal management pressures, and rely on software or instruments that did not provide up-to-date or believable control information for the actual circumstances that existed.

1–2 July Due to other work, the radar system at FCC Zurich operated in 'fallback' mode, so there was no auto correlation of flight targets possible and the optical STCA was not displayed. The schedule of the work was unknown before to the ATCs in Zurich and there was no indication it would affect ATC operations.

18:48 The TU takes off from Moscow: the crew is experienced but has never had simulator TCAS training.

21:06 The B757 takes off from Bergamo.

21:21:50 B757 radio contact with ACC Zurich.

21:21:56 B757 transponder code assigned by ACC.

21:23–21:34:37 Direct phone connection to adjacent ATC units not available at ACC Zurich and no bypass system.

21:29:50 B757 assigned flying height attained at 36,000 feet.

21:30:11 TU radio contact with ACC Zurich.

21:30:33 TU transponder code assigned by ACC.

Both TU and B757 TCAS systems are working.

21:33:18 to 21:34:41 TU crew discusses B757 on right as detected by TCAS display, at a distance of 27 miles. This is about one minute before they collide.

21:33:34 Radar control at Karlsruhe alerted of potential problem, and ATC there tries to contact ACC Zurich by phone but is unable to make connection. The phones are down, and four calls in succession failed to connect.

21:34:25 to 21:34:55 TU banks right as a course correction.

21:34:36 TU pilot sights B757, saying 'Here visually'.

The TU has now seen the B757, from its strobe light, but it is nighttime and visually it is hard to judge distance and position.

*Phase (3)* results when the escalation occurs during the repeated and continuing emphasis and attempts to ensure that everything remains more or less understood, when it is not and/or far from normal. Suffering from 'pressonitis', we continue on rather than isolating the failed parts of the system, addressing those first, rather than pressing on with the day's seemingly necessary tasks that further compound the situation.

21:34:39 B757 pilot leaves seat to go to toilet. Separation of planes was 13.6 miles.

21:34:42 TU TCAS alarm 'Traffic, traffic' and acknowledged verbally by the crew B757 TCAS alarm 'Traffic, traffic' also.

21:34:44 B757 Auto pilot turned off in response to TCAS alert, engine thrust reduced, descent at 1500 ft/min.

21:34:49 TU instructed to descend to 35,000 feet by ACC saying to TU: 'I have crossing traffic' since the planes were then only 5.5 miles apart, and 'descend', which ATC instruction was already too late to ensure adequate separation from the B757 (7 miles and 1,000 feet vertically).

This key fact of inadequate separation had not been noticed by the ATC, partly because the ATC was actually unable to read the B757's new flight level on the monitor until a radar image refresh occurred later at 21:35:24. The previous (current) image showed adequate separation.

The job seemingly done, the ATC now turns attention to an A320 on another monitor. Dealing with this flight is time consuming, as the needed telephones are inoperable.

21:34:56 TU control column forward, engine thrust reduced and descends.

21:34:56 TU TCAS alert 'Climb, climb' conflicting with earlier advice to descend. B757 TCAS alert 'Descend, descend'. Required separation of 7 miles infringed.

21:34:58 B757 autopilot turned off in response to TCAS alert.

21:34:59 TU co-pilot reports TCAS alert to climb, but does not gain attention as the pilot answers that ACC has asked for descent. No one mentions that TCAS has priority over ATC according to the 'rules'.

21:35:00 Auto alarm (STCA) by ACC Zurich computer to ATC workstation, but this was not noticed in Control Room as the ATC was dealing on another workstation with another A320 flight.

21:35:02 TU rate of descent reduced.

21:35:03 TU engine thrust reduced more and rate of descent ~1,500 ft/min. TU crew advised by ACC ATC to 'expedite' descent to 35,000 feet.

21:35:04 TU auto pilot turned off in response.

21:35:05 TU descent rate increased by pilot to 2,000 ft/min. The ATC in Zurich turns attention back to the A320 again who had called in twice.

21:35:05 B757 CVR records crew's visual sighting of TU.

21:35:10 B757 TCAS alert 'Increase descent, increase descent' and descent rate increased by crew to 2600 ft/min, the correct reaction to the alert.

21:35:14 B757 Master aural warning in cockpit because preset cruise altitude had been left.

21:35:19 Both B757 Crew and TU crew tell ATC of their TCAS warning to descend, but this is not noticed by controller ACC Zurich. Delay of 23 seconds from TCAS warning is considered as too long by BFU, but was due to the blocked communication by the ATC talking to the other A320 on another frequency.

21:35:24 TU TCAS alert 'Increase climb' and affirmed and repeated by co-pilot

21:35:26-30 B757 Co-pilot ask PIC to 'descend, (expletive), descend hard', as the TU is now in sight on a collision course.

21:35:27 TU pilot tries to climb to avoid collision also.

21:35:30 B757 Control column hard forward to dive to avoid collision.

21:35:32 B757 Collision at 34,890 feet with the TU and the B757 at about right angles.

21:36:01 Having finally dealt with the A320 flight, the ATC now calls the TU three times without an answer, the B757 having disappeared from the monitor.

*Phase (4)* finally denial is evident from all the humans involved, where they do not realise their full responsibility and contribution, and how it happened. Also management and society believes that actions taken or not, could have saved the day (thus saving the investment), and others are to blame for whatever happened, while in fact all were and are an integral part of the shared problem.

The ATC at Zurich had sole responsibility for the airspace, including assuming radar planning, executive and approach controller, plus some supervisory tasks. Other staff, if available, could and should have monitored the two tracks on the radar. But the ATC had no time to do that or to delegate, as he was handling another aircraft simultaneously (the A320) as well as those on their collision course.

Without up to date data and some help, the flights were doomed.

The staffing of the night shift did not allow for continuous workstation (monitor) coverage. The ATC was not solely at fault.

The BFU stated opinion in their Report [2] is that the ATC at Zurich was not 'in a position to safely execute the transferred and additionally assumed tasks'. Additionally, it was: 'the duty of management and the QA of the air navigation service company (the contractor for Zurich's ATC) to realise these deficiencies and to take appropriate corrective actions (author note e.g., properly staff the shift). In addition the (management and air navigation service company) tolerated the current practice applied to the conduct of the night shift'.

The auto-warning systems worked so well, but were ignored. As the BFU report [2] says: 'according to general conviction, the TCAS only makes sense if worldwide all crews rely on the system and comply with the advisories.' But also they note: 'the intended purpose (of TCAS) can only be achieved with human assistance'.

This of course raises again the question as to what degree we should automate systems, and the role of the human operator as advisor, supervisor and ultimate decision maker. We have a HTS that is inseparable when it comes to effectiveness in practice, and learning in reality. The conundrums of automation become even more evident the more we use it.

The BFU have asked, in their recommendations [2], for the International body (ICAO) to change the requirements so that pilots are *required* to obey and follow TCAS advisories regardless of contrary ATC instructions, 'unless it is too dangerous to comply'. A certain risk balancing act is still needed by the crew.

So here we have all the piece of the puzzle. With management's tacit approval, on the ground there was an ineffective, understaffed air traffic control, with inadequate data and communications. In the air, there were crews using a new technological system that is only partially integrated with their thinking, and an automatic system that allow warnings to be ignored. Communication everywhere breaks down, and inadequate situational assessment and advisory tools allow the collision outcome to occur.

As a tragic and highly personal footnote, it was reported by the press on 26th February 2004, that the air traffic controller (ATC) on duty that night was stabbed to death at home, apparently in revenge by someone related to one of accident victims, who then served a short prison term. Two managers were also later indicted and convicted for allowing the inadequate staffing of the control tower.

## References

[1] Duffey, R.B. and Saull, J.W., 2002, 'Know the Risk', First Edition, Butterworth and Heinemann, Boston, USA.
[2] Bundesstelle für Flugunfalluntersuchung (BFU), 2004, German Federal Bureau of Aircraft Accident Investigation Report, AX001-2/02, May.

# Appendix F

## Risk from the Number of Outcomes We Observe: How Many are There?

*'It is no use arguing with a prophet; you can only disbelieve him.'*

*Winston Churchill*

The more outcomes we have, the greater our risk. We show here a number of useful relationships between the probability of outcomes and the number that we might actually observe. This mathematical development also enables us to show a link back to 'conventional' statistical analysis as derived from sampling theory, and also illustrates the consistency of our MERE derived probability of an outcome with the frequency and number of outcome observations. It also provides a theoretical basis for the Jar of Life analogy, where we sampled outcomes by blindly drawing balls from the Jar that represented outcomes or non-outcomes.

Recall that we defined our probability as the Laplace definition for the CDF, $p(\varepsilon) = n/N$, being the number of outcomes we observe in our experience interval, $n$, divided by all the possible ones, $N$. In his original terminology, all the $N$ outcomes were 'equally possible' so, as we have shown, the chance of drawing any one outcome is simply $1/N$ for a uniform distribution. We also know this is consistent with our observing many different possible patterns of outcomes, even in the presence of learning.

It is reasonable to ask the question backwards. Having defined and derived the probability of an outcome, *how many outcomes* might we actually observe? Recall our analogy in the Introduction to drawing from Bernoulli's urn, which we called the Jar of Life. We sample or observe, in our $j$th observation interval, just $n$ outcomes from among the many (unknown) $N$, total ones, and we also have $m$ non-outcomes out of $M$ total, which we may or may not record or observe. What are the mathematical and physical relations between these outcomes and the non-outcomes, if any? What is our risk of observing or having the n outcomes? And given we have observed the $n$th of the outcomes, what then is the risk of our having

---

*Managing Risk: The Human Element*   Romney B. Duffey and John W. Saull
Copyright © 2005 and 2008 Romney B. Duffey and John W. Saull, Published by John Wiley & Sons, Ltd

(observing) the very next, $(n + 1)^{th}$ one? After all having a probability is all very well, but we want to:

a) know the risk of how many outcomes we might actually have or expect, so we have a rate and learning curve, and
b) manage the risk by evaluating the information entropy for safety management purposes using the distribution of the number(s) of outcomes observed.

The analysis we present here is derived directly as a variation from the analysis by Jaynes, 2003 [1] in 'Probability Theory', where the derivations of the sampling distribution are given with some care. The standard statistics textbooks, for example by Hays, 1988 [2] and Bulmer, 1979 [3] also enable the same result to be more indirectly derived. The analysis presented here demonstrates the link between observing outcomes as they emerge from the Jar of Life, and the conventional distribution of outcomes derived from statistical sampling. We adapt the nomenclature to that used here for outcomes and learning from experience.

## The Number of Outcomes: The Hypergeometric Distribution

The analogy of observing outcomes or non-outcomes, both good or bad, which represent risk or no risk, is to the drawing of colored balls from a jar. This is classic binomial sampling. We cannot see into the jar, and do not know what precisely is in it but only make estimates from what we happen to take out and observe. The jar analogy is a convenient way to describe how we are observing outcomes and making informed choices and decisions about the future based on what we have observed in the past. We observe the pattern of outcomes – the black balls – as if sampled from the jar, and expect to make some prediction about how many more there are and when they will appear, and in what pattern or sequence. Interspersed with the, '$n$' outcomes we observe are the '$m$' non-outcomes – the white balls – which we may or may not record. (See Figure A-F1.)

In the Introduction, we adapted this conceptual model of the Bernoulli urn to the world of physically observed events, the Jar of Life. The action of drawing from the Jar is equivalent to just the appearance or not, one by one, of similar independent events or outcomes. In the Jar, by this analogy, there are a total of $N$ black balls (which represent outcomes) and $M$ white balls (non-outcomes), but we do not know how many of each, but there must be $N + M$ outcomes and non-outcomes in total. We make choices from the Jar, and may pull out many white balls, $m$, representing non-outcomes, so many that the few, $n$, black balls (events) might even seem quite rare. If we were to replace them all back into the Jar, provided the number of outcomes is relatively small the probability (chance) of drawing an outcome is almost unchanged.

So we have come up with, $n$, discrete outcomes, observed and recorded as a sequence of black balls in our observation interval. There are, $n^N$, different sequences possible of just the outcomes, which could be a huge number. Presumably, we observe the most probable in our observation interval; after all it is the one that occurred. There are standard geometric formulas for the probability of a given sequence, but only if we know something about the number and order of the prior, $n$, (outcomes) black and of the, $m$, (non-outcomes) white balls. In Appendix B, we show how the maximum likelihood or most probable outcome also actually corresponds to the learning curve.

Clearly if we knew nothing, we would expect the overall probability of any outcome to be given by the ratio of the number of all the outcomes to the total number of all the possible outcomes and non-outcomes:

$$P(N) = N/(M + N)$$

Indeed, we do not know these numbers, $M$ and $N$, so what do we do?

We have sampled, $n$, outcomes, and, $m$, non-outcomes from the Jar in our observation interval. Obviously, $n < N$ and, $m < M$. We do not know the numbers unless we have a given

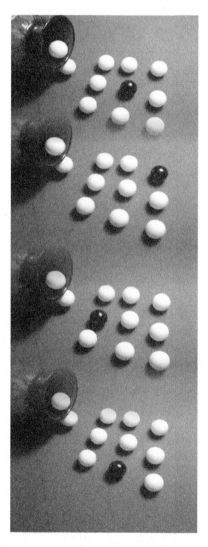

**Figure A-F1.** The black ball outcome could have appeared in any one of many different positions or possible sequences among the non-outcomes, the white balls, like in some of the patterns shown

number of total outcomes, which we do not have, unlike the case of reliability testing of a fixed number of components. In our sample of the total number of observations (draws) from the Jar of, $(m + n)$, we could have observed any of all the different possible combinations of outcome and non-outcome sequences, as there is nothing special or pre-determined about our chosen or actual observation interval, or about the observed sequence.

The prediction of the outcome probability also has great importance in the prediction and detection of defects or quality by defined sampling of industrial components, process streams and manufacturing products (i.e., for the chance of, $n$, defects being found in a sample of, $(n + m)$, out of, $(N + M)$, produced).

The probability of observing $n$ outcomes in any order in the $n + m$ draws (the prior observed or recorded $n$ outcomes plus the $m$ non-outcomes) is given by the classic hypergeometric distribution function (see Jaynes, pp. 68–69). This may be written:

$$P(n) = \frac{\binom{N}{n}\binom{M}{m}}{\binom{M+N}{m+n}}$$

where $P(n)$ is the probability of observing $n$ outcomes in exactly $(m + n)$ observations of outcomes and non-outcomes; and as an example of the standard notation, $^{N}C_{n} = \binom{N}{n}$ is the number of combinations of $N$ outcomes observed $n$ at a time $\equiv \left( \frac{N!}{n!(N-n)!} \right)$ In our notation for observations in experience space, $N \equiv N_{T} = \Sigma_{j}\, N_{j}$ and $n \equiv N_{j} = \Sigma n_{i}$.

To illustrate the power and behaviour of this function, let us look in more detail at the case shown in Figure A-F1 where outcomes are relatively rare. Of the balls that have fully emerged, there has been one outcome (one black ball) observed so far, $n = 1$, along with eight non-outcomes (white balls). We have missed and do not count the one non-outcome still near the Jar. So the total sample of outcomes and non-outcomes in this chosen $j$th observation interval is, $n + m = 9$, and, $n < m$. We do not know how many more outcomes and non-outcomes are in the Jar of Life, so, $N + M$, is unknown.

What is the risk of seeing one or more outcomes out of the unknown total number in any such observation interval?

The evaluation of the hypergeometric probability can be performed using the Excel xls. statistical function routine for the $P(n)$ formula. Results for a range of possible number of outcomes from one to four are shown in the Figure A-F2, where, of course, the $n = 1$ case corresponds to the rare outcome limit. The calculations are for any sample observation, $(n + m)$, of nine from among the range of possible $(N + M)$ totals, which shows the sensitivity to how many there may be in the Jar.

What we see is revealing: the chance of seeing more than one outcome is small at first, and then grows as the total increases above about 30 being possible. The probability of observing any number of outcomes, $n = 1, 2 \ldots$, then falls away monotonically like constant risk lines, $CR$, of slope, $-1$, on the log–log plot as the total number of possible possibilities increases. We are more likely, $(P(n)\uparrow)$, to observe more outcomes, $(n \uparrow)$, for any given large number of total possibilities, since in this chosen case, $P(n) \propto n/(N + M)$.

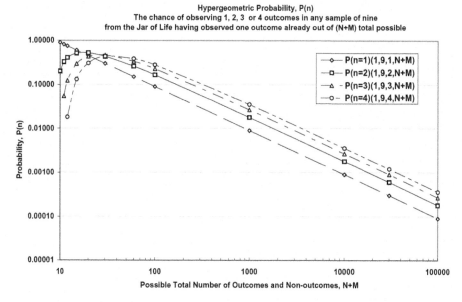

**Figure A-F2.** The hypergeometric function for the outcome probability

Indeed if $(N + M)$ is taken as a measure of our total learning experience, as we show later, the total number of non-outcomes clearly could have a large effect on reducing the perceived or apparent outcome probability. This type of trend is also exactly what we see reflected in the data.

The hypergeometric distribution[1] is the most general sampling result, but requires a knowledge of both the number of outcomes and non-outcomes. In a fixed sample of components, these would be known, but not for any HTS. So we need to examine some special cases and limits to gain insight into the answer.

## Few Outcomes and Many Non-Outcomes: The Binomial and Poisson Distributions

In life, we are observing a sample of outcomes or a slice of experience space. But in the limit of large numbers of non-outcomes, or an effectively infinite Jar, then, $M + N \rightarrow \infty$ and

---

[1]For the more general case of say, $k$, different outcome types (cf. colours), 1, 2, ... $k$, then for any number of outcomes, $\Sigma n_k$, of the, $k$ types, the hypergeometric formula is Hays, p. 147 [2]:

$$P\left(\sum n_k\right) = \frac{\Pi_k \binom{N_k}{n_k}}{\binom{\sum_k N_k}{\sum_k n_k}}$$

For the present outcome versus non-outcome case, we have $k = 1, 2$, hence we have, $P(\Sigma n_k) \equiv P(n)$, with, $N_{k=1} = N$, $n_{k=1} = n$, $N_{k=2} = M$, and $n_{k=2} = m$, corresponding to the current notation for, $(N, n)$, outcomes and $(M, m)$, non-outcomes.

$M \to \infty$, and with relatively few outcomes, $M \gg N$ and $m \gg n$, so the hypergeometric result becomes

$$P(n) \to \binom{n+m}{n}\left(\frac{N}{M+N}\right)^n \left\{1-\frac{N}{M+N}\right\}^m$$

$$P(n) \to \frac{1}{n!}\left\{\{p(N)\}^n \{1-p(N)\}^m\right\}$$

where, $p(N) = N/(N+M)$, as before. For the case when outcomes are relatively rare so that, $M \gg N$, $p(N) \sim N/M$, giving a probability only if we knew the number of non-outcomes.

This expression for $P(n)$ for this limit is the usual *binomial distribution* for two outcome possibilities (an outcome or a non-outcome), which in statistical analysis is often called the chance of either a failure or a success. The standard cases that are often discussed in statistics textbooks when deriving this type of distribution are a series of $n$ coin tosses (choosing heads or tails, with $p(N) = 1/2$ and $M = N$); or for $n$ dice throws (chance of, say, making a six, with $p(N) = 1/6$, since $N = 1$ and $M = 5$). In these special and interesting cases, $M$ is known.

Provided that we have $mp(N) \ll 1$, we can write the second term in brackets as an exponential, so we have a Poisson-type distribution:

$$P(n) \approx \frac{e^{-mp(N)}}{n!} \{p(N)\}^n$$

This result is a major hint for us to compare the Jar result to the standard textbook derivation of the probabilities for observing outcomes for a finite sample. Suppose we have observed a sample of a finite and known number of outcomes, $n$, and known or unknown non-outcomes, $m$. The number of finite outcomes in $(n + m)$ samples or draws from the Jar (just like the number of coin tosses) gives the probability of the $n$ outcomes, $P(n)$. This is the product of three terms:

1) The first is the number of possible combinations of the outcomes among the $(n + m)$ total outcomes and non-outcomes, taken or observed $n$ at a time, or $\binom{n+m}{n}$.

2) The second is the probability of the $n$ outcomes, which is the probability of one outcome, $p(\varepsilon) = n/N$, occurring independently $n$ times, or $\{p(\varepsilon)\}^n$.

3) The third is the probability of the $m$ non-outcomes occurring, which is the reliability, or $\{1 - p(\varepsilon)\}^m$.

So multiplying (1), (2) and (3), we have the usual *binomial distribution* for the probability of exactly $n$ outcomes as,

$$P(n) = \binom{n+m}{n}\{p(\varepsilon)\}^n \{1-p(\varepsilon)\}^m$$

This is the form that was first derived and discussed by Bayes in 1763. In the same limit of large numbers of non-outcomes and few outcomes, when $m \gg n$,

$$P(n) \to \frac{1}{n!}\left\{ \{p(\varepsilon)\}^n \{1 - p(\varepsilon)\}^m \right\}$$

This limit result is again related to the binomial distribution, and is identical in form to that derived above for sampling from the Jar of Life. The unknown (CDF) probability of an outcome, $p(N)$, is now replaced by the *known* (CDF) probability, $p(\varepsilon)$, based on our prior sample.

Substituting from the MERE expression for $p(\varepsilon)$, we can evaluate the probability of observing any number, $n$, of outcomes as a function of experience but only if we if have some idea about or estimate of the number, $m$, of non-outcomes. But we also recall that non-outcomes are not usually recorded or known.

Provided, $mp(\varepsilon) \ll 1$, for few observed outcomes and small outcome probability, we can approximate and write the second term in brackets as an exponential so,

$$P(n) \approx \frac{e^{-mp(\varepsilon)}}{n!}\{p(\varepsilon)\}^n$$

which is again a Poisson-type distribution.

If we do not have many outcomes, $(n \ll m)$, in some instances we may use the number of non-outcomes as a direct measure of the experience, since we learn from the non-outcomes too. In this special case, the number of non-outcomes is proportional to the experience, $m \propto \varepsilon$, which we measure in 'tau' units, $\tau$, so for that case this result may be approximated as:

$$P(n) \approx \frac{e^{-\tau \cdot p(\varepsilon)}}{n!}\{p(\varepsilon)\}^n$$

The exponential term can also be expanded to give,

$$P(n) \approx (1/n!)\{p(\varepsilon)\}^n \{1 - mp(\varepsilon) + \cdots \text{higher-order terms}\}$$

For small probabilities and for observed numbers of non-outcomes such that $mp(\varepsilon) \ll 1$, we have the equivalent simple limit distribution:

$$P(n) \to \frac{1}{n!}\{p(\varepsilon)\}^n$$

which is solely a function of the number of outcomes, $n$, for a given probability.

Translated into a Bayesian formulation, this probability, $P(n)$, can be regarded as:

$$P(n) \equiv p(\mathrm{P}) = p(\varepsilon)^{n-1} \times p(\mathrm{L}) = p(\varepsilon)^{n-1} \times p(\varepsilon)/n!$$

In words, $P(n)$ is then equivalent to a posterior probability, $p(\mathrm{P})$, for the $n$th outcome given the prior probability, $p(\varepsilon)^{n-1}$, of all the previous, $(n-1)$, outcomes times the factorial likelihood, $p(\mathrm{L}) \equiv p(\varepsilon)/n!$, of the $n^{\text{th}}$ outcome.

## The Number of Outcomes: In the Limit

The two (finite and infinite) limits for the probability should trend to the same answer as the number of non-outcomes, $m$, becomes larger. So for the two cases of sampling from the Jar, the two binomial probabilities, $P(n)$, should become equal. Equating the two results we have:

$$\frac{1}{n!}\left\{\{p(N)\}^n\{1-p(N)\}^m\right\} = \frac{1}{n!}\{p(\varepsilon)\}^n\{1-p(\varepsilon)\}^m$$

which implies, of course, that for the same and any finite $n$ and $m$ values, we must have

$$p(\varepsilon) \rightarrow p(N)$$

Insofar as $p(N)$ is the true value at some infinite future, then $p(\varepsilon)$ *constitutes a prediction based on our prior observed outcomes*. So, in the limit of large numbers of non-outcomes, $m$, the CDF ($p = n/N$), is related to the numbers of outcomes and non-outcomes by:

$$p(\varepsilon) = n/N \equiv N/(M+N) = n!\sqrt[n]{P(n)}$$

This argument and sampling equivalence justifies the choice of the Laplace prior probability measure, $p = n/N$, for an observed sample of outcomes, and links us back to standard statistical sampling theory for predicting the probability of any number of outcomes. The analysis also shows that finite but large sampling is a reasonable approximation to the case where we do not know the numbers of all the outcomes, $N$, and non-outcomes, $M$.

For large numbers of non-outcomes, or an effectively infinite Jar, where $M + N \rightarrow \infty$ and $M \rightarrow \infty$, with relatively few outcomes, so $M \gg N$ and $m \gg n$, and small probability of an outcome such that $mp(\varepsilon) \ll 1$, we derived above the simple (approximate) limit for the posterior probability as:

$$P(n) \approx \frac{1}{n!}\{p(\varepsilon)\}^n$$

This is simply a normalised expression for the probability of observing a number, $n$, of independent outcomes. As a guide to our thinking, we can evaluate this expression for $P(n)$ for any number of outcomes, $n$, to determine the observation probability for a given prior probability $p(\varepsilon)$ at any experience. The higher values of prior probability strictly violate our constraint ($mp(\varepsilon) \ll 1$) if there are too many non-outcomes, but are still useful for relative comparison purposes.

There is a much smaller probability of observing or having outcomes as $p(\varepsilon)$ decreases, consistent with *the reduction of risk with increased experience and by having a learning environment*. Recalling that actually we have a double exponential for the MERE 'human bathtub', this gives the CDF (prior probability) as:

$$p(\varepsilon) = 1 - \exp\{(\lambda - \lambda_m)/k - \lambda(\varepsilon_0 - \varepsilon)\}$$

Here, $\lambda(\varepsilon) = \lambda_m + (\lambda_0 - \lambda_m)\exp - k(\varepsilon - \varepsilon_0)$, and $\lambda(\varepsilon_0) = \lambda_0 = n/\varepsilon$, at the initial experience, $\varepsilon_0$, accumulated for the initial $n$-outcome(s); and for the first event $n \sim 1$. We take our usual

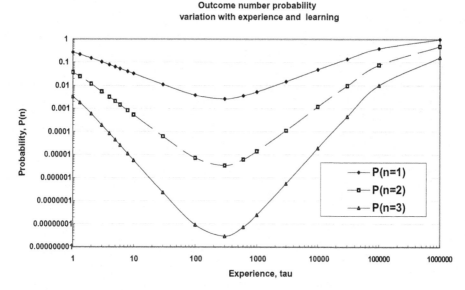

**Figure A-F3.** The MERE probability of observing a specific number of outcomes calculated as a function of increasing experience

experience measure as $\varepsilon \equiv \tau$ unit and thus symbolically, referenced to some initial probability at zero experience, we have

$$p(\varepsilon) = 1 - (1 - p(\tau_0))\exp[\{\lambda_m(\tau - \tau_0)\} + \{\lambda_0 - \lambda_m\}/k]^{e^{-k(\varepsilon - \varepsilon_0)}}$$

giving the MERE posterior probability of observing $n$ outcomes as a function of experience and learning as,

$$P(n) \approx \frac{1}{n!}\left\{1 - (1 - p(\tau_0))\exp[\{\lambda_m(\tau - \tau_0)\} + \{(\lambda_0 - \lambda_m)/k\}]^{e^{-k(\varepsilon - \varepsilon_0)}}\right\}^n$$

This approximate result is plotted in Figure A-F3 also, to illustrate the variation with experience for a range of possible outcome numbers, $n$, using our 'best' MERE values. The probability, $P(n)$, of observing any given number of outcomes, $n$, is shown on the $y$-axis versus the experience on the $x$-axis.

We can see that, unsurprisingly, there is a 100% chance of not observing an outcome, since $P(0) = 1$; but indeed we may expect *one* outcome, ($n = 1$), when, $P(n) \equiv P(1) = p(\varepsilon)$, exactly the prior MERE probability. Thus, the $P(n = 1)$ line for, $n = 1$, overlays the MERE probability result: we expect one outcome, but the risk of observing more outcomes than that is ten (10) times less likely.

## The Perfect Learning Limit: Learning from Non-Outcomes

In the psychological literature, it is recognised that individual human learning behaviour and response also can involve so-called 'incidental learning', which is not necessarily just learning from error correction. In other words, we may learn something from what goes right (the non-outcomes), as well as from what goes wrong (the outcomes). We also found an approximate solution to this special case, which was of Poisson exponential form for low probabilities and small numbers of outcomes, ($n \ll m$), compared to non-outcomes. In this 'perfect learning' case, we can also take the number of non-outcomes as a measure of the experience. This assumption implies the ideal of learning from all the non-outcomes, not just the (rare) outcomes. Expressing experience in arbitrary units, tau $\tau$, the perfect learning probability, $P(n)$, for any number, $n$, of outcomes is given by the Poisson-type distribution:

$$P(n) \approx \frac{e^{-\tau.p(\tau)}}{n!} \{p(\tau)\}^n$$

and is a function now only of experience.

Now the prior probability, $p(\varepsilon) \equiv p(\tau)$, is itself a double exponential corresponding to the 'human bathtub' of the, $P(n = 1)$, line shown in Figure A-F3. Hence the expression above for the 'perfect learning' probability, $P(n)$, is actually a *triple exponential*! This is a new result that corresponds to a so-called extreme value distribution. The evaluation of this Poisson-type perfect learning expression using the best MERE best values is shown in Figure A-F4, superimposed on the previous bathtub curves.

The dramatic cliff-edge decline due to the $e^{e^e}$ variation in probability is obvious. What is shown is quite intriguing, partly as a result of the mathematical limits chosen. At low experience, this special case of a 'perfect learning' Poisson-type result follows closely the large number, low probability, small number of outcomes ($1 \leq n \leq 3$) bathtub results shown also in Figures A-F3 and A-F4. It is therefore a good approximation at small experience.

Suddenly, at a larger experience between $100 < \tau < 1,000$, which apparently depends on the number of outcomes, $n$, the perfect learning probability, $P(n)$, plummets to effectively zero. *No more outcomes are likely whatever experience is gained – we have learned enough at this Perfect Learning Limit.*

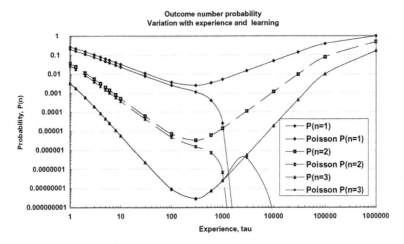

**Figure A-F4.**   The special case of learning from non-outcomes

This result could have been anticipated from the limit, $P(n) \to 0$, which occurs when

$$p(\tau)^n e^{-\tau p(\tau)} \ll n!$$

For the small exponent expansion, $\tau p(\tau) \ll 1$, this limit equation gives the condition for an effectively zero probability as the perfect *Learning Limit:*

$$\tau \sim 0\{1/p(\tau)\}.$$

Since here, $p(\tau) = 1/\tau$, and is the rare event case for, $n = 1$, clearly this limit result is only as good as our assumptions, and strictly conflicts with the expansion approximation. The result places a limit on our use of a Poisson-type probability distribution to only small experience and many non-outcomes. The Perfect Learning limit fails as soon as we have an event, as it should. So, the equation also has a useful simple physical interpretation, which is that: (a) we learn from non-outcomes the same way we learn from outcomes, as we have assumed; (b) the perfect learning ends as soon as we have just a single outcome; and (c) the influence of the finite minimum rate is then lost.

## The Relative Change in Risk When Operating Multiple Sites

Suppose we operate multiple systems that have risk opportunities but, by operating safely or by luck, actually have observed no outcomes so far. We would like to estimate the relative increase in risk due to the many manufacturing units, sites, factories or systems based on the operating experience. Now we know the probability of having an outcome is, $p(\varepsilon)$, at any experience for any one HTS. So the probability of *not* having or observing an outcome, $p(n = 0)$ for that system is given by the statistical trick of using the converse of actually having or observing an outcome, i.e., by the reliability:

$$p(n = 0) = (1 - p(\varepsilon))$$

We now suppose that as we gain experience although we have observed no outcomes, $(n = 0)$, we have observed a number of non-outcomes, $m$, each being an independent event. These may all be considered as learning opportunities, either because we utilise them for subconscious unlearning, error correction and forgetting, or have an integrated set of safety and risk management systems. Hence, at any experience the probability of having the $m$ non-outcomes is the multiplicand of the probabilities of each separate one:

$$p(m) = \Pi_m p(n = 0) = \{p(n = 0)\}^m = \{1 - p(\varepsilon)\}^m$$

So the probability of observing or having at least one outcome, $(n > 0)$, is given by the converse of not having any outcomes among the $m$ non-outcomes, or

$$p(n > 0, m) = 1 - p(m)$$

or,

$$p(n > 0, m) = 1 - \{1 - p(\varepsilon)\}^m$$

From the MERE result, the probability of an outcome in any HTS is, of course,

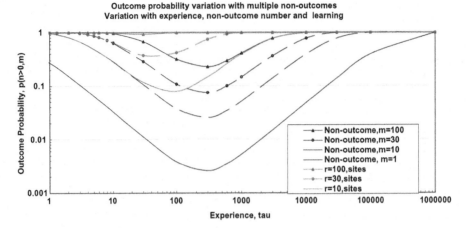

**Figure A-F5.** Calculated risk of at least one outcome with the number of non-outcomes and experience

$$p(\varepsilon) = 1 - \exp\{(\lambda - \lambda_m)/k - \lambda(\varepsilon_0 - \varepsilon)\}$$

Assuming that we gain experience from the non-outcomes as well as from the outcomes, taking all the $m$ non-outcomes as learning opportunities or risk exposure, then we may increase the experience measure proportionally as, $\varepsilon \equiv m\tau$. Since we include this extra experience from all the $m$ non-outcomes in the overall or accumulated experience, the failure rate will also be changed. Thus, the relative probability of having at least one outcome, $n > 0$, in all the, $m$, opportunities or chances is written as:

$$p(n > 0, m) = 1 - \{1 - p(m\tau)\}^m$$

with,

$$p(m\tau) = 1 - \exp\{(\lambda - \lambda_m)/k + \lambda m\tau)\}$$

where, for the case of accumulating this experience at, $r$, separate sites or systems,

$$\lambda(\tau) = \lambda_m + (\lambda_0 - \lambda_m)\exp - kr\tau$$

We show the calculated results in Figure A-F5 for various assumed numbers for $m$ and $r$. As we might have expected, the relative risk or probability of an outcome compared to the base case of $m = 1$, $r = 1$ increases with the number of non-outcomes or sites for any given amount of experience.

## References

[1] Jaynes, E.T., 2003, 'Probability Theory: The Logic of Science', First Edition, Cambridge University Press, Cambridge, UK, Edited by G.L. Bretthorst.
[2] Hays, W.L., 1988, 'Statistics', Holt, Rinehart and Winston, Inc., Fourth Edition.
[3] Bulmer, M.G., 1979, 'Principles of Statistics', Dover Publications, Inc., New York, p. 170.

# Appendix G

## Mixing in a Tank: The D.D. Williamson Vessel Explosion

Information source:

U.S. Chemical Safety and Hazard Investigation Board, Investigation Report No. 2003-11-I-KY, March 2004, D. D. Williamson & Co., Inc., Louisville, Kentucky, 11 April 2003

### Errors in Mixing in a Tank at the Caramel Factory: The Facts

On 11 April 2003, at about 2:10 a.m., a vessel ruptured at the D.D. Williamson & Co., Inc. (DDW), plant in Louisville, Kentucky, killing one operator. The explosion and debris damaged the western end of the facility, and released 26,000 pounds of ammonia solution in water from another nearby storage tank, forcing the evacuation of as many as 26 residents and requiring 1,500 people to shelter-in-place.

It is reported by the US CSB that DDW is the world's largest producer of caramel colouring for food products, including cola drinks, sauces, and seasonings: the Company's website (www.caramel.com) states that they are the 'world leader in caramel colour'. The Company's website (http://www.caramel.com/aboutus.asp) also notes in 2005 that: 'Our operations in North America, Europe Asia and Africa have earned the rigorous ISO 9002 certification'. This Louisville plant employed approximately 45 people and had been in operation since 1948. We do not know if there had been any previous events, but assuming this to be the only one gives a maximum interval of about 1 in ~300,000 working hours, somewhat larger than, but roughly in accord with, our minimum rate expectations.

For this outcome in Kentucky the US Chemical Safety and Hazard Investigation Board (CSB) issued a technical report. This is the source from which all the sequence and causal information given here is extracted (CSB, 2004) [1], supplemented by some of our own explanatory notes and literature research.

## The Prior Knowledge

*Phase (1)* of the early unfolding precursors which were known to happen but unrecognised as to their significance by the humans who built, use, insure and operate the system.

Food processing and chemical facilities are extremely common, and use many hazardous and potentially explosive fluids, chemicals, mixtures and reactants in their piping, pressure vessels and process lines. Explosions, vessel failures and process fires seem to be fairly commonplace in industrial process plants, but it is hard to get the data as they are often confidential and scattered around between the various agencies and among the chemical, pipeline, oil, gas, waste, pharmaceutical, packaging, paint, plastics, food and other industries. In the USA, many of these industries and facilities are regulated, investigated and inspected by multiple and different local and government agencies and entities responsible for hazard assessment and analysis, environmental safety, insurance codes and standards, plus industrial and worker safety. These federal agencies include the CSB, EPA, NTSB, USCG, MSHA and OSHA, with jurisdiction and reporting requirements that depend historically on the type and nature of the facility process and its hazards.

The vessel that failed was a feed tank, most likely as a result of overheating the caramel colour liquid inside, which generated excessive (vapor) pressure. The tanks were being used as unregistered and un-inspected pressure vessels. Failures and explosions of boilers and pressure vessels (B&PV) have been known since the start of the Industrial Revolution and the use of steam-powered machinery some 200 years ago. Stringent materials, inspections, safety measures, codes and standards have been developed nationally to cover the *mechanical* aspects of vessel design, manufacture and operation.

But failures of B&PV in HTS still occur. The B&PV data reported to a modern database was analysed in 'Know the Risk' (Duffey and Saull, 2002) [2], which covered over 1,500 B&PV failures and in-service defects in an observation interval of just two years (1998 and 1999). The DSM analysis of this experience base resulted in a maximum failure interval of one failure per 175,000 boiler-hours occurring for recent outcomes in HTS.

The US CSB has released a 'reactive hazards' data report covering only those chemicals considered hazardous by the US EPA. That report lists 167 outcomes ($N_j$) from using EPA listed reactive chemicals alone, in an observation interval of just 22 years from 1980 to 2001. The various outcomes are stated to have caused in total over 100 deaths and many $100M in damage (US CSB, 2003) [3].

It is clear that carefully gathered prior data are incomplete, flawed and under reported as the CSB state:

> *CSB staff identified that progress on preventing reactive accidents was hampered by a general lack of reliable data – including information on root causes and lessons learned. They also noted that the tally of 167 reactive incidents was almost certainly an underestimate due to data deficiencies.*

So precursors are known, but may go unreported, unknown or be invisible to operators of different facilities. Before their arrival in Louisville, both (feed) tanks had been used in the manufacture of ammonium bisulfite, a raw material for caramel colour. The tanks were operated (before) at atmospheric pressure and were equipped with pressure relief devices at that time. The CSB also learned that Tank #2 had been deformed on two previous occasions due to the misapplication of vacuum (absolute pressure reduction), and was then refitted and returned to service. Details of these repairs were not available; however, one employee recalled that the tank welds were not x-rayed to ensure tank integrity (which is the usual practice for pressure vessels).

DDW staff (including management) did not consider the feed tanks to be pressure vessels. So the plant owner/operator did not notify the Commonwealth of Kentucky that it was bringing the two tanks into the State, as required by Kentucky boiler and pressure vessel regulations, nor did DDW register the tanks with the State. Interestingly, since this notification procedure is a self-motivated purely paper rule or requirement, other than formally it does not actually require a state physical licence or inspection prior to operation. Because of its low operating pressure, the tanks also fell below the limit required for risk planning by the EPA: no one recognised or analysed the significance of the potential risk.

*Phase (2)* where the confluence occurred of developing failures and events where, despite the humans nominally being in control, they actually had no choice but to make decisions based on inadequate data, commercial or fiscal management pressures, and rely on software or instruments that did not provide up-to-date or believable control information for the actual circumstances that existed.

It began with the day shift on 10 April 2003, and the spray dryer operators at the caramel manufacturing plant had completed processing one dried product and had begun preparing the system for the next product. It was essentially a manual mixing and heating operation, and had been done many times before.

The two vessels used in the mixing process were for the manufacture of food-grade caramel colouring and functioned as a feed tank for a spray dryer that produced powdered colourants. The feed tanks, which were heated with steam and pressurised with air, were operated manually. To ensure that the filling, heating, and material transfer processes stayed within operating limits, operators relied on their experience and on physical readouts from local temperature and pressure indicators (gauges and dials).

The two ~2000 gallon tanks (feed Tank #1 and feed Tank #2) fed a spray dryer. These stainless-steel pressure vessels were equipped with coils for heating with steam or cooling with water and with agitators for mixing the product. To prepare the spray dryer feed, the tanks were partially filled with caramel colour liquid and about 10% carrying agent with water added was mixed in to improve spray dryer performance. The product being prepared at the time of the incident had a very high viscosity. So the mixture had to be and was heated to $160\,^\circ F$ using steam on the feed tank coils to lower the viscosity and improved the ability to pump the mixture to the spray dryer and force it through the dryer nozzles.

To also assist in the transfer of material from the feed tank to the spray dryer feed pump, the feed tank was also pressurised with air at approximately 22 psi (pounds per square inch) using the compressed air system. Each feed tank had a 1-inch vent line with valve tied into the airline, but it was necessary to close the vent valve to add pressure to the feed tank.

When the feed tank was emptied, the vent (pipe)line was opened to allow the pressure to bleed off. A pump raised the pressure of the emptying mixture to more than 4,000 psi to force the liquid through the atomiser nozzles at the top of the spray dryer and create the desired particle size. The material fell 25 feet through the spray dryer chamber, while air heated to $600\,°F$ flowed up, so by the time the material reached the bottom of the chamber, it was dried to powder.

Unknown to the workers and the regulator, this mixing and pre-spraying procedure violated both the rules and vessel licence, since the feed tanks violated the Kentucky boiler and pressure vessel safety requirements. As installed, the feed tanks had no safety valves or rupture disks (to protect against overpressure by venting the tanks). Each tank was equipped with a 1-inch vent line, terminating in a (single) manually operated valve, which operators used to relieve pressure and often shut off. (If functioning as a normal pressure vessel, the tanks would also follow the usual practice of having safety valves, alarms, and trips; plus automatic control of the various heating, mixing and transfer operations with multiple and perhaps remote readings of pressure and temperature; plus extensive operator training, written procedures, safety reviews and periodic inspections).

*Phase (3)* results when the escalation occurs during the repeated and continuing emphasis and attempts to ensure that everything remains more or less understood, when it is not and/or far from normal. Suffering from 'pressonitis', we continue on rather than isolating the failed parts of the system, addressing those first, rather than pressing on with the day's seemingly necessary tasks that further compound the situation.

The tanks were placed on weigh cells to measure batch quantities; there was no other automatic instrumentation. A temperature gauge located midway up the tank shell and a pressure gauge on the air feed manifold were the only instruments associated with the tanks.

DDW written procedures did not explain the risks of overheating the feed tanks when the vent valves were closed. *Operators relied on their experience* to judge the length of time necessary to heat a feed tank; practices differed slightly among operators. At DDW, a new operator was paired with an experienced operator to learn the required job assignments (so called on-the-job-training, or OJT). Safety meetings were held to explain general safety concepts, such as fire safety, hazard communication, and emergency plans.

On the night of the incident, the lead operator, with five years experience, was teamed with a new operator hired three months earlier. On each shift, the two operators worked in the spray dryer area of the plant. In addition to producing the spray-dried product detailed above, the operators filled and labeled product containers (typically plastic bags placed inside cardboard boxes), and moved them to warehouse areas using forklift trucks.

This task involved cleaning out the spray dryer and the two feed tanks with hot water. The day shift operators then filled feed Tank #1, the smaller of the two tanks, with caramel colour liquid and the carrying agent, and heated the tank to $160\,°F$. They also cleaned and emptied feed Tank #2 before their work shift ended.

The night-shift lead operator in the spray dryer area arrived at the plant at 6:30 p.m. The second spray dryer operator arrived at 7:00 p.m. Based on interviews, the lead operator slept from 7:00 p.m. until approximately 10:00 p.m., at which time the two operators reassembled the spray dryer system and began spray-drying material fed from Tank #1. They also began preparing the next batch of material in Tank#2. To ensure a continuous flow of liquid to the spray dryer, the operators typically alternated the feed tanks, feeding out of one tank while the second one was prepared, then switching tanks as the in-service tank ran empty.

In preparing Tank #2, the operators added the caramel liquid and the agent, and then began heating the mixture to usual 160 °F. *But early in the shift, while the two operators were packaging the spray-dried product from tank #1 (in 50-pound plastic bags inside cardboard boxes), they placed incorrect labels on the shipping boxes. After discovering this error, they began to re-label the boxes while tank #2 was heating.*

At approximately 2:00 a.m., the second operator observed caramel colour product running out of the agitator shaft seal at the top of Tank #2 and down the sides. This indicated excess temperature and pressure on the tank (forcing the product out past the shaft seal). It is likely that the caramel liquid also flowed into the 1-inch vent line pipe, filling and plugging it. The operator called the lead operator over from the packaging area (to see what was happening) and, as they were discussing the situation, one of the tank insulation retaining bands snapped (indicating possible overpressure). The lead operator asked the second operator to get the night-shift maintenance mechanic (presumably to seal the shaft) and then moved to the southwest side of Tank #2, (presumably to read the temperature) where the only temperature gauge was located.

As the second operator left the spray dryer area to locate the maintenance mechanic, Tank #2 exploded. The lead operator's death was caused by massive trauma (from the consequences of the explosion).

The explosion extensively damaged the western end of the DDW facility. The five-story-tall spray dryer was toppled over, and debris was (thrown and) scattered up to 150 yards from the source of the explosion. The top head of the feed tank separated at the weld seam and was propelled approximately 100 yards to the west, landing on the CSX rail line on the north side of the facility. The tank shell split open in a roughly vertical line. It appears that the tank was propelled off its foundation and struck the 12,000-gallon aqua ammonia storage tank, located 15 feet away; and then ricocheted approximately 20 feet before hitting the bottom of the spray dryer structure and toppling it.

When the aqua-ammonia storage tank was knocked off its foundation the piping was ripped loose, which resulted in the 26,000-pound aqua ammonia leak. An ammonia vapor cloud traveled southwest from the storage tank, towards neighbouring homes, forcing later evacuation. (See Plate 8)

The (surviving) second operator and two other employees, standing two rooms away from the source of the explosion, were unable to return to the area due to debris, the sparking of electrical connections, steam leaks and the strong smell of natural gas from a broken fuel line. After calling the Louisville 911 centre to report the incident, they immediately proceeded to isolate and shut down the area. The plant's automatic alarm system had already notified the DDW alarm service, which contacted the Louisville Fire Department. The employees turned off the steam, shut down the plant boilers, and isolated the area before leaving, at which time the Louisville Fire and Police Departments had arrived on scene. Automatic valves on the natural gas system worked as intended, and there was no fire as a result of the explosion.

*Phase (4)* finally denial is evident from all the humans involved, where they do not realise their full responsibility and contribution, and how it happened. Also management and society believes that actions taken or not, could have saved the day (thus saving the investment), and others are to blame for whatever happened, while in fact all were and are an integral part of the shared problem.

The CSB determined and stated the following causes that feed Tank #2 most likely failed as a result of:

(a)  overheating of the caramel liquid, which generated pressure; and
(b)  plugging of the vessel vent valve, since the tank had no overpressure protection.

The facility was built, operated in the Commonwealth of Kentucky and covered by state law. The law requires that all pressure vessels be certified by an inspector, registered with the National Board, and registered with the state. In addition, for used vessels, such as the DDW feed tanks, Kentucky Administration Regulations state:

> '. . . before a vessel is brought into Kentucky for use, it shall be inspected by a boiler inspector or a special boiler inspector and the data shall be filed by the owner or user of the boiler or pressure vessel with the Boiler Inspection Section for approval.'

(As noted above) DDW staff did not consider the feed tanks to be pressure vessels. As a result, DDW did not notify the State when the feed tanks were brought into Kentucky, nor did it identify the tanks as pressure vessels for insurance purposes. State officials explained that proper notification triggers an inspection. In this instance, *State inspectors stated that they would have rejected the vessels for lack of National Board registration.* Insurance company inspections occurred regularly at DDW; however, they focused on the two packaged boiler units and the pressure vessels in which the caramel liquid is produced.

In a CSB survey, the US state officials surveyed agreed that unregistered vessels, and the states' inability to know of their use, are an ongoing problem.

DDW used contract-engineering services, when necessary, for environmental permitting, installation and subsequent modification of the spray dryer system, and development of the EPA required Risk Management Program (RMP) package for the aqua ammonia tank. DDW also relied on insurance audits (by others) as a check on its engineering practices. As noted earlier, these inspections and services did not note the use of the feed tanks as pressure vessels.

The CSB conclusions found that DDW did not have:

(a)  effective programs in place to determine if equipment and processes met basic process and plant engineering requirements;
(b)  adequate hazard analysis systems to identify feed tank hazards, nor did it effectively use contractors and consultants to evaluate and respond to associated risks; and
(c)  adequate operating procedures or adequate training programs to ensure that operators were aware of the risks of allowing the spray dryer feed tanks to overheat and knew how to respond appropriately.

## Another Echo

In another extraordinary, but by now expected Echo, in early 2006 another explosion but this time in North Carolina killed one worker and injured 14 others due to mixing an excess of reactive chemicals which caused a runaway chemical reaction (US CSB, 2007) [4]. The excellent summary report by the US Chemical Safety board is brief but clear.

In an eerily similar accident to those explosions at JCO, Kean Canyon and DDW, the Synthron plant accident was yet another case of management failure, inadequate training, and worker unawareness with the usual litany of a confluence of causes. A different batch of chemicals was mixed just by scaling up using 'experience' rather than knowledge, and without due consideration of the resulting heat loads and safety implications, and with everyone involved proceeded seemingly totally unaware of the dangers.

The Lessons Learned issued by the CSB speak volumes about what should really be by now common, accepted and required practices, and clearly exhibit insufficient learning from the many prior, indeed similar outcomes.

*'Manufacturers should take a comprehensive approach, and:*

- *identify and characterize reactive hazards;*
- *systematically evaluate what can go wrong, including mis-charging of reagents, loss of cooling, instrument malfunction, and other credible failure scenarios;*
- *implement, document, and maintain adequate safeguards against the identified failure scenarios; and*
- *multiple, independent safeguards may be needed to reliably ensure the safety of the reactive process.*

*Chemical manufacturers and others with reactive chemistry operations should control changes to batch recipes, including key operating conditions, such as:*

- *the quantities, proportions, and sequencing of reactor feeds;*
- *reaction temperature;*
- *conditions that could cause initiator or monomer accumulation; and*
- *conditions that could affect the deactivation of monomer inhibitors*
- *or stabilizers.*

*Manufacturers with reactive chemistry operations should:*

- *document the performance requirements and capabilities of*
- *process equipment, such as the reactor condenser at Synthron;*
- *periodically inspect and service process equipment, including the*
- *water side of heat exchangers, to maintain appropriate safety margins; and*
- *train personnel on hazards and procedures.*

*Manufacturers should ensure that worker training includes:*

- *the nature of the reactive hazards, including process safety margins; and*
- *operating procedures, including appropriate cautions and warnings, the consequences of deviations, recognition of deviations and abnormal operations, and the appropriate responses to control or mitigate their effects.*

*Manufacturers should:*

- *implement an effective emergency plan;*
- *train employees on the plan;*

- *install an evacuation alarm system that is audible and/or visible throughout the facility;*
- *conduct regular exercises to help ensure rapid evacuation to a safe location in an emergency; and*
- *coordinate their emergency planning with offsite response organizations.'*

It seems from the outcome data and from these findings and recommendations that we humans are indeed doomed to repeat our mistakes.

## References

[1] US Chemical Safety and Hazard Investigation Board (CSB), 2004, Investigation Report No. 2003-11-I-KY, March 2004, Catastrophic Vessel Failure: D.D. Williamson & Co., Inc., Louisville, Kentucky, 11 April 2003, NTIS number PB2004-103035.
[2] Duffey, R.B. and Saull, J.W., 2002, 'Know the Risk', First Edition, Butterworth and Heinemann, Boston, USA.
[3] US Chemical Safety and Hazard Investigation Board (CSB), 2003, Report No. 2003-15-D, Incident Data: Reactive Hazard Investigation -Investigation Data Release, September.
[4] US Chemical Safety and Hazard Investigation Board (CSB), 2007, Report No. 2006-04-I-NC, 31 July 2007 Case Study, Runaway Chemical Reaction and Vapor Cloud Explosion, Synthron, LLC, Morganton, NC.

# Appendix H

## Never Happening Again

*'The Future is not what it was.'*

*B. Levin*

### The Risk of an Echo, or of a Repeat Event

We have already seen that nearly identical events can reoccur, or outcomes repeat themselves that are seemingly very similar or almost identical (see the Appendices describing actual events and the Four Echoes). Having already had one outcome, what is our risk or chance of having another one, exactly or very similar to the one that already happened? It is the probability of an Echo.

Of course, after some disaster, accident, event or failure, everyone would like to make sure we do not have another one; and many often express the desire to ensure that it will or can 'never happen again'. The reduction of repeat risk is the usual purpose of all the inquiries, reports, lawsuits, studies and analyses into the accident and event cause. So we try to eliminate all the identified causes, being the faults, the sequence, the failures, the logic, the design problems and errors, the maintenance issues, the management failings, plus the everyday items that have all combined to make it happen. That is the present basis for societal and human learning to reduce or indeed eliminate the risk.

But even if we address all this litany of causes, even if we are learning from them, how likely are we to have another similar such event, an error or an outcome? Fortunately there is a way to estimate an answer to this question too[1]. To do that, we first turn again to the Jar of Life analogy, knowing that somewhere in the Jar are the other black balls (the unknown outcomes) still waiting to appear.

---

[1] This 'never happening again' problem is the direct analogy of the classic 'birthmate matching' problem extensively discussed in the stimulating, intriguing and entertaining text by Mosteller [1] to which we are indebted. In his Problem #32, the total possible number for $N$ is 365, being the days of the year or opportunities for matching; and $n$ is the number of people available for possible matching to these days and to each other.

---

We assume that we can make or label the (black ball) outcomes so they are actually *distinguishable* types. Then we can tell them apart, or at least we would recognise two that were or are effectively the same, or at least very similar. After all, no two accidents are exactly or absolutely identical in every possible way. Although all the events are nominally the same, being simply outcomes, let us treat them as if each one is distinct or identifiable. For the moment, consider the outcome types $n_k = 1,2,3 \ldots N$, and we have observed just, $n = \Sigma_j n_k$, in total so far. But as usual, we may not know the magnitude of $N$, and we have not tampered or changed any of the remaining $(N - n)$ outcomes as only the $n$ outcomes have occurred and the rest still have not appeared.

We examine this prior information for the moment and try to make a Bayesian-type estimate of the chance of another outcome. Consistently, from Bulmer and Jaynes, we have, as before, the conditional relation for the probability of any future event:

Posterior probability, $[p(\mathrm{P})]$ is proportional to the Prior probabiltiy, $[p(\varepsilon)]$
times the Likelihood of another outcome, $[p(\mathrm{L})]$

or, symbolically,

$$\text{Future } p(\mathrm{P}) \propto \text{Past } p(\varepsilon) \times \text{Likelihood } p(\mathrm{L})$$

Assuming there are a total of $N$ outcomes possible, the equivalent probability of any past or prior outcome is, as usual,

$$p(\varepsilon) = \sum\nolimits_j n_k \Big/ \sum\nolimits_N n_k = n/N .$$

We may take the number of outcome types observed so far in the $j$th observation interval, $\Sigma_j n_k = n$, such that for any one more, or for the very next outcome the number of outcome types is then $\Sigma_j n_{k+1} = n + 1$. So for the very next or the, $(n + 1)$th outcome, the future risk is given by:

$$p(\mathrm{P}) \equiv p(n+1) \propto p(\varepsilon) \times p(\mathrm{L})$$

Having already observed $n$ of such outcomes before, the future risk or chance of the *one* next observed outcome, $n + 1$, then comes from the posterior or future estimate:

$$\begin{aligned} p(\mathrm{P}) \equiv p(n+1) &= p(\varepsilon) \times [f(\varepsilon)/p(\varepsilon)] \\ &= p(\varepsilon) \times [(1/N)/(n/N)] \\ &= (n/N) \times (1/n) = 1/N \end{aligned}$$

Thus, since $N$ is constant, even if unknown, the posterior, $p(\mathrm{P}) \equiv f(\varepsilon) = p(n + 1)$, is also the constant probability, $p(\mathrm{P}) \sim 1/N$.

To establish the likelihood, $p(\mathrm{L})$, of the very next outcome, the incremental chance of having any outcome derives interchangeably from using Sveshnikov's 'generalised Bayes formula'. Based on the prior outcomes having already occurred with this prior probability, $p(\varepsilon)$, the probability or Likelihood of the next outcome, $p(\mathrm{L})$, in our present experience-based notation is then given by the fractional relation:

$$p(\mathrm{L}) = p(\mathrm{P}) = \frac{(f(\varepsilon), \text{ probability that the very next outcome will occur})}{(p(\varepsilon), \text{ probability that the outcome has already occurred})}$$
$$= (1/N)/(n/N) = 1/n$$

Therefore, it does not matter how many outcomes have already occurred, the posterior or future probability, $p(\text{P})$, of the next one remains unchanged and uniform, $1/N$, even while the likelihood, $p(\text{L})$, decreases as $1/n$.

This future or posterior probability, $p(\text{P}) = 1/N$ is by now very familiar. As might have been expected, it is precisely the LaPlace–Bayes result, being exactly the (uniform) chance of having or observing any one outcome in the first place. But we must still answer our question regarding the chance of a repeat event using this information and insight.

## The Matching Probability for an Echo

We want to know the chance of having any two of these outcomes as being similar or effectively identical, which is the matching problem for an Echo. In other words, we want the probability that any two of the observed, $n_k$, outcomes are similar. The probability of any *one* such event is always the usual Laplace–Bayes result, $p(\text{P}) \sim 1/N$, for the posterior probability of a uniform risk as was just derived above. The chance of any one of all the possible, $N$ outcome types *not* matching, $r = 0$, or *not* being similar or identical to any of all the remaining $(N - 1)$ other types is the failure to match probability, $P(r = 0, 1)$. This failure (or non-outcome) probability is given by the converse of the probability of observing any one outcome, $p(\text{P})$, since if we do not have even one outcome it cannot match any other anyway, hence:

$$P(r = 0, 1) = 1 - p(\text{P}) = 1 - (1/N)$$
$$= (N - 1)/N$$

For all the prior outcomes, $n$, that have actually been observed so far out of the total possible, $N$, we assume the chance of not matching any one to any other is the same for all (being the uniform similarity choice). Therefore, the probability that *none* of them match any one other outcome is this single failure to match probability, $P(r = 0, 1)$ occurring just $n$-times over, so,

$$P(r = 0, n) = \{(N - 1)/N\}^n$$

The probability of *at least one* match or Echo, $r > 0$, existing among the actual, $n$, prior outcome types observed is simply the complement of not having any matches at all, $r = 0$, or:

$$P(r > 0, n) = 1 - P(r = 0, n)$$
$$= 1 - \{(N - 1)/N\}^n$$
$$= 1 - \{(1 - 1/N)\}^n$$

Since $N$ is potentially large, $1/N \ll 1$, so $(1 - 1/N) \approx e^{-1/N}$, and hence,

$$P(r > 0, n) \approx 1 - \{e^{-1/N}\}^n$$
$$= 1 - e^{-n/N}$$

which probability is also identical to Mosteller's result for birthmate matching. The outcome probability expression also mirrors, of course, the outcome (failure) rate relation introduced and adopted in Chapter 1, where equivalently,

$$p(\varepsilon) \equiv P(r > 0, n) = 1 - e^{-\int \lambda d\varepsilon} = 1 - e^{-n/N}$$

So, equating the exponents, the equivalent *matching opportunity rate* is the outcome rate, $\lambda = \{1/(N-n)\}dn/d\varepsilon$, precisely as expected and representing a common-sense check.

There is a corresponding change in the matching probability as the chance of a non-match varies, according to the exponential of the ratio of the actual number available or observed, $n$, to the total number of the many possible opportunities, $N$. If we use our usual LaPlace–Bernoulli definition of the probability of an outcome as given by the ratio of those observed $n$, to the total possible $N$, then the exponent becomes,

$$P(r>0, n(\varepsilon)) = 1 - e^{-p}$$

If, as might be expected, we also have many more potential outcomes so, $n \sim N$, or even unknown rare events, then asymptotically, $p \rightarrow 1$, and of course the risk of an Echo tends to,

$$p(r>0, n) \rightarrow 1 - 1/e = 0.63$$

There is therefore a large risk of the *existence* of another similar outcome, and the myth of 'never happening again' is exposed. We just cannot fight the probabilities as we are doomed to repeat at least one outcome among many, and Echoes *will* occur. This counter intuitive result we have seen before in Appendix F in a different guise: there it was the risk or opportunity of actually having a rare event, if we try often enough so that potentially, $N$, is comparatively large. So even for rare events, when we have, $n = 1$, so that $p(\varepsilon) \rightarrow 1/N$, the same result still holds, and the paradox is that *low probability rare events can also reoccur*. As is often said, lightning can and does strike twice in the same place.

Of course, this is what we might have expected before doing all this algebra and reasoning about matching similar outcomes. They can be rare too, but they do exist, and having had one outcome type, we might as well expect another.

## The Impact of Learning and Experience on Managing the Risk of Repeat Events

We can safely assume that we learn from the outcomes we observe, and hence, try to reduce the probability of an outcome as we gain experience. After all, that hypothesis and approach is the entire premise behind the existence of the ULC and of effective modern safety management methods. The influence of learning can now be explicitly included. Recall the probability, $p(\varepsilon)$, at any outcome at experience, $\varepsilon$, is based on observing $n(\varepsilon)$ prior outcomes, which is now a function of our experience, out of the total of $N$ possible ones.

But the probability of an outcome, failure or error occurring in or taking less than $\varepsilon$ is just the cumulative distribution function, CDF, also conventionally written as $F(\varepsilon)$. The CDF is related to the failure rate, $\lambda(\varepsilon)$, where the number of observed outcomes now varies with experience as we descend the learning curve:

$$p(\varepsilon) \equiv F(\varepsilon) = n(\varepsilon)/N = 1 - e^{-\int \lambda(\varepsilon)d\varepsilon}$$

So the probability, $p(\varepsilon)$, is itself a double exponential in experience because of the exponential form of the outcome (failure) rate, $\lambda(\varepsilon)$, arising from the learning hypothesis and the MERE solution which is:

$$\lambda(\varepsilon) = \lambda_{\mathrm{m}} + (\lambda_0 - \lambda_{\mathrm{m}})\exp{-k\varepsilon}$$

Carrying out the integration from an initial experience, $\varepsilon_0$, out to any interval, $\varepsilon$, we obtained the probability as the double exponential:

$$p(\varepsilon) = 1 - \exp\{(\lambda - \lambda_{\mathrm{m}})/k - \lambda(\varepsilon_0 - \varepsilon)\}$$

Therefore, the probability of matching, $P(r > 0, n)$, or having *at least one* outcome or event recur as we gain experience, is given by a *triple* exponential variation,

$$P(r > 0, n(\varepsilon)) \approx 1 - \mathrm{e}^{-p(\varepsilon)}$$

This result becomes, after explicitly including the impact of learning on the matching probability,

$$P(r > 0, n(\varepsilon)) = 1 - \mathrm{e}^{-\{1-\exp\{(\lambda_0 - \lambda_{\mathrm{m}})/k - \lambda(\varepsilon_0 - \varepsilon)\}\}}$$

The numerical values for this equation for the risk of 'happening again', $P(r > 0, n(\varepsilon))$, or the matching probability, can be derived using our 'best' MERE estimates for, $k$ and $\lambda_{\mathrm{m}}$, as a function of accumulated experience represented in the usual $\tau$ units. The result is shown in Figure A-H1 and gives the probability of an Echo. Somewhat perversely and also paradoxically, this purely statistical approach shows that there is indeed a high risk of something similar 'happening again' at any accumulated experience, no matter how rare the outcome. In fact, as we might have expected, the risk actually increases as we gain experience, before the impact of attaining the minimum outcome rate eventually takes effect and the risk declines dramatically. The probability of happening again as given by the matching probability, $P(r > 0, n(\varepsilon))$ at a given experience, is about ~0.3 (a 1-in-3 chance) and then *rises* to a maximum of $1 - 1/\mathrm{e} \sim 0.63$, before it then plunges towards zero at very large experience.

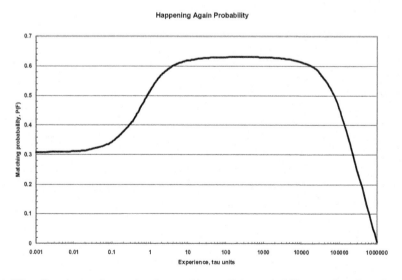

**Figure A-H1.** Ever happening again: the matching or Echo probability as a function of experience

The matching probability curve in Figure A-H1 is effectively the numerical inverse (or the complement) of the 'human bathtub' probability; it shows we should *not* be surprised by Echoes and by having repeated or similar events. In managing risk and using learning, apparently we should actually *expect* that similar things are quite likely to have a risk of happening more than once.

## The Theory of Evidence: Belief and Risk Equivalence

When the past outcome information is not exact or complete, or we are just unsure, there is another means available for predicting the possibility of an outcome occurring or one reoccurring. Semantically, this enters us into the realm of belief as well as of chance, and a subtle shift in terminology.

We may not know exactly what has happened before in the past, and perhaps even less about what might happen again in the future. Therefore, in reaching judgements about future likelihood we must weigh the past or existing evidence, which in this case is the imperfect outcome data. To reflect the degree of belief about possible outcomes, both past and future, the formal mathematical Theory of Evidence assigns *ranges* between 0 to 1 for the chance (probability) of certain outcomes occurring or not depending on the belief (Shafer, 1976) [2]. Thus, the theory defines and uses a mathematical expression that is given by:

$$s = 1 - e^{-w}$$

where, in the notation of evidence theory, $s$ is called a 'belief support function' and $w$ is called the 'weight of evidence'. This specific algebraic form is derived from the condition of simply being able to additively combine the belief and weight functions.

Recall that the risk probability of an outcome, failure or error occurring in or less than any experience, $\varepsilon$, is just the cumulative distribution function, CDF, also conventionally written as $F(\varepsilon)$. The CDF is related to the failure rate, $\lambda(\varepsilon)$, by:

$$p(\varepsilon) \equiv F(\varepsilon) = n(\varepsilon)/N = 1 - e^{-\int \lambda(\varepsilon)d\varepsilon}$$

This expression is derivable from conventional Reliability Theory and we can see by inspection that the expression for $p(\varepsilon)$ is identical in form and equivalent to the expression for $s$ in the Theory of Evidence. Therefore, by physical analogy, we presume here that the Theory of Evidence is simply describing formally the range of *belief* in the risk assessment that determines the *probability* of what we may already know or do not know. Both the belief and the probability are based on our partial knowledge and experience of prior outcomes.

Thus, *physically* we may equate these equivalent probability and belief expressions separately obtained from these apparently disparate theories of Reliability and of Evidence, respectively. Hence, by analogy, we obtain the risk equivalences that:

$$s \equiv p(\varepsilon) \equiv F(\varepsilon) = n(\varepsilon)/N$$

and

$$w \equiv \int \lambda(\varepsilon)d\varepsilon$$

In other words, *physically* the support belief function, *s*, serves the purpose of assigning a prior probability statement; and the weight, *w*, represents the evidence afforded by the effective number of prior integrated outcomes up to any experience, $\varepsilon$, based on a known or assumed hazard or failure rate. Insofar as any prior outcomes may be known or have been actually observed, mathematically the *belief and evidence weight combine* such that outcomes indeed have a finite chance of occurring again, precisely according to the range of outcome numbers and rates that have already been observed. In the fuzzy logic but precise parlance of Evidence Theory, we do not need unique information in order to make a predictive probability estimate of an outcome reoccurring.

## References

[1] Mosteller, F., 1987, 'Fifty Challenging Problems in Probability', Dover Publications, New York, pp. 46–49.
[2] Shafer, G., 1976, 'A Mathematical Theory of Evidence', Princeton University Press, NJ, p. 8.

# Appendix I

## A Heuristic Organisational Risk Stability Criterion

*'If we've learned one thing from this tragedy it's the need for humility.'*

*John Mogford, 2006*

### Order and Disorder in Physical and Management Systems

The discussion we give here is new and postulates a new numerical measure for managing risk and predicting success. The argument given below is not mathematically exact and heuristically assumes that an equivalence or analogy exists between the emergence of order (i.e., learning patterns) in physical, mathematical and homo-technological systems (HTSs). By a physical analogy, the approach links the emergence of learning in human organizations and entities with recent ideas of the emergence of order and structure from chaos in the physical sciences.

As eloquently suggested by Ilya Prigogine and his co-workers (Kondepudi and Prigogine, 1998) [1], a non-equilibrium and statistically fluctuating system can evolve towards an ordered state. Paradoxically, the fluctuations at the unobserved microscopic atomic and molecular level that characterise the non-equilibrium themselves provide the *necessary* opportunity for structure and order to emerge as distributions at the observed macroscopic level.

Professor Yuri Kirillov pointed out to us these developments in non-equilibrium entropy, suggesting that we may examine the creation of structure from disorder in HTS as well as for the purely physical and chemical systems discussed in Prigogine's work. The question is then whether there is an implied relationship between these two apparently vastly different fields.

In our technological world, we have the same phenomenon and, by analogy, the same randomness and disorder that must exist for order and learning to occur. Managers, executives, employees, procedures, training and individual skill acquisition also intend to achieve the creation of order in any HTS or corporate organisation from the natural disorder. The

*Managing Risk: The Human Element*   Romney B. Duffey and John W. Saull

Copyright © 2005 and 2008 Romney B. Duffey and John W. Saull, Published by John Wiley & Sons, Ltd

system learns how to behave macroscopically (externally and organisationally), when in fact it is a collection of a myriad of microscopic (internally and individually) fluctuating and unpredictable interactions (e.g., in discussions, meetings, rules, procedures, communications, training, one-on-ones, coffee breaks, lunch groups, hallway gatherings, rumour mills . . .). In practice in the 'real' world, multitudinous random and informal learning opportunities exist in addition to the purely formal and official ones, and result in error state distributions based on knowledge and experience that affect and reflect in actual decision making.

We would like to believe and know that the management and safety system are both producing order and results (profit and low risk) and is stable against short-term fluctuations and risk pressures (failure and collapse). Just as in all fluctuating systems, the correct measure of order is the information entropy, the $H$-factor, which represents the uncertainty in the observed outcome distribution as the emergent result of the unobserved learning and error correction processes. As in physical systems, it is necessary to have the randomness, fluctuations and disorder for the learning, structure and knowledge patterns (or distributions) to actually emerge. One key question is not only is the organisation or HTS learning, but also is it stable? – that is, heading in the right direction of decreasing risk that results from the increased order, pattern recognition and emergent structure.

This same question and issue of system stability also has direct application to the subjective concept of 'resilience engineering', where '. . . *resilience is the intrinsic ability of an organisation (system) to maintain or regain a dynamically stable state, which allows it to continue operation after a major mishap and/or the presence of a continuous stress*' (Hollnagel E. et al., 2006) [2]. But 'resilience' has not been actually measured or quantified anywhere: it is simply a desirable property. We develop here the numerical and objective criterion that is precisely applicable to the quantification of 'resilience', hence incidentally unifying that empirical concept with the general theory and practice of managing risk through learning. This criterion is also relevant to 'crisis management' policies and procedures, and emergency response centres in major corporations, facilities and industries.

## Stability Criterion

The measure of order adopted in physical systems is also entropy, and the stability condition simply represents how a molecular system responds dynamically to thermodynamic entropy changes. Thus, for stability the incremental change in the thermodynamic entropy, $dS$, must be negative (Kondepudi and Prigogine, 1998) [1], so in any *time* increment:

$$dS/dt \leq 0$$

We can postulate a direct analogy with the risk outcomes and measures for an HTS to define our equivalent organisational risk stability criterion (ORSC). Simply from the fact that the incremental change in risk (information entropy, $H$) with changes in probability must be negative, in any *experience* increment we must have:

$$dH/dp \leq 0$$

This condition requires that a maximum ('peak') or minimum ('trough') exists in our changing information (error state) distribution, so that what we actually observe is the most likely. Now many others and we have derived the relation for the Information Entropy as:

$$H = -\sum p \ln p$$

Assuming a continuous probability distribution indeed exists, we can write this summation as an integral function:

$$H = -\int p \ln p \, dp$$

So,

$$dH/dp = -p \ln p$$

Interestingly, there is a parallel requirement for convergence in iterative computational learning machines, which is termed 'empirical risk minimisation'. In such machines, using learning 'algorithms' for successive trials, the approximations and sequential rules are sought, which are intended to mimic or model the neural learning processes, but by using a computer. It has been shown that a necessary condition for convergence is for the equivalent computational entropy measure to vanish in the limit of many observations or samples, meaning as $n \to \infty$ (Vlapnik, 2000) [3]. So the equivalent numerical convergence theorem or requirement is such that the ratio:

$$\mathrm{Lim}_{n \to \infty}(H/n) = 0$$

We postulate that this is equivalent to Prigogine's approach, being an incremental stability condition for any system (i.e., where order is emerging from chaos). For incremental changes, and since $p = n/N$, assuming a sufficient numbers of outcomes,

$$dH/dp \to 0, \text{ as } n \to \infty.$$

We know from the SEST analysis of fluctuating outcome distributions that in any observation interval the outcome probability varies with depth of experience nearly as,

$$P \approx p_0 e^{-\beta \varepsilon}$$

Hence, since $dH/dp = -p \ln p$, then,

$$dH/dp = p_0 e^{-\beta \varepsilon}(\beta \varepsilon - \ln p_0)$$

where, as usual, the probability, $p_0 = n_0/N_j$, is the ratio of relative zeroth error state occupancy number to the total observed, and $\beta$, is the learning shape parameter.

We can assert that for any observed HTS to be stable, the necessary stability condition (ORSC) is given by evaluating the condition for convergence[1]. For the above stability inequality to exist requires that:

$$\beta \varepsilon - \ln p_0 \to 0$$

---

[1] We are tempted to call this the Kirillov Stability Condition, simply to reflect his keen and original insight.

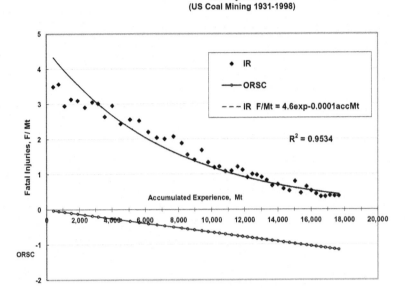

**Figure A-I1.**   Example stability criterion calculation

Physically, we can say that the ratio of error reduction by learning to the number of irreducible errors, at any moment of experience, must be such that for increasingly large outcome numbers, $n$:

$$\{\beta\varepsilon/\ln p_0\} \leq 1$$

This ratio can be postulated to be the Organizational Risk Stability Number, also and incidentally representing the quantification of 'resilience', and for stability and/or convergence must have a value that is less than unity. Once again, the requirement is that we must measure and quantify the probability of outcomes, using actual data, and determine the variation of the *distribution* with experience.

To demonstrate the ORSC principle, we use real data for a simple and well-defined dataset, in this particular case for coal mining fatalities. The variation of the number of fatalities, $F$, with depth of experience (accumulated millions of tons mined, Mt) was used to provide the working estimate for the learning exponent, $\beta$; and the value for $p_0$ was calculated to be ~0.046 from the numbers of fatalities. Figure A-I1 shows the resulting ORSC simply added below the plot of the instantaneous rate, *IR*. It can be seen clearly that the estimated value of $\{\beta\varepsilon/\ln p_0\} \leq 1$ and is stable for this purely illustrative example.

## References

[1]  Kondepudi, D. and Prigogine, I., 1998, 'Modern Thermodynamics: From Heat Engines to Dissipative Structures', John Wiley & Sons, New York.

[2] Hollnagel, E, Woods, D.W., and Leveson, N. (Editors), 2006, 'Resilience Engineering: Concepts and Precepts', Ashgate Publishing, Aldershot, England, Chapter 1, Resilience – the Challenge of the Unstable, pp. 9–16.

[3] Vlapnik, V.N., 2000, 'The Nature of Statistical Learning Theory', 2nd edition, Springer-Verlag, New York, pp. 43–45.

# Appendix J

## New Laws of Practice for Learning and Error Correction

*That all our knowledge begins with experience, there is no doubt . . .*

*Immanuel Kant*

### Individual Learning and Practice

We provide the detailed comparison of our new learning and statistical theories for system outcome data with the traditional analysis of the learning curves obtained from tests with individual human subjects. The results provide a consistent predictive basis for the learning trends emerging all the way from timescales of many years in large technological system outcomes to actions that occur in about a tenth of a second for individual human decisions. Hence, we demonstrate both the common influence of the human element and the importance of statistical reasoning and analysis.

Understanding human learning behaviour and processes has fascinated psychologists and others for many years. From extensive observations of the skill and learning process in individuals, the number of successful outcomes from learning is known to be determined by the amount of 'practice', or number of trials. We show this is equivalent to our use of 'experience'. The learning rate has been measured by counting the number of error free outcomes with increasing trials; and by the reduction in response time, $RT$, to achieve a given outcome or successful task performance with increasing practice. There has also been an extended, continuing and not very fruitful debate over whether power laws or exponential functions give better fits to the laboratory data using stylised human trials.

We examine here comparisons with the data and empirical analysis that underpins the use of empirical learning curve correlations to describe individual skill and learning. These correlations of experimental data determine separately and independently the error rate for repetitive tasks, and the instantaneous response time reductions for recognising patterns and recall for successive trials. Interestingly, the dependence of the learning trend on the number of trials, $t$, is different for each type. The fundamental technical questions are then

*Managing Risk: The Human Element*   Romney B. Duffey and John W. Saull
Copyright © 2005 and 2008 Romney B. Duffey and John W. Saull, Published by John Wiley & Sons, Ltd

not only why the learning curves have the dependencies they have, but also why they are different.

We assume that they represent just two distinct types of learning behaviour. For error reductions that depend on prior learning of repetitive skills, we postulate that the error correction *rate* (systematic learning and unlearning) is due to the learning hypothesis, and hence, the error or success rate varies with the *accumulated* experience or practice. But for the different response time reductions that depend on an instantaneous judgement or learned response, we postulate that the error correction *probability* (faster solution and the most likely) is due to discerning order and patterns, and hence, the error or success rate varies with the *depth* of experience or practice.

With the present work, the empirical but highly successful correlations that have been developed in psychology and the cognitive sciences are therefore placed on a firmer theoretical and practical basis. Importantly, the new results also link the learning processes in all homo-technological systems (HTSs) and, conversely, show that the human element indeed inexorably dominates the system behaviour. The individual using past experience forms learning patterns and prior learning determines the probability of error. The instantaneous decisions from the resulting skill, knowledge and rule acquisition are reflected in the distribution of the outcomes we observe externally from the systems they inhabit, decreasing with practice and experience. This is consistent with Ohlsson's Theory of Error Correction (Ohlsson, 1996) [1], where rule correction and unlearning provide the mechanisms for error correction and skill acquisition at the individual level.

Therefore, we now compare our new and predictive general theory to these published correlations[1].

## Comparison to Error Reduction Data

Consider the first case when the number of successes increases, or failures decrease, with increased repetitive learning. Our analysis for predicting the outcome rates from HTSs is based on the Learning Hypothesis where the rate of reduction of the error rate with experience is proportional to the error rate. The result is an exponential form for the failure rate and for the Universal Learning Curve (ULC). The best representation of the world data is in Know the Risk (Duffey and Saull, 2002) [2]:

$$E^* = \exp - 3N^* \qquad (J1)$$

Here, $E^* = (1 - \lambda/\lambda_m)/(1 - \lambda_0/\lambda_m)$, the ratio of the failure rate, $\lambda$, at any experience, $\varepsilon$, to the failure rate, $\lambda_0$, at the initial experience, and to the minimum failure rate, $\lambda_m$, achieved at the maximum experience, $\varepsilon_T$, and $N^*$ is the non-dimensional experience, $\varepsilon/\varepsilon_T$. For correlating all the disparate data, the maximum experience can also be taken as either that at which the minimum outcome rate was attained, or as the most experience achieved with that system. The learning rate constant or slope factor, $-3$, is obtained from a fit to some 200 years of outcomes covering some 800 data points from multiple technological systems.

The observed result of skill testing on human subjects shows a non-linear relation exists between practice and the amount of error reduction, or conversely the increasing numbers of

[1] The authors thank Professor Stellan Ohlsson for providing the referenced papers and data sources for this analysis.

**Table A-J1.** Practice correlation values for data fits given by Stevens and Savin ($N_S = at^m$)

| Task | Constant, $a$ | Slope, $m$ | Start, $t_0$ | Stop, $t_T$ | Units |
|------|------|------|------|------|------|
| Syllables | 5.7 | 1.56 | 1 | 20 | # Trials |
| Ball tosses | 0.0356 | 1.25 | 200 | 20,000 | # Tosses |
| Typesetting | 46.4 | 1.10 | 12.7 | 1,227 | # Hours |
| Invert writing | 25 | 1.18 | 1 | 70 | # Minutes |
| Coding | 16 | 1.18 | 1 | 20 | # Minutes |

successes, $N_S$. This ubiquitous relation has been termed the 'law of practice'. In fact, Stevens and Savin, 1962 [3] studied many such learning experiments which examined the improvement in success with practice for stylised tasks like learning to run a maze, write upside down, toss balls at a target, typeset words, memorise word strings, etc., etc.

Stevens and Savin [3] fitted all these datasets with a series of *totally* empirical 'power laws' that correlated the number of successful or correct responses, $N_S$, as a function of practice, $t$:

$$N_S = at^m \tag{J2}$$

where the fitting constants are $a$ and $m$, with the number of trials, $t$, as the practice measure. Generally, success improves with practice ('practice makes nearly perfect'), and predicting this 'power law' form has now been taken as a necessary test of any psychological learning theory.

For analysis, we chose several task types with a large apparent spread in the values, slopes and ranges for these human learning activities. The experimental results, practice range and fitted values for $a$ and $m$, for this selection of tasks are shown in Table A-J1.

In order to compare these 'success' data to the Learning Hypothesis, we really need a failure rate, $\lambda$, or conversely an effective *rate* of successful outcomes. Now the failure rate is not given explicitly in the Stevens and Savin paper, nor is the number of failures, $N_F$. But we can determine the needed non-dimensional error rate, $E^*$, by working backwards from the correlations, given the fact that the rate of failures with increasing trials, $t$, is related straightforwardly to the differential rate of the number of successes, $N_S$, by:

$$dN_F/dt = -dN_S/dt = -amt^{m-1} \tag{J3}$$

By definition, this differential rate of failure with increasing trials, $dN_F/dt$, is proportional to, $\lambda$, the usual failure rate, so also,

$$dN_F/dt \propto \lambda(a, m, t). \tag{J4}$$

To obtain the differentials that give the failure rates, we assume the $(a,m,t)$ correlations given for, $N_S$, do indeed fit the data well to a very high degree, as shown in the Figure given in the original Stevens and Savin paper (the actual data were plotted but not tabulated). Hence, we can take the fitted $(a,m,t)$ power laws for $N_S$ as reasonable substitutes for the original data points, which they are by definition. Noting that the minimum failure rate, $\lambda_m$, occurs at the

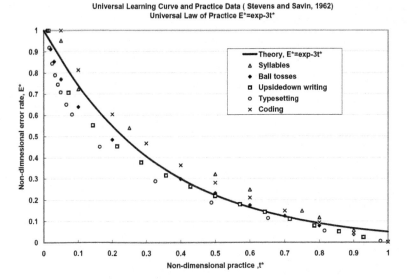

**Figure A-J1.** The Universal Law of Practice, $E^* = \exp - 3t^*$

maximum practice $t_T$, the equivalent expression for the non-dimensional error rate ratio, $E^*$, for any amount of practice, $t$, from the power law correlation becomes,

$$E^* = \frac{(1 - \lambda/\lambda_m)}{(1 - \lambda_0/\lambda_m)} \Rightarrow \frac{\left(1 - \{t/t_T\}^{m-1}\right)}{\left(1 - \{t_0/t_T\}^{m-1}\right)} \tag{J5}$$

Here, $t_0$ is the initial and $t_T$, the maximum amount of practice, $t^* = t/t_T$, is the non-dimensional practice for any number of trials, and the constant product, $am$, has cancelled out everywhere.

The needed values of $t_0$, $t_T$ and $m$ are all reported for the empirical correlations (see Table A-J1), so we can back-calculate $E^*$ for any given non-dimensional practice, $t^*$. The result is shown in the Figure A-J1, where the points are actually typical values calculated from Table A-J1 correlations for the entire ranges of practice given.

We observe an *extraordinary* fact. The individual practice curves align almost *exactly* with the totally independently derived Universal Learning Curve that fits all the world's HTS outcome data based on the Learning Hypothesis (see Chapter 1 and [2]). The experience parameter in the ULC is simply transformed to the non-dimensional practice, $t^*$, so the non-dimensional error *rate* ratio is,

$$E^* = \exp - 3t^* \tag{J6}$$

Formally, this result has established the equivalence between 'accumulated experience' for a system and 'practice' for an individual as the relevant and corresponding measures for learning rate trends. Because of its extraordinarily general basis, we may call this new curve the Universal Law of Practice (ULP). The major implication is then that the failure rate and bathtub-shaped error probability for the *individual* have exactly the same forms and dependencies on experience (practice) as derived for the *system* outcomes in Appendix A and Chapter 4. The individual is indeed an integral part of the system, so much so that *the system behaviour mirrors precisely the same learning trends.*

In addition, this comparison shows a key point: the learning behaviour at the system level is *exactly the same form* as that which occurs at the individual level. The Learning Hypothesis holds true and is independently validated.

## Comparison to Response Time Data and the Consistent Law of Practice

Consider now the second case where the response time is an instantaneous measure of how quickly new things or tasks are learned or recognised. Our prediction of the variation of learning response time with experience is based on the statistical theory that shows the probability distribution of errors is exponential with depth of experience. Based on the statistical treatment of outcomes, the distribution with experience that emerges is also the most likely from the statistical error state theory. From that distribution, we derived the Information Entropy as a measure of the degree of order and uncertainty in the emergence of learning patterns (see Chapter 5 and Duffey and Saull, 2004) [6]. We coupled this result with the known Hick–Hyman Law for the observed effects of Information Entropy on learning response time, $RT$ (see Duffey and Saull, 2006 [4] and Duffey and Ohlsson, tbp [5]).

The Hick–Hyman expression (see Chapter 8) represents the response time as a function of the information entropy or random stimulus. Thus, we now know that the response time varies explicitly with the experience depth, $\varepsilon$, in any interval as,

$$RT_j(\varepsilon) = a_j + b_j(p_0 + p_0^* e^{-\beta\varepsilon})^2(\frac{1}{4} - \frac{1}{2}\ln\{p_0 + p_0^* e^{-\beta\varepsilon}\}) \tag{J7}$$

where the $a$ and $b$ constants derive from the Hick–Hyman law. Physically *and hence mentally*, the terms in brackets represent the most probable *distribution* of outcome errors with depth of experience. The parameters that are observation interval dependent are the probabilities of error state occupancy, $p_0$ and $p_0^*$, and the learning constant, $\beta$, for the most probable (i.e., observed) distribution. By grouping the constant terms ($a_j$, $b_j$, $p_0$, etc.) together we may write this expression as:

$$RT_j(\varepsilon) = A_j + B_j e^{-\beta\varepsilon} + C_j e^{-2\beta\varepsilon} \tag{J8}$$

where $A_j$, $B_j$ and $C_j$ are constants and the logarithmic term is taken to be relatively small.

The observed result from tests using human subjects is also a non-linear relation between practice and the response time reduction. This relation has also been termed the 'law of practice', and is ubiquitous. The major study by Heathcote et al., 2000 [7] examined 40 studies with over 7,900 learning series from 475 subjects of such learning experiments. These tests were for many different learning situations, measuring improvement in response time with practice for stylised tasks like memory search, counting, mental arithmetic, visual search, motor learning, etc., etc. They correlated the response times, $RT$s, using a *totally* empirical exponential and/or power law function assumed to be of the form, using the same notation as above:

$$RT(t) = A + \left(Be^{-mt}\right)/t^c \tag{J9}$$

where $A$, $B$ and $c$ are constants. The forms chosen were justified by heuristic reasoning about the type and nature of the presumed learning processes. The options are for an exponential choice, $c = 0$; for a power law choice, $m = 0$; or for a mixed variation. The values of the 'constants' varied with the experiment and were fitted to each test series. The relative reduction in response time from the initial value, $RT(0) \rightarrow B/t^c$ when $t \rightarrow 0$ is,

$$RT(t)/RT(0) = \left(At^c + Be^{-mt}\right)/B \tag{J10}$$

Moreover, they showed that – at least for the $RT$ data reviewed – an exponential (with $c = 0$) was generally a somewhat better fit than a power law (with $m = 0$), contrary to the previous wisdom and conventional choices. This exponential form is very similar to the MERE failure rate expression, but the basis and application is entirely different. Our result is based on the statistical analysis of outcomes, where the exponential probability distribution with experience naturally emerges from the uncertainty.

The comparable statistical entropy theory result for the $RT$ can be derived by substituting numbers of trials or practice, $t$, as the $\tau$ units of the depth of experience/practice variable, $\varepsilon$. So we have the $ABC$ Law of Practice:

$$RT(t) = A_j + B_j e^{-\beta t} + C_j e^{-2\beta t} \tag{J11}$$

Physically and mentally, the exponential terms now reflect the uncertainty due to the probability distribution of outcomes with the amount of practice, which varies with the learning parameter, $\beta$. The relative reduction from the initial value, $RT(0) = (A_j + B_j + C_j)$, when $t \rightarrow 0$ is the $ABC$ ratio equation,

$$RT(t)/RT(0) = \left\{A_j + B_j e^{-\beta t} + C_j e^{-2\beta t}\right\}/\left(A_j + B_j + C_j\right) \tag{J12}$$

By inspection, these two $RT$ 'laws of practice' (the empirical exponential fit equation (J9) and the information entropy theory equation (J11)) have extraordinarily similar forms. There are enough 'constants' to fit almost any data, but we have now given them a consistent theoretical basis and physical meaning. Essentially, identical fits to data can be obtained when we self-evidently take $\beta \equiv m$, assuming that 'depth of experience', $\varepsilon$, equivalent to 'practice', $t$. To prove that fact directly preferably requires access to, and analysis of, all the original data, which we do not have. But the excellent agreement can be shown conclusively in principle as follows.

There was one subset test for counting (Heathcote et al.'s Figure 4, Count 3 dataset), with some 12,000 trials, where the numerical values for $A$ and $B$ were listed for an exponential correlation ($c = 0$). Again ,we have made the entirely reasonable assumption that the published correlation fits to, and is an acceptable substitute for, the actual data points for the present purpose of establishing the comparison in the learning trends. As a direct numerical test, the present entropy theory was therefore fitted to Heathcote et al.'s $RT$ data correlation curve adopting the same slope, $m$, and by normalising the $A$, $B$ and $C$ values to the published values.

In Figure A-J2, for this specific counting case, we plot the non-dimensional $RT/RT(0)$ response time ratios calculated both by the exponential correlation ($c = 0$ in equation (J10)) and by the entropy theory (equation (J12)) against the non-dimensional practice, $t^*$.

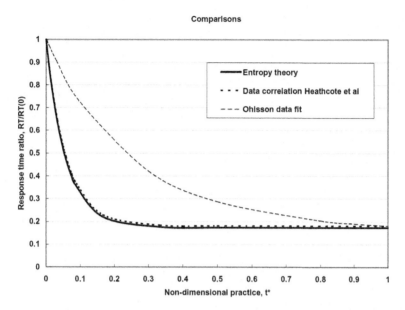

**Figure AJ-2.** The consistent law of practice: Comparison of entropy theory with *RT* data correlation

The curves from the two expressions are clearly totally indistinguishable. Just to show other generally similar trends, for comparison, we show the correlation of Ohlsson's *RT* data that was completely independently developed.

Recently, to account for differing data and models, Brown has proposed yet another more complex but still empirical form for the response time, RT (Brown, 2002) [8]. This form is actually a ratio of exponential terms which, using the same notation as above, can be written as:

$$RT(t) = A + B \left\{ \frac{(1-C)e^{-mt}}{(1-Ce^{-mt})} \right\} \tag{J13}$$

where as usual, *m, A, B* and *C* are constants, and $RT(0) = (A + B)$ as $t \to 0$.

Expanding the exponential term in the denominator, multiplying out the terms and regrouping the resulting constants, this can then be written as the infinite series,

$$RT(t) = A' + B'e^{-mt} + C'e^{-2mt} + \ldots \ldots \tag{J14}$$

This series in equation (J14) is also *identical* in form to our approximate expression equation (J8) for *RT* that was derived from the information entropy, using the Hick–Hyman *RT* law. The implication is that *the instantaneous decision making and error correction observed for individuals is reflected in the outcome learning trends observed for the entire system.*

## Reconciling the Laws

As an incidental benefit, we can now also reconcile some of the controversy in psychology between apparently competing power law and exponential fits for the Laws of Practice. We observe that the mathematical form of the learning curve and response time functions are both essentially the same. That is, from equation (J6) for the ULC/ULP,

$$E^* = \frac{(1-\lambda/\lambda_m)}{(1-\lambda_0/\lambda_m)} \Rightarrow \frac{\left(1-\{t/t_T\}^{m-1}\right)}{\left(1-\{t_0/t_T\}^{m-1}\right)} = e^{-3t^*} \tag{J6}$$

Rearranging and using the facts that, from equation (J4), $dN_S/dt \, \alpha - \lambda$, and $t^* \alpha t$, we have the rate of success with increasing trials varying with number of trials as,

$$dN_S/dt \, \alpha \, (dN_S/dt)_m + \{(dN_S/dt)_0 - (dN_S/dt)_m\}e^{-3t} \tag{J15}$$

or, say,

$$dN_S/dt = A_S + B_S e^{-mt} \tag{J16}$$

where $A_S$ and $B_S$ are constants representing the final and initial success rates for a given set of trials. Now, from equation (J11) for the response time, $RT$, variation with the number of trials we have,

$$RT(t) = A_j + B_j e^{-\beta t} + C_j e^{-2\beta t} \tag{J11}$$

Trials and experience being equivalent, the success rate (equation (J16)) and the response time (equation (J11)) are both generally *exponential* functions with the first two terms being *identical in functional form*. Of course, there will be differing values derived for the many and various fitting 'constants', $A_S$, $B_S$, $A_j$, $B_j$, $C_j$, $\beta$ and $m$ depending on the actual tests and trials performed and on the data range that is fitted, and may well be approximated by other power laws, series and/or polynomials.


## Conclusions

In a sweeping generalisation, we have shown a consistent relationship between human performance in learning with the outcomes, errors and accidents in technological systems. Moreover, the distinctly different dependencies on practice (experience) are explained for repetitive learning and instantaneous response time experiments.

Utilising the Learning Hypothesis and the statistical information entropy in the presence of learning, we provide a technical rationale for the form of the previously developed empirical correlations and 'laws of practice' used for fitting error reduction and response time data.

The consistent and new Universal Law of Practice for error reduction, skill acquisition, and system outcome *rates* is proposed as:

$$E^* = \exp - 3t^* \tag{J17}$$

where, $t^*$, is the non-dimensional practice, and is equivalent to the 'accumulated experience', $N^*$, for all HTSs. This form and trend of reducing errors with practice is identical to the Universal Learning Curve for HTSs outcomes reducing with experience, and established the importance of accumulated experience on learning and error correction.

For the response time, $RT$ variation, we propose the new consistent Law of Practice, as given by the probability distribution from the statistical error state theory coupled with the Hick–Hyman law:

$$RT_j = a_j + b_j(p_0 + p_0^* \mathrm{e}^{-\beta\varepsilon})^2\left(\frac{1}{4} - \frac{1}{2}\ln\{p_0 + p_0^* \mathrm{e}^{-\beta\varepsilon}\}\right) \qquad (J18)$$

It is clear that we may use the approximate simplified expression as a new correlating consistent ABC Law of Practice, without any loss of accuracy for fitting to any RT response *time* data,:

$$RT_j = A_j + B_j\mathrm{e}^{-\beta t} + C_j\mathrm{e}^{-2\beta t} \qquad (J19)$$

where $A_j$, $B_j$ and $C_j$ are constants determined from and by comparison to the data, as usual, but also derived here from a firm basis of theoretical reasoning. The practice number of trials, $t$, is equivalent to the 'depth of experience' for HTSs, $\varepsilon$.

These new results are also consistent with the vast body of data reported for human subjects, and the empirical forms of practice correlations adopted to date. An additional and powerful reason for using this new approach is the entire theoretical concept and basis that suggests and requires that order (learning curves) emerge from the disorder and random (neural) learning processes. This concept is also consistent with and derived from the established Hick–Hyman model, and there is an equivalence shown between 'depth of experience' and 'practice' in instantaneous cognitive decision making by individuals.

Thus, we have successfully linked the mental learning processes with the observed physical error distributions of outcomes using the information entropy measure. These conclusions, analysis and results all clearly support the present learning hypothesis and statistical learning theory approach in any and all HTSs, as does the validation shown against all the published data trends.

## References

[1] Stellan Ohlsson, 'Learning from Performance Errors', Psychological Review, 1996, Vol. 103, No. 2, pp. 241–262.

[2] Duffey, R.B. and Saull, J.W., 2002, 'Know the Risk', First Edition, Butterworth and Heinemann, Boston, MA.

[3] Stevens, J.C. and Savin, H.B., 1962, 'On the form of learning curves', J. Experimental Analysis of Behavior, 5,1, pp. 15–18.

[4] Duffey, R.B. & Saull, J.W. Measuring and Predicting Organizational Learning and Safety Culture, Proc. International Conference on Probabilistic Safety Assessment and Management, PSAM 8, 2006, New Orleans, LA.

[5] Duffey, R.B. and Ohlsson, S., tbp, 'Learning and Risk Reduction by Error Correction: On the Scaling from Individuals to Collectives'.

[6] Duffey, R.B. and Saull J.W., 2004, 'Reliability and Failures of Engineering Systems Due to Human Errors', in Proc. The First Cappadocia Int. Mechanical Engineering Symposium (CMES'-04), Cappadocia, Turkey.

[7] Heathcote, A, Brown, S. and Mewhort, D.J.K., 2000, 'The Power Law Repealed: The Case for an Exponential Law of Practice', Psychonomic Bulletin and Review, 7,2, pp. 185–207.

[8] Brown, S., 2002, Ph.D. Thesis, University of Newcastle, Psychology Department, available for download at www.newcastle.edu.au/psychology/ncl.

# Appendix K

## Predicting Rocket Launch Reliability – Case Study

### Summary

Improving rocket reliability is a key issue for the architecture and risk of future manned and unmanned space missions (NASA, 2005) [1] and (Hsu and Duffey, 2006) [2]. In Chapter 3, we examined the chance of a Space Shuttle loss, and to reduce that risk, NASA is examining alternate crew survival vehicles and new system 'architectures'. In subsequent chapters, we provided ideas and methods to predict the risk, so we now apply these to make a prediction using the extensive data given (S. Go, 2007) [3] for NASA's RL-10 rocket launch failures between 1962 and 2005[1]. We re-analysed the failure rates, failure probability and learning rates for these upper stage tests. The probability of failure was compared to our new theory, to other existing world data and to traditional statistical methods. As a result, we show the predictions and uncertainty for the future reliability trends.

### Theory of Rocket Reliability

Consider a series of a number of rocket launches, $L$, where, $n$, rockets fail during the series, giving a total of, $n = N_j$, failures occur during the total number of launches, $\Sigma L$. In Go's original analysis [3], the instantaneous failure fraction, $n/L$, during the launch series was equated to the failure probability, and the reliability was then estimated. Here, we derive a failure rate, $\lambda$, for the same data, and use that rate to estimate the failure probability, $p(n)$, for any number of failures, $n$, in any accumulated number of launches, $L$. We check this analysis against Go's result, and with the predictions from the Learning Hypothesis theory as based on the world data trends for failures in multiple technologies.

By definition, the CDF, $F(L)$, is actually given by the ratio of the accumulated number of failures, $n$, observed in any number of launches, $L$, to the total possible number of failures, $N$,

---

[1]We are grateful to Professor Joseph Fragola and Dr Suzie Go for providing access to this unique information.

$$p(n) = F(L) = n/N$$

Conventionally, from the theory of engineering reliability for the failure rate of components, this failure probability for any number of launches, $L$, is also given by,

$$F(L) = p(L) = 1 - e^{-\int \lambda dL}$$

where $\lambda$ is the failure rate per launch[2]. Assuming learning from failures occur and the failure rate is a function of experience, the experience measure for the failure rate integration is the accumulated number of launches, $L$, extending from the first, $L = 1$, up to any final total of, $\Sigma L$, launches.

The failure probability, $p(L)$, implies the reliability, $R(L)$, as given by the converse expression:

$$R(L) = 1 - p(L)$$

To determine the needed failure rate, $\lambda$, and hence, the probability for any launch number, $L$, we actually have two choices, using the known dataset given by Go [3] for the $RL$-10 rocket launches from 1962–2005.

## a)  Unknown Total Number of Launches and Failures

The first and more usual situation is of observing failures during a number of launches, in a series when the total numbers of launches and failures are initially unknown *a priori*. We have a changing failure probability as experience is gained from more and more launches and failures. After observing $n$ failures out of any number of launches, $L$, the instantaneous failure rate $\lambda(L)$ *per number of successful launches* is:

$$\lambda(L) = \{dn/dL\}/(L - n)$$

where the numerator is the instantaneous *differential* of the fractional count of launch failures. In the denominator, the running count of the number of failures, $n$, has been subtracted from the instantaneous launch running total, $L$, in order to correct the failure *rate* for the past failures already observed in the increasing and varying number of launches. The exponent in the failure rate integral, $e^{-\int \lambda dL}$, can now be written as,

$$-\int \lambda(L) dL = -\int \{dn\}/(L - n) = -\ln(1 - n/L)$$

So, the resulting failure probability reduces to,

$$p(n) \equiv p(L) = 1 - e^{-\int \lambda dL} = 1 - e^{-\ln(1-n/L)} = n/L,$$

---

[2]Note that the failure rates could be estimated as a rate per unit (rocket) burn time instead of per launch, but the information readily available to us was not sufficient to derive this value. Anyway, using an average burn time is simply proportional and equivalent to using the number of launches. Which experience measure is more relevant to the actual failure mode is then another question to consider based on the data, as we will show.

which is exactly the failure fraction expression used by Go [3], and also justifies using the differential failure rate expression.

The RL-10 data can also be evaluated numerically from the finite and discrete series when we count the numbers, $n$, of failures in $L$, launches, since integration presumes a continuous failure rate function. For the series of discrete outcomes in the present example, the failure rate exponent, $\int \lambda dL$, can be written instead as the summation, $\Sigma \lambda \Delta L$, taken over any finite differential number of launches, $\Delta L$.[3]

## b) Known Total Number of Launches and Failures

The second case is when the total number of launches in a series, $\Sigma L$, and the total number of failures observed, $N_j$, are both known *a posteriori*, as for after a fixed data or test sample. After $n$ failures occurring out of any number of launches, $L$, the overall failure rate, $\lambda(N)$, *per total number of successful launches*, is the approximation:

$$\lambda(N) = \{n/N_j\}/(\sum L - N_j)$$

where the numerator corresponds to the *integral* fractional count of launch failures, $p(n)$. Note that in the denominator, the total number of failures, $N_j$, has been subtracted from the total launches, $\Sigma L$, in order to correctly estimate the failure *rate*, which is particularly important if there are many failures. The limits of the failure rate for $n = 0$ and $n = N_j$ are self-evident.

The failure rates, $\lambda(L)$ and $\lambda(N)$, give two distinct probability estimates for $p(n)$, corresponding to the usual running or instantaneous probability, $p(n) \equiv p(L)$, and the overall total probability, $p(N)$, respectively.

In addition, as derived elsewhere (see: Chapter 5, Appendix A and Appendix F), we can *predict* the posterior (future) probability, $P(n)$, of any further number of failures, based on the accumulated experience, $\tau$. So indeed, presuming that learning from launch experience is still occurring, we may expect *one* more failure, $(n = 1)$, with exactly the prior MERE probability as given by,

$$P(n) \rightarrow P(1) \equiv p(n) = 1 - \exp\left\{\left(\lambda - \lambda_{\sum L}\right)/k - \lambda(\tau - \tau_0)\right\}$$

We can also make a direct comparison to the learning trends suggested by the Universal Learning Curve (ULC) (Chapter 1). As derived from the Learning Hypothesis, the ULC is given by the correlation between the non-dimensional error rate, $E^*$, and a non-dimensional measure of experience, $N^*$, where:

---

[3]For a discrete series, we must approximate the failure count differential as, $d \equiv \Delta n = n_L + n_{L-1}$, being the subtraction of the preceding, $n_{L-1}$, from the current, $n_L$, counts of the number of failures; and write the corresponding launch differential as $dL \equiv \Delta L = L_L - L_{L-1}$, being the subtraction of the previous, $L - 1$, count from the current $L$ count of the corresponding number of launches. So, numerically,

$$\lambda(L) \rightarrow \{\Delta n/\Delta L\}/(L - n) = \{(n_L - n_{L-1})/(L_L - L_{L-1})\}/(L_L - n_L)$$

The failure rate summation is now written as $\Sigma \lambda \Delta L = \Sigma \lambda(L_L - L_{L-1}) = \Sigma(n_L - n_{L-1})/(L_L - n_L)$, which is the discrete approximation that is equivalent to the exact integral result given above.

$$E^* = \exp - 3N^*$$

Here, $E^*$ is the non-dimensional error (failure) rate, normalised to the initial highest rate, $\lambda_{n=1} \equiv \lambda_0$, and the lowest attained rate, $\lambda\Sigma_L \equiv \lambda_m$, so:

$$E^* = \left\{ \lambda(N) - \lambda_{\Sigma L} \right\} / \left\{ \lambda_{n=1} - \lambda_{\Sigma L} \right\}$$

The $N^*$ term above is some non-dimensional experience measure, usually proportional to $L/\Sigma L$, and the numerical factor of three (3) in the exponent is derived from comparisons against the learning trend from two centuries of failure and outcome data.

## Results

The basic RL-10 rocket data [3] are shown as running totals in Table A-K1. The count of the number of failures, $n$, for a given number of launches, $L$, was given for a series total count of $\Sigma L = 185$ launches for the total count of $N_j = 22$ launch failures of various kinds and types occurring during the series. Given this information, we can now calculate the failure rates, $\lambda(L,N)$, and probabilities $p(L,N)$, and validate the theory by comparison to the prior and independent analyses of other outcome data.

**Table A-K1.**  RL-10 Launch and failure counts and theoretical results

| Launches, L | Failures, n | Fraction, n/L | 0.01 N* | n/185 | Failure Rate (L) | p(L) approx | p(L) exact | Failure Rate (N) | p(N) |
|---|---|---|---|---|---|---|---|---|---|
| 2 | 1 | 0.5000 | 6.19E-08 | 0.0054 | 0.50000 | 0.6321 | 0.5000 | 0.00272 | 0.0054 |
| 3 | 2 | 0.6667 | 9.28E-08 | 0.0108 | 1.00000 | 0.8045 | 0.6667 | 0.00364 | 0.0036 |
| 5 | 3 | 0.6000 | 1.55E-07 | 0.0162 | 0.25000 | 0.7287 | 0.6000 | 0.00330 | 0.0066 |
| 8 | 4 | 0.5000 | 2.47E-07 | 0.0216 | 0.08333 | 0.6242 | 0.5000 | 0.00276 | 0.0083 |
| 10 | 5 | 0.5000 | 3.09E-07 | 0.0270 | 0.10000 | 0.5614 | 0.5000 | 0.00278 | 0.0055 |
| 20 | 6 | 0.3000 | 6.19E-07 | 0.0324 | 0.00714 | 0.4689 | 0.3000 | 0.00168 | 0.0166 |
| 25 | 7 | 0.2800 | 7.73E-07 | 0.0378 | 0.01111 | 0.4081 | 0.2800 | 0.00157 | 0.0078 |
| 27 | 8 | 0.2963 | 8.35E-07 | 0.0432 | 0.02632 | 0.3692 | 0.2963 | 0.00167 | 0.0033 |
| 38 | 9 | 0.2368 | 1.18E-06 | 0.0486 | 0.00313 | 0.3321 | 0.2368 | 0.00135 | 0.0147 |
| 40 | 10 | 0.2500 | 1.24E-06 | 0.0541 | 0.01667 | 0.3061 | 0.2500 | 0.00143 | 0.0029 |
| 52 | 11 | 0.2115 | 1.61E-06 | 0.0595 | 0.00203 | 0.2815 | 0.2115 | 0.00122 | 0.0145 |
| 70 | 12 | 0.1714 | 2.17E-06 | 0.0649 | 0.00096 | 0.2582 | 0.1714 | 0.00099 | 0.0177 |
| 78 | 13 | 0.1667 | 2.41E-06 | 0.0703 | 0.00192 | 0.2394 | 0.1667 | 0.00097 | 0.0077 |
| 80 | 14 | 0.1750 | 2.47E-06 | 0.0757 | 0.00758 | 0.2247 | 0.1750 | 0.00102 | 0.0020 |
| 82 | 15 | 0.1829 | 2.54E-06 | 0.0811 | 0.00746 | 0.2131 | 0.1829 | 0.00108 | 0.0021 |
| 90 | 16 | 0.1778 | 2.78E-06 | 0.0865 | 0.00169 | 0.2028 | 0.1778 | 0.00105 | 0.0084 |
| 92 | 17 | 0.1848 | 2.85E-06 | 0.0919 | 0.00667 | 0.1943 | 0.1848 | 0.00110 | 0.0022 |
| 140 | 18 | 0.1286 | 4.33E-06 | 0.0973 | 0.00017 | 0.1833 | 0.1286 | 0.00077 | 0.0363 |
| 142 | 19 | 0.1338 | 4.39E-06 | 0.1027 | 0.00407 | 0.1743 | 0.1338 | 0.00081 | 0.0016 |
| 145 | 20 | 0.1379 | 4.49E-06 | 0.1081 | 0.00267 | 0.1666 | 0.1379 | 0.00084 | 0.0025 |
| 146 | 21 | 0.1438 | 4.52E-06 | 0.1135 | 0.00800 | 0.1602 | 0.1438 | 0.00088 | 0.0009 |
| 185 | 22 | 0.1189 | 5.72E-06 | 0.1189 | 0.00016 | 0.1533 | 0.1189 | 0.00073 | 0.0281 |

The principle calculated results are also shown in the Table A-K1, taken directly from our .xls worksheet 'NASA.RL-10', where the counts of the running number of launches, $L$, and corresponding number of failures, $n$, are listed in the first two columns.

The Columns 7 and 10 in Table A-K1 contain the instantaneous, $p(L)$, and overall, $p(N)$, failure probabilities, as derived from the failure probability expression using the exact integral, $p(L)$, and the discrete summation, $p(L,N)) \equiv 1 - e^{-\Sigma\lambda(L,N)\Delta L}$, knowing the instantaneous and total failure rate values, $\lambda(L,N)$ from Columns 6 and 9, respectively.

The exact probability value, $p(L)$, in Table A-K1 Column 8 is calculated using the instantaneous failure rate, $\lambda(L)$, and is precisely the failure fraction, $n/L$, (in Table A-K1, Column 3), as used by Go [3] for the original reliability estimates. There are numerical differences using the approximate discrete formula for, $p(L)$ as in Column 7. The overall agreement suggests additional comparisons and validation for both the failure rate assumptions and the probability, as follows.

## Measures of Experience

We presume that learning from each launch failure occurs throughout the launch series and that is evident in the succession of corrective design measures listed by Go [3]. As usual, we now need to determine a non-dimensional basis for the overall experience, $N^*$, that reflects the error correction process based on the experience with this particular RL-10 rocket type.

The simplest measure is to adopt the ratio of the number of launches to the total number, $N^* = L/\Sigma L$, where $\Sigma L = 185$, reflecting just the overall launch experience. More generally, we know that failures also occur during the launch process, the rocket lift-off and the full acceleration time. In order to compare to other data for probability purposes, the question arises as to what should be taken as the 'correct' measure for the experience units, $\tau$, for estimating the instantaneous non-dimensional experience, $N^*(\tau)$. We would expect the launch failure probability to be some function of system operational experience units, $\tau$, which are related both to the number of rockets made and launched, and for how long they were used (also known as the burn time). Specifically, for launch failures, we have the general but unknown functional form of the burn time and rocket launch experience, both good and bad:

$$N^*(\tau) = f\left(n, N_j, L, \sum L, \text{burn time} \ldots\right)$$

We need guidance for an empirical estimate or guess (which is not yet proven) to take into account the experience gained from the whole system as well as that from the individual rocket launches. As the first and somewhat crude estimate, we choose as the relevant experience measure the multiplication of the ratio of the fractional launch numbers and burn times for any number of failures, $n$, after, $L$, launches, to the total numbers and burn times for all the rocket launches, $\Sigma L$. Therefore, we take $N^*(\tau)$ as varying as the product of the launch number and burn time ratios,

$N^*(t) \, \alpha$ (Fractional numbers of rockets launched to the total tested, $L^*$)×(Fractional average burn time per rocket to the total burn time, $BT^*$)

$$\alpha \left(L/\sum L\right) \times BT^*$$

In the Go [3] data report, a total burn time was given as 155,523 seconds for RL-10 rockets with an average burn time of about 89 seconds for each RL-10 rocket (the design value is given as 120 seconds), so BT* = 89/155,523.

For fitting purposes we adopt the simplest and direct proportionality factor, $\Phi$, so numerically for the RL-10 series of 185 launches,

$$N^*(\tau) = \Phi \times (L/185) \times (89/155,523).$$

We can then vary the $\Phi$-factor multiplier empirically as may be needed to reflect: (i) our lack of knowledge; (ii) to improve the data fit; and (iii) to account for uncertainty or variations in the experience ratios. The key test of how well this or any other assumption works is to compare it against the actual data.

## Comparison to World Data

We now compare the failure fraction or probability, $n/L$ (number of failures, $n \equiv F$, per number of launches, $L$), using the data reported by Pate-Cornell, 2000 [4], and to the MERE fit given in Chapter 3. This comparison is shown in Figure A-K1 as a function of the accumulated count of the number of launches, $L$.

The comparison is reasonable, suggesting consistency of approach (and even perhaps of the database). The predicted minimum is about a 17% failure fraction according to the, $F/L$, line shown, which was originally fitted to the Pate-Cornell dataset in Chapter 3. It is evident that the number of launches is a relevant experience measure from this comparison.

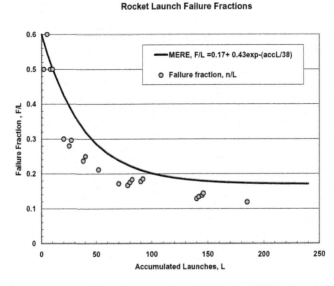

Rocket Launch Failure Fractions

**Figure A-K1.** Comparison of RL-10 launch failure fraction to the MERE fit by Duffey and Saull for the data of Pate-Cornell

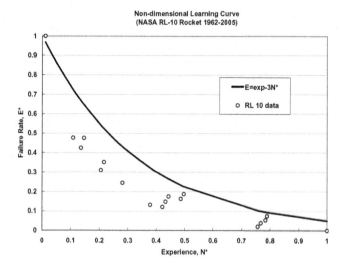

**Figure A-K2.** Comparison of RL-10 data to the ULC

Next we compare to the existing ULC trends. The $N^*$ experience values for this ULC case are always normalised to the maximum total experience, so very conveniently, $N^*$ reduces to the simple ratio of the number of launches, $L$, to the known total number:

$$N^* = \Phi\{(L_L^* \times BT^*)\}/\Phi\{(L_{\sum L}^* \times BT^*)\} = L/\sum L = L/185,$$

where the common factors $\Phi$, $\Sigma L$ and $BT^*$ have all cancelled out. The corresponding non-dimensional failure rate, $E^*$, was derived from the failure rate, $\lambda(N)$, in Table A-K1, Column 9, based consistently on the *total* number of launches. The result is shown in Figure A-K2, where the ULC line shown of $E^* = \exp - 3N^*$ is taken directly from our previous work (Chapter 1) and (Duffey and Saull, 2002) [5].

The agreement is quite reasonable, implying that the overall learning trend is indeed accurately captured by the overall failure rate, $\lambda(N)$, and that continuous learning and error correction was occurring throughout all the series of launches and launch failures. It is evident that the non-dimensional launch ratio, $L/\Sigma L$, is also a relevant measure for experience from this comparison for a known total launch sample.

## Predicting the Probability of Failure

Lastly, and most importantly, we compare to the probability *prediction* based on the assumption that learning from failures continues to occur. From the Learning Hypothesis, and from the MERE result for the failure probability (Chapter 4 and Appendix A), we note that the equivalent probability expression is now of the form:

$$p(L) = 1 - \exp\left\{\left(\lambda - \lambda_{\sum L}\right)/k - \lambda\left(\tau - \tau_0\right)\right\}$$

where,

**Probability Prediction Compared to Commercial Airline Crashes, Space Shuttle Losses ,
Rocket Launch Failures, Large Oil Spills and Nuclear Plant Latent Errors**

**Figure A-K3.** Comparison of the RL-10 failure probability to other data and to the MERE bathtub result

$$\lambda - \lambda_{\sum L} = \left(\lambda_{n=1} - \lambda_{\sum L}\right)\exp-(k(\tau - \tau_0))$$

and, $\lambda_{n=1}$ and $\lambda_{\Sigma L}$, correspond to the initial (highest) and final (lowest) failure rates at the relevant experience units, $\tau_0$ and $\tau$, respectively. For this comparison, we use our best experience, $N^*(\tau)$, values, which are straightforwardly calculated using the assumed 'launch times burn-time' experience ratio formula:

$$N^*(\tau) = \Phi\left(L/\sum L\right)BT^* = \Phi \times (L/185) \times (89/155{,}523)$$

The resulting $N^*$ values calculated using this assumption are given in Table A-K1 Column 4, where as an initial working estimate we have taken a constant value for, $\Phi \approx 10^{-2}$. In Figure A-K3, the comparison is shown of the corresponding exact *instantaneous* probability, $p(L)$, values (from Column 8 in Table A-K1) to the original MERE bathtub, $p(n)$, (see Chapters 5 and 9). Also shown are the independent datasets we have already analysed for commercial aircraft fatal accidents, oil spills at sea, and non-detection of latent errors, where the non-dimensional experience units are appropriately referenced to the total millions of flights taken, millions of tons shipped, and elapsed transient time, respectively.

The expected trend is clear of a steadily decreasing launch risk with increasing launch experience and of general agreement with the MERE theory and with these other data. The agreement is rather better than we might have expected. If the $\Phi$-factor value is order-of-magnitude correct, it would literally imply that only about a 1% fraction of the total experience is relevant to the learning trends. However, it is evident that both launch number *and* burn time are relevant measures for experience from this comparison.

The *prediction* for the posterior (future) probability is that a further reduction in RL-10 launch failure probability of about one order of magnitude is possible before reaching the minimum of the bathtub, as shown by Figure A-K3. This factor of 10 reduction in the *predicted* failure probability, or conversely the maximum reliability, could be attained after at least some ten (10) times more experience in total launches and/or burn time (i.e., after about another 1,800 or so RL-10 launches). Any new design or system architecture variant should be expected to follow this same bathtub curve.

## Statistical Estimates of the Failure Probability for the Very 'Next' Launch

Just for completeness, we now provide what sampling from the Jar of Life might predict (Chapter 1 et seq.), using more traditional statistical methods. These methods are restricted when predicting the failure probability of future launches as they cannot explicitly account for learning, in effect assuming that the prior known failure ratio, $n/L$, is essentially unchanged for the very next launch (see also Chapter 3). Although varying with launch count, the prior failure fraction is used to extrapolate to any future number but without correcting for learning effects. Having already observed or recorded, $n$, launch failures among the, $(L-n)$, prior successful launches, we can calculate the hypergeometric probability after each launch of observing the next, or $(n+1)$th, failure in the very next, $(L+1)$th, launch. From Appendix F and Jaynes, 2003 [6] (pp. 68–69), noting that we now write that, $(M+N) \equiv L$, the instantaneous total number of launches, the probability for the, $(n+1)$th, failure is then given by:

$$P(n+1, n>0)) = \frac{\binom{N}{n}\binom{M}{m}}{\binom{M+N}{m+n}} \equiv \frac{\binom{n+1}{n}}{\binom{L}{L+1}} \rightarrow (n+1)/(L+1)$$

Here, $P(n+1)$, is the probability of observing, $n+1$, failures in exactly, $L+1$, launches having already seen, $n>0$, failures in $L$, launches, and essentially assumes that the failure/success ratio remains unaltered.

We recall that LaPlace's Rule of Succession (Chapter 8) asserts that the probability of the 'next' outcome has a very similar result,

$$P(\text{LaP}, n+1) = (n+1)/(L+2).$$

From Appendix F, the binomial probability prediction for this same situation, but for, $L \rightarrow \infty$, and relatively few failures, $n \ll L$, gives the updated probability estimate after each, $L$th, launch and, $n$th, failure as:

$$P(n+1) = \{n/L\}^{n+1}\{1-(n/L)\}^{L+1}\},$$

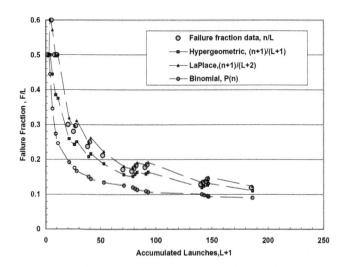

**Figure A-K4.** The running statistical estimates just for the probability of the very next ($n$ + 1)th launch failure on the very next $(L + 1)^{th}$ launch, as derived from the failure data

where we take, $p(L) = n/L$, which assumes the unchanging or prior failure probability for the very next launch[4]. We could also take $p(L) = p(n + 1) \sim (n + 1)/(L + 1)$ as another estimate for the future (next launch) probability, but the resulting numerical values are essentially identical once both, $n, L \gg 1$.

These one-by-one launch-by-launch calculations, and those from using the standard xls. worksheet binomial function, are shown in Figure A-K4 by the smoothed fitted (dashed) lines which in effect compares the, $L$th, data point to the prediction for the very next, or $(L + 1)$th, launch.

The 'next launch failure probability' lines show bumps and humps due to updating the individual random failures, which seem to come in groups. The results demonstrate that LaPlace's classic Rule follows the data the best, followed by the hypergeometric estimate. The deviations between the three estimates are due to the differing constant probability or constant failure ratio assumptions, and to the finite sample size, since the launch number is not sufficiently large or infinite. But this comparison shows clearly that these sampling formulae while providing a reasonable updated failure estimate, by definition do not provide a smooth predictive trend but are simply a *post hoc* running estimate. We have already shown the effect of learning in Appendix F, where including the MERE probability into the binomial expression correctly predicts the human bathtub curve.

---

[4]Instead of just for the next launch, we can also calculate the running binomial probability, $P(\Sigma L)$, of one more failure, $(n + 1)$, for every future launch for all of the remaining launches, $\Sigma L - L - 1$ (or $185 - L - 1$), assuming either the currently observed failure probability, $p(L) = n/L$, or a presumed future probability, $p(L) = (n + 1)/ (L + 1)$, when there is a known or predicted total number of future launches, $\Sigma L$, in this case of up to 185.

Not shown is the xls. binomial prediction for, $P(L = 185)$, made after each launch, $L$, for all $(185 - L - 1)$ successful launches remaining, assuming a probability of $(n + 1)/(L + 1)$, throughout for one more failure. This gives the trivial prediction of an equal risk or chance of the next failure occurring in each half of the launches, before and after 92 launches.

For comparison, the range given by our predictive estimates in Chapter 3 for the risk or probability of failure of the very next Space Shuttle is:

$$0.002 < P(\text{next}) < 0.03$$

These Shuttle loss values are within the above MERE bathtub *predictions* for the RL-10 when including the benefits of learning from experience, and are much smaller than the purely prior-based statistical estimates of ~0.1. These ranges and differences represent strictly an additional uncertainty for any risk estimate,

## Independent Validation of the MERE Launch Failure Curve

In addition to RL-10 data, Professor Joseph Fragola supplied us with the 1980–2005 data for over 1,900 launches of 13 international rocket types with 93 failures[5]. This enables a true test against yet another set of independent data. The comparison of the MERE curve from the data for just 240 launches to the failure fraction data, $n/L$, for five more major rocket types is shown in the Figure A-K5. The greatest number of accumulated launches (765) is

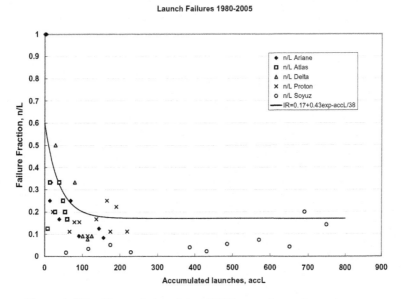

**Figure A-K5.** Extrapolation of the MERE curve fit to other rocket types

---

[5]The authors are very grateful to Professor Fragola for supplying this novel and very complete information.

for the Russian Soyuz type. Whilst not claiming exactitude, the trends are clearly very similar for all types, and the minimum failure fraction does not decline significantly.

## Observations

We have examined the NASA rocket launch failure data given by Go for 1962–2005. In this analysis, we have shown that the prior RL-10 rocket launch failure data are consistent with the world's information and predictions with regard to both learning rate and failure probability. The agreement between theory and data is achieved using an empirical launch number ratio times burn time ratio for the learning experience measure. These quantities are self-evidently expected to be relevant for error correction and to learning from failures, and hence need to be carefully tracked.

Alternatively, and in principle, we have shown that the learning hypothesis can also be utilised as a basis for *predicting* the potential reduction of the chance of future failures or outcomes for this major technological system, and hence for any new design variant as improvements are made and implemented from learning.

## References

[1] NASA, 'Exploration Systems Architecture Study (ESAS)', 2005, Final Report, NASA-TM-2005-214062, November (Available: www.sti.nasa.gov).

[2] Hsu, F. and Duffey, R.B., 2006, 'Managing Risks on the Space Frontier', Chapter 30, Beyond Earth: The Future of Humans in Space, Editor: Bob Krone, Apogee Books, Burlington, Canada.

[3] Go, S., 2007, 'A Historical Survey with Success and Maturity Estimates of Launch Systems with RL-10 Upper Stage Engines', Proceedings RAMS 2007 Symposium, Las Vegas, NV.

[4] Paté-Cornell, E. and Dillon, R., 2000, 'Probabilistic Risk Analysis for the NASA Space Shuttle: A Brief History and Current Work', Submitted for publication in Reliability Engineering and System Safety, April.

[5] Duffey, R.B. and Saull, J.W., 2002, 'Know the Risk', First Edition, Butterworth and Heinemann, Boston, MA.

[6] Jaynes, E.T., 2003, 'Probability Theory: The Logic of Science', First Edition, Cambridge University Press, Cambridge, UK, Edited by G.L. Bretthorst.

# Index

Page references followed by 't' denote tables; 'f' denote figures; common organizational or usual working abbreviations in parentheses.

CPSIA information can be obtained
at www.ICGtesting.com
Printed in the USA
BVOW10*1657070916

PP7399900001B/1/P